María de los Ángeles Gómez González and Teresa Sánchez Roura
English Pronunciation for Speakers of Spanish

María de los Ángeles Gómez González
Teresa Sánchez Roura

English Pronunciation for Speakers of Spanish

From Theory to Practice

DE GRUYTER
MOUTON

ISBN 978-1-5015-1096-0
e-ISBN (PDF) 978-1-5015-1097-7
e-ISBN (EPUB) 978-1-5015-0294-1

Library of Congress Cataloging-in-Publication Data
A CIP catalog record for this book has been applied for at the Library of Congress.

Bibliographic information published by the Deutsche Nationalbibliothek
The Deutsche Nationalbibliothek lists this publication in the Deutsche Nationalbibliografie; detailed bibliographic data are available on the Internet at http://dnb.dnb.de.

Cover image: Bram Janssens/Hemera/thinkstock
Typesetting: RoyalStandard, Hong Kong
Printing and binding: CPI books GmbH, Leck
♾ Printed on acid-free paper
Printed in Germany

www.degruyter.com

Table of Contents

Acknowledgements

We wish to acknowledge the unswerving support that many colleagues and students, as well as friends and family members, have given us in the process of preparing this book and its accompanying website. Special mention must be made of the following people and institutions.

To devise the *EPSS Multimedia Lab*, the website that accompanies this textbook (http://www.usc.es/multimlab/index.html), we benefited greatly from the technical expertise of Alejandro Carbajo and Santiago Fernández, as well as from the premises provided by *A Casa do Rock* and *SERVIMAV*, the Audiovisual Media Service of the University of Santiago de Compostela. Our gratitude also extends to Milagros Torrado Cespón, Patrick Ashcroft, Charlotte Astley, Eithne Keane, Andrew Rollings and Rachel Sammons, who allowed us to record and video-tape them as native speakers of Spanish and British English. Likewise, our heartfelt thanks go to our colleagues María Dolores Gómez Penas, Susana María Doval Suárez and Andrew Rollings, who took their time to contribute to the production of the contents of the website (information concerning the Spanish language) and the book (Chapters five and seven). Grateful thanks are also due to Milagros Torrado Cespón and Alba Ágata Dias Fernández, who assisted us in both the formatting and compilation of the material included in this volume and the EPSS Multimedia lab. We would also like to acknowledge the collaboration of the following scholars: Mercedes Cabrera Abreu, Francisco Gallardo del Puerto, Mª Luisa García Lecumberri, Mark Huckvale, Rafael Monroy Casas and Francisco Vizcaíno Ortega for having provided us with useful material on (acoustic) phonetics and on the acquisition of English pronunciation by Spanish-speaking learners, which contributed greatly to the completeness of these aspects of the manual; and last, but not least, J. Lachlan Mackenzie, Francisco Gonzálvez, Susana Doval Suárez, Elsa González Álvarez, Laura Alba Juez and Mike Hannay, to whom we are also much indebted for giving so generously their time to read earlier versions of the volume and providing constructive suggestions and corrections. We hereby thank these scholars for their input and absolve them of any responsibility for what follows.

The International Phonetic Alphabet (2005) is reproduced by kind permission of the International Phonetic Association (Department of Theoretical and Applied Linguistics, School of English, Aristotle University of Thessaloniki, Thessaloniki 54124, Greece). Thanks are also due to University of Chicago Press (Figure 4) and Hodder Education (Figure 26). The publishers will make arrangements with any copyright-holder that has not been contacted, although every effort has been made to trace and acknowledge ownership of copyright.

Finally, for years of financial support, we would also like to thank the *Spanish Ministry of Science and Innovation* (MICINN) and the *European Funds for Regional Development* (EFRE) (FFI2010-19380), as well as the Xunta de Galicia (INCITE09 204 155PR and GRC2015/002 GI-1924).

List of Tables

List of Figures

Audio Tracks

All the listening material accompanying this book, whether **audio exercises** or **audio illustrations**, is available in the companion website of this book, EPSS Multimedia Lab (http://www.usc.es/multimlab/index.html).

You can visit the Lab for your own choice of audio exercises as you proceed through the material in the book. Audio illustrations (listed below) are marked where relevant throughout the book with the icon and a reference number, so that AI 1.3 means 'Audio Illustration 3 in Chapter 1'. You can easily find and listen to them in the EPSS Multimedia Lab under the "Audio Illustrations" tab in the main menu.

Audio Illustrations Chapter 1

Audio Illustrations Chapter 2

Audio Illustrations Chapter 3

Audio Illustrations Chapter 4

List of Abbreviations and Phonetic Symbols

Abbreviations	Meaning
af	after/following
bf	before/followed by
C	consonant
CV	Cardinal Vowel
CVS	Cardinal Vowel Scale
dB	decibel(s)
EFL	English as a Foreign Language
EPD	(Cambridge) English Pronunciation Dictionary
F	formant(s)
F_0	fundamental frequency
F_1	first formant
F_2	second formant
Fr	French
GA	General American
Hz	Hertz
IPA	International Phonetic Alphabet
Lat	Latin
L1	First language
L2	Second language
LPD	Longman Pronunciation Dictionary
msecs	milliseconds
n	noun
NLM	Native Language Magnet
NP	normal pronunciation
NRP	non-regional pronunciation
OBR	openness, backness and lip rounding
OLD	Oxford Learner's Dictionary
PAM	Perceptual Assimilation Model
pl	plural
post-alv	post-alveolar
PSp	Peninsular Spanish
PresE	Present-day English

RP	Received Pronunciation
SFS	Speech Filing System
SID	Speech Internet Dictionary
sg	singular
Sp	Spanish
SR	Speech Recognition
SSBE	Standard Southern British English
SSE	Standard Scottish English
SSLE	Spanish-speaking learners of English
usu	usually
V	vowel
v	verb
VT	Vocal tract

Phonetic Symbols	Meaning	Examples
a	Cardinal Vowel no. 4 (open front unrounded)	First element of the RP diphthong /aɪ/ <i> in *idle* [ˈaɪdl̩]
ɐ	near-open central vowel	Scottish English pronunciation of the vowels in *bud* or *putt*
æ	raised open front vowel	<a> in *cat* [kæt]
ɑ	Cardinal Vowel no. 5 (open back unrounded)	Fr *pas* ‘but’
ɑː	long open back unrounded vowel	<ar> in *card* [kɑːd]
ɒ	Cardinal Vowel no. 13 (open back rounded)	<o> in *pot* [pɒt]
b	voiced bilabial plosive	<b> in *bib* [bɪb]
β	voiced bilabial fricative	<v> in PSp *ave* [ˈaβ̞e] ‘bird’
ɔ	Cardinal Vowel no. 6 (open-mid back rounded)	First element of the RP diphthong /ɔɪ/ <oy> in *boy* [bɔɪ]
ɔː	long open-mid back rounded vowel	<or> in *port* [pɔːt]
d	voiced alveolar plosive	<d> in *dear* [dɪə]
ʤ	voiced postalveolar affricate	<dg> in *bridge* [brɪʤ]
ð	voiced dental fricative	<th> in *this* [ðɪs]

e	Cardinal Vowel no. 2 (close-mid front unrounded)	<e> in *dress* [dres]
ə	central unrounded vowel: "schwa"	post-nuclear and pre-nuclear <a> in *banana* [bəˈnɑːnə]
ɛ	Cardinal Vowel no. 3 (open-mid front unrounded)	<e> in Fr *père* 'father'
ɜː	long open-mid central unrounded vowel	<er> in *herb* [hɜːb]
f	voiceless labio-dental fricative	<f> in *fair* [feə]
g	voiced velar plosive	<g> in *hug* [hʌg]
h	voiceless glottal fricative	<h> in *hip* [hɪp]
ɦ	voiced glottal fricative	<h> in *ahead* [əˈɦed]
i	Cardinal Vowel no. 1 (close front unrounded)	<i> in PSp *isla* [ˈisla] 'island' and RP /i/ <y> in *noisy* [ˈnɔɪzi]
iː	long close front unrounded vowel	<ee> in *seed* [siːd]
ɪ	lax close front unrounded vowel	<i> in *this* [ðɪs]
ʝ	voiced palatal fricative	<y> in PSp <yeso> [ˈʝeso] 'plaster'
k	voiceless velar plosive	<c> in *cap* [kæp]
l	voiced alveolar lateral approximant	<l> in *eleven* [ɪˈlevn̩]
ɫ	velarised voiced alveolar lateral/ dark l	<l> in *peel* [piːɫ]
m	bilabial (realisation of a) nasal	<m> in *mother* [ˈmʌðə]
ɱ	labio-dental (realisation of a) nasal	<m> in *comfort* [ˈkʌɱfət]
ɯ	Cardinal Vowel no. 16 (close back unrounded)	RP /uː/ with spread lips
n	alveolar nasal	<n> in *plan* [plæn]
ŋ	velar (realisation of a) nasal	<ng> in *sing* [sɪŋ]
ɲ	palatal nasal	<ñ> in PSp *caña* [ˈkaɲa] 'cane'
o	Cardinal Vowel no. 7 (close-mid back rounded)	<o> in PSp *no* [no] 'not'
ø	Cardinal Vowel no. 10 (close-mid front rounded)	<eu> in Fr *peu* 'little'

œ	Cardinal Vowel no. 11 (open-mid front rounded)	<eu> in Fr *peur* ‘fear’
Œ	Cardinal Vowel no. 12 (open front rounded vowel)	It has not been found to exist as a separate phoneme.
θ	voiceless dental fricative	<th> in *thin* [θɪn]
p	voiceless bilabial plosive	<p> in *pet* [pet]
r/ɹ	voiced post-alveolar approximant	<r> in *red* [red] or [ɹed]
r	voiced alveolar trill or multiple vibrant	<rr> in PSp *carro* [ˈkaro] ‘cart’
ɾ	voiced alveolar tap	<r> in PSp *caro* [ˈkaɾo] ‘expensive’
s	voiceless alveolar fricative	<ss> in *miss* [mɪs]
ʃ	voiceless postalveolar fricative	<sh> in *ship* [ʃɪp]
t	voiceless alveolar plosive	<t> in *tin* [tɪn]
ʧ	voiceless postalveolar affricate	<ch> in *choose* [ʧu:z]
u	Cardinal Vowel no. 8 (close back rounded)	<u> in PSp *útil* [ˈutil] ‘useful’
u:	long close back rounded vowel	<oo> in *food* [fu:d]
ʊ	lax close back rounded vowel	<u> in *put* [pʊt]
v	voiceless labio-dental fricative	<v> in *very* [ˈveri]
ʌ	Cardinal Vowel no. 14 (open-mid back unrounded)	<u> in *mud* [mʌd]
w	voiced labial-velar central approximant semivowel	<w> in *white* [waɪt]
x	voiceless velar fricative	<j> in PSp *jarra* [ˈxara] ‘jar’
y	Cardinal Vowel no. 9 (close front rounded)	<u> in Fr *du* ‘from’
ʎ	voiced palatal lateral	<ll> in PSp *llama* [ˈʎama] ‘flame’
ɤ	Cardinal Vowel no. 15 (close-mid back unrounded)	Realisation of PresE /ʊ/ in some dialects
z	voiced alveolar fricative	<z> in *zoo* [zu:]
ʒ	voiced postalveolar fricative	<s> in *measure* [ˈmeʒəʳ)]
ʔ	glottal stop	<tt> in *button* [bʌʔn̩]

ʘ	bilabial click	
!	alveolar click	
ǁ	velar click	
Diacritics	**Meaning**	**Examples**
ʰ [pʰ]	aspirated	<p> in *peel* [pʰiːɫ]
⁼ [p⁼]	unaspirated	<p> in *spider* [ˈsp⁼aɪdəʳ]
̬ [t̬]	voiced	<t> in *matter* [ˈmæt̬əʳ]
˚ [ŋ̊] [d̥]	voiceless or devoiced	<d> in *did* [d̥ɪd̥]
ʲ [kʲ]	palatalised consonant	<k> and <n> in *keen* [kʲiːnʲ]
ʷ [pʷ]	labialised consonant (lip rounding)	<p> and <t> in *put* [pʷʊtʷ]
̪ [d̪]	dental	<n> in PSp *monte* [ˈmõn̪te] 'hill'
ˡ [dˡ]	lateral release	<d> in *middle* [ˈmɪdˡl̩]
ⁿ [tⁿ]	nasal release	<t> in *catnap* [ˈkætⁿnæp]
ᵐ [pᵐ]	nasal release	<p> in *topmost* [ˈtopᵐməʊst]
˜ [ẽ]	nasalised	<e> in *ten* [tẽn]
˺ [g˺]	non-audible release	<g> in *big* [bɪg˺]
ˆ [pˆ]	unreleased	First <p> in *top post* [ˌtʰɒpˆ ˈpʰəʊst⁼]"
₊ [k̟]	advanced (consonants)	<k> in *key* [k̟iːː] or [k₊iːː]
˖ [u̟]	advanced (vowels)	Quality of RP [uː]
¯ p̄	retracted (consonants)	<p> in *pool* [p̄ːu ɫ] or [p-ːuɫ]
˗ [ɑ̠]	retracted (vowels)	[ɑ̠ː] retracted variant of RP [ɑː]
¨ [ä]	centralised	Quality of RP [ɑː]
˕ [ɪ̞]	lowered or more open	<i> in *sit* [sɪ̞t]
˔ [ɪ̝]	raised or closer	<i> in *bit* [bɪ̝t]
̯ [i̯]	non-syllabic	<ai> in PSp *aire* [ˈai̯re] 'air'
̩ [n̩]	syllabic	<n> in *eleven* [ɪˈlevn̩]
ːː	extra-length	<ee> in *bee* [biːː]
ˑ	half-length	<ea> in *beat* [biˑt]
ː	normal length	<or> in *cord* [kɔːd]
ˈ	primary stress	*computer* [kəmˈpjuːtəʳ]
ˌ	secondary stress	*understand* [ˌʌndəˈstænd]

/ /	phonemic transcription	*post* /pəʊst/
[ ]	allophonic/phonetic transcription	*post* [pʰəˈʊst⁼]
*	ungrammatical/wrong pronunciation	*earliest* *[ˈɜːlɪst]
.	syllable boundary	PSp *reyes* [re.ɹes] 'kings'
|	tone unit boundary	
||	pause	
_#	word-finally	
#_	word-initially	

Purpose and Scope of the Book

English Pronunciation for Speakers of Spanish. From Theory to Practice (EPSS) is aimed at meeting the needs of speakers of Spanish who want to learn or teach English **phonetics** and **phonology** at universities and teacher-training institutes, or otherwise wish to improve their English **pronunciation** and their skills in **transcribing** English phonetically. To be covered in one or preferably two semesters, the volume can be used in a course on English Phonetics and Phonology and/or on English Pronunciation. In addition, the book may be useful to anyone interested in gaining insight into the differences and similarities that exist between English and Spanish pronunciation to prepare the ground for more advanced and extensive reading in the field.

EPSS is supported by a companion website called **EPSS Multimedia Lab** available at http://www.usc.es/multimlab/index.html. It contains the **audio files** (audio illustrations or audio exercises) accompanying the book, with entries for each numbered soundtrack in its corresponding unit and tab, sampling the voices of **five native speakers** of **British English** (three female and two male) and **one** female speaker of **Peninsular Spanish**, as well as **animations, videos** and **additional material** that can be used in combination with this manual or independently, including: (1) an **Animated Sound Bank of English-Spanish** (with phonemic transcriptions and original recordings), (2) **Glossaries and Dictionaries of Phonetics and English Pronunciation**, (3) **Downloadable and Recorded Exercises** (with their keys), and (4) **Other Resources to Teach and Learn English Phonetics and Pronunciation.**

The term **pronunciation** in the title is a cover term for the contents of both the book and the website. EPSS provides a down-to-earth introduction to the basic principles, most significant concepts and terminology of English phonetics, adopting an essentially practical **contrastive** approach. Our intention is to show how practical phonetics can be effectively used both to learn English phonetics and pronunciation and to teach it to non-natives, in particular to **Spanish-speaking learners of English** (SSLE) by helping them to represent, perceive and reproduce the sounds of English as compared to those of Spanish. To this effect, the sounds of British English, more specifically the **Received Pronunciation** (RP) accent, are contrasted with those of Spanish, particularly **Peninsular Spanish** (PSp). Separate units are devoted to the discussion of **vowels, vowel glides, consonants**, and features of **connected speech**, including such phenomena as co-articulation, assimilation, elision, linking and prosody (stress, rhythm, intonation), as well as to the description of **sound/spelling relationships** in English. In addition, the volume also offers SSLE guidance on how to pronounce and talk in conversations. To provide such guidance is of paramount importance to us, because after years of experience as teachers of English phonetics to Spanish university students we agree with Coe (2001: 91) that "European Spanish speakers, in particular, probably find English pronunciation harder than speakers of any other European language".

Accordingly, taking a **communicative approach**, the book highlights the phonetic and phonemic contrasts and specific cues that are most important to aiding comprehension in English. Likewise, the features of English pronunciation that are potentially problematic for speakers of Spanish are emphasised so as to prevent misconceptions and avoid, whenever possible, the presence of a **foreign accent**, which may result from a variety of factors, ranging from **language universal** and (L1 and L2) **language-specific constraints** (taking into account the learner's native language or linguistic variety and its linguistic similarity to the target accent) to **individual**-dependent **characteristics** (age, instruction, phonetic and auditory abilities, as well as such affective factors as attitude, identity and concern for good pronunciation) (Kenworthy 1987; Morley 1991; Lecumberri 1999; Moyer 1999). As we are aware that these factors mean that SSLE are unlikely to start on the study of phonetics with a native-like pronunciation but are likely to carry the signature of the phonological structure and "articulatory setting" (position of articulators) of Spanish, specific sections of this book are devoted to serving as a guide towards "correct" pronunciation habits. Our purpose is to help SSLE **sound as close as possible to native English** or, at least, **acquire an intelligible RP pronunciation** (being able to produce the sound patterns of English). By achieving **comprehensibility** (so that the meaning of what is said is understood) and **interpretability** (so that the purpose of what is said is understood), they will satisfy their communicative needs in any situation (**functional communicability**) and increase their self-confidence while also fostering their monitoring abilities and speech strategies (Burn 2003). Nevertheless, it should be noted that intelligibility may be affected by other factors besides pronunciation (Fayer and Krasinski 1987), such as **grammatical correctness** (Varonis and Gass 1981), the **fluidity** and **rhythm of speech** (Anderson-Hsieb and Kehler 1988), **familiarity** with the topic discussed (Gass and Varonis 1984) and background or ambient **noise** (Munro 1998).

The book contains **seven chapters**. Each begins with a general introduction to the topic named in its title, followed by detailed analyses of the relevant issues, which are regularly interspersed with illustrative **audio illustrations**, **examples** and **diagrams** (e.g. waveforms, spectrograms, midsagittal sections of facial diagrams, Tables, Figures and other kinds of artwork). At the end of each chapter, there are also sections with recommendations for **Further Reading** and a battery of **Exercises** of different kinds. The proposed activities are devised not only to help the reader gain practice in ear-training, oral production and phonetic transcription using the symbols and diacritics provided by the **International Phonetic Alphabet**, but also to encourage scientific thinking about phonetic issues. Although all the chapters can be read in any order, we recommend following the order given, since both the explanations and the exercises are cumulative in that later chapters are based on the contents explained in earlier ones so that previously presented technical terms are used without any further explanation.

Chapter 1 gives an overview of the fields of **phonetics** and **phonology**, paying particular attention to the notions of phoneme and allophone and to the structure of the syllable and syllabic sounds. After this, the sounds of RP are presented as a pronunciation model for SSLE in comparison with those of PSp. In addition, the main differences between broad (or phonemic) and narrow (or allophonic) transcriptions are noted, and practical tips are given on how to represent speech sounds more accurately in transcriptions than would be possible using ordinary spelling, bearing in mind the complex and often unpredictable relationship between spelling and pronunciation.

Chapter 2 summarises the principles of **articulatory phonetics**, describing the process that takes place between our lungs and our lips in the production of speech sounds. The organs of speech are described in relation to the function each plays in the articulation of speech sounds, noting that these organs are also involved in the realisation of other primary biological functions (e.g. breathing, licking and biting), as well as in the production of noises which are not speech sounds (e.g. coughing, sneezing and whistling). Descriptions are also provided of the speech organs and the air-stream mechanisms that are used to produce (pulmonic, glottalic and velaric) speech sounds, noting the action of the vocal cords that is responsible for the distinction between voiced and voiceless sounds. The chapter closes with a characterisation and classification of speech sounds in terms of their articulatory and acoustic features.

Chapter 3 describes RP **pure vowels** and **complex vowels** (or **vowel glides**) in comparison with those of PSp, while **Chapter 4** focuses on **consonants**, distinguishing four main groups: plosives, fricatives, affricates and approximants. In these two chapters each RP sound is described according to nine parameters: (1) **IPA symbol**, (2) **Identification**, (3) list of **Allophones**, (4) articulatory **Description**, (5) **Environment and main allophonic realisations**, offering a description of the main contexts of appearance of the sound in question as well as of its main realisations, (6) **Spellings**, (7) **Regional and social variants**, mentioning the most important alternative pronunciations of each sound in RP and other accents in order to show that pronunciation is not monolithic (see § 1.5), (8) **Comparison with Spanish and advice**, providing pronunciation tips that are essential for intelligibility or otherwise may be relevant to the imitation of a native-like accent, and (9) **Further practice**, which includes recorded (and transcribed) examples (extracted from our Sound Bank). The exercises included in these two chapters are specially devised to facilitate improvement targetting the potential weaknesses that speakers of Spanish may have to improve in their production and perception of RP sounds (e.g. difficult or subtle phonemic contrasts, sounds that exist in English but not in Spanish, and so on).

Chapter 5 explains common phenomena of **connected speech** in English: **coarticulation**, **assimilation**, **elision**, **linking**, **juncture** and **gradation**, the latter referring to the different realisations of sounds (i.e. weak vs. strong) that result from the metrical structure of speech and their position in the syllable. The chapter summarises the main variants (or **allophones**) of **RP phonemes** arising from the aforementioned phenomena with their corresponding notation conventions or diacritics, which show how sounds influence one another when put together in words, phrases, sentences and speech sequences. Roughly, what happens is that the faster we speak, the less carefully and clearly we distinguish the beginning of one word from the end of the previous one, and some features of final and initial sounds start merging together because of economy of articulatory effort (i.e. laziness).

In close connection with the above mentioned phenomena, **Chapter 6** concentrates on **stress**, **rhythm** and **intonation**. We shall see how words are stressed in isolation and in the stream of speech. Likewise, tonality, tonicity and tone are examined closely as the main constituents of intonation, and their functions are explained in detail.

Lastly, **Chapter 7** explores both the systematic and the unsystematic relationships between the **written** and **spoken forms** of English words. We believe it is important to know at least the main spelling patterns of each of the English phonemes because they can be used as predictors for pronunciation, although exceptions to general tendencies are also pointed out.

The **Answer Key** at the end of the book provides sample answers for the written exercises included in each chapter, as well as the phonetic transcriptions of the texts that are proposed as further transcription practice. These are complemented, as already noted, with the (audio) activities (and their keys), as well as the resources that are available on the **EPSS Multimedia Lab**. The volume closes with a **Reference** section listing the sources that are either cited throughout the text or included in the **Further Reading Section** of each chapter.

Given its practical orientation, the theory in the book has been kept as simple and accessible as possible. Our comparison of English and Spanish is based on prior literature but also on our own experience and observation over the years as university teachers of this subject. We accept responsibility for any weaknesses and errors in this respect. To find out more about the issues raised in EPSS the reader is referred to such textbooks as *Gimson's introduction to the pronunciation of English* (Cruttenden 2014), *English phonetics and phonology: an introduction* (Carr 2012), *Understanding phonetics* (Ashby 2011), *Practical phonetics and phonology* (Collins and Mees 2009), *An introduction to phonetics and phonology* (Clark *et al.* 2007), *Speech sounds* (Ashby 2006), *English phonetics and phonology* (Roach 2005), and *A manual of English phonetics and phonology* (Skandera and Burleigh 2005), to mention but a few. Other accounts of English phonetics and pronunciation that are specifically addressed to SSLE can be found in *La pronunciación del inglés británico simplificada* (Monroy Casas 2012), *Teach yourself English pronunciation* (Estebas Vilaplana 2009), *English phonetics and phonology for Spanish speakers* (Mott 2005), *Fonética inglesa para españoles* (Alcaraz and Moody 1993), *La pronunciación del inglés RP para hablantes de español* (Monroy Casas 1980), *A course in English phonetics for Spanish speakers* (Finch and Ortiz Lira 1982), *Manual de pronunciación inglesa comparada con la española* (Sánchez Benedicto 1980), *The sounds of English and Spanish* (Stockwell and Bowen 1965), and *Una comparación entre los sistemas fónicos del ingles y del español* (Lado 1965); while studies contrasting English with other languages are, for instance, *The phonetics of English and Dutch* (Collins and Mees 2003) and *Comparing the phonetic features of English, French, German, and Spanish* (Delattre 1965). Turning to texts on Spanish phonetics and phonology, we recommend *Manual de fonética española. Articulaciones y sonidos del español* (Martínez Celdrán and Fernández Planas 2007), *Tratado de fonología y fonética españolas* by Quilis (1993, 1985), *Estudios de fonología española* by Navarro Tomás (1966 [1946], 1991[1918]) and *Fonología española* (Alarcos LLorach 1961 [1983]).

With respect to the phonetic transcription system used, it is very similar to that utilised by Peter Roach, James Hartman and Jane Setter in their different editions of Daniel Jones's (*Cambridge*) *English Pronouncing Dictionary* (EPD) (2011; 15th, 16th and 17th edns. 1997, 2003, 2006) and by J. C. Wells in his *Longman Pronunciation Dictionary* (LPD) (2008; 1st and 2nd edns. 1990, 2000). If you are interested in transcription manuals in particular, we recommend Tench (2011), Lillo (2009), Monroy Casas (2001) and García Lecumberri and Maidment (2000), but if what you want is to practise English pronunciation, some classic books are Baker (2007), Arnold and Gimson (1976) and Gimson (1980).

EPSS provides transcriptions of English words that are frequent and/or somehow troublesome for foreign learners, as well as passages that illustrate the common processes of connected speech, with the intention of providing a natural and accurate representation of how native speakers sound. Phonetic transcription is necessary to raise awareness of the target that should be aimed at, as well as of the possible pronunciations to be expected from native speakers. But this is a skill that can be best mastered by regular practice. So, whether working alone or in a group (where you can learn from others), SSLE are encouraged to engage in the task itself as often as possible, first transcribing sets of words and then checking their progress with the help of the answers provided in the Appendix and the website, before moving on to more advanced transcriptions. It should be borne in mind, however, that the transcription keys provided are only model answers. This means that they are always acceptable, but not necessarily the only possible ones as there may be other alternatives since pronunciation is subject to more variation than any other aspect of language.

Finally, on the issue of speech analysis, we have used Speech Filing System (SFS 4.7 and SFS/WASP Version 1.54) for spectrographic and waveform analysis (Huckvale 2008), freely available at http://www.phon.ucl.ac.uk/resource/sfs/wasp.htm, while PRAAT 5.0.20 may be used for intonation curve analysis (Boersma and Weenink 2008), which can also be freely downloaded at http://www.fon.hum.uva.nl/praat/. Learners are advised to record their own pronunciation to use these audio files for reference and checking. Additional information and resources may be found in the corresponding sections of the EPSS Multimedia Lab.

Chapter 1
1 Phonetics and Phonology

1.1 Introduction

If we simplify the distinctions within the whole of linguistic science we can say that basically there are two kinds of branches: **external** and **internal** ones. External branches of linguistics deal with disciplines that can influence or be influenced by language (e.g. sociolinguistics, ethnolinguistics, psycholinguistics, neurolinguistics, etc.). In contrast, internal branches are concerned with the study of different aspects of language itself, such as **morphology** (the analysis of morphemes), **lexicology** (the study of words), **syntax** (the study of how words are used to create phrases, clauses and sentences), **semantics** (the exploration of meaning), or **pragmatics** and **discourse** (the analysis of individual utterances and of organised sets of utterances or text units in context).

Although in terms of methods they are certainly very different from the rest, **phonetics** and **phonology** can be regarded as two further interrelated internal fields of linguistics in that, broadly, both explore the **phonic** or **sound component** of language, an indispensable foundation of linguistic enquiry.[1] We do believe that the boundary between phonetics and phonology need not be sharply drawn, nor should it be constructed on assumptions about the primacy of one over the other. For, although we analyse speech by breaking it down into its several aspects, the reality is one of integration because speech sounds cannot be thoroughly studied exclusively in isolation without looking at their linguistic function and context, in much the same way that their function cannot be properly analysed without considering their articulatory and/or acoustic features (Lass 1984: 1). However, we shall distinguish phonetics from phonology for methodological reasons and because it seems true that phonetics can be studied without really exploring phonology, while phonology is closely dependent on phonetics for the data on which it relies to pursue its arguments (Gussenhoven and Jacobs 2005).

Ultimately, what this book shows is that one thing is to speak without deliberately pondering on what we are doing, and another is to study this process systematically for the purpose of its scientific analysis, as it happens in phonetics and phonology, two fields of linguistics that are being constantly updated and extended.

---

1 Other dimensions of phonetic and phonological analysis are: (1) the combinatory possibilities of the sounds (the **phonotactics** or syllable structure, see § 1.3.3); (2) the **prosody** of the language (pitch, loudness, length, accent, rhythm, intonation, see Chapter 6); and (3) the relationship between sounds and letters (**graphology** or **graphemics**, see Chapter 7).

1.2 Phonetics

Often depending more on data, scaled measurements, instruments and technologies than other areas of linguistics, **phonetics** is an empirical science (based on the observation of facts) which studies the concrete characteristics of human sound-making, especially **speech sounds**[2] but also involuntary noises (e.g. hiccups and coughing) as well as other aspects of voice. For the phonetician, sounds are phenomena in the physical world and phonetics provides information on their physical properties, allowing us to devise methods of sound description, classification and transcription (Crystal 2008: 363–364). Phonetic categories are thus generally defined using terms which have their origins in external disciplines such as anatomy, physiology and acoustics, so that consonant sounds, for example, are usually described by making reference to anatomical place of articulation (dental, palatal, etc.) and their physical makeup (the frequency and amplitude of consonantal sound waves). The discipline is often referred to as **general phonetics** because it is based on the assumption that the methods of analysis are equally applicable to the sounds of any language in the world, which reflects the phoneticians' attempts to discover the universal principles underlying the nature and use of speech sounds. **Experimental phonetics** is another term used to emphasise the "pure" scientific endeavour of general phonetics.

General phonetics, interpreted as involving general studies of speech sounds, is usually distinguished from **functional phonetics**, which investigates the phonetic properties of specific languages or how the sounds are used within the pronunciation system of a language, an approach which is usually carried out under the heading of **phonology**, which will be further described in section 1.3.

Three branches of phonetics are generally recognised depending on which phase of the **speech chain** (the process in which humans produce and hear speech) is being described: **articulatory, acoustic** and **auditory**. Our ability to communicate is apparently an easy and unremarkable action, but beneath the surface there are five complex processes at work labelled A to E in Figure 1 below (adapted from Denes and Pinson 1993: 5). Stages A and E involve the formulation and interpretation of the message in the brains of speaker and listener respectively, forming the link between phonetics and **psycholinguistics**. We are constantly monitoring our own speech by listening to our performance, a process termed **audio-feedback**, which is represented in the diagram as the

---

2 Speech sounds are a small subset of all the noises which humans can produce with their vocal apparatus in order to form words.

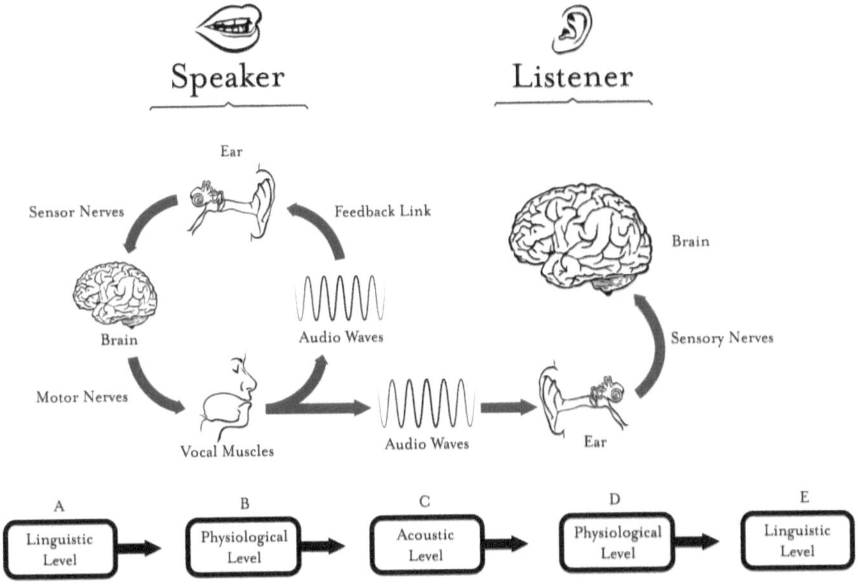

Figure 1: The speech chain

feedback link. Stage B symbolises the bodily function that is responsible for the production of speech sounds (**articulatory phonetics**). In Stage C the physical nature of speech sounds can be examined, as well as how they are transmitted through the air as sound waves (**acoustic phonetics**). Stage D corresponds to the way in which the addressee's ear perceives the speech signal (**auditory phonetics**).

We can thus conclude that phonetics analyses the anatomy and physiology of speech sounds, integrating the three aspects mentioned above, i.e. articulatory, acoustic and auditory/perceptual. The study of any of these aspects, involving appropriate instrumental analysis techniques (e.g. airflow measurement, speech synthesis, sound wave analysis, sampling, averaging, etc.) is covered by the umbrella term **instrumental phonetics**.

Phonetics plays an important role in the teaching of foreign languages and is also useful in the acquisition of good diction, in speech therapy for people with speech and hearing impediments, as well as in sound transmission and forensic linguistics. In what follows, separate sections will be devoted to describing articulatory, acoustic and auditory phonetics. The emphasis of this book is mainly on **articulatory phonetics**, but whenever necessary, acoustic and/or auditory considerations are also incorporated.

1.2.1 Articulatory Phonetics

Articulatory phonetics explores the nature and limits of the human ability to use the speech organs to articulate speech, despite organic differences, transforming aerodynamic energy into acoustic energy or **sound waves**, which are then perceived by the human auditory system as **speech sounds** (Laver 1994). Speakers differ organically from each other in anatomical factors such as the dimensions, mass and geometry of their vocal organs (e.g. the shape and size of the articulators and the speech cavities), and yet they may be judged to be producing linguistically and paralingistically identical utterances that are perceived as speech sounds. As a producer of speech sounds, you may be already aware, even if intuitively, of some aspects of articulatory phonetics. Now you need to deepen your awareness of the movements, gestures and feelings occurring in your **vocal tract** (VT) when producing speech sounds, and learn some specialised vocabulary to be able to verbalise such knowledge. For instance, we shall see that from an articulatory point of view the RP sound /p/ is a voiceless bilabial plosive because its production involves no vibration of the vocal cords, but a close compression of the lips and generally a palpable puff of air upon release from the mouth (see § 4.2.1.1).

Articulatory phonetics is the branch of phonetics most widely taught, underpinning both acoustic and auditory phonetics, in such wide-ranging disciplines as languages and linguistics, speech and language therapy, medical science, voice and singing studies, and drama, among others (Ashby 2011: 9). The principles and details of articulatory phonetics are further detailed in Chapters 2 to 5 when examining the production of speech, English vowels and consonants in comparison with those of Spanish, and connected speech phenomena, respectively.

1.2.2 Acoustic Phonetics

Acoustic phonetics studies the physical properties of speech sounds (e.g. frequency, amplitude, rate, etc.) as transmitted between mouth and ear (Crystal 2008: 7–8). Two instances of the same spoken sequence made by the same speaker are in fact most unlikely to be acoustically identical despite their phonetic likeness. Likewise, identical utterances from two different speakers are bound to be even more acoustically different. Acoustic measurements serve to support these and other articulatory or auditory judgements, the most widely used being those provided by **waveforms** and **spectrograms**.

The **waveform** of a sound represents a moving airstream which is modified by the articulators as it travels through the VT. Displaced particles of air move away from rest position and back to it, displacing other particles and causing them to repeat the same vibratory pendulum-like movement. This pattern of movement has the shape of a wave, and its acoustic representation is called a **sine** or **sinusoidal wave** on the grounds of certain mathematical properties that it has. Figure 2 below plots examples of sine waves, where the x axis indicates **time** in seconds or milliseconds (.001 second or 1 millisecond), and the y axis relative **intensity** in arbitrary units.

Waveforms may be **periodic** (as in Figure 2 (a) below) or **aperiodic** (as in Figure 2(b)). **Aperiodic waveforms** have no identifiable periodicity, and are characteristic of what we call **noise** (e.g. that produced by thunder, clapping hands and splashing water). **Periodic waveforms,** on the other hand, are more characteristic of speech, singing and birdsong, and can be described in terms of amplitude, intensity and frequency. The **amplitude** of the wave is the maximum distance that a particle moves in each direction from its starting point, that is the distance from the base line to the highest point of the curve. In general the greater the amplitude, the louder the sound is perceived to be. Amplitude correlates with **intensity**, which is measured in **decibels (dB)**. In Figure 2 (a) below we can see that the two sine waves have identical amplitude and intensity (vertical axis).

The **frequency** of a sound wave is the number of cycles (movement from rest position to position 2, back to position 3 and back to rest again) completed within a given limit of time (usually one second). Frequency is measured in **Hertz (Hz)**: one Hz equals one cycle per second. A cycle can be measured from any point on a wave to the next point. The **fundamental frequency** (**F_0**) of a sinewave is the number of times per second the vocal folds vibrate. At the same time as producing the fundamental frequency, a range of other higher frequencies called **overtones** or **harmonics** are also produced, which arise from the complex wave effects that occur when the vocal folds vibrate, a movement that can be viewed on stroboscopic images of vocal fold vibration and is often referred to as the **mucosal wave** (see § 2.2.2).

Harmonics are multiples of the fundamental frequency and contribute to the resonant **quality** or **timbre** of the sound. The arrow in Figure 2 (a) points to where the oscillation repeats itself at 0.004 seconds. This indicates that one cycle of this wave lasts 0.004 seconds, so its F_0 equals 1/0.004 seconds or 250 Hz. Then the second harmonic will be at approximately 500 Hz, the third at 750 and so on. These peaks of intensity are called **formants (F)** or VT resonances, and they are numbered upwards from the lowest in frequency. We shall see that the first two formants, F1 (**first formant**) and F2 (**second formant**) are related to vowel articulation (section 2.4.1). We perceive frequency as **pitch**. Pitch variation is produced primarily by stretching the length of the vocal folds which results in

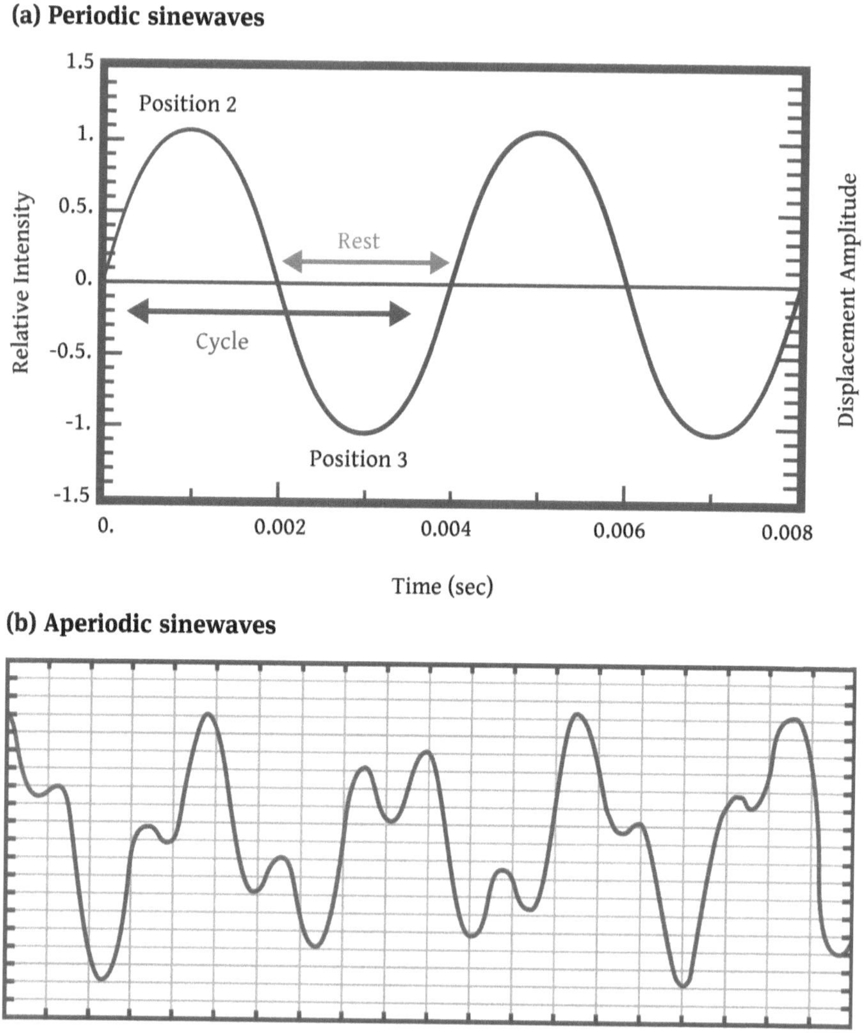

Figure 2: Periodic and aperiodic sinewaves

different intonation patterns and tonal distinctions on vowels. The higher the frequency, the higher the pitch. The range of pitch found in speech is about 60–500 Hz (men between 100 and 150 Hz, women between 200 and 325 Hz, and children around 265 Hz), although we do not usually use the entire range in speaking.

In Figure 3 below, sinewaves (a) and (b) have the same frequency (200 Hz) but different amplitudes, low (a) and higher (b); while sinewaves (c) and (d) share approximately the same amplitude, but differ in frequency: (c) has a low frequency and (d) a much higher one.

Figure 3: Sinewaves with different amplitudes and frequencies

In addition, periodic waveforms can be **simple sinewaves** or **complex** ones, which consist of more than one sinewave and can be broken down into these component waves. In speech all periodic waveforms are complex, an illustration of which is presented in Figure 4 below, consisting of three sinewaves with different amplitudes and frequencies (viz. 100Hz with the greatest amplitude, 200Hz with the smallest amplitude, and 300Hz with a medium one) (Ladefoged 1996).

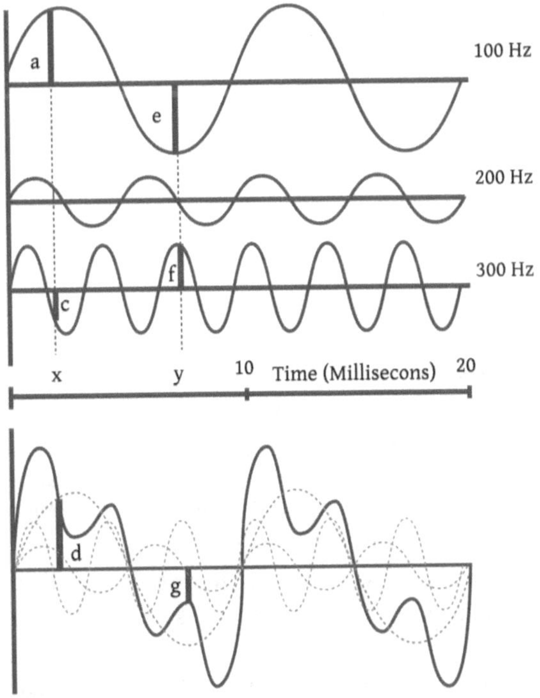

Figure 4: Constructing a complex wave

Spectrograms, on the other hand (also known as **spectral waterfalls**, **sonograms**, **voiceprints**, or **voicegrams**), are time-varying spectral representations (i.e. forming an image) that show how the spectral density of a sound varies with time. The instrument that generates a spectrogram is called a **spectrograph**. Spectrograms have a three-dimensional display. The horizontal axis represents **time**, the vertical axis **frequency**, and a third dimension indicates the **amplitude** of a particular frequency at a particular time, which is represented by the intensity, or concentration of energy at particular frequency bands (the formants) that stand out in darker colour in the image. Figure 5 below illustrates the speech waveform and wideband spectrogram for one realisation of the utterance "passed London".

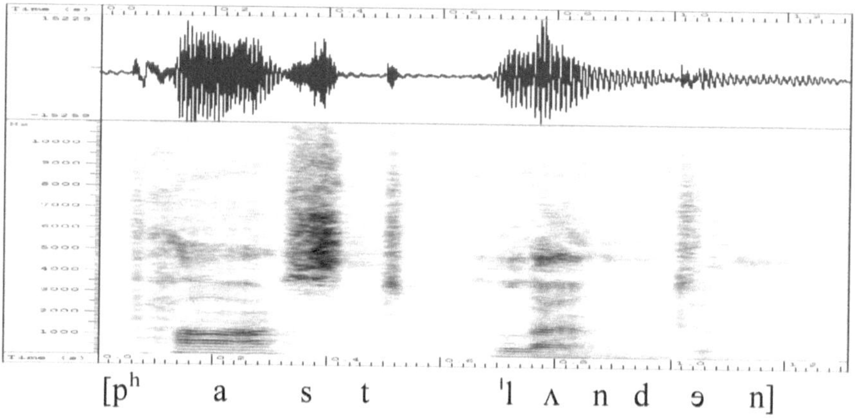

Figure 5: Speech waveform and spectrogram of "passed London"

Speech spectrograms are called **wideband** or **narrowband** depending on what window length is used, as shown in Figure 6 below containing the spectrographic representation of /m/ *in "machali"* (adapted from Jawale 2010).

The shorter the window, the larger its bandwidth. So if the window is shorter, the spectrogram is called **wideband**, and if the window is larger, **narrowband**. Wideband spectrograms are widely used in phonetics because they reflect a crucial feature of speech sounds, namely their **formant structure** (i.e. amplitude peak in the frequency spectrum of a sound); whereas narrowband spectrograms are less often used because they reveal **harmonic structure** (pitch), a kind of information which is of comparatively less importance to learners.

Acoustic measurements like those provided in Figure 6 below can be obtained quite easily using a computer, a microphone and freely downloadable

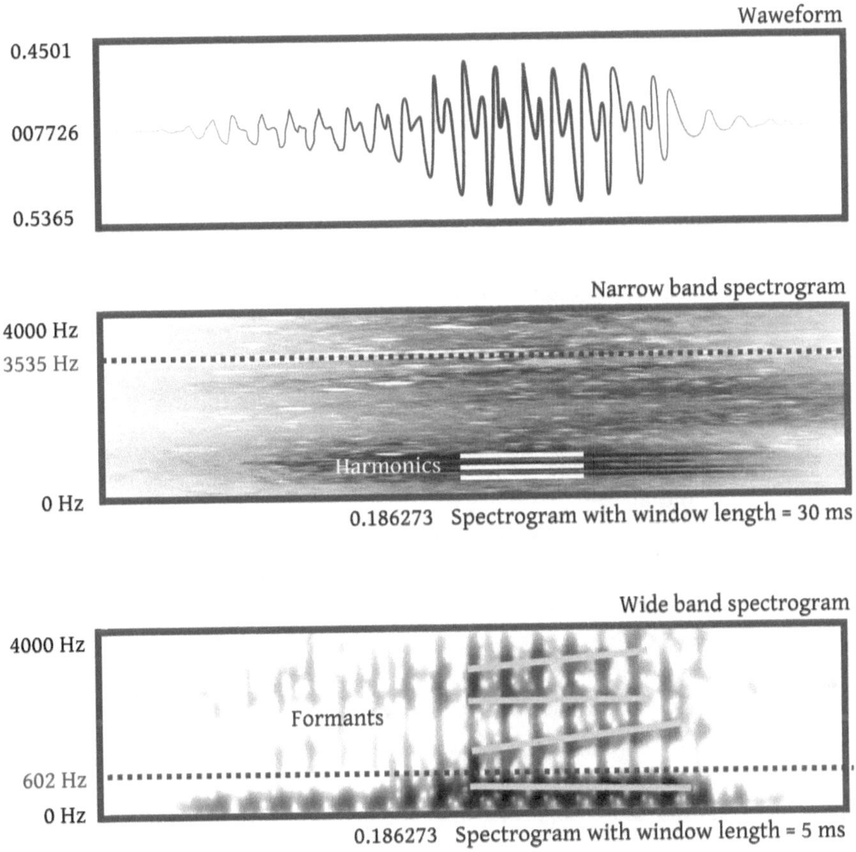

Figure 6: Narrowband and wideband spectrograms

software such as WASP or Praat. These programs allow us to process and analyse the acoustic recordings of speech. Increasingly today this kind of acoustic measurements and interactive displays are used in different disciplines such as forensics, psychology, speech therapy, pronunciation training, and language teaching, where interactive displays based on speech waveform analysis are increasingly used to assist specially foreign language learners in fine-tuning their pronunciations (Ashby 2011: 10), as in the case of Cabrera Abreu and Vizcaíno Ortega (2009). Chapter 2 offers acoustic representations of vowels and consonants (waveforms and spectrograms) and summarises the acoustic features of these speech sounds.

1.2.3 Auditory Phonetics

Phonetics is just as much about how we hear or perceive what is said as about how we say what we say. **Auditory phonetics** investigates the perceptual response to speech sounds, as mediated by ear, auditory nerve and brain (Crystal 2008: 44). Although the mental processes linked to the perception of speech are still largely unknown, we do know that the human ear can only hear sounds having certain characteristics. So the main interest of auditory phonetics lies in determining the processes whereby speakers discriminate speech sounds based on the perception of: (1) their temporal characteristics (i.e. perceived length); (2) their prosodic attributes (pitch, tone and loudness); and (3) the way these facets are interrelated with rhythm and stress in conformity with the metrical structure of speech.

Auditory phonetics underpins much of ear-training as well as practical phonetic training and accent coaching, which prove very useful for improving the pronunciation of a foreign language. So you would do well to try and identify (and reproduce) all the sounds of RP in comparison with those of PSp, as well as with the other sounds (and corresponding symbols) included in the IPA chart. At a more theoretical level, another dimension of auditory phonetics is the study of **speech perception** involving such aspects as the hearing mechanism and the effects of sounds on the brain which are explored by audiologists, psychologists, neurologists, and other specialists (Ashby 2011: 10).

1.2.4 The interface of the auditory, acoustic and articulatory levels

The categories recognised in auditory phonetics have correlates in acoustic and articulatory phonetics. Thus, as shown in Table 1 below (adapted from Alcaraz and Moody 1993: 13), we can say that pitch is articulatorily related to the position of the vocal folds and to the different articulations of speech sounds, on the one hand, and acoustically to the different formant structure of the spectrographic representation of such sounds, on the other.

Table 1: The interface of the auditory, acoustic and articulatory levels

Articulatory Phonetics	Acoustic phonetics	Auditory phonetics
Articulators	Formants	Pitch
Vocal folds	Frequency (n° cycles; wave; Hertz)	Tone
Effort/Intensity	Amplitude (intensity)	Loudness
Quantity/Duration	Rate / Tempo (pace delivery)	Length

Likewise, tone is articulatorily related with the action of the vocal cords, and acoustically, with the frequency of vibration of these organs; while loudness is in principle associated with articulatory effort and, acoustically, with amplitude. Lastly, length or duration relates to articulatory quantity and to rate or tempo in acoustic phonetics.

To summarise, remember that pitch, tone, loudness and length are psychological, perceptual characteristics, whereas formant structure, frequency, amplitude and rate are physical properties of speech sounds.

1.3 Phonology

Phonology is a branch of linguistics that studies the **systems** and **structures** of speech (Crystal 2008: 365–366) and intends to show how sounds function in a **systemic** way in a given language (Cruttenden 2014: 3). The term **system** indicates that we operate with the finite options that are available in a given language. The significance of any particular selection within a system lies in the contrast between what is selected and what could have been selected. Accordingly, in a phonological system, for example, the choices are limited and make sense only by reference to the system itself, a point which has long been recognised in discussion of **phonological distinctiveness** (Ball and Quayle 2009).

In contrast, the term **structure** suggests that choices are made within a "structured" scheme or framework, but sometimes it refers to the linear organisation of language. In this second sense, structure can be contrasted with **system**, reflecting the two dimensions of linguistic organisation that are often referred to as **paradigmatic** and **syntagmatic**, respectively. Paradigmatic relations are those that exist among the options in a system, for example between a phoneme and the other phonemes to which it is opposed. Syntagmatic relations, on the other hand, are linear or sequential, operative for example in the coarticulation or assimilation of adjacent sounds or in the organisation of alliteration or rhyme across longer stretches of language.

Sound systems comprise the meaningful relations and distinctions that exist among speech sounds across and within languages. Speech sounds are organised into a system of contrasts, which are analysed in terms of phonemes, distinctive features, combinations of sounds (sound structures such as syllables, words, etc.) or other phonological units according to the theory adopted. As a result, phonology is often said to be marked by abstraction and generality. It investigates what properties of speech sounds have a functional, communicative value. The aim of **phonologists** is to demonstrate the existence of distinctive sounds and patterns in a language, to investigate their function, behaviour and organisation, and to spell out the principles and rules underlying phonetic relationships, making as general statements as possible about the nature of sound systems.

If phonetics provides descriptions of sounds and ways of classifying them, phonology is a kind of functional phonetics which employs these data to classify the speech sounds of a language into a system of contrasts. For example, the English words, *pan, tan, can, ban, Dan, fan, van* and *ran*, illustrate a meaning-bearing or **contrastive opposition** that is triggered by their initial consonants /p t k b d f v r/. These consonants create a **phonological system** because they stand in potential distinctive opposition to each other. **Phonologists** are interested in determining such oppositions and use such terms as **distinctive, functional, contrastive** or **information-bearing** to refer to them.

Two branches of the subject are usually recognised: segmental and suprasegmental phonology. **Segmental phonology** analyses speech into discrete segments or sounds (e.g. (semi)vowels, (semi)consonants), while **suprasegmental or non-segmental phonology** analyses those features which extend over more than one segment, such as intonation patterns. A further distinction is made between **diachronic** and **synchronic phonology**: the former explores patterns of sound change in the history of language, while the latter investigates sound patterns regardless of the processes of historical change.

In the following sections we shall address key issues in phonological theory: (1) the difference between **phoneme** and **allophone** (Section 1.3.1); (2) some basic principles of **phonological analysis** (Section 1.3.2); and (3) the basics of the **syllable**, its **structure** in English and Spanish and **syllabic consonants** (Section 1.3.3).

1.3.1 Phone, phoneme and allophone

A **phone** (enclosed between square brackets, as in [p]) is a single phonetic segment, viewed in terms of its phonetic character without regard to its possible phonological status. The term "phone" is related to "phoneme" in the same way "morph" is related to "morpheme". A **phoneme** (enclosed between slant brackets, as in /p/) is an abstract segment in the phonological system of a particular language or speech variety that is generally described as the smallest linguistic unit which can make a difference in meaning (Jones 1967/1976). The notion originated from the need to establish patterns of organisation out of the indefinitely large range of sounds that may be used in languages. Phonemes stand in **constrastive distribution**, that is, they can occur in the same phonetic context and if they do, they produce a change of meaning. For example /d/ and /t/ are phonemes in English because both can occur word-finally and substituting one by the other (**substitution test**) triggers a change of meaning as in e.g. *bed – bet* /bed/ – /bet/. Such pairs of words (usually with different meanings) that differ only in one phoneme are called **minimal pairs.**

Closely related with this, another feature of phonemes is that they can be **contrasted**, that is, they can be characterised and opposed to or distinguished from the rest, in terms of the values they have as regards a limited set of **phonological features** (e.g. voice, place of articulation, manner of articulation, lip-rounding, back, central, etc.): different phonemes will have different phonological features.

A third feature of phonemes is that they are **limited** or fixed in number. We can only speak of the phonemes of some particular speech variety or a particular accent of a given language, because the number of phonemes varies from one language to another. Thus, in section 1.5 (see Table 4) it will be shown that RP has forty-nine phonemes, and PSp forty-two.

AI 1.1 Identification of phonemes

In addition, the notion of phoneme allows linguists to group together sets of phonetically similar phones as variants, or "members", of the same underlying unit. **Phones** are said to be realisations of one phoneme, and the variants are referred to as **allophones** of the phonemes. **Allophones** (represented between square brackets, as in [p^h]) are phonetically distinct realisations of a single phoneme that are contextually determined. There are two kinds of allophones:

(1) **intrinsic**, when they occur spontaneously as a result of the phonetic context (such as the nasalisations of vowels when followed by a nasal consonant); or
(2) **extrinsic**, which are produced systematically (without a physiological reason) by speakers of a certain language, as in the case of aspirated voiceless plosives at the beginning of stressed syllables in English (Tatham and Morton 2011).

Whether intrinsic or extrinsic, the allophones of a phoneme display three main characteristics:

(1) they exhibit **phonetic similarity**, that is, they show a similar phonetic make-up that allows us to relate them as variations of a particular phoneme;
(2) they do **not entail a change of meaning**; and

(3) they may stand in either **complementary distribution** or in **free variation.** Allophones are in complementary distribution when they occur in different, or mutually exclusive, phonetic environments (e.g. aspirated and unaspirated plosives in English); and they stand in free variation when they occur in the same phonetic context, usually as a result of regional, register or social pronunciation variants (see § 1.3.2).

To summarise, the phoneme can be described as an indivisible and minimally abstract structureless unit that has identifiable phonetic characteristics and may be realised in speech by phonetically different phones (its allophones) in the same or in different environments (Trask 2012). It is in this sense that phonemes may be viewed as a set of sounds: each member of this set is an allophone of the phoneme. The allophones of a phoneme, on the other hand, are united within it by their shared phonetic similarity and they may stand either in complementary distribution or in free variation.

The most important thing for communication is to be able to recognise and use not only the full set of phonemes of the language being used, but also its allophones, particularly those that stand in complementary distribution as they can cause intelligibility problems or otherwise can result in a foreign accent. For instance, an untrained English speaker can tell by simply listening that the two instances of [l] in *little* are not the same (clear [l] vs. dark [ɫ]), and yet s/he is aware that they correspond to one *l*-sound in English. Likewise, a Spanish speaker may not be aware of the fact that the two occurrences of [d] in the word *dedo* 'finger' are phonetically different ([dental plosive [d̪] vs. dental fricative [ð]), but s/he will certainly tell that the two phones correspond to one *d*-sound in Spanish. This can only be adequately explained by considering how speech sounds are produced (phonetics) in combination with how they function in a given language (phonology), which reinforces the idea presented in the Introduction, that phonetics and phonology are integrated.

1.3.2 Phonological analysis

A basic principle of phonological analysis consists in distinguishing **phonemes** from **allophones** (Crystal 2008: 361–362). By way of illustration, we can say that in RP /t/ and /p/ are two consonantal **phonemes** because they stand in **parallel** or **contrastive distribution**, as illustrated by a minimal pair such as *tin* – *pin*: if /t/ is replaced by /p/ (or vice versa) (**substitution test**) at the beginning of the segment *-in*, then we obtain two different English words, which have two different meanings.

AI 1.2 Contrastive distribution of phonemes in RP

In addition, in English /t/ has different **allophones** or realisational variants depending on the phonetic context in which this phoneme occurs and which therefore are said to be in **complementary distribution**, such as [t^h] ('aspirated'), [$t^{=}$] ('unaspirated'), [t^n] ('nasalised'), [t̬] ('voiced'), etc. We could then work out a phonological realisation rule that indicates the actual pronunciation of this phoneme in a number of contexts:

/t/ → [t^h] 'aspirated' /#_] 'word-initially' (one of the possible contexts)
→ [$t^{=}$] 'unaspirated' / [s_] 'after s'
→ [t^n] 'nasalised' / [_n] 'before nasal consonants'
→ [t̬] 'voiced' / V_V 'between vowels or in intervocalic position'

Figure 7: Realisation rule for some allophones of /t/

In Figure 7, the arrow head following the curly bracket means 'is realised as' or 'is pronounced as', while the slant line (/) separates the operation of the rule (to the left of it) from the environment (to the right), and the underscore (or underdash) (_) represents the position of the sound itself in relation to its environment. In addition, the "number sign", [#], indicates a word boundary; therefore (#_) means 'immediately after a word-boundary' and (_#) 'immediately before one'. Finally, [V_V] means 'between two vowels', and we can say "elsewhere" to cover all the other phonetic environments that fall outside the environments specified in a phonological rule. In section 1.4 more indications will be provided to help you transcribe English phonemes and their allophones.

For any particular system **biuniqueness** is a requirement. This implies that phones, phonemes and allophones can be unambiguously assigned to each other by means of general rules or strategies of pronunciation rather than by idiosyncratic adjustments to individual phonemes. Phonological relationships, however, are not always biunique. One phenomenon contributing to this lack of biuniqueness is **neutralisation**. A neutralisation occurs when two (or more) closely related phonemes that are in contrast with each other in most positions are non-contrastive in certain other positions. When this happens, the "opposition" between the two phonemes is said to be "neutralised". In English, for example, the voicing contrast is neutralised after initial [s-]. By way of illustration, [t, d] contrast in most environments: initially (*tip* – *dip* [tɪp, dɪp]), finally (*cat* – *cad* [kæt, kæd]), after [l] (*colt* – *cold* [kɒlt], [kəʊld]), and after nasals (*shunt* – *shunned* [ʃʌnt, ʃʌnd]). But after initial [s-], the voicing opposition is neutralised because only a voiceless (or devoiced) consonant may occur in this context, and as a result the contrast between [t] and [d] in that phonetic context does not exist, nor, similarly, is there a contrast between [p] and [b] or [k] and [g] in this environment (*sting* [stɪŋ], – *sdin]). A further neutralisation of the phonemic contrast between [s] and [z] can be observed in the formation of English plurals. After voiceless sounds, only the voiceless fricative [s] is possible (e.g. [-ps] *ropes*, [-ts] *bits*, [-ks] *docks*, [-fs] *waifs*, [-θs]) *breaths*); whereas after voiced sounds, only the voiced counterpart [z] occurs (e.g. [-bz] *robes*, [-dz] *bids*, [-gz] *dogs*, [-vz] *waves*, [-ðz] *lathes*). The [s] – [z] contrast is also neutralised in verb-endings (e.g. *laughs*, *waits*, *lives*) and in possessives (e.g. *John's*, *Jack's*). But in this case the environment is restricted to **obstruents**,[3] since [s, z] may still contrast after a **sonorant**[4] (e.g. *pence* – *pens* [pens, penz], *since* – *sins* [sins, sinz], *else* – *sells* [els, selz]).

The effect of a neutralisation, then, is the narrowing of a set of contrasts in a particular environment. There exist three main types of neutralisation. The first takes place when a language has a certain contrast but only one of the relevant phonemes in contexts of neutralisation. This is the case of English voiced [b, d, g] and voiceless plosives [p, t, k]. They occur in word-initial and word-medial positions, but only voiceless or devoiced plosives occur word-finally. Therefore, it can be concluded that the contrast of voicing is inoperative or neutralised word-finally (e.g. *tack* [tæk] – *tag* [tæg̊]). The second type of neutralisation may be represented by some kind of variation or alternation among the otherwise contrasting phonemes. For example, in English a nasal consonant tends to be **homorganic** (i.e. produced in the same place of articulation) with a following stop within a word, and so we can say that when this happens the contrast with other non-homorganic nasals is neutralised in this context (nasal + plosive). Take, for example, the case of the homorganic series bilabial nasal and plosive [mb, mp] (*co<u>mb</u>at, i<u>mp</u>lausible*). In this context the contrast between [m] and [n] is neutralised because non-homorganic series [nb, np] are not possible (**co**nb**at*, **in**p**lausible*).

Alternatively, neutralisation may be represented by **free variation**, or "either or relations". Free variation occurs when two (or more) sounds or phones appear in the same environment (**parallel distribution**) without a change in

---

3 **Obstruent** is cover-term for sounds produced with a constriction which impedes the flow of air through nose or mouth, as in **plosives**, **fricatives** and **affricates** (Crystal 2008: 338).

4 **Sonorant** sounds are defined articulatorily, as those produced with a relatively free airflow and vocal fold vibration (voiced), as in **vowels**, **liquids**, **nasals** and **laterals** (Crystal 2008: 442).

meaning and without being considered incorrect by native speakers, as in alternative pronunciations of the same words in regional, register or social variants (e.g. ***either*** [eɪðə] vs. [iːðə]) or in individual speakers' variants ("prestige", personal style, pathologies, etc.) (e.g. as when speakers articulate the word *pit* with a released or an unreleased plosive) (see Sections 4.2.1.1 and 5.2.6 for a discussion of the types of plosive release and released sounds, respectively). The phonemes and realisations of phonemes (allophones) that stand in parallel distribution are called **free variants** as opposed to **contrastive variants** and **contextual variants** which are found in cases of contrastive (phonemes) and complementary distribution (allophones), respectively (see § 1.3.1).

In terms of phonological analysis, there are three ways of treating neutralisations:

(1) to abandon biuniqueness (no indeterminacy when invoking grammatical or semantic relationships);
(2) to insist that sounds representing neutralisations must be treated as allophones of a phoneme (e.g. word-final voiceless plosives are taken at face value): voiced plosives do not occur word-finally; or
(3) to recognise the notion of **archiphoneme**, which consists of the shared features of two (or more) closely-related phonemes, but excludes the feature which distinguishes them (Trubetzkoy 1969: 79). Thus the archiphoneme of [p b] consists of the features [bilabial and plosive] (but excludes voicing, which separates them); the archiphoneme of [s z] is [alveolar, fricative]; the archiphoneme of [m n ŋ] is [nasal]; and so on. For transcription purposes, the symbols [P T K] can be used to represent the archiphonemes of [p b], [t d] and [k g], respectively.

The concept of neutralisation must be distinguished from a superficially similar phenomenon known as **defective distribution**. Defective distribution means that a sound does not occur in all possible environments and as a result its distribution is said to be "incomplete". Three examples of sounds showing defective distributions are RP [ŋ], [h] and [f]. [ŋ] may follow a short vowel, but not a long vowel, and it can occur finally, but not initially. On the other hand, [h] can occur initially in a syllable, but not finally, and it can precede a glide consonant ([hj-, hw-]), but not a **liquid**[5] (*[hl-] *[hr-]); while [f] can occur initially (*fine*), medially (*wafer*) and finally (*knife*), but not before another obstruent word-initially (e.g. *[fp-], *[ft-]).

5 The term **liquid** is used collectively to refer all the apico-alveolar sounds (made by placing the tip of the tongue in the alveolar ridge) of the types [l] and [r] (Crystal 2008: 286).

The following series of words illustrate the realisation of the phonemic contrasts between English /t/ and /d/ and Spanish /m/ and /n/ in various word positions, as well as the neutralisation processes that occur both in English and Spanish concerning /t/ – /d/, /p/ – /b/, /k/ – /g/ and /m/ – /n/.

English:

/t/ – /d/ as distinct phonemes: ***t**ip* – ***d**ip*; *ca**t*** – *ca**d***; *col**t*** – *col**d***; *shun**t*** – *shunne**d**.*

/t/ – /d/ as neutralised phonemes: *s**t**rain* – *its **d**rain.*

/p/ – /b/ as neutralised phonemes: *s**p**eak* – *its **b**eak.*

/k/ – /g/ as neutralised phonemes: *s**c**ore* – *it's **g**ore.*

Spanish:

/m/ – /n/ as distinct phonemes: ***m**apa* 'map' – ***n**apa* 'synthetic leather', *ma**m**á* 'mom' – *ma**n**á* 'manna'.

/m/ – /n/ as neutralised phonemes: hoNbre 'man'.

1.3.3 Phonological structure

Most native speakers of a language can usually give a quick answer if asked to count the number of syllables in a given word. However, although this division seems quite simple and straightforward, it is very frequent to find disagreement among speakers on the syllabic division of certain "problematic" words, and problems also arise when trying to provide a definition of this linguistic concept that is unanimously agreed upon.

Section 1.3.3.1 offers a brief summary of the main definitions of the **syllable**. After this, Section 1.3.3.2 gives an overview of the **phonotactic possibilities** of English and Spanish, that is, the vowel-consonant combinations which are possible in syllable-initial and syllable-final positions in these two languages, and it also provides advice to SSLE on the acquisition of English consonant clusters. Closing our description of phonological structure, Section 1.3.3.3 focuses on a specific syllable type, that having a **syllabic consonant** as a nucleus.

1.3.3.1 The syllable

Words can differ from each other not only in terms of which sounds they consist of, but also in terms of the particular sequence of consonants and vowels that gives them their structural shape. Languages have different restrictions on the **combinatory possibilities** and **distribution** of speech sounds within words, and this is the major concern of **phonotactics**: a discipline of linguistics that explores the combinatorial constraints and possibilities within **syllable structure**, as already noted in the introduction.

The syllable has been defined as a "unit at a higher level than that of the phoneme or sound segment, yet distinct from that of the word or morpheme" (Gimson 1980: 55–57). Two types of approaches have been adopted to define the term:

(1) a **phonetic** approach, which tries to provide a universal definition of the concept; and
(2) a **linguistic** or **functional** approach, which makes reference to the structure of a particular language.

In the phonetic approach, syllables are generally described as consisting of a **centre** (**nucleus** or **peak**), which involves little or no obstruction to the airflow and is perceived as comparatively loud (Roach 2005: 67). This **nuclear place** is generally realised by **vowels** although in some circumstances it may also be filled by a **consonant**, as in the third syllable of the word *eleven* [ɪˈlevn̩] (Section 1.3.3.2).[6] **Minimum syllables** consist only of a nucleus (e.g. /ɑː/ *are*, /ɔː/ *or*). In addition, before or after the nucleus, that is, at the beginning (**onset**) or end (**coda**) of the syllable, there may also be greater obstruction to the airflow and/or less sound. Syllables may thus consist of an **onset**, followed by a **nucleus** and a **coda** (e.g. /gʊd/ *good*), or else they may just consist of either an **onset** and a **nucleus** (e.g. /tiː/ *tea*) or a **nucleus** and a **coda** (e.g. /ɪz/ *is*). The notion of **rhyme**, comprising the peak (or non-consonantal segment(s)) and the coda (the final consonantal segment(s)), is used to postulate a close relationship between these two elements that is distinct from the onset (initial consonantal segment(s)) because, among other things, word stress is assigned considering only the elements of the rhyme (**rhyme projection principle**), as shown in Figure 8 which plots the relative prominence and boundaries of the three syllables in the word *forbidden*.

6 Sounds are usually represented along a "sonority hierarchy" depending on their "carrying power" or relative sonority: at the top are open vowels, followed by close vowels, laterals, nasals, approximants, trills, fricatives, affricates and plosives, and flaps at the end; and, generally, voiced sounds are more prominent than voiceless ones (Cruttenden 2014) (see § 1.3.3.3).

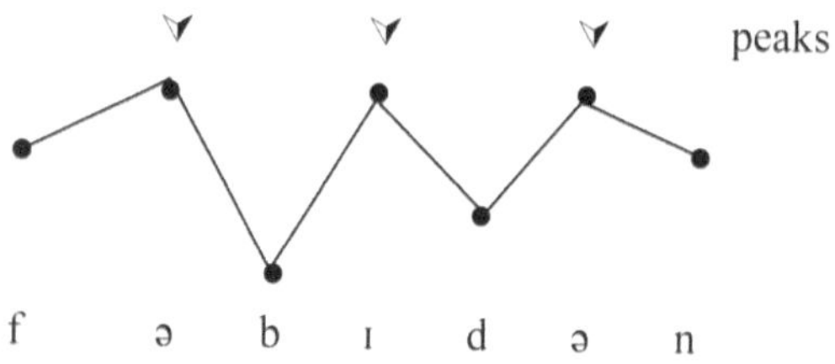

Figure 8: Plotting syllable prominence and syllable boundaries

AI 1.3 Identification of a short vowel as syllabic nucleus

In the linguistic (functional or phonological) approach, syllables are examined taking into account the possible combinations of phonemes that occur in a given language. **Syllabic structure** differs from one language to another in terms of such parameters as how many consonants can occur in the onsets and codas of syllables, or whether vowels can occur without consonantal onsets (**syllables with zero onsets**), or whether both **open syllables** (those ending in a vowel) and **closed** or **checked syllables** (those ending in a vowel) are possible.[7]

As an illustration, the three English words /tʌk/ *tuck*, /trʌk/ *truck*, and /strʌk/ *struck* are all structurally different. Using C to mean 'a consonant' and V to mean 'a vowel' (a diphthong is considered as one unit and is thus represented as a single V), structural formulae for these three words are CVC, CCVC and CCCVC, respectively. Series of two Cs or more indicate the presence of a **consonant cluster**, that is, a group of consonant sounds that appear together without an intervening vowel in any possible position in a word. Formulae of this sort are usually used to comment on the phonological structure of individual syllables. If we go back now to the notion of minimal pair, in the light of syllable structure, we could say that, while /pæn/ *pan* and /tæn/ *tan*, both of CVC structure, form a minimal pair in English, /pæn/ *pan* and /tæp/ *tap* do not because, although both are also of CVC structure, they differ in more than one structural place. The words /spæn/ *span* and /tæn/ *tan* do not form a minimal pair either, because their structures (CCVC and CVC) are not identical.

1.3.3.2 Syllabic patterns in English and Spanish and advice

Now let us compare the syllabic patterns of English and Spanish outlined in Table 2 below (adapted from Gallardo del Puerto 2005: 208–225; see also Gimson 1984: 237; Roach 2005: 73–77; Cruttenden 2014: 259–267).

7 **Checked vowels** are those that occur in checked or closed syllables (Crystal 2008: 74).

Table 2: Syllable patterns in English (RP) and Spanish (PSp)

PATTERNS			ENGLISH	SPANISH
			Open syllables	
1	V		/eɪ/ *a*	/i/ *y*
2	CV		/peɪ/ *pay*	/mi/ *mi*
3	CCV		/preɪ/ *pray*	/tri/ *triturar*
4	CCCV		/spreɪ/ *spray*	
			Closed syllables	
1	VC		/iːt/ *eat*	/ar/ *árbol*
2	VCC		/iːts/ *eats*	/eks/ *extra*
3	VCCC		/ɑːskt/ *asked*	
4	CVC		/biːt/ *beat*	/sol/ *sol*
5	CVCC		/biːts/ *beats*	/teks/ *texto*
6	CVCCC		/θæŋks/ *thanks*	
7	CVCCCC		/teksts/ *texts*	
8	CCVC		/kwiːn/ *queen*	/tren/ *tren*
9	CCVCC		/kwiːnz/ *queens*	/trans/ *transcribir*
10	CCVCCC		/trʌŋks/ *trunks*	
11	CCCVC		/striːt/ *street*	
12	CCCVCC		/striːts/ *streets*	
13	CCCVCCC		/stræŋgl̩/ *strangle*	
14	CCCVCCCC		/stræŋgl̩d/ *strangled*	
Initial clusters	**CC**	/tw/	*tweed*	*tuétano*
		/kw/	*question*	*cueva*
		/pj/	*pure*	*pié*
		/tj/	*tube*	*tiene*
		/kj/	*cure*	*quiere*
		/pr/	*prime*	*preso*
		/br/	*brie*	*brasa*
		/tr/	*tree*	*triturar*
		/dr/	*draw*	*dragón*
		/kr/	*crew*	*cruz*
		/gr/	*green*	*gramo*
		/pl/	*plant*	*pleno*
		/bl/	*blue*	*blusa*
		/kl/	*clue*	*cloro*
		/gl/	*glue*	*glucosa*
		/fr/	*free*	*Francia*
		/θr/	*three*	X
		/ʃr/	*shrink*	X
		/fl/	*flee*	*flojo*
		/sp/	*spy*	X
		/st/	*stay*	X
		/sk/	*sky*	X

Table 2: (continued)

PATTERNS			ENGLISH	SPANISH
		/sf/	*sphere*	X
		/sm/	*smog*	X
		/sn/	*snake*	X
		/sl/	*slay*	X
		/sw/	*swim*	*suave*
		/sj/	*assume*	*siento*
Initial clusters	**CCC**	/spl/	*splash*	X
		/spr/	*spray*	X
		/str/	*street*	X
		/skr/	*screen*	X
		/spj/	*spurious*	X
		/stj/	*stew*	X
		/skw/	*squid*	X
		/skj/	*skew*	X
Final clusters	**CC**	/pt/	*opt*	X
		/bd/	*described*	X
		/kt/	*sect*	X
		/gd/	*begged*	X
		/θt/	*earthed*	X
		/ðd/	*breathed*	X
		/ft/	*soft*	X
		/vd/	*curved*	X
		/st/	*fast*	X
		/zd/	*raised*	X
		/ʃt/	*washed*	X
		/ʒd/	*camouflaged*	X
		/sk/	*ask*	X
		/sp/	*wasp*	X
		/tʃt/	*watched*	X
		/dʒd/	*judged*	X
		/mp/	*camp*	X
		/nt/	*ant*	X
		/ŋk/	*think*	X
		/nd/	*and*	X
		/md/	*seemed*	X
		/ŋd/	*longed*	X
		/lt/	*belt*	X
		/lp/	*help*	X
		/lk/	*milk*	X
		/tθ/	*eighth*	X
		/dθ/	*width*	X
		/ps/	*cops*	X

Table 2: (continued)

PATTERNS			ENGLISH	SPANISH
		/bz/	*jobs*	X
		/bs/	X	*substraer*
		/ts/	*cuts*	X
		/dz/	*beds*	X
		/ds/	X	*adscrito*
		/ks/	*sex*	*exponer*
		/gz/	*legs*	X
		/fθ/	*fifth*	X
		/fs/	*cliffs*	X
		/vz/	*halves*	X
		/θs/	*baths*	X
		/ðz/	*bathes*	X
		/nθ/	*tenth*	*Sánz*
		/ŋθ/	*length*	X
		/mf/	*triumph*	X
		/ns/	*sense*	*instinto*
		/nz/	*cans*	X
		/mz/	*comes*	X
		/ŋz/	*songs*	X
		/lf/	*golf*	*golf*
		/lv/	*twelve*	X
		/ls/	*else*	*vals*
		/lz/	*tells*	X
		/lθ/	*wealth*	X
		/lʃ/	*Welsh*	X
		/ntʃ/	*branch*	X
		/ndʒ/	*change*	X
		/tn/	*button*	X
		/dn/	*garden*	X
		/lm/	*elm*	X
		/tl/	*battle*	X
		/dl/	*pedal*	X
		/rs/	X	*perspicacia*
Final clusters	**CCC**	/spt/	*grasped*	X
		/skt/	*asked*	X
		/mpt/	*bumped*	X
		/ŋkt/	*linked*	X
		/lpt/	*helped*	X
		/lkt/	*milked*	X
		/ntʃt/	*launched*	X
		/ndʒd/	*changed*	X
		/ltʃt	*filched*	X
		/ldʒd/	*divulged*	X

Table 2: (continued)

PATTERNS		ENGLISH	SPANISH
	/pst/	*eclipsed*	X
	/tst/	*mightst*	X
	/dst/	*midst*	X
	/kst/	*text*	X
	/mft/	*triumphed*	X
	/lvd/	*involved*	X
	/lst/	*whilst*	X
	/dnt/	*hadn't*	X
	/znt/	*hasn't*	X
	/vnt/	*haven't*	X
	/pts/	*opts*	X
	/kts/	*products*	X
	/sps/	*grasps*	X
	/sts/	*atheists*	X
	/sks/	*masks*	X
	/fts/	*lifts*	X
	/mps/	*camps*	X
	/nts/	*ants*	X
	/ndz/	*winds*	X
	/ŋks/	*thanks*	X
	/lps/	*helps*	X
	/lbz/	*bulbs*	X
	/lts/	*belts*	X
	/ldz/	*worlds*	X
	/lks/	*silks*	X
	/pθs/	*depths*	X
	/tθs/	*eighths*	X
	/dθs/	*widths*	X
	/ksθ/	*sixth*	X
	/fθs/	*fifths*	X
	/mfs/	*triumphs*	X
	/nθs/	*months*	X
	/lfs/	*Ralph's*	X
	/lvz/	*wolves*	X
	/lθs/	*wealths*	X
	/lfθ/	*twelfth*	X
	/lmz/	*films*	X

In Table 2 you can see that neither English nor Spanish exploit all the possible combinations of phonemes within the syllable because they are not allowed by the phonological patterns (or **phonotactics**) of these two languages. It can also be observed that English has a wider range of syllable patterns than Spanish. As will be explained, besides three-consonant codas, English also admits the possibility of four-consonant codas generally resulting from the addition of tense and/or number endings to three-consonant codas (*glimpsed* /glɪmpst/, *twelfths* /twelfθs/). Neither coda type is found in Spanish and two-consonant codas are very infrequent (Gallardo del Puerto 2005: 208–225).

English permits open syllables with a maximum of three consonants in their onsets, and closed syllables with up to four consonants in their codas, which makes at least eighteen syllabic patterns: four onset and fourteen coda patterns (Gimson 1984: 237; Roach 2005: 73–77; Cruttenden 2014: 259–267). The **four onset patterns** that may occur in **open syllables** are listed as patterns 1 to 4 in Table 2. Now some specifications should be made about patterns 3 and 4. In **pattern 3, CCV** (/pleɪ/ *play*), CC is either /s/ + /t w m/ (/steɪ/ *stay*, /swæm/ *swam*, /smæʃ/ *smash*) or C + /l r w j/ (/kleɪ/ *clay*, /traɪ/ *try*, /kwɪk/ *quick*, /ˈfjuːəl/ *fuel*). This suggests that that initial two-consonant clusters may follow one of two possible patterns: /s/ + /t w m/ or C (one of a set of fourteen consonants) + /l r w j/. Turning to **pattern 4**, CCCV = /s/ + /p t k/ + /l r j w/ (/sprei/ *spray*, /stjuːd/ *stewed*, /skwɔːk/ *squawk*, /skwiːl/ *squeal*). This specification indicates that onsets with three-consonant clusters have to consist of initial /s/, followed by one element of the /p t k/ set, and a third one from /r l j w/. Note that there is a constraint to the effect that when the third consonant is /w/, the first two consonants must be /s/ and /k/ (/skwɔːk/ *squawk*, /skwiːl/ *squeal*). Further combinatorial constraints on CCCV patterns determine that /spr/ and /str/ are both permitted, but /spw/ and /stw/ are not.

Turning to **closed syllables**, Table 2 above lists the **fourteen coda patterns** that occur in English. However, there exist a number of restrictions regarding the types of consonants that may be combined in closed syllables, the most important ones being:

(1) /r h j w/ do not combine with other consonants in final positions.

(2) **CC coda clusters** result from the following combinations: /p t k/ + /t s θ/ (/biːts/ *beats*, /striːts/ *streets*, /iːts/ *eats*)), /b d g/ + /d z/ (/begd/ *begged*), /tʃ/ + /t/ (/bliːtʃt/ *bleached*), /ʤ/ + /d/ (/brɪʤd/ *bridged*), nasal + plosive, fricative or affricate (/kwiːnz/ *queens*), fricative + plosive (/briːðd/ *breathed*), /l/ + stops (plosives or nasals) or fricatives (/kɔːld/ *called*).

(3) **CCC coda clusters** predominantly follow short vowels and result from three main patterns: /p t d k/ + /ts st θs sθ/ (/siksθ/ *sixth*), nasal or /l/ + a plosive-plosive, plosive-fricative, fricative/affricate-plosive (/θæŋks/ *thanks*, /trʌŋks/

trunks, /stræŋgl̩/ *strangle*), and /s/ + a plosive-plosive or a plosive-fricative combinations (ɑːskt/ *asked*).

(4) **CCCC coda clusters** occur only rarely and are the result of attaching /t/ or /s/ morphemes to CCC (/teksts/ *texts*, /siksθs/ *sixths*, /glɪmpst/ *glimpsed*).

Recapitulating what has been just described, Figure 9 below represents the structure of the syllable in English. It shows that slots 1, 2 and 6 tend to be occupied by "pure" consonants, whereas slots 3 and 5 are filled by one approximant /l r w j/ (see Sections 2.3.2.3 and 4.2.4) or the homorganic nasal phoneme /n/; while slot 4 is occupied by a vocalic element (or a sequence of them), and positions 7 and 8 are usually realised by morphological endings (e.g. /s z/, /t d/) (Knowles 1974).

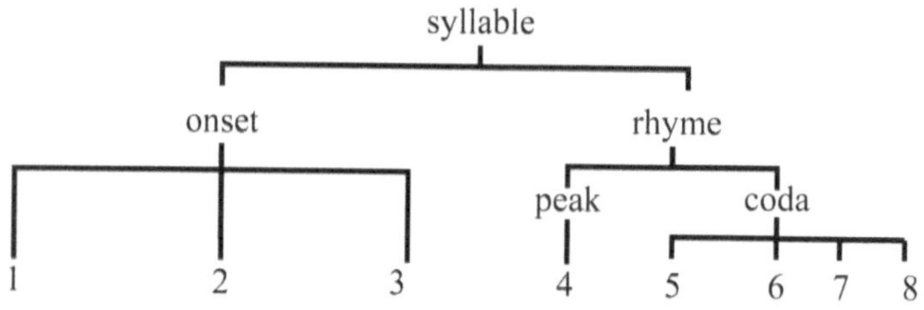

Figure 9: The structure of the syllable in English

Spanish, on the other hand, permits open and closed syllables with up to two consonants in their onsets and codas, which adds to at least nine possible syllable patterns: **three onset** and **six coda patterns**, which are illustrated in Table 2 and are reproduced below for clarity of exposition as (1) to (3) and (4) to (9) below, respectively (Quilis 1993; Quilis and Fernández 1996):

(1) **V** (/i/ *y* 'and', /oi/ *hoy* 'today')
(2) **CV** (/mi/ *mi* 'my', /su/ *su* 'his, her')
(3) **CCV** (/fru-/ as in *triturar* 'grind', *fruta* 'fruit')
(4) **VC** (/ar/ as in *arbol* 'tree');
(5) **VCC** (/eks/ as in *extra* 'extra');
(6) **CVC** (/sol/ *sol* 'sun');
(7) **CVCC** (/teks/ as in *texto* 'text');
(8) **CCVC** (/tren/ *tren* 'train');
(9) **CCVCC** (/trans/ as in *transcribir* 'transcribe').

Taking the above into account we can conclude that in English there is a predominance of closed syllables and there exists a wider variety of syllable structures (17 vs. 9), favouring consonantal clusters in both onsets and codas that are not allowed in Spanish. In Spanish, on the other hand, open syllables are strongly favoured and syllables ending with consonants are less common, the dominant syllable pattern being CV, followed by CVC. Onset and coda clusters have a maximum of two consonants, words having two consonants in coda position being mostly of foreign origin (*duplex*).

Spanish learners are thus advised to pay particular attention to the eight English syllabic patterns that have no correlate in Spanish: CCCV, VCCC, CVCCC, CVCCCC, CCVCCC, CCCVC, CCCVCC and CCCVCCC. Yet another difference between English and Spanish is that, while in Spanish the V element of the syllable can only be a vowel, in English it can quite frequently be a **sonorant consonant** /**l r m n ŋ**/, which therefore becomes **syllabic**, as is explained in Section 1.3.3.3.

Consonant clusters may be problematic for SSLE (Sedláčková 2010; Gallardo del Puerto 2005: 316–322; 356–358, 373–375, 407–427, 437–450; Estebas Vilaplana 2009: 63, 98–117). In principle, initial consonant clusters that are shared by both languages should pose little or no difficulty: /**pl**/ (*plant – planta*), /**pr**/ (*promise – promesa*), /**bl**/ (*blouse – blusa*), /**br**/ (*broccoli – brócoli*), /**tr**/ (*trace – traza*), /**dr**/ (*drug – droga*), /**kl**/ (*class – clase*), /**kr**/ (*crisis – crisis*), /**gl**/ (*glory – gloria*), /**gr**/ (*great – grande*), /**fl**/ (*flower – flor*) and /**fr**/ (*frank – franco/a*). If the same consonant appears twice in spelling, the pronunciation only involves one sound (*le**tt**er* /ˈletə/). There are two exceptions to this tendency. One is when the same affricate is pronounced twice in a sequence, as in *ri**ch** **ch**urch* /rɪtʃ tʃɜːtʃ/, *oran**g**e **j**am* /ˈɒrɪndʒ dʒæm/; and the other is when the two consonants belong to different grammatical categories, as in *mi**dd**ay* /ˌmɪdˈdeɪ/ (prefix + root), *drunke**nn**ess* /ˈdrʌŋkənnəs/ (root + suffix), *par**t-t**ime* /ˌpɑːt ˈtaɪm/ (compound), *la**te** **t**rain* /ˈleɪt ˈtreɪn/, in which case double sounds are pronounced like single sounds but with longer duration, even though two sounds appear in transcriptions.

More troublesome seem to be those consonant clusters that exist in English but do not occur in Spanish, in which case SSLE usually opt for either **cluster reduction** (**simplification**) or the **substitution** or **adjustment** of the sound that is alien to them so as to come "closer" to Spanish pronunciation. In the former case frequently the final consonant(s), generally /t/, /d/, /k/ or /s/, are omitted so that such words as *tex**ts*** /teksts/, *talke**d*** /tɔːkt/ and *complaine**d*** /kəmˈpleɪnd/ may be mispronounced as *[teks], *[tɔːk] and *[kəmˈpleɪn] and the listener will understand a singular referent and present actions rather than plural referents and past actions, respectively. But there may be cases in which the middle consonant (*chil**d**'s* *[tʃaɪlz], *ni**n**e years* *[naɪjɪəz]) or the last two consonants (*hol**ds*** *[xol]) are dropped.

Turning to adjustments, the most common one is that of initial English clusters beginning with /s/, not found in Spanish, which tend to be wrongly pronounced with a preceding **epenthetic**, or "added", /e/ sound. As a result, such words as *star* and *smart* may be mispronounced as *[esˈtar] and *[esmart], instead of /stɑː/ and /smɑːt/ (Carlisle 1998; Sedláčková 2010). Otherwise, a vowel, usually [e], may also be inserted between the two final consonants, and so words such as *strangle* /stræŋgl̩/ and *talked* /tɔːlkt/ may be wrongly pronounced as *[ˈstræŋgel] and *[ˈtɔːlked], causing a strong foreign accent effect because either a pronunciation with [ə] or preferably one with no vowel between the consonants would sound closer to native.

Other phenomena resulting from universal co-articulatory tendencies may also occur such as **devocing** of word-final sounds (*climbed* *[klaɪmt], *love* *[lʌf], *years* *[jɪəs], *matches* *[mætʃɪs], *evenings* *[iːvnɪŋks], *mornings* *[mɔːnɪŋks], *pads* *[pæts], *always* *[ɔːlweɪs], *lose* *[luːs]), **fricativisation** of word-final plosives (*helped* *[xelps]), and **metathesis**, or the alteration of the order of phonemes in a word (*last* *[lats]).

SSLE should be aware of these mispronunciations and should try to pronounce English consonant clusters appropriately so as to avoid communication and intelligibility problems. This is particularly relevant for speakers of some Spanish accents, such as the Andalusian accent, in which word-final consonants, especially [s], tend to be dropped.

1.3.3.3 Syllabic consonants

Syllabic consonants are widely produced in various registers in English (Jones 1967/1976; Roach, Sergeant and Miller 1992) but they do not occur in Spanish (Finch and Ortiz Lira 1982). Marked with a short vertical stroke beneath the consonant symbol [n̩], syllabic consonants frequently occur in CC̩ syllabic patterns that generally result from the weakening, or reduction, of CəC syllables (*eleven* [ɪˈlevn̩]). Such syllabics are pronounced as the centre of the syllable instead of a vowel, after a preceding consonant in post-tonic unstressed positions and almost always just before a morpheme boundary, as in, for instance, [ˈbɒtl̴̩ŋ] *bottle* and [ˈbɒtl̴̩ŋɪŋ] *bottling*. In RP there are four consonants that can be syllabic: [ɫ̩] /l̩/, perhaps the most noticeable example, and [n̩ m̩ ŋ̍]. /r/ may also be syllabic in rhotic accents,[8] but in RP it becomes syllabic only in some sporadic cases, generally as a result of /ə/ deletion in rapid speech which may leave either syllabic [ɹ̩] or pre-vocalic non-syllabic /r/ pronunciations (*generous* [ˈdʒenəɹəs] → [ˈdʒenɹ̩əs] – [ˈdʒenɹəs], *memory* [ˈmeməri] → [ˈmemɹ̩i] – [ˈmemɹi]) (Roach 2005: 86–90, 125–127).

---

8 Rhotic accents, languages and dialects are those in which /r/ is pronounced following a vowel (such as Spanish, as in *par* /par/ ‘pair’). In contrast, varieties which do not have this feature are **non-rhotic** (such as RP as in *par* /pɑː/ and *park* /pɑːk/) (Crystal 2008: 417).

Concerning **syllabic** [ɫ̩] /l̩/, it produces laterally released preceding consonants (with lowered side-rims of the tongue allowing the airflow to escape over them) and is found word-medially and word-finally, corresponding to the following spellings: <**al**> (*petal* [ˈpetɫ̩]), <**el**> (*panel* [ˈpænɫ̩]), <**le**> (e.g. *bottle* [ˈbɒtɫ̩], *couple* [ˈkʌpɫ̩] *struggle* [ˈstrʌgɫ̩], *cattle* [ˈkætɫ̩]) and <**les**> (mostly in plural nouns and third personal singular present verbal forms, as in e.g. *wrestles* [ˈresɫ̩z]). In words with final <**le**> in their base forms, if a suffix beginning with a vowel is attached, then the [l] generally remains syllabic but the letter <e> is lost (e.g. *struggling* [ˈstrʌgŋ̩ɫɪŋ] and *bottling* [ˈbɒtɫ̩ɪŋ]). On the other hand, similar words that are not formed in this way do not have syllabic [ɫ̩] and therefore reflect a grammatical contrast such as the one existing between [ˈkɒdɫ̩ɪŋ] *coddling*, participial form of the verb *coddle*, and [ˈkɒdlɪŋ] *codling* meaning 'small cod'.

Turning to the nasal group, **syllabic** [n̩] is the most frequent of all. It usually occurs word-medially and word-finally after alveolar plosives and fricatives, which are nasally released by lowering the soft palate, as in *threaten* [ˈθretn̩], *threatening* [ˈθretn̩ɪŋ], *seven* [ˈsevn̩], *often* [ˈɒfn̩], *heaven* [ˈhevn̩]. But [n̩] does not occur after [l tʃ ʤ], and so such words as *sullen*, *Christian*, and *pigeon*, for example, must be pronounced [ˈsʌlən], [ˈkrɪstʃən], and [ˈpɪʤən]. Similarly, after velar consonants in syllables spelt *-an* or *-on*, [n̩] is rarely heard (e.g. *toboggan* [təˈbɒgən], *wagon* [ˈwægən]), while after bilabial consonants [n̩] and [ən] pronunciations alternate (*happen* [ˈhæpn̩], [ˈhæpən], *happening* [ˈhæpn̩ɪŋ], [ˈhæpənɪŋ]).

Lastly, **syllabic** [m̩ ŋ̍] usually result from progressive assimilatory and elision processes as it occurs when preceding a bilabial (*ribbon* [ˈɹɪbm̩], *happen* [ˈhæpm̩]) or a velar plosive (*thicken* [ˈθɪkŋ̍], *dragon* [ˈdrægŋ̍]), as will be further explained in Section 5.2.7.

AI 1.4 Syllabic consonants in RP

It should be kept in mind that, although every CÇ has a corresponding CəC alternative, not every CəC has a corresponding CÇ counterpart. These alternations can be explained by resorting a phonological rule that is related to the **sonority hierarchy principle** (Jones 1975), illustrated in Figure 10:

SONORITY

– ⟵⟶ +

plosives - affricates – fricatives – nasals – liquids – glide consonants – close vowels - open vowels

Figure 10: Sonority scale or sonority hierarchy

Although there is some argument about its details, the main tenets of the sonority hierarchy principle are widely accepted. Based on the principle that the more open the VT, the more sonorous or prominent the speech sound is, the sonority hierarchy suggests that consonants are perceived as less sonorous than vowels, and that plosives are the less sonorous of speech sounds as opposed to open vowels, which are the most sonorous speech sounds, while the rest show increasing degrees of sonority from left to right in the sonority hierarchy.

Applying the sonority hierarchy principle to English syllabicity the following phonological rule emerges: C_x ə C_y (V) → C_x C̩$_y$ (V) #, under the conditions that (a) C̩ is post-tonic, (b) C_y = non-glide sonorant consonant, (c) $C_x < C_y$ (where "<" means 'is less sonorous') or C_x = /r/, and (d) V = unstressed. The following are illustrations that confirm this **syllabic sonorant creation principle**:

(1) Cx < Cy, where alternative pronunciations with and without syllabic consonants may be heard: *bakery* [ˈbeɪkəɹi] – [ˈbeɪkɹ̩i], *penal* [ˈpiːnəɫ] – [ˈpiːnɫ̩], *chancellor* [ˈtʃɑːnsələ] – [ˈtʃɑːnsɫ̩ə], *generous* [ˈdʒenəɹəs] – [ˈdʒenɹ̩əs]

(2) Cx = /r/, where pronunciations with and without syllabic consonants also fluctuate: *barren* [ˈbæɹən] – [ˈbæɹn̩], *irony* [ˈaɪəɹəni] – [ˈaɪəɹn̩i], *Carolyn* [ˈkæɹəlɪn] – [ˈkæɹɫ̩ən].

(3) Cx > Cy, which contravenes the syllabic sonorant creation principle barring syllabic consonant pronunciations: *venom* [ˈvenəm], *melon* [ˈmelən], *enemy* [ˈenəmi], *felony* [ˈfeləni].

In semiformal registers of RP, syllabic consonants are often regarded as obligatory, in so far as non-syllabic pronunciations may be considered as mispronunciations: for example, saying [ˈpiːpəɫ] rather than [ˈpiːpɫ̩] for *people*, or [ˈkætəɫ] rather than [ˈkætɫ̩] for *cattle*. In more technical and less common words, however, syllabic and non-syllabic pronunciations oscillate more freely, although syllabics are usually preferred (e.g. *missal* [ˈmɪsɫ̩], [ˈmɪsəɫ], *acquittal* [əˈkwɪtɫ̩], [əˈkwɪtəɫ]).[9] In pronunciation dictionaries (LPD, EPD), alternative pronunciations with or without syllabic consonants are transcribed with a superscript schwa [ᵊ], as in the case of *awful* [ˈɔːfᵊɫ], while syllabics are marked when that is the preferred pronunciation (for further details on /l/ pronunciations see § 4.2.5.1).

What the above examples of syllabics have in common is that all of them result in unstressed two-consonant clusters, where the syllabic one is the second element. This seems to suggest that three-consonant clusters with a third (or second and third) syllabic element are disfavoured in RP, although they may

9 Note that the word-final ending <-ile> (*fer**tile**, fu**tile**, mis**sile**, rep**tile***) is pronounced [aɪɫ] in RP, but in American English is reduced to syllabic dark [ɫ̩].

also be possible in some words (including those with two syllabics in a row, [CC̩C̩], as in e.g. *national* [ˈnæʃn̩ɫ̩], *veteran* [ˈvetr̩n̩]), and *optional* [ˈɒpʃn̩ɫ̩]). Instead, alternative pronunciations are preferred such as:

(1) [CCəC] (e.g. *abandon* [əˈbændən], *Boston* [ˈbɒstən], *Camden* [ˈkæmdən], *lantern* [ˈlæntən], *London* [ˈlʌndən], *veteran* [ˈvetrən]), *optional* [ˈɒpʃnəɫ];

(2) [CəCC̩] (e.g. [ˈvetərn̩]);

(3) [CəCəCə] (e.g. [ˈvetərən]).

1.4 Phonetic transcription

One of the chief resources of phonetics is **phonetic transcription**, where the term "phonetic" is used in a broad sense to refer to the representation of speech using phonetic symbols. In what follows we shall see the phonetic symbols that are used to represent sounds as presented in the **International Phonetic Alphabet** (section 1.4.1); the two main types of phonetic transcription that are used to represent speech sounds, **broad** and **narrow transcription** (section 1.4.2); and some **practical guidelines** to help you transcribe better (section 1.4.3).

1.4.1 The International Phonetic Alphabet (IPA)

The International Phonetic Alphabet (IPA)[10] (Table 3 below) is the best-known and most widely accepted set of phonetic symbols that are used to classify speech sounds. In addition, the IPA provides many **diacritics**, which are small additional symbols that are added to the main symbol shapes to modify the sound being represented. Diacritics may be of two kinds: (1) those representing **suprasegmental information** (primary and secondary stress marks and so on), and (2) those representing different **articulatory features** (e.g. tongue advancement and retraction, nasalisations, degrees of lip rounding and voicing, among many others), which depending on the shape of the phoneme symbol may be placed either above or below it and which are necessary to represent the degree of allophonic detail that is provided in **narrow transcriptions**, as will be explained in Section 1.4.2 and Chapter 5.

10 The acronym IPA is used to refer to both the association and to its alphabet.

Table 3: The symbols of the IPA

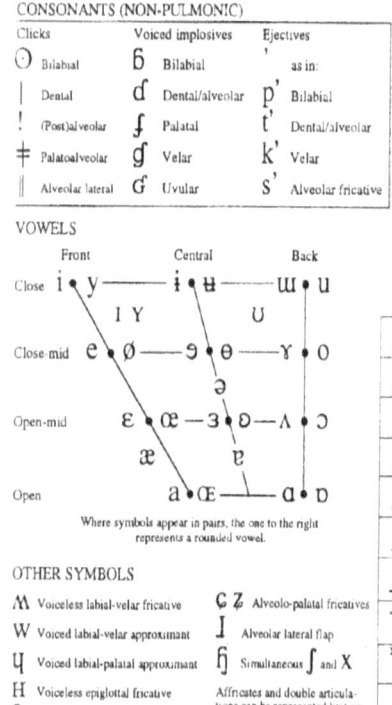

THE INTERNATIONAL PHONETIC ALPHABET (revised to 1993)

CONSONANTS (PULMONIC)

	Bilabial	Labiodental	Dental	Alveolar	Postalveolar	Retroflex	Palatal	Velar	Uvular	Pharyngeal	Glottal
Plosive	p b			t d		ʈ ɖ	c ɟ	k g	q ɢ		ʔ
Nasal	m	ɱ		n		ɳ	ɲ	ŋ	ɴ		
Trill	ʙ			r					ʀ		
Tap or Flap				ɾ		ɽ					
Fricative	ɸ β	f v	θ ð	s z	ʃ ʒ	ʂ ʐ	ç ʝ	x ɣ	χ ʁ	ħ ʕ	h ɦ
Lateral fricative				ɬ ɮ							
Approximant		ʋ		ɹ		ɻ	j	ɰ			
Lateral approximant				l		ɭ	ʎ	ʟ			

Where symbols appear in pairs, the one to the right represents a voiced consonant. Shaded areas denote articulations judged impossible.

CONSONANTS (NON-PULMONIC)

Clicks		Voiced implosives		Ejectives	
				ʼ	as in:
ʘ	Bilabial	ɓ	Bilabial	pʼ	Bilabial
ǀ	Dental	ɗ	Dental/alveolar	tʼ	Dental/alveolar
ǃ	(Post)alveolar	ʄ	Palatal	kʼ	Velar
ǂ	Palatoalveolar	ɠ	Velar	sʼ	Alveolar fricative
ǁ	Alveolar lateral	ʛ	Uvular		

VOWELS

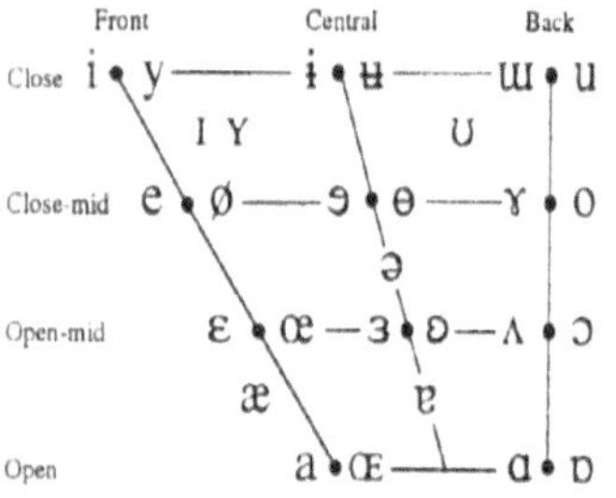

Where symbols appear in pairs, the one to the right represents a rounded vowel.

OTHER SYMBOLS

ʍ	Voiceless labial-velar fricative	ɕ ʑ	Alveolo-palatal fricatives
w	Voiced labial-velar approximant	ɺ	Alveolar lateral flap
ɥ	Voiced labial-palatal approximant	ɧ	Simultaneous ʃ and x
ʜ	Voiceless epiglottal fricative		
ʢ	Voiced epiglottal fricative		
ʡ	Epiglottal plosive		

Affricates and double articulations can be represented by two symbols joined by a tie bar if necessary. k͡p t͡s

SUPRASEGMENTALS

ˈ	Primary stress	ˌfoʊnəˈtɪʃən
ˌ	Secondary stress	
ː	Long	eː
ˑ	Half-long	eˑ
˘	Extra-short	ĕ
.	Syllable break	ɹi.ækt
|	Minor (foot) group	
‖	Major (intonation) group	
‿	Linking (absence of a break)	

TONES & WORD ACCENTS

LEVEL		CONTOUR	
e̋ or ˥	Extra high	ě or ˩˥	Rising
é ˦	High	ê ˥˩	Falling
ē ˧	Mid	e᷄ ˦˥	High rising
è ˨	Low	e᷅ ˩˨	Low rising
ȅ ˩	Extra low	e᷈ ˧˦˧	Rising-falling
↓	Downstep	↗	Global rise
↑	Upstep	↘	Global fall

etc.

DIACRITICS Diacritics may be placed above a symbol with a descender, e.g. ŋ̊

̥ Voiceless	n̥ d̥	̤ Breathy voiced	b̤ a̤	̪ Dental	t̪ d̪
̬ Voiced	s̬ t̬	̰ Creaky voiced	b̰ a̰	̺ Apical	t̺ d̺
ʰ Aspirated	tʰ dʰ	̼ Linguolabial	t̼ d̼	̻ Laminal	t̻ d̻
̹ More rounded	ɔ̹	ʷ Labialized	tʷ dʷ	̃ Nasalized	ẽ
̜ Less rounded	ɔ̜	ʲ Palatalized	tʲ dʲ	ⁿ Nasal release	dⁿ
̟ Advanced	u̟	ˠ Velarized	tˠ dˠ	ˡ Lateral release	dˡ
̠ Retracted	i̠	ˤ Pharyngealized	tˤ dˤ	̚ No audible release	d̚
̈ Centralized	ë	̴ Velarized or pharyngealized	ɫ		
̽ Mid-centralized	e̽	̝ Raised	e̝ (ɹ̝ = voiced alveolar fricative)		
̩ Syllabic	ɹ̩	̞ Lowered	e̞ (β̞ = voiced bilabial approximant)		
̯ Non-syllabic	e̯	̘ Advanced Tongue Root	e̘		
˞ Rhoticity	ɚ	̙ Retracted Tongue Root	e̙		

AI 1.5 Becoming familiar with the IPA

Phoneticians use a larger set of symbols when they want to represent sounds more accurately, and/or including non-speech sounds. Table 3 shows that in the IPA, **cardinal vowels** are included in a vowel quadrilateral chart (Section 2.3.1.3), while **consonants** are arranged in a table according to **place of articulation, manner of articulation** and **voicing** (Section 2.3.2).

1.4.2 Types of phonetic transcription

Transcription can be in either of two "directions". From what we hear spoken, or what we read from "spelt" text (i.e. in ordinary writing), we can write a so-called **direct transcription** into phonemic or phonetic text, while from phonetic symbols we can write a **reversed transcription** into spelt text. Direct is more often needed than indirect.

We must also be clear about another distinction (that has just been mentioned in passing). Very often we do not need to indicate the pronunciation of a word very precisely, but just enough to distinguish it, for example, from other words that are fairly similar but perhaps spelt the same in ordinary writing. *Tear* is pronounced /tɪə/ when referring to a teardrop that comes from your eye (Sp. *lágrima*) but /teə/ when meaning 'to damage something by pulling it apart or into pieces or by cutting it on something sharp' (OLD) (Sp. *rasgar*). Such basic transcriptions are variously called **broad, phonemic** or **phonological** and show very little phonetic detail and especially not detail which is predictable from general phonetic principles or from the phonological properties of the language in question (SID). Thus, aspiration of plosives or nasalisation of vowels would not be shown in a broad transcription of English, but would be shown in languages where these features are phonologically contrastive, i.e. when they imply a change of meaning. In broad transcriptions we work with phonemes and they are enclosed between **slant bars** (e.g. *ten* /ten/) (Sections 1.3.1 and 1.5). The number, identity and membership of phonemes differs from language to language, and from accent to accent within a given language. Phonemic transcriptions therefore record the order in which phonemes occur using a set of symbols and a series of conventions and principles which must be studied in order to assign each symbol its correct value, the basic operating principle being that of using one symbol for phoneme. Thus, in Section 1.5. it will be shown that to produce a phonemic transcription of RP, for instance, forty-four symbols will be used: twenty for vowels and vowel glides, and twenty-four for consonants.

Narrow transcription, on the other hand, shows a large amount of phonetic detail (even non-contrastive), using additional diacritics to give extra information about the realisation of each sound in a particular context (such as nasalisations, (de)voicings, dentalisations, and length reductions), and it is enclosed between **square brackets** (e.g. *ten* [tʰẽn̊]). For this reason this kind of transcription is also called **phonetic** or **allophonic**. The latter label derives from **allophone**, meaning that in narrow transcriptions we include information about the allophonic realisations of phonemes (see section 1.3.1. and Chapters 3 to 5). Allophonic transcriptions therefore record the actual realisations of each phoneme in its precise context of occurrence, employing a set of phonetic symbols and diacritics. For ease and clarity of exposition, except for Chapter 5, we mostly show just the **phonetic** (or **allophonic**) **detail of one segment** in an otherwise phonemic transcription. These transcriptions are enclosed between square brackets ([tʰen]), because slant bars are restricted to phonemic transcriptions (/ten/).

In the past, broad and narrow transcriptions were identified with phonemic and allophonic transcriptions, respectively, but nowadays, while the tendency is still for phonemic transcription to be always broad, phonetic transcriptions may be relatively broad or narrow, depending on the amount of phonetic detail provided. All types of transcriptions are useful for phonetic analysis. A phonemic transcription is more economical and it is the one given in pronunciation dictionaries. But mastery in allophonic transcription is also essential for both foreign language teachers and learners, not only to refer to the actual nature of the target sounds which in many cases involve very subtle differences, but also to avoid mispronunciations (e.g. *tree* should be pronounced [t̠ɹ̥i::] not *[tɾ̥i:]) (Chapters 4 and 5). In this book, however, targeting mostly phonemic contrasts, emphasis is laid on broad (direct or reversed) transcription as it includes all (and only) the information that is necessary to meaning or otherwise that is most relevant in one particular context. Narrow transcriptions are also used in Chapters 3 to 5 in order to explain the variations of RP phonemes that are contextually determined and the mispronunciations of SSLE.

AI 1.6 An example of broad transcription

An example of broad and narrow transcriptions
Consider the examples of broad and narrow transcriptions presented below, which are preceded by their orthographic version. Look at the text, trying to match the written words and the symbols.

Although in terms of methods they are certainly very different from the rest, ***phonetics*** *and* ***phonology*** *can be regarded as two further interrelated internal* *fields of linguistics in that, broadly, both are concerned with the same object of study: the phonic or sound component of language, an indispensable foundation of linguistic enquiry.*

|| ɔːlˈðəʊ ɪn tɜːmz əv ˈmeθədz ˈðeɪ ə ˈsɜːtnli ˈveri ˈdɪfrənt frəm ðə rest | fəˈnetɪks ənd fəˈnɒlədʒi kən bi rɪˈgɑːdɪd əz tuː ˈfɜːðər ˌɪntərɪˈleɪtɪd ɪnˈtɜːnl̩ fiːldz əv lɪŋˈgwɪstɪks ɪn ðæt | ˈbrɔːdli | bəʊθ ə kənˈsɜːnd wɪð ðə seɪm ˈɒbdʒekt əv ˈstʌdi | ðə ˈfɒnɪk ɔː ˈsaʊnd kəmˈpəʊnənt əv ˈlæŋgwɪdʒ | ən ˌɪndɪˈspensəbl̩ faʊnˈdeɪʃn̩ əv lɪŋˈgwɪstɪk ɪnˈkwaɪəri ||

A phone is a single phonetic segment viewed in terms of its phonetic character without regard to its possible phonological status. The term 'phone' is related to 'phoneme' in the same way 'morph' is related to 'morpheme'.

|| ə fəːʊ̃n ɪz ə ˈsʲĩŋgˡɫ̩ fə̃ˈnet̬ʲɪk ˈsegⁿmə̃nt vʲjuːd ĩn tʰɜ̃ːmz əv ɪts fə̃ˈnet̬ʲɪk ˈkæɹək˺tə wɪˈðaˑʊt ɹʲɪˈgɑːd tʰə ɪts ˈp̠ʰʷɒs̬ʲɪbˡɫ̩ ˌfəːʊ̃nəˈl̠ʷɒdʒʲɪk̬ˡɫ̩ ˈsteˑɪt̬əs || ðə tʰɜ̃ːm fəːʊ̃n ɪz ɹʲɪˈleˑɪt̬əd tʰə ˈfəːʊ̃nʲĩːm ĩn̺ ðə s̬eːĩm weːːɹ m̠ʷɔːf ɪz ɹʲɪˈleˑɪt̬əd tʰə ˈm̠ʷɔːf̬ʲĩːm ||

1.5 Received Pronunciation (RP) and Peninsular Spanish (PSp)

This manual describes **Received Pronunciation** (RP for short), also known as **BBC English, Oxford English**, or the **Queen's English** (Jones 1967/1976; Gimson 1980, 1984, 1994; Wells 1982). A widely established term, RP is endorsed here to refer to the standard prestige variety of British English that is "received" through the mass media, particularly the BBC (but it is not obligatory), and socially, it is associated with the upper and upper-middle class (public school education, stockbrokers, diplomats, etc.). RP originated in the Southeast, and probably it is still associated with this area by people from Northern, Central and Western England.[11] There are two main reasons to choose RP as the model accent:

(1) It is a neutral accent that is universally understood by both native and foreign speakers alike; and
(2) It is the accent of reference that is described in most books and materials of EFL, especially in Europe, and so it should also be familiar to Spanish learners of English.[12]

11 RP does not designate a monolithic accent, but rather is an umbrella term that is used to refer to a number of varieties such as: **U-RP** (**upper-crust RP**) (old-fashioned upper class accent, almost a caricature), **Conservative RP** (characteristic of older generations), **Mainstream RP** ("regular" accent of native RP speakers), **Adoptive RP** (spoken by adults who did not speak RP as children) or **Near-RP** (an accent that does not adjust itself to the definition of RP because it includes some regionalisms) (Wells 1982; Hughes *et al.* 2013).

12 Other manuals prefer to speak about **Standard Southern British English** (SSBE) (Mott 2005) in compliance with the recommendation of the *Handbook of the International Phonetic Association* (1999: 4) that is best to use the label "standard", whereas such terms as **General**

Table 4 below shows that the sound system of **RP** consists of **forty-nine sounds**, twelve vowels, eight diphthongs, five diphthong + /ə/ combinations and twenty-four consonants (Cruttenden 2014; Roach 2005), whereas the sound inventory of **PSp** has **forty-two sounds**, five vowels, fourteen diphthongs, four triphthongs and nineteen consonants (Navarro Tomás 1966 [1946], 1991 [1918]). Now listen to all the sounds of English RP and Peninsular Spanish displayed in Table 4.

AI 1.7 The sound systems of RP and PSp

The layout of Table 4 is intended to show phoneme correspondences or closest sound equivalences between RP and PSp. Accordingly, blank lines are used when no exact matchings occur (as in the case of RP /ŋ/ that has no equivalent phoneme in Spanish), while the use of different phonemic symbols across the two languages shows that the sound(s) in question exhibit some phonetic similarity, but not close phonetic likeness (as in the case of RP /h/ and PSp /x/, which are both fricative sounds but the former is glottal while the latter is velar) (Gallardo del Puerto 2005).

A detailed description of the phoneme inventory of RP in comparison with that of PSp is provided in Chapters 3 (examining vowels, diphthongs and triphthongs individually) and 4 (consonants). At this early stage it should only be noted that our comparison is not systematic, but rather it focuses on the differences and parallelisms that exist between the sound inventories of these two languages that are felt useful to better grasp English phonetics and pronunciation by speakers of Spanish. Consequently, no individual description is offered for those phonemes that occur only in Spanish (e.g. [ʎ] or [ɲ] in *llama* 'flame' or *caña* 'rode', respectively), but observations about allophonic and phonemic realisations in varieties of Spanish and the languages spoken in Spain are included whenever necessary to clarify the discussion or aid learners to gain pronunciation strategies and skills.

British (GB) (Cruttenden 2014: 4–5) and **non-regional pronunciation** (NRP) (Collins and Mees 2009: 4–6) are also employed to refer to an allegedly more updated and more encompassing neutral type of modern English with no local accent features. In addition, it has also been claimed that **Standard Scottish English** (SSE) is an easier accent for foreign learners than RP on the grounds that it is a rhotic accent (Cruttenden 2014: 326), while other models are used to represent the target pronunciation in situations in which English is used as a *lingua franca*, as in the case of **Amalgam English** (which incorporates the more easily learnable characteristics of various Englishes and some features that are common to subcontinental varieties, e.g. Bangladesh, India and Pakistan) and **International English** (which reduces the inventory of English sounds even more to what is felt more easily learnable). Finally, those countries that have been traditionally influenced by the U.S. tend to take **General American** (GA) as a model.

Table 4: The sound systems of RP and PSp

English Sounds Examples (49)		**Spanish Sounds Examples (42)**	
Vowels (12)		**Vowels (5)**	
æ	*bad* [bæd]		
ʌ	*cut* [kʌt]	a	*cama* [ˈkama] ‘bed’
ɑː	*bard* [bɑːd]		
e	*bed* [bed]	e	*mesa* [ˈmesa] ‘table’
ə	*colour* [ˈkʌlə]		
ɜː	*herb* [hɜːb]		
ɪ	*sit* [sɪt]		
iː	*seat* [siːt]	i	*sin* [sin] ‘without’
ɒ	*cod* [kɒd]		
ɔː	*cord* [kɔːd]	o	*amor* [aˈmor] ‘love’
ʊ	*pull* [pʊl]		
uː	*pool* [puːl]	u	*uso* [ˈuso] ‘usage’
Dipthongs (8)		**Diphthongs (14)**	
aɪ	*life* [laɪf]	ai̯	*aire* [ˈai̯re] ‘air’
eɪ	*grey* [greɪ]	ei̯	*rey* [rei̯] ‘king’
ɔɪ	*boil* [bɔɪl]	oi̯	*hoy* [oi̯] ‘today’
aʊ	*cow* [kaʊ]	au̯	*pausa* [ˈpau̯sa] ‘pause’
əʊ	*so* [səʊ]		
		eu̯	*neutro* [ˈneu̯tro] ‘neutral’
		ou̯	*bou* [bou̯] ‘type of fishing’
eə	*bear* [beə]		
ɪə	*beer* [bɪə]		
		ja	*viaje* [ˈbjaxe] ‘trip’
		je	*diente* [ˈdjen̪te] ‘tooth’
		jo	*radio* [ˈraðjo] ‘radio’
		ju	*viuda* [ˈbjuða] ‘widow’
ʊə	*sure* [ʃʊə]		
		wa	*cuadro* [ˈkwaðro] ‘painting’
		we	*bueno* [ˈbweno] ‘good’
		wo	*asiduo* [aˈsidwo] ‘assiduous’
		wi	*fuimos* [ˈfwimos] ‘(We) went’
Diphthongs + [ə] / Triphthongs (5)		**Diphthongs + [ə] / Triphthongs (4)**	
eɪə	*player* [pleɪə]		
aɪə	*tyre* [taɪə]		
ɔɪə	*employer* [ɪmˈplɔɪə]		
əʊə	*slower* [sləʊə]		
aʊə	*hour* [aʊə]		
		wei̯	*buey* [bwei̯] ‘ox’
		wai̯	*averigüáis* [aβeriˈɣwai̯s] ‘(You) find out’
		jei̯	*vieira* [ˈbjei̯ra] ‘scallop’
		jai̯	*saciáis* [saˈθjai̯s] ‘(You) satisfy’

Table 4: (continued)

Consonants (24)		**Consonants (19)**	
p	*pin* [pɪn]	p	*pan* [pan] 'bread'
b	*bin* [bɪn]	b	*bien* [bjen] 'well'
t	*tin* [tɪn]	t	*tan* [tan] 'so'
d	*day* [deɪ]	d	*dos* [dos] 'two'
k	*kiss* [kɪs]	k	*acto* ['akto] 'act'
g	*good* [gʊd]	g	*gol* [gol] 'goal'
f	*fame* [feɪm]	f	*fumo* ['fumo] '(I) smoke'
v	*visit* ['vɪzɪt]		
θ	*thin* [θɪn]	θ	*zumo* ['θumo] 'juice'
ð	*rather* ['rɑːðəʳ]		
s	*miss* [mɪs]	s	*sumo* ['sumo] '(I) add'
z	*zoo* [zuː]		
ʃ	*cash* [kæʃ]		
ʒ	*vision* ['vɪʒn]		
h	*ham* [hæm]		
		x	*jamón* [xa'mon] 'ham
ʧ	*match* [mæʧ]	ʧ	*chico* ['ʧiko] 'boy'/'small'
ʤ	*bridge* [brɪʤ]		
		ʝ	*yeso* ['ʝeso] 'plaster'
m	*mum* [mʌm]	m	*cama* ['kama] 'bed'
n	*night* [naɪt]	n	*cana* ['kana] 'grey hair'
ŋ	*thing* [θɪŋ]		
		ɲ	*caña* ['kaɲa] 'cane'
l	*like* [laɪk]	l	*lata* ['lata] 'tin'
		ʎ	*llama* ['ʎama] 'flame'
r [ɹ]	*rise* [raɪz]		
		r [r̄]	*carro* ['karo] 'cart'
		ɾ	*caro* ['karo] 'expensive'
j	*yet* [jet]		
w	*wet* [wet]		

1.6 A guide to phonetic transcription of RP and PSp

The following brief notes and tips should help you to transcribe, and/or to copy transcriptions correctly, as well as to improve your pronunciation.

(1) Never join symbols as in spelling. Never use capitals.

(2) Mark primary stress with ['] immediately before the stressed syllable, and secondary stress with [ˌ] (e.g. ˌfəʊtə'græfɪk).

(3) Punctuation: [|] is equivalent to [,] and [||] is equivalent to [.] Never use other marks for punctuation. The apostrophe is not used to indicate contracted forms.

(4) Write symbols in their correct form and clearly. Symbols that are ordinary letters must, in most cases, resemble the typed or printed form rather than certain common hand-written forms. Especially [**b f g l r s v z**]. In these

cases Roman symbols are used as phonetic symbols to represent phonemes because they are not already in use. This explains why, although [ɹ] is the IPA symbol that represents the most common pronunciation of the initial phoneme of *run* in English, /**r**/ is used instead in phonemic transcriptions. Likewise, in addition to the five Roman letters/symbols [a e i o u] that represent the Spanish vowel phonemes, eight additional non-Roman symbols [**ɑ æ ɜ ə ɪ ɔ ɒ ʊ**] are also used because they are necessary to represent the vocalic qualities of RP vowels and vocalic glides.

(5) Never write <c>, <q>, <x>, <y>, nor [i, u] in diphthongs, nor [r] before a consonant or after a vowel at the end of a word unless transcribing a **rhotic dialect** (e.g. GA) or to indicate **linking** with a following word-initial vowel in the same phrase (see fn 8 and Section 5.5 for further details).

(6) Note that [**z**] represents the first sound in English <zoo>, not the one in *thin* /θɪn/ or Spanish *zoo* /θoo/. However, [**j**] represents the first sound in *yes* /jes/, not the one in *jet* /ʤet/.

(7) We can also analyse the **logic of symbols**. As regards consonants, the first sound in *thin* is made with the tip of the tongue between the teeth and the symbol [**θ**] is like a picture of a tongue in a mouth. [**ð**] retains the curved shape of a medieval scribe's <d> with a cross-stroke added to indicate that, unlike [**d**], this is a fricative sound for the production of which the tip of the tongue again protrudes between the teeth and lips. The sounds [**z ʒ**] are somewhat similar to each other, and the same applies to [**s ʃ**]. The symbol [**ʒ**] is a mixture of [z] and the lower part of [g] which indicates the more retracted (palatal) quality of the former; whereas [**ʃ**] has the shape of a stretched [s]. The sound spelt <ch> consists of [t] followed by [ʃ], so the symbol is [**ʧ**]. The same applies to the voiced version [**ʤ**] (consisting of [d] + [z]) and sounds a bit like Spanish <d + ll>. The symbol [**ŋ**], a mixture of letters <n> and <g>, represents the sound spelt <ng>.

As for vowels, the vowel in *ten* [**e**] is virtually the same in English and Spanish. The vowel in *been* [**iː**] is the same as Spanish [i] except that it is a long sound, as indicated by the length marks, also called **triangular colons** [ː]. The symbols for vowels that do not exist in Spanish are based on, or are modified versions of, the spellings of the most similar Spanish sounds. The symbol [**ɪ**] is a small capital *I*. [**ʌ**] is a small capital *A* with the horizontal line omitted. [**æ**] is a mixture of *a* and *e*, and [**ə**] is *e* turned round so that it looks a bit like *a*. RP [**ɑ**], called **script alpha**, represents a much more retracted realisation than Sp [a̟]. Its rounded counterpart [**ɒ**], **turned script ɑ**, is basically the letter <o> with a bit added, while [**ɔː**] is <o> with a bit missing. [**ʊ**] is like *u* but with "wings" instead of a "foot", and [**uː**], though similar in shape, sounds different from Spanish /u/ (longer and closer).

(8) It should also be emphasised that the distinction between "broad" and "narrow" transcription is neither a black-and-white one nor a hard-and-fast rule. We can find moderately broad and narrow transcriptions. Here syllabic consonants [C̩] will be marked both in broad and narrow transcriptions. Thus, syllabic *l*, for example, will be marked as /l̩/ in broad transcriptions, but as [ɫ̩] in narrow transcriptions. Besides syllabicity, both broad and narrow transcriptions will include, when appropriate: happy-tensing *i* (Section 3.2.1), linking *r* (Section 5.5) and weak forms (Section 5.7.1).

(9) Transcriptions should always be checked in a (pronunciation) dictionary such as LPD or EPD, whose set of phonetic symbols conforms or deviates only in minor details from the one used here following Wells' or Jones' models.

(10) As they are a tool to learn pronunciation, practise reading phonetic transcriptions aloud without referring to the orthographic transcript. Likewise, do as many transcriptions as possible and do not be discouraged if you make some mistakes. The more you practice, the fewer mistakes you will make.

Further reading

The range of books and articles devoted to the pronunciation of British English is wide. Some well-known ones are Cruttenden (2014), Gimson (1984, 1994) and Kreidler (1989). The first is a revised version of the second, Gimson's approach, and both have been two major inspirations for this book, while the last one is more focused on phonology and phonological processes. Of the early works on generative phonology, the main one is Chomsky and Halle (1968), although you may find a more accessible introduction to this approach in Brengelman (1970). Two historical books worth mentioning are: Baugh and Cable (1993) and Scragg (1974), but the latter concerns spelling rather than pronunciation.

Introductory accounts of speech and phonetics (including its branches, i.e. articulatory, acoustic and auditory or perceptual) can be found in a number of textbooks such as Cruttenden (2014, Chapters 1 and 3), Ashby (2005, Chapters 1 and 2; 2011, Chapter 1), Roach (2005, Chapters 1 and 2), Ashby and Maidment (2005, Chapter 5), Ladefoged (2001, Chapter 2), Ladefoged (2003, Chapters 6 to 8), Ball and Rahilly (1999, Chapters 9 to 12), and Laver (1994, Part 1). Lodge (2009) and Katz (2013), on the other hand, offer a critical and a simplified overview of the field, respectively. For more advanced descriptions of the basic principles of (English) phonology (and phonetics), the reader is referred to Carr (2012), Clark *et al.* (2007), Gussenhoven and Jacobs (2005), Roca and Johnson

(1999), Giegerich (1992), Katamba (1989) and Lass (1984), to mention but a few. The structure of the syllable in English is dealt with in Cruttenden (2014, Chapter 5), Roach (2005, Chapter 8), Goldsmith (1990, Chapter 3), Katamba (1989, Chapter 9) and Hogg and McCully (1987, Chapter 2).

Moving on to Spanish, classic analyses of syllable structure may be found in Alcina and Blecua (1975) and RAE (1973), while other classic books that describe the sounds of PSp are, as already noted in the introduction, Quilis (1985, 1993), Alarcos LLorach (1961 [1983]), Navarro Tomás (1991[1918], 1966 [1946]). More recent approaches may be found in Martínez Celdrán and Fernández Planas (2007), Gil (2007), Hualde (2005) and Martínez Celdrán *et al.* (2003), whereas Colina (2009) presents Spanish phonology from a syllabic perspective. Other thorough introductions to Spanish phonetics and phonology for teachers and speakers of other languages may be found in Quilis and Fernández (1996), Núñez Méndez (2005) and Arteaga and Llorente (2009), among others.

To compare the sounds of English and Spanish, some basic references also mentioned in the introduction are Stockwell and Bowen (1965), Alcaraz and Moody (1993), Finch and Ortiz Lira (1982) and Mott (2011), as well as Cabrera Abreu and Vizcaíno Ortega (2009), who propose an acoustically-based method to explain English phonetics and phonology to Spanish speakers.

Exercises

1. What is the difference between producing "noises" and "speech sounds", i.e. between meaningless physical sounds and linguistic sounds? Think of a baby: the human being takes approximately one year before producing intelligible speech sounds, and yet s/he is not silent during that time. What makes the difference?
2. Would you justify seeing phonetics as a branch of linguistics? If so, how? Now, in a forensic phonetics investigation: how important is it that the specialist has linguistic knowledge as well – i.e. that s/he is a phonologist as well as a phonetician? Justify your answer.
3. Using the word *pit* as a basis, explain the difference between contrastive distribution (phonemes) and complementary distribution (allophones).
4. Think of the sequence given in Section 1.3.: *pan, tan, can, ban, Dan, fan, van, ran*. How would you justify that /s/ is a phoneme of English?
5. Look at the following sequences from the films 'Pink Panther' (the "I want to buy a hamburger" scene at http://www.youtube.com/watch?v=9q_aXttJduk) and 'My fair lady' (the 'Accent training' scene at http://www.youtube.com/watch?v=l8CID-bXgo4&feature=related). Comment on Inspector

Clouseau and Eliza Doolittle's training sessions aiming at good pronunciation: are these sessions phonetic or phonological in nature?

6. Given the following two utterances, in English and in Spanish, identify those phonemes that are likely to sound foreign when pronounced by a non-native speaker. Explain in your own words why they would sound foreign.
   (1) We have some ham sandwiches ready for tea in the garden
   (2) El perro está en la jaula y no quiere comer.
7. Give the syllabic pattern of the following words: *three, tax, table, awe, checking.*
8. Provide one monosyllabic word for each of the RP English phonemes below, using minimal pairs where possible:

   /æ ɑː ɜː ɪ ɔː ʊ əʊ eə t g v θ ʃ ʤ h r j/
9. Give the phonetic symbol as required:

initial consonant	1. car	2. school	3. yes	4. this
medial consonant	5. cushion	6. button	7. branches	8. over
final consonant	9. sing	10. axe	11. faith	12. bottle
vowel	13. war	14. blood	15. earn	16. kiss

10. Initial consonant clusters. The following consonant clusters do not occur in Spanish. Pronounce the following words, paying special attention to the initial consonant clusters. Transcribe them.

    /θr/: threat three thrill through thrive throat throw

    /ʃr/: shred shriek shrimp shrug shrine
11. /s/-initial clusters are particularly difficult for Spanish speakers. Pronounce the following words trying not to insert an extra /e/ sound before the initial cluster. Transcribe them.

    /sk/: scab sketch skin score school skirt skull skate scare scout square squeeze

    /sl/: slam slender sleep slob slew slurp slave slide slow slogan

    /sm/: smart smell smith smog small smile smoke

    /sn/: snap sniff sneeze snob snail snare snow

    /sf/: sphere

    /sp/: spam spa special spend speak spark spin spirit speed speech sport spoon Spain spare spice spoil spoke

    /st/: stack stand star steady stem steam stick still steal stock stop storm stool student stir study stay stile stone

    /skr/: scrap script screw scream screen

/spl/: splash split splendid

/spr/: sprang spread spring spray

/str/: strap stress street strict strong strange strike

12. Final consonant clusters are particularly difficult for Spanish speakers, especially those ending in a plosive. Pronounce the following words carefully, paying special attention to the endings. Then transcribe them.

    /ft/: draft left gift soft

    /kt/: act affect depict deduct

    /lt/: belt built fault

    /ld/: build field old cold gold told child wild world

    /nt/: can't sent tent mint want hunt saint pint point

    /nd/: hand send friend wind pond fund find found sound pound

13. Render the following passage into ordinary spelling:

    / fəˈnetɪks ɪz ə brɑːntʃ əv lɪŋˈgwɪstɪks ðət kəmˈpraɪzɪz ðə ˈstʌdi əv ðə ˈsaʊndz əv ˈhjuːmən spiːtʃ / ɔːr ɪn ðə keɪs əv saɪn ˈlæŋgwɪdʒɪz ði ɪˈkwɪvələnt ˈæspekts əv saɪn // ɪt s kənˈsɜːnd wɪð ðə ˈfɪzɪkl̩ ˈprɒpətɪz əv spiːtʃ ˈsaʊndz ɔː saɪnz / fəʊnz / ðeə ˌfɪzɪəˈlɒdʒɪkl̩ prəˈdʌkʃn̩ / əˈkuːstɪk ˈprɒpətɪz / ˈɔːdɪtəri pəˈsepʃn̩ / ənd ˈnjʊəˌrəʊˌfɪzɪəˈlɒdʒɪkl̩ ˈsteɪtəs // fɒˈnɒlədʒi / ɒn ði ˈʌðə hænd / ɪz kənˈsɜːnd wɪð ði ˈæbstrækt / grəˈmætɪkl̩ ˌkærəktəraɪˈzeɪʃn̩ əv ˈsɪstəmz əv ˈsaʊndz ɔː saɪnz //

Chapter 2

2 The Production and Classification of Speech Sounds

2.1 Introduction

This chapter describes the way human speech is produced (Section 2.2), what articulatory parameters are generally used to classify vowels (Section 2.3.1) and consonants (Section 2.3.2), as well as what the acoustic features of (RP, PSp) speech sounds are (Section 2.4).

2.2 The organs of speech

All the organs involved in the production of speech sounds can be arranged into three groups, or systems: the **respiratory system**, where the initial breathing process is initiated; the **phonatory system**, where vibration, or **phonation**, takes place, and the **articulatory system**, where resonance is modified in the VT, as illustrated in Figure 11.

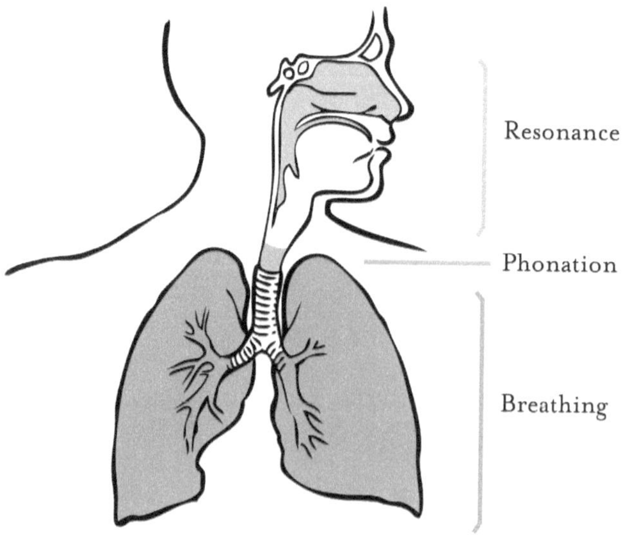

Figure 11: Systems involved in the production of speech

Three main **airstream mechanisms** or ways of initiating airflow to produce sounds are recognised depending on the source of the airstream: **pulmonic** if the source is in the respiratory system (the lungs), **glottalic** when the airflow proceeds from the phonatory system and **velaric** if the airstream is generated in the articulatory system (Pike 1943; Abercrombie 1975; Clark *et al.* 2007). A further distinction involves the direction of the airstream: if the air flows outward, then **egressive sounds** are produced, while **ingressive sounds** are those in which the airstream flows inward through the mouth or nose.

Speech sounds in English and Spanish are produced with an **eggressive** (or outgoing) **pulmonic airstream** (or column of air), which moves upwards from the lungs (breathing) through the larynx (phonation) and outwards through the **vocal tract cavity** (resonance) consisting of the **pharyngeal**, **oral** and **nasal cavities**, where a series of articulators come into play. None of these organs conforming the three systems involved in speech production have speech as their main original function (e.g. the lungs are for breathing, the vocal cords are for preventing choking, the tongue is for eating and tasting, the nose for breathing and smelling, and so on), but they have been adapted to produce communicative sounds, as will be explained in what follows.

2.2.1 The respiratory system and pulmonic sounds

The main organs in the respiratory system are the **lungs**, which are connected with the exterior by means of the bronchial tubes and the **trachea** (or **windpipe**). The lungs are contained within the thoracic cavity, protected by the rib cage and separated from the abdominal cavity by the **diaphragm**. The breathing cycle (Figure 12) involves the **expansion** and **contraction** of the lungs in a controlled manner, a process which normally takes four seconds. The rib cage expands by lowering the diaphragm, which results in air flowing into the lungs (**inspiration** or **inhalation**).

After filling with air, the lungs collapse under their own heavy weight, so the diaphragm muscle is raised and the chest contracts so that an outgoing flow of air (**expiration** or **exhalation**) is started.

AI 2.1 Ingressive and egressive airstream

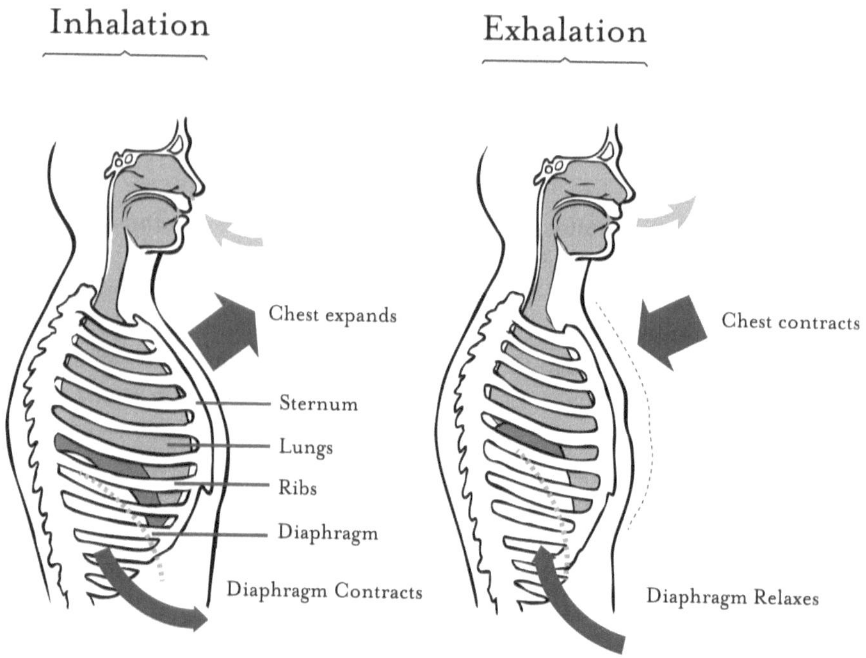

Figure 12: The breathing cycle

In many languages, such as English or Spanish, as already noted, all the speech sounds are articulated during the exhalation process with eggressive pulmonic airstream. This means our utterances are partly shaped by the physiological capacities imposed by our lungs and by the muscles that control their actions. When we speak we are forced to make pauses in order to refill our lungs with air and this will to some extent determine the division of speech into intonational phrases (see the discussion of tonality in Section 6.3).

Pulmonic ingressive sounds are also possible. They are produced when the airflow is going into the lungs, which alters the voice quality considerably. But it is unclear whether ingressive pulmonic sounds occur as normal speech sounds. Fuller (1990) claims to have recorded one speaker of Tsou, an Austronesian language of Taiwan, using pulmonic ingressive fricatives in word-initial position, but Ladefoged and Zeitoun (1993) were unable to attest this with other speakers from the same village. The only cases of pulmonic ingressives as normal speech sounds are apparently those used by women with other women in certain situations in Tohono O'odham (Papago) (Hill and Zepeda 1999). It seems that pulmonic ingressives (**inhaled speech**) are mostly employed **paralinguistically,**[13] as in the case of Japanese ingressive [s] (produced when the speaker is upset), the Scandinavian languages (usually with feedback words (*yes*, *no*) or cries of pain or sobbing), the English ingressive interjection *heuh!* (used to express surprise or empathy when someone is hurt), in Portuguese (also in interjections) or in Brazilian *falar para dentro* ('talking to the inside') (produced when speakers talk to themselves when they are alone or manifesting discomfort). Also, when we snore we produce a sound with an ingressive pulmonic airstream.

2.2.2 The phonatory system, phonation modes and glottalic sounds

The phonatory system includes the **laryngeal structures** through which **phonation** is achieved, regulating the air flow to create both **voiced and voiceless segments** (in addition to other **phonation types**), and it is the source of air pressure used to produce **glottalic sounds.**

The **larynx,** colloquially known as the **voicebox** or **Adam's Apple,** is a casing ring situated at the top of the trachea that consists of nine separate cartilages and is bigger in males than in females (Figures 13 and 14). Through the use of certain laryngeal muscles, it can be moved slightly upwards or downwards, producing different voice quality effects and aiding in the process of bringing up air from the lungs and through the trachea.

Within the larynx, running from the arytenoids forward to the interior of the front of the thyroid cartilage, are the **vocal folds,** or more commonly **vocal cords,** two whitish bands of ligament that are typically about 17 to 22 mm long in males and about 16 mm in females (Clark *et al.* 2007: 178; Ball and Rahilly 1999: 8–11).

The action of the vocal cords is controlled by forward, backward and side-to-side movements of the two **arytenoid cartilages. Backward and forward** movements of the arytenoid cartilages adjust the **tension** of the vocal cords. The more tense the vocal folds are, the higher the perceived **pitch** of speech sounds. In contrast, **side-to-side movements** of the arytenoids achieved by using the posterior cricoarytenoid muscles, either separate (or **abduct**) or bring

13 **Paralanguage** refers to the conscious or unconscious use of non-verbal elements (gestures, giggling and the like) to modify meaning, convey emotion or signal an attitude or a social role. The term **paralinguistics** is restricted to vocally produced sounds or variations in tone of voice (with breathy or creaky voice or by adopting secondary articulations such as nasalizations or labializations) which produce the same effect and seem to be less systematic than prosodic features (intonation and stress) (Crystal 2008: 349).

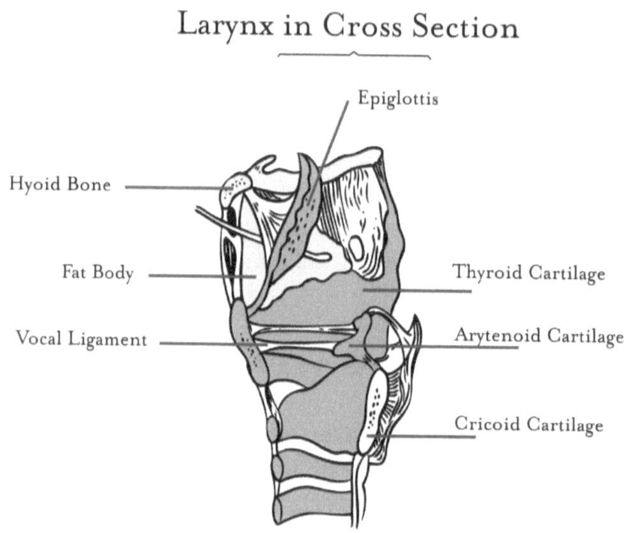

Figure 13: Larynx in cross section

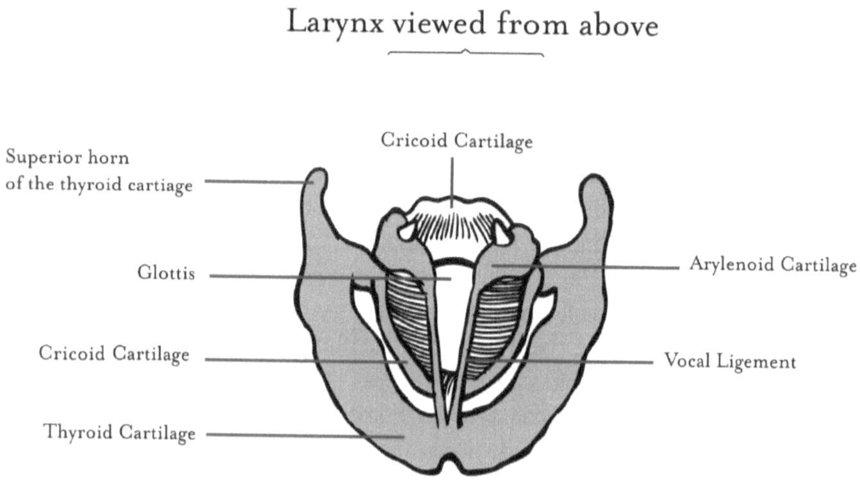

Figure 14: Larynx viewed from above

together (or **adduct**) the vocal folds. When the vocal folds are abducted, or held wide apart, as shown in Figure 15 (a), a clear passage for the airstream is allowed so that no vibration occurs. This is what happens in normal breathing or when voiceless consonants are produced. If the vocal folds are adducted, or brought together (or nearly so) along most of their length, as in Figure 15 (b) below, they vibrate when the airstream passes through them producing **voice**, as it occurs in the production of vowel sounds and voiced consonants. In addition, the vocal folds may be set together leaving a small opening between them.

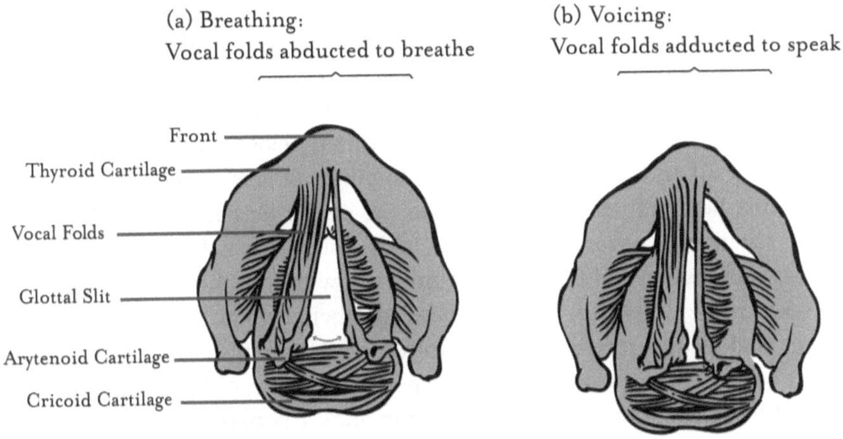

Figure 15: Human larynx and vocal folds

Normally, the vocal cords come together rapidly but part more slowly, so that the opening phase is comparatively longer than the closing stage. The space that is left between the vocal folds is called the **glottis**, or the **glottal slit**, which may be opened or closed to varying degrees. Considering the different degrees of aperture and tension of the glottis, **seven** main **phonation modes** can be recognised, as represented in Figure 16 below: (a) **voice** or **modal voice**, (b) **unvoiced** or **pulmonic**, (c) **glottal stop**, (d) **creak**, (e) **creaky voice**, (f) **whisper**, and (g) **breathy voice**. The first three apply to the production of certain individual sounds of the language, whereas the last four refer to the whole chain of connected speech, regardless of the various voiced, voiceless or glottal sounds in it. But in all seven phonation types, **eggresive pulmonic airflow** passes through the glottis within the larynx, so that a series of modifications take place involving the vocal folds, the arytenoids and other laryngeal muscles. These seven phonation types are explained in what follows, but they can be best observed with a **laryngoscope**, which gives a stationary mirrored image of the glottis, or through **stroboscopic techniques**, which allow to obtain a moving record and high speed films of the vocal cords in action.

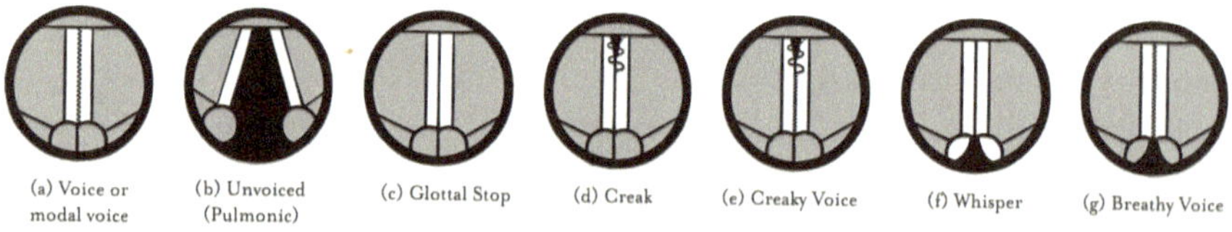

Figure 16: Phonation modes

The mechanism of **voicing** (**voice**) reflects the so-called **Bernoulli principle**, according to which a moving stream of gas or liquid tends to pull objects from the sides of the stream to the middle. The faster the stream goes, the stronger the pull. In voicing, the vocal folds are held fairly close together, as shown in Figures 15 (b) and 16 (a) above. When the pulmonic airstream passes between them, the Bernoulli effect, together with the elastic tension of the folds, pulls them together. As soon as the vocal folds are together, the Bernoulli effect ceases and the force of the airstream from below pushes them apart again, but as soon as they are apart, they are pulled together again as a result of Bernoulli effect, and so the process continues. Voiced phonation, then, involves expelling short puffs of air very rapidly by the repeated vibration of the vocal folds. The rate of these vibrations controls the **fundamental frequency** of a sound, which is, on average, 120–130 times per second in an adult male speaker, and about 220–230 times per second for an adult female. This determines what we perceive as **pitch**, whereby sounds are recognised as being **high** or **low**: the faster the vibration of the vocal folds, the higher the pitch of the sound. Slow vibration, resulting in a deeper pitch, may result from longer and larger vocal folds as in the bigger larynxes of males.

Voicelessness (adjective **unvoiced**, but also **pulmonic**) is a specific adjustment of the glottis and not just the absence of voicing. It refers to the abduction of the vocal folds that results in the opening of the glottis, as represented in Figures 15 (a) and 16 (b) above. The vocal cords (and the arytenoids) are open at between 60% and 95% of its maximal opening, and the pulmonic eggressive airstream flows relatively freely through the larynx. This kind of airflow is characterised by **nil phonation**.

All languages have both voiceless and voiced sounds contrasting in their phonological systems. Interestingly enough, in most European languages, like English and Spanish, voiced sounds are in general three times more common than voiceless ones; but other languages may have ratios that are more balanced (Dutch), or even voiceless sounds occurring more often than voiced ones (Korean). In English and Spanish, sonorants and vowels are rarely voiceless, whereas obstruents are commonly found voiceless, although they can also occur voiced.

Somewhat resembling a weak cough or a cork pulled out of a champagne bottle, the **glottal stop** [ʔ], illustrated in Figure 16 (c) above, is produced by bringing together the vocal folds (and the arytenoids) blocking the airstream coming from the lungs behind them for a moment, followed by the sudden release of this pressurised air. In some languages, glottal stops are actual phonemes, as in Arabic and Persian, while in English they can occur both segmentally (e.g. as a realisation of final [p], [t] and [k], as in *clap*, *what* and *cock*) and prosodically (e.g. as a hiatus blocker or pause marker in *co-operate*) (see § 5.2.8.2 for further details).

AI 2.2 Glottal stop

In addition, there exist other **glottalic sounds** that are produced with an airstream coming from or to the larynx, by closing the vocal folds tightly shut so that no air can pass through the glottis. **Glottalic egressive sounds** (produced with an outgoing airstream and a closed glottis as well as with a supralaryngeal closure gesture) are called **ejectives** and they are especially common in the native languages of North America (Pacific Northwest) but are very infrequent in Europe (except in the Caucusus region, at the border of Europe and Asia). Less common than ejectives, **glottalic ingressive sounds** (produced with an ingoing airstream) are called **implosives** and they are especially common in Africa and Central America (Mayan languages).

Creak, also termed **glottal fry** or **vocal fry** because of the sputtering effect it produces, consists of pulses of air passing through the glottis with the arytenoids tightly closed, allowing only the front portion of the vocal folds to vibrate and producing a succession of glottal stops, as shown in Figure 16 (d) above. Creak has low sub-glottal pressure and low volume velocity air flow; and the frequency of vocal fold vibration can be in the region of 30–50 pulses per second. **Creaky voice**, represented in Figure 16 (e), combines creak with voice. It is often used by English speakers paralinguistically (replacing modal voice) either to suggest boredom, authority, avoid disturbing people, or to keep a conversation private. Some people use this voice idiosyncratically as a sign of affectation.

AI 2.3 Creaky voice

Whisper, also known as **library voice**, requires the glottis to be closed by about 25% and the vocal folds to be closer together than for voicelessness, especially the anterior section of the folds, whereas the triangular-shaped opening takes place at the back, so that a considerable amount of air escapes at the arytenoids, as illustrated in Figure 16 (f). Air flow is strongly turbulent, which produces the characteristic hushing quality of whisper. This phonation type is used contrastively in some languages, but we are more used to thinking of whisper as an extra-linguistic device to disguise the voice or, at least, to reduce its volume.

Breathy voice, in Figure 16 (g), is a combination of whisper and voice. Although the vocal cords are open, the expulsion of air is so strong that they are made to vibrate. This is the voice associated with "sexy" voices, and is also known as "bedroom voice", sometimes used by singers as a special effect.

Finally, we should mention **falsetto voice**, which is produced when the thyroarytenoid muscle contracts to hold the vocal folds very tightly, allowing vibration at the edges. The glottis is kept slightly open and sub-glottal pressure is relatively low. The resultant phonation is characterised by very high frequency vocal fold vibration (between 275 and 634 pulses per second for an adult male). Falsetto is not used linguistically in any known language, but has a variety of extralinguistic functions dependant on the culture concerned (e.g. greeting in Tzeltal, Mexico). Falsetto voice is pertinent to males, as women's voices are generally higher pitch anyway, and is used in singing more often than in speaking.

2.2.3 The articulatory system and velaric sounds

The articulatory system, also known as **vocal tract** (VT), consists of various elements distributed in three supralaryngeal, or supraglottal, cavities that are illustrated in Figure 17: the **pharynx** (throat in everyday language), the **nasal cavity** (nose) and the **oral cavity** (mouth), which act as resonators and alter the sound produced by the vibration at the vocal folds, by providing the necessary amplification or diminishing it. Sounds, particularly the vowels, can also be modified in these cavities by the alterations in shape which they can adopt, and also, particularly the consonants, by means of the various articulators within: the **soft palate** or **velum**, the **hard palate**, the **alveolar ridge**, the **tongue**, the **teeth** and the **lips**. A description of each of these three articulatory cavities is provided in turn. In addition, at the end of this section, we shall also see that the articulatory system, or to be more precise the **tongue**, is the source of air pressure that is necessary to produce **velaric sounds**.

Forming the rostral boundary of the larynx, the **epiglottis** is a small movable muscle whose function is to prevent food from going down the trachea into the lungs and so divert it to the **oesophagus** down to the stomach. The **pharynx** is a tube about 7 to 8 cm long, which runs from the top of the larynx up to the back of the nasal and oral cavities. The lower area of the pharynx, nearer the oral cavity, is called **oropharynx**, and the upper part, nearer the nasal cavity, is the **nasopharynx**. The section of the pharynx which is immediately above the larynx is called **laryngopharynx**, and the **epilarynx** is the area of contact between them. The size and shape of the pharynx can be altered in a number of ways. The overall volume of the pharynx may be reduced, by raising the larynx, or it may be reduced besides adding an obstruction to the airflow, if the root of the tongue and the epiglottis are retracted into the oropharynx, or even its back wall can be contracted, by drawing the side walls to each other. These different articulatory gestures result in corresponding alterations of the quality of the voice.

Access to the **nasal cavity**, which can be touched by the back of the tongue, is triggered at the **velopharyngeal port** by **lowering the soft palate**, or **velum**, so that the outgoing body of air is released through the **nares**, or **nostrils** (although it may also simultaneously flow through the oral cavity), and nasal resonance is provided. This is what happens in the articulation of **nasal** and **nasalised** sounds. But in normal breathing and to produce **oral** speech sounds **the velum is raised**, so that the airstream is liberated through the mouth without entering the nasal cavity.

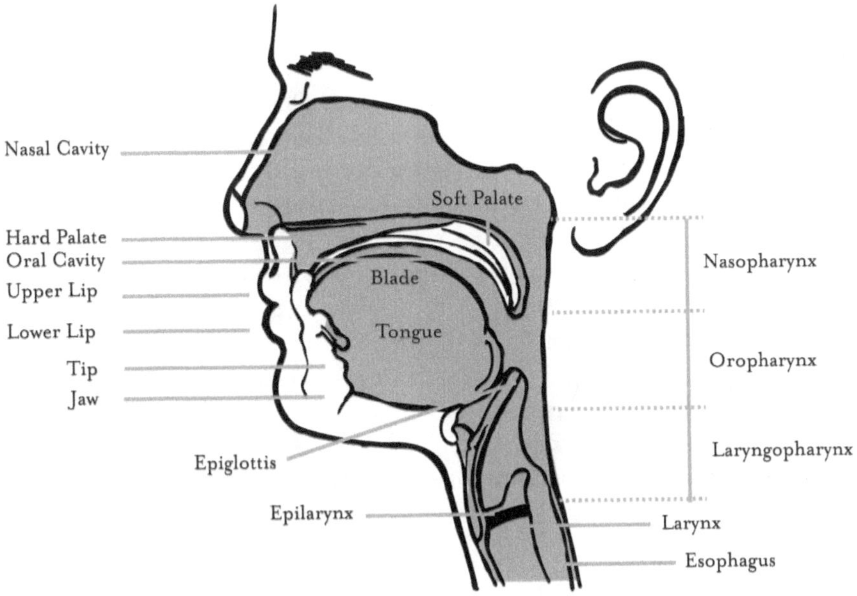

Figure 17: The articulatory system

Let us focus on the **oral cavity**, the most versatile of the three supralaryngeal cavities. The mouth may be closed or opened by raising or lowering the **lower jaw**, or **mandible**. The **upper** and **lower lips** are flexible and can adopt a variety of positions. They can be in a **neutral** shape, or they can be **open** (or held apart), **closed** (or brought together), or **rounded** in different degrees. So we can say, for instance, that the lips are either **closely rounded**, or **tightly rounded** (vs. **slightly rounded** or **loosely rounded**), or **spread apart** (either loosely or tightly). They can also come into contact with the **teeth**, which are fixed in position and act as obstacles to the airstream. The **tongue**, on the other hand, is the most flexible of the articulators within the supralaryngeal system. It can adopt many different shapes and can also come into contact with many other articulators. The **tip** (adjective **apical**) and **blade** (adjective **laminal**) can either approximate or touch the **upper teeth**, and the **alveolar ridge**, the section between the upper teeth and the hard palate; but they can also bend upwards and backwards so that their underside can touch the **roof of the mouth**, or **hard palate**,[14] which can also be touched by the **front** of the tongue. The **back** of the tongue can be raised against the **velum** and the **uvula**, whereas its **root** (or **base**) can be retracted into the **pharynx**. The area where the front and back of the tongue meet is known as **centre** (adjective **central**). Likewise, the front, centre and root of the tongue are sometimes collectively known as the **body** of the tongue, while the edges of the tongue are called **rims**.

We shall see that sound descriptions necessarily refer to (1) the height of the tonge, that is, whether it is raised or touches the teeth, alveolar ridge, and so on, because different places of articulation produce different sounds, and (2) the position of the tongue in the mouth, that is, whether it is advanced or retracted, which affects the size of the oropharyngeal cavity, and consequently, influences the quality of the sounds produced (especially vowels).

Before closing this section, let us consider **velaric sounds**. These are made by the body of the tongue trapping a volume of air between two closures in the mouth, one at the velum (the back of the tongue is placed against the soft palate), and one further forward (the tip, blade and rims of the tongue are placed against the teeth and the alveolar ridge). Velaric egressive sounds (produced with an outgoing airstream) are physically impossible because it is not possible to compress the portion of the oral tract between the velar closure and the anterior closure. **Velaric ingressive sounds** (produced with an ingressive airstream) are called **clicks** and tend to be used paralinguistically (mainly as

---

14 **Palatography** and **electropalatography**, studying the kind and extent of the area of contact between the tongue and the roof of the mouth, provide a practical way of recording tongue movements and illustrating the articulation of speech sounds.

interjections). In English and Spanish, the kissing sound that people make is a bilabial click ([ʘ]), whereas the alveolar click [!] is used to express disapproval or annoyance and the velar click [||] is the sound produced to encourage horses. The only languages that use clicks as regular speech sounds are found in Southern Africa, to be more precise the Khoi and San languages, as well as some of the Southern Bantu languages.

2.3 Articulatory features and classification of phonemes

When the egressive pulmonic air passes through the phonatory system and reaches the articulatory system of the oral and nasal cavities, it is modified by certain organs that move against others and may be released in different ways, depending on the degree of aperture of the mouth. In this section we shall see that vowels, vowel glides and consonant sounds are produced differently and therefore need different parameters of classification.

2.3.1 Vowels and vowel glides

A complete characterisation of **vowels**, or **vocalic sounds**, and **vowel glides** involves three types of features: (1) functional (or phonological), (2) acoustic/auditory and (3) articulatory. Functionally, vowels are syllabic, that is, they are the nucleus of the syllable, thereby getting intonational prominence (unlike **semivowels** or **semiconsonants**[15] and **approximants** (see Sections 2.3.2.3 and 4.2.4)), which tend to be marginal in the syllable. From an acoustic point of view, vowels and vowel glides are characterised by homogenous and regular formant structure patterns, as will be further discussed in Sections 2.4.1 and 2.4.2. Articulatorily speaking, vowels are characterised by having no obstruction in the VT: the air-stream comes through the mouth (or through the mouth and nose), centrally over the tongue and meets a stricture of open approximation, in other words, there is a considerable space between the articulators in their production. Seven other articulatory features determining **vowel quality** are

15 The terms **semi-consonant** and **semi-vowel** may be used interchangeably although they bring different ideas to the fore. The label semi-consonant highlights the consonantal quality of segments that function as a syllabic margin (e.g. English [j] and [w] in [j + é], *yet* /jet/, [j + ɪ] *year* /jɪə/, [w + é] *wet* /wet/) but are not the nucleus or peak (i.e. the most prominent or sonorous part) of the syllable. In contrast, the label semi-vowel reinforces the idea that the segment has the phonetic (articulatory, auditory and acoustic) characteristics of a vowel, but the phonological behaviour of a consonant (it occurs in syllable margins) (Crystal 2008: 431).

observed in relation to the action of the vocal folds, the soft palate, the tongue and the lips, as well as the muscular effort employed in their articulation:

(1) The **action of the vocal cords** during phonation: generally all vowels and vowel glides are **voiced** (i.e. produced with vibration of the vocal folds), but they may be **devoiced**, especially when occurring next to a voiceless plosive (as in the second vowel of *carpeting* or *multiple*) (for more details on the devoicing of RP vowels, see § 5.2.2);

(2) The **action of the velum** or soft palate: **raised**, in oral articulations, or **lowered**, in nasal(ised) articulations;[16] generally all vowels in RP and PSp are oral (i.e. the air escapes through the mouth), but they can be nasalised, especially if followed by nasal consonants (like [e] in *ten* [tẽn] or [a] in PSp *pan* [pãn] 'bread') (for further details on the nasalisation of RP vowels see § 5.2.4);

(3) **Tongue height**, which refers to how close the tongue is to the roof of the mouth, and consequently determines the degree of openness of the mouth and of the vowels according to four values: **close (high)**, **half-close (high-mid)**, **half-open (low-mid)** and **open (low)**. This parameter is further discussed in Section 2.3.1.1.

(4) **Tongue backness**, which refers to the part of the tongue that is highest in the articulation of a vowel (**tip**, **blade**, **front** or **back**, see Fig. 16 above) rendering three values of vocalic description: **front**, **central** and **back**. These values are further explained in Section 2.3.1.1.

(5) **Lip shape**, basically involving three positions **(slightly/tightly) rounded**, **spread** and **neutral**, as will be explained in Section 2.3.1.2.

(6) **Duration**, or the length of the vowel, and **energy of articulation**, that is, the muscular effort required to articulate a vowel, more details of which are given in Section 2.3.1.4.

(7) Whether **vowel quality** is relatively **sustained** (i.e. the tongue remains in a more or less steady position), or whether there is a **transition** or **glide** from one vocalic element to another (or others) within the same syllable, as will be noted in Section 2.3.1.5.

In what follows, further details are given about the articulatory features and classification of vowels and vowel glides, as well as about their relation to the system of cardinal vowels (Section 2.3.1.3). Chapter 3 (Sections 3.2 and 3.3) offers

---

16 The terms ending *–ised* (adj.)/*–isation* (n.) generally refer to a secondary articulation (see § 2.3.2.5.). That is, any articulation which accompanies another (primary) articulation and which normally involves a less radical constriction than the primary one (e.g. nasalised-nasalisation, palatalised-palatalisation, etc.).

a detailed description of the vowels and vowel glides of RP in comparison to those of PSp, while Chapter 5 summarises their main realisational or allophonic variants.

AI 2.4 Vowels and glides of English RP

2.3.1.1 Tongue shape

There are two parameters involved in vowel articulation that concern the tongue: tongue height and tongue backness. The position of the highest point is used to determine vowel height and backness. **Tongue height** indicates how close the tongue is to the roof of the mouth. If the upper tongue surface is close to the roof of the mouth (like /iː/ in *fleece* and /uː/ in *goose*), then the sounds are called **close vowels**, or **high vowels**. By contrast, when vowels are made with an open mouth cavity, with the tongue far away from the roof of the mouth (like /æ/ in *trap* and /ɑː/ in *palm*), then they are termed **open vowels**, or **low vowels**. There are two further intermediate values between these two: **half-close (high-mid)** and **half-open (low-mid)**, which represent a vowel height between close and half-open in the former case, and between open and half-close in the latter (see also Section 2.3.1.3 on cardinal vowels).

In RP there are four close/high vowel phonemes /**iː ɪ ʊ uː**/, three open/low vowels /**æ ɑː ɒ**/ and five mid vowels /**e ʌ ɜː ə ɔː**/; while PSp has two close/high vowel phonemes /**i u**/, one open/low vowel /**a**/, and two mid vowels /**e o**/. The degree of openness or closeness of vowels may be further specified by means of two diacritics: [˔] (*bit* [bɪ̝t]) and [˕] (*sit* [sɪ̝t]), which indicate respectively raised (closer) or lowered (more open) realisations of vowels within these four values.

Tongue backness, in turn, identifies which part of the tongue is highest in the articulation of the vowel sound: if the front of the tongue is highest, we speak of **front vowels** (like /iː/ in *fleece*); if the back of the tongue is the highest part, we have what are called **back vowels** (like /ɔː/ in *cord* or /uː/ in *clue*). **Central vowels** are articulated with the tongue in a neutral position, neither pushed forward nor pulled back, but it may be raised to the degrees mentioned above (like /ə/ in the second syllable of *venom*, which represents a central vowel between half-open and half-close).

In RP there are three central vowels /**ʌ ə ɜː**/, four front vowel phonemes /**iː ɪ e æ**/, and five back vowel phonemes /**ɑː ɔː ɒ ʊ uː**/, whereas PSp has two front vowels /**i e**/, one central vowel /**a**/ and two back vowels /**o u**/. The degree of frontness or backness of vowels may be further specified by means of the diacritics [+] [–], which express more retracted or more advanced vocalic realisations within these four values. Both are usually placed above the vowel symbol, but they may also follow it, as will be illustrated in Chapter 5.

Testing RP close and open vowels

To test close and open vowels, say the English vowel /ɑː/ as in *palm*. Put your finger in your mouth. Now say the vowel /iː/ as in *fleece*. Feel inside your mouth again. Look in a mirror and see how the front of the tongue lowers from being close to the roof of the mouth for /iː/ to being far away for /ɑː/. Now say these English vowels: /iː/, /ɜː/ and /æ/. Can you feel the tongue moving down? Then say them in the reversed order and feel the tongue moving up.

Testing RP front and back vowels

To test front and back vowels, take another set of English vowels: /ɑː/ and /ɔː/ and /uː/. Notice how it is the back of the tongue that raises for /ɔː/ and /uː/, whereas for /ɑː/ the tongue is fairly flat.

2.3.1.2 Lip shape

The second parameter used to describe different vowel qualities is the shape of the lips. We will consider mainly three possibilities:

(1) tightly or slightly **rounded**, or **pursed**: the corners of the lips are brought towards each other and the lips pushed forwards ([u]);
(2) tightly or slightly **spread**: the corners of the lips are moved away from each other, as for a smile ([i]); and
(3) **neutral**: the lips are not noticeably rounded or spread – as in the noise most English people make when they hesitate, spelt *er*.

The main effect of lip-rounding is the enlargement of the mouth cavity and the decrease in size of the opening of the mouth, both of which deepen the pitch and increase the resonance of the front oral cavity. Lip shape affects vowel quality significantly. A typical pattern is found in most languages of the world, whereby front and open vowels have spread to neutral position, whereas back vowels have rounded lips (although reverse positions are also possible, as in the French vowel in *neuf*, for example).

In RP all **front** and **central vowels** are **unrounded**, while all **back vowels** (except /**ɑː**/) are **rounded**, and the same applies to PSp. This seems to be the general tendency according to which every language has at least some unrounded front vowels and some rounded back vowels. Lip rounding makes back vowels sound more different from front vowels and have greater perceptual contrasts. In addition, it should be noted that labialised variants of consonants occur (annotated with a superscript [ʷ]) in the vicinity of a rounded vowel, as in the /p/ and /t/ of *put* [pʷʊtʷ]. Further details on the lip positions of RP and PSp vowels, as well as on the phenomenon of labialisation, are offered in Chapters 3 and 5 respectively.

2.3.1.3 The cardinal vowels and the Cardinal Vowel Scale

We have established the closest and most front vowel [i]; the closest and most back vowel [u]; the most open front vowel [a] and the most open and most back vowel [ɒ]. These degrees of aperture plus the front-back distinction define 8 **reference points** based on a combination of articulatory and auditory criteria, which represent eight different vocalic qualities represented in Figures 18 (a) and 18 (b).

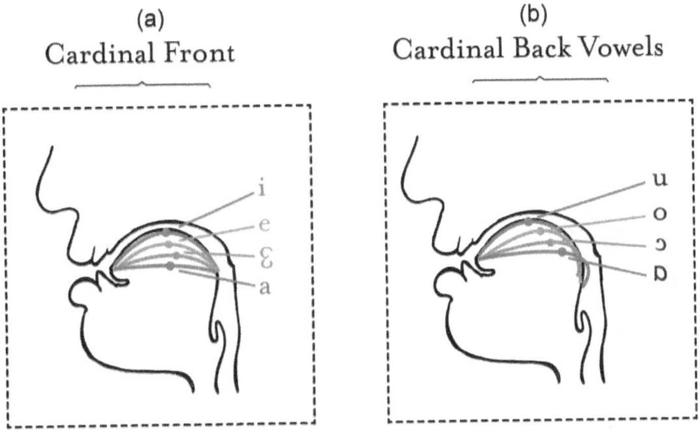

Figure 18: Highest tongue positions for (a) cardinal front and (b) cardinal back vowels

The **cardinal vowels** (CV) (termed after the cardinal points of the compass) indicate the upper and lower vowel limits beyond which the tongue cannot rise, in relation to the roof of the mouth, without friction or tongue depression, as shown in Figure 19 below. The vowels at the upper vowel limit are the front vowel [i] and the back vowel [u]; the vowels at the lower vowel limit are the front vowel [a] and the back vowel [ɒ].

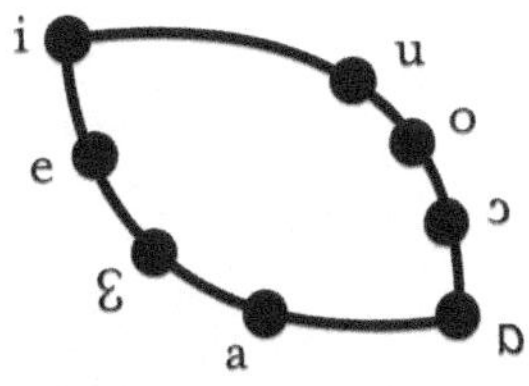

Figure 19: Relative highest and lowest points of the tongue for cardinal vowels

Taking the aforementioned into account, in 1917 the English phonetician Daniel Jones devised the **Cardinal Vowel Scale** (CVS), also called **Cardinal Vowel Quadrilateral**, or **Cardinal Vowel Trapezium**, which is presented in Figure 20 below (see also the vowel matrix on the IPA, reproduced as Table 3 in Section 1.4.1).

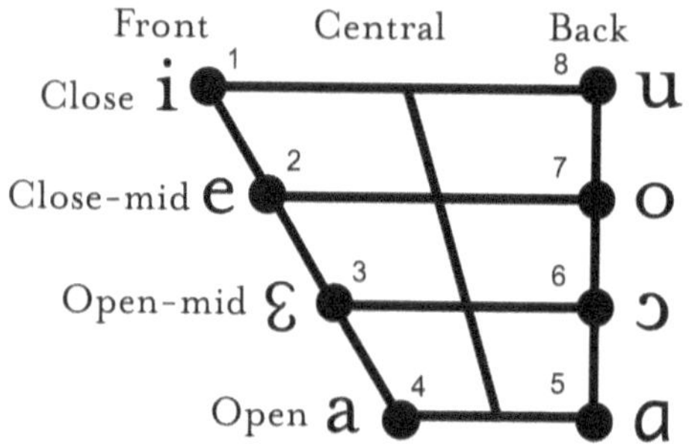

Figure 20: The Cardinal Vowel Scale

The **primary cardinal vowels**, CV 1 to CV 8 in Figure 20 above, should be distinguished from corresponding **secondary cardinal vowels**, which are derived from corresponding primary cardinal vowels by reversing the lip-rounding, from CV 9 to CV 18 which are represented in grey in Figure 21 below. Thus, primary CVs 1 to 5 are unrounded, and 6 to 8 are rounded; whereas secondary CVs 9 to 13 are rounded, and 14 to 16 unrounded.

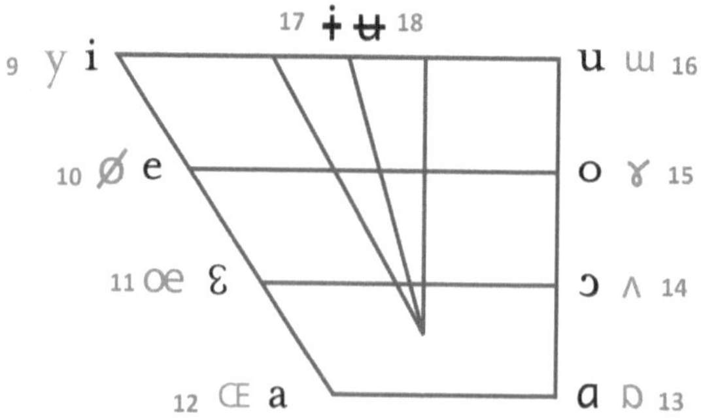

Figure 21: Primary cardinal vowels vs. secondary cardinal vowels

Table 5 below revises the identification and description of the primary cardinal vowels in terms of tongue height and lip shape. There is no agreed abbreviation to describe vowels, but our habit is to speak of **OBR labels (openness, backness** and **lip rounding**). Notice also that cardinal vowels do not refer to the vowels of a particular language, but rather are a set of reference vowels used by phoneticians in describing the sounds of languages in general. In Chapter 3 the vowels of RP will be allocated in the relevant places of the CVS.

Table 5: Primary Cardinal Vowels

CV	IPA	Identification	Description
1	[i]	close front unrounded	At the top left corner of the CVS, CV 1 stands for an articulation in which the lips are unrounded, and the front of the tongue is located as high as possible.
2	[e]	close-mid front unrounded	It stands for a more open articulation than CV 1, in which the lips are also unrounded, but the front of the tongue is lowered somewhat from the CV 1 position.
3	[ɛ]	open-mid front unrounded	It stands for a more open articulation than CV 2, keeping the same lip shape and degree of frontness, but with the tongue lowered to the half-open position.
4	[a]	open front unrounded	It stands for an even more open articulation than CV 3, in which the lips remain unrounded, but the tongue is moved as far to the front of the vowel space as possible while remaining as low as possible.
5	[ɑ]	open back unrounded	At the bottom right-hand corner of the CVS, it stands for an articulation in which the lips are again unrounded and the body of the tongue is again as low as possible, but as far back as possible in the vowel space, without causing friction.
6	[ɔ]	open-mid back rounded	Immediately above CV 5, CV 6 stands for a closer and rounded articulation. The lips are rounded and the tongue is raised as far back as possible to the half-open position in the vowel space, without causing friction.
7	[o]	close-mid back rounded	Immediately above CV 6, CV 7 retains the same degree of backness and a higher degree of lip-rounding, but the tongue height is raised to the half-close position.
8	[u]	close back rounded vowel	At the top right-hand corner of the CVS, CV 8 stands for an articulation in which the lips are tightly rounded and the tongue is as high and as far back as possible without causing friction.

2.3.1.4 Duration and energy of articulation

Duration means the time each sound takes to be pronounced, which is only of linguistic significance if the relative duration of sounds is considered. The **pace of delivery** in the production of speech sounds is auditorily perceived as **length**, involving in the case of vowels the **short** and **long** distinction (**vocalic quantity**). In PSp this difference does not entail a phonemic contrast in the vocalic system, but in other languages the duration of the production of a vowel has a phonemic contrast, which is often combined with vowel quality, and this is the case of RP (see § 3.2 for further details). In RP there are five **long vowels** /**ɑː ɜː iː ɔː uː**/ and seven **short vowels** /**æ ʌ e ɪ ə ɒ ʊ**/. But the relative duration of a long phoneme may be lengthened or reduced, depending on the phonetic context in which it occurs. In the first case we speak of **(extra) lengthening** and it is indicated with double length marks [ːː], as in the realisation of [iː] in *tea* [tiːː], especially when the word is emphatic; whereas cases of vowel length reduction are referred to under the umbrella term **clipping**, which is marked with only a single length mark or triangular colon [ˑ], as in the realisation of [iː] in *leap* [liˑp]). For further details on vowel allophones involving differences in length, the reader is referred to Sections 2.3.2.4 and 5.2.1.

Now turning to the amount of muscular tension required to produce vowels, if they are articulated in extreme positions, they are more tense (like /iː/ in *tea* or /uː/ in *blue*) than those articulated nearer the centre of the mouth which are lax (like /ə/ in the second syllable of *venom*). In RP the five long vowels are **tense** /**ɑː ɜː iː ɔː uː**/ and the remaining short vowels are **lax** /**æ e ɪ ə ʌ ɒ ʊ**/, while in Spanish all vowels are tense (Monroy Casas 1980, 1981, 2012) (see § 3.2 for further details). SSLE should know that in English both tense and lax vowels can occur in closed syllables, but (apart from unstressed vowels) only tense vowels can occur in open syllables (Ladefoged 2001).

2.3.1.5 Steadiness of articulatory gesture

A final classification of vowel sounds involves the steadiness of the articulatory gesture adopted in vowel production. If the positions of the tongue and lips are held steady during production of a vowel sound, the resulting sound is known as a **steady-state vowel, pure vowel**, or **monophthong**. As already seen in Table 4, in RP there are twelve pure vowels /**æ e ɪ ə ʌ ɒ ʊ ɑː ɜː iː ɔː uː**/, which in Chapter 3 (Section 3.2) will be further described and compared with the five vowels of PSp /**a e i o u**/.

If there is a clear change, or **glide**, in the tongue or lip shape we speak of **diphthongs** or **triphthongs**, in which the glide is carried out in one single movement from one vocalic position to another within the syllable. As already displayed in Table 4, in RP there exist eight diphthongs **/aɪ eɪ ɔɪ aʊ əʊ eə ɪə ʊə/** and five triphthongs **/eɪə aɪə ɔɪə əʊə aʊə/**, which in Chapter 3 (Section 3.3) receive independent treatment and are compared with the fourteen diphthongs **/ai̯ ei̯ oi̯ au̯ eu̯ ou̯ wa we wo wi ja je jo ju/** and four triphthongs **/wei̯ wai̯ jei̯ jai̯/** of Psp.

2.3.2 Consonants

While vowels are produced with no obstruction to the airflow as it passes through the VT, for the articulation of consonants this obstruction does exist (Hooke and Rowell 1982). Consonants are identified according to **three-term VPM** labels standing for **Voice, Place** and **Manner of articulation**, which together give the consonant its distinctive quality. The **voiced/voiceless** opposition, as well as the **fortis/lenis** contrast are related to **phonation**, and are discussed in Section 2.3.2.1. Place of articulation and manner of articulation are explained in Sections 2.3.2.2 and Section 2.3.2.3, respectively, the latter including the subservient feature of **orality**, which is described separately in Section 2.3.2.4. Thus, in order to describe and classify consonant sounds according to production, we have to speak of these four parameters, in addition to that of **secondary articulation**, which is discussed in Section 2.3.2.5.

From an **acoustic** point of view, consonants may be broadly characterised as having non-homogenous and irregular formant structure patterns, as will be further discussed in Section 2.4.3. A detailed description of RP consonants as compared to those of PSp is offered in Chapter 4, while Chapter 5 summarises their main realisational or allophonic variants.

2.3.2.1 Voicing and energy of articulation

Voice is a fundamental term used in the phonetic classification of speech sounds, referring to the auditory result of the vibration of the vocal cords. Sounds produced while the vocal cords are vibrating are **voiced sounds**; those produced with no such vibration are **voiceless** or **unvoiced**. If a sound which is normally voiced is, in a particular phonetic environment, produced with less voice than elsewhere, or with no voice at all, it is said to be **devoiced**. This quality is a matter of degree. In other words, there are contexts in which the devoicing of a particular voiced sound is complete, whereas in other phonetic contexts its voicing is only partially diminished. Be that as it may, there only exists one symbol to indicate devoicing: a small circle [˚] that is placed beneath (**under-ring**) [d̥] or above (**over-ring**) [ŋ̊] the consonant symbol. As already noted in Section 1.3.2, an example of devoicing is that which occurs with voiced plosives in word-final positions such as the [g] of *tag* [tæg̊]. By the same token, voiceless phonemes may show different degrees of vocal fold vibration when occurring next to voiced sounds or in intervocalic positions. This phenomenon is known as **voicing** and is symbolised with a [̬] above or below the phonetic symbol, as in [t] in *matter* [ˈmæt̬ə]. More details on the devoicing or voicing of RP consonants are offered in section 5.2.2.

According to the **voice-voiceless** distinction the phonemes of RP and PSp can be classified as either voiced or voiceless, as shown in Table 6 below (see also the consonant matrix on the IPA, reproduced as Table 3 in Section 1.4.1). Broadly speaking, voiceless consonants are longer and are articulated with greater muscular effort and breath-force than their voiced counterparts, causing a reduction of the preceding vowels or sonorant consonants while the voiced series do not have such an effect (see Chapter 4 for further details).

Now turning to energy of articulation, the **fortis/lenis** contrast refers to the relatively strong or weak degree of muscular force that a sound is made with. In fortis consonants articulation is stronger and more energetic than in lenis ones. **Fortis** consonants are voiceless and **lenis** consonants are not always voiced, since some voicing is lost in initial and final positions, and final consonants are typically almost totally devoiced. Medially – i.e. between vowels or other voiced sounds – lenis consonants have full voicing. When initial in a stressed syllable, fortis plosives /p t k/ have strong aspiration (with a brief puff of air), as in ***pea*** [pʰiː], whereas lenis plosives are always unaspirated, as in ***bib*** [bɪb] (see § 4.2.1 and 5.2.5). Vowels are shortened before a final fortis consonant, as in ***beat*** [biˑt], whereas they have full length before a final lenis consonant, as in ***bead*** [biːd]. This phenomenon is known as **pre-fortis clipping**, which was introduced in Section 2.3.1.4 and will be further discussed in Section 5.2.1. In addition, syllable-final fortis stops often have a reinforcing glottal stop, as in *set down* [seʔt daʊn], whereas syllable-final lenis stops never have one, as in ***said*** /sed/ (see § 5.2.8).

🎧 **AI 2.5 Voiced and voiceless consonants**

Table 6: Voiced and voiceless consonants in RP and PSp

RP		PSp	
Voiceless	**Voiced**	**Voiceless**	**Voiced**
p t k	b d g	p t k	b d g
	m n ŋ		m n ɲ
			r
			ɾ
f θ s ʃ h	v ð z ʒ	f θ s x	ʝ
ʧ	ʤ	ʧ	
	w j r (ɹ)		
	l		l ʎ

2.3.2.2 Place of articulation

The **place of articulation** (also **point of articulation**) of a consonant is the point of contact where an obstruction occurs in the VT between an **active articulator,** i.e. an organ that moves (typically some part of the tongue or the lips), and a passive location or **passive articulator,** i.e. the target of the articulation, or the place towards which the active articulator moves, whether there is actual contact between them or not. Passive articulators are: the **teeth,** the **gums,** and the **roof of the mouth** comprising **alveolar ridge, hard palate** and **soft palate** to the back of the throat. Note that the **glottis** and **epiglottis** are movable places of articulation that are not reached by any organs in the mouth. The labels used to describe phonemes according to place of articulation are usually based on the passive articulator. From the front of the mouth towards the back, the places of articulation involved in the production of RP sounds are: (1) **bilabial,** (2) **labio-dental,** (3) **dental,** (4) **alveolar,** (5) **palato-alveolar,** (6) **palatal,** (7) **velar** and (8) **glottal,** which, except for (8), are shown in Figure 22 below.[17]

17 There exist two additional places of articulation that are necessary to describe consonants across the languages of the world: **uvular,** or sounds articulated with a constriction between the back of the tongue and the uvula (e.g. the uvular trill [R] in French as in *rouge* 'red'); and **pharyngeal,** attributed to sounds articulated with a primary stricture occurring in the pharynx (e.g. the pharyngeal fricatives /ħ/ and /ʕ/ in Somali as in [ʕa:di] 'normal', [ħol] 'cane', although pharyngeal sounds may also occur in English in disordered speech).

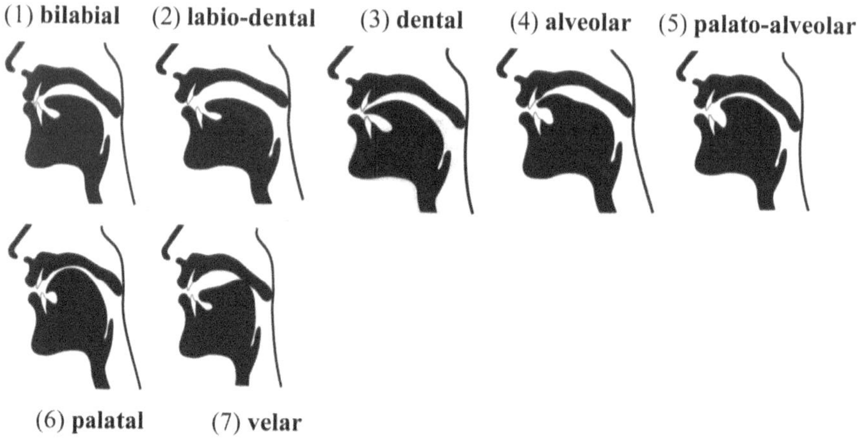

Figure 22: Seven places of articulation relevant for English

Bilabial articulations involve the **lower lip** and **upper lip**, so that bilabial sounds are sounds made by the coming together of both lips. In RP and PSp there are three bilabial sounds: /**p b m**/. The articulators in **labio-dental** sounds are the **lower lip** and the **upper front teeth** in such a way that the lower lip is actively in contact with the upper teeth, as in the production of RP /**f v**/ and PSp /**f**/. The articulators operating in **dental sounds** are the **tip of tongue** and the rear of the **upper front teeth. Dental consonants** are made by the tip of the tongue against the teeth. PSp has three dental consonants /**t d θ**/, whereas RP has only two /**θ ð**/, which should be more appropriately identified as "interdental" because in their articulation the tip of the tongue protrudes between the upper and lower teeth.

Alveolar, on the other hand, refers to a point of articulation in which the **tip/blade** of the tongue is in contact with the **alveolar ridge**, as occurs in the pronunciation of the six alveolar phonemes of RP /**t d s z n l**/ and the five alveolar consonants of PSp /**s n l ɾ r**/. In a **palato-alveolar** (or **alveolo-palatal** or **post-alveolar**) place of articulation the articulators are the **blade/front** of the tongue and the **front of the hard palate.** The sounds produced in this place require a double movement of the tongue towards the area between the alveolar ridge and hard palate: the blade of the tongue makes contact with the alveolar ridge, while the front of the tongue is raised in the direction of the hard palate. This applies to the five **palato-alveolar** phonemes found in RP /**ʃ ʒ ʧ ʤ r**/ and the only palato-alveolar phoneme of PSp /**ʧ**/.

To produce palatal sounds the front of the tongue is in contact with or approaches the **hard palate.** In RP there is one palatal consonant phoneme, /**j**/ (the initial sound of *yet* /jet/), whereas in PSp there are three palatal consonants /**ʝ ɲ ʎ**/. Other palatalised sounds may be heard as variants of a phoneme (marked with a superscript small J [ʲ]), such as [k] in *keep* [kʲiːp]) (Section 2.3.2.5). Velar sounds are made by raising the **back of the tongue** against the **soft palate.** There are three velar phonemes in RP /**k g ŋ**/, and also three in PSp /**k g x**/. Lastly, **glottal** articulations are made in the larynx, due to the closure or narrowing of the glottis, the aperture between the vocal cords. The audible release of a complete closure at the glottis is known as a glottal stop /**ʔ**/. Figure 23 locates RP consonant phonemes in their corresponding places of articulation (see also the consonant matrix on the IPA, reproduced as Table 3 in Section 1.4.1).[18]

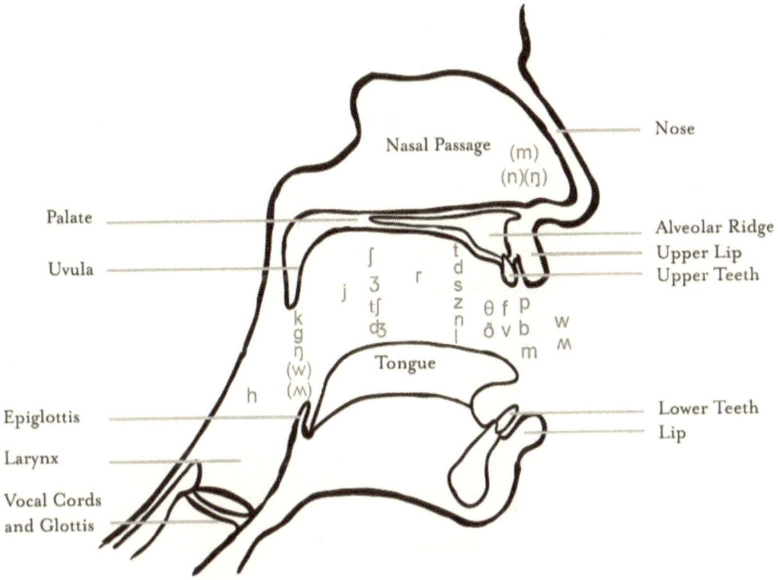

Figure 23: Places of articulation for RP consonants

2.3.2.3 Manner of articulation

Manner of articulation means how the sound is produced. Articulation involves a stricture, or narrowing of the VT, which affects the airstream. There are three

---

18 There exist two additional places of articulation that are necessary to describe consonants across the languages of the world: **uvular**, or sounds articulated with a constriction between the back of the tongue and the uvula (e.g. the uvular trill [R] in French as in *rouge* 'red'); and **pharyngeal**, attributed to sounds articulated with a primary stricture occurring in the pharynx (e.g. the pharyngeal fricatives /ħ/ and /ʕ/ in Somali as in [ʕaːdi] 'normal', [ħol] 'cane', although pharyngeal sounds may also occur in English in disordered speech).

possible types of stricture, which are, along a scale from greatest to least narrowing, as follows:

(1) **Complete closure**, or **occlusion**, with complete blocking of airflow; this stricture produces sounds known as **stops** (**plosives** and **nasals**), trills and taps.

(2) **Close approximation** is a narrowing that gives rise to friction, producing sounds known as **fricatives** or **spirants**.

(3) **Open approximation** forms no obstruction but changes the shape of the VT, thereby altering the nature of the resonance; this gives rise to the production of **(central) approximants** and **lateral approximants**. Note that as in the production of vowels, the airflow is also fully unimpeded.

Note that affricate sounds often behave as if they were intermediate between stops and fricatives, but phonetically they are sequences of stop plus fricative. Therefore six possible manners of articulation should be identified: (1) **plosives**, (2) **nasals**, (3) **fricatives**, (4) **affricates**, (5) central and lateral **approximants** and (6) **taps** and **trills** (see also the consonant matrix on the IPA, reproduced as Table 2 in section 1.4.1).

For the articulation of plosives, like RP and PSp **/p b t d k g/** (as well as **[ʔ]** in English), a complete closure is made in the VT that is suddenly released; the air pressure which had built up behind the closure rushes out with an explosive sound, as illustrated in Figure 24 below.

AI 2.6 RP plosives

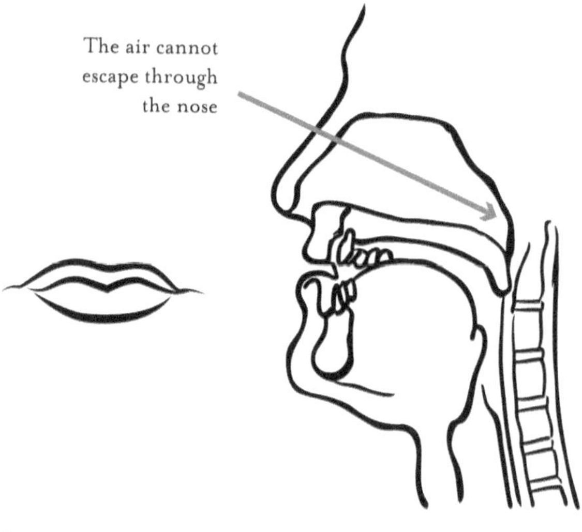

Figure 24: Manner of articulation for plosive stops

Nasal sounds are produced with a stricture of complete closure in the oral cavity, but with the soft palate being lowered so that the airflow can escape through the nasal cavity, as represented in Figure 25 below.

AI 2.7 RP nasals

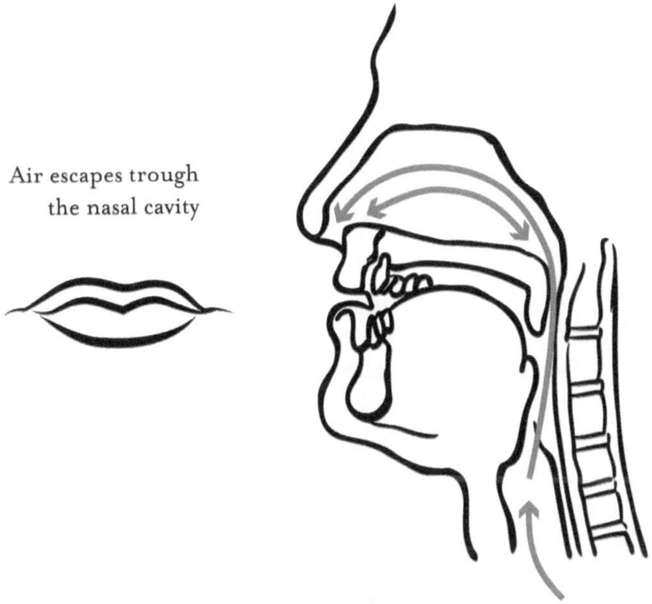

Figure 25: Manner of articulation for nasal stops

The closure may be produced in different places of the VT, which determines the production of different nasal sounds. Depending on the location of the closure, nasals are classified as: bilabial (produced by the lips), as in RP and PSp /**m**/, alveolar (produced between tip of the tongue and the alveolar ridge), as in RP and PSp /**n**/, velar (produced by the back of the tongue and the velum), as in RP /**ŋ**/, or palatal (articulated with the middle or back part of the tongue raised to the hard palate), as in PSp /**ɲ**/.

Fricative sounds are made when two organs come so close together that the air moving between them produces audible friction. There is no complete closure between the organs, simply a stricture or narrowing. In RP there are nine fricatives, /**f v θ ð s z ʃ ʒ h**/, and in PSp, five /**f θ s x ʝ**/. An additional distinction is usually made in fricative articulation depending on the shape of the aperture produced to release the airflow, as shown in Figure 26 below (Cruttenden 2014: 198–205).

AI 2.8 RP fricatives

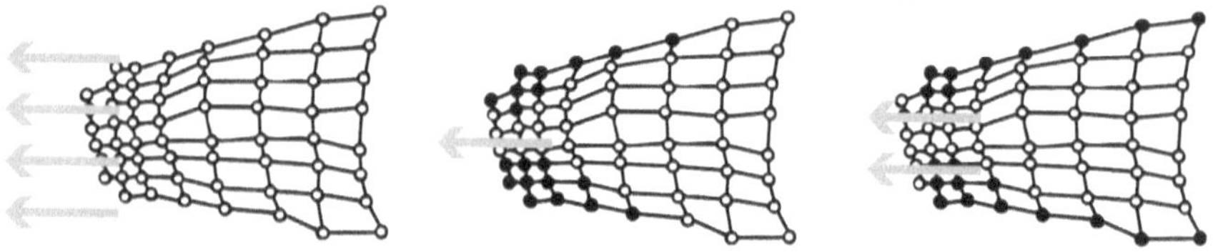

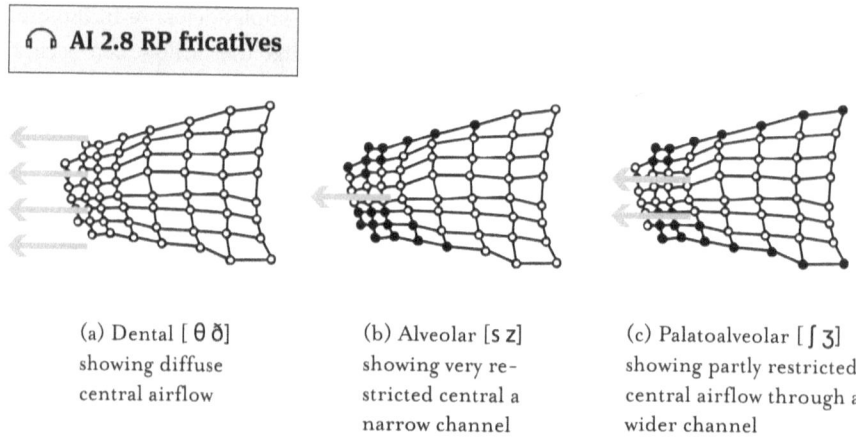

(a) Dental [θ ð] showing diffuse central airflow

(b) Alveolar [s z] showing very restricted central a narrow channel

(c) Palatoalveolar [ʃ ʒ] showing partly restricted central airflow through a wider channel

Figure 26: Palatograms of fricative articulations

Palatogram[19] (a) in Figure 26 above shows that for the articulation of RP dental fricatives /**θ ð**/, the airflow is diffusively released through an opening that is technically termed **slit**, which means that the upper surface of the tongue is smooth. By contrast, palatograms (b) and (c) show that in the production of both RP alveolar (/**s z**/) and palato-alveolar /**ʃ ʒ**/ fricatives, the tongue has a median depression, termed **groove**, so that the outgoing stream of air is channelled along this central groove, which is quite narrow in the case of the alveolars, but a little broader for the palato-alveolars. Grooved fricatives are collectively known as **sibilants**, in RP /**s z ʃ ʒ**/ and /**s**/ in PSp, because they are produced with much noisier, stronger friction than the slit, dental fricatives.

Affricate sounds are produced when the air pressure behind a complete closure in the VT is gradually released: the initial release produces a plosive, but the separation that follows is sufficiently slow to produce audible friction, and there is thus a fricative element in the sound also. However, the duration of the friction is usually not as long as would be the case for an independent fricative sound. In RP only /t/ and /d/ are released in this way, producing /**ʧ**/ and /**ʤ**/, respectively; while PSp has only one affricate phoneme /**ʧ**/.

AI 2.9 RP affricates

For the articulation of (central) approximants one articulator approaches another in such a way that the space between them is wide enough to allow the airstream

19 A **palatogram** is a graphic representation of the area of the palate contacted by the tongue that is used in articulatory phonetics to study articulations made against the palate (Crystal 2008: 348).

through with no audible friction. In RP there are three central approximant phonemes, /**w j r** (or ɹ)/, in addition to all vowels and vowel glides. Although the status of [**w j**] in PSp is a debatable issue, here we shall consider them as allophones of /u/ and /i/ respectively (Navarro Tomás 1966 [1946], 1991 [1918]; Quilis and Fernández 1996).

AI 2.10 RP approximants

A lateral (approximant) is made where the air escapes around one or both sides of a closure made in the mouth, as in the various types of /**l**/ in RP and PSp. Typically this is produced with the centre of the tongue forming a closure with the roof of the mouth but the sides lowered and the air escaping without friction. PSp has an additional palatal lateral phoneme /**ʎ**/, for the articulation of which there is extensive linguo-palatal contact that is, overall, less posterior than that of /**ɲ**/.

To close this section, a distinction should be made between trills and taps. A **trill** is a sound made by the rapid percussive action of an active articulator against a passive one. The two types of trill that most frequently occur in languages are alveolar (the tongue-tip striking the alveolar ridge, as in the PSp /**r**/ of *carro* 'cart') and uvular (the uvula striking the back of the tongue, as in French). A single rapid percussive movement – i.e. one beat of a trill – is termed a **tap**, as in the PSp /**ɾ**/ of *caro* 'expensive'.

2.3.2.4 Orality

Related to manner of articulation, this feature concerns the distinction between oral sounds (produced with a raised velum) and nasal sounds, which are uttered by lowering the soft palate. All consonants are oral except for the three nasal phonemes in RP /**m n ŋ**/ and PSp /**m n ɲ**/. However, as already noted for vowels (Section 2.3.1), consonants may have nasalised variants, represented with a [^{n}] [^{m}] when followed by a nasal consonant, as in the case of [t] in *ca**t**nip* ['kæt^{n}nɪp] or [p] in *to**p**most* ['top^{m}məʊst]. Further details on nasalisation may be found in Sections 2.3.2.5 and 5.2.4.

AI 2.11 Nasal versus oral sounds

2.3.2.5 Secondary articulation

The basic production of a speech sound may be modified by means of what is known as **secondary articulation**. These processes include the following: (1)

labialisation, (2) **palatalisation**, (3) **velarisation**, (4) **glottalisation** and (5) **nasalisation** (Lass 1984; Cohn 1990; Barry 1992; Ladefoged and Maddieson 1996).

Labialisation (indicated with a superscript [ʷ]) involves the addition of lip-rounding and the elevation of the tongue back. It is used as a cover term for **labialised consonants** (i.e. those occurring in the vicinity of rounded vowels, especially consonants preceding them in an accented syllable) such as [kʷ] and [ɫʷ] in ***cool*** [kʷuːɫʷ], as well as sequences of the form Cw, as in *quantity* [kʷwɒntəti] (see § 5.2.3). **Palatalisation** (symbolised with a superscript [ʲ]), on the other hand, refers to the addition of front tongue raising to hard palate – i.e. the tongue takes on an [i]-like shape with a possible [j] off-glide. This what happens to the *u*-sounds of words like ***t**une*, ***d**une*, ***n**ew*, *a**ss**ume*, ***b**eautiful*, which are therefore pronounced [juː] (/tjuːn/, /djuːn/, /njuː/, /əˈsjuːm/, /ˈbjuːtəfl̩/). As a result, the preceding consonants are represented in narrow transcriptions as **palatalised** [**tʲ dʲ nʲ sʲ bʲ**]. Contrast the /m/ in ***m**e* and ***m**ore*: in the first case it is palatalised [mʲiː], and in the second labialised [mʷɔː]. In addition to the notion of adding an "i-colour", palatalisation also refers to the process whereby a non-palatal sounds becomes palatal (see § 5.2.3, 5.3.4). **Velarisation** means the addition of back-of-the-tongue raising towards the velum – i.e. the tongue takes on an [u]-like shape. This is typical of what is known as *dark l*, represented as [ɫ], as in *sti**ll***, *te**ll***, *sha**ll***, *bu**ll***. **Glottalisation** refers to the addition of a reinforcing glottal stop [**ʔ**]. The English fortis plosives /p t k ʧ/ are regularly glottalised when syllable-final, as in *li**p**stick* [ˈlɪʔpstɪʔk] (see § 5.2.8.2). Finally, **nasalisation** (marked with [˜]) represents the addition of nasal resonance through lowering the soft palate. In English, vowels preceding nasals are often nasalised as in *stro**ng*** [strɒ̃ŋ], ***m**a**n*** [mæ̃n] (see § 5.2 and 5.2.4).

Some details on these allophonic variants of phonemes have already been given in Section 2.3.2.2, but a more thorough discussion is presented in Chapters 3 and 4, when dealing with the allophonic variants of each of the RP vowels and consonants, and in Chapter 5 when giving an overview of connected speech phenomena.

2.4 Acoustic features of speech sounds

In this section we will look at the acoustic features of speech sounds, using waveforms and spectrograms (SFS/WASP Version 1.54), which represent the size and shape of the VT during their production. There also exist specific computer programs that have been devised to test the computer production and recognition of speech sounds as well as to do speech synthesis, but these different dimensions of speech processing lie well beyond the scope of this manual. For further details on such programs and/or speech processing techniques and applications, two good overviews are offered in Ladefoged (1996) and Coleman (2005).

Now, if we are to describe speech sounds from an acoustic point of view, broadly it can be said that the larynx is their **source** and the VT is a system of acoustic **filters**. In Section 1.2.2, we have seen that the glottal wave is a periodic complex wave (a pulse wave) with different alignments of prominence, or energy peaks, at specific frequencies resulting from VT resonance, known as **formants**, which represent the strongest ("loudest") components in the signal with the greatest amplitude and are composed of fundamental frequency (F_0) and a range of harmonics. Variations with respect to the direction in which the F_0 changes with time (roughly between 60-500Hz) are responsible for **intonation** (Section 6.4). The filtering function of resonators (nasal cavity and oral cavity) reduce the amplitude of certain ranges of frequency while allowing other frequency bands to pass with very little reduction of amplitude. The output of the resonance system always has the Fo of the glottal wave, while the formants F1, F2, F3 are imposed by the VT, and so there exists a correlation between articulation and formant structure. Thus, the sound waves radiated at the lips and the nostrils are a result of the modifications imposed by this resonating system on the sound waves coming from the larynx, where vocal fold vibration switching on and off triggers phonemic differences and contrasts (degrees of voicing and voicelessness). By way of illustration, the response of the VT (with the tongue in neutral position) is such that it imposes a pattern of certain natural frequency regions (e.g. 500 Hz-1500 Hz-2500 Hz for a VT 17cm in length) and reduces the amplitude of the remaining harmonics of the glottal wave, which results in the articulation of a schwa vowel. The respective peaks of energy (formants F1 – F2 – F3) are retained regardless of variations in Fo of the larynx pulse wave. Further modification of formant structure can be obtained by altering tongue and lip shapes. Rounded and protruded lips, for instance, lengthen the "horizontal" resonance chamber and hence lower its resonating properties, thereby lowering F values.

Section 2.4.1 below explains that each vowel sound has a different and unique arrangement of formants, which therefore determine its identifying acoustic characteristics. Likewise, the spectrographic peculiarities of vowel glides and consonants are summarised in Sections 2.4.2 and 2.4.3, respectively.

2.4.1 Vowels

All vowels are **voiced**, as shown by the vertical striations in the spectrograms, and this means that they contain a **voicing** or **voice bar**, i.e. a dark band running parallel to the bottom of the spectrogram indicating presence of energy at fundamental frequency associated with voicing, usually in the region of 100–200 Hz depending on speaker-specific characteristics. This can be seen in Figure 27 below, extracted from Katz (2013: 197), which presents the spectographic image of the clause *Buy Spot food!* produced by a male American speaker (assuming that Spot is hungry).

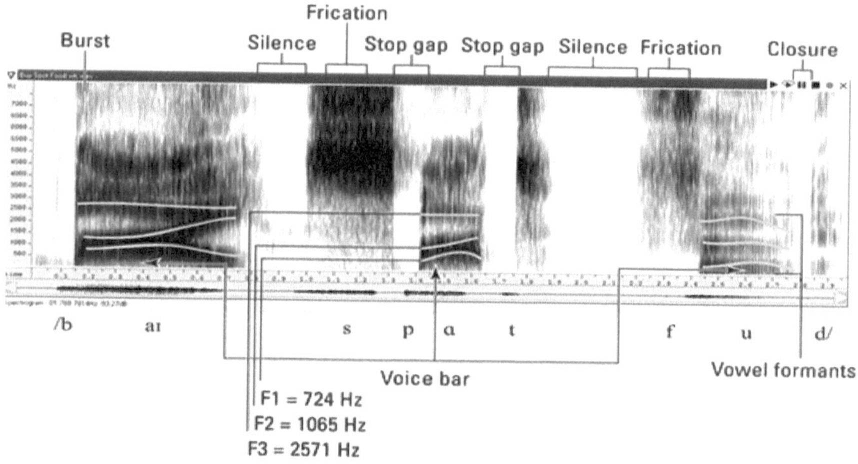

Figure 27: Reading a spectrogram

Note that in Figure 27 vowels, vowel glides and voiced consonants [b d] do have a voice bar, whereas voiceless sounds [p s t d] do not. **Vowel formants**, in turn, show up on the spectrogram as dark bands running roughly horizontal with the bottom of the page. Modifications of formant structure can be obtained by altering the shape of the VT, simply by varying the height and backness of the tongue as well as the position of the lips. Furthermore, there exists a correlation between the values of **F1** (**first formant**), the centre frequency of the lowest resonance of the VT, and the articulatory and/or perceptual dimension of **vowel height** (high vs. low vowels, or close vs. open vowels), on the one hand, and between the **backness of the tongue** and **F2** (**second formant**), reflecting the place of maximal constriction during the production of the vowel, on the other. The correlation of vowel height (closeness) is inversely proportional to F1 values so that closer vowels have lower F1 values than open vowels and vice versa; whereas front vowels have higher F2 values than back values, lip-rounding having the effect of lowering the overall energy throughout the formants. So, in Figure 27 we can see that the value of F1 is higher for [ɑ], an open vowel, than for [u], a close vowel, while the [ɪ] sound of [aɪ], a front vowel, has a higher F2 value than [ɑ] and [u], two back vowels, but the latter displays an overall lowering of its formant pattern as a result of its lip-rounding.

The adult male formant frequencies for all RP vowels as collected by John Wells around 1960 are presented in Table 7 below, where you can see that:

(1) the F1 value for close vowels is around 300 Hz and it rises to 600 and 800 from close-mid to open vowels;
(2) F2 values are highest (over 2500 Hz) for front vowels; and
(3) F3 values correlate with those of F2.

Table 7: Formant frequencies of RP vowels

Vowel	F1(Hz)	F2(Hz)	F3(Hz)
iː	280	2620	3380
ɪ	360	2220	2960
e	600	2060	2840
æ	800	1760	2500
ʌ	760	1320	2500
ɑː	740	1180	2640
ɒ	560	920	2560
ɔː	480	760	2620
ʊ	380	940	2300
uː	320	920	2200
ɜː	560	1480	2520

In addition, there are four other features of vowel production with an acoustic correlate that must be observed in spectrograms. Two of them relate to the relative length of the vowel, **pre-fortis clipping** and **rhythmic clipping** (Section 5.2.1), and another two reflect whether the vowel has **non-delayed onset to voicing** or **delayed onset to voicing** (Section 5.2.2). In cases of pre-fortis clipping, vowels (especially long ones) have a shorter duration of vocal fold activity as a result of their being followed by voiceless consonants in the same syllable, e.g. [i·] in ***leak*** [li·k], which is spectrographically represented by a voice bar and striations with a shorter duration. The same acoustic effect occurs in instances of rhythmic clipping, where (long) vowels are followed by more than one syllable in the same rhythmic unit, like the first vowel of ***leakage*** [ˈlĭ·kɪʤ] [ĭ·], which is even shorter than the vowel of *leak*. Now compare the spectrograms in Figure 28 below.

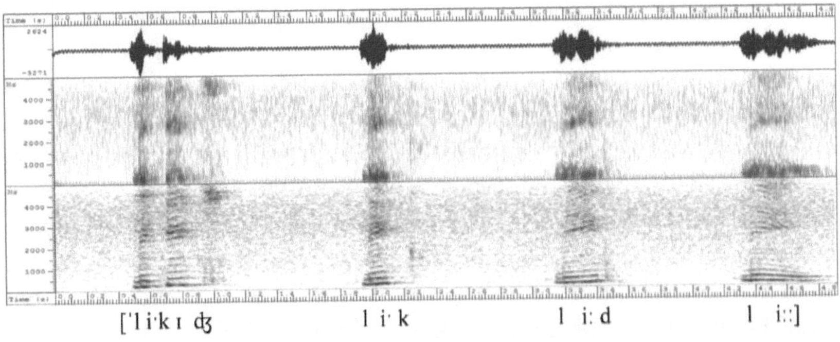

Figure 28: Waveforms and spectrograms of "leakage", "leak", "lead" and "lee"

In Figure 28 you can see that the four instances of [i] differ in length: the sound is shortest [ĭˑ] in *leakage* (rhythmic and pre-fortis clipping); it is clipped [iˑ] in *leak* (pre-fortis clipping); it has normal length [i:] in *lead* before a voiced consonant; and it is extra-long [i::] in *lee*, a word that is in an open word-final syllable.

Non-delayed onset to voicing, on the other hand, is observed in vowels preceded by syllable-initial voiced consonants, as in ***bee*** [bi::], which means that they show vocal fold activity immediately after the release of the consonant, with a voice bar and striations being observed immediately after a short explosion bar. By contrast, if a vowel is preceded by a voiceless consonant, as in ***pea*** [p^{h}i::], then it has a delayed onset to voicing: this means that vocal fold activity begins a while later, after the release of the consonant, and the voice bar and striations begin a while after the explosion bar, with weak random energy being observed along the frequency axis. The spectrographic representation of non-delayed [i], as in ***bee*** [bi::], and delayed [i], as in ***pea*** [p^{h}i::] [i] are illustrated in Figure 29 below.

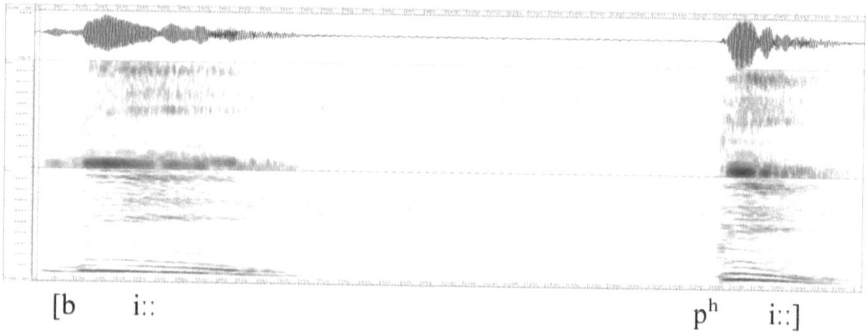

Figure 29: Waveforms and spectrograms of "bee" and "pea"

2.4.2 Vowel glides

We have seen that in glides the tongue moves in order to produce one vowel quality followed by another, thereby modifying the shape and size of the oral cavity. The tongue movement that takes place during the production of vowel glides is represented spectrographically by a **transition** in the formant pattern from the first to the second vowel pointing in the direction of which the glide is made, as shown in the production of [aɪ] in Figure 27 above, and the spectrograms of the eight RP **diphthongs** in Figure 30 below. In some cases the slight bends of formant structures indicate how the speaker has diphthongised the vowel sound in question.

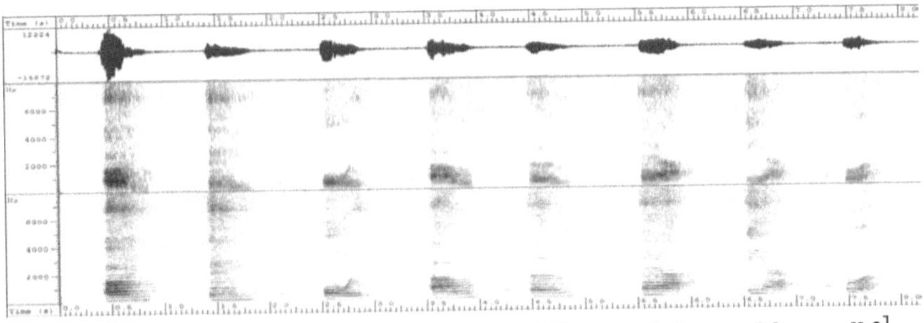

Figure 30: Waveforms and spectrograms of [aɪ, eɪ, ɔɪ, aʊ, əʊ, eə, ɪə, ʊə]

2.4.3 Consonants

Consonants can be best spotted in spectrograms at **transitions**, i.e. the edges of the vowels that are next to the consonants, the time period when the mouth is changing shape between consonant and vowel. We have already seen that voiced consonants have a voice bar and show vertical striations in spectrograms corresponding to vocal fold vibration, whereas no such acoustic cues occur during stop articulation, while in aspiration or frication there is a noise component, as shown in Figure 27 above. Now focusing on the acoustic correlates of place of articulation, bilabial sounds display a weak and diffuse spectrum, and the values of F2 and F3 are comparatively low: the locus of F2 is about 700~1200Hz. Alveolar sounds, in turn, show a diffuse rising spectrum and have an F2 value of approximately 1700~1800Hz, while velar sounds display a compact spectrum in which the second and third formant structures have a common origin, the value of F2 usually being high (about 3000 Hz).

Let us analyse the acoustic correlates of manner of articulation. **Obstruents** (plosives, fricatives and affricates, see § 1.3.2, fn 3) involve a complete or almost complete obstruction to the airflow in the VT, and these different degrees of stoppage have clear acoustic correlates. Thus, the three articulatory phases of **plosives** [**p b t d k g**], closure of the articulators, the build-up of air behind them, and the final release, are reflected in spectrograms as a gap in the pattern (the first two stages). Figure 31 below shows that, in voiceless stops [**p t k**] there is a voiceless silent interval (70–140 ms), which is long if unaspirated, and is followed by a burst if aspirated, in which case the formants may be seen in noise. In voiced stops [**b d g**], the closure is generally shorter, they have a voice bar during closure and the release burst is weaker and has no aspiration.

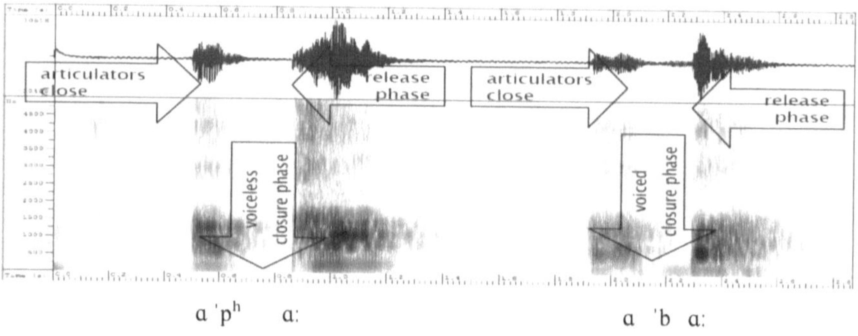

Figure 31: Acoustic phases of plosives in [apʰa:] and [aba:]

In **fricatives** the body of air is forced through a relatively narrow passage involving friction, which acoustically results in a continuous high-frequency noise component (random energy pattern with striations) that is easily identifiable on the spectrogram, as shown in Figure 32: alveolar fricatives [**s z**] have frequencies concentrated in the high range, at 3600–8000 Hz; the palato-alveolar fricatives [**ʃ ʒ**] are somewhat lower, in the range of 2000–7000 Hz; labio-dental [**f v**] and dentals [**θ ð**] have similar values (1500–7000 Hz vs 1400–8000 Hz); and the glottal fricative [**h**] has the lowest values (500–6500 Hz), its spectral pattern being likely to mirror that of the following vowel.

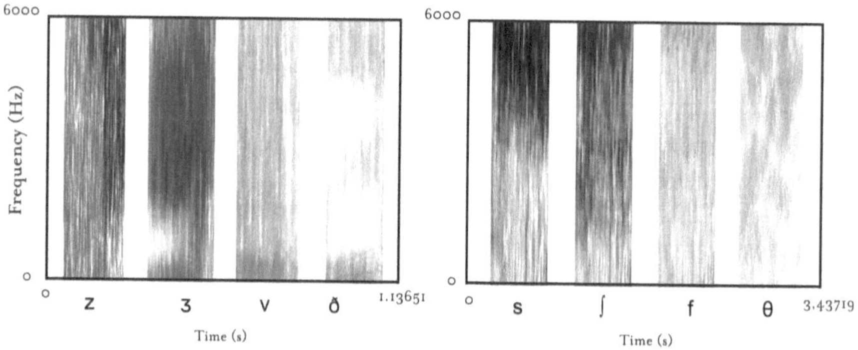

Figure 32: Spectrograms showing the noise patterns of fricatives

In addition, **voiceless fricatives** [**f θ s ʃ h**] have **noise** only, which is much stronger in the case of **sibilants** [**s ʃ**], and they are generally longer than their **voiced counterparts** [**z ʒ**], which show weaker noise and voicing bar, although **non-sibilant ones** [**v ð**] may have **no noise** at all. All in all, the friction of voiced fricatives is shorter than that the voiceless series.

The spectrographic representations of **affricates** [**ʤ ʧ**] in Figure 33 below shows the characteristics of their components: a break for the stop combined with a high-frequency noise for the fricative, although the stop transition may have a palatalised component, which is not present in alveolar stops, or alternatively there may be brief intervening alveolar friction [s z] before the fricative component of the affricates [ʃ ʒ] (Cruttenden 2014: 188–209).

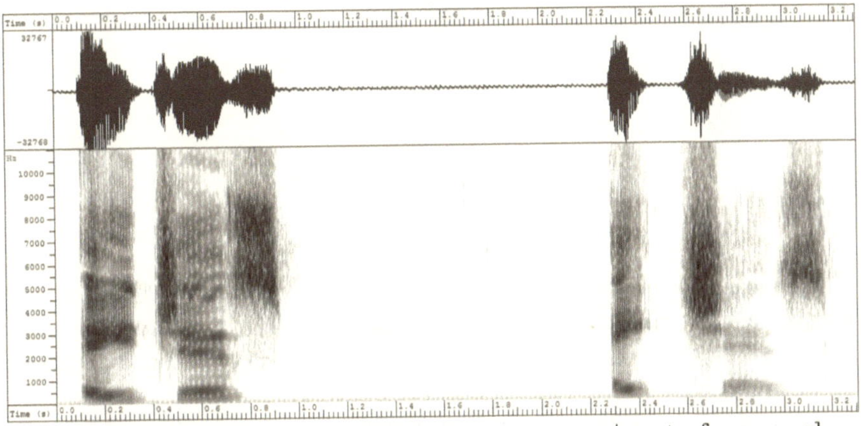

Figure 33: Spectrograms of "ages" [ˈeɪʤɪz] and "h's" [ˈeɪʧɪz]

Moving on to **sonorant** consonants (see § 1.3.2, fn 4), including **nasals** [**m n ŋ**], **liquids** [**l r**] and the **approximants** [**w j**], acoustically they behave like vowels (especially in intervocalic positions) in that they exhibit a voicing bar along with formant-like structures. As regards the spectrographic picture of nasals, the manner cues include the absence of an explosion bar, with absence of energy around 1000 Hz, as well as the presence of a low-frequency resonance or "murmur" below 500Hz, with nasal formants at about 250, 2500 and 3250 Mhz. There are also abrupt transitions from and into the neighbouring sounds involving the rapid fall and rise in energy as the nasal is made and released, due to additional nasal cavity resonance that results from lowering the soft-palate (velum).

The spectral shape of each nasal, particularly in connection with the second and third formant transitions to and from F2 and F3, varies slightly with the place of the obstruction in the VT, as for homorganic plosives: minus transitions for /**m**/, slight plus transitions for /**n**/, and plus transitions of F2 and minus transitions of F3 for /**ŋ**/ (Cruttenden 2014: 209–210). Furthermore, experimental research has shown that a key acoustic feature to distinguish bilabial from alveolar nasals is the relative proportion of energy that is present: 395–770 Hz for **bilabials** and 1265–2310 Hz for **alveolars** (Kurowski 1987; Ohde 1994). Spectrograms of /m n ŋ/ in ***sim***, ***sin*** and ***sing*** are shown in Figure 34 below.

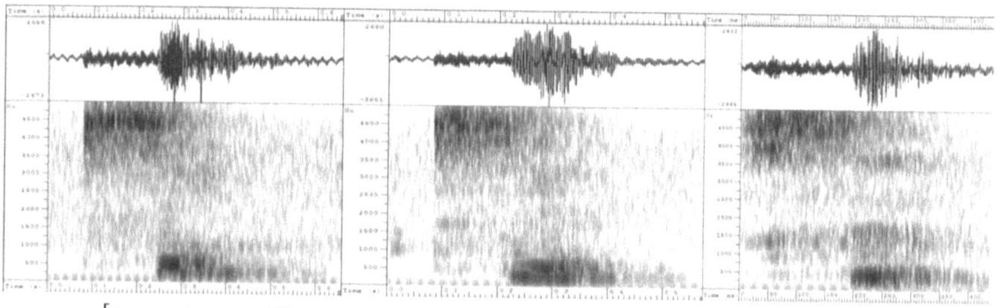

Figure 34: Spectrograms of "sim" [sɪm], "sin" [sɪn] and "sing" [sɪŋ]

The nasalisation of vowels is cued by the presence of a low-frequency resonance and an increase in **formant damping**, that is, the sound waves get weaker as they progress in time, reducing the vibratory movement and amplitude of the sound.

Like nasals, **laterals** exhibit a discontinuity in formant amplitude from adjacent vowels and also have a vowel-like formant structure with weak amplitude, but the values are in the neighbourhood of 250, 1200 and 2400 Hz. The difference between **clear** [l] (in syllable-initial positions) and **dark** or **velar** [ɫ] (in syllable final positions) lies in the fact that they have respectively the timbre of a close front vowel and a close back vowel: as a result, in [l] the values of F1 (low) and F2 (weak) are quite far apart (around 300 and 1600 Hz), whereas they are close together in [ɫ] (around 400 and 600 Hz). For both realisations of /l/ F3 is high and weak (around 2500 Hz). Transitions from and to vowels tend to be slower than those for nasals.

Lastly, the formants of **non-lateral approximants** show, in general, stronger amplitude than laterals and nasals, and exhibit the corresponding vowels but with lower amplitude and lower F1 (all consonants have lower F1 than vowels), as illustrated in Figure 35. The F1 of [ɹ] is between 120 and 600 Hz, the lower the frequency the greater the lip-rounding, while F2 and particularly F3 display lower values between 700 Hz and 1200 Hz. The tap variant [ɾ], in contrast, has very short closure duration (around 30ms). Turning to the **glide consonants**, the starting point in both cases is that of [u:] or [i:], i.e. about 240 Hz, but [**w**] has low F2 (within the range of 360–840 Hz) and weak low F3, whereas [**j**] has high values for both F2 and F3 (within the range of 2280–3600 Hz).

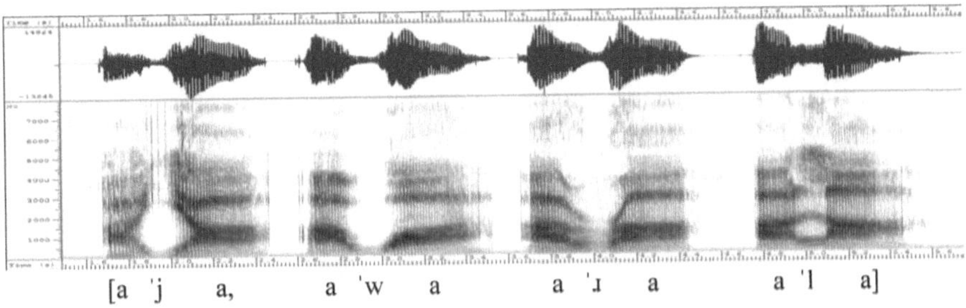

Figure 35: Spectrograms of [a'ja], [a'wa], [a'ɹa], [a'la]

Further reading

As in the previous chapter, for an overview of the physics of speech we recommend phonetics texts such as Cruttenden (2014, Chapter 2), Lodge (2009, Chapters 2 and 9), Ashby (2005, Chapter 3; 2011, Chapters 1 to 8), Ogden (2009, Chapter 4), Ashby and Maidment (2005, Chapters 2 to 6), Ball and Rahilly (1999, Chapters 1 to 3), and Laver (1994, Chapter 7).

The issues of airstream mechanisms and phonation types are covered at a basic level in a variety of volumes, including Ogden (2009, Chapter 10), Ashby and Maidment (2005, Chapter 7), Ashby (2005, Chapter 6), Ladefoged (2001, Chapter 6), and Ball and Rahilly (1999, Chapters 2 and 4). Slightly more advanced discussion of non-pulmonic consonants can be found in Laver (1994, Chapter 6), and detailed accounts of clicks, ejectives and implosives may be found in Ladefoged (2005, Chapters 1 and 14) and Ladefoged and Maddieson (1996, Chapters 8 and Chapter 3).

Accessible accounts of vowel classification, albeit focused on English, are presented in, for instance, Cruttenden (2014, Chapters 4 and 8), Ashby (2011, Chapters 6 and 7), Ashby and Maidment (2005, Chapter 5), and Ladefoged (2001, Chapter 4), whereas Hayward (2000, Chapter 6) provides a detailed analysis of vowel acoustics. Turning to consonants, their classification in VPM terms is addressed in Cruttenden (2014, Chapters 4 and 9), Ashby (2005, Chapters 3 and 5; 2011, Chapter 8), Lodge (2009, Chapter 2), Ashby and Maidment (2005, Chapters 3 and 4), and Ladefoged (2001, Chapter 7). Other advanced readings are Ashby (2006, Chapters 3 to 7), Ladefoged and Maddieson (1996) and Laver (1994, Chapters 8 to 10), among many others. Additional bibliographic recommendations concerning (English and Spanish) vowels and consonants are offered in Chapters 3 and 4, respectively.

Good introductions to acoustic phonetics may be found in Katz (2013, Chapters 12 to 14), Hewlett and Beck (2006, Chapter 17), Ladefoged (2003), Kent and Read (2002, Chapter 5), and Ball and Rahilly (1999, Chapter 9), whereas Cabrera Abreu and Vizcaíno Ortega (2009) propose an acoustically-based method to explain English phonetics and phonology to SSLE.

Exercises

1. Ingressive sounds are those that are produced on an airstream flowing inward through the mouth or nose. Can you give some examples? Do some languages produce this kind of speech sounds?
2. Voice disorders are those medical conditions that can affect the production of speech. Otolaryngology or ENT (ear, nose, and throat) is the branch of medicine and surgery that specialises in their diagnosis and treatment. Vocal injury is not infrequent. It is claimed that, strictly speaking, only 5% to 10% of the population has a completely normal speech and healthy voice. Can you think which are the main disorders that can affect voice?
3. Speech-Language Pathology professionals (Speech-Language Pathologists (SLPs), or informally, speech therapists) specialise in communication disorders as well as swallowing disorders. What are the main conditions that a speech therapist has to deal with in connection with the production of speech sounds?
4. An articulation disorder involves difficulty in producing sounds. A child with speech sound disorders will be hard to understand, which has serious implications, not only in his/her intelligibility but also in his/her socialisation process. Examine and discuss the following examples of errors children can produce and classify them according to what type of speech disorder you think it represents.

1. *I go to coo on the buh	(I go to school on the bus)
2. *I have a wosy wabbit	(I have a rosy rabbit)
3. *I am a dood dirl	(I am a good girl)
4. *I saw a wittle wamb	(I saw a little lamb)
5. *I ree a boo	(I read a book)
6. *My poo i boken	(My spoon is broken)
7. *I have a wed wadio	(I have a red radio)
8. *The tar is toming	(The car is coming)

5. Speech recognition (SR) is a computer science which translates spoken words into text. Think of applications of this area of study in everyday life.

6. Think of the differences between singing, shouting or speaking quietly, and explain them in phonetic terms. How do rapping or chanting differ from these?
7. Are the phonation and articulation processes independent from each other? If so, what are the consequences?
8. Phonetically speaking, what is the difference between a consonant sound and a vowel? And phonemically?
9. Watch the scene from the Pink Panther again, which was mentioned in Chapter 1, exercise 5. Why do you think *would* was the word chosen for a close-up of Steve Martin? When dubbed into Spanish, what word should be chosen here in order to achieve the same effect?
10. Look at the sequences in Chapter 1, exercise 6 again. Now explain from a detailed articulatory point of view what might cause the foreignness effect.

Chapter 3

3 Vowels and Vowel Glides

3.1 Introduction

In this and the following chapter, the sounds of RP are contrasted with each other as well as with those of Spanish. Accordingly, using the articulatory features (basically tongue shape and height, lip shape and duration) and the acoustic measurements already introduced, this chapter compares and contrasts the **vowel systems** of RP and PSp. The vowel system of **RP** consists of **twenty sounds**, of which **twelve** are **monophthongs** (seven short /**ɪ e ʌ æ ə ɒ ʊ**/ and five long /**iː ɜː ɑː ɔː uː**/) and **eight** are **diphthongs** /**aɪ eɪ ɔɪ əʊ aʊ ɪə eə ʊə**/). **PSp**, on the other hand, has **nineteen sounds**, **five** of which are pure **vowels** /**a e i o u**/ and **fourteen** are **diphthongs** (/**ei̯ ai̯ oi̯ au̯ eu̯ ou̯ ja je jo ju wa we wo wi**/). In addition, in RP there are five diphthongs + [ə] combinations ([**eɪə aɪə ɔɪə əʊə aʊə**]) that have no equivalents in the Spanish triphthongs ([**wei̯ wai̯ jei̯ jai̯**]), as already noted (see § 1.5, Table 4).

The **contrastive approach** has been adopted for three main reasons. Firstly, it allows us to take into account the **interlanguage phonological system** of learners, considering both the first language (L1) and the (perception of the) second language (L2) sound systems, as well as additional factors at work such as markedness and other universal phonetic principles (Ellis 1985, 1994).

Empirical studies show that, on the one hand, prior language experiences have an impact on the way a language is learned (Flege 1991, 1995, 2003; Kuhl *et al.* 1992; Kuhl 1993; Best 1994, 1995; Best and Tyler 2007; Boomershine 2013), and, on the other, a better awareness of sound perception may help improve production and understanding (Flege 2003; Flege and MacKay 2004). Focusing on L2 vowel production and perception, studies conducted within the **Perceptual Assimilation Model** (PAM), for example, have found that the structure of listerners' vowel space is significantly affected by their L1 vowel inventory and that native-language/second-language perceptual similarity acts as a predictor of difficulties in the discrimination of non-native contrasts (Flege 1991; Best 1994, 1995; Best and Tyler 2007; Boomershine 2013). Likewise, Flege's (1995, 2003) **Speech Learning Model** suggests that patterns of learning are predictable from assimilation of L2 sounds to L1 ones, so that vowels that are weakly assimilated into L1 categories should be easier to learn than vowels that are more strongly assimilated. Compatible with these two models is the **Native Language Magnet** (NLM) observation that sound prototypes have a "**perceptual magnet**" **effect** with respect to other sounds, so that sounds in the vicinity of a "prototype" in L1 (e.g. one of the five Spanish vowels) are not as easily discriminated as are sounds of equivalent auditory difference that are not located near a sound prototype (Kuhl *et al.* 1992; Kuhl 1993).

In what follows it will be shown that, although there are additional factors at work, NLM predictions broadly hold true for SSLE. RP sounds /**ʌ æ ɑː**/, /**e ɜː ə**/, /**iː ɪ**/, /**ɔː ɒ**/, /**uː ʊ**/, which resemble the L1 PSp prototypes /**a**/, /**e**/, /**i**/, /**o**/ and /**u**/ respectively, are difficult to distinguish from their corresponding prototypes because the latter attract to themselves perceptions of sounds that fall under their scope the way a magnet would, and consequently single category assimilations occur. Likewise, PAM predictions seem to be confirmed in that different types of category assimilations (good exemplar, acceptable but not ideal exemplar, or deviant, as opposed to uncategorisable instances) are influenced by the phonemic inventory of L1, among other factors (Cortés Pomacóndor 1999, 2000; Gallardo del Puerto 2005). Moreover, as duration and the tense-lax distinctions are not contrastive features in Spanish, SSLE are expected to be less sensitive than English natives to such cues (García Lecumberri and Cenoz Iragui 1997; Escudero and Chládková 2010).

Secondly, by adopting a contrastive approach that notes the existing differences and similarities between the sound inventories of RP and PSp, we can anticipate and thereby help to circumvent the difficulties that SSLE may encounter when producing and hearing RP sounds, as hypothesised in **contrastive** or **error analysis** (Lado 1957). Although learning is in general facilitated where there are equivalent features between L1 and L2, this and the following chapters will show that the equivalences that exist between the sound systems and the suprasegmental features of English and Spanish are rarely exact but mostly similar. As a result, so-called **interference** or **transfer mispronunciations** are common in the interlanguage of SSLE, who, assuming a more complete correspondence than exists, carry over Spanish sound patterns in cases where English has in fact no parallel sounds or features.

In addition to the L1 influence and speaker-dependent variables mentioned above (anatomic and psychological features and capabilities, age, sex, grammatical correctness, rhythmic adequacy, etc.), there exist two additional factors that may affect the way a sound is perceived and produced which therefore should be considered: **phonetic context** and **orthographic pronunciation**. It will be shown that, depending on which phonetic context it occurs in, a sound may have different realisations and, as result, it may be categorised differently (Peperkamp et al. 2006; Altenberg 2005; Quilis and Esgueva 1983; Mann and Repp 1980). For instance, we shall see that SSLE may assimilate RP /**dʒ**/ in such words as ***gin*** to Spanish [**ʝ**] because this language has a voiced palatal fricative word-initially, while in ***age*** it can be perceived as [**tʃ**] owing to the devoicing of word-final voiced sounds that takes place in English (García Lecumberri and Cenoz 2003).

Similarly, SSLE's mispronunciations of unstressed syllables generally result from orthographic pronunciations reflecting the spelling of words (*final* *[ˈfaɪnal], *silence* *[saɪlens], rather than vowel weakening (/ˈfaɪnl̩/, /ˈsaɪləns/) (Gallardo del Puerto 2005: 416; García Lecumberri and Gallardo 2003).

But, notwithstanding the difficulties involved in learning English pronunciation, it is nonetheless true that experimental research suggests that perceptual processes improve gradually as production capabilities are developed, which underscores the dynamic or changing nature of the learner's interlanguage during L2 acquisition (Flege *et al.* 1994, 1997; Fox *et al.* 1995; Allen *et al.* 1995; Chang *et al.* 2009). Hence, in order to improve perceptual and production capabilities, Spanish speaking (and all other) EFL learners are advised to practise as much as possible. For this purpose, plenty of practice material is included in this book and the supporting EPSS Multimedia Lab.

Our third intention in adopting a contrastive approach is to favour holistic learning. Our aim is that the details of each English sound may be learned all at once and simultaneously compared and contrasted not only with those of Spanish as an L1, but also with each other, on the grounds of both primary and secondary cues. In the case of vowels, for instance, primary cues are articulatory features and F1/F2 targets (Flege *et al.* 1994), as well as sound-orthography correlations (Chapter 7), whereas formant movement and duration are secondary cues (Fox *et al.* 1995, Iverson and Evans 2007).

In what follows a detailed description is offered of **RP vowels** (Section 3.2) and **vowel sequences** including diphthongs and triphthongs (Section 3.3) along nine main parameters:

(1) **IPA symbols**, giving the names of the phonetic symbols.
(2) **Identification**, providing the identification of RP sounds in OBR labels.
(3) **Position in the CVS**, plotting the location of RP and PSp sounds in the CVS.
(4) **Description**, describing the articulation of RP sounds.
(5) **Environment**, noting the main contexts of appearance of RP sounds.
(6) **Spellings** (with transcribed examples), listing the spellings of RP sounds in decreasing frequency and noting the most remarkable exceptions (if any).[20]
(7) **Regional and social variants**, mentioning the most important alternative pronunciations in RP, making only sporadic references to other accents that

20 In this subsection, the relevance of silent letters and alternative pronunciations of the same spellings are mentioned in passing, as a more detailed account of the relationship between spelling and pronunciation is offered in Unit 7, where one spelling at a time will be dealt with, together with the various sounds (including absence of sound) that it represents. Incidentally, spellings with and without <r> such as <o> and <ea> vs. <or> and <ear>, are presented as different spellings because they represent different sets of sounds.

are close to it; whereas the **allophonic realisations** of RP sounds, i.e. their contextually conditioned phonetic variants, are described separately in Chapter 5.

(8) **Comparison with Spanish and advice**, where the sounds of RP are compared and contrasted with those of PSp and some advice on pronunciation for Spanish learners is provided, including comments about which aspects of RP are essential for intelligibility and which features are only relevant to the imitation of a native-like accent.

(9) **Further practice**, presenting recorded (and transcribed) examples extracted from our Sound Bank. As already explained, the Sound Bank, as well as additional keyed audio exercises and all the listening and support material accompanying this book are available at the companion website EPSS Multimedia Lab.

3.2 A comparison of English and Spanish pure vowels

Like other Germanic languages, (RP) English shows a relatively "crowded" vowel-space comprising, as already noted, **twelve** steady-state or **pure vowels** that are normally plotted in a trapezium and are usually described in OBR terms as follows:

/iː/ Close, front, tightly-spread, tense and long (free), as in ***beans*** /biːnz/.

/ɪ/ Near-close, near-front, slightly-spread, lax and short (checked) (see fn. 7), as in ***bins*** /bɪnz/.

/e/ Between close-mid and open-mid, front, slightly-spread, lax and short (checked), as in ***sell*** /sel/.

/ɜː/ Between close-mid and open-mid, central, neutrally spread, tense and long (free), as in ***first*** /fɜːst/.

/ə/ Between close-mid and open-mid (in non-final positions) and open-mid (in final positions), central, neutral lip shape, lax and short (checked), as in ***alone*** /əˈləʊn/, ***doctor*** /ˈdɒktə/.

/ʌ/ Between open-mid and open, central, neutral, lax and short (checked), as in ***drugs*** /drʌgz/.

/æ/ Between open-mid and open, front, neutral, checked (but longer, in many words, than the other short vowels), neither lax nor tense, as in ***ham*** /hæm/.

/ɑː/ Open, near-back, neutral, tense and long (free), as in ***bark*** /bɑːk/.

/ɒ/ Open, back, slightly-rounded, lax and short (checked), as in ***dock*** /dɒk/.

/ɔː/ Between open-mid and close-mid, back, medium lip-rounding, tense and long (free), as in ***port*** /pɔːt/.

/ʊ/ Close-mid, back, closed lip-rounding, lax and short (checked), as in *cook* /kʊk/.

/uː/ Close, back, very closed lip-rounding, tense and long (free), as in *roof* /ruːf/.

By contrast, like most Romance languages, Spanish has a more simple vowel system with only **five pure vowels /a e i o u/** that are usually symmetrically arranged in an inverted triangle as there is no front-back opposition at the open position. Table 8 below summarises the similarities and differences that exist between the RP and PSp vowel systems along the OBR parameters that define vocalic quality, examples for each vowel phoneme having been already provided in Table 4 (Section 1.5).

Table 8: Classification of the vowels of RP and PSp

Tongue Height	**RP**						**PSp**		
	Tongue position						Tongue position		
	Front		Central		Back		Front	Central	Back
	Tense	Lax	Tense	Lax	Tense	Lax	Tense	Tense	Tense
Close/high	iː	ɪ			uː	ʊ	i		u
Mid		e	ɜː	ə	ɔː		e		o
Open/low		æ		ʌ	ɑː	ɒ		a	

From an **articulatory point of view,** we can say that English vowels are distributed in both the periphery and the central sections of the CVS. They are distinguished according to the tense-lax and long-short oppositions and generally begin abruptly with a strong vibration of the vocal cords that dies away slowly (Stockwell and Bowen 1965; Flege 1989). In Spanish the opposite happens as vocal cord vibration begins gently and stops brusquely. Besides, SSLE may find it difficult to produce or even perceive the tense-lax and long-short distinctions because these contrasts have no phonemic status in Spanish. All Spanish vowels can be considered to be tense and short, and generally to be closer and pronounced more to the front of the mouth than the English short counterparts, without producing the diphthongisations, or vowel glides to [i], [u] or [ə] (Delattre 1965; Stockwell and Bowen 1965; Monroy Casas 1980, 1981, 2012; Fox *et al.* 1995). Experimental studies have shown that Spanish vowels have roughly the same length as English short vowels, while English long vowels may be twice as long (García Lecumberri and Elorduy 1994), although in some phonetic contexts a reduced long vowel and short vowel may have a similar duration (***beat*** [biˑt] – ***bid*** [bɪd]; see § 2.3.1.4).

None of the Spanish vowels exactly coincides with the area of articulation of English vowels. As already noted, four RP vowels /**iː e ɔː uː**/ could be regarded as near equivalents of Spanish /**i e o u**/, even though English /**iː uː**/ are more centralised, while /**e**/ and /**ɔː**/ are more open and closer than their Spanish counterparts, respectively. In Spanish there also exists an allophone of /**a**/ occurring in closed syllables and before /u/ (*baúl* 'trunk') which approximates RP /**ɑː**/ (Navarro Tomás 1991; García Lecumberri and Elorduy 1994). Consequently, SSLE should pay special attention to RP /**ə ɜː ɪ ʊ ɒ**/, not only because of the potential difficulty involved in their production and perception as Spanish does not have central and lax vowels in its phoneme inventory, but also due to their high frequency of occurrence (especially /ə ɪ/) (Monroy Casas 1980, 1981, 2012; Sedláčková 2010; Helman 2004; Swan and Smith 2001; Finch and Ortiz Lira 1982). Likewise, such contrasts as /**iː**/ – /**ɪ**/, /**e**/ – /**æ**/, /**æ**/ – /**ʌ**/, /**ɔː**/ – /**əʊ**/ should also be emphasised, not only because they can prove particularly problematic for SSLE, but also because they are present in all varieties of English native pronunciation (Wells 2005).

From an **acoustic point of view**, English vowels are intrinsically longer (Monroy Casas 1980, 2012)[21] and are also generally higher in F2 than their Spanish counterparts, which manifests the already noted tendency for RP vowels to be articulated with a fronted tongue position as compared to PSp vowels (Bradlow 1995; Disner 1983). In addition, while English speakers use three dimensions of spectral information, high-low, front-back and duration, SSLE only use the first two, and so they must be able to not only distinguish a larger number of vowels, but also make use of duration and spectral cues that are not normally relevant for Spanish vowel perception (Quilis 1981; Martínez Celdrán 1996; Morrison 2006).[22]

Turning to their **distribution**, Spanish shows a higher proportion of vowels than English (43.49% vs. 39.21%). The predominant vowels in Spanish are the most **fronted** ones /**a e o**/, and the **central** ones in English (33.65% vs. 23.98%), as already remarked (Finch and Ortiz Lira 1982; Cruttenden 2014). In

---

21 According to Lehiste (1970: 18), there exists a correlation across languages between vocalic quantity and vowel height so that low or open vowels tend to be longer than high or close vowels.

22 Although it is true that in Spanish there may exist length differences between the vowels of such words as *azar-azahar* ('chance' – 'orange blossom'), ***pelé-peleé*** ('(I) peeled' – '(I) fought'), ***le-lee*** ('to him/her' – 's/he reads'), this difference does not involve a paradigmatic contrast (a choice between two different vowels that triggers a change of meaning), but rather it results from the pronunciation of one or two consecutive instances of the same vowel.

addition, while all Spanish vowels may occur and are pronounced in all three positions in the word, initial, medial and final, both in unstressed and stressed syllables (Navarro Tomás 1968), English exhibits **stress-determined** and **syllable-determined constraints** on the appearance of certain vowels, the most relevant of such constraints being listed below (Fry 1947; Finch and Ortiz Lira 1982):

(1) /**ə**/ is restricted to unstressed syllables unless as part of a vowel glide (e.g. /ɪə eə ʊə/)
(2) Lax vowels, /**e æ ɒ ʊ ʌ**/, never occur in word-final open syllables, whereas tense vowels and diphthongs can appear in such contexts.
(3) Tense vowels and diphthongs can never appear before /ŋ/, while lax vowels show no constraints with regard to codas.
(4) /**ʊ ʊə**/ almost never occur word-initially (apart from *oomph* /ʊmf/, *umlaut* /ˈʊmlaʊt/ and *Uruguay* /ˈjʊərəgwaɪ/).
(5) /**iː e ɜː**/ very rarely appear in unstressed word-initial syllables.

One last difference concerns the **sound-spelling correspondences**, which, in the case of English, are mentioned in what follows and are further detailed in Chapter 7 in order to help (Spanish) EFL learners build up systematic associations between sounds and spellings. At this stage, suffice it to say that, although both languages use the Latin alphabet, the English alphabet consists of **26 Roman letters**, whereas the Spanish one also includes the letter ***ñ*** and the digraphs ***ch*** and ***ll***, even though the letters ***k*** and ***w*** do not appear very often in Spanish words (Helman 2004). Confusion can arise when the letters used to represent sounds differ between languages, and this is especially common in the case of English and Spanish vowels. Furthermore, sound-spelling correspondences are much more complex in English than in Spanish: the **twelve RP vowels** may be represented with **seventy regular spellings**, apart from **another seventy** that are less common, while Spanish vowels may correspond to only fourteen different spellings (Finch and Ortiz Lira 1982: 41).

Given the relative simplicity of the Spanish vowel-space, for SSLE to be able to produce English vowels correctly, they not only must learn new categories, but also need to be able to "hear" and "see" the differences that distinguish the two sound inventories to avoid confusing them. To ease this task, this book departs from the usual practice of describing each RP vowel individually, based on the tense/lax or long/short distinction and moving counter-clockwise around the CVS. Instead, as represented below in Figure 36, which superimposes the vowel triangle of the five PSp vowels (marked with [○]) and the vowel trapezium of RP vowels (marked with [•]) in the CVS, we classify RP and PSp vowels together into five groups corresponding to the **five mappings of perceptual vowel-space** (represented with dotted lines) that SSLE tend to make, as already noted in the introduction of this chapter (Finch 1982; Alcaraz and Moody 1993; García Lecumberri and Cenoz Iragui 1997; Iverson and Evans 2007; Iverson *et al.* 2006; Iverson and Evans 2007; Gallardo del Puerto 2005; Escudero and Chládková 2010):

(1) **Group 1**, RP /**iː ɪ**/ vs. PSp /**i**/, comprising three vowels situated in the close front section of the CVS.
(2) **Group 2**, RP /**e ə ɜː**/ vs. PSp /**e**/, grouping together four vowels that are located in the front or central, between half-close and half-open quadrant of the CVS.
(3) **Group 3**, RP /**æ ʌ ɑː**/ vs. PSp /**a**/, bringing together four vowels that are articulated within the front, central or back, between half-open and open section of the CVS.
(4) **Group 4**, RP /**ɒ ɔː**/ vs. PSp /**o**/, consisting of three rounded vowels produced in the back, open or just below the half close regions of the CVS.
(5) **Group 5**, RP /**ʊ uː**/ vs. PSp /**u**/, relating three rounded vowels produced in the back, close or just above the half close regions of the CVS.

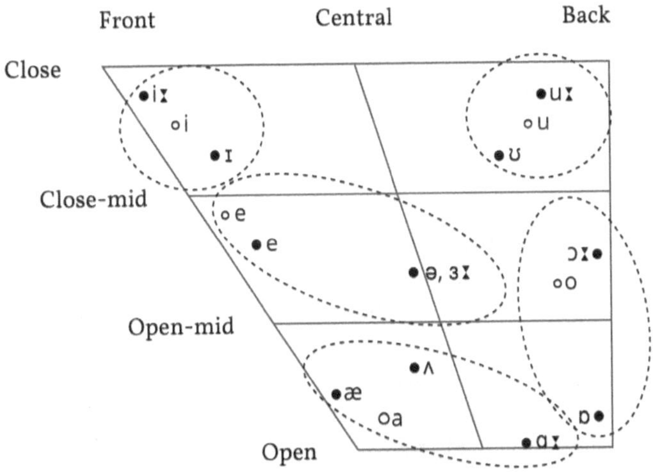

Figure 36: The vowels of RP and PSp in the CVS

3.2.1 Group 1: RP /iː ɪ/ vs. PSp /i/

IPA Symbols

i Lower-case I (or Latin small letter I).
ɪ Small capital I (or Latin letter small capital I).

Identification

/**iː**/ Close, front, tightly spread, tense and long (free).

/**ɪ**/ Near-close, near-front, slightly-spread, lax and short (checked).

Position in CVS

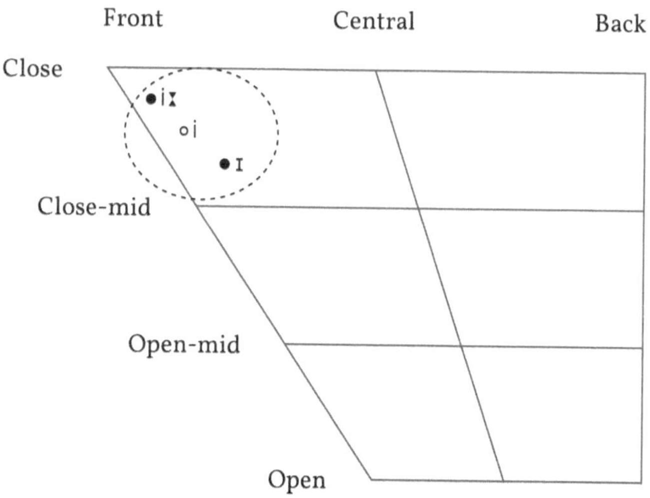

Figure 37: RP /iː ɪ/ vs. PSp /i/ in the CVS

Description

For the articulation of RP /**iː**/ the front of the tongue is raised just below and just behind the front close (or high) position. The lips are spread and the tongue is tense, with the side rims making a firm contact with the upper molars. The quality is that of a centralised and slightly lowered CV [i̞].

RP /**ɪ**/, on the other hand, is articulated by raising a part of the tongue that is nearer to the centre than the front, to just above the close-mid (or half-close) position. The lips are slightly spread, the tongue is lax (compared with the tension for /iː/), and the side rims make a light contact with the upper molars. The quality is a centralised and closer CV 2 [e] = [ë̝]

See the animations and **videos under RP /iː/ and /ɪ/ (compared with Spanish /i/) in the Sound Bank of the EPSS Multimedia Lab** (see also e.g. Gimson 1984: 101–105; Gimson 1994: 97–100; Roach 2005: 16, 20; Collins and Mees 2009: 100; Cruttenden 2014: 111–115).

Environment

/iː/ occurs in open and closed syllables, but not before /ŋ/, whereas /ɪ/ may occur in all positions of the word, including final open syllables, although note the HappY-tensing process mentioned below.

Spellings

Table 9: The spellings of RP /iː ɪ/

/iː/ (in stressed syllables)	/ɪ/ (in stressed or unstressed syllables)
<ee>[23] see /siː/, cheese /ʧiːz/	<i> is /ɪz/, sit /sɪt/, igloo /ˈɪgluː/
<e>[24] be /biː/, these /ðiːz/	<y> rhythm /ˈrɪðᵊm/, symbol /ˈsɪmbl̩/
<ea> sea /siː/, beans /biːnz/, leaf /liːf/	<e>[25] added /ˈædɪd/, faces /ˈfeɪsɪz/
<ie>[26] piece /piːs/, believe /bɪˈliːv/	<ie> sieve /sɪv/, mischief /ˈmɪsʧɪf/
<ei, ey>[27] seize /siːz/, key /kiː/, geyser /ˈgiːzə/	<a> orange /ˈɒrɪnʤ/, palace /pælɪs/
<i> ski /skiː/, police /pəˈliːs/	<u> busy /ˈbɪzi/, lettuce /ˈletɪs/
<ae> aedile /ˈiːdʌɪl/, aeolic /iːˈɒlɪk/	<ui> built /bɪlt/, circuit /ˈsɜːkɪt/
Rare spellings <eo> people /ˈpiːpl̩/ oecumenic /ˌiːkjuːˈmenɪk/ <ay> quay /kiː/ <is> debris /ˈdeɪbriː/, precis/ˈpreɪsiː/	**Rare spellings** <o> women /ˈwɪmɪn/ <ee> breeches /briːˈʧɪz/ (or /brɪˈʧɪz/)

23 However, if the <ee> spelling is followed by <r> in stressed syllables, then its **normal pronunciation** (NP) is /ɪə/, e.g. b**ee**r /bɪə/.
24 /iː/ pronunciation corresponds to the <e> spelling usually in stressed syllables that are followed by silent <e> or other vowel letter, as in ***e**ve* /iːv/ (*compl**e**te, l**e**gal*).
25 Note that the NP of <-ed> is /-ɪd/ in adjectives (e.g. *sacr**e**d* /ˈseɪkrɪd/, wick**e**d /ˈwɪkɪd/), as well as in the past and past participle of regular verbs ending in <-t> /-tɪd/ or <-d> /-dɪd/ (e.g. *want**e**d, land**e**d*). Similarly, the plural noun inflectional ending <-es> is /-ɪz/ (e.g. *fish**e**s, fac**e**s*), only if the singular form ends in /s, z, ʃ, ʧ, dʒ/ final sound (e.g. *mass**e**s, priz**e**s, fish**e**s, witch**e**s, judg**e**s*).
26 Note that the NP of <ie> is /iː/ in medial position, but it is /aɪ/ word-finally: ***lie*** /laɪ/, ***die*** /daɪ/.
27 The frequent combination <–cei–> is pronounced /siː/, but the NP of the <ei> spelling is /eɪ/, as in ***ei**ght* /eit/, *w**ei**ght* /weit/, and less likely /aɪ/ as in *h**ei**ght* /haɪt/.

Note that a shorter variety of /iː/, [i] (transcribed without the length mark [ː]), occurs in unstressed word- and stem-final syllables with the spellings listed below:

<y> happ**y** /ˈhæpi/, cit**y** /ˈsɪti/, carr**y**ing /ˈkæriɪŋ/
<ay> Sund**ay** /ˈsʌndi/ (which can also be pronounced /eɪ/, /ˈsʌndeɪ/)
<ey> motl**ey** /ˈmɒtli/
<ie> sweet**ie** /ˈswiːti/, lad**ie**s /ˈleɪdiz/
<i> ant**i**dote /ˈæntidəʊt/, hand**i**cap /ˈhændikæp/
<e> h**e** /hi/, sh**e** /ʃi/, w**e** /wi/, m**e** /mi/, b**e** /bi/
<ea> Chels**ea** /ˈʧelsi/, Swans**ea** /ˈswɒnzi/

The first case, involving the pronunciation of word final <y> as [i] rather than [ɪ], illustrates what has been called **HappY-tensing** (or **Y-tensing**) (Wells 1982), which originated in southern British accents, but nowadays has become the standard RP pronunciation to such an extent that [ɪ] pronunciations are regarded as somewhat old-fashioned and as a characteristic of Conservative RP (Cruttenden 2014: 331).[28]

Likewise, [i] may also correspond to <i>, <e>, <ie> spellings in or immediately before the following unaccented word endings:

<-ation> substant**i**ation /səbˌstænʃiˈeɪʃn̩/, cr**e**ation /kriˈeɪʃn̩/
<-eal> cer**e**al /ˈsɪəriəl/
<-ean> Guin**e**an /ˈgɪniən/
<-ear> nucl**e**ar /ˈnjuːkliə/
<-ia> med**i**a /miːdiə/
<-ial> gen**i**al /ˈʤiːniəl/
<-ian> Armen**i**an /ɑːˈmiːniən/
<-iance> dev**i**ance /ˈdiːviəns/
<-iate> substant**i**ate /səbˈstænʃieɪt/
<-ience> aud**i**ence /ˈɔːdiəns/
<-ient> amb**i**ent /ˈæmbiənt/
<-ied> stud**ie**d /ˈstʌdid/
<-ior> infer**i**or /ˈɪnˈfɪəriə/
<-ious> glor**i**ous /ˈglɔːriəs/
<-ium> atr**i**um /ˈeɪtriəm/
<-ius> gen**i**us /ˈʤiːniəs/

28 An exception to this HappY-tensing tendency concerns the stem-final <y> of *-ly* adverbs, which tends to be pronounced either [ɪ] or [ə] (rather than /i/), although the suffix itself does conform to the HappY-tensing tendency, as in the case of e.g. *easily* /ˈiːzəli/, *tidily* /ˈtaɪdɪli/)

Finally, [i] can also be found word-medially, usually before a strong vowel in unstressed syllables with the spellings:

<i> or**i**ent /ˈɔːriənt/, per**i**odic /ˌpɪəriˈɒdɪk/, conc**i**erge /kɒnsiˈeəʒ/
<e> archa**e**ological /ˌɑːkiəˈlɒdʒɪkl̩/, nucl**e**i /ˈnjuːkliaɪ/, cr**e**ate /kriˈeɪt/

Regional and social variants

In the spelling subsection we have already seen that in final unaccented position the contrast between /**ɪ**/ and /**iː**/ is **neutralised** because the general tendency is to pronounce [**i**], a shorter variant of /iː/. Also common among RP speakers is the diphthongisation of /iː/ so that a slight vowel glide tends to be made from a position near to [ɪ], [ɪi], especially in stressed open syllables and in final position. Likewise, as a result of the "Southern diphthong shift", typical of London, Cockney, Birmingham, the South and Midlands of England, /iː/ may be pronounced as [əɪ].

Turning to /ɪ/, the degree of closeness and centralisation of its variants depends on the accentual force falling upon them and their position in the word. It tends to be pronounced [ə] in some final unaccented endings such as *-ate, -em, -ible, -itive, -ily, -ity*, as in *chocol**ate*** /ˈtʃɒklət/, *syst**em*** /ˈsɪstəm/, *poss**ible*** /ˈpɒsəbl/, *pos**itive*** /ˈpɒzətɪv/, *eas**ily*** /ˈiːzəli/, and *qual**ity*** /ˈkwɒləti/. In contrast, some other unstressed endings such as *-ace, -ess* have both /ɪ/ and /ə/ pronuncaitions, as in *pal**ace*** /ˈpæləs/ and *usel**ess*** /ˈjuːsləs/, but the general trend is for /ɪ/ to remain the predominant pronunciation as in: *-age* /ɪdʒ/ *vill**age*** /ˈvɪlɪdʒ/, *-et* /ɪt/ -especially following /k, g, tʃ, dʒ/- *pock**et*** /ˈpɒkɪt/, *targ**et*** /ˈtɑːgɪt/, *budg**et*** /ˈbʌdʒɪt/, *hatch**et*** /ˈhætʃɪt/ (except *-let, -ret*> /ət/, e.g. *scarl**et*** /ˈskɑːlət/, *clar**et*** /ˈklærət/), and *be-* /bɪ/, e.g. ***be**come* /bɪˈkʌm/). Lastly, where the difference between /ɪ/ and /ə/ reflects a contrast in (grammatical) meaning, RP tends to retain the /ɪ/-/ə/ distinction (e.g. *off**ices*** /ˈɒfɪsɪz/ versus *offic**ers*** /ˈɒfisəz/), which is also the case of the /ɪt/, /ət/-/eɪt/ pronounciations of the spelling <-ate> (e.g. *estim**ate*** (n) /ˈestimət/ vs. *estim**ate*** (v) /ˈestimeɪt/). The neutralisation of these oppositions suggests a non-RP pronunciation.

Comparison with Spanish and advice

RP /**iː**/ is longer and slightly closer than PSp /**i**/, while RP /**ɪ**/ has different spectral features: it is not so tense and it is closer and more retracted. SSLE (normally in the initial learning stages) tend to confuse English /i/ and /ɪ/, assimilating both phonemes to the single L1 category /i/. This assimilation derives from a combination of factors: (1) the phonetic similarity and close proximity of these vowels in vowel-space; (2) the fact that Spanish does not have [ɪ] in its inventory, and (3) orthographic reasons since both English /i/ and /ɪ/ may correspond to <i> in spelling, which is the letter that represents Spanish /i/ (García Lecumberri and Cenoz Iragui 1997; Escudero 2000; Escudero and

Boersma 2004; Flege *et al.* 1997; Morrison 2002; Iverson and Evans 2007). However, other SSLE (probably in later learning stages) tend to rate /ɪ/ as closer to Spanish /e/ because of their higher spectral similarity, the strongest cue in their L1, and yet a minority of learners can categorise it as closer to Spanish /u/ (Flege 1991; Escudero 2000; Escudero and Boersma 2004; Morrison 2006, 2008; Boomershine 2013; Escudero and Chládková 2010).

Learners are thus advised to practise the RP /**iː**/ – /**ɪ**/ contrast in order to be able to perceive and produce their different spectral characteristics (tense vs. lax, long vs. short, closer and more advanced vs. more open and retracted). To produce RP /iː/, SSLE should try to utter a longer sound than their usual Spanish /i/, but the tongue should be in a position somewhat more retracted towards the pharyngeal cavity and the tongue tip should be in contact with the lower incisors; whereas the quality of English [i] (in unstressed syllables and cases of HappY-tensing) is similar to that of Spanish [i]. Turning to RP /ɪ/, to pronounce it Spanish speakers should try to make a shorter sound that is closer to the vowel of the Spanish word *mes* 'month' than to the vowel of *mis* 'my' (Monroy Casas 1980, 2012; Estebas Vilaplana 2009).

Further practice

AI 3.1. The spellings of RP /iː/. Further practice

b**ee** /biː/	lad**ie**s /ˈleɪdiz/	sh**ee**p /ʃiːp/
bel**ie**ve /bɪˈliːv/	l**ea**d /liːd/	th**e**se /ðiːz/
everybod**y** /ˈevribɒdi/	l**ea**t /liːt/	

Pl**ea**se, take th**e**se s**ea**ts.
||ˈpliːz | ˈteɪk ðiːz ˈsiːts||

J**ea**n, can you f**ee**l th**e**se?
||ˈʤiːn | kən ju ˈfiːl ˈðiːz||

Sh**e** bel**ie**ves discr**ee**t p**eo**ple perc**ei**ved the sc**e**ne.
||ʃi bɪˈliːvz dɪˈskriːt ˈpiːpl̩ pəˈsiːvd ðə siːn||

The qu**ee**n in gr**ee**n scr**ea**med.
||ðə ˈkwiːn ɪn ˈgriːn ˈskriːmd||

My **ee**l's m**ea**l is a p**ie**ce of m**ea**t with a bit of ch**ee**se.
||maɪ ˈiːlz ˈmiːl ɪz ə ˈpiːs əv ˈmiːt wɪð ə bɪt əv ˈʧiːz||

At l**ea**st, Den**i**se could sn**ee**ze and f**ee**d and fr**ee**ze the fl**ea**s.
||ət ˈliːst | dəˈniːz kəd ˈsniːz ənd ˈfiːd ənd ˈfriːz ðə ˈfliːz||

Through thr**ee** ch**ee**se tr**ee**s thr**ee** fr**ee** fl**ea**s flew.
||θruː ˈθriː ˈtʃiːz ˈtriːz ˈθriː ˈfriː ˈfliːz ˈfluː||

AI 3.2 The spellings of RP /ɪ/. Further practice

believe /bɪˈliːv/ lid /lɪd/ ship /ʃɪp/
illicit /ɪˈlɪsɪt/ lit /lɪt/ this /ðɪs/
lettuce /ˈletɪs/ private /ˈpraɪvɪt/

Can you fill this?
||kən ju ˈfɪl ˈðɪs||

When did you begin to build a gym in England?
||ˈwen dɪd ju bɪˈgɪn tə ˈbɪld ə ʤɪm ɪn ˈɪŋglənd||

Although she was busy, she managed to fix the bin in the kitchen.
||ɔːlˈðəʊ ʃi wəz ˈbɪzi | ʃi ˈmænɪʤd tə fɪks ðə bɪn ɪn ðə ˈkɪʧɪn||

Imagining managing an imaginary menagerie.
||ɪˈmæʤɪnɪŋ ˈmænɪʤɪŋ ən ɪˈmæʤɪnəri mɪˈnæʤəri||

Six sick hicks nick six slick bricks with picks and sticks.
||sɪks sɪk hɪks nɪk sɪks slɪk brɪks wɪð pɪks ənd stɪks||

A cricket critic.
||ə ˈkrɪkɪt ˈkrɪtɪk||

3.2.2 Group 2: RP /e ɜː ə/ vs. PSp /e/

IPA Symbols

e Lower-case E (or Latin small letter E).
ɜ Reversed Epsilon (or Latin small letter reversed open E).
ə Schwa (or Latin small letter Schwa).

Identification

/e/ Between close-mid and open-mid, front, slightly-spread, lax and short (checked).
/ɜː/ Between close-mid and open-mid, central, neutrally spread, tense and long (free).
/ə/ Between close-mid and open-mid (in non-final positions) and open-mid (in final positions), central, neutral lip shape, lax and short (checked).

Position in the CVS

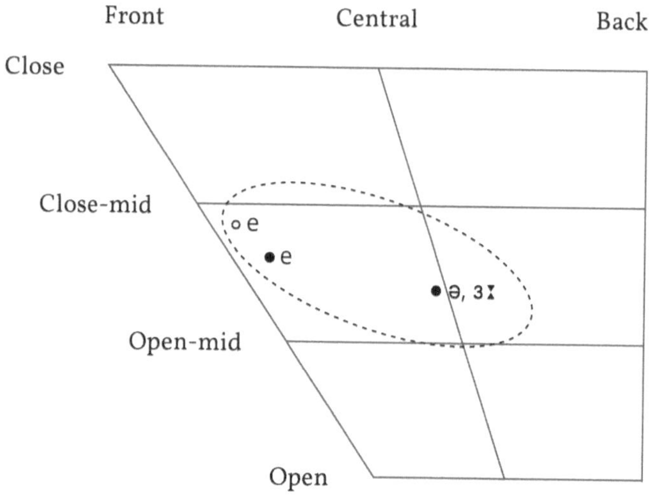

Figure 38: RP /e, ɜː, ə/ vs. PSp /e/

Description

For the articulation of RP /**e**/, the front of the tongue is raised below the close-mid position. The lips are slightly spread and slightly wider apart than for /ɪ/. The tongue may have more tension than in the case of /ɪ/, the side rims making a light contact with the upper molars. The quality lies between that of CV 2 [e] and that of CV 3 [ɛ] = [e̞] or [ɛ̝].

RP /**ɜː**/ is articulated with the centre of the tongue raised between close-mid and open-mid position, the side rims making no firm contact with the upper molars. The lips are neutral. The quality is remote from all peripheral Cardinal Vowel values.

Often coinciding in quality with /ɜː/ but differing in length and tension, RP /**ə**/ is produced with the centre of the tongue being raised between the close-mid and open-mid positions in non-final contexts, but in final positions the vowel tends to be articulated in the open-mid central region or even lower [ɐ] (near-open central vowel). The lips are neutral. Like that of /ɜː/, the quality of RP schwa is remote from all peripheral Cardinal Vowel values and its acoustic formants are similar to those for /ɛː/ and /ʌ/.

See the animations and **videos under RP /e/, /ɜː/ and /ə/ (compared with Spanish /e/) in the Sound Bank of the EPSS Multimedia Lab** (see also e.g. Gimson 1984: 101–105; Gimson 1994: 101, 115–118; Roach 2005: 16, 20; Collins and Mees 2009: 100; Cruttenden 2014: 111–115).

Environment

/e/ is never pronounced in word-final, open syllables. Nearly all cases of /ɜː/ occur in stressed syllables that have an *r* in the spelling, so care must be taken to avoid post-vocalic /r/ (unless in instances of liaison as described in Section 5.5). Lastly, /ə/ has a very high frequency because it may result from the pronunciation of any vowel or vowel glide in unstressed syllables, as explained in the spelling subsection. However, /ə/ may also occur in stressed syllables as part of a centring glide, /ɪə/, /eə/, /ʊə/ (e.g. ***dear*** /dɪə/, ***where*** /weə/, **tou**rist /ˈtʊərɪst/), or a triphthong, /aɪə/, /eɪə/, /ɔɪə/, /aʊə/, /əʊə/ (e.g. ***liar*** /laɪə/, ***player*** /pleɪə/, ***coyer*** /kɔɪə/, ***our*** /aʊə/, ***slower*** /sləʊə/).

Spellings

In addition to the spellings listed in Table 10, /ə/ is the NP of unstressed function words such as ***a***, *an*, *and*, *the*, ***for*** (Section 5.7), and it is also frequent in **unstressed prefixes** and **suffixes**, as well as in a large number of **unstressed place-names suffixes** such as the following:

<ad->	**a**dmonish /ədˈmɒnɪʃ/
<-borough>	Flamb**orough** /ˈflæmbərə/
<-burgh>	Edinb**urgh** /ˈedɪnbrə/
<-bury, -bery>	Newb**u**ry, Newb**e**ry /ˈnjuːbəri/
<-folk>	Norf**olk** /ˈnɔːfək/
<-ford>	Oxf**ord** /ˈɒksfəd/
<-ham>	Birming**ham** /ˈbɜːmɪŋəm/
<-land>	Irel**and** /ˈaɪələnd/
<-ment>	establishm**e**nt /ɪˈstæblɪʃmənt/
<-mouth>	Bournem**ou**th /ˈbɔːnməθ/
<-stone>	Maidst**o**ne /ˈmeidstən/
<suc->	s**u**cceed /səkˈsiːd/

In contrast, less common or more learned words tend to have a full vowel, unreduced to schwa, in unstressed syllables as in the examples below; while word final <-ow> (as in *tomorr**ow**, yell**ow***) and <-o> (as in *potat**o**, phot**o***) are normally pronounced [əʊ], schwa reduction being regarded as a very substandard:

asph**alt** /ˈæsfælt/
c**ar**nation /kɑːˈneɪʃn̩/
cha**os** /ˈkeɪɒs/
contr**act** (n) /ˈkɒntrækt/
conv**er**t (n.) /ˈkɒnvɜːt/
ep**o**ch /ˈiːpɒk/
esquire /esˈkwaɪə/, /ɪˈskwaɪə/
ferm**ent** /ˈfɜːment/ (n) (vs. /fəˈment/ (v))
handic**ap** /ˈhændɪkæp/
m**u**scology /mʌsˈkɒlədʒi/
N**or**wegian /nɔːˈwiːdʒn̩/
pr**e**stige /presˈtiːʒ/, /presˈtiːdʒ/
stat**u**te /ˈstætjuːt/, /ˈstætʃuːt/
torm**e**nt /ˈtɔːment/(n) /tɔːˈment/ (v)
zodi**ac** /ˈzəʊdiæk/

Table 10: The spellings of RP /e ɜː ə/

/e/ (in stressed syllables)	/ɜː/ (in stressed syllables)	/ə/ (in unstressed syllables)
<e> wet /wet/ pencil /ˈpensl̩/	<er> herb /hɜːb/ Berkley /ˈbɜːkli/	Any vowel or vowel sequence in unstressed position (esp. <a>, <o>, <e(r)>) policeman /pəˈliːsmən/ possible /ˈpɒsəbl̩/ August /ˈɔːgəst/ chieftain /ˈʧiːftən/ tortoise /ˈtɔːtəs/ ancient /ˈeɪnʃənt/ vengeance /ˈvenʤəns/
<ea>[29] head /hed/, breath /breθ/	<err> err /ɜː/	
<a> any /ˈeni/, ate /et/	<ur> Thursday /ˈθɜːzdeɪ/	
<ai> said /sed/ against /əˈgenst/	<urr> purr /pɜː/	
<ay> says /sez/	<ir> first /fɜːst/	
<ei> Leicester /ˈlestə/	<irr> whirr / wɜː/	Unstressed sequences of vowel(s) plus <r> figure /ˈfɪgə/ colour /ˈkʌlə/ forget /fəˈget/ surpass /səˈpɑːs/
<eo> leopard /ˈlepəd/	<yr> myrtle /ˈmɜːtl̩/	
<u> bury /ˈberi/, burial /ˈberɪəl/	<yrr> myrrh /mɜː/	
	<w> + <or> world /wɜːld/, worse /wɜːs/, worth /wɜːθ/, worthy /wɜːði/	Unstressed spelling <re> centre /ˈsentə/ genre /ˈʒɑːnrə/
	<ear> earth /ɜːθ/, earn /ɜːn/	
	<our> journey /ˈʤɜːni/	
	French loanwords <eu> milieu /ˈmiːljɜː/ Richelieu /ˈriːʃəˌliɜː/ <eur> voyeur /vwɑːˈjɜː/	
	Rare spellings <ere> were /wɜː/ <olo> colonel /ˈkɜːnl̩/	

29 In the stressed syllables of approximately sixty words because the NP of <ea> is /iː/.

Lastly, schwa is often lost in many positions (only if leaving an acceptable consonant sequence) as a consequence of the syncopated rhythm of English, as illustrated in the examples below, where you can see that this is quite normal before /l/, /r/ and /n/, which become syllabic. In general, schwa elision and vowel reduction depend a great deal on speed of delivery, so that in rapid speech many reductions occur which would be unusual in slower speech. By contrast, schwa tends to be kept between nasals (*Germany* /ˈdʒɜːməni/) and between a nasal and a homorganic consonant (*London* /ˈlʌndən/) (see also section 1.3.3.3 on syllabic consonants).

asp**i**rin /ˈæspr̩in/
fact**o**ry /ˈfæktr̩i/
nurs**e**ry /ˈnɜːsr̩i/
comf**or**table /ˈkʌmftəbl̩/
gen**e**rally /ˈdʒenr̩əli/
op**e**ning /ˈəʊpn̩ɪŋ/
comp**a**rable /ˈkɒmpr̩əbl̩/
gen**e**rous /ˈdʒenr̩əs/
consid**e**rable /kənˈsɪdr̩əbl̩/
hist**o**ry /ˈhɪstr̩i/
reas**o**nable /ˈriːzn̩əbl̩/
dec**o**rative /ˈdekr̩ətɪv/
lit**e**rature /ˈlɪtrətʃə/
temp**e**rature /ˈtemprətʃə/
def**i**nitely /ˈdefn̩ətli/
mod**e**rate /ˈmɒdr̩ət/
veg**e**table, /ˈvedʒtəbl̩/
ev**e**ry /ˈevr̩i/

Regional and social variants

Generally RP /e/ tends to have an open quality ([e̞]) that is more similar to CV 3 [ɛ] than to CV 2 [e]; and central diphthongisations of the vowel (e.g. [meᵊn] [weᵊt]) are characteristic of affected RP pronunciation.

As regards the other two central vowels, in Refined RP a more open variant of [ɜ̞ː] tends to be produced, while the degree of openness of /ə/ ranges widely depending on the context of appearance. The closest realisation, in the close-mid central region of the CVS, occurs in the vicinity of velar consonants /k, g, ŋ/ (e.g. *long **a**go* /ˈlɒŋəˈgəʊ/). A more open variant with tongue-raising between close-mid and open-mid is produced in non-final positions (e.g. ***a**lone* /əˈləʊn/, *f**a**tigue* /fəˈtiːg/, *dec**o**rative* /ˈdekərətɪv/, *aft**e**rw**a**rds* /ˈɑːftəwədz/), while the most open realisation, with the tongue in the open-mid central position, occurs in final positions (e.g. *doct**o**r* /ˈdɒktə/, *moth**e**r* /ˈmʌðə/, *ov**e**r* /ˈəʊvə/, *pict**u**re* /ˈpɪktʃə/). In this context, refined RP speakers tend to produce an even more open [ɐ] and retracted variant [ɑ̟]. In Irish English, many speakers insert schwa between clusters of sonorants, usually /lm/, e.g. /fɪlm/ → /fɪl.əm/. This process leads to resyllabification and is known as **schwa epenthesis**. For further contexts of schwa pronunciation the reader is referred to Section 5.7 on vowel gradation.

Comparison with Spanish and advice

Spanish /e/ is much closer to RP /e/ than to /ɜː/, the other **e**-type vowel of English. RP /**e**/ is between PSp /e/ and /a/ for F1 but much nearer to the former for F2, and probably for that reason Spanish learners tend to equate it with the Spanish prototype /e/, although less frequently it is also identified with [æ] (García Lecumberri and Cenoz Iragui 1997; Finch and Ortiz Lira 1982). However, despite being quite similar in quantity and despite being transcribed with the same symbol, the quality of Spanish and English /e/ is rather different: RP /e/ is a bit more open and retracted and, to produce it, Spanish learners should try and utter a long Spanish [eː] (especially before voiced consonants) but in the middle the mouth should be opened a bit more by lowering the jaw and the tongue, the tongue tip being in contact with the lower incisors. Its quality is very similar to the Galician **e**-sound in such words as *terra* 'earth' or *tes* '(you) have', or the Catalan **e**-sound in *pera* 'pear' or *mel* 'honey' (Monroy Casas 1980, 2012; Estebas Vilaplana 2009).

Turning to /**ɜː**/ and /**ə**/, these are the two RP vowels that least resemble any of the PSp vowels, and for this reason they may be difficult for SSLE according to error analysis (Lado 1965). By contrast, the NLM theory hypothesises the opposite: that these two phonemes should be highly distinctive and easy to perceive because there are no similar prototypes in Spanish to be confused with them. Experimental research, however, confirms the error analysis prediction for these two central vowels, as they display a large amount of wrong identifications resulting from assimilations with almost all prototypical vowels of Spanish: some SSLE learners perceive them as similar to [ʌ] -a retracted kind of Spanish [a̙]-, while others assimilate them to a kind of [æ] or to [o], and a minority to a kind of [u] (Finch and Ortiz Lira 1982; García Lecumberri and Cenoz Iragui 1997; Iverson and Evans 2007; Escudero and Chládková 2010). This is probably due to the fact that both the F1 and F2 of the central RP vowels are closest to PSp /a/ (although F1 is also near to PSp /e/ and /o/), in addition to the learners' tendency to refer to closest sounding and/or similarly spelt L1 vowels. Another important factor involved in this confusion is the fact that Spanish is a syllable-rhythm language whereas English is a stressed-rhythm language, so SSLE have a tendency to pronounce one of the Spanish vowels (when similarly spelt) in each and every syllable (e.g. *revelatory* */r[e]v[e]ˈl[a]t[o]r[i]/), while English has schwas in most unstressed syllables if they are not **smoothed** or **compressed** (e.g. /ˌrevəˈleitᵊri/) (see also Sections 3.3.3 and 5.7).

In order to avoid having a strong foreign accent, it is therefore crucial for EFL learners to pay special attention to the pronunciation and perception of /ɜː/ and /ə/, the latter in particular because it is by far the most frequently used vowel in English (Finch and Ortiz Lira 1982: 79). It has been noted that /ɜː/ and /ə/ are very similar in quality, the only difference being that /ɜː/ is much longer than /ə/. For their articulation, the lips should be neutral and the mouth should be open very little, adopting a mid-centralised tongue position slightly higher than for the articulation of Spanish /a/, as in mouth breathing, and then, without moving any of the articulators, the two sounds should be uttered as when thinking aloud (*eeehhh*), exerting more tension and longer duration in the case of /ɜː/. English /ə/ is very close to the Catalan vowel at the end of such words as *hola* 'hallo' or *mare* 'mother' (Monroy Casas 1980, 2012; Estebas Vilaplana 2009).

Further practice

AI 3.3. The spellings of RP /e/. Further practice

friend /frend/	leopard /ˈlepəd/	tech /tek/
health /helθ/	let /let/	then /ðen/
led /led/	perfect (vb) /pəˈfekt/	

Geoffrey Reynolds, my friend, help me bury the dead.
||ˈʤefri ˈrenəldz | maɪ ˈfrend | ˈhelp mi ˈberi ðə ˈded||

The wretch, concentered all in self.
||ðə ˈreʧ ˌkənˈsentədˈ ɔːl ɪn ˈself||

His head leant on a fence.
||hɪz ˈhed ˈlent ɒn ə ˈfens||

Many an anemone ate an enemy anemone.
||ˈmeni ən əˈneməni et ən ˈenəmi əˈneməni||

Send toast to ten tense stout saints' ten tall tents.
||ˈsend ˈtəʊst tə ˈten ˈtens ˈstaʊt ˈseɪnts ˈten ˈtɔːl ˈtents||

Seventy seven benevolent elephants.
||ˈsev^{ə}nti ˈsevn̩ bəˈnevələnt ˈelɪfənts||

AI 3.4. The spellings of RP /ɜː/. Further practice

attorney /əˈtɜːni/	serve /sɜːv/	word /wɜːd/
journal /ˈʤɜːn^{ə}l	sir /sɜː/	worth /wɜːθ/
journey /ˈʤɜːni/	Turk /tɜːk/	

The nurse prefers the turquoise purse.
||ðə ˈnɜːs prɪˈfɜːz ðə ˈtɜːkwɒɪz ˈpɜːs||

The court adjourned the trial for the murder of the Turkish merchant, which surprised the world.
||ðə ˈkɔːt əˈʤɜːnd ðə ˈtraɪəl fə ðə ˈmɜːdər əv ðə ˈtɜːkɪʃ ˈmɜːʧənt | wɪʧ səˈpraɪzd ðə wɜːld||

The c**ur**ly-haired g**ir**l's f**ir**st b**ir**thday is on the th**ir**d Th**ur**sday of this month.
||ðə ˌkɜːliˈheəd ˈgɜːlz ˌfɜːst ˈbɜːθdeɪ ˈɪz ɒn ðə ˈθɜːd ˈθɜːzdi əv ðɪs ˈmʌnθ||

A t**ur**bot's not a b**ur**bot, for a t**ur**bot's a butt, but a b**ur**bot's not.
||ə ˈtɜːbətz nɒt ə ˈbɜːbət | fər ə ˈtɜːbət z ə ˈbʌt | bət ə ˈbɜːbət s ˈnɒt||

How much m**yr**tle would a t**ur**tle h**ur**dle if a t**ur**tle could h**ur**dle m**yr**tle?
||ˈhaʊ ˈmʌʧ ˈmɜːtl̩ wʊd ə ˈtɜːtl̩ ˈhɜːdl̩ ɪf ə ˈtɜːtl̩ kəd ˈhɜːdl̩ ˈmɜːtl̩||

AI 3.5. The spellings of RP /ə/. Further practice

attack /əˈtæk/	Belg**iu**m /ˈbelʤəm/	questi**o**n /ˈkwesʧən/
b**a**nan**a** /bəˈnɑːnə/	butt**o**ck /ˈbʌtək/	s**ur**pass /səˈpɑːs/

See y**ou** lat**er**!
||ˈsiː jə ˈleɪtə||

Hundr**e**ds **o**f students **are** taking **a** miser**a**ble breakf**a**st.
||ˈhʌndrədz əv ˈstjuːdn̩ts ə ˈteɪkɪŋ ə ˈmɪzrəbl̩ ˈbrekfəst||

There's **a** formal pr**o**posal to s**u**spend the sent**e**nce.
||ðeəz ə ˈfɔːml̩ prəˈpəʊzl̩ tə səˈspend ðə ˈsentəns||

Th**e** pres**e**nt f**or** my broth**er** is **a** book **a**bout **a** wiz**ar**d.
||ðə ˈprezənt fə maɪ ˈbrʌðər ɪz ə bʊk əˈbaʊt ə ˈwɪzəd||

Upp**er** roll**er**, low**er** roll**er**.
||ˈʌpə ˈrəʊlə | ˈləʊə ˈrəʊlə||

3.2.3 Group 3: RP /ʌ æ ɑː/ vs. PSp /a/

IPA Symbols

ʌ Turned V (or Latin small letter turned V).
æ Ash.
ɑ Script A (or Latin small letter Alpha).
a Lower-case A (or Latin Small letter A).

Identification

/**ʌ**/ Between open-mid and open, central, neutral, lax and short (checked).
/**æ**/ Between open-mid and open, front, neutral, checked (but longer than the other short vowels in such words as *mad*, *rag*, *ham*, *sand*), neither lax nor tense.
/**ɑː**/ Open, near-back, neutral, tense and long (free).

Position in the CVS

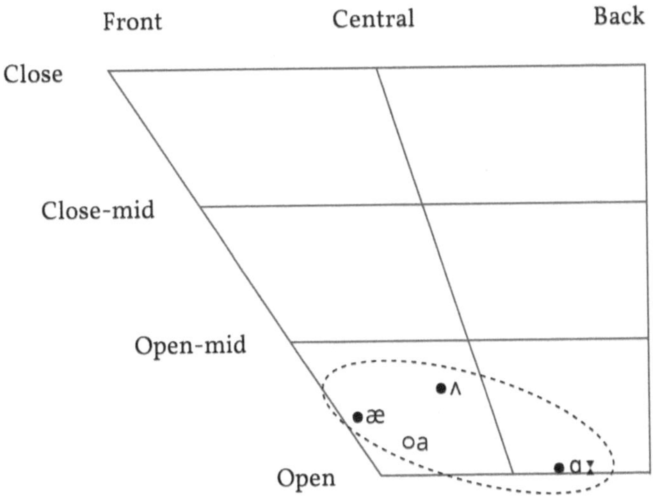

Figure 39: RP /ʌ, æ, ɑː/ vs. PSp /a/

Description

In order to pronounce RP /**ʌ**/, the jaws are considerably separated and the centre of the tongue is raised just above the fully open position. The lips are neutral and no contact is made between the tongue and the upper molars. Its quality is similar to CV 4 /a/, but slightly centralised and closer: [ä̝] [ɐ].

For the articulation of RP /**æ**/, on the other hand, the front of the tongue is raised between the open-mid and open positions, with the side rims making a very firm contact with the back upper molars. The lips are neutrally unrounded. The mouth is more open than for /e/. The quality of RP/æ/ is nowadays nearer CV 4 [a] (front open) than CV 3 [ɛ] (front open-mid).

RP /**ɑ**ː/, in turn, is articulated with the centre and back of the tongue in the fully open position. The lips are neutrally open and no contact is made between the side rims and the upper molars. The quality is that of a centralised CV 5 [ɑ] = [ɑ̈]. Length reduction as a result of pre-fortis and rhythmic clipping is not as noticeable as in the other long vowels (see § 5.2.1).

See the animations and **videos under RP /ʌ/, /æ/ and /ɑː/ (compared with Spanish /a/) in the Sound Bank of the EPSS Multimedia Lab** (see also e.g. Gimson 1984: 110–112; Gimson 1994: 102–107; Roach 2005: 16, 20; Collins and Mees 2009: 98–101; Cruttenden 2014: 119–125).

Table 11: The spellings of RP /ʌ æ ɑː/

/ʌ/ (in stressed and some unstressed syllables)	/æ/ (in stressed syllables)	/ɑː/ (in stressed syllables)
<u> cupboard /ˈkʌbəd/ hiccup /ˈhɪkʌp/	<a> / <-aphic> angry /ˈæŋgri/ gnat /næt/ photographic /fəʊtəˈgræfɪk/	<a> + <ff>[30] staff /stɑːf/
<o>[31] Monday /ˈmʌndeɪ/		<a> + <ft> after /ˈɑːftə/, craft /ˈkrɑːft/
<ou> + <gh> / <ght>[32] enough /ɪˈnʌf/ tough /tʌf/ hiccough /ˈhɪkʌp/	<ai> plaid /plæd/ plait /plæt/	<a> + <nt> can't /kɑːnt/ shan't /ʃɑːnt/
<oo>[33] blood /blʌd/ flood /flʌd/		<a> + <nd> demand /dɪˈmɑːnd/
		<a> + <nce> dance /dɑːns/
		<a> + <nch> branch /brɑːntʃ/
		<a> + <sp> gasp /gɑːsp/
		<a> + <st> last /lɑːst/
		<a> + <sk> asked /ɑːskt/
		<a> + <ss> pass /pɑːs/
		<a> + <th> path /pɑːθ/
		<a> + <lm> (silent l) almond /ˈɑːmənd/
		<a> + <lf> (silent l) half /hɑːf/
		<ar>[34] car /kɑː/, yard /jɑːd/
		<er> clerk /klɑːk/ Derby /ˈdɑːbi/
		<ear>[35] heart /hɑːt/
		<au>, <au> + <gh>[36] draught /drɑːft/, laugh /lɑːf/
Rare spellings <oe> does /dʌz/ <wo> twopence /ˈtʌpəns/	**French loanwords** <i> lingerie /ˈlænʒəri/ timbre /ˈtæmbrə/ meringue /məˈræŋ/ <ei> reveille /rɪˈvæli/	**French loanwords** <oi> /wɑː/ repertoire /ˈrepətwɑː/ <aa(r)> bazaar /bəˈzɑː/ <a> moustache /məˈstɑːʃ/ camouflage /ˈkæməflɑːʒ/ pyjamas /pəˈdʒɑːməz/

Environment

/ʌ æ/ do not occur in open-word final syllables, while /ɑː/ does not appear before /ŋ/. Although /ʌ/ normally occurs in stressed syllables, it can also be found in unstressed ones, as in *hiccough* (/ˈhɪkʌp/), *uphold* (/ʌpˈhəʊld/) and *unfortunate* (/ʌnˈfɔːʧənət/).

Spellings

In addition, attention should be paid to the following exceptions to the most common spellings of RP /ɑː/ noted in Table 11:

h**al**fpenny /ˈheɪpeni/ <a> + <lf>
h**al**fpence /heɪpənts/

sc**ar**ce /skeəs/ <a> + <r>
-w**ar**ds /wədz/

aspect /ˈæspekt/ <a> + <sp>
aspirin /ˈæsprɪn/

cl**a**ssic /ˈklæsɪk/ <a> + <ss>
p**a**ssage /ˈpæsɪʤ/

C**a**therine /ˈkæθrɪn/ <a> + <th>
g**a**ther /ˈgæðə/
sw**a**th /swɔːθ/
wr**a**th /rɒθ/

Regional and social variants

A closer and retracted realisation of /**ʌ**/, [ʌ̝̈], is typical of Refined RP. Also an /ʌ/-/ɒ/ alternation may be found in RP when the stressed spelling <o> is followed by a nasal as in *constable* /ˈkʌnstəbl/ or /ˈkɒnstəbl/ (also accomplish, comrade).

Like /ʌ/, a closer variety of /æ/, [ɛ], is preferred in Refined RP, but it may also be diphthongised to [ɛᵊ] so that such words as *bad* and *sad* may be pronounced [bɛᵊd] and [sɛᵊd]. In addition, it must be noted that this vowel is now generally longer than the other RP short vowels /ɪ, e, ə, ʌ, ɒ, ʊ/. This lengthening effect is (particularly) noticeable before voiced consonants (e.g. *bad*, *bag*, *can*), in which case /æ/ approaches /ɑː/ in length, and even more so in the South of England.

Turning to /**ɑ**ː/, a back variant of [ɑ̠] is typical of Refined RP, as is the case of [ɑː] pronunciations instead of [æ] in some words such as *gymnastic* [ʤɪmˈnɑːstɪk] and *Atlantic* [əˈtlɑːntɪk]. In a number of other words [æ] and [ɑː] pronunciations alternate. But a pronunciation with /ɑː/ seems to be perceived as Refined RP: (1) in tonic position, *lather* [ˈlɑːðə], [ˈlæðə], *masque* [mæsk], [mɑːsk], *massage*

[ˈmæsɑːʒ], [məˈsɑːʒ]; (2) in words having the ending *-aph* (and all its derivates), *photogr**aph*** [ˈfəʊtəgræf], [ˈfəʊtəgrɑːf], *telegr**aph*** [ˈtɛlɪgræf], [ˈtɛlɪgrɑːf]; and (3) the words beginning with *trans-*, ***trans**fer* [ˈtrænsfə], [ˈtrɑːnsfə]), ***trans**form* [ˈtrænsfɔːm], [ˈtrɑːnsfɔːm], ***trans**mission* [trænzˈmɪʃən], [trɑːnzˈmɪʃən], etc. Note, however, that in some of these cases different pronunciations change the meaning of the word: *m**a**ss* /mɑːs/ (religious service 'misa'), /mæs/ (uncountable noun 'masa'); *ass* /ɑːs/ ('backside'), /æs/ ('donkey').

Comparison with Spanish and advice

The quality of RP /**ʌ**/ is quite similar to PSp /a/, but it is shorter and more different from it than RP /ɑː/, so it tends to be perceived as a non-prototypical [a] sound by SSLE, who, in some cases, also identify it with [æ] or even with PSp [o] (Finch and Ortiz Lira 1982; García Lecumberri and Cenoz Iragui 1997; Escudero and Chládková 2010). RP /ʌ/ is more centralised and closer than PSp /a/, but we could say that particularly when followed by voiced consonants, as in words such as *n**o**thing* /ˈnʌθɪŋ/, *m**o**ther* /ˈmʌðə/, *b**o**rough* /ˈbʌrə/, it sounds close to the Spanish [a] sound appearing in such words as *n**a**zi*, *m**a**dera* 'wood' or *v**a**ra* 'stick'.

For the articulation of /**æ**/, the lower jaw is in a closer position than for Spanish /a/, the tongue is more advanced and the lips are more spread and tense, producing a quality that is half-way between Spanish /a/ and /e/. Tightening of the pharynx may provide useful pronunciation practice. /æ/ is nearest to Sp /a/ in F1 and to PSp /e/ in F2 /a/. But, as the Fl distance between RP /æ/ and PSp /a/ is smaller than that between RP /æ/ and PSp /e/, SSLE tend to assimilate it more with PSp /a/ (García Lecumberri and Cenoz Iragui 1997; Escudero and Chládková 2010).

RP /**ɑː**/ is longer than /ʌ/ and more open, with the lips in a neutral position. Although it is the vowel of this group that comes closest to the Spanish prototype /a/ with regard to formants and in fact sets the closest relationship between

---

30 In this and the following spellings, <a> is pronounced /ɑː/ in stressed syllables followed by two consonant letters, the first being <f, n, s> or silent <l>.

31 <o> is usually pronounced /ʌ/ in the vicinity of <u, m, n, w, v, th>.

32 However, the NP of <ou> is /aʊ/.

33 But note that the NP of <oo> is /uː/.

34 <ar> is pronounced /ɑː/ in stressed word-final syllables (whether followed by a consonant or not).

35 The NP of stressed <er> is /ɜː/, and that of <ear> is /ɪə/ as in ***beard*** /bɪəd/, ***hear*** /hɪə/, or less frequently, /eə/ (***pear*** /peə/), or /ɜː/ (***heard*** /hɜːd/).

36 Note that the NP of stressed <au(gh)> is /ɒ/.

the vowels in the two languages, the tongue is more central and retracted than for PSp /a̟/, and in both cases it is as low as possible (even more so in English), as when yawning, gargling or saying “aaaa” for a throat exploration (Finch and Ortiz Lira 1982; García Lecumberri and Cenoz Iragui 1997; Escudero and Chládková 2010). Note, however, that the backness of /ɑː/ must not reach that of CV 5, since that will sound affected.

To avoid misunderstandings and not to confuse RP /**ʌ æ ɑː**/, SSLE should therefore keep the following in mind (Monroy Casas 1980, 2012; Estebas Vilaplana 2009):

(1) /ʌ/ is the shortest and /ɑː/ the longest a-type vowels in English, while /æ/ has an in-between duration, but it is the longest of short RP vowels.

(2) RP /ʌ/ is unrounded as well as closer and more advanced than /ɒ/, which is more open and retracted, and rounded.

(3) RP /æ/ is more open and advanced than /ʌ/ and its quality is between Spanish /e/ and /a/: for its articulation the mouth must have a similar degree of opening as for Spanish /a/ but the position of the lips is similar to Spanish /e/. Spanish learners should avoid the common mistake of producing [æ] too close to [e]. Special attention should therefore be paid to the vowel distinctions illustrated in words like *marry* /ˈmæri/, *merry* /ˈmeri/, *Mary* /ˈmeəri/, and ***cup*** /kʌp/, ***cap*** /kæp/ and ***cop*** /kɒp/. Galician and Catalan speakers should have no difficulty in producing this sound because they have it in the phonetic inventories of these two languages.

(4) /ʌ/ and /ɑː/ are the two English phonemes that come closest to Spanish /a/, their main difference being length: the former is short, and the latter, long. So it is crucial to maintain especially the length difference between /ʌ/-/ɑː/ for the right pronunciation of such minimal pairs as ***bun*** – ***barn; cut*** – ***cart; lust*** – ***last; must*** – ***mast; stuff*** – ***staff.***

Further Practice

🎧 AI 3.6. The spellings of RP /ʌ/. Further practice

an**o**ther /əˈnʌðə/	**o**nion /ˈʌnjən/	tw**o**pence /ˈtʌpəns/
bl**oo**d /blʌd/	t**u**ck /tʌk/	w**o**nder /ˈwʌndə/
d**oe**sn't /ˈdʌznt/	t**u**g /tʌg/	

Get r**ou**gh and **u**nusual st**u**ff in our w**o**nderful c**o**mpanies in D**u**blin and L**o**ndon.

||ˈget ˈrʌf ənd ʌnˈjuːʒʊəl ˈstʌf ɪn ˈaʊə ˈwʌndəfəl ˈkʌmpəniz ɪn ˈdʌblɪn ənd ˈlʌndən||

The bel**o**ved m**o**ther and s**o**n j**u**mped **u**p j**u**st **o**nce and had en**ou**gh f**u**n **u**nder the s**u**n on M**o**nday.
||ðə bɪˈlʌvɪd ˈmʌðər ənd sʌn ʤʌmpt ʌp ʤʌst wʌns ənd həd ɪˈnʌf fʌn ˈʌndə ðə sʌn ɒn ˈmʌndeɪ||

D**ou**ble b**u**bble g**u**m, b**u**bbles d**ou**ble.
||ˈdʌbl̩ ˈbʌbl̩ ˌgʌm | ˈbʌbl̩z ˈdʌbl̩||

M**u**mmies make m**o**ney and a d**o**zen b**u**ns and m**u**ffins.
||ˈmʌmiz ˈmeɪk ˈmʌni ənd ə ˈdʌzn̩ ˈbʌnz ənd ˈmʌfɪnz||

R**u**gged r**u**bber baby b**u**ggy b**u**mpers.
||ˈrʌgɪd ˈrʌbə ˈbeɪbi ˌbʌgi ˈbʌmpəz||

Mrs H**u**nt had a c**ou**ntry c**u**t fr**o**nt in the fr**o**nt of her c**ou**ntry c**u**t pettycoat.
||ˈmɪsɪz ˈhʌnt həd ə ˌkʌntri ˈkʌt ˈfrʌnt ɪn ðə ˈfrʌnt əv hə ˌkʌntri ˈkʌt ˈpetikəʊt||

AI 3.7. The spellings of RP /æ/. Further practice

album /ˈælbəm/
ex**a**m /ɪgˈzæm/
h**a**ndb**a**g /ˈhændbæg/
h**a**t /hæt/
h**a**ve /hæv/
pl**ai**d /plæd/
pl**ai**t /plæt/
t**a**ck /tæk/

P**a**t is gl**a**d she's passed her ex**a**m.
||pæt s glæd ʃiz pɑːst hər ɪgˈzæm||

As a m**a**tter of f**a**ct, it was a fl**a**sh in the p**a**n.
||əz ə ˈmætər əv fækt | ɪt wəz ə flæʃ ɪn ðə pæn||

How can an **a**nt run so fast?
||ˈhaʊ kən ən ˈænt ˈrʌn ˈsəʊ ˈfɑːst||

I g**a**ther that the s**a**lad on the bl**a**ck m**a**t h**a**s **a**pples, c**a**rrots, mer**i**ngue and a s**a**ndwich.
||aɪ ˈgæðə ðət ðə ˈsæləd ɒn ðə ˈblæk ˈmæt hæz ˈæpl̩z | ˈkærəts | ˈməˈræŋ ənd ə ˈsænwɪʤ||

If you can't c**a**n any c**a**ndy c**a**n, how many c**a**ndy c**a**ns can a c**a**ndy c**a**nner c**a**n if he can c**a**n c**a**ndy c**a**ns?
||ɪf ju ˈkɑːnt ˈkæn ˈeni ˈkændi ˈkæn | ˈhaʊ ˈmeni ˈkændi ˈkænz kən ə ˈkændi ˈkænə ˈkæn ɪf hi kən ˈkæn ˈkændi ˈkænz||

AI 3.8. The spellings of RP /ɑ:/. Further practice

asking /ˈɑ:skɪŋ/	hard /hɑ:d/	marvellous /ˈmɑ:vləs/
calm /kɑ:m/	heart /hɑ:t/	tar /tɑ:/
clerk /klɑ:k/	laugh /lɑ:f/	

Ah! Barbara, Martha and Charles are dancing in the bar in the dark while Margaret is playing the guitar.
||ɑ: | ˈbɑ:brə | ˈmɑ:θə ənd ˈʧɑ:lz ə ˈdɑ:nsɪŋ ɪn ðə ˈbɑ:r ɪn ðə ˈdɑ:k waɪl ˈmɑ:grɪt ɪs ˈpleɪɪŋ ðə gɪˈtɑ:||

What a funny dancer Barbara is!
||ˈwɒt ə ˈfʌni ˈdɑ:nsə ˈbɑ:brə ˈɪz||

Let's take a fast photograph.
||ˈlets ˈteɪk ə ˌfɑ:st ˈfəʊtəgrɑ:f||

We can't.
||wi ˈkɑ:nt||

It's too dark.
||ɪts ˈtu: ˈdɑ:k||

Stay calm!
||ˈsteɪ ˈkɑ:m||

No need for alarm.
||ˈnəʊ ˈni:d fər əˈlɑ:m||

The giraffe doesn't harm.
||ðə ʤɪˈrɑ:f ˈdʌznt ˈhɑ:m||

3.2.4 Group 4: RP /ɔ: ɒ/ vs. PSp /o/

IPA Symbols

ɒ Turned script A (or Latin small letter turned alpha).
ɔ Latin small letter open O.
o Latin small letter O.

Identification

/ɔ:/ Between open-mid and close-mid, back, medium lip rounding, tense and long (free).
/ɒ/ Open, back, slightly-rounded, lax and short (checked).

Location in the CVS

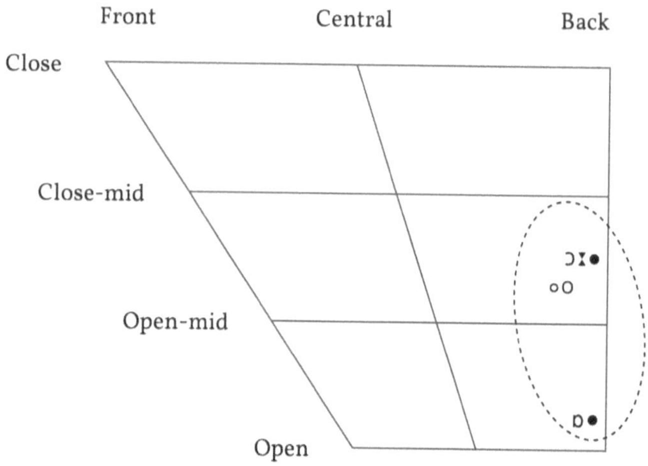

Figure 40: RP /ɒ ɔː/ vs. PSp /o/

Description

For the articulation of RP /ɔː/ the back of the tongue is raised between the open-mid and close-mid position and no contact is made between the tongue and the upper molars. There is medium lip-rounding. Its quality lies between CV 6 [ɔ] and CV 7 [o], i.e. [ɔ̝] or [o̞].

RP /ɒ/ is articulated with the back of the tongue in the fully open position. The lips are slightly rounded and no contact is made between the tongue and the upper molars. The quality is that of an open lip-rounded CV 5 [ɑ] = secondary CV 13 [ɒ].

See the animations and **videos under RP /ɔː/ and / ɒ / (compared with Spanish /o/) in the Sound Bank of the EPSS Multimedia Lab** (see also e.g. Gimson 1984: 114–118; Gimson 1994: 108–111; Roach 2005: 16, 20; Collins and Mees 2009: 98–101; Cruttenden 2014: 99, 102).

Environment

/ɒ/ never occurs word-finally, and /ɔː/ does not appear before /ŋ/.

Spellings

Table 12: The spellings of RP /ɔː ɒ/

/ɔː/ (in stressed syllables)	/ɒ/ (in stressed and unstressed syllables)
<ar> **war** /wɔː/, **quart** /kwɔːt/ **toward** /təˈwɔːd/	<o>[37] **cod** /kɒd/, **dock** /ˈdɒk/, **response** /rɪˈspɒns/
<or> **sword** /sɔːd/ **forward** /ˈfɔːwəd/	<w>/<wh>/<qu> + <a>[38] **was** /wɒz/, **what** /ˈwɒt/ **quarrel** /ˈkwɒrəl/
<ore> <ure> **sore** /sɔː/, **sure** /ʃɔː/	<ou>, <ow> **cough** /kɒf/, **knowledge** /ˈnɒlɪdʒ/
<our>, <oar>, <oor>[39] **four** /fɔː/, **board** /bɔːd/ **poor** /pɔː/	<au> **because** /bɪˈkɒz/, **cauliflower** /ˈkɒlɪflaʊə/
<aw>, <au>, <au> + silent <gh> **awful** /ˈɔːfᵊl/, **cause** /kɔːz/ **daughter** /ˈdɔːtə/	
<a> + <ll>/<lt>/<ld>/<lk>/<ls>[40] **all** /ɔːl/, **salt** /sɔːlt/ **stalk** /ˈstɔːk/, **also** /ˈɔːlsəʊ/	
<ou> + silent <gh>[41] **ought** /ˈɔːt/, **fought** /ˈfɔːt/	
<oa> **broad** /brɔːd/, **abroad** /əˈbrɔːd/	
Rare spellings <awer> **drawer** /drɔː/ ('sliding box') <aw> **drawer** /drɔːə/ ('person who draws') <awe> **awe** /ɔː/	**Rare spellings** <a> + silent <ch> **yacht** /jɒt/ <eau> **bureaucracy** /bjʊəˈrɒkrəsi/

37 Stressed <o> is pronounced /ɒ/ in the following cases: (1) monosyllabic words ending in one or two consonants; (2) words ending in two consonants + silent <e> (e.g. *response* [rɪˈspɒns], *involve* [ɪnˈvɒlv]); (3) two-syllable words in which stressed <o> is followed by two consonants or more (e.g. *doctor* [ˈdɒktə], *constant* [ˈkɒnstənt], *across* [əˈkrɒs]) (4) polysyllabic words with the primary stress on <o> (e.g. *crocodile* [ˈkrɒkədaɪl], *dominate* [ˈdɒmɪneɪt], *positive* [ˈpɒzɪtɪv], *poverty* [ˈpɒvəti], *solitary* [ˈsɒlɪtəri]); and (5) words ending in <-ic>, <-ical> (e.g. *comic* [ˈkɒmɪk], *methodical* [məˈθɒdɪkl]).

The following common English words, however, do not conform to the spelling tendencies just described for RP /ɔː/:

sh**a**ll /ʃæl/ (strong form)
dr**au**ght /drɑːft/
l**au**gh /lɑːf/

Regional and social variants

With respect to **/ɔː/**, as noted in fn 36, this phoneme used to contrast with /ɔə/, normally in words derived from <[ɒ]/[ɔː] + r> in RP, so that *saw* and *sore* were pronounced differently. Nowadays this contrast is generally not made, except by some older speakers. In addition, a number of words which formerly had only /ʊə/ in RP have now acquired an alternative pronunciation with /ɔː/ (e.g. ***sure***, ***poor***, ***your***). Note also the SSBE tendency for /ɔː/ to cover both /ɔː/ and /ɒ/, so that, for example, the words *c**augh**t* and *c**o**t* may be pronounced [kɔːt]. In addition, alternative /ɔː/-/ɑː/ pronunciations are observed in some French loanwords such as *l**au**nch* [lɔːnʃ], [lɑːnʃ] and *j**au**ndice* [ˈdʒɔːndɪs], [ˈdʒɑndɪs].

/ɒ/, in turn, has very little variation in RP (and generally in British English), apart from the preference of some Refined RP speakers to pronounce [ɔː] instead of [ɒ] in a number of words, usually preceding consonant clusters headed by /l, s, θ, f/ (e.g. *acr**o**ss* [əˈkrɔːs], [əˈkrɒs], ***Au**stralia* [ɔːsˈtreɪlɪə], [ɒsˈtreɪlɪə], ***Au**stria* [ˈɔːstrɪə], [ˈɒstrɪə], ***au**sterity* [ɔːˈstɛrɪti], [ɒˈstɛrɪti], ***au**spice* [ˈɔːspɪs], [ˈɒspɪs], ***au**thority* [ɔːˈθɒrɪti], [ɒˈθɒrɪti], *cl**o**th* [klɔːθ], [klɒθ], ***o**ff* [ɔːf], [ɒf], *s**a**lt* [sɔːlt], [sɒlt], *f**a**lse* [fɔːls], [fɒls]).

Comparison with Spanish and advice

RP /ɒ/ and /ɔː/ show acoustic features that place them in the region of Spanish /o/, although the English sounds involve a more retracted realisation, **/ɒ/** being more open than /**o**/, and **/ɔː/** closer. Some SSLE, however, may rate [ɒ] as a type of PSp [e] probably due to their close F2 value, and in some cases [ɒ] and [ɔː] may be confused as a result of the inability to perceive the lax-tense and length

---

38 /ɒ/ is the NP of <wa>, <wha>, <qua> in stressed syllables and when these combinations occur before one or more final non-velar sounds. Nevertheless, the letter <a> has its NP /eɪ/ when these spellings precede: (1) a single consonant + silent <e>, (2) a single consonant + a pronounced vowel, or (3) a velar consonant /k, g, ŋ/ (e.g. *wh**a**le* [weɪl], *w**a**ge* [weɪdʒ], *equ**a**tor* [ɪˈkweɪtə], *qu**a**ke* [kweɪk]).

39 Formerly this spelling was pronounced [ɔə], but today this is regarded as conservative pronunciation in regional accents.

40 Also in compounds and derivatives in which <l> is single.

41 In stressed syllables of around 30 words; this spelling has many different pronunciations.

cues that distinguish these two sounds (Finch and Ortiz Lira 1982; García Lecumberri and Cenoz Iragui 1997; Escudero and Chládková 2010).

Accordingly, for the articulation of these two rounded vowels learners are advised to pay special attention to the perception and production of the lax-tense and short-long contrasts, in addition to their different degrees of lip-rounding, which seems to be the crucial feature to distinguish the three sounds (Monroy Casas 1980, 2012; Ward 1972: 96). To practice RP /**ɔ:**/, as in *call* /kɔ:l/, SSLE may try to produce the vowel of *col* 'cabbage' but with longer duration; its quality is close to that of Galician or Catalan [o] in final positions. To target RP /**ɒ**/, on the other hand, a good practice may be to utter a long Spanish [o] but in the middle the mouth should be opened a bit more by lowering the jaw and the tongue (Monroy Casas 1980, 2012; Estebas Vilaplana 2009). Remember that RP /ɒ/ is shorter and more open than RP /ɔ:/, while Spanish /o/ has an in-between quality.

Further Practice

AI 3.9. The spellings of RP /ɔ:/. Further practice

always /ˈɔ:lweɪz/	bef**ore** /bɪˈfɔ:/	sw**or**d /sɔ:d/
author /ˈɔ:θə/	l**aw** /lɔ:/	w**a**ter /ˈwɔ:tə/
b**al**d /bɔ:ld/	s**ough**t /ˈsɔ:t/	

Sean's d**augh**ter, L**au**ra, ad**ore**s sm**all** t**or**toises and footb**all**.
||ˈʃɒnz ˈdɔ:tə | ˈlɔ:rə | əˈdɔ:z ˈsmɔ:l ˈtɔ:təsɪz ənd ˈfʊtbɔ:l||/

Paul th**ough**t going to M**al**ta in **Au**gust or in **au**tumn is a b**ore.**
||ˈpɔ:l ˈθɔ:t ˈgəʊɪŋ tə ˈmɔ:ltə ɪn ˈɔ:gəst ɔ:r ɪn ˈɔ:təm ˈɪz ə ˈbɔ:||

The **au**thor of the st**o**ry, Ge**or**ge, has **al**ready gone in the yacht for a f**our**teen minute sail in the cold w**a**ter.
||ði ˈɔ:θər əv ðə ˈstɔ:ri | ˈdʒɔ:dʒ | həz ɔ:lˈredi ˈgɒn ɪn ðə ˈjɒt fər ə ˌfɔ:ti:n ˌmɪnɪt ˈseɪl ɪn ðə ˈkəʊld ˈwɔ:tə||

Knife and a f**or**k, bottle and a c**or**k that is the way you spell New Y**or**k.
||naɪf ənd ə fɔ:k | ˈbɒtl̩ ənd ə ˈkɔ:k ˈðæt ɪs ðə ˈweɪ ju ˈspel ˌnju: ˈjɔ:k||

Does this shop sp**or**t c**or**ds and sh**or**t socks with spots?
||dəz ðɪs ˈʃɒp ˈspɔ:t ˌkɔ:dz ənd ˌʃɔ:t ˈsɒks wɪð ˈspɒts||

I s**aw** a s**aw** in W**ar**s**aw** that could outs**aw** any s**aw** that I ever s**aw**.
||ˈaɪ ˈsɔ: ə ˈsɔ: ɪn ˈwɔ:sɔ: ðət kəd ˌaʊtˈsɔ: ˈeni ˈsɔ: ðət ˈaɪ ˈevə ˈsɔ:||

AI 3.10. The spellings of RP /ɒ/. Further practice

because /bɪˈkɒz/ knowledge /ˈnɒlɪʤ/ tog /ˈtɒg/
cough /kɒf/ revolver /rɪˈvɒlvə/ wander /ˈwɒndə/
donkey /ˈdɒŋki/ rock /ˈrɒk/

Tommy and Polly wandered around Gloucester and Oxford.
||ˈtɒmi ənd ˈpɒli ˈwɒndəd əˈraʊnd ˈglɒstər ənd ˈɒksfəd||/

Sorry, what's wrong with washing socks?
||ˈsɒri | ˈwɒts ˈrɒŋ wɪð ˈwɒʃɪŋ ˈsɒks||/

Everybody would want a long holiday in Australia.
||ˈevrɪbɒdi wʊd ˈwɒnt ə ˌlɒŋ ˈhɒlədeɪ ɪn ɒsˈtreɪliə||/

If pros and cons are opposite, is progress the opposite of congress?
||ɪf ˈprəʊz ənd ˈkɒnz ər ˈɒpəzɪt | ˈɪz ˈprəʊgres ði ˈɒpəzɪt əv ˈkɒŋgres||

Top chopsticks shops stock top chopsticks.
||ˌtɒp ˌʧɒpstɪks ˈʃɒps ˈstɒk ˌtɒp ˈʧɒpstɪks||/

3.2.5 Group 5: RP /uː ʊ/ vs. PSp /u/

IPA Symbols

u Latin small letter U.
ʊ Upsilon (or Greek small letter Upsilon).

Identification

/uː/ Close, back, very closed lip rounding, tense and long (free).
/ʊ/ Close-mid, back, closed lip rounding, lax and short (checked).

Location in the CVS

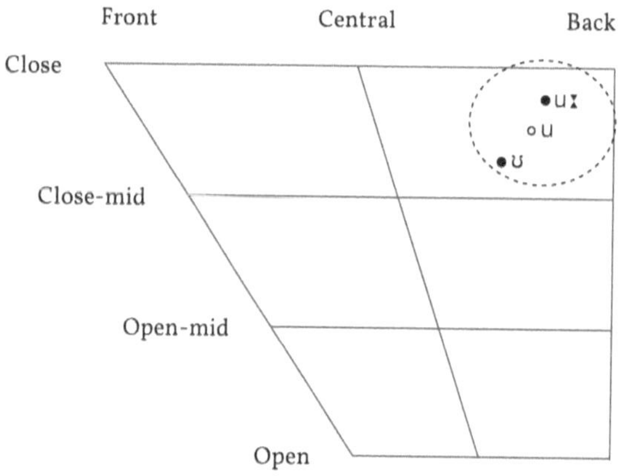

Figure 41: RP /ʊ, uː/ vs. PSp /u/

Description

For the articulation of RP /**u:**/ a part of the tongue somewhat centralised from true back is raised just below closed position, in a symmetrical back relationship with the front vowel /i:/. The articulation is tense compared to that of /ʊ/ and no firm contact is made between the tongue and the upper molars. The lips tend to be very closely rounded or trumpet-shaped. The quality is that of a slightly lowered and centralised CV 8 [u] = [ü̞].

RP /**ʊ**/ is articulated with a part of the tongue nearer the centre than the back raised just above the close-mid position, in a symmetrical back relationship with the front vowel /ɪ/. There is close lip-rounding. The tongue is lax (compared with the tenser /u:/) and no firm contact is made between the side rims and the upper molars. The quality is a centralised and closer CV 7 [o] with closer rip-rounding = [ö̝].

See the animations and **videos under RP /u:/ and /ʊ/ (compared with Spanish /u/) in the Sound Bank of the EPSS Multimedia Lab** (see also e.g. Gimson 1984: 119–122; Gimson 1994: 112–114; Roach 2005: 16, 20; Collins and Mees 2009: 98–101; Cruttenden 2014: 130–134).

Environment

[ʊ] is found in both accented and unaccented syllables, but it does not occur in word-initial positions nor before final /ŋ/, and finally only in the unaccented form of *to* [tʊ] and *you* [jʊ]. RP /u:/ is never pronounced before /ŋ/, either.

Spellings

Note that a shorter variety of [u] (without the length marks [:]) occurs in unstressed syllables, especially after [j] (*circ**u**lar* /ˈsɜ:kjulə/), [**tj**] when it results from the merging of [t] and [j] (*situation* /sɪtjuˈeɪʃən/ – /sɪʧuˈeɪʃən/, as well as in unstressed word- and stem-final spellings listed below.

<ou> y**ou** /ju/, thr**ou**ghout /θruˈaʊt/
<o> t**o** /tu/, int**o** /ˈɪntu/, wh**o** /hu:/

[u] can also occur word-medially, usually before a stressed vowel with the spellings:

<ew> intervi**ew**ee /ˌɪntəvjuˈi:/
<u> infl**u**enza /ˌɪnfluˈenzə/, virt**u**osity /ˌvɜ:ʧuˈɒsəti/
gen**u**ine /ˈʤenjuɪn/

Table 13: The spellings of RP /uː ʊ/

/uː/ (mostly in stressed syllables)	/ʊ/ (in stressed and unstressed syllables)
<u> cr**u**cial /kruːʃəl/, fl**u**te /fluːt/ fl**u**ency /ˈfluːənsi/, fl**u**or /fluːə/	<u>[42] p**u**t /ˈpʊt/, c**u**shion /ˈkʊʃən/, s**u**gar /ˈʃʊgə/
<oo>[43] t**oo** /tuː/, m**oo**n /muːn/	<oo> l**oo**k /lʊk/, w**oo**l /wʊl/
<o> d**o** /duː/, m**o**ve /muːv/	<o> w**o**man /ˈwʊmən/ W**o**lverhampton /ˈwʊlvəˌhæmptən/
<ou>[44] gr**ou**p /gruːp/, w**ou**nd /wuːnd/ thr**ou**gh /θruː/	<ou> c**ou**ld /kʊd/, sh**ou**ld /ʃʊd/
<ew>, <ue>, <ui>[45] fl**ew** /fluː/, bl**ue** /bluː/ virt**ue** /ˈvɜːʧuː/, s**ui**t /suːt/	
<oe> can**oe** /kəˈnuː/	

Finally, [u] / [ju] / [jʊ] pronunciations may also be heard in the <u> spellings of such word endings as:

<-ua(r)>	jag**ua**rs /ˈʤægjuəz/
<-ual(ly)>	cas**ua**l /ˈkæʒjuəl/, act**ua**lly /ˈækʧuəli/
<-uenc(e/y)>	confl**ue**nce /ˈkɒnfluənts/
<-uent, -uance>	infl**ue**nt /ˈɪnfluənt/, contin**ua**nce /kənˈtɪnjuəns/
<-uary>	Febr**ua**ry /ˈfebruəri/ – /ˈfebjʊəri/, mort**ua**ry /ˈmɔːʧuəri/
<-uate(ion)>	insin**ua**te /ɪnˈsɪnjueɪt/, sit**ua**tion /ˌsɪtjuˈeɪʃn̩/

42 <u> is pronounced /ʊ/ in the stressed syllables of about 30 words of common use.

43 <oo> is pronounced /uː/ in stressed syllables, except when followed by <r>, in which case its NP is /ɔː/.

44 The NP of <ou> is /aʊ/.

45 The NP of the spellings <u>, <ew>, <eu>, <ue>, <ui>, <oe> is /uː/ in stressed syllables, and normally after /tʃ dʒ r l/). Note, however, that these spellings are pronounced [juː] when they are preceded by: (1) plosives /b d p t k/ (e.g. *t**u**ne* [tjuːn], *d**u**ke* [djuːk], *arg**ue*** [ˈɑːgjuː], *bea**u**ty* [ˈbjuːti], *ask**ew*** [əˈskjuː]; (2) nasals /m n/ (e.g. *m**u**sic* [ˈmjuːzɪk], *n**eu**ter* [ˈnjuːtə], *n**ew*** [njuː], *n**ui**sance* [ˈnjuːsns]); (3) fricatives /f v h/ (e.g. *f**eu**d* [fjuːd], *f**ue**l* [ˈfjuːəl], *f**ew*** [fjuː], *h**ue*** [hjuː]); and (4) <l>, if preceded by a stressed vowel (e.g. *val**ue*** [ˈvaljuː]). But both /uː/ and /juː/ are heard when the spellings <u>, <ue>, <ui>, <ew> are preceded by: (1) /s z θ/ (e.g. *enth**u**siasm* [enˈθuːzɪæz(ə)m], [enˈθjuːzɪæz(ə)m], *s**ui**t* [suːt], [sjuːt]), and (2) syllable-initial /l/ or when /l/ is preceded by an unstressed vowel (e.g. *absol**u**te* [ˈabsəluːt], [ˈabsəljuːt], *l**u**te* [luːt], [ljuːt]).

Regional and social variants

Apart from variation in rounding and variation between /ʊ/ and /u:/ in some words (e.g. ***broom*** [brʊm], [bru:m], ***groom*** [grʊm], [gru:m], ***room*** [rʊm], [ru:m], ***tooth*** [tʊθ], [tu:θ]), little striking variety is found in RP /**ʊ**/. There exists an increasing tendency for [ʊ] to be unrounded in such common words as e.g. ***could*** [kʊd], ***should*** [ʃʊd], ***would*** [wʊd], which have a schwa in their unaccented forms, so if we take into account its unrounding process, it is coming closer to its unrounded equivalent, that is secondary CV 15 [ɤ]. Throughout the north of England no contrast is made between /ʊ/ and /ʌ/, and a vowel in the region of [ʊ] is used for both.

Turning to RP /**u:**/, there are two main variants: (1) more centralised realisations or fronted variants if following [j] (e.g. ***beauty*** [ˈbjüˑti], ***youth*** [jü:θ); and (2) different kinds of diphthongisation [ʊu], [əʊ], particularly in final position (e.g. ***do*** [dʊu], [dəʊ], ***shoe*** [ʃʊu], [ʃəʊ], ***who*** [hʊu], [həʊ]) in Cockney. In SSE, as there is no /ʊ/-/u:/ contrast, both vowels are covered by a centralised kind of CV8 [u] = [ü], or by a centralised vowel with a very slight lip-rounding [ÿ].

Comparison with Spanish and advice

Both RP /u:/ and /ʊ/ tend to be identified with PSp /u/, which make it hard for Spanish speakers to be able to distinguish such English words as *fool* /fu:l/ and *full* /fʊl/ (Finch and Ortiz Lira 1982; García Lecumberri and Cenoz Iragui 1997; Escudero and Chládková 2010). However, the quality and duration of both RP sounds differ from their Spanish counterpart.

/**u:**/ is longer and has more tension and correspondingly more lip-rounding and a closer realisation than PSp /u/. To produce English /u:/, Spanish speakers should utter a lengthened Spanish [u], as the vowel of the word *uva* 'grape', whereas the quality of English [u] (in unstressed syllables) is similar to that of Spanish [u]. RP /**ʊ**/, in turn, is shorter than /u:/ and more open than PSp /u/, its quality lies between Spanish [u] and [e]. For its pronunciation a good practice may be to utter a long Spanish [u], but in the middle the mouth should be opened a bit and the lips should be relaxed so as to have a bit less lip rounding. As /ʊ/ is half-way between RP /u/ and /ə/, any error in its quality should be in the direction of /ə/ (Monroy Casas 1980, 2012; Estebas Vilaplana 2009).

Further Practice

AI 3.11. The spellings of RP /u:/. Further practice

after**noo**n /ˌɑ:ftəˈnu:n/	l**o**se /lu:z/	s**u**pernatural /ˌsu:pəˈnætʃrəl/
fl**u** /flu:/	rh**eu**matism /ˈru:mətɪzəm/	tiss**ue** /ˈtɪʃu:/
l**oo**se /lu:s/	s**ui**t /su:t/	

Hugh and S**ue** were tr**u**ly tr**u**ants and liked c**oo**l, good f**oo**d.
||ˈhjuː ənd ˈsuː wə ˈtruːli ˈtruːənts ənd ˈlaɪkt ˈkuːl | ˈgʊd ˈfuːd||

Exc**u**se me, Andr**ew**, do you have ch**ew**ing gum and some fr**ui**t j**ui**ce?
||ɪkˈskjuːz ˈmiː | ˈændruː | də ju ˈhæv ˈʧuːɪŋ ˌgʌm ənd səm ˌfruːt ˈʤuːs||

My w**ou**nds were **oo**zing pus and I had to resched**u**le the j**u**nior tr**oo**p meeting.
||ˈmaɪ ˈwuːndz wər ˈuːzɪŋ ˈpʌs ənd ˈaɪ ˈhæd tə ˌriːˈʃedjuːl ðə ˈʤuːnɪə truːp ˈmiːtɪŋ||

J**u**ne ass**u**mes that by looking at the manual she'll prod**u**ce a sol**u**tion with a bl**ue** coloration.
||ˈʤuːn əˈsjuːmz ðət ˈbaɪ ˈlʊkɪŋ ət ðə ˈmænjʊəl ʃil prəˈdjuːs ə səˈluːʃn̩ wɪð ə ˌbluː ˌkʌləˈreɪʃn̩||

A T**u**dor wh**o** t**oo**ted the fl**u**te tried to t**u**tor t**wo** t**oo**ters to t**oo**t.
||ə ˈtjuːdə huˈtuːtɪd ðə ˈfluːt ˈtraɪd tə ˈtjuːtə ˈtuː ˈtuːtəz tə tuːt||

AI 3.12. The spellings of RP /ʊ/. Further practice

b**u**tcher /ˈbʊʧə/	R**ou**mania /rʊˈmeɪnɪə/	w**oo**ls /wʊlz/
neighbourh**oo**d /ˈneɪbəhʊd/	s**u**gar /ˈʃʊgə/	w**or**sted /ˈwʊstɪd/
p**u**dding /ˈpʊdɪŋ/	w**o**lf /wʊlf/	

Please, p**u**t the c**oo**kery b**oo**ks on the b**oo**kshelf in the dining-room, w**ou**ld you?
||pliːz | ˈpʊt ðə ˈkʊkəri ˌbʊks ɒn ðə ˈbʊkʃelf ɪn ðə ˈdaɪnɪŋ ˌruːm | wʊd ˈjuː||

The w**o**man from W**or**cester suffered from b**o**som related problems.
||ðə ˈwʊmən frəm ˈwʊstə ˈsʌfəd frəm ˌbʊzəm rɪˈleɪtɪd ˈprɒbləmz||

Hugh first st**oo**d l**oo**king at the b**oo**ks, and then p**u**lled the covers of P**u**ss in Boots, threw them to the br**oo**k and told the truth, without beating about the b**u**sh.
||ˈhjuː ˈfɜːst ˈstʊd ˈlʊkɪŋ ət ðə ˈbʊks | ənd ˈðen ˈpʊld ðə ˈkʌvəz əv ˈpʊs ɪn ˈbuːts | ˈθruː ðəm tə ðə ˈbrʊk ənd ˈtəʊld ðə ˈtruːθ | wɪðˈaʊt ˈbiːtɪŋ əˈbaʊt ðə ˈbʊʃ||

Esau W**oo**d saw a w**oo**d saw, saw w**oo**d, as no w**oo**d saw w**ou**ld saw w**oo**d.
||ˈɪsɔː ˈwʊd ˈsɔː ə ˌwʊd ˈsɔː | ˈsɔː ˈwʊd | əz ˈnəʊ ˌwʊd ˈsɔː wʊd ˈsɔː ˈwʊd||

3.3 A comparison of English and Spanish vowel glides

Glides are articulatorily described as movements from a given vocalic starting point towards an end-point alluding to two main parameters:

(1) **Tongue shape**, including tongue backness and height, which refers to which part of the tongue is raised and how close it comes to the roof of the mouth (e.g. (just, slightly) above, below, behind, forward of, front/centre/back, (half) open/close position);

(2) **Lip shape**, which generally changes during glides in accordance with the lip spreading/rounding associated with the vowel elements involved, though the amount of lip shape change is often less than might be expected.

Accordingly, under the term **diphthong** are included sequences of two vocalic elements forming a movement or glide within one syllable from a **first element**, or **starting point**, towards a **second element**, or **end-point**, as opposed to pure vowels which remain constant and do not glide. Diphthongs are usually classified articulatorily and auditorily according to three main parameters:

(1) The **direction** of the movement of the tongue, distinguishing **closing** (if the glide is in the direction of a closer vocalic position), **opening** (if the movements is towards a more open position) or **centring** diphthongs (if there is a glide from a peripheral to a more centralised vocalic position);
(2) The **distance** the tongue travels, according to which diphthongs can be articulatorily labelled **narrow** (if the glide is short) and **wide** (if the glide is long);
(3) The **prominence** of their elements, which determines whether diphthongs are auditorily **falling** (when most of the length and stress associated with the glide is concentrated on the first element, the second element being only slightly sounded) or **rising** (when the prominence increases as we pass from the first to the second element).

Focusing on English and Spanish, the diphthongal space shows the reverse situation than that found for vowels because RP has fewer diphthongs than PSp, as already noted in the introduction of this chapter (see also § 1.5 Table 4).

RP has only eight diphthongs, /**ɪə eə ʊə əʊ aʊ eɪ əʊ**/, with their first element in the general region of [ɪ e a ə ʊ] and the second element in the area of [ɪ ʊ ə]. Considering the direction of the glide, the RP set is classified into three **centring diphthongs**, /**ɪə eə ʊə**/, in which the articulation moves from the periphery of the CVS towards a mid-central neutral vowel [ə], and five **closing diphthongs**, in which the articulation either moves towards the near front, close, spread vowel [ɪ], /**aɪ eɪ ɔɪ**/, or towards the near close back rounded vowel [ʊ], /**əʊ aʊ**/. Turning to distance, RP has only three **wide diphthongs**, /**aɪ ɔɪ aʊ**/, where the distance between the two elements of the glide is bigger than in **narrow diphthongs**, which is the case of all the other RP diphthongs, whether centring, /**ɪə eə ʊə**/, or closing, /**eɪ əʊ**/. If we move on to prominence, all RP diphthongs are **falling**, that is, most of the length and stress associated with the glide is concentrated on the first element, the second element being only slightly sounded. Note also that /**eɪ aɪ ɪə eə**/ have **unrounded lips** throughout their articulation, while in the diphthongs /**ɔɪ ʊə**/ they change from **rounded to unrounded**, and in /**əʊ aʊ**/ they move from **unrounded to rounded.**

In addition, the following generalisations may be applied to all the RP diphthongs:

(1) With the exception of /ɔɪ/, they principally derive from former (typically long) pure vowels.
(2) They are particularly susceptible to variation regionally and socially in both elements. The exact end-point of the glide depends on context, and can vary from speaker to speaker.
(3) No diphthong occurs before /ŋ/, except where word-final /n/ is assimilated to /ŋ/ in connected speech, e.g. *own* [əʊŋ] in *own car.*
(4) Before **dark l** [ɫ] diphthongs tend to be reduced to their corresponding first element (a normally long monophthong) plus a slight glide to [ᵊ] or [ᵘ], as in the case of e.g. *failed* [feᵊɫd], *male* [meᵊɫ], *pail* [peᵊɫ], *sails* [seᵊɫz]; *aisle* [aᵊɫ], *mild* [maᵊɫd], *mile* [maᵊɫ], *piles* [paᵊɫz]; *cowl* (n) [kaᵁɫ], *foul* [faᵁɫ], *owl* [aʊɫ]; *bolt* [bəʊɫt], *hole* [həʊɫ], *moult* [məʊɫt], *roll* [rəᵁɫ], *poles* [pəʊɫz]; *boils* [bɔᵊɫz], *coil* [kɔᵊɫ], *soil* [sɔᵊɫ]; *real* [rɪᵊɫ]; *cruel* [ˈkruːᵊɫ] (see also fn 58 in § 3.3.3 on **levelling** or **smoothing**).
(5) Note that, though very widespread, not all the speakers of British English use the diphthong [ʊə]. Instead, some use the long vowel [ɔː], or other diphthongs [ɔə].

Besides falling diphthongs, English also has **rising glides**, which arise when the first element (transcribed in LPD [j] or [w]) becomes the less prominent segment of the glide and is compressed with the following vowel into a single syllable. This occurs in the second syllable of such words as *lenient* and *influence* when they are pronounced fast: [ˈlɪːnjənt], [ˈɪnflwəns]. Faster or compressed pronunciations are more usual in frequently-used words, in fast or casual speech, and if the word has already been used in the discourse. Alternatively, in slower pronunciations, especially those involving centring glides in which the schwa element represents a morphological ending, diphthongs tend to be realised as **hiatuses** with the two elements of the glide being pronounced over two different syllables and the first elements of /ɪə/ and /ʊə/ having a tense [i] and [u] realisation respectively. Accordingly, a slow pronunciation of *lenient* and *influence* would be [ˈlɪːni.ənt] and [ˈɪnflu.əns].

Another point worth of mention is that of hiatuses involving two instances of two similar vowel phonemes, which in English are neither fused or reduced. In such cases, foreign learners should be aware to pronounce two consecutive vowels, one tense and the other lax, as in, for instance, *earliest* /ˈɜːliɪst/ and emplo**yee** /ɪmˈplɔɪiː/, rather than just one vowel (*[ˈɜːlɪst]) or a palatal semi-consonant plus a vowel (*[ɪmˈplɔjiː]).

Lastly, it should be kept it mind that English tends to avoid the repetition of two identical vowels both within and between words. A good illustration of this is provided by the definite and the indefinite articles: to reinforce the hiatus that should exist between word boundaries, *the* is pronounced [ði], rather than [ðə], if followed by vowels (*the annoyance* [ði əˈnɔɪəns], *the apple* [ði ˈapl]); whereas, in the same context, the indefinite article *a* [ə]/[eɪ] requires the presence of an alveolar nasal to demarcate word boundaries, and thereby becomes *an* [ən]/[æn] (*an annoyance* [ən/æn əˈnɔɪəns], *an apple* [ən/æn ˈapl]).

Turning to Spanish, it has fourteen diphthongs, /**ai̯ ei̯ oi̯ au̯ eu̯ ou̯ wa we wo wi ja je jo ju**/, which are classified according to the closing-opening and falling-rising oppositions. Six are **falling-closing** /**ai̯ ei̯ oi̯**, **au̯ eu̯ ou̯**], with the pattern V + semi-vowel, and the other eight are **rising** [**ja je ju jo wa we wi wo**], with the pattern semi-consonant + V, which are also **opening** except for [**ju wi**] (Quilis 1981; Quilis and Fernández 1982; Martínez Celdrán 1986). In addition, while English diphthongs have the phonological status of a long vowel and can be described as indivisible diphthongal nuclei that cannot be split by any phonological rule, Spanish diphthongs can be characterised as complex syllable nuclei consisting a sequence of a vowel + semivowel (falling-closing) or a semi-consonant + vowel (rising) that can be divided by a word-internal boundary (e.g. *rey* 'king' [rei̯] → *reyes* 'kings' [re.ʝes]). Besides, in English [j w] are classified as two semi-consonant phonemes which can cluster with other consonants in onset clusters (e.g. [tw] in ***tw**enty* /ˈtwenti/) and do not form diphthongs when followed by vowels (e.g. [jiː] ***yi**eld* /jiːld/, [wʊ] ***woo**d* /wʊd/); in Spanish, by contrast, [j w] together with [i̯] and [u̯] are generally regarded as allophonic realisations of /i/ and /u/ respectively and may create a diphthong or a triphthongs if followed by other vowels (e.g. *rad**io*** 'radio' [ˈraðjo], ***cua**dro* [ˈkwaðro], ***buey*** 'ox' [bu̯ei̯]) (Alarcos LLorach 1961 [1983]; Navarro Tomás 1966 [1946], 1991 [1918]; Quilis 1981; Martínez Celdrán 1986; Calvo Shadid 2008). Moreover, in Spanish diphthongs can also be pronounced as a result of resyllabification across words (e.g. *jug**ó y** comió* 'he played and ate', [xu.ɣoi̯.ko.mio]), or they may even disappear when the accent shifts (e.g. ***fia**rás* '(you) will trust' vs. ***fía**s* '(you) trust'). Nevertheless, despite that it may be tempting to believe that the Spanish sequences <ía> (*d**ía*** 'day', *hab**ía*** 'there was'), <ea> (*tar**ea*** 'task', *pel**ea*** 'fight') and <úa> (*p**úa*** 'spike', 'pick', *gr**úa*** 'crane') come close to the English vowel glides [ɪə], [eə] and [ʊə], respectively, they are in fact **hiatuses**, rather than diphthongs (Navarro Tomás 1991; Hualde 2005; Hualde and Prieto 2002).[46] Triphthongs also occur in Spanish. They consist of two close vowels with a more open one in the middle and have the pattern semi-consonant + V + semi-vowel. They generally appear in verbs and result from the addition of inflectional endings (*averig**üéi**s* [aβeriˈɣwei̯s] 'you find out' (pl pres subj), *acaric**iái**s* [akariˈθjai̯s] 'you caress' (pl pres ind)) (Quilis and Fernández 1982).

46 The diphthong-hiatus distinction is based on changes in formant trajectories (especially of F2) and duration: hiatuses show a greater degree of curvature of the F2 trajectory and also longer duration than diphthongs, and as a consequence the vowels in a hiatus sequence, unlike those of diphthongs, belong to different syllables (Aguilar 1999: 72).

Figures 42 and 43 display starting points and directions for diphthongal vowel glides in RP and PSp, respectively. In what follows RP diphthongs and triphthongs are described along the same subsections that were considered for the description of vowels in Section 3.2. Note, however, that only RP **closing diphthongs** (Section 3.3.1) are contrasted with their PSp **falling counterparts** because **centring diphthongs** and **triphthongs** have **no correlates in Spanish**, as already advanced in Table 4 (Section 1.5).[47] It will be shown that four RP diphthongs /**aʊ eɪ aɪ ɔɪ**/ seem to present no difficulties for SSLE as they tend to be assimilated with their Spanish counterparts /**au̯ ai̯ ei̯ oi̯**/, whereas RP /**əʊ**/ is identified either with Spanish /**ou**/ or /**o**/ (Finch and Ortiz Lira 1982: 42; Gallardo del Puerto 2005: 186). Nevertheless, mispronunciations or communication flaws may arise broadly for three main reasons (Monroy Casas 2012, 1980; Estebas Vilaplana 2009; Swan and Smith 2001):

(1) because more emphasis is laid on the second rather than on the first vowel of diphthongs due to the influence of Spanish;
(2) because the last element of centring diphthongs (/**ɪə ʊə eə**/) is replaced by a flap [ɾ], probably due to the fact that most of these diphthongs are spelt with an <r>, even though RP is a non-rhotic accent, in addition to the aforementioned difficulties of Spanish speakers in pronouncing the English schwa /ə/;
(3) or because vowel glides, particularly closing diphthongs (/**eɪ ɔɪ aɪ əʊ aʊ**/), are monophthongised as a result of smoothing, despite the fact that, as already noted, this phenomenon affects the pronunciation of most glides amongst native speakers of English, especially in rapid speech.

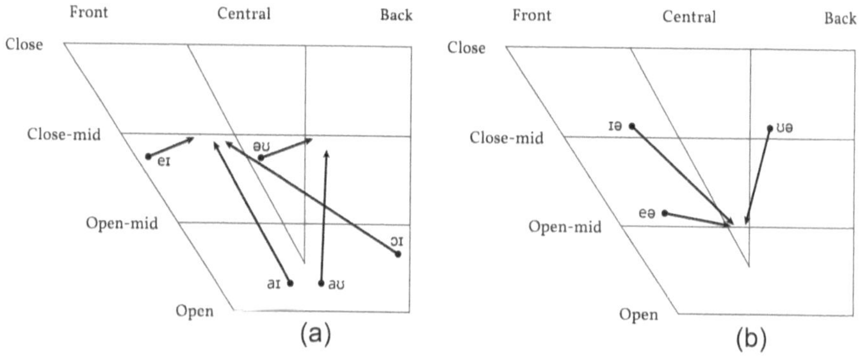

Figure 42: RP diphthongs: (a) closing (b) centring

47 It could be argued that RP /ʊə/ is close to the PSp diphthong [wa] (e.g. ***suave*** 'soft', ***guante*** 'glove'). However, this comparison is disregarded here because of their dissimilar nature: the Spanish diphthong is rising and the first element is less prominent, and the second element is more prominent, more open and fronted than in English.

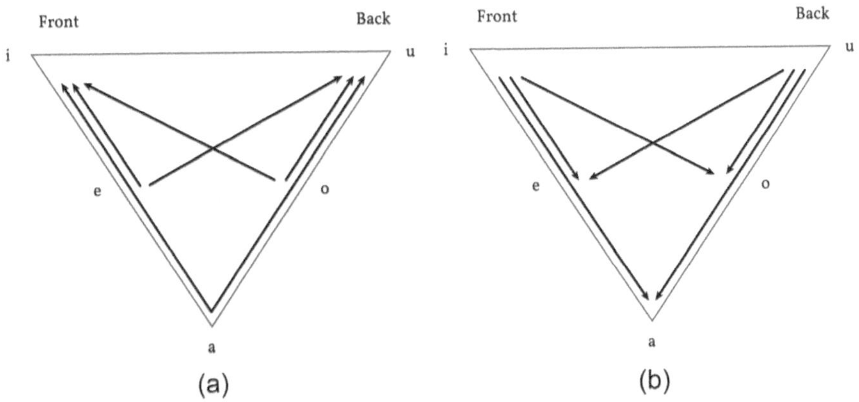

Figure 43: PSp diphthongs: (a) falling (b) rising

3.3.1 Closing diphthongs

This section focuses on RP five closing diphthongs. Section 3.3.1.1 describes [ɪ]-diphthongs, /**eɪ aɪ ɔɪ**/, displayed in Figure 44 along with their PSp counterparts, in which the articulation moves towards the near front, close, spread vowel [ɪ] or [i]. Section 3.3.1.2, on the other hand, characterises [ʊ]-diphthongs, [**əʊ aʊ**], presented in Figure 45 in comparison with their PSp counterparts, where there is a vowel glide towards the near close back rounded vowel [ʊ] or [u].

Note that /eɪ, aɪ/ have unrounded lips throughout their articulation, while in /ɔɪ ʊə/ they change from rounded to unrounded and in /əʊ aʊ/ they move from unrounded to rounded.

3.3.1.1 RP /eɪ aɪ ɔɪ/ vs. PSp /ei̯ ai̯ oi̯/

IPA Symbols

eɪ Lower-case E (or Latin small letter E) plus Small capital I (or Latin letter small capital I) combination.

aɪ Lower-case A (or Latin Small letter A) plus Small capital I (or Latin letter small capital I) combination.

ɔɪ Latin small letter open O (or Latin small letter E) plus Small capital I (or Latin letter small capital I) combination.

ei̯ Lower-case E (or Latin small letter E) plus plus reduced Lower case I (or Latin small letter I) combination.

ai̯ Lower-case A (or Latin Small letter A) plus plus reduced Lower case I (or Latin small letter I) combination.

oi̯ Latin small letter O plus reduced Lower-case I (or Latin small letter I) combination.

Identification

[**eɪ**] Near-close front, falling, narrow, closing diphthong (unrounded).

[**aɪ**] Near-close front, falling, wide, closing diphthong (unrounded).

[**ɔɪ**] Near-close front, falling, wide, closing diphthong (rounded to unrounded).

Position in the CVS

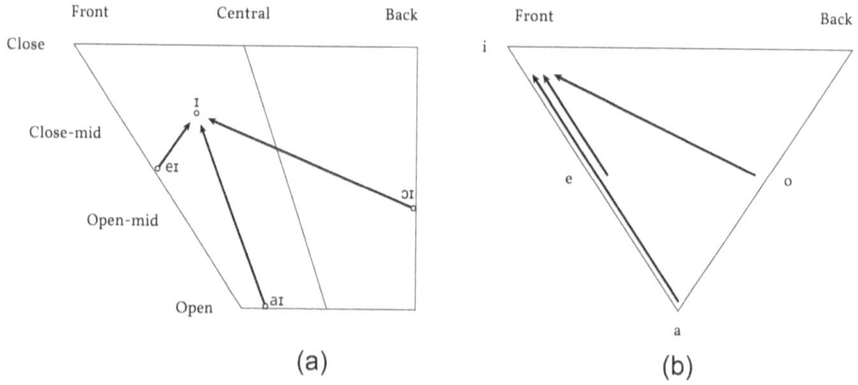

Figure 44: [ɪ/i] diphthongs in RP (a) and PSp (b)

Description

For the articulation of RP /**eɪ**/, the glide begins from slightly below the half-close front position [e̞] and moves in the direction of RP /ɪ/, there being a slight closing movement of the lower jaw. The lips are spread throughout.

RP /**aɪ**/, on the other hand, begins at a point slightly behind the front open position [ä], approaching RP /ɑ/, and moves in the direction of RP /ɪ/ nearer to a centralised half-close position [ë̞]. The closing movement of the lower jaw is obvious and the lips change from a neutral to a loosely spread position.

RP /ɔɪ/, in turn, starts with the centre of the tongue raised between half-open and half-close, and then it moves in the direction of RP /ɪ/ nearer to a centralised half-close position [ë̞]. There is a slight closing movement of the lower jaw, and the lips are neutral for the first element but have a tendency to round on the second segment. The starting point may have a tongue position similar to RP /ɒ/.

See the animations and **videos under RP /eɪ/, /aɪ/ and /ɔɪ/ (compared with Spanish /ei̯ ai̯ oi̯/) in the Sound Bank of the EPSS Multimedia Lab** (see also e.g. Gimson 1984: 128–133, 134–138; Gimson 1994: 120–123, 124–127; Roach 2005: 21–23; Collins and Mees 2009: 102–104; Cruttenden 2014: 140–149).

Spellings

Table 14: The spellings of RP /eɪ aɪ ɔɪ/

/eɪ/ (in stressed syllables)	/aɪ/ (in stressed syllables)	/ɔɪ/ (in stressed syllables)
<a>[48] **A**pril /ˈeɪprəl/ C**a**mbridge /ˈkeɪmbrɪʤ/ ch**a**os /ˈkeɪɒs/	<i>[49] **i**dle /ˈaɪdl̩/, l**i**fe /laɪf/	<oi> b**oi**l /bɔɪl/, t**oi**let /ˈtɔɪlɪt/
<ai, ay>[50] j**ai**l /ʤeɪl/, r**ai**n /reɪn/ cr**ay**on /ˈkreɪən/	<ie, ye, y>[51] l**ie** /laɪ/ b**ye** /baɪ/, dr**y** /draɪ/ as**y**lum /əˈsaɪləm/ sc**y**the /saɪð/	<oy> j**oy** /ˈʤɔɪ/, **oy**sters /ˈɔɪstəz/
<ei, ey>[52] gr**ey** /greɪ/ ob**ey** /əˈbeɪ/	<ei, ey(e)> **ei**ther /ˈaɪðə/ n**ei**ther /ˈnaɪðə/ **eye** /aɪ/	
<ea>[53] gr**ea**t /ˈgreɪt/ st**ea**k /steɪk/	<i> + silent <gh>[54] br**igh**t /braɪt/ h**igh** /haɪ/	
<ei> + silent <gh> sl**eigh** /sleɪ/, **eigh**t /eɪt/	<uy> b**uy** /baɪ/, g**uy** /gaɪ/	
<a> in <-ate>[55] gradu**ate** /ˈgræʤueɪt/ approxim**ate** /əˈprɒksɪmeɪt/ estim**ate** /ˈestimeɪt/	<-i> (Lat, pl) alumn**i** /əˈlʌmnaɪ/ termin**i** /ˈtɜːmɪnaɪ/ radi**i** /ˈreɪdɪaɪ/	
French loanwords <e, é, ê> d**e**but /ˈdeɪbjuː/ caf**é** /ˈkæfeɪ/ cr**e**pe /kreɪp/ <ee, ée> matin**ee** /ˈmætɪneɪ/ toup**ee** /ˈtuːpeɪ/ <et> ball**et** /ˈbæleɪ/ chal**et** /ˈʃæleɪ/ <-er> dossi**er** /ˈdɒsɪeɪ/ foy**er** /ˈfɔɪeɪ/		**German names and loanwords** Kr**eu**tzer /ˈkrɔɪtsə/ Plattd**eu**tsch /ˈplætdɔɪʧ/

Table 14: (Continued)

/eɪ/ (in stressed syllables)	/aɪ/ (in stressed syllables)	/ɔɪ/ (in stressed syllables)
Rare cases <ae> G**ae**lic /ˈgeɪlɪk/ <ao> g**ao**l /ʤeɪl/ <au> g**au**ge /geɪʤ/	**Rare cases** <ae> m**ae**stro /ˈmaɪstrəʊ/ <ai> **ai**sle /aɪl/ <aye> **aye** /aɪ/ <ui> g**ui**se /gaɪz/	**Rare cases** <uoy> b**uoy** /bɔɪ/
Exceptions qu**ay** /kɪː/ s**ai**d /sed/ s**ay**s /sez/	**Exceptions** bew**i**lder /bɪˈwɪlda/ ch**i**ldren /ˈtʃɪldr^{ə}n/ w**i**lderness /ˈwɪldənɪs/ w**i**nd /wɪnd/ (n) (vs. w**i**nd /waɪnd/ (vb))	**Exceptions** ch**oi**r /kwaɪə/

Regional and social variants

The [ɪ] element of the vowel glides /eɪ, aɪ, ɔɪ/ tends to be absorbed into an [ə] or [ʊ] glide before dark [ɫ], as in ***sail*** [seəɫ]), ***tile*** [taːəɫ]) and ***boil*** [bɔːəɫ]. In the case of /eɪ/, older speakers may have a closer starting point nearer to CV2 [2], whereas Refined RP speakers prefer a more open starting point nearer to CV3 [ɛ]. In addition, as a result of the "Southern diphthong shift", typical of London, Cockney, Birmingham, the South and Midlands of England, [eɪ] may be pronounced as [aɪ], [aɪ] as [ɑɪ] or [əɪ], and [ɔɪ] as [oi]. Besides, in Refined RP and Cockney (as well as in the so-called **mid-Atlantic pronunciation**) a very back starting point for [aɪ] is most common, [ɑ̈ɪ], which may sometimes involve the elimination of the glide, leaving a long monophthong [ɑɑː] (e.g. pop singers usually reduce *I* and *my* to [ɑː] and [mɑː]), while in a wide area of South-west

---

48 Note the different pronunciations and meaning of *bass* /beɪs/ ('instrument') and /bæs/ ('fish').

49 /aɪ/ is the NP of <i> when it is followed by a simple C + silent <e>. This is also the NP of <i> in usually word-final <-ind> (e.g. ***f**i**nd*** /faɪnd/, ***bl**i**nd*** /blaɪnd/, ***h**i**nd*** /haɪnd/), final <-ild> (e.g. ***ch**i**ld*** /ʧaɪld/, ***w**i**ld*** /waɪld/, ***m**i**ld*** /maɪld/), and <i> when followed by a silent <g+n>, usually in word-final position (e.g. ***s**i**gn*** /saɪn/, ***mal**i**gn*** /məˈlaɪn/, ***des**i**gn*** /diˈzaɪn/). Note that if <g> is not silent, then the pronunciation is /ɪ/ (e.g. ***s**i**gnal*** /ˈsɪgnl/, ***s**i**gnature*** /ˈsɪgnəʧə/).

50 If the sequences <ai, ay> are followed by <r>, their NP is /eə/.

51 <ie, ye, y> are pronounced [aɪ] usually in word-final position, but also in some medial cases (e.g. *c**y**cle* /ˈsaɪk(ə)l/, *as**y**lum* /əˈsaɪləm/).

52 The spelling <ei> can also be pronounced /iː/ (e.g. *conc**ei**ve* /kənˈsiːv/, *perc**ei**ve* /pəˈsiːv/).

53 The NP of <ea> is /iː/ (e.g. *j**ea**ns* /dʒiːnz/, *J**ea**n* / /dʒiːn/ (female name) vs. /dʒɑːn/ (male name).

54 <igh, eigh> are pronounced [aɪ] usually in word-final position and/or before <t>.

55 Beware that <a> in the <-ate> suffix is pronounced /eɪ/ in verbs, but in nouns and adjectives its pronunciation is /ət/ (e.g. /ˈgrædʒuət/, /əˈprɒksɪmət/, /ˈestimət/).

and South-central England prefer [əɪ] pronunciations, with unrounded, raised, and centralised starting points. This is also the quality of refined RP pronunciations of /ɔɪ/, [əɪ] or [ɑɪ], which are characterised by unrounded, raised, and centralised starting points.

Comparison with Spanish and advice

It can be said that the three English [ɪ]-diphthongs, /**eɪ**/ (*lay* /leɪ/), /**aɪ**/ (*high* /haɪ/) and /**ɔɪ**/ (*boy* /bɔɪ/), approximate in quality to the Spanish ones, /**ei̯**/ (*ley* 'law' [lei]), /**ai̯**/ (*hay* 'there is' [ai̯]) and /**oi̯**/ (*voy* '(I) go' [boi̯]). RP /aɪ aʊ/, in particular, start in an area that is quite similar to that of Spanish /a/ and the starting points of /ai̯ au̯/. RP /eɪ ɔɪ/, however, start in a lower area of the CVS than their Spanish counterparts /ei̯ oi̯/. But the main difference between the two languages resides in the second element: in Spanish it has a clear [i] quality, whereas in English the [ɪ] sound is more relaxed and open, between Spanish [i] and [e]. However, no misunderstandings will occur if a Spanish [i] type of vowel is uttered as the end point of these three diphthongs (Monroy Casas 1980, 2012; Gallardo del Puerto 2005: 184–186; Estebas Vilaplana 2009).

Further practice

AI 3.13. The spellings of RP /eɪ/. Further practice

ch**a**os /ˈkeɪɒs/	pl**a**te /pleɪt/	sl**ei**ghing /ˈsleɪɪŋ/
conv**ey** /kənˈveɪ/	pl**ay**ed /pleɪd/	th**ey** /ˈðeɪ/
expl**ai**n /ɪkˈspleɪn/	r**ai**lw**ay** /ˈreɪlweɪ/	

The mayor says he's afr**ai**d th**ey** elabor**a**te a deliberate plan to r**ai**se riot in B**a**ker street.
||ðə ˈmeə ˈsez hiz əˈfreɪd ðeɪ ɪˈlæbəreɪt ə dɪˈlɪbᵊrət ˈplæn tə ˈreɪz ˈraɪət ɪn ˈbeɪkə ˈstriːt||

I don't like this m**ay**onnaise. M**ay** I ch**a**nge it?
||ˈaɪ dəʊnt ˈlaɪk ðɪs ˌmeɪəˈneɪz || ˈmeɪ aɪ ˈʧeɪndʒ ɪt ||

Tod**ay**, at a quarter to **ei**ght, I'm going aw**ay** to Sp**ai**n by pl**a**ne.
||təˈdeɪ | ət ə ˈkwɔːtə tu ˈeɪt | aɪm ˌgəʊɪŋ əˈweɪ tə ˈspeɪn baɪ ˈpleɪn||

That's a bit d**a**ngerous at your **a**ge.
||ˈðæts ə bɪt ˈdeɪndʒərəs ət jər ˈeɪdʒ||

Six slimy sn**ai**ls s**ai**led silently.
||ˈsɪks ˌslaɪmi ˈsneɪlz ˈseɪld ˈsaɪləntli||

On a l**a**zy l**a**ser r**ai**ser lies a l**a**ser r**ay** er**a**ser.
||ɒn ə ˈleɪzi leɪzə ˈreɪzə ˈlaɪz ə ˈleɪzə reɪ ɪˈreɪzə||

AI 3.14. The spellings of RP /aɪ/. Further practice

I /aɪ/	**i**ce /aɪs/	t**igh**t /taɪt/
eyes /aɪz/	**i**sland /ˈaɪlənd/	tr**ie**d /traɪd/
h**ei**ght /haɪt/	p**ie** /ˈpaɪ/	t**y**pewr**i**ter /ˈtaɪpraɪtə/

V**i**olet l**i**kes rock-cl**i**mbing, horse-r**i**ding, and **i**ce-skating.

||ˈvaɪələt ˈlaɪks ˈrɒkˌklaɪmɪŋ | ˈhɔːsˌraɪdɪŋ | ənd ˈaɪsˌskeɪtɪŋ||

M**i**ke is going b**i**cycle-r**i**ding with M**i**les next Fr**i**day.

||ˈmaɪk s ˈɡəʊɪŋ ˈbaɪsɪkl̩ˌraɪdɪŋ wɪð ˈmaɪlz ˌnekst ˈfraɪdi||

I'll ask the l**i**brarian if there are intriguing sc**i**-f**i** and ps**y**cho movies on DVD.

||aɪl ˈɑːsk ðə laɪˈbreərɪən ɪf ðər ər ɪnˈtriːɡɪŋ ˈsaɪˌfaɪ ənd ˌsaɪkəʊ ˈmuːvɪz ɒn ˌdiviˈdiː||

Birdie birdie in the sk**y** laid a turdie in m**y** **eye**.

||ˈbɜːdi ˈbɜːdi ɪn ðə ˈskaɪ ˈleɪd ə ˈtɜːdi ɪn maɪ ˈaɪ||

If cows could fl**y**, **I**'d have a cow p**ie** in m**y** **eye**.

||ɪf ˈkaʊz kəd ˈflaɪ | aɪd ˈhæv ə ˌkaʊ ˈpaɪ ɪn maɪ ˈaɪ||

AI 3.15. The spellings of RP /ɔɪ/. Further practice

destr**oy**ed /dɪˈstrɔɪd/	n**oi**se /nɔɪz/	t**oy** /tɔɪ/
flamb**oy**ant /flæmˈbɔɪənt/	**oy**ster /ˈɔɪstə/	v**oi**ce /vɔɪs/
Fr**eu**d /frɔɪd/	tabl**oi**d /ˈtæblɔɪd/	v**oy**age /ˈvɔɪɪdʒ/

The engine of J**oy**ce's Rolls R**oy**ce makes an ann**oy**ing n**oi**se, which is probably due to lack of **oi**l.

||ði ˈendʒɪn əv ˈdʒɔɪsəz ˌrəʊlz ˈrɔɪs ˈmeɪks ən əˈnɔɪɪŋ ˈnɔɪz | wɪtʃ ɪz ˈprɒbəbli djuː tə ˈlæk əv ˈɔɪl||

Sp**oi**lt b**oy**s usually enj**oy** destr**oy**ing n**oi**sy t**oy**s.

||ˌspɔɪlt ˈbɔɪz ˈjuːʒəli ɪnˈdʒɔɪ dɪˈstrɔɪɪŋ ˌnɔɪzi ˈtɔɪz||

What n**oi**se ann**oy**s an **oy**ster most? A n**oi**sy n**oi**se ann**oy**s an **oy**ster most.

||ˈwɒt ˈnɔɪz əˈnɔɪz ən ˈɔɪstə ˈməʊst|| ə ˌnɔɪzi ˈnɔɪz əˈnɔɪz ən ˈɔɪstə ˈməʊst||

3.3.1.2 RP /əʊ aʊ/ vs. PSp /eu̯ ou̯ au̯/

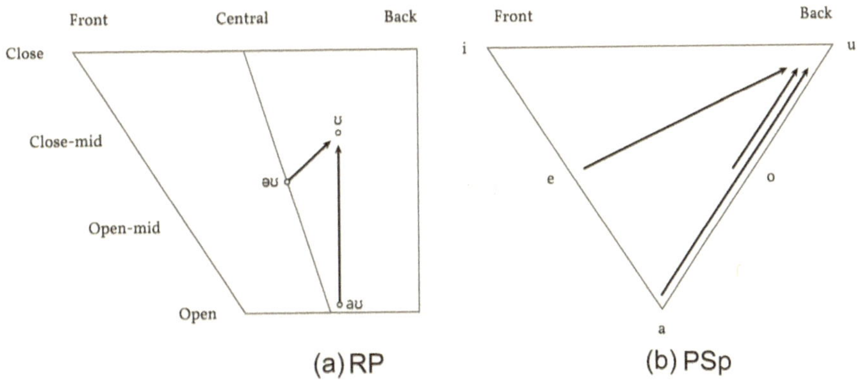

Figure 45: [ʊ/u] diphthongs in (a) RP and (b) PSp

IPA Symbols

əʊ Schwa and Lower-case Upsilon combination.

aʊ Lower-case A and Lower-case Upsilon combination.

eu̯ Lower-case E (or Latin small letter E) and reduced Latin small letter U combination.

ou̯ Latin small letter O and reduced Latin small letter U combination.

au̯ Lower-case A (or Latin Small letter A) and reduced Latin small letter U combination.

Identification

[əʊ] Near-close back, falling, back, closing, narrow diphthong (unrounded to rounded).

[aʊ] Near-close back, falling, back, closing, wide diphthong (unrounded to rounded).

Description

For the articulation of RP /**əʊ**/ the tongue moves from a centralised, between half-open and half-close position towards that of RP /ʊ/. There is a slight closing movement of the lower jaw, and the lips are neutral for the first element but tend to round on the second element. The starting point may have a tongue position similar to RP /ɜː/.

By contrast, RP /**aʊ**/ begins at a point between the back and front open positions, slightly more fronted than the position for RP /ɑː/, and moves in the direction of RP /ʊ/ approaching the half-close level [ö]. The glide is much more extensive than that used for /əʊ/ and is symmetrically opposed to the front RP diphthong /aɪ/. The lips change from neutrally open to weakly rounded.

See the animations and videos under RP /əʊ/ and /aʊ/ (compared with Spanish /eu̯ ou̯ au̯/) in the Sound Bank of the EPSS Multimedia Lab (see also e.g. Gimson 1984: 128–133, 134–138; Gimson 1994: 120–123, 124–127; Roach 2005: 21–23; Collins and Mees 2009: 102–104; Cruttenden 2014: 140–149).

Spellings

Table 15: The spellings of RP /əʊ aʊ/

/əʊ/ (in stressed syllables)	/aʊ/ (in stressed syllables)
<o> cold /kəʊld/, won't /wəʊnt/	<ou> council /ˈkaʊnsil/, loud /laʊd/
<oe> doe /dəʊ/, woe /wəʊ/	<ow> frown /fraʊn/, bow /baʊ/
<ou> / <ou> + silent <gh>, ow shoulder /ˈʃəʊldə/, poultry /ˈpəʊltri/ though /ðəʊ/, sparrow /ˈspærəʊ/	<ou> + silent <gh> drought /draʊt/, slough /slaʊ/
<oa> load /ləʊd/, oatmeal /ˈəʊtmiːl/	
French loanwords <eau> château /ˈʃætəʊ/, plateau /ˈplætəʊ/ bureau /ˈbjʊərəʊ/ <au> mauve /məʊv/, au pair /əʊ peə/ gauche /gəʊʃ/ <ot> argot /ˈɑːgəʊ/ , tarot /ˈtærəʊ/	
Rare cases <ew> sew /səʊ/ <oo> brooch /brəʊʧ/ <ao> Pharaoh /ˈferəʊ/	**Rare cases** <eo> MacLeod /məˈklaʊd/

Regional and social variants

English /**əʊ**/ involves a lot of variation. Conservative RP uses a rounded first element [öʊ], while Refined RP tends to produce an unrounded and advanced first element, between half-close and half-open, and centralised from front [ɛ̈ʊ]. Alternatively, an unrounded central monophthong can also be found [əː] (especially where [ɫ] follows). /əʊ/ is regularly kept in RP in unaccented syllables, but in colloquial speech and other “substandard” dialects it is generally reduced to

/ə/ (e.g. *fellow* [ˈfelə], *obey* [əˈbeɪ], *phonetics* [fəˈnetɪks], *window* [ˈwɪndə]). This latter tendency results in the production of a number of **homophones**, that is, words with different spellings that have an identical pronunciation, in colloquial speech that are distinct in a more formal style: *ferment – foment* [fəˈment], *hypertension – hypotension* [haɪpəˈtenʃən] (see also Chapters 4 and 7). In addition, Refined RP, Cockney and Australian English have [æ̈ʊ], even [æʏ̈], with fronting of the first element and unrounding spreading to the second element, whereas other accents (SSE), in much of the north of England and GA) have a relatively pure vowel around CV [o], which is close to the [oː] pronunciation that may also be heard in Cockney and is typical of London Regional RP.

Moving on to /**aʊ**/, RP variants mainly involve the fronting ([a̟]) or retraction ([ɑ]) of the starting point, but it can also entail its raising ([æ], [ɛ], [ə], [ʌ], [uː]). Fronting is typical of popular regional forms of speech (the London region included), while in Cockney and Australian English, the first element is fronted and raised to the [æ] or [e] varieties. Alternatively, in Cockney /aʊ/ may also be monophthongised to long [aː]. Refined RP also prefers an [aːː] extra-long realisation of the first element, especially in those contexts in which the diphthong has its fully long form.

Comparison with Spanish and advice

The pronunciation of RP /**əʊ**/ may be problematic for Spanish learners because [ə] does not form part of the Spanish vocalic system. Spanish speakers tend to produce this diphthong with an initial [o], thereby resembling the pronunciation of the Spanish diphthong [ou̯] found in the word ***bou*** [bou̯] ('type of fishing'). This is an acceptable pronunciation in GA, in which the normal pronunciation of this diphthong is [oʊ] instead of [əʊ]. But in RP such pronunciations have a strong foreign accent. Accordingly, in order to sound like RP speakers, Spanish learners should strive to start this diphthong with an [ə]-sound, with a slight opening of the mouth as if for mouth breathing, the articulators moving in the direction of a relaxed type of [u] in the end-point. The closest Spanish diphthong to RP [əʊ] is /eu̯/ (e.g. ***neutro*** [ˈneu̯tro] 'neutral') but the first element of the RP glide is more central and the second more relaxed.

RP /**aʊ**/, on the other hand, should have no problem for Spanish learners since it is similar to the Spanish diphthong [au̯] found in the word ***pausa*** [ˈpau̯sa] ('pause'), the only difference being that the starting point is more retracted and the end-point less relaxed in Spanish. However, the pronunciation of a Spanish [u] as the end-point of these two diphthongs should not cause intelligibility problems (Monroy Casas 1980, 2012; Gallardo del Puerto 2005; Estebas Vilaplana 2009).

Further practice

AI 3.16. The spellings of RP /əʊ/. Further practice

br**oo**ch /brəʊʧ/ gr**o**ss /grəʊs/ s**o** /ˈsəʊ/
f**oe** /fəʊ/ neur**o**sis /njʊəˈrəʊsɪs/ s**o**ldier /ˈsəʊldʒə/
gr**ow**s /grəʊz/ repr**oa**ch /rɪˈprəʊʧ/ th**ough** /ðəʊ/

Alth**ough** you offered J**oe** J**o**nes a soup b**ow**l full of chocolate scones, he's j**o**king he'll make a sn**ow**ball and will thr**ow** it at your n**o**se.
||ɔːlˈðəʊ ju ˈɒfəd ˈdʒəʊ ˈdʒəʊnz ə ˌsuːp ˈbəʊl ˈfʊl əv ˌʧɒklət ˈskɒnz | hiz ˈdʒəʊkɪŋ hil ˈmeɪk ə ˈsnəʊbɑːl ənd wɪl ˈθrəʊ ɪt ət jə ˈnəʊz||

Hell**o**, J**oa**n, do you kn**ow** that you can see the v**o**cal f**o**lds with this microsc**o**pe?
||həˈləʊ | ˈdʒəʊn | də ju ˈnəʊ ðət ju kən ˈsiː ðə ˌvəʊkl̩ ˈfəʊldz wɪð ðɪs ˈmaɪkrəskəʊp||

Oh! M**o**ses supp**o**ses his t**oe**ses are r**o**ses, but M**o**ses supp**o**ses err**o**neously.
||ˈəʊ | ˈməʊzɪz səˈpəʊzɪz ɪz ˈtəʊzɪz ə ˈrəʊzɪz | bət ˈməʊzɪz səˈpəʊzɪz ɪˈrəʊnɪəsli||

The two-t**oe**d tree t**oa**d tried to tread where the three-t**oe**d tree t**oa**d trod.
||ðə ˌtuːtəʊd triː ˈtəʊd ˈtraɪd tə ˈtred weə ðə ˌθriːtəʊd triː ˈtəʊd ˈtrɒd||

AI 3.17. The spellings of RP /aʊ/. Further practice

a l**ou**se /ə laʊs/ h**ow** /haʊ/ pron**ou**nce /prəˈnaʊns/
all**ow**s /əˈlaʊz/ m**ou**ntain /ˈmaʊntɪn/ ren**ow**n /rɪˈnaʊn/
dr**ou**ght /ˈdraʊt/ m**ou**the /ˈmaʊð/ r**ou**nd-eyed /raʊndaɪd/

'Turn the br**ow**n c**ou**ch upside-d**ow**n with**ou**t d**ou**bts', sh**ou**ted Paul as l**ou**dly as he could.
||tɜːn ðə braʊn kaʊʧ ˈʌpsaɪd daʊn wɪðˈaʊt daʊts | ˈʃaʊtɪd pɔːl əz ˈlaʊdli əz hi kʊd||

The d**ou**ghty cl**ow**n raised his eye-br**ow**s when he was all**ow**ed to take the pl**ou**gh by the b**ou**gh, and then br**ow**sed his f**ou**l task.
||ðə ˈdaʊti klaʊn reɪzd ɪz aɪ braʊz wen hi wəz əˈlaʊd tə teɪk ðə plaʊ baɪ ðə baʊ | ənd ðen braʊzd ɪz faʊl tɑːsk||

How much gr**ou**nd would a gr**ou**ndhog hog, if a gr**ou**ndhog could hog gr**ou**nd?
||ˈhaʊ ˈmʌʧ graʊnd wʊd ə ˈgraʊndˌhɑːg hɒg | ɪf ə ˈgraʊndˌhɑːg kəd hɒg graʊnd||

3.3.2 Centring diphthongs: RP /ɪə eə ʊə/

This section concentrates on the three RP centring diphthongs, **/ɪə/**, **/eə/**, **/ʊə/**, in which the articulation moves from the periphery of the CVS towards a mid-central neutral vowel [ə]. The lips are unrounded throughout the articulation of /ɪə, eə/ and change from rounded to unrounded in /ʊə/ (see also e.g. Gimson

1984: 142–145; Gimson 1994: 131–134; Roach 2005: 22; Collins and Mees 2009: 104; Cruttenden 2014: 153–156).

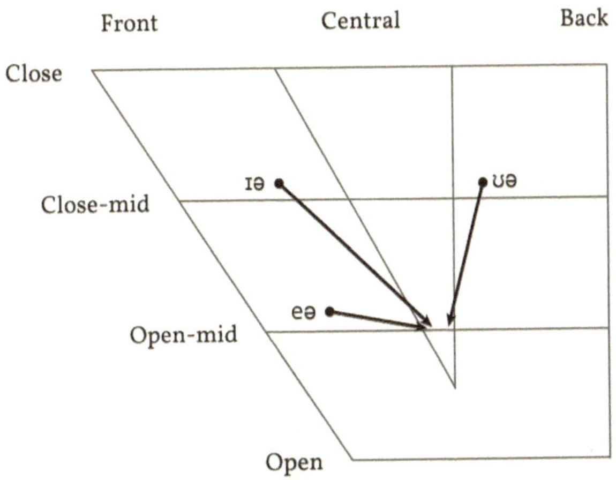

Figure 46: Centring diphthongs in RP

IPA Symbols

ɪə Small capital I (or Latin letter small capital I) and Schwa combination.

eə Lower-case E and Schwa combination.

ʊə Lower-case Upsilon and Schwa combination.

Identification

[**ɪə**] Centring, falling, narrow (unrounded).

[**eə**] Centring, falling, narrow (unrounded).

[**ʊə**] Centring, falling, narrow (rounded to unrounded).

Description

The glide of RP /**ɪə**/ moves from a half-close and centralised front tongue position (as for RP /ɪ/) in the direction of the more open variety of /ə/ in word final positions, or to a mid type of /ə/ in non final contexts. The lips change from slightly spread to neutrally open.

For RP /**eə**/, in turn, the glide begins from slightly above the half-open front position [ɛ] and moves in the direction of the more open variety of /ə/, especially word-finally. There is a very slight opening movement of the lower jaw and the lips are neutrally open throughout. The starting point is a bit closer than RP /æ/.

For the articulation of RP /**ʊə**/ the tongue glides from a position similar to that used for /ʊ/ towards the more open type of /ə/ when occurring word-finally, and to a closer variety of /ə/ word medially. The lips change from weakly rounded to neutrally spread as the glide progresses.

See the animations and videos under RP /ɪə/, /eə/ and /ʊə/ in the Sound Bank of the EPSS Multimedia Lab (see also e.g. Gimson 1984: 142–145; Gimson 1994: 131–134; Roach 2005: 22; Collins and Mees 2009: 104; Crutenden 2014: 153–156).

Spellings

Table 16: The spellings of RP /ɪə eə ʊə/

/ɪə/ (in stressed syllables)	/eə/ (in stressed syllables)	/ʊə/ (in stressed syllables)
<e> + <r> / <er(e)> **he**ro /ˈhɪərəʊ/, **er**a /ˈɪərə/ **mere** /mɪə/, **que**ry /ˈkwɪəri/ exp**er**ience /ɪkˈspɪərɪəns/	<a> + <r> / <ae> + <r> / <are> M**ar**y /ˈmeəri/, **aer**obic /eəˈrəʊbɪk/ **care** /keə/	<ure> / <u> + <r> **sure** /ʃʊə/, **cure** /kjʊə/ **jur**y /ˈʤʊəri/
<eer> **beer** /bɪə/ engin**eer** /ˌenʤɪˈnɪə/	<air> **air** /eə/, **fair** /feə/	<oor> **boor** /bʊə/ **spoor** /spʊə/
<ear> **year** /jɜː/, **tear** (n) /ˈtɪə/ **beard** /bɪəd/	<ear> **pear** /peə/, **tear** (v) /ˈteə/ **wear** /weə/	<e>[56] **eur**o /ˈjʊərəʊ/ **Eur**ope /ˈjʊərəp/
<ier, eir, ir> chandel**ier** /ˌʃændəˈlɪə/ **weir**d /wɪəd/ em**ir** /eˈmɪə/ Algec**ir**as /ˌælʒɪˈsɪərəs/	<eir> **heir** /eə/, **their** /ðeə/	
	<ere> **there** /ðeə/, **where** /weə/	
French loanwords <ir> souven**ir** /ˌsuːvəˈnɪə/ **Classical languages loanwords** <eo> th**eo**logical /ˌθiəˈlɒʤɪkl̩/ <eou> spontan**eous** /spɒnˈteɪniəs/ <eu> petrol**eum** /pɪˈtrəʊliəm/ <io, iou> un**ion** /ˈjuːniən/ prev**ious** /ˈpriːviəs/ <iu> stad**ium** /ˈsteɪdiəm/ delir**ium** /dɪˈlɪriəm/	**French loanwords** <ere> prem**iere** /ˈpremieə/ **Spanish loanwords** <e> sombr**ero** /sɒmˈbreərəʊ/	**French loanwords** <our> **tour** /tʊə/, **dour** /dʊə/ **bour**geois /ˈbʊəʒwɑː/ **cour**gette /kʊəˈʒet/ **gour**met /ˈgʊəmeɪ/ **gourd** /gʊəd/ <e> liq**ueur** /lɪˈkjʊə/

56 Here we can see that the pronunciations [jʊə] – [juːə] with /j/ preceding /ʊə/ correspond to the letter <e> followed and/or preceded by the previous spellings.

Table 16: (Continued)

/ɪə/ (in stressed syllables)	/eə/ (in stressed syllables)	/ʊə/ (in stressed syllables)
	Rare cases <ayor> ma**yor** /meə/ <ayer> pra**yer** /preə/ <e> V**e**rdi /ˈveədi/	**Rare cases** <ewer> **sewer** 'drain' /ˈsʊə/
Exceptions there /weə/ where /ðeə/	**Exceptions** **are** /ɑː/ **weir** /wɪə/ **weird** /wɪəd/	**Exceptions** truant /ˈtruːənt/

Note that in the case of /ʊə/, many of the words ending in <ure>, <oor> <our> may also be pronounced [ɔə] or [ɔː] (e.g. ***poor*** [pʊə], [pɔː] (like *paw* (n, v)); ***sure*** [ʃʊə], [ʃɔə], [ʃɔː] (like *shore, Shaw*)).

Regional and social variants

In unaccented syllables where the schwa element usually representing a suffix with morphemic status, the starting point of /ɪə/ and /ʊə/ may be pronounced as a closer and more tense vowel [iə] (e.g. *easier, serious*) and [uə] or [juːə] (e.g. *influence, valuable, vacuum, eventual*), which seems to suggest a hiatus of the vowels in sequence.

Nowadays, these three diphthongs are increasingly monophthongised in RP. /**ɪə**/ tends to be pronounced [ɜː] or [ɑː] in Refined RP, especially in accented final syllables, which contrasts with the glide from a relatively close to an almost open position that may be heard in Cockney, sometimes with an intervening [j], i.e. [ijä]. /**eə**/ has a completely acceptable open monophthongal realisation [ɛ] in General RP, although Refined RP keeps the diphthong but with a more open starting point [æə̞], which contrasts with the closer starting point [e̝ə] of Cockney. With regard to /**ʊə**/, it is being gradually replaced by the long monophthong /ɔː/, although [ɔə] pronunciations may also be heard. Accordingly, the pronunciations of such words as *Shaw*, ***sure***, ***shore*** may still be kept distinct by some speakers [ʃɔː], [ʃʊə], [ʃɔə], or they may be levelled to [ʃɔː] by others; likewise, ***you're*** may be realised as [jʊə] (most frequently) or as [jɔː] (identical with ***your***). Nevertheless, commonly used monosyllabic words (e.g. ***dour*** /dʊə/, ***gourd*** /gʊəd/), the [uːə]/[uə]/[ʊə] derived from /uː/ plus /ə/ (e.g. ***pursuer*** /pəˈsuːə/), and words with a preceding [j] (e.g. ***bureau*** [ˈbjʊərəʊ], ***cure*** [kjʊə], ***curious*** [ˈkjʊərɪəs], ***endure*** [ɪnˈdjʊə], ***puerile*** [ˈpjʊəraɪl], ***secure*** [sɪˈkjʊə]) are generally not subject to lowerings or monophthongisations.

Comparison with Spanish and advice

Spanish has no centring diphthongs,[57] but approximate realisations of RP /ɪə/, /eə/ and /ʊə/ may be found in the hiatus sequence [ía] (e.g. ***día*** 'day', ***vía*** 'way', ***mía*** 'mine' (fem. sing.)), [eə] (e.g. *pel**ea*** 'fight', *grag**ea*** 'pill') and [úa] (e.g. ***púa*** 'spike'), the starting point being closer, and the end-point, more prominent and more open and advanced in Spanish so that the glide is longer in Spanish than in English (Finch and Ortiz Lira 1982: 42; Gallardo del Puerto 2005: 186).

Nevertheless, if the aim is to produce centring diphthongs with an RP accent, Spanish learners should pay particular attention to two aspects of pronunciation (Monroy Casas 1980, 2012; Estebas Vilaplana 2009):

(1) to avoid the production of final flap [ɾ] because in most cases centring diphthongs are spelt with an <r> and RP is a non-rhotic accent; and

(2) to pronounce an [ə] vowel as the end-point of these diphthongs, which is produced with almost no movements of the articulators apart from the narrow opening of the mouth, instead of the vowels [e] or [a], which would be the cause of a strong foreign accent.

Further practice

AI 3.18. The spellings of RP /ɪə/. Further practice

d**ear** /dɪə/	f**ier**ce /fɪəs/	p**eri**od /ˈpɪərɪəd/
fak**ir** /ˈfeɪkɪə/	mat**eri**al /məˈtɪərɪəl/	sinc**ere** /sɪnˈsɪə/
f**ear**s /fɪəz/	mus**eu**m /mjuːˈzɪəm/	z**er**o /ˈzɪərəʊ/

'What about having a b**ee**r and some c**ere**al h**ere**, in the same place as last y**ear**?' said Mr L**ea**r to the Austrian, white b**ear**ded mountain**eer**.
||ˈwɒt əˈbaʊt ˈhævɪŋ ə ˈbɪər ənd səm ˈsɪərɪəl ˈhɪə | ɪn ðə seɪm ˈpleɪs əz ˌlɑːst ˈjɪə| ˈsed ˈmɪstə ˈlɪə tə ði ˌɒstriən | ˌwaɪtbɪədɪd ˌmaʊntɪˈnɪə||

Good id**ea**, the atmosph**ere** is id**ea**l!
||ˈgʊd aɪˈdɪə | ði ˈætməsfɪə z aɪˈdɪəl||

H**ere** come the b**ee**rs, ch**ee**rs!
||ˈhɪə ˈkʌm ðə ˈbɪəz| ˈʧɪəz||

R**ea**l w**eir**d r**ear** wheels!
||ˌrɪəl wɪəd ˌrɪə ˈwiːlz||

---

57 English rhotic accents such as Scottish English or GA have no centring diphthongos either. Instead, they have the first element of the glide followed by /r/ in those words which have an <r> in the spelling before consonants and before a pause: /ɪə/ is pronounced /ɪ/ or /i/ + /r/; /eə/ results in /e/ or /eɪ/ + /r/ combinations; and /ʊə/ is realized as /uː/ or /ʊ/ + /r/.

D**eer**, d**eer**, oh d**ear**, your car**eer** as a d**eer** is over h**ere**.
||ˈdɪə | ˈdɪə | əʊ ˈdɪə | jə kəˈrɪər əz ə ˈdɪə z ˈəʊvə hɪə||

N**ear** an **ear**, a n**ear**er **ear**, a n**ear**ly **ee**rie **ear**.
||ˈnɪər ən ˈɪə | ə ˌnɪərər ˈɪə | ə ˈnɪəli ˌɪəri ˈɪə||

AI 3.19. The spellings of RP /eə/. Further practice

aqu**aa**rium /əˈkweəriəm/
b**ear** /beə/
bol**e**ros /bəˈleərəʊz/
m**ayor** /meə/
million**aire** /ˌmɪlɪəˈneə/
pr**ayer**s (thing) /preəz/
sc**ar**ce /skeəs/
sc**ar**es /skeəz/
wh**ere** /weə/

Cl**aire** has c**are**fully looked for her squ**are** h**air**brushes everywh**ere**, upst**airs** and downst**airs**, but th**ey're** nowh**ere**.
||ˈkleə həz ˈkeəfəli ˈlʊkt fə hə ˌskweə ˈheəbrʌʃɪz ˈevrɪweə | ˌʌpˈsteəz ən ˌdaʊnˈsteəz | bət ˈðeə ˈnəʊweə||

My p**a**rents found it weird that a r**are** can**a**ry, a h**a**re and a m**a**re were eating a p**ai**r of th**eir** p**ea**rs on the pier.
||maɪ ˈpeərənts ˈfaʊnd ɪt ˈwɪəd ðət ə ˌreə kəˈneəri | ə ˈheər ənd ə ˈmeə wər ˈiːtɪŋ ə ˈpeər əv ðeə ˈpeəz ɒn ðə ˈpɪə||

Fuzzy Wuzzy was a b**ear**, Fuzzy Wuzzy had no h**air**.
||ˈfʌzi ˈwʌzi wəz ə ˈbeə | ˈfʌzi ˈwʌzi həd nəʊ ˈheə||

AI 3.20. The spellings of RP /ʊə/. Further practice

act**ua**lly /ˈækʧuəli/ /ˈæktjuəli/
end**ur**ance /ɪnˈdjʊərəns/
j**ew**el /ˈʤuːəl/
n**eur**ological /ˌnjʊərəˈlɒʤɪkl̩/
p**oor** /pʊə/
p**ue**rile /ˈpjʊəraɪl/
rit**ua**l /ˈrɪʧʊəl/
sp**ur**ious /ˈspjʊəriəs/
t**our**ney /ˈtʊəni/

D**ur**ing my visit to the aestheticist to check my eye-cont**our** and my manic**ure** it was pouring rain in the m**oor**s.
||ˈdjʊərɪŋ maɪ ˈvɪzɪt tə ðə iːsˈθetɪcɪst tə ˈʧek maɪ ˌaɪˈkɒntʊə ənd maɪ ˈmænɪkjʊər ɪt wəz ˈpɔːrɪŋ ˈreɪn ɪn ðə ˈmʊəz||

C**ur**iously D**ur**acell batteries seem to have more end**ur**ance.
||ˈkjʊərɪəsli ˈdjʊərəˌsel ˈbætriz ˈsiːm tə ˈhæv mɔːr ɪnˈdjʊərəns||

The f**ur**ious soldier's shoulder s**ure**ly got hurt in the t**our** and probably will have no c**ure**.
||ðə ˈfjʊərɪəs ˌsolʤərz ˈʃəʊldə ˈʃʊəli gɒt ˈhɜːt ɪn ðə ˈtʊər ənd ˈprɒbəbli wl ˈhæv nəʊ ˈkjʊə||

3.3.3 Diphthongs + [ə]

Closing diphthongs, /eɪ aɪ ɔɪ əʊ aʊ/, may be followed by /ə/, either as an inseparable part of the word (e.g. ***rayon*** /reɪən/, ***fire*** [faɪə], ***Noah*** [ˈnəʊə], ***soya*** [ˈsɔɪə], ***hour*** [ˈaʊə],) or as a morpheme that is appended to a root (e.g. ***gayer*** [geiə], ***higher*** [haɪə], ***slower*** [sləʊə], ***employer*** /ɪmˈplɔɪə/), in which case the second element /ɪ, ʊ/ is less prominent than the first and last.

Five vowel glides may be obtained in this way: [**eɪə aɪə ɔɪə əʊə aʊə**]. In all of them the tongue begins a glide in the direction of the second element, but then the direction changes again towards a final central position, as shown in Figure 47 below (see also e.g. Gimson 1984: 139–142; Gimson 1994: 128–130; Roach 2005: 24–26; Collins and Mees 2009: 102, 103; Crutenden 2014: 150–152).

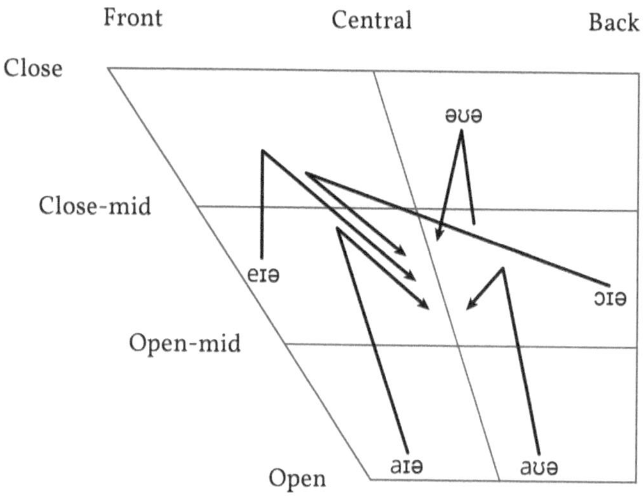

Figure 47: Diphthongs + [ə] in RP

It should be noted, however, that in those cases in which these glides spread over two syllables or more (e.g. *gayer, player, slower*), it would be inaccurate to regard them as a triphthongs, as they rather behave as hiatuses.

Description

In the phonemic combination in which the diphthong /**eɪ**/ is followed by /**ə**/ (as in ***gayer*** [geɪə]), the diphthongal glide is abruptly interrupted, and then the tongue moves with an audible glide to a relatively open variety of /ə/. In turn, when the diphthong /**aɪ**/ is followed by /**ə**/ (as in ***fire*** [ˈfaɪə]), the tongue glides from a position just behind and above front open, the lips being neutral, towards a centralised front position just above half close, the lips becoming gradually slightly spread; but before reaching the half close height, the tongue then glides to a central position just below half open, the lips returning to a neutral position at the end of the glide. The movement of the tongue is therefore extensive.

In the case of [**ɔɪə**] (as in *joyous* [ˈʤɔɪəs]) and [**əʊə**] (as in ***slower*** [sləʊə]), the diphthongal glides ([ɔɪ], [əʊ]) are abruptly interrupted, and then the tongue moves with an audible glide to a relatively open variety of /ə/. In the case of [ɔɪə], the lips change from open rounded to neutral, and from neutral to round and then back to neutral in [əʊə]. In both the movement of the tongue is not extensive.

Lastly, for the articulation of [**aʊə**] (as in *power* [ˈpaʊə]), the tongue glides from just above a centralised open position towards a centralised back position just above half close, but before reaching the half close height, the tongue then glides to a central position just below half open. The lips change from neutrally open to weakly rounded and back to neutral at the end of the glide. The movement of the tongue is therefore extensive.

See the animations and videos under RP /eɪə/, /aɪə/, /ɔɪə/, /əʊə/ and /aʊə/ in the Sound Bank of the EPSS Multimedia Lab (see also e.g. Gimson 1984: 139–142; Gimson 1994: 128–130; Roach 2005: 24–26; Collins and Mees 2009: 102, 103; Cruttenden 2014: 150–152).

Spellings

Table 17: The spellings of RP diphthongs + [ə]

Diphthongs + [ə]	Spellings	
/eɪə/	**player** /pleɪə/, **layer** /ˈleɪə/	
/aɪə/	<ire> **tired** /ˈtaɪəd/ <yre> **tyre** /ˈtaɪə/, **lyre** /ˈlaɪə/ <ier> **flier** /ˈflaɪə/ <ia> **via** /ˈvaɪə/	**Rare cases** <oir> **choir** /ˈkwaɪə/ <i> **virus** /ˈvaɪərəs/
/ɔɪə/	<oyer> destr**oyer** /dɪˈstrɔɪə/ empl**oyer** /ɪmˈplɔɪə/ <oya> enj**oya**ble /ɪnˈʤɔɪəbl̩/	
/əʊə/	<ower> m**ower** /ˈməʊə/, sl**ower** /ˈsləʊə/	
/aʊə/	**<owe(r)>** sh**ower** /ˈʃaʊə/ **<our>** fl**our** /ˈflaʊə/, h**our** /ˈaʊə/	

Regional and social variants

Given that the second element of these vowel glides is very weak, there is a tendency in General RP and in Refined RP, especially if spoken rapidly, to drop this second element thereby reducing the glide to two elements (diphthong) or to one element (monophthong) so that such words as *layer* and *lair* may be pronounced as [lɛ:] and [la:], respectively. This process is referred to as **levelling** or **smoothing**[58] and it results in the following realisations:

(1) **[aɪə]** → **[a:ə]** as in ***buyer*** [ˈba:ə], ***choir*** [ˈkwa:ə], ***fire*** [fa:ə], ***higher*** [ˈha:ə], ***liar*** [ˈla:ə], ***liable*** [ˈla:əb(ə)l], ***lyre*** [la:ə], ***society*** [səˈsa:əti], ***shyer*** [ˈʃa:ə], ***tyre*** [ta:ə]. Diphthongal pronunciations are often reduced to the long monophthong [**a:**].

(2) **[aʊə]** → **[ɑ:ə]** as in ***coward*** [ˈkɑ:əd], ***nowadays*** [ˈnɑ:ədeɪz], ***our*** [ˈɑ:ə], ***shower*** [ˈʃɑ:ə]. The qualitative difference distinguishing the first element of [a:ə] and [ɑ:ə] is often levelled out to one central open vowel, resulting in the production of such homophones as ***sire-sour; shire-shower; tyre-tower***. Further reductions may also occur so that [aʊə] may be pronounced as the long monophthong [**ɑ:**]. In accents with a more extensive levelling (such as affected RP), this is also the pronunciation of the monophthongisations in (1) above, and as a result such [ɑ:]-homophones may be heard: ***byre-buyer-bower-bar*** [bɑ:]; ***shire-shower-Shah*** [ʃɑ:]; ***tyre-tower-tar*** [tɑ:].

(3) **[eɪə]** → **[e:ə]** / **[eə]**, as in ***conveyor*** [kənˈve:ə], ***greyer*** [gre:ə], ***layer*** [le:ə], ***payer*** [ˈpe:ə], while a monophthongisation to [**ɛ:**] is a completely acceptable alternative in General RP.

(4) **[əʊə]** → [ɜ:ə] → [**ɜ:**],[59] so that in General RP homophones may be produced such as *mower-myrrh* [ˈmɜ:]; *slower-slur* [slɜ:].

(5) **[ɔɪə]** → **[ɔ:ə]**, as in ***buoyant*** [ˈbɔ:ənt], ***employer*** [ɪmˈplɔ:ə], ***enjoyable*** [ɪnˈdʒɔ:əb(ə)l], ***joyous*** [ˈdʒɔ:əs].

(6) Likewise, /eɪ, aɪ, ɔɪ/ tend to lose the [ɪ] element when followed by /i:/ or /ɪ/ both between and within words (e.g. ***playing, buy it***).

Comparison with Spanish and advice with PSp and advice

58 **Smoothing**, or the loss of the second part of a diphthong or triphthong, should be distinguished from the phenomenon of **compression**, or the squashing of the two syllables into one syllable. Both processes are optional, or stylistically determined. Hence, for instance, given the disyllabic starting point *power* [paʊ.ə], the word can be smoothed to disyllabic [pa.ə], and then the result can be compressed to [paə] or even further to a monophthong [pa:]. Similarly, *going* [gəʊ.ɪŋ] can be smoothed to [gə.ɪŋ] and then compressed to [gəɪŋ].

59 Note that when the first vowel of the triphthong is [ə] and it is levelled, the corresponding long monophthong is transcribed as [ɜˑ], because [ə] can only occur alone in unstressed syllables and therefore the sequence [əˑə] is reinterpreted as [ɜˑə].

As it happened with centring diphthongs, the main problem that RP triphthongs pose to Spanish speakers is grasping the correct pronunciation of the [ə] end-point, for which special attention should be paid to: (1) avoiding the production of a final [ɾ̄] when an <r> is present in spelling, and (2) ending these glides with an [ə] vowel, by relaxing the articulators and opening the mouth slightly, instead of pronouncing the vowels [e] or [a] (in such words as *tower* or *loyal*), which would be the cause of a strong foreign accent (Monroy Casas 1980, 2012; Estebas Vilaplana 2009). Also, it is important that learners resist the phonotactic tendency of Spanish to palatalise [j] or velarise [w] the second element of the glide ([ɪ], [ʊ]) (as in *fire* *[ˈfajə], *employer* *[emˈplɔjə] and *tower* *[ˈtawə], which would amount to a foreign accent.

Foreign learners should be aware of the reductions described above in order to be able to understand colloquial English, as well as to be able to reproduce the reductions that are normal among educated speakers. Nevertheless, as these reductions are often stigmatised as vulgarisms, extreme forms of levelling (monophthongisations) should be avoided, while unreduced pronunciations should be preferred in those cases in which the [ə] element corresponds to a suffix with a definite meaning, as in such words as *high**er*** /haɪə/ or *plough**er*** /plaʊə/.

Further practice

AI 3.21. The spellings of RP /eɪə/. Further practice

conv**eyor** /kənˈveɪə/	l**ayer** /ˈleɪə/	pr**ayer** (person) /ˈpreɪə/
g**aia**ty /ˈɡeɪəti/	m**ayo**nnaise /meɪəneɪz/	st**ayer** /ˈsteɪə/
gr**eyer** /ˈɡreɪə/	pl**ayer** /ˈpleɪə/	r**ayo**n /reɪən/

The pr**aye**r and the pl**aye**r agreed that the Bible has multiple l**aye**rs of meaning.
||ðə ˈpreɪər ənd ðə ˈpleɪər əˈɡriːd ðət ðə ˈbaɪbl̩ həz ˈmʌltɪpl̩ ˈleɪəz əv ˈmiːnɪŋ||

The p**ayer** in r**ayo**n is really a st**ayer** but not a betr**ayer**.
||ðə ˈpeɪər ɪn ˈreɪən z ˈrɪəli ə ˈsteɪə bət nɒt ə bɪˈtreɪə||

AI 3.22. The spellings of RP /aɪə/. Further practice

att**ire** /əˈtaɪə/	**iron** /ˈaɪən/	sc**ie**nce /ˈsaɪəns/
b**uyer** /ˈbaɪə/	l**iar** /ˈlaɪə/	t**yre** /ˈtaɪə/
fl**ier** /ˈflaɪə/	psych**ia**trist /sɪˈkaɪətrɪst/	w**ire** /ˈwaɪə/

The cl**ie**nts found some **iron wire** in this **tyre**.
||ðə ˈklaɪənts faʊnd səm ˈaɪən ˈwaɪər ɪn ðɪs ˈtaɪə||

In **Ire**land some b**uyer**s h**ire**d a car to a l**iar** without finding out if the price was higher or lower.
||ɪn ˈaɪələnd səm ˈbaɪəz ˈhaɪəd ə kɑː tu ə ˈlaɪə wɪðˈaʊt ˈfaɪndɪŋ aʊt ɪf ðə praɪs wəz ˈhaɪər ɔː ˈləʊə||

AI 3.23. The spellings of RP /ɔɪə/. Further practice

bu**oya**nt /ˈbɔɪənt/	enj**oya**ble /ɪnˈdʒɔɪəbl̩/	l**oya**l /lɔɪəl/
destr**oyer** /dɪˈstrɔɪə/	f**oyer** /ˈfɔɪə/	s**oya** /ˈsɔɪə/
empl**oyer** /ɪmˈplɔɪə/	j**oyou**s /ˈdʒɔɪəs/	T**oya** /ˈtɔɪə/

Roger met his j**oyou**s and flamb**oya**nt lawyer in the f**oyer**.
||ˈrɒdʒə met ɪz ˈdʒɔɪəs ənd flæmˈbɔɪənt ˈlɔːjər ɪn ðə ˈfɔɪə||

Being an empl**oyer** or an employee these days is not something enj**oya**ble.
||ˈbiːɪŋ ən ɪmˈplɔɪər ɔːr ən ˌemplɔɪˈiː ðiːz deɪz ɪz nɒt ˈsʌmθɪŋ ɪnˈdʒɔɪəbl̩||

AI 3.24. The spellings of RP /əʊə/. Further practice

bl**ower** /ˈbləʊə/	m**oa** /ˈməʊə/	sh**ower** /ʃəʊə/ 'one who shows'
g**oer** /ˈgəʊə/	m**ower** /ˈməʊə/	s**ower** /ˈsəʊə/
l**ower** /ˈləʊə/	r**ower** /ˈrəʊə/	s**ewer** /ˈsəʊə/ 'one who sews'

This r**ower** is sl**ower** than the other.
||ðɪs ˈrəʊə z ˈsləʊə ðən ði ˈʌðə||

Meeting-g**oer**s and homeowners were offered bl**ower**s, lawn-m**ower**s and shower-head nozzles at l**ower** prices.
||ˈmiːtɪŋ ˈgəʊərz ənd ˈhəʊməʊnəz wər ˈɒfəd ˈbləʊəz | lɔːn ˈməʊəz ənd ˈʃəʊə hed ˈnɒzl̩z ət ˈləʊə ˈpraɪsɪz||

AI 3.25. The spellings of RP /aʊə/. Further practice

c**owa**rd /ˈkaʊəd/	**our** /ˈaʊə/	t**owe**l /ˈtaʊəl/
fl**ower** /ˈflaʊə/	p**ower** /ˈpaʊə/	t**ower** /ˈtaʊə/
fl**our** /ˈflaʊə/	s**our** /ˈsaʊə/	v**owe**l /ˈvaʊəl/

The soldier with the beard that we saw in the b**ower** market is not a hero, but a c**owa**rd.
||ðə ˈsəʊldʒə wɪð ðə bɪəd ðət wi ˈsɔː ɪn ðə ˈbaʊə ˈmɑːkɪt s nɒt ə ˈhɪərəʊ | bət ə ˈkaʊəd||

Don't put the milk by the fire because it may go s**our.**
||dəʊnt ˈpʊt ðə mɪlk baɪ ðə ˈfaɪə bɪˈkɒz ɪt meɪ gəʊ ˈsaʊə||

The Shah always uses **our** fl**ow**ery t**ow**el after the sh**ower.**
||ðə ʃɑː ˈɔːlweɪz ˈjuːsɪz ˈaʊə ˈflaʊəri ˈtaʊəl ˈɑːftə ðə ˈʃaʊə||

Further reading

There exist many volumes that devote specific chapters or sections to the description of English vowels and vocalic glides. Again, we recommend Cruttenden (2014, Chapter 8), Ogden (2009, Chapter 5), Ladefoged (2001, Chapter 9; 2005, Chapter 15), Roach (2005, Chapters 2 and 3), Collins and Mees (2003, pp. 89–126), Ladefoged and Maddieson (1996, Chapter 9) and Gimson (1984, Chapter 7), among others. A more advanced account of the acoustic features of vowels and vowel glides is offered by Hayward (2000, Chapter 6).

Turning to Spanish, in addition to Cabrera Abreu and Vizcaíno Ortega's (2009) acoustic-based analysis, classic descriptions of the acoustic features of Spanish vowels and vowel glides may be found in Martínez Celdrán (1998) and Quilis (1981), while more general descriptions are provided in Martínez Celdrán and Fernández Planas (2007), Navarro Tomás (1991 [1918], 1966 [1946]), Quilis and Fernández (1982), Quilis (1985, 1993), and Alarcos Llorach (1961 [1983]).

Among the recommended texts that describe RP vowels specifically oriented to SSLE are, as already noted in the introduction, Monroy Casas (1980, 2012, Chapters1 and 2), Estebas Vilaplana (2009, Chapter 1), Mott (2011, Chapters 5 and 12) and Finch and Ortiz Lira (1982, Chapter 6), Lillo (2009, Chapter 2) and García Lecumberri and Maidment (2000: 8-16) providing transcription practice material.

Finally, more detailed accounts concerning the acquisition of English vowels by speakers of Spanish are offered in Escudero and Chládková (2010), Gallardo del Puerto (2005), Escudero (2000), García Lecumberri and Cenoz Iragui (1997), and Dale and Poms (1985), to mention but a few.

Exercises

1. Passive transcription. Read aloud the following passage given in broad transcription, paying special attention to the vowel sounds. Then write it out in ordinary spelling.
   / nʌn əv ði ˈɔːgənz kənˈfɔːmɪŋ ðə θriː ˈsɪstəmz ɪnˈvɒlvd ɪn spiːtʃ prəˈdʌkʃn̩ hæv spiːtʃ əz ðeə meɪn əˈrɪdʒn̩əl ˈfʌŋkʃn̩ //fər ɪgˈzɑːmpl̩ / ðə lʌŋz ɑː fə ˈbriːðɪŋ / ðə ˈvəʊkl̩ kɔːdz ɑː fə prɪˈventɪŋ ˈtʃəʊkɪŋ / ðə tʌŋ ɪz fər ˈiːtɪŋ ənd ˈteɪstɪŋ / ðə nəʊz

fə ˈbriːðɪŋ ən ˈsmelɪŋ / ən ˈsəʊ ɒn / bət ˈðeɪ həv biːn əˈdæptɪd tə prəˈdjuːs kə ˈmjuːnɪkətɪv ˈsaʊndz / əz ɪz ɪkˈspleɪnd ɪn ˈwɒt ˈfɒləʊz //

2. Explain the difference between the vowels of /fɪl/ – /fiːl/ and – /fʊl/ – /fuːl/. Why do we actually use two different symbols -i.e. /ɪ/ – /iː/ and /ʊ/ – /uː/- to represent these vowel sounds, instead of just one, with or without the duration mark?
3. Group 1: /ɪ/ and /iː/. Read aloud the following words given in broad transcription and then write them out in ordinary spelling.

1. /ʧiːz/	2. /ˈbɪskɪt/	3. /piːʧ/	4. /stɪl/
5. /bɪʧ/	6. /wiːk/	7. /ʤiːnz/	8. /ˈletɪs/
9. /liːv/	10. /kiːn/	11. /ˈiːvnɪŋ/	12. /piːs/
13. /ðiːz/	14. /ˈfɪzɪks/	15. /mɪst/	16. /gɪlt/
17. /pəˈliːs/	18. /ˈliːdə/	19. /kiː/	20. /liːp/

4. Group 1: /ɪ/ and /iː/. Give a phonemic transcription of the words below and then classify them into two columns. Note that there is one word which does not fit in either column.

women	wanted	please	village	minute
key	rich	Sunday	complete	tip
reach	private	tea	piece	city
meat	receive	people	build	field
sheet	busy	pleasure	pretty	sleep

5. Group 2: /e/, /ə/ and /ɜː/. Read aloud the following words and then write them out in ordinary spelling.

1. /ˈnekləs/	2. /ˈɒnə/	3. /ˈprefəs/
4. /ˈbrekfəst/	5. /ɜːn/	6. /hɜːd/
7. /bɜːθ/	8. /ɜːθ/	9. /wɜːk/
10. /ˈberɪ/	11. /gɜːl/	12. /ˈweðə/
13. /wɜːd/	14. /red/	15. /ˈʤɜːnɪ/
16. /ˈkʌlə/	17. /ˈmʌðə/	18. /ɜːʤ/
19. /bɜːd/	20. /ʧɜːʧ/	21. /pɜːl/

6. Group 2: /e/, /ə/ and /ɜː/. Give a phonemic transcription of the words below and then classify them into three columns. Note that there is one word which does not fit in any column.

nurse	best	world	stomach	turn
river	skirt	head	mother	friend
many	bury	thirst	pearl	work
journey	search	person	them	worm
church	afraid	dead	breath	conservation

7. Group 3: /æ/, /ɑ:/ and /ʌ/. Read aloud the following words given in broad transcription and then write them out in ordinary spelling.

1. /stʌf/	2. /ˈfɑ:ðə /	3. /ˈæplz/
4. /ˈbʌrə/	5. /stɑ:f/	6. /blʌd/
7. /bæŋk/	8. /lʌv/	9. /rɪˈmɑ:ks/
10. /ɑ:nt/	11. /dræŋk/	12. /nʌn/
13. /sʌn/	14. /ˈbɑ:skɪt/	15. /ˈɑ:nsə/
16. /wʌn/	17. /ˈsæmən/	18. /ænt/
19. /drʌŋk/	20. /ˈkʌntri/	21. /lɑ:fs/

8. Group 3: /æ/, /ɑ:/ and /ʌ/. Give a phonemic transcription of the words below and then classify them into three columns. Note that there is one word which does not fit in any columns.

duck	aunt	badge	hard	packet
month	hut	Monday	laugh	garden
bad	bother	uncle	blood	bath
love	past	man	half	father
grass	park	country	glass	heart

9. Group 4: /ɒ/ and /ɔ:/. Read aloud the following words given in broad transcription and then write them out in ordinary spelling.

1. /pɔ:t/	2. /kɔ:s/	3. /swɒn/
4. /ˈwɔ:tə/	5. /sɔ:/	6. /gɒn/
7. /tɔ:k/	8. /kɔ:t/	9. /wɔ:d/
10. /ˈɔ:ltə/	11. /rɔ:/	12. /wɒt/
13. /wɔ:k/	14. /kɒst/	15. /sɒlt/
16. /bɔ:/	17. /ɔ:/	18. /bɪˈkɒz/
19. /pɔ:/	20. /wɔ:n/	21. /jɔ:/

10. Group 4: /ɒ/ and /ɔ:/. Give a phonemic transcription of the words below and then classify them into two columns. Note that there is one word which does not fit in either column.

horse	doctor	law	forty	wander
porter	potter	salt	caught	war
cause	sausage	wonder	bought	wash
because	fault	watch	daughter	knowledge

11. Group 5: /ʊ/ and /uː/. Read aloud the following words given in broad transcription and then write them out in ordinary spelling.

1. /pʊl/	2. /fluː/	3. /ruːt/
4. /gruːp/	5. /bʊk/	6. /suːn/
7. /fruːt/	8. /ruːd/	9. /wʊlf/
10. /gʊd/	11. /luːk/	12. /lʊk/
13. /wʊd/	14. /fʊt/	15. /ʃuː/
16. /bʊʃ/	17. /ʤuːs/	18. /fuːd/
19. /ʧuːz/	20. /θruː/	21. /kruːz/

12. Group 5: /ʊ/ and /uː/. Give a phonemic transcription of the words below and then classify them into two columns. Note that there is one word which does not fit in either column.

butcher	wolf	full	butler	fruit
foot	pull	June	true	rude
put	soon	move	food	cook
pool	clue	grew	sugar	woman
moon	good	fool	cushion	Jew

13. Closing diphthongs: /eɪ/, /aɪ/, /ɔɪ/, /əʊ/ and /aʊ/. Read aloud the following words given in broad transcription and then write them out in ordinary spelling.

1. /reɪn/	2. /taɪm/	3. /nɔɪz/
4. /həʊm/	5. /haʊs/	6. /laʊd/
7. /əʊn/	8. /braʊn/	9. /θrəʊ/
10. /rəʊd/	11. /bɔɪ/	12. /deɪ/
13. /ðeɪ/	14. /weɪt/	15. /daɪ/
16. /kraɪ/	17. /fraɪt/	18. /kɔɪn/
19. /heɪt/	20. /aɪl/	21. /eɪt/

14. Closing diphthongs: /eɪ/, /aɪ/, /ɔɪ/, /əʊ/ and /aʊ/. Give a phonemic transcription of the words below and then classify them into columns. Note that there is one word which does not fit in any column.

break	favour	plough	weight	sign
toy	mile	road	voice	boy
sky	point	toe	height	aid
plain	said	buy	know	mouse
though	town	around	say	brown

15. Centring diphthongs: /ɪə/, /eə/ and /ʊə/. Read aloud the following words given in broad transcription and then write them out in ordinary spelling.

1. /dɪə/	2. /beə/	3. /pʊə/
4. /weə/	5. /peə/	6. /feə/
7. /ʃʊə/	8. /hɪə/	9. /bɪəd/
10. /fɪə/	11. /heə/	12. /reə/
13. /mʊə/	14. /ˈhɪərəʊ/	15. /tʊə/

16. Centring diphthongs: /ɪə/, /eə/ and /ʊə/. Give a phonemic transcription of the words below and then classify them into three columns. Note that there is one word which does not fit in any column.

real	share	jewel	idea	weird
mayor	jury	cruel	year	cure
where	stare	sure	fierce	cheer
parents	clean	peer	hair	tour

17. Diphthongs + [ə]: /aɪə/, /eɪə/, /ɔɪə/, /əʊə/ and /aʊə/. Read aloud the following words given in broad transcription and then write them out in ordinary spelling.

1. /ˈfraɪə/	2. /ˈpleɪə/	3. /ˈləʊə/
4. /ˈlɔɪəl/	5. /ˈtaʊə/	6. /ˈleɪə/
7. /ˈflaʊə/	8. /ˈrɔɪəl/	9. /ˈaɪən/
10. /ˈsləʊə/	11. /ˈdraɪə/	12. /ˈgreɪə/

18. Diphthongs + [ə]: /aɪə/, /eɪə/, /ɔɪə/, /əʊə/ and /aʊə/. Give a phonemic transcription of the words below and then classify them into columns. Note that there is one word which does not fit in any column.

liar	layer	higher	quite	towel
joyous	sour	fire	mower	gayer
shower	hire	quiet	soya	widower

19. Transcribe the following sentences:
    1. She was pretty busy in her leisure time serving tea to English teachers.
    2. She had the leather jacket cleaned but kept the sweater on.
    3. My aunt asked the man who had put the apples in the basket and he answered back.
    4. My uncle and my younger cousin ran past me.
    5. The monk did not have any money for the bus to Gloucester.
    6. My tongue and my stomach would love that honey.
20. Homophones. The following transcriptions represent a pair of homophones (unless otherwise stated). Give their spellings.

1. /nɒt/	2. /fɔːt/	3. /ɜːn/	4. /juː/(3)	5. /θruː/
6. /ruːt/	7. /luːz/	8. /wʊd/	9. /kɔːs/	10. /wɒt/
11. /stiːl/	12. /kɔːt/	13. /ˈkɜːnl/	14. /wɔːn/	15. /kruːz/

Chapter 4
4 Consonants

4.1 Introduction

This chapter describes RP consonants based on the acoustic, auditory and articulatory features (basically place and manner of articulation, position of the vocal folds, as well as force or energy of articulation) previously detailed in Chapters 1 and 2 (see under § 1.2, 2.3.2 and 2.4.3). As already noted, acoustically, consonants are characterised by irregular formant patterns, and articulatorily, they differ from vowels in that their production involves some sort of impediment or stricture in the VT, which is not present in vowel articulation. Here, in line with other reference books (Gimson 1980, 1984, 1994; Cruttenden 2008, 2014; Colina 2009), consonants are classified into two main groups, **obstruents** and **sonorants**, according to their **sonority**, that is, the correlation that exists between the degree of openness of the VT that is necessary for their articulation and the relative loudness with which they are perceived (see § 1.3.3.2 for details on the **sonority hierarchy principle**).

Obstruents include three kinds of consonants that are produced with different types of obstruction to the airflow having resonance above that point of constriction (see fn 3). In the case of **plosives** the stricture impedes the airflow through nose or mouth; in **fricatives** the stricture causes friction; and in **affricates** there is a combination of both articulations. Articulatorily, obstruents show a distinctive opposition between **fortis** and **lenis** types; and acoustically they are typically associated with a noise component and with irregular formant structure patterns that show higher frequency. Phonologically, they tend to be "non-syllabic" or marginal in the syllable.

Sonorants, on the other hand, are articulatorily defined as frictionless sounds that are produced with a relatively free, or unimpeded, oral or nasal airflow, having a vocal fold position such that spontaneous voicing is possible (see fn 4). They resonate throughout the VT. To this group belong four groups of consonants differing in manner of articulation, **nasals, approximants** (including glide consonants and liquids), **taps** and **trills**, which share many phonetic characteristics with vowels. Acoustically sonorants are characterised by the absence of a noise component and by homogeneous formant structure patterns that are lower in frequency. Some sonorants (nasals and liquids) may also be syllabic (see § 1.3.3.3).

As already explained, consonants are identified according to **three-term VPM labels** related to:

(1) **Voicing**, i.e. whether or not the vocal cords vibrate in their articulation (voiced-voiceless) (see § 2.3.2.4).

(2) **Place of articulation**, alluding to where the obstruction or stricture occurs with regard to eleven possible locations in the VT (bilabial, labio-dental, dental, alveolar, post-alveolar, palato-alveolar, palatal, velar, uvular, pharyngeal, and glottal) (see § 2.3.2.2); and

(3) **Manner of articulation**, considering the type of **obstruction** that exists in the VT: broadly, plosives, affricates and nasals involve a complete closure of the oral tract; taps and trills are articulated with intermittent closures; laterals are produced with a partial oral closure; and fricatives need a stricture of close approximation (see § 2.3.2.1).

Consistent with the contrastive standpoint justified in Chapter 3, section 4.2 compares the consonant systems of RP and PSp, focusing on the five groups that may be established according to their sonority and manner of articulation: **plosives, fricatives, affricates** – which make up the **obstruent** class –, **nasals** and **approximants** – which constitute the **sonorant** class. The members of each group are characterised along nine parameters:

(1) **IPA symbols**, giving the names of the phonetic symbols related to each consonant phoneme.

(2) **Identification** of RP consonants according to the VPM labels.

(3) **Allophones**, listing the main allophonic realisations with their corresponding IPA symbols and meanings.

(4) **Description**, describing the articulation of RP consonants.

(5) **Environment and main allophonic realisations**, offering a description of the main contexts of appearance of RP consonants, as well as an explanation of their most relevant **allophonic realisations**, which are recapitulated in Chapter 5.

(6) **Spellings** (with transcribed examples), listing the spellings of RP consonants in decreasing frequency and noting the most remarkable exceptions (if any).

(7) **Regional and social variants**, mentioning the most important alternative pronunciations of consonants in RP and other related accents.

(8) **Comparison with Spanish and advice**, where each RP consonant or consonant group is contrasted with the equivalent sounds in PSp providing pronunciation tips that are essential for intelligibility or otherwise may be relevant to the imitation of a native-like accent.

(9) **Further practice**, which includes recorded (and transcribed) examples (extracted from our Sound Bank). The reader is referred also to the Audio Units (exercises) to be listened to and practised. Remember that all the listening material is available in the companion EPSS Multimedia Lab.

4.2 A comparison of English and Spanish consonants

The RP consonant system (annotated in bold type in Table 18 below) consists of **twenty-four** phonemes: six plosives /**p t k b d g**/, nine fricatives /**f v θ ð s z ʃ ʒ h**/, two affricates /**tʃ dʒ**/, three nasals /**m n ŋ**/ and four approximants /**j w l r**/. The voiceless velar fricative [**x**] and the glottal plosive [**ʔ**] are excluded from Table 18 because the former occurs exceptionally in some Scottish pronunciations of some words such as *loch* [lɒx] (vs. [lɒk]), whereas the glottal stop is not phonetically distinctive in RP, nor does it exist in the phonetic inventory of PSp. It will be explained that in RP [**ʔ**] is mostly used as a reinforcement for vowels or as an allophone of plosives (see § 5.2.8). It should also be clarified that [**w**] appears twice in Table 18 to reflect its double labial-velar articulation, the former being placed between brackets due to its secondary nature (see § 4.2.5.2).

As already remarked, only obstruents participate in the **fortis** /**p t k f θ s ʃ tʃ**/ – **lenis** /**b d g v ð z ʒ dʒ**/ opposition,[60] which is an important one for the repercussion it may have on the articulation of neighbouring sounds basically in terms of length and voicing (see § 2.3.2.1). The most remarkable are the two effects produced by fortis consonants. One is the reduction in length of previous vowels and sonorants (**pre-fortis clipping**, see § 2.3.1.4, 2.3.2.4, 5.2.1). As an illustration, compare *ro**p**e* [rəˑʊp], *hur**t*** [hɜˑt], *lea**k*** [liˑk], *sen**t*** [senˑt], *sel**f*** [seɫˑf], with reduced pre-fortis vowels and sonorants, with *ro**b**e* [rəːʊb], *hear**d*** [hɜːd], *lea**g**ue* [liːg], *sen**d*** [senːd], sel**v**es [ˈseɫːvz], which have fully long vowels and sonorants. The other effect exerted by fortis plosives is the devoicing of a subsequent sonorant in consonantal clusters, as in e.g. *quiet* [ˈkw̥aɪət] *try* [tɹ̥aɪ], *play* [pl̥eɪ], *pure* [pj̥ ʊə], where the four approximants are devoiced because they follow a fortis consonant in a stressed syllable (for more details see § 5.2.2).

Now examining the phonemic oppositions that exist between the consonant systems of English and Spanish, it will be seen from Table 18 that while RP has twenty-four distinctive consonants, PSp only has nineteen (see also Table 4 in § 5.1), although these totals do not include allophonic or dialectal variations within either language (see § 1.3.1 and 5.2). Both languages have seven sonorant

---

60 /h/ constitutes a special case because it does not participate in the fortis-lenis opposition, like sonorants, but it lacks the voicing feature typical of the sonorant group.

Table 18: The distinctive consonants of RP and PSp

Place of articulation ⇒			LABIAL		(Inter)-Dental	CORONAL[61]				Velar	Glottal
			Bilabial	**Labio-dental**		**Alveolar**	**Post-alveolar**	**Palato-alveolar**	**Palatal**		
Manner of articulation ⇓ Language			Two lips together	Lower lips and upper teeth	Tongue blade against upper teeth / between teeth	Tongue tip against alveolar ridge		Midway between palatals and alveolars	Tongue blade towards hard palate	Tongue body against velum	Between vocal cords
OBSTRUENTS Obstruction to the airflow, voiced or voiceless	**Plosives** (oral stops) 3 stages: closing, compression release	**RP**	**p** **b**		t d	**t** **d**				**k** **g**	
		PSp	p b							k g	
	Fricatives Narrow opening friction	**RP**		**f** **v**	**θ** **ð**	**s** **z**		**ʃ** **ʒ**			**h**
		PSp		f	θ	s			ʝ	x	
	Affricates Begin as plosives, but end as fricatives	**RP**						**ʧ** **ʤ**			
		PSp						ʧ			

61 'Coronal' is a articulatorily cover-term for alveolar, dental and palato-alveolar consonants referring to sounds that are produced with the blade of the tongue raised from its neutral position. Its opposite, 'non-coronal', alludes to sounds that are articulated with the tongue blade in neutral position, as in labial and velar consonants (Crystal 2008: 117).

Table 18: (Continued)

Place of articulation ⇒				**LABIAL**		**(Inter)-Dental**	**CORONAL**				**Velar**	**Glottal**
				Bilabial	**Labio-dental**		**Alveolar**	**Post-alveolar**	**Palato-alveolar**	**Palatal**		
Manner of articulation ⇓ Language				Two lips together	Lower lips and upper teeth	Tongue blade against upper teeth / between teeth	Tongue tip against alveolar ridge		Midway between palatals and alveolars	Tongue blade towards hard palate	Tongue body against velum	Between vocal cords
SONORANTS Greater degree of resonance, all voiced	**Nasals** Velum lowered, airflow through nose		**RP**	**m**			**n**				**ŋ**	
			PSp	**m**			**n**			ɲ		
	Approximants No closure or friction	**Glides**	**RP**	**(w)**						**j**	**w**	
			PSp									
		Liquids	**RP**				**l**	**r [ɹ]**				
			PSp				l			ʎ		
	Taps		**RP**									
			PSp					ɾ				
	Trill		**RP**									
			PSp					r				

consonants, RP /**m n ŋ l r w j**/ and PSp /**m n ɲ l ʎ ɾ r**/, whereas the rest are obstruents: seventeen in RP /**p b t d g k f v θ ð s z ʃ ʒ h ʧ ʤ**/ and twelve in PSp /**p b t d g k f θ s ʝ x ʧ**/. Moreover, while both RP and PSp have six plosives and three nasals, they differ as to the number of phonemes consigned in the other manners of articulation, as summarised in Table 19.

Table 19: Differences between the consonantal phonemic systems of English and Spanish

English 24 consonants	**Spanish** 19 consonants
6 plosives /**p t k b d g**/	6 plosives /**p t k b d g**/
9 fricatives /**f v θ ð s z ʃ ʒ h**/	5 fricatives /**f θ s ʝ x**/
2 affricates /**tʃ ʤ**/	1 affricate /**tʃ**/
3 nasals /**m n ŋ**/	3 nasals /**m n ɲ**/
1 lateral /**l**/	2 laterals /**l ʎ**/
3 approximants /**r w j**/[62]	1 flap /**ɾ**/
	1 trill /**r**/[63]

In addition, the tables reveal that only **eleven** RP consonant phonemes have equivalent ones in PSp: /**p b k g f θ s tʃ m n l**/. The other thirteen RP consonants have no exact equivalent phonemes in Spanish, /**t d ʤ v ð z ʃ ʒ h ŋ r j w**/. For this reason particular attention should be paid to these sounds as they can project possible phonemic difficulties for SSLE, as explained in Chapter 3, even though some of them may still appear in the phonetic or allophonic inventories of some dialects of Spanish.

Nine belong to the obstruent category (see § 8.2.2). Firstly, although both languages have six plosives, /**t d**/ are dental in PSp, but alveolar in RP. Secondly, Spanish has only the voiceless affricate /tʃ/, while English has one pair, voiceless /tʃ/ (***church*** /tʃɜːtʃ/) and voiced /**ʤ**/ (***bridge*** [brɪʤ]). The other six obstruents that only occur in English belong to the fricative paradigm, /**f v θ ð s z ʃ ʒ h**/, which contains four voiceless-voiced pairs, as against only five single fricatives in PSp

62 Although here the wide-spread practice is adopted to annotate RP post-alveolar approximant as /r/, the IPA symbol that denotes this characterization is [ɹ] "Latin small letter turned R", and so the latter will be used in narrow transcriptions to represent the post-alveolar approximant.
63 The IPA symbol /r/ stands for an alveolar trill, which corresponds to the description of the consonantal phoneme found in Spanish (as in *perro* 'dog'), although other symbols have also been used to represent it such as /r̄/ or /R/ (mostly to denote all *r* types).

/f θ s ʝ x/: the voiced labio-dental /**v**/ (*visit* /ˈvɪzɪt/), dental /**ð**/ (*rather* /ˈrɑːðəʳ/) and alveolar /**z**/ (*zoo* /zuː/) fricatives, both the voiced /**ʒ**/ (*vision* /ˈvɪʒn/) and unvoiced /**ʃ**/ (*cash* /kæʃ/) palato-alveolar fricatives, and the voiceless glottal fricative /**h**/ (*ham* /hæm/). The latter should not be confused with the spelling <h> in Spanish, which is always silent, and so compare e.g. ***hola*** 'hi' /ˈola/ with ***hello*** /həˈləʊ/. The remaining four RP consonant phonemes that cannot be found in the phonemic inventory of Spanish belong to the sonorant group: the velar nasal /**ŋ**/ (*thing* /θɪŋ/), the postalveolar approximant /**r**/ [ɹ] (*rise* /raɪz/ [ɹaɪz]), and the glide consonants /**j w**/, which are here regarded as (semi-)consonants in RP, but as allophones of the vowels [i] and [u] in Spanish (see § 4.2.5.3 and 4.2.5.4).

PSp, on the other hand, has **six** consonant phonemes that do not occur in RP: the palatal nasal /**ɲ**/ (*caña* /ˈkaɲa/ 'cane', close to /nj/ as in *knew*), the voiceless velar fricative /**x**/ (*jamón* /xaˈmon/ 'ham'), which comes close to RP /h/ but has a different place of articulation, the voiced palatal fricative /**ʝ**/ (*yeso* /ˈʝeso/ 'plaster') and the palatal lateral approximant /**ʎ**/ (***llama*** /ˈʎama/ 'flame', close to /lj/ as in in *million*), the latter two resembling RP /ʒ/ and /ʤ/ but with a different place and manner of articulation, respectively. Lastly, while in Spanish there are two *r* types that have phonemic status, the alveolar tap /**ɾ**/ (*pero* 'but') and the alveolar trill /**r**/ (*perro* 'dog'), in English [ɾ] is an allophone of /r/ (*very* [ˈveɾi]) and /t/ (*butter* [ˈbʌɾə]).

Also relevant to the comparison between the consonant systems of English and Spanish are the following points (Fry 1947; Delatre 1965: 41; Navarro Tomás 1968; Monroy Casas 1980: 75; 2012; Finch and Ortiz Lira 1982: 62-65; Helman 2004; Swan and Smith 2001):

(1) Generally speaking, **Spanish consonants are shorter** and are articulated with less muscular tension than their English counterparts, and are usually **not so strongly released**; as a result, variation of length of the consonant itself and of the preceding vowel is not used in Spanish as a cue to identify consonant quality as it occurs in English (***bead*** [biːd] vs. *beat* [biˑt]).

(2) Consonants in both English and Spanish show similar **oscillations in place of articulation** depending on their phonetic contexts of occurrence (see § 5.2.7). This is particularly so in the case of **alveolars**, but it also applies to velars and /**m n**/, which may have pre- or post-alveolar, pre- or post-velar, and labio-dental realisations ([ɱ]) if followed by /f v/, respectively. Likewise, in Castilian Spanish, though not in Latin American Spanish, /l n/ can have dental allophones [̪], if they precede /θ ð/, as in *calzado* 'footwear', as it occurs in English.

(3) Turning to **frequency counts**, consonants occur **more frequently in English** than in Spanish, /**s z**/ and /**k**/ showing top frequency in the former, but

in the two languages the most common places of articulation are **alveolar** followed by **velar**. Note that this tendency is more skewed in English because seven consonant phonemes are articulated in the (post)alveolar region, as against only three in Spanish.

(4) Considering **distribution**, it should be noted that only six consonants have a restricted distribution in RP: /**ʒ h ŋ r w j**/. Both /ʒ/ and /ŋ/ are **barred from word initial position**, whereas /**h r w j**/ **do not appear word finally**. All the other consonants can occur word initially, medially and finally. In Spanish, on the other hand, consonants show a more restricted distribution as they are more frequently found in initial than in final positions, the latter being restricted to /d s n l/ and flapped *r*. As a result, speakers of Spanish may fail to pronounce final consonants accurately or strongly enough due to the higher number of consonants which may occur in that position in English. Especially problematic may be those English words ending in a consonant that does not exist or is barred from that position in Spanish.

(5) In terms of **syllable structure**, we have seen that while in English **onsets** and **codas** may have up to **three and four consonants**, respectively (***spr**ay* /sprei/, *si**xths*** /sɪksθs/), Spanish exhibits a maximum of two consonants in both slots (***trans**-cribir* 'transcribe') (see § 1.3.3.1).

(6) An examination of the **spellings** of consonants shows that English has over **one hundred and twenty spellings** for its inventory of twenty-four phonemes, whereas Spanish has twenty eight spellings to represent nineteen (see Chapter 7).

(7) Lastly, considering **accent variation**, in English it is **vowels that vary the most** from one regional variety to another, but in Spanish it is mainly consonants. In both languages, however, consonants have more allophonic variants than vowels.

Speakers of Spanish should make selective use of distinctive cues when learning English consonants taking into account their different L1 phonemic and phonetic inventories as they may give rise to pronunciation problems. Moreover, every effort should be made to accurately apprehend and reproduce the differences so far described, the most outstanding involving (1) phonemes that are common to English and Spanish but have different realisations (e.g. fortis plosives), (2) sounds which are phonemes in one language but allophones in the other (e.g. English /ð z/ vs. Spanish [ð z]), and (3) phonemes that occur only in English and therefore should be learnt anew by speakers of Spanish. The following are specific areas of difficulty and common replacements/mispronunciations detected in the pronunciation of SSLE, which are further discussed in the subsequent sections in connection with the particular phonemes ascribed to each consonant group (Sedláčková 2010; Estebas Vilaplana 2009; Helman 2004; Gallardo del Puerto 2005; Finch and Ortiz Lira 1982; Coe-Guerrero 1981):

(1) /**p**/ tends to be pronounced as unaspirated and as a result it may sound almost like [b], which can result in miscommunication. The same is applies to /k/ (which may be confused with [g]) and /t/ (which may be replaced by [d]).

(2) The /**b**/ – /**v**/ contrast that exists in English can be problematic. Whereas in English /b/ is always a stop, SSLE tend to pronounce [β], the approximant allophone of /b/, between voiced sounds, and also very frequently in replacement of RP /v/, especially in word-initial position. Moreover, in word-final position RP /b/ may be devoiced to [p] (as when *cu**b*** is pronounced [kʌp] instead of /kʌb/). This replacement may similarly take place in the case of word-final /g/ (which may become [k]) and /d/ (which may be realised as [t]).

(3) In addition to being unaspirated, RP /**t**/ tends to be pronounced as dental (instead of alveolar) to match Spanish /t/. For the same reason, dental realisations of /**d**/ are also frequent, causing confusion with (and replacement by) [ð].

(4) Since the phoneme /**ð**/ does not exist in Spanish, it is often replaced by /d/.

(5) RP /**z**/ is frequently pronounced as a voiceless fricative [s], or even as [θ] if pronunciation is misled by the common grapheme <z>.

(6) Due to its absence in Spanish, RP /**ʃ**/ is often replaced by [s] or [ʧ]. But, if the EFL learner knows how to pronounce the phoneme, s/he may overuse it and replace RP /**ʧ**/ by [ʃ] in some contexts.

(7) RP /**ʒ**/ may be replaced by [ʃ], [ʧ] or even [s].

(8) RP /**h**/ may be dropped, or otherwise it may be pronounced with a hissing sound or be replaced by Spanish [x].

(9) RP /**ʤ**/ tends to be confused with and replaced by [ʝ], [ʎ] and [j], or even by [ʧ].

(10) In word-final positions RP /**m**/ may be replaced by [n] or [ŋ].

(11) As RP /**ŋ**/ does not occur in Spanish, it may be replaced by [n], [ng] or [nk].

(12) Learners may have trouble pronouncing dark *l* [**ɫ**].

(13) While in RP the post-alveolar approximant [**ɹ**] is a continuant sound, SSLE usually replace it by the Spanish flap [ɾ] or trill [r].

(14) RP /**j**/ may be confused with (or it can replace) [ʤ], as mentioned in (9) above, but due to the influence of Spanish it may also be mispronounced as a voiced palatal fricative [ʝ] or a palatal lateral [ʎ], instead of as a palatal approximant.

(15) RP /**w**/ may be mispronounced as a [b], or quite frequently, [g] may be inserted before the sound itself.

4.2.1 Plosives

In English there are six plosive consonants, /**p b t d k g**/, which can be also referred to as pulmonic, egressive, **oral stops**. Their articulation involves three successive stages (see also e.g. Gimson 1984: 152–171; Gimson 1994: 139–156; Roach 2005: 32–35; Collins and Mees 2003: 149–163; Collins and Mees 2009: 81–87; Cruttenden 2014: 162–185):

(1) **Closing, closure** or **approach stage**, during which the active articulator raises towards the passive articulator in order to form a complete closure or obstruction to the airstream. This is the defining characteristic of **stops**; if there is no closure, then there is no stop.
(2) **Hold** or **compression** stage, during which, the lung air cannot go out of the mouth as it is stopped at the point where the two articulators meet. When we pronounce plosives the soft palate is in its raised position, and as a result the lung air cannot be released through the nose either (unless a nasal consonant follows the plosive). The vocal folds may or may not vibrate.
(3) **Release** or **explosion** stage, during which the two articulators are abruptly separated so that the lung air goes out of the mouth producing a kind of explosion (hence the term **plosive**). If the vocal folds vibrate in the compression stage, they continue to do so in the release stage; but if stage (2) is voiceless, then stage (3) may either be also voiceless (**aspirated**) or it may be the onset of vocal fold vibration. There exists an off-glide, or transition, from the plosive to the following sound.

In addition, the plosive paradigm can be further classified according to the three-term VPM series used to classify consonants:

(1) **Position of the vocal folds**, either they do not vibrate in **voiceless** or **unvoiced** plosives /**p t k**/, or they do vibrate, when pronouncing the **voiced** ones /**b d g**/. There exists allophonic variation involving different degrees of **devoicing** [b̥ d̥ g̊] or **voicing** [p̌ t̬ k̬] in the case of voiced and voiceless plosives, respectively. Devoiced realisations of voiced plosives occur in initial and especially in final positions (*Did* [d̥ɪd̥]); while fully voiced realisations, left unmarked in allophonic transcriptions, arise in word-medial, intervocalic position (*labour* [ˈleibə]. In the latter phonetic context voiceless plosives have voiced realisational variants (*matter* [ˈmæt̬ə] (see § 1.3.2 and 2.3.2.1).
(2) **Place of articulation**: /**p b**/ are **bilabial**, the two articulators that are used when we pronounce them are the two lips, the lower lip, the active articulator, and the upper lip, the passive articulator. /**t d**/ are **alveolar** because the two articulators are the tip of the tongue, the active articulator, and the

alveolar ridge, the passive articulator. Finally, **/k g/** are **velar**, the back of the tongue and the soft palate acting as the active and passive articulator, respectively.

(3) **Force or energy of articulation: /p t k/** are **fortis** or strong consonants because they are pronounced with more muscular force or energy than **/b d g/**, which are **lenis** or weak consonants. As already remarked, long vowels and diphthongs are shortened or clipped when followed by a fortis consonant either within the word or in the following word. For example, in *see**k*** the vowel is shortened [si·k], while in *wee**d*** [wi:d], the vowel is fully long. This shortening helps to differentiate many word-pairs such as *mate* [me·it] and *made* [me:id].

Three additional features must be taken into account to characterise the plosive group: **release type, aspiration** and their **Voice Onset Time** (VOT) values. Considering the type of release, plosives may have three different allophonic variants depending on their position in the word and on the consonant that follows them:

(1) **Non audible release**, annotated in narrow transcriptions with a **superscript high-tone mark** [p˺ t˺ k˺ b˺ d˺ g˺], is attributed to the allophones of so-called **incomplete plosives** in the sense that the third (release or explosion) stage is either non-audible or it does not exist. More common in the velar pair than in the bilabial or alveolar ones (Byrd 1992), incomplete plosives are restricted to two main contexts: word-finally, particularly before a silence and in rapid speech (*roa**d*** [rəʊd˺]), and in consonantal clusters, where incomplete plosives occur if they are followed by another plosive or by an affricate either within a word, both in the same or a different syllable, or between words, as shown in the following examples: *a**c**t* [æk˺t], *pi**c**ture* [ˈpɪk˺tʃə], *tra**ck** tape* [ˈtɹæk˺ ˈteip], *bi**g** ball* [ˈbɪg˺ ˈbɔ:l], *we**b**cast* [ˈweb˺kʰɑ:st]. Accordingly, the articulatory steps that are necessary to pronounce, for instance, incomplete [b] in the [b˺k] sequence of the last example would be as follows. In the first stage, the two articulators, the two lips, come into contact in order to produce [b], the soft palate is in its raised position. In the second stage, the lung air cannot go out through the nasal passage and it is compressed in the mouth just behind the closure made by the two articulators, the back of the tongue is placed close to the soft palate. In the third stage, the articulators are separated and the lung air goes out of the mouth producing a kind of explosion. Two plosives are pronounced but there is only one explosion.

In addition, cases of **gemination** (i.e. sequences of identical stops, as in *to**p** **p**ost, goo**d** **d**ay*)[64] and series of **homorganic plosives** (i.e. with the same place of articulation) that differ in voicing (*to**p** **b**rand, tha**t** **d**ay, bi**g** **c**oach*) involve only one closing stage and one release stage with an approximately double-length compression stage. In the case of homorganic plosive clusters, the first plosive is more accurately termed **unreleased** and is annotated with a **superscript up arrowhead** [ˆ]: [ˈtʰɒpˆ ˈpʰəʊst⁼], [ˈgʊdˆ ˈdeɪ], [ˈtɒpˆ ˈbɹænd] [ðətˆ ˈdeɪ], [bɪgˆ kəʊtʃ]). Cues for the recognition of voiceless or voiced sounds are provided by onset or cessation of voice, if voiced, and, if voiceless, by the presence of aspiration and the shortening of previous sonorants.

Finally, in the event of clusters with three plosives, the first two plosives are incomplete (or unreleased in homorganic plosive clusters). For in addition to the omission of the third stage of the first plosive, the central plosive has non-audible first and third stages (*ru**bbed** **p**ork* [rʌb˺d˺ pɔːk]), and if that slot is occupied by [p t k], then the second stage is manifested by a silence of certain duration (*sto**pped** **b**egging* [ˈstɒp˺t˺ ˈbegɪŋ]).

As will be apparent from the transcribed examples, incomplete fortis plosives are always unaspirated because they lack the release stage when aspiration is produced.

(2) **Nasal release,** annotated with a superscript lower-case N [**pⁿ tⁿ kⁿ bⁿ dⁿ gⁿ**], takes place when the plosive is followed by a nasal consonant, both within and between words, as illustrated in the following cases: *to**pm**ost* [ˈtɒpᵐməʊst], *su**bm**erge* [səbᵐˈmɜːdʒ], *chu**tn**ey* [ˈtʃʌtⁿni], *chi**ck**en* [ˈtʃɪkⁿŋ̍], *chea**p** **m**attress* [tʃiːpᵐ ˈmætɹɪs]. If the nasal is homorganic, what we do is just to keep the two articulators together in the oral chamber while lowering the soft palate so that the compressed air is liberated through the nasal passage. But if the nasal is not homorganic (*bi**g** **m**all* [bɪgᵐ mɔːl]), then the plosive is not released until the articulatory movements for the nasal consonants are performed (change of place of articulation in the oral chamber and lowering of the soft palate); otherwise, some oral release may be perceived.

(3) **Lateral release,** transcribed with a superscript lower-case L [**pˡ tˡ kˡ bˡ dˡ gˡ**], occurs when a plosive is followed by a lateral consonant. The plosive is then said to be released laterally, both between and within words, either when

---

64 The only case where geminated letters are pronounced as double sounds is when they occur across words (*ca**n** **n**ever* /kən ˈnevə/) or when they correspond to two different grammatical categories within words: (1) prefix + word (*mi**dd**ay* /ˌmɪdˈdeɪ/), (2) word + suffix (*lea**nn**ess* /ˈliːnnəs/), (3) compounds (*ho**p-p**ole* /ˈhɒp pəʊl/). Even though two sounds appear in transcription, most of the times double sounds are pronounced as single sounds, except that they last longer. An exception to this are the series consisting of two affricates, in which case the sounds are produced twice (*ri**ch** **ch**urch* /ˈrɪtʃ ˈtʃɜːtʃ/ *oran**ge** **j**uice* /ˈɒrɪndʒ dʒuːs/).

the plosive is followed by **syllabic** [ɫ̩], as in *little* [ˈlɪtˡɫ̩], or when [**l**] is initial in the next syllable or word, as in ***bad*** *leg* [bædˡ leg]. This means that the lung air goes out laterally because one or the two sides of the tongue are lowered to allow the air to escape to pronounce [l], the plosive contact remaining. A distinction can be made between "true lateral release", occurring in homorganic plosive-nasal sequences [tˡl], [dˡl], where there is no intervening removal of the tongue contact on the alveolar ridge so that the air cannot escape centrally over the tongue, and the other laterally released plosives in [**p b k g**] + [**l**] sequences, where the escape of air is lateral in the sense that the partial alveolar contact for [l] is made before or at the time of the release of the plosive (***apple*** [ˈæpˡɫ̩] *fake leg* [ˈfeɪkˡ ˈleg], ***g**low* [gˡləʊ]) (Cruttenden 2014: 172).

Let us now turn to the other two features that characterise plosives: aspiration and VOT. **Aspiration** (annotated with superscript lower-case H) is an articulatory feature that may be present in the release stage of RP fortis plosives in a specific context. In Section 2.3.2.1 it was explained that, when occurring in stressed syllable-initial position, fortis plosives are **aspirated** [**pʰ tʰ kʰ**], i.e. they are articulated with a brief puff of air (Crystal 2008: 38–39), as in ***p**an* [pʰæn], *tan* [tʰæn] and *can* [kʰæn]. In all other contexts fortis plosives are either **unaspirated** [**p⁼ t⁼ k⁼**], after /s/ as in *ski* [sk⁼iː], or otherwise have a **relatively weak aspiration**, in unaccented syllables (***p**olice* [p⁼əˈliːs]) and in both word and syllable final positions (*ta**p*** [tʰæp⁼]). Notice, however, that when fortis plosives are followed by approximants, especially in syllable-initial stressed position, aspiration is manifested regardless of its degree as approximant devoicing [l̥ ɹ̥ j̊ w̥] (e.g. *play* [pl̥eɪ], s**pl**endid [ˈspl̥endɪd], ***t**ry* [tɹ̥aɪ], *strange* [stɹ̥eɪndʒ], *obs**c**ure* [əbˈskj̊ʊə], ***q**uite* [kw̥aɪt⁼]) (see § 5.5.2).

The acoustic correlate of aspiration, VOT, measures in milliseconds the interval between the release burst stage and the onset of voicing (Lisker and Abramson 1964; Ladefoged, 2001: 120; Cruttenden 2014: 164–165). Broadly, aspirated voiceless plosives [**pʰ tʰ kʰ**], as [pʰ] in ***p**ea* [pʰiː], exhibit **positive VOTs**, or **voicing lags** (i.e. the vocal-fold activity starts after the release of the plosive); whereas unaspirated voiceless plosives [**p⁼ t⁼ k⁼**], as in *ski* [sk⁼iː], have a **zero VOT** (i.e. the plosive release and the onset of vocal-fold vibration are simultaneous). The VOT values for voiceless plosives have been found to increase the further back the place of articulation is from labial to velar (Docherty 1992; Volatis and Miller 1992). In contrast, fully voiced [**b d g**] and devoiced voiced plosives [**b̥ d̥ g̊**] have long and short **negative VOTs** or **voicing leads** (i.e. the voicing starts before the release or explosion stage) respectively. These VOT differences of plosives are graphically represented in Figures 48 and 49, where

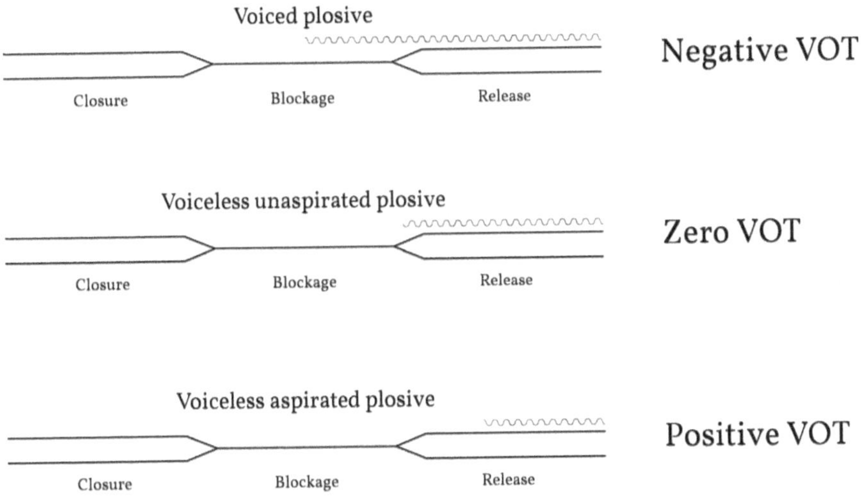

Figure 48: VOT values for RP plosives

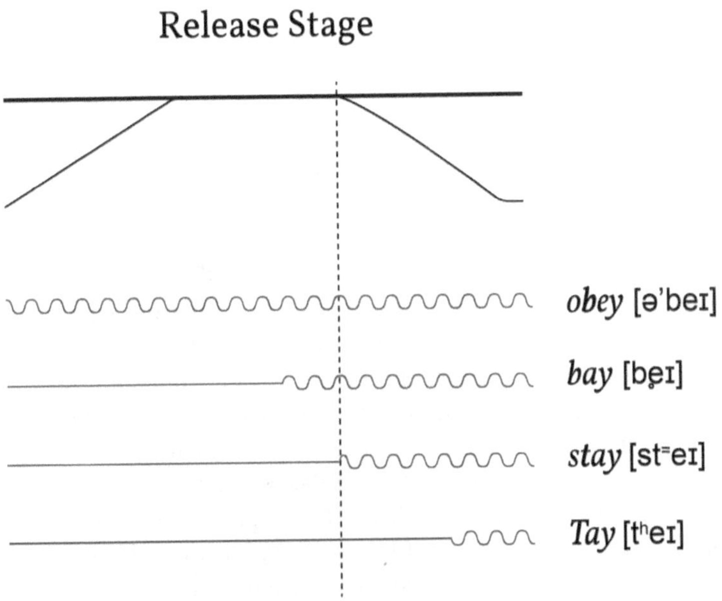

Figure 49: Examples of illustrating the VOT values for RP plosives

one can see the impact that VOT values have on the articulation of the subsequent sound. Differences reside mainly in the point at which voicing starts in relation to the release stage of plosives. (De)voiced and unaspirated voiceless plosives trigger **non-delayed onsets to voicing:** voiced plosives have "unbroken voicing" for which no VOT values can be specified (*o**b**ey* [əˈbeɪ]); devoiced lenis plosives have negative VOTs (***b**ay* [b̥eɪ]); and unaspirated voiceless plosives have zero VOTs (*s**t**ay* [st⁼eɪ]). Aspirated voiceless plosives, in contrast, with positive VOTs are followed by sounds showing **delayed onsets to voicing** (**T**ay [tʰeɪ]). Further details on VOT differences may be found in Sections 2.4.1 and 2.4.3, where the acoustic features of vowels and plosives are discussed. It was explained that fortis plosives have a voiceless silent interval, which is long if unaspirated, and is followed by a burst if aspirated. Voiced stops, in contrast, have generally a shorter closure during which there is a voice bar and the release burst is weaker and has no aspiration.

More details about the allophonic variants of English plosives (e.g. place of articulation, **lenition** and **fortition**), as well as the effects they exert on the neighbouring sounds are offered in Chapter 5 (see § 5.2 and 5.3).

To conclude this introduction to the plosive group, let us focus on the major differences and pronunciation difficulties that they may pose for speakers of Spanish (Finch and Ortiz Lira 1982: 62–65; Estebas Vilaplana 2009: 49–64; Cruttenden 2014: 173, 328). Learners can become aware of the different nature of RP phonemes by means of ear training and oral practice. As already advanced, particular attention should be paid to the **aspiration** of RP fortis plosives in syllable-initial stressed position because failure to do so can lead to intelligibility or otherwise can result in a foreign accent. While aspiration is the main distinguishing cue to differentiate [**p t k**] from [**b d g**] in initial acquisition stages by native speakers of English (Macken and Barton 1980), this feature may be considered as non-existent in Spanish, where the contrast between plosive pairs relies exclusively on the presence-absence of voice. Consequently, SSLE have a tendency to pronounce words like *pen* as *[pen] (without aspiration), instead of [pʰen] (with aspiration), which may be misunderstood by English listeners as *Ben* [ben] since they interpret lack of aspiration as a mark of voiced [b] (Stockwell and Bowen 1965; Monroy Casas 1980; Dale and Poms 1986: 81; Swan and Smith 2001; Catford 1987; Avery and Ehrlich 1992; Gallardo del Puerto 2005: 196–197; Sedláčková 2010: 59; Mott 2011; Gleason 2012). Likewise, if learners do not devoice sonorants after fortis obstruents (plosives and fricatives), an English ear may interpret, for instance, that a lenis rather than a fortis plosive is produced (e.g. ***g**lue*, ***b**ride* and ***d**une* instead of ***c**lue*, ***p**ride* and ***t**une*), leading to miscommunication or misunderstandings. In fact, VOT duration is one of the factors that have most influenced on the native English speakers' perception of a foreign accent in SSLE's pronunciation (Flege 1991; Flege and Eefting 1988). To practice this feature, visual reinforcement can be obtained by holding a piece of paper in front of your mouth, which should move at the production of an aspirated fortis plosive. Aspiration of lenis plosives should be avoided. This feature has been traced in some speakers of Spanish resulting from hypercorrection and an effort to sound less Spanish.

Other characteristics of plosive realisation that tend to be mastered last but should also be attended to by learners who aim at a near approximation to RP are: (1) the **nasal** and **lateral release** of **alveolar plosives** followed by homorganic [**n**] and [**l**], without any intervening [^{h}] or [^{ə}]; (2) the production of **incomplete plosives** following other plosives or affricates; and (3) the **devoicing of sonorants** following a plosive. Although in Spanish plosives may also have a nasal release (e.g. [t^{n}] [k^{n}] in *é**t**nico* 'ethnic' and *té**c**nico* 'technical' 'technician') or a lateral release (e.g. [t^{l}l] [b^{l}l] in *a**t**las* 'atlas' and *sa**b**le* 'sable'), the production of alveolar plosives with nasal or lateral release within the same syllable may be potentially complicated. Learners are advised to keep their tongue against the alveolar ridge so as to avoid the insertion of a vowel.

The production of incomplete plosives may also be difficult for speakers of Spanish because in this language plosives do not normally occur together (but notice such series as [p˺t] and [k˺t] in *a**pt**o* and *a**ct**o*), and they never appear in final position. In addition, SSLE should be careful not to fricativise English plosives in contexts in which this is not allowed in English. Whereas in English [b d g] are largely realised as plosives (albeit the affricated allophones discussed in Section 5.2.8.1), in Spanish they only have a plosive realisation before a pause and after nasals (e.g. [mb] *ca**mb**io* 'change') and /l/ (e.g. *Ma**ld**ivas*), being fricativised elsewhere. Thus, if a lenis plosive intervenes in a plosive cluster or is followed by a sonorant, then it is realised as a fricative in accordance with the commonest tendency of Spanish to realise voiced plosives [b d g] as corresponding voiced fricatives or approximants [**β ð ɣ**] in most contexts (e.g. [ðɣ] *E**dg**ardo*, [βð] *a**bd**icar* 'abdicate', [ðm] *a**dm**irar* 'admire', [ɣm] *do**gm**a* 'dogma') (Stockwell and Bowen 1965; Navarro Tomás 1966; Quilis and Fernández 1982; Finch and Ortiz Lira 1982; Mott 2011). As these fricative sounds have an allophonic, but not phonemic status in Spanish, it may be the case that in English sequences where there is an initial fricative and an intervocalic plosive (***th**ey **d**o* /ðeɪ ˈduː/) SSLE reverse the order of these two sounds (*[deɪ ˈðu]) which should be avoided in order not to sound foreign (Gallardo del Puerto 2005: 197).

4.2.1.1 Bilabial plosives /p b/

IPA Symbols

p Lower-case P.
b Lower-case B.

Identification

/**p**/ Fortis voiceless bilabial plosive.
/**b**/ Lenis voiced bilabial plosive.

Allophones

/**p**/	/**b**/
[**p**^{h}] 'aspirated'	
[**p**$^=$] 'unaspirated'	
[**ʔ**] 'glottalised'	
[**p̌**] 'voiced'	[**b̥**] 'devoiced'
[**p**˺] 'non-audible release'	[**b**˺] 'non-audible release'
[**p**ˆ] 'unreleased'	[**b**ˆ] 'unreleased'
[**p**^{n}] 'nasal release'	[**b**^{n}] 'nasal release'
[**p**^{l}] 'lateral release'	[**b**^{l}] 'lateral release'
[**p̪**] 'labio-dental'	[**b̪**] 'labio-dental'
[**p̠**] 'more retracted'	[**b̠**] more retracted'
[**p**^{w}] 'labialised'	[**b**^{w}] 'labialised'
[**p**^{j}] 'palatalised'	[**p**^{j}] 'palatalised'
[**ɸ**] 'voiceless bilabial fricative'	[**β**] 'voiced bilabial fricative'

Description

When we pronounce /**p**/ the two lips form a closure and the lung air is stopped behind it; the soft palate is in its raised position, so that there are two closures. In the release stage, the two articulators are separated and the lung air goes out of the oral cavity producing a kind of explosion. The vocal folds do not vibrate, they are apart. /p/ is produced with more muscular energy than its voiced counterpart, and it shortens the vocalic sounds that precede it (***beep*** [bi·p]).

/**b**/ is pronounced in the same way as /p/ but with less muscular energy, and the vocal folds may vibrate for all or part of the compression stage. Aspiration does not take place in the production of this sound, nor does it affect the length of the preceding vocalic or sonorant sound (*ur**b*** [ˈɜːb]).

See the animations and videos under RP /p/ and /b/ (compared with Spanish /p b/) in the Sound Bank of the EPSS Multimedia Lab.

Environment and main allophonic realisations

RP /p b/ can appear in all possible contexts. Initially in a stressed syllable /p/ is aspirated [**p**^{h}] (***p**an* [p^{h}æn], *a**pp**ear* [əˈp^{h}ɪə]). Finally in the word, it loses some of that aspiration [p$^=$] (*ta**p*** [t^{h}æp$^=$]), and when preceded by /s/ it is unaspirated [**p**$^=$] (*s**p**ider* [ˈsp$^=$aɪdə^r]). Considering voice, between voiced consonants /p/ may be voiced [**p̌**] (*A**p**ril* [ˈeɪp̌ɹəl], *u**p**on* [əˈp̌ɒn]) and /b/ is fully voiced (*ra**bb**it* [ˈɹæbɪt], *ru**bb**er* [ˈɹʌbəʳ], *hus**b**and* [ˈhʌzbənd]), but the latter loses some of its voicing when it occurs in initial position (***b**ig* [b̥ɪg]) and is completely **devoiced** in final position (*ro**b*** [ɹɒb̥]). /t/ may also be **glottalised** [ʔ] word-medially (*su**pp**er* [ˈsʌʔə]) and in homorganic consonant clusters that occur word-finally or at close-knit word-boundaries (*soa**p** powder* [ˈsəʊʔ ˈpaʊdə] (see Regional variants and Section 5.2.8.2).

In consonantal clusters, both plosives are **incomplete**, with **non-audible release** [p̚ b̚], if followed by another plosive or by an affricate (*sto**pp**ed* [stɒp̚t], ru**bb**ed [rʌb̚d]), or **unreleased** [p˄ b˄], if followed by a homorganic plosive (*to**p** **b**rand* [ˈtɒp˄ ˈbɹænd]). They may also be produced with **nasal release** [p^{n} b^{n}], nasal plosion being heard, when followed by a nasal consonant (*shi**p**mate* [ˈʃɪp^{m}meɪt], *kee**p** narrating* [kiːp^{n} nəˈreɪtɪŋ], *su**b**mit* [səb^{m}ˈmɪt]). The plosion will be lateral and they will have a **lateral release** [pˡ bˡ], if followed by a lateral consonant (***p**lay* [pˡleɪ], ***b**lue* [bˡluː]). Besides, in the above examples and elsewhere sonorants are devoiced after /p/ (***p**lay* [pl̥eɪ]).

Both stops are often produced with a **labio-dental** [p̪ b̪] rather than a bilabial closure when they are followed by a labio-dental fricative /f v/ (*cu**p**ful* [ˈkʌp̪fʊl], *o**b**viate* [ˈɒb̪vɪeɪt]). Likewise, more **retracted realisations** occur, especially in consonantal clusters, when a following sound has a more retracted place of articulation, as in ***p**rice* [p̠ɹaɪs] and ***b**rush* [b̠ɹʌʃ] (see § 5.2.7). In addition to the glottalised and affricated variants discussed in Section 5.2.8, other allophonic realisations show different degrees of **lip-rounding** (***b**og* [bʷɒg) or **lip-spreading** (***p**ea* [pʲiː]) in the vicinity of rounded and spread vowels respectively (see § 5.2.3).

Spellings

Table 20: The spellings of RP /p b/

/p/	/b/
<p> ho**p** /hɒp/, ho**p**e /həʊp/ ho**p**ing /ˈhəʊpɪŋ/	<b> ru**b** /rʌb/, **b**ack /bæk/
<pp> ho**pp**ing /ˈhɒpɪŋ/, su**pp**er /ˈsʌpəʳ/	<bb> ru**bb**er /ˈrʌbəʳ/, e**bb** /eb/
<ph> shep**h**erd /ˈʃepəd/	
Rare cases <gh> hiccou**gh** /ˈhɪkʌp/	**Rare cases** silent <p> + <b> cu**pb**oard /ˈkʌbəd/

The letter *p* is silent when it occurs before *n*, *s* or *t* in several words of Greek origin:

pneumonia /njuːˈməʊnɪə/	**p**sychology /saɪˈkɒlədʒi/)
pseudo /ˈsjuːdəʊ/	**p**terodactyl /ˌterəˈdæktɪl/

In addition, *p* is silent in *cu**p**board*, where it is followed by pronounced /b/ as already noted in Table 20, and in the following words:

cor**ps** /kɔː/	ras**p**berry /ˈrɑːzbəri/
cou**p** /kuː/	recei**p**t /rɪˈsiːt/

In <mpt> spellings *p* may or may not be silent, and so alternative pronunciations occur with and without it (e.g. *attem**p**t* /əˈtempt/ – /əˈtemt/, *tem**p**t* /tempt/ – /temt/, *em**p**ty* /ˈempti/ – /ˈemti/).

The letter *b*, on the other hand, is silent in <mb> and <bt> combinations, mostly in final position, as in:

clim**b** /klaɪm/	plum**b**er /plʌmə^{r}/	de**b**t /det/
com**b** /kəʊm/	Woolacom**be** /ˈwʊləkəm/	dou**b**t /daʊt/
crum**b** /krʌm/		su**b**tle /ˈsʌtl̩/
lam**b** /læm/		
num**b** /nʌm/		
plum**b** /plʌm/		
thum**b** /θʌm/		
tom**b** /tuːm/		

Regional and social variants

Both the amount of aspiration given to /p/ and the degree of devoicing associated with /b/ varies between speakers (Cruttenden 2014: 175). In some dialects (Southern Irish, Highland Scottish) /p/ shows stronger aspiration, while in others it has only little aspiration (Lancashire). In RP it is increasingly typical to reinforce word-final fortis plosives with a glottal closure (see § 5.2.8.2 **glottal reinforcement**). Some speakers may also devoice /b/ in intervocalic positions.

Comparison with Spanish and advice

There are two issues that Spanish speakers should attend to in this group: the distinction between /p/ and /b/ in initial and final positions, and the fully voiced realisation of intervocalic /b/ (Cruttenden 2014: 175; Estebas Vilaplana 2009: 49–62).

Whereas in Spanish /b/ is always voiced, in English it is devoiced [b̥] in initial and final positions, and so in these two contexts [b] sounds close to [p]. Accordingly, in order to not sound foreign and not to affect the intelligibility of the two bilabial plosives, it is essential that SSLE pronounce [**pʰ**] with aspiration in stressed syllable-initial position (***appear*** [əˈpʰɪə]); otherwise, as already explained, they will sound foreign and communication problems may arise because the absence of aspiration suggests /b/ to an English ear, and so words such as ***pen*** may be misunderstood as ***Ben***, ***pin*** as ***bin*** and the like. Furthermore, the main cue to distinguish /**p**/ and /**b**/ when they precede /**l r w j**/, as in ***plead*** – ***bleed***, ***pray*** – ***bray***, is the devoicing of the latter only when they follow accented syllable initial aspirated /p/, giving the following contrasts [pl̥iːd] – [bliːd], [pɹ̥eɪ] – [bɹeɪ] (Dale and Poms 1986; Swan and Smith 2001; Avery and Ehrlich 1992; Gleason 2012; Cruttenden 2014: 328–329). In final positions, no problems seem to arise because speakers of Spanish tend to pronounce [b] as [p]. In this context, the major distinguishing cue that native English speakers use is not aspiration because /p/ tends to be unaspirated, but rather the length of the preceding vowel: it is shorter if followed by [**p˭**] (*ro**p**e* [ɹəˈʊp˭]) than when the following sound is devoiced (*ro**b**e* [ɹəːʊb̥]). Nevertheless, SSLE should take special care not to pronounce word-final /b/ as [f] in such words as ***pub*** *[paf], which may occur as an interference from the tendency of Spanish to fricativise final plosives (Gallardo del Puerto 2005: 200).

Another aspect that causes a strong foreign accent is the tendency that Spanish speakers have to produce a voiced bilabial fricative [β] in intervocalic position, as in *ro**b**o* 'theft' [ˈroβo], when this is the only environment in which RP /b/ is a fully voiced bilabial stop (*ro**bb**er* [ˈɹɒbəʳ]). To overcome this pronunciation problem, Spanish learners are advised to produce English intervocalic [b] as the initial sound of the word ***b**ola* 'ball'.

Further practice

AI 4.1 The spellings of RP /p/. Further practice

pack /pæk/	**p**lay /pleɪ/	ta**p**er /ˈteɪpə/
sim**ple** /ˈsɪmpl̩/	**pepp**er /ˈpepə/	ho**pp**ing /ˈhɒpɪŋ/
ca**p** /kæp/	ta**p** /tæp/	

Perha**p**s you can **p**ay for the sho**pp**ing?
/pəˈhæps ju kən peɪ fə ðə ˈʃɒpɪŋ/

She **p**lays the **p**iano **p**erfectly.
/ʃi pleɪz ðə pɪˈænəʊ ˈpɜːfɪktli/

Peter **P**i**p**er **p**icked a **p**eck of **p**ickled **pepp**ers.
/ˈpiːtə ˈpaɪpə pɪkt ə pek əv ˈpɪkl̩d ˈpepəz/

AI 4.2 The spellings of RP /b/. Further practice

back /bæk/	**b**in /bɪn/	clu**b** /klʌb/
sym**b**ol /ˈsɪmbl̩/	a**b**road /əˈbrɔːd/	ra**bb**it /ˈræbɪt/
ca**b** /kæb/	ru**bb**er /ˈrʌbə/	

Betty **b**rought **b**ags of **b**eautiful pe**bb**les.
/ˈbeti ˈbrɔːt bægz əv ˈbjuːtəfl̩ ˈpebl̩z/

My **b**rown ra**bb**it eats ca**bb**age and **b**ananas.
/maɪ braʊn ˈræbɪt iːts ˈkæbɪdʒ ənd bəˈnɑːnəz/

We'd **b**etter **b**ook a ca**b**.
/wid ˈbetə bʊk ə kæb/

Betty and **B**o**b** **b**rought **b**ack **b**lue **b**alloons from the **b**ig **b**azaar.
/ˈbeti ənd bɒb ˈbrɔːt bæk bluː bəˈluːnz frəm ðə bɪg bəˈzɑː/

4.2.1.2 Alveolar plosives /t d/

IPA Symbols

t Lower-case T.
d Lower-case D.

Identification

/**t**/ Fortis voiceless alveolar plosive.
/**d**/ Lenis voiced alveolar plosive.

Allophones

/**t**/	/**d**/
[**tʰ**] 'aspirated'	
[**t˭**] 'unaspirated'	
[**ʔ**] 'glottalised'	
[**ɾ**] 'alveolar tap'	
[**t̬**] 'voiced'	[**d̥**] 'devoiced'
[**t̚**] 'non-audible release'	[**d̚**] 'non-audible release'
[**t˄**] 'unreleased'	[**d˄**] 'unreleased'
[**tⁿ**] 'nasal release'	[**dⁿ**] 'nasal release'
[**tˡ**] 'lateral release'	[**dˡ**] 'lateral release'
[**t̪͆**] 'labio-dental'	[**d̪͆**] 'labio-dental'
[**t̠**] 'retracted' 'post-alveolar'	[**d̠**] 'retracted' 'post-alveolar'
[**tʷ**] 'labialised'	[**dʷ**] 'labialised'
[**tʲ**] 'palatalised'	[**dʲ**] 'palatalised'
[**s**] 'voiceless alveolar fricative'	[**z**] 'voiced alveolar fricative'

Description

When we pronounce /**t**/, the soft palate is in its raised position and the tip of the tongue comes into contact with the alveolar ridge so that a closure is formed and the lung air is blocked at that point. The air escapes upon the sudden separation of the alveolar closure producing a kind of explosion. The vocal folds do not vibrate, but are wide apart. /t/ is produced with more muscular energy than its voiced counterpart and it reduces the length of preceding vocalic and sonorant sounds (*beat* [biˑt]).

/**d**/ is articulated in the same way as /t/, but with less muscular energy, and the vocal folds may vibrate for all or part of the compression stage. Aspiration does not take place in the production of this sound, nor does it shorten the length of preceding vocalic or sonorant sounds (*bead* [biːd]).

See the animations and videos under RP /t/ and /d/ (compared with Spanish /t d/) in the Sound Bank of the EPSS Multimedia Lab.

Environment and main allophonic realisations

RP /t d/ can appear in all possible contexts. In syllable-initial stressed position /t/ is **aspirated** [**t^h**] (tea [t^{h}iː], *attire* [əˈt^{h}aɪə]). Finally in the word, it loses some of that aspiration [**t$^=$**] (*cat* [k^{h}æt$^=$]), and when preceded by /s/ it is **unaspirated** [**t$^=$**] (*stay* [ˈst$^=$eɪ]). Considering voice, between voiced sounds /t/ acquires some **voicing** [t̬] (*attain* [əˈt̬eɪn], *spitting* [ˈspɪt̬ɪŋ]) and /d/ is **fully voiced** (*addition* [əˈdɪʃn̩], *London* [ˈlʌndən], *ladder* [ˈlædə^r]), but the latter loses some of its voicing [**d̥**] when it occurs in initial position (*day* [d̥eɪ]) and is completely devoiced in final position (*cod* [kɒd̥]). In syllable-final positions, /t/ is commonly reinforced or replaced by a glottal closure (*late* [leɪʔt] [leɪʔ], *bent* [benʔt] [benʔ]) (for further details see § 5.2.8.2 on **glottalisation** and **glottaling**). In addition, in weakly accented contexts /t d/ are especially liable to **affrication** [**t^s d^z**] (*time* [ˈt^{s}aɪm], *dime* [d^{s}aɪm]) or even replacement by corresponding fricatives (*important* [ɪmˈpɔːt^{s}n̩t] [ɪmˈpɔːsn̩t]) (see § 5.2.8.1 on **affrication** and **fricativisation**).

In consonantal clusters, both plosives are incomplete, with non-**audible release** [**t˺ d˺**], if followed by another plosive or by an affricate (*football* [ˈfʊt˺bɔːl], *white chalk* [ˈwaɪt ˈtʃɔːk], *bad play* [ˈbæd˺ ˈpleɪ], *bed changes* [ˈbed˺ ˈtʃeɪndʒɪz]), or **unreleased** [**t^ d^**], if followed by a homorganic plosive (*white doll* [waɪt^ dɒl], *bad tan* [ˈbæd^ tæn]). They may also be produced with **nasal release** [**t^n d^n**] and nasal plosion will be heard, when followed by a (homorganic) nasal consonant (*curtness* [ˈkɜːt^{n}nəs], *nutmeg* [ˈnʌt^{m}meg], *not now* [nɒt^n naʊ], *admit* [əd^{m}ˈmɪt], *red notebook* [ˈred^n ˈnəʊtbʊk]). Lateral plosion will be heard if [l] follows, in which case alveolar plosives have a homorganic **lateral release** [**t^l d^l**] (*at least* [ət^l liːst] *middle* [ˈmɪd^{l}l̩]), that is, only part of the alveolar obstruction is removed as the tongue-tip contact remains. Note also that in the above examples and elsewhere sonorants are devoiced after /t/ (*try* [tɹ̥aɪ]).

The alveolar contact is the most sensitive to the place of articulation of a subsequent sound (see § 5.2.7), which is demonstrated by the ease with which alveolar consonants, particularly /t d/, may be elided in consonantal clusters (see § 5.4). Thus, alveolar stops may have **post-alveolar** realisations [̠], if followed by /r/, which is realised as a voiced fricative [ɹ̝] after /d/, but as a voiceless fricative after /t/, so that the two allophonic series are pronounced [**d̠ɹ̝**] [**t̠ɹ̝̊**] (***dry*** [d̠ɹaɪ], ***tray*** [t̠ɹ̥eɪ]). **Dental** allophones [**t̪ d̪**] are produced before /θ ð/ (***not*** *those* [ˈnɒt̪ ðəʊz], ***hide*** *this* [ˈhaɪd̪ðɪs]).

The lip position for the articulation of /t d/ will also be conditioned by that of the adjacent sounds. Thus, allophonic realisations show different degrees of anticipatory **lip-rounding** (***t****oo* [tʷuː], ***t****wice* [tʷwaɪs], ***d****oor* [dʷɔː], ***d****windle* [ˈdʷwɪndl̩]) or **lip-spreading** (***t****ea* [tʲiː], ***d****uty* [ˈdʲjuːti]) in the vicinity of rounded and spread vowels or semi-vowels, respectively (see § 5.2.3).

Spellings

Table 21: The spellings of RP /t d/

/**t**/	/**d**/
<t> vi**t**al /ˈvaɪtl̩/, **t**ell /tel/, ca**t** /kæt/	<d> ma**d** /mæd/, **d**ate /deɪt/, me**d**al /ˈmedl̩/
<tt> hi**tt**ing /ˈhɪtɪŋ/, a**tt**ack /əˈtæk/	<dd> a**dd**ed /ˈædɪd/, E**dd**y /ˈedi/
<th>[65] **Th**ames /temz/, **Th**omas /ˈtɒməs/ **th**yme /taɪm/, **Th**ailand /ˈtaɪlænd/	
<-ed> wash**ed** /wɒʃt/, laugh**ed** /lɑːft/	<-ed> open**ed** /ˈəʊpᵊnd/, bomb**ed** /bɒmd/
<-d> type**d** /taɪpt/	
<tte> cigare**tte** /ˌsɪgəˈret/	
silent <gh> + <t> brou**ght** /ˈbrɔːt/	
Rare cases <tw> **tw**o /tuː/ silent <ch> + <t> ya**cht** /jɒt/	**Rare cases** silent <l> + <d> wou**ld** /wʊd/

65 Note that the NP of <th> spellings is /θ/ or /ð/ (see § 4.2.2.2), although they may also be silent (*as***th***ma* /ˈæsmə/).

Table 21 shows that the inflectional ending <-ed> for past tenses and past participles of regular verbs ending in a voiced sound other than /d/ is pronounced /d/ (*seiz**ed*** /siːzd/, *play**ed*** /pleɪd/); but if they end in a voiceless consonant other than /t/, then it is pronounced /t/ (*pack**ed*** /pækt/, *stretch**ed*** /stretʃt/). When the last sound of the stem of such verbal forms is a /d/ or a /t/, the inflectional ending is pronounced /ɪd/ (*land**ed*** /ˈlændɪd/, *wait**ed*** /ˈweɪtɪd/).

Adjectives ending in <-ed>, on the other hand, follow the same pronunciation principles as those at work in the pronunciation of the verbs from which they derive: /ɪd/ or /əd/ after /t/ or /d/ (*excit**ed*** /ɪkˈsaɪtɪd/ – /ɪkˈsaɪtəd/), /d/ after voiced consonants other than /d/ (*surpris**ed*** /səˈpraɪzd/), and /t/ after voiceless consonants other than /t/ (*embarrass**ed*** /ɪmˈbærəst/). There are a number of adjectives, however, that contravene these principles and have different pronunciations for the verbal and adjectival uses of the same <*-ed*> forms, as shown below:

Spelling	**Adjective**	**Verb**
ag**ed**	/ˈeɪdʒɪd/ – /ˈeɪdʒd/	/eɪdʒd/
bless**ed**	/ˈblesɪd/ – /ˈblesəd/	/blest/
crabb**ed**	/ˈkræbɪd/ – /ˈkræbd/	/kræbd/
crook**ed**	/ˈkrʊkɪd/	/krʊkt/
dogg**ed**	/ˈdɒgɪd/	/dɒgd/
jagg**ed**	/ˈdʒægɪd/	/dʒægd/
learn**ed**	/ˈlɜːnɪd/	/lɜːnd/
ragg**ed**	/ˈrægɪd/	/rægd/
rugg**ed**	/ˈrʌgɪd/	
-legg**ed**	/ˈlegɪd/ – ˈlegd/	
nak**ed**	/ˈneɪkɪd/	
sacr**ed**	/ˈseɪkrɪd/	
wick**ed**	/ˈwɪkɪd/	
wretch**ed**	/ˈretʃɪd/	

In addition, the letter *t* is silent in the combinations <-f**t**en>, <-s**t**en>, <-s**t**le>, and in several words of French origin, as shown in the word lists below, while in a few common words pronunciations may be found with /t/, or more frequently, without it: *of**t**en* (/ˈɒftᵊn/, /ˈɒfᵊn/), *ches**t**nut* (/ˈtʃestnʌt/, /ˈtʃesnʌt/), and *Chris**t**mas* (/ˈkrɪstməs/, ˈkrɪsməs/).

chas**t**en /ˈtʃeɪsᵊn/
chris**t**en /ˈkrɪsᵊn/
fas**t**en /ˈfɑːsᵊn/
glis**t**en /ˈɡlɪsᵊn/
has**t**en /ˈheɪsᵊn/
lis**t**en /ˈlɪsᵊn/
mois**t**en /ˈmɔɪsᵊn/

apos**t**le /əˈpɒsl̩/
cas**t**le /ˈkɑːsl̩/
jos**t**le /ˈdʒɒsl̩/
nes**t**le /ˈnesl̩/
rus**t**le /ˈrʌsl̩/
this**t**le /ˈθɪsl̩/
whis**t**le /ˈwɪsl̩/

French loanwords
buffe**t** /ˈbʊfeɪ/
gourme**t** /ˈɡʊəmeɪ/
mor**t**gage /ˈmɔːɡɪdʒ/
nouga**t** /ˈnuːɡɑː/
parque**t** /ˈpɑːkeɪ/
rappor**t** /ræˈpɔː/
taro**t** /ˈtærəʊ/
pencha**nt** /ˈpɑːnʃɑːn/[66]

Turning to instances of silent *d* spellings, they occur in such common words as *han**d**kerchief* (/ˈhæŋkətʃɪf/) and *han**d**some* ˈ(hænsəm), while *san**d**wich* and *We**d**nesday* have alternative pronunciations with or without /d/, the latter being more common (/ˈsændwɪdʒ/, /ˈsænwɪdʒ/, /ˈwednzdeɪ/, /ˈwenzdeɪ/).

In rapid colloquial speech /tj/ and /dj/ are frequently reduced to [tʃ] and [dʒ], so that no contrast is made between words like ***due*** and ***J**ew*, the first syllable of ***T**uesday* and the initial sound in ***ch**oose*.

Regional and social variants

The main variants of English alveolar plosives concern /**t**/, involving its **glottalisation**, the amount of **aspiration** associated with it, as well as its realisation as a brief **alveolar tap** [ɾ] in intervocalic positions, the latter being a particularly common realisation in high frequency words and expressions (*be**tt**er* [ˈberə]) (Collins and Mees 2003: 162; Cruttenden 2014: 178). Unlike American English, in RP there is no tendency to neutralise the /t/ – /d/ contrast in pairs such as *coa**t**ing – co**d**ing, ra**t**ing – rai**d**ing, whi**t**er – wi**d**er*.

While the absence of glottal effects is a feature of Conservative RP, the use of **glottalised** [**ʔt**] or the replacement of /t/ by a glottal stop [**ʔ**] is now acceptable in **Estuary English**[67] (***get off*** [ˈgeʔtɒf] [ˈgeʔɒf], ***got it*** [ˈgɒʔtɪt] [ˈgɒʔɪt]). Likewise, the production of [ʔ] preceding syllabic [ɫ̩] (***kettle*** [ˈkeʔɫ̩], ***bottle*** [ˈboʔɫ̩]) and especially in unaccented intervocalic word-medial positions (*la**t**er* [ˈleɪʔə]) is typical of regional varieties such as Cockney and Glasgow English (see § 5.2.8.2).

The amount of aspiration associated with /t/ also varies considerably across accents of English. It is higher in Irish, Indian English and in Welsh- or Gaelic-influenced English (e.g. Western Highlands) than in RP, but there is generally

---

66 As we have seen in Section 3.3.1 and you can also see here, the endings <-et> and <-ot> of French loanwords have diphthongal values.

67 **Estuary English** refers to a variety of British English spoken in the counties adjacent to the estuary of the River Thames, and thus displaying the influence of London regional speech, especially in pronunciation (Crystal 2008: 173–174).

little aspiration in Lancashire, South African and Scottish English. In addition, tap [ɾ] realisations of /t/ in post-accented intervocalic positions, both within words and at close-knit word boundaries, are typical of GA (*butter* [ˈbʌɾə], *put it* [ˈpʊɾɪt]), but they may also be heard in South African English and in Southern Irish English, as well as in Cockney as an alternative to [ʔ].

Three other allophonic realisations may also be heard: as post-alveolar approximant [ɹ], in some urban varieties of South Lancashire and West Yorkshire, as **retroflex**[68] [ʈ], in Indian English, whereas in Irish English both /t/ and /d/ are realised as **apico-alveolar fricatives** [t̞ d̞] whenever it appears in syllable coda between vowels (*bottom* [ˈbɑt̞əm] and word-finally (*but* [bʌt̞], *wood* [wud̞]) (Hickey 2007: 3128)

Comparison with Spanish and advice

SSLE should pay particular attention to five issues concerning the articulation of /t/ and /d/ to aim at a native-like pronunciation: (1) adopt an alveolar place of articulation, (2) aspirate [tʰ] in stressed syllable-initial positions, (3) distinguish word final /t/ and /d/, (4) produce /d/ as a plosive in medial and final positions, and (5) not omit /t/ or /d/ in consonant clusters (Finch and Ortiz Lira 1982: 68; Gallardo del Puerto 2005: 196–197; Estebas Vilaplana 2009: 49–62; Mott 2011: 256; Cruttenden 2014: 179).

A common pronunciation problem of SSLE is the confusion of the place of articulation /t d/, which is alveolar in RP, the tip of the tongue being in contact with the alveolar ridge, but dental in Spanish, the closure being made between the tip of the tongue and the upper teeth. This is an extremely noticeable error due to the high frequency of these two sounds. In order to master their fluent use in connected speech, SSLE should practice the alveolar stricture, whose recognition and production should not be difficult as it is the same one used to pronounce Spanish /n/. To this effect it can also be helpful to practise homorganic affricated forms of /t d/, [tˢ dᶻ], (*time* [ˈtˢaɪm], *dime* [ˈdˢaɪm]), avoiding heterorganic dental affrications of the [tθ dð] type (see § 5.2.8.1).

Similarly, every effort should be made to produce an aspirated [**tʰ**] in stressed syllable initial position (*tea* [tʰiː]), as well as to avoid word-final plosive replacement of /t/ for /d/ keeping in mind that final /t/, but not final /d/ despite being devoiced [d̥], reduces the length of the previous vowel or sonorant (*beat* [biˑt]) (Dale and Poms 1986; Swan and Smith 2001; Catford 1987; Avery and Ehrlich 1992; Gleason 2012).

68 The label **retroflex** refers to a place of articulation in which the tip of the tongue is curled back in the direction of the front part of the hard palate (Crystal 2008: 415).

Another aspect that causes a strong foreign accent is the tendency that SSLE have to produce a voiced dental fricative [ð] in intervocalic position, as in ***lado*** 'side' [ˈlaðo], when this is the only environment in which RP /**d**/ is a fully voiced alveolar stop (*la**dd**er* [ˈlædəʳ]). Similarly, in word final positions SSLE may mispronounce word-final /d/ as a voiced [ð] or voiceless [θ] fricative because these are the realisations that occur in Spanish (*bonda**d*** 'goodness' [bonðað], [bonðaθ]). This mispronuciation of [ð] for [d] may cause communication problems derived from the loss of the /d/ – /ð/ contrast that distinguishes many English words (*bree**d*** [ˈbriːd] – *brea**th*** [ˈbriːð], *ri**d**e* /ˈraɪd/ – *wri**th**e* /ˈraɪð/). To overcome this pronunciation problem, SSLE are advised to produce English intervocalic and word-final [d] as the initial sound of the word ***d**ota* 'supply', although English /d/ is more retracted.

Lastly, the **omission** of /**t**/ and /**d**/ in **consonant clusters**, especially when they represent grammatical categories such as negation or tense, or when /t/ and /d/ precede homorganic /s/ and /z/ should be avoided as this is one of the factors that most influence the intelligibility and comprehensibility of SSLE. Accordingly, special care should be taken to pronounce final consonants, as for instance in *don'**t**, walke**d**, robbe**d**, Fre**d**'s car, i**t**'s true, wha**t**'s this* as [dəʊnt], [wɔːkt], [rɒbd], [ˈfredz kɑː], [ɪts ˈtruː] [wɒts ˈðɪs], instead of *[don], *[wɔːk], *[rɒb], *[ˈfrez kɑː], *[ɪs ˈtruː], *[wɒs ˈðɪs]).

Further practice

AI 4.3 The spellings of RP /t/. Further practice

tin /tɪn/	**t**ry /traɪ/	**t**rain /treɪn/
me**t**al /ˈmetl̩/	**t**wen**t**y /ˈtwenti/	kno**t** /nɒt/
be**t** /bet/	deb**t** /det/	

I**t**'s **t**wen**t**y **t**o **t**wo.
/ɪts ˈtwenti tə tuː/

Wha**t** have you go**t** in your pocke**t**?
/ˈwɒt həv ju ˈgɒt ɪn jə ˈpɒkɪt/

Try in**t**erne**t**.
/traɪ ˈɪntənet/

The **t**wo-**t**wen**t**y-**t**wo **t**rain **t**ore through the **t**unnel.
/ðə tuː ˈtwenti tuː treɪn ˈtɔː θruː ðə ˈtʌnl̩/

AI 4.4 The spellings of RP /d/. Further practice

din /dɪn/	**d**rive /draɪv/	opene**d** /ˈəʊpənd/
me**d**al /ˈmedl̩/	a**dd**e**d** /ˈædɪd/	mi**dd**le /ˈmɪdl̩/
be**d** /bed/	**d**inner /ˈdɪnə/	

Don't **d**rink and **d**rive, it's ba**d**.
/dəʊnt drɪŋk ənd draɪv | ɪts bæd/

Dinner will be serve**d** **d**ownstairs before mi**d**night.
/ˈdɪnə wɪl bi sɜːvd ˌdaʊnˈsteəz bɪˈfɔː ˈmɪdnaɪt/

A **d**ozen **d**ouble **d**amask **d**inner napkins.
/ə ˈdʌzn̩ ˈdʌbl̩ ˈdæməsk ˈdɪnə ˈnæpkɪnz/

Donal**d** **D**uck was a **D**isney character **d**ressed in **d**ark blue and re**d**.
/ˈdɒnl̩d dʌk wəz ə ˈdɪzni ˈkærəktə drest ɪn dɑːk bluː ənd red/

4.2.1.3 Velar plosives /k g/

IPA Symbols

k Lower-case K.
g Opentail G.

Identification

/**k**/ Fortis voiceless velar plosive.
/**g**/ Lenis voiced velar plosive.

Allophones

/k/	/g/
[kʰ] 'aspirated'	
[k⁼] 'unaspirated'	
[ʔ] 'glottalised'	
[k̬] 'voiced'	[g̊] 'devoiced'
[k˺] 'non-audible release'	[g˺] 'non-audible release'
[k^] 'unreleased'	[g^] 'unreleased'
[kⁿ] 'nasal release'	[gⁿ] 'nasal release'
[kˡ] 'lateral release'	[gˡ] 'lateral release'
[k̟] 'advanced' 'pre-velar'	[g̟] 'advanced' 'pre-velar'
[k̠] 'retracted' 'post-velar'	[g̠] 'retracted' 'post-velar'
[kʷ] 'labialised'	[gʷ] 'labialised'
[tʲ] 'palatalised'	[gʲ] 'palatalised'
[x] 'voiceless velar fricative'	[ɣ] 'voiced velar fricative'

Description

When we pronounce /**k**/ the two articulators, the back of the tongue and the soft palate, form a complete closure so that the lung airstream is stopped behind it. As the soft palate is in its raised position, there are two closures. In the release stage the two articulators are separated and the lung air goes out of the mouth producing a kind of explosion. The vocal folds are wide apart and do not vibrate. /k/ is produced with more muscular energy than its voiced counterpart, and it shortens the vocalic and sonorant sounds preceding it (*leak* [liˑk]).

/**g**/ is pronounced in the same way as /k/ but with less muscular effort, and the vocal folds may vibrate for all or part of the compression stage. Aspiration does not take place in the production of this sound, nor does it shorten the length of preceding vocalic or sonorant sounds (*league* [liːg]).

See the animations and videos under RP /k/ and /g/ (compared with Spanish /k g/) in the Sound Bank of the EPSS Multimedia Lab.

Environment and main allophonic realisations

RP /k g/ can occur in all positions in a word. Initially in a stressed syllable /k/ is **aspirated** [k^{h}] (*key* [k^{h}iː], *accustomed* [əˈk^{h}ʌstəmd]), but it loses some of that aspiration [k$^{=}$] in word-final positions (*tick* [tɪk$^{=}$]), and is **unaspirated** [k$^{=}$] when preceded by /s/ (*scum* [ˈsk$^{=}$ʌm]). Considering voicing, betwen voiced sounds the voiceless velar plosive has a **voiced** realisation (*akin* [əˈk̬ɪn]) whereas the voiced velar plosive is **fully voiced** (*anger* [ˈæŋgə], *argue* [ˈɑːgjuː], *eager* [ˈiːgə], *buggy* [ˈbʌgi]), but /g/ **loses** some of its **voicing** [g̊] when occurring in initial position (*goat* [g̊əʊt]) and it is completely devoiced in final position (*dog* [dɒg̊]). /k/ may also be reinforced by **glottalisation** [ʔ] (*actor* [ˈæ͜ʔktə]) when a vowel, nasal or lateral precedes it and it is followed by another consonant or a pause; and in Cockney and other regional (South East) urban dialects /k/ is replaced by the glottal stop word-medially and in consonant clusters (*ticket* [ˈtɪʔɪt]) (see 5.2.8.2).

In addition to the affricated variants (discussed in Section 5.2.8.1), other allophonic variants of both plosives are those with **non-audible release** [**k**̚ **g**̚], if followed by another plosive or by an affricate (*locked* [ˈlɒk̚t], *thick door* [ˈθɪk̚ dɔː], *rugby* [ˈrʌg̚bi], *big gesture* [ˈbɪg̚ ˈdʒestʃə]), or those that are **unreleased** [**k**ˆ **g**ˆ], if followed by a homorganic plosive (*dark grey* [dɑːkˆ greɪ], *big game* [bɪgˆ geɪm]). They will be produced with nasal plosion and **nasal release** [**k**^{n} **g**^{n}], if followed by a nasal consonant (*acknowledge* [ək^{n}ˈnɒlɪdʒ], *back movement* [ˈbæk^{m} ˈmuːvmənt], *dogma* [ˈdɒg^{m}mə], *big novel* [ˈbɪg^{n} ˈnɒvl̩]), and they will have a lateral plosion and lateral **release** [**k**^{l} **g**^{l}] before [l], with the airstream escaping laterally round the point of alveolar closure (*clean* [k^{l}liːn], *struggle* [ˈstrʌg^{l}l̩]). In the above examples and elsewhere, notice also that /k/ has a devoicing effect on an adjacent sonorant (*acknowledge* [ək^{n}ˈn̥ɒlɪdʒ], *clean* [kˡl̥iːn], *equal* [ˈiːkʷw̥əl], *dockyard* [ˈdɒkj̊ɑːd]).

Finally, it should be borne in mind that the velar contact is affected by the place of articulation of a subsequent sound (see § 5.2.7). Hence, velar stops will have **post-velar** realisations [̠], if followed by a back vowel [uː ʊ ɒ ɔː] or semi-vowel [**w**] (*cool* [k̠uːɫ], *good* [ḡʊd], or **pre-velar** realisations [̟], before a **front** vowel [iː ɪ] or glide consonant [j] (*king* [k̟ɪŋ̟], *geese* [g̟iːs]). Similarly, lip position will also vary depending on the articulatory gesture adopted for the adjacent sound. Hence, /k d/ will have allophonic realisations with **lip-rounding** (*cool* [kʷuːɫ], *quite* [kʷwaɪt], *goose* [gʷuːs]) or **lip-spreading** (*kit* [kʲɪt], *geese* [g̟ʲiːs], *cure* [kʲjʊə], *argue* [ˈɑːgʲjuː]) in the vicinity of rounded and spread vowels or semi-vowels, respectively (see § 5.2.3).

Spellings

Table 22: The spellings of RP /k g/

/k/	/g/
<k> / <k> + silent <h> **k**ey /kiː/, tur**k**ey /ˈtɜːki/ ma**k**e /ˈmeɪk/ gym**kh**ana /dʒɪmˈkɑːnə/, **kh**aki /ˈkɑːki/	<g> hu**g** /hʌg/, **g**lad /glæd/
<c>[69] **c**at /kæt/, **c**old /kəʊld/, a**c**t /ækt/	<gg> hu**gg**ed /hʌgd/, e**gg** /eg/
<ck> / <ch> / <che> sa**ck** /sæk/, bla**ck**board /ˈblækbɔːd/ **ch**aracter /ˈkærəktə/, a**che** /eik/	<gu> / <gue> **gu**ide /gaɪd/ lea**gue** /liːg/
<cc> + <a, o, u> / <s> + <c> o**cc**upy /ˈɒkjʊpaɪ/, a**cc**ount /əˈkaʊnt/[70] s**c**are /skeəʳ/, dis**c**uss /dɪˈskʌs/	<g> + silent <h> **gh**astly /ˈgɑːstli/ **gh**etto /ˈgetəʊ/

69 The words ***Celt*** and ***Celtic*** are pronounced /kelt/ and /ˈkeltik/, but in Scotland they are pronounced /selt/ and /ˈseltɪk/. The names of the Glasgow football (***Celtic***) and Boston basketball (***Celtics***) teams also have the latter /s/ pronunciation.

70 Note, however, /ks/ pronunciations of <cc> spellings word-medially followed by <i> or <e> as in such words as ***accent*** /ˈæksənt/, ***succeed*** /səkˈsiːd/ and ***accident*** /ˈæksɪdənt/. In addition, other words like ***flaccid*** may have two possible pronunciations /ˈflæk.sɪd/ or /ˈflæs.ɪd/, while words borrowed from Italian may have /ʧ/, as in *cappuccino* /ˌkæpʊˈʧiːnəʊ/.

<q> + <u>[71] **qu**een /kwiːn/, **qu**irk /kwɜːk/ li**qu**id /ˈlɪkwɪd/, *con**qu**est* /ˈkɒŋkwest/	
<x> /<xe> /ks/ si**x** /sɪks/, a**x**le /æksl̩/ a**xe** /æks/	<x> /gz/ e**x**am /ɪgˈzæm/, e**x**ist /ɪgˈzɪst/ Ale**x**ander /ˌælɪgˈzɑːndə/
French / Spanish loanwords <qu> / <que> **que**ue /kjuː/, li**qu**or /ˈlɪkəʳ/ con**qu**er /ˈkɒŋkəʳ/, **qu**iche /kiːʃ/ mos**qu**ito /məˈskiːtəʊ/, **qu**ay /kiː/ bouti**que** /buːˈtiːk/, bou**qu**et /bʊˈkeɪ/ <cqu> la**cqu**er /ˈlækə/, ra**cqu**et /ˈrækɪt/ <cq> + <u> a**cq**uire /əˈkwaɪə/, a**cq**uaint /əˈkweɪnt/	**French loanwords** <gu> / <gue> **gu**itar /gɪˈtɑː/ fati**gue** /fəˈtiːg/
Rare cases A**kk**adian /əˈkeɪdiən/	

It should be remembered that spellings with both *k/c* and *g* may be silent. The spelling *k/c* is silent in the <**kn**> and <s**c**> digraphs, as illustrated in the word lists below, as well as in a few other words involving <**c**t> and <**ck**> clusters: *indi**c**t* /ɪnˈdaɪt/, vi**c**tual(s) /ˈvɪtl̩/, /ˈvɪtl̩z/, *Conne**c**ticut* /kəˈnetɪkət/, *bla**ck**guard* /ˈblægɑːd/, *Co**ck**burn* /ˈkəʊbɜːn/, /ˈkəʊbən/.

knife /naɪf/ corpus**c**le /ˈkɔːpʌsl̩/
knight /naɪt/ mus**c**le /ˈmʌsl̩/
know /nəʊ/ s**c**eptre /ˈseptə/
knuckle /ˈnʌkl̩/ s**c**ene /siːn/

Turning to <g>, this spelling is silent in the initial and final digraph <**g**n> and in the final cluster <**g**m>.[72]

71 The digraph <qu> is pronounced /kw/ in such words as the aforementioned, but it can also be pronounced /k/ in medial position, especially in words of French or Spanish origin as also illustrated in Table 22.

72 Nevertheless, the *g* of <gm> cluster is pronounced in the following derived words: *paradig-matic* /ˌpærədɪgˈmatɪk/, *phle**g**matic* /flegˈmætɪk, *si**g**nal* /sɪgnl̩/, *si**g**natory* /ˈsɪgnətr̩i/, *assi**g**nation* /ˌæsɪgˈneɪʃn̩/, *resi**g**nation* /ˌrezɪgˈneɪʃn̩/.

gnaw /nɔː/
gnostic /ˈnɒstɪk/
gnocchi /njɒki/
ali**g**n /əˈlaɪn/
assi**g**n /əˈsaɪn/
beni**g**n /bəˈnaɪn
campai**g**n /kæmˈpeɪn/
champa**g**ne /ʃæmˈpeɪn/
desi**g**n /dɪˈzaɪn/
physio**g**nomy /ˌfɪzɪˈɒnəmi/
resi**g**n /rɪˈzaɪn/
sovere**ig**n /ˈsɒvrɪn/
diaphra**g**m /ˈdaɪəfræm/
paradi**g**m /ˈpærədaɪm/
phle**g**m /flem/
synta**g**m /ˈsɪntæm/

Regional and social variants
The main variants of velar plosives concern the degrees of aspiration associated with /k/ (Cruttenden 2014: 182). As in the case of /p t/, more aspiration than in RP is heard in the areas of Celtic influence (Scottish Highlands, Wales and Southern Ireland) and Indian English, whereas lesser aspiration is typical of Lancashire accent.

Comparison with Spanish and advice
It is essential that SSLE pronounce [**kʰ**] with aspiration in **stressed syllable-initial position** ***key*** [kʰiː], taking care to reduce the length of the preceding vowel or sonorant when /k/ occurs word finally (***leak*** [liˑk]), in which case aspiration is optional, but generally it is not produced (Dale and Poms 1986; Swan and Smith 2001; Catford 1987; Avery and Ehrlich 1992; Gleason 2012).

SSLE should also avoid weakening intervocalic /**g**/ to a fricative [ɣ], as in *lago* 'lake' [ˈlaɣo], when this is the only environment in which RP /g/ is a fully voiced velar stop (*lager* [ˈlɑːgəʳ]), as already noted about the other voiced plosives. In addition, learners should refrain from pronouncing initial [w] as [g] in words such as ***wo****man* /ˈwʊmən/, which tend to be wrongly pronounced with initial [gu-], [ɣu-] or [u-] (Finch and Ortiz Lira 1982: 64, 71; Cruttenden 2014: 182; Estebas Vilaplana 2009: 49–62).

Further practice

AI 4.5 The spellings of RP /k/. Further practice

came /keɪm/	**ck**ed /kɪkt/	o**cc**upy /ˈɒkjʊpaɪ/
a**c**tive /ˈæktɪv/	a**cq**uire /əˈkwaɪə/	
ba**ck** /bæk/	ma**k**e /ˈmeɪk/	

I've got **c**a**k**e and bis**c**uits.
/aɪv ˈgɒt keɪk ənd ˈbɪskɪts/

I'll **c**oo**k** the por**k** at si**x** o'clo**ck**.
/aɪl kʊk ðə pɔːk ət sɪks əˈklɒk/

That **c**ruel **c**riminal **kick**ed the **c**at
/ðət krʊəl ˈkrɪmɪnl̩ kɪkt ðə kæt/

Crisp **c**rusts **c**ra**ck**le **c**runchily.
/krɪsp krʌsts ˈkrækl̩ ˈkrʌntʃɪli/

AI 4.6 The spellings of RP /g/. Further practice

game /geɪm/	**g**at /gəʊt/	**gu**itar /gɪˈtɑː/
a**g**nostic /ægˈnɒstɪk/	hu**gg**ing /ˈhʌgɪŋ/	bi**gg**er /ˈbɪgə/
ba**g** /bæg/	fati**gue** /fəˈtiːg/	

Give me a bi**gg**er book.
/gɪv miː ə ˈbɪgə bʊk/

He's **g**one to **g**et a **g**reen ba**g**.
/hiz gɒn tə ˈget ə griːn bæg/

The **g**round will look **g**reener when the **g**rass has **g**rown.
/ðə graʊnd wɪl lʊk ˈgriːnə wen ðə grɑːs həz grəʊn/

Cows **g**raze in **g**roves on **g**rass which **g**rows in **g**rooves in **g**roves.
/kaʊz greɪz ɪn grəʊvz ɒn grɑːs wɪtʃ grəʊz ɪn gruːvz ɪn grəʊvz/

4.2.2 Fricatives

RP fricatives /**f v θ ð s z ʃ ʒ h**/ can be characterised along the following four articulatorily parameters (see also e.g. Gimson 1984: 178–192; Roach 2005: 49–54; Collins and Mees 2003: 139–148; Collins and Mees 2009: 88–90; Cruttenden 2014: 192–208):

(1) **Manner of articulation**: to pronounce a fricative consonant the two articulators used in their production do not come into contact as for the plosives. So, when going out of the mouth through the passage formed by the articulators the lung air produces air turbulence, or a kind of **friction** or "hissing sound" (Roach 2005: 48). The soft palate is in its raised position thereby closing the nasal passage and releasing the lung air through the oral tract. There is an on/off-glide with respect to the adjacent sound (manifested acoustically by formant transitions), which is more noticeable in the case of vowels.

(2) **Place of articulation** involves five possible points, which is rare in the world's languages (Maddieson 1984: 43) and is in general a more important distinctive cue than the distinctions between voiced and voiceless pairs of each place of articulation. /**f v**/ are **labio-dental** because the two articulators used to produce them are the lower lip, the active articulator, and the upper front teeth, the passive articulator. /**s z**/ are **alveolar**, and so the tip of the tongue, the active articulator, rises towards the alveolar ridge, the passive articulator, the airstream escaping along a **groove**; in contrast /**θ ð**/ use a flatter configuration, the airstream escaping through the dental **slit** that is left between the tip of the tongue, the active articulator, and the upper front teeth. /**ʃ ʒ**/ use a **palato-alveolar**[73] closure that is left between blade of the tongue and the palato-alveolar region, with flat tongue tip and blade and grooving further back, but the latter is not as deep as the one used in /**s z**/. Finally, /**h**/ is glottal. This means that the lung air produces friction when it goes out through the glottis and throughout the oral tract, while the articulators are ready in order to produce the following vowel. Phonetically, /h/ can be described as "a voiceless vowel with the quality of the voiced vowel that follows it" (Roach 2005: 60).

(3) **Position of the vocal folds**: the vocal folds do not vibrate when /**f θ s ʃ h**/ are pronounced, and so these fricative consonants are **voiceless** or unvoiced. In contrast, when /**v ð z ʒ**/ are pronounced the vocal folds usually vibrate, but these sounds may lose some of their voicing if they occur initially or finally in the word, and are fully voiced between voiced sounds (Haggard 1978; Docherty 1992).

(4) **Force of articulation and length**: /**f θ s ʃ h**/ are pronounced with more muscular force or energy than /**v ð z ʒ**/. So these two subgroups of fricatives are described as **fortis** or **strong**, and **lenis** or **weak** consonants, respectively. As mentioned before, this feature is quite important because it affects

73 Although in the latest version of the IPA alphabet the fricatives /ʃ ʒ/ and by extension the affricates /tʃ dʒ/ are classified as post-alveolar (see Table 3), in this book the former IPA label **palato-alveolar** is retained to better reflect the palatalized alveolar nature of these sounds.

the length of the preceding vocalic or sonorant sound, which is shortened when followed by a fortis consonant, either within the word or at word-boundaries. For instance, in ***loath*** [ləˑʊθ] and ***roof*** [ruˑf] the vowel is reduced; while in ***loathe*** [ləːʊð] and ***those*** [ðəːʊz] the diphthong is fully long because it is followed by lenis [ð] and [z] (see § 2.3.1.4 and 2.3.2.4). Note, however, that although voiceless fricatives shorten the vowels and sonorants that precede them, they are themselves longer than their voiced counterparts (Subtelny *et al.* 1966; Malécot 1968).

Acoustically, as already detailed in Section 2.4.3, fricative consonants are characterised by **high-frequency noise** (random energy pattern with striations), which is especially strong in voiceless fricatives /**f θ s ʃ h**/, and even more so in the case of the two sibilants /**s ʃ**/. Voiced fricatives, on the other hand, show weaker noise and voicing bar, there may being no noise at all when producing the non-sibilant ones /**v ð**/ (see § 2.4.3). Auditorily, sibilants /**s z ʃ ʒ**/ are characterised by sound intensity, i.e. they are louder and longer compared to non-sibilants /**f v θ ð h**/.

Under each place of articulation below it will be shown that the main allophones of fricatives concern different degrees of voicing or devoicing (see also § 5.2 and 5.3), as well as the affrication of plosives with [ɸ β s z x ɣ] and the fricativisation of approximants /r l w j/ that are explained in Section § 5.2.8.1. Finally, as regards advice to SSLE, attention should be centred on reproducing with precision the place of articulation required for labio-dental, dental, alveolar and palato-alveolar articulations, and on the reduction of length that fortis fricatives exert on preceding vowel and sonorant sounds (Finch and Ortiz Lira 1982: 59, 60, 68–70; Estebas Vilaplana 2009: 64–81; Cruttenden 2014: 194).

4.2.2.1 Labio-dental fricatives: RP /f v/ vs. PSp /f/ /f v/

IPA Symbols

f Lower-case F.
v Lower-case V.

Identification

/**f**/ Fortis voiceless labio-dental fricative.
/**v**/ Lenis voiced labio-dental fricative.

Allophones

/f/	/v/
[f̬] 'voiced'	[v̥] 'devoiced'
[f̟] 'advanced'	[v̟] 'advanced'
[f̠] 'retracted'	[v̠] 'retracted'
[fʷ] 'labialised'	[vʷ] 'labialised'
[fʲ] 'palatalised'	[vʲ] 'palatalised'
[v] 'voiced labio-dental fricative'	[f] 'voiceless labio-dental fricative'

Description

When we pronounce /**f**/ the lower lip approximates to the upper front teeth, a small passage is formed, and the soft palate is in its raised position. As a result, when the lung air goes out through that passage it produces friction, a kind of hissing sound. The vocal folds are apart and do not vibrate. /f/ is produced with more muscular energy than its voiced counterpart and it shortens the vocalic sounds that precede it (***leaf*** [liˑf], ***laugh*** [lɑˑf], ***life*** [laˑɪf]).

/v/ is pronounced in the same way as /f/, but, in this case, the vocal folds show different degrees of vocal fold vibration, depending on its phonetic context. /v/ is also produced with less energy than its voiceless counterpart, and it does not shorten the length of preceding vocalic or sonorant sounds (***leave*** [liːv], *carve* [kɑːv], ***cave*** [keːɪv]).

See the animations and videos under RP /f/ and /v/ (compared with Spanish /f/) in the Sound Bank of the EPSS Multimedia Lab.

Environment and main allophonic realisations

RP /f v/ can occur in all word positions. /**f**/ remains voiceless initially (***fit*** [fɪt]) and finally (***cough*** [kɒf], but between voiced sounds it acquires some voicing (***offer*** [ˈɒf̬ə]). /**v**/ is **fully voiced** betwen voiced sounds (*ever* [ˈevəʳ], *canvas* [ˈkænvəs], *silver* [ˈsɪlvə]), but it loses some of its voicing [v̥] when occurring in initial position (***voice*** [v̥ɔɪs]) and it is completely devoiced in final position (***give*** [gɪv̥]). Besides, /v/ may be realised as [**f**] before a voiceless consonant at close-knit word-boundaries, regularly in ***have to*** and more rarely in other sequences (*give to*, ***have ten***), or it may be **elided** in rapid, colloquial speech in the unaccented forms of ***have*** and ***of*** regardless of the following sound (*could have played* [kəd ə ˈpleɪd], *lots **of** men* [ˈlɒts ə ˈmen]).

In addition, the labio-dental contact is affected by the place of articulation of a subsequent sound (see § 5.2.7). Hence, labio-dental fricatives will have **retracted** realisations [̠], in the vicinity of a bilabial plosive or a back vowel [uː ʊ ɒ ɔː] or semivowel [w] (*obvious* [ˈɒbv̠ ɪəs] ***fool*** [f̠uːɫ]), or **advanced** realisations [̟], before a **front** vowel [i: ɪ] or glide consonant [j] (*feel* [f̟i̟:ɫ], *veal* [v̟i:ɫ]). Similarly, lip position will also vary depending on the articulatory gesture adopted for the adjacent sound. Hence, /f v/ will have allophonic realisations with **lip-rounding** (*food* [fʷu:d], *vodka* [ˈvʷɒdkə],) or **lip-spreading** (*feet* [fʲi·t], *vehicle* [ˈvʲi·ɪkɫ]) in the vicinity of rounded and spread vowels or semi-vowels, respectively (see § 5.2.3).

Spellings

Table 23: The spellings of RP /f v/

/f/	/v/
<f> / <fe> pre**f**er /prɪˈfɜ:ʳ/, **f**eet /fi:t/ li**fe** /laɪf/	<v> / <ve> **v**ery /ˈveri/, **v**ulgar /ˈvʌlgə/ gi**ve** /gɪv/, li**ve** /lɪv/
<ff> / <ffe> o**ff**er /ˈɒfə/, ba**ff**le /ˈbæfl̩/, gira**ffe** /dʒɪˈrɑ:f/	<vv> na**vv**y /ˈnævi/, sa**vv**y /ˈsævi/
<ph>, <pph> **ph**oto /ˈfəʊtəʊ/, **ph**rase /freɪz/ di**ph**thong /ˈdifθɒŋ/, ne**ph**ew /ˈnefju:/ sa**pph**ire /ˈsæfaɪə/	<ph> Ste**ph**en /ˈstevn̩/
<gh> enou**gh** /ɪˈnʌf/, drau**gh**t /drɑ:ft/	
Rare cases silent <l> + <f> ha**lf** /hɑ:f/ <f> + silent <t> so**ft**en /ˈsɒfn̩/	**Rare cases** <f> o**f** /əv/ <lve> ha**lve** /hɑ:v/

Regional and social variants

/f v/ register no important variants in RP, other than the pronunciation of /f/ as [v] word-initially in South-west England speech (Cruttenden 2014: 197).

Comparison with Spanish and advice

SLE should avoid pronouncing /v/ as either [b], a voiced bilabial plosive, or [β], a voiced bilabial fricative (Stockwell and Bowen 1965; García Lecumberri 1999, 2000). While in Spanish <b> and <v> spellings correspond to one phoneme, /b/ voiced bilabial plosive (*visita* 'visit' [biˈsita]), in English they represent two different phonemes, voiced bilabial plosive /b/ and voiced labio-dental fricative /v/, respectively. As a result, a common mistake of SSLE is to pronounce such words as *very* /ˈveri/ or *visit* /ˈvɪzɪt/ with a voiced bilabial plosive (*[ˈberi], *[ˈbɪsɪt]), instead of a voiced labio-dental fricative, which may lead to misunderstandings resulting from the loss of the /**b**/ – /**v**/ contrasts that exists in English (*very* /ˈveri/ – **b**erry /ˈberi/).

Care should, therefore, be taken to distinguish /f/, /b/ and /v/ sounds, in ***fail*** /feɪl/ – ***bail*** /beɪl/ – ***veil*** /veɪl/, the last two in particular as they prove to be the most problematic for SSLE. In addition, as discussed in other pairs of consonants, every effort should be made to distinguish word-final [f] and [v̥] by reducing the duration of the vowel or vocalic glide that precedes [f] (***leaf*** /liˑf/ – ***leave*** [liːv], ***safe*** [seˑɪf] – ***save*** [seːɪv̥]) (Finch and Ortiz Lira 1982: 64, 71; Dale and Poms 1986; Swan and Smith 2001; Catford 1987; Avery and Ehrlich 1992; Cruttenden 2014: 182; Estebas Vilaplana 2009: 80–82; Gleason 2012).

Further practice

AI 4.7 The spellings of RP /f/. Further practice

fat /fæt/	**f**amily /ˈfæməli/	**ph**oto /ˈfəʊtəʊ/
ri**f**le /ˈraɪfəl/	o**ff**er /ˈɒfə/	gira**ffe** /dʒɪˈrɑːf/
lea**f** /liːf/	o**ff** /ɒf/	

We **f**inally voted on **F**riday at **f**ive **f**i**f**teen.
/wi ˈfaɪnəli ˈvəʊtɪd ɒn ˈfraɪdi ət faɪv ˌfɪfˈtiːn/

My ne**ph**ew lau**gh**s at **f**unny jokes about **f**ishing.
/maɪ ˈnevjuː lɑːfs ət ˈfʌni dʒəʊks əˈbaʊt ˈfɪʃɪŋ/

I live with **f**ive **f**riends in a **f**i**f**th-**f**loor **f**urnished **f**lat.
/ˈaɪ ˈlɪv wɪð faɪv frendz ɪn ə fɪfθ flɔː ˈfɜːnɪʃt flæt/

Four **f**urious **f**riends **f**ought **f**or the **ph**one.
/fɔː ˈfjʊərɪəs frendz ˈfɔːt fə ðə fəʊn/

Fred **f**ed Ted bread, and Ted **f**ed **F**red bread.
/fred fed ted bred | ənd ted fed fred bred/

AI 4.8 The spellings of RP /v/. Further practice

vat /væt/	**v**ery /ˈveri/	**v**iew /vjuː/
ri**v**al /ˈraɪvəl/	tra**v**el /ˈtrævl̩/	se**v**en /ˈsevn̩/
lea**ve** /liːv/	gi**ve** /gɪv/	

Various student groups tra**v**elled to **V**enice in the **v**acation.
/ˈveərɪəs ˈstjuːdnt gruːps ˈtrævl̩d tə ˈvenɪs ɪn ðə vəˈkeɪʃn̩/

A **v**ery wide **v**ariety o**f** people came.
/ə ˈveri waɪd vəˈraɪəti əv ˈpiːpl̩ keɪm/

I lo**ve** the nice **v**iew o**v**er the **v**illage.
/| ˈaɪ lʌv ðə naɪs vjuː ˈəʊvə ðə ˈvɪlɪdʒ/

That **v**et looks after **v**irtually all the li**v**estock in the **v**alley.
/ðət vet lʊks ˈɑːftə ˈvɜːtʃʊəli ɔːl ðə ˈlaɪvstɒk ɪn ðə ˈvæli/.

Vincent **v**owed **v**engeance **v**ery **v**ehemently.
/ˈvɪnsn̩t vaʊd ˈvendʒəns ˈveri ˈviːəməntli/

Se**v**enty se**v**en bene**v**olent elephants.
/ˈsevn̩ti ˈsevn̩ bəˈnevələnt ˈelɪfənts/

4.2.2.2 Dental fricatives: RP /θ ð/ vs. PSp /θ/

IPA Symbols

θ Theta.
ð Eth.

Identification

/**θ**/ Fortis voiceless dental fricative.
/**ð**/ Lenis voiced dental fricative.

Allophones

/**θ**/
[**θ̬**] 'voiced'
[**θ^w**] 'labialised'
[**θ^j**] 'palatalised'
[**ð**] 'voiced dental fricative'
[**f**] 'voiceless labio-dental fricative'

/**ð**/
[**ð̥**] 'devoiced'
[**$\eth^w$**] 'labialised'
[**$\eth^j$**] 'palatalised'
[**θ**] 'voiceless dental fricative'
[**v**] 'voiced labio-dental fricative'
[**z**] 'voiced alveolar fricative'
[**l**] 'alveolar lateral approximant'

Description

To pronounce /**θ**/ the soft palate is in its raised position, and the tip of the tongue makes a light contact with the edge and inner surface of the upper incisors so that a small passage is formed, through which the outgoing airflow is released producing a slight friction. The vocal folds do not vibrate, but are wide apart. /θ/ is produced with more muscular energy than its counterpart, and it shortens the vocalic sounds that precede it (***birth*** [bɜˑθ], ***wreath*** [ɹiˑθ],

oath [ə'ʊθ]). /**ð**/, on the other hand, is pronounced in the same way as /θ/, but with less energy and with the vocal folds showing different degrees of vibration depending on its context of occurrence. It does not shorten the length of preceding vocalic or sonorant sounds (*wrea**the*** [ɹiːð]).

For the articulation of both /θ ð/ the tongue is quite flat, and as a result, the passage through which the lung air is released has "the nature of a slit rather than a groove" (Gimson 1994: 168; Cruttenden 2014: 199; Collins and Mees 2003: 141). For this reason these two dental consonants are technically known as **slit fricatives** (Stone 1990; Stone et al. 1992) (see § 2.3.2.3).

See the animations and videos under RP /θ/ and /ð/ (compared with Spanish /θ/) in the Sound Bank of the EPSS Multimedia Lab.

Environment and main allophonic realisations

RP /θ ð/ can occur in all word positions. /**θ**/ remains voiceless initially (***th**ick* [θɪk]) and finally (*brea**th*** [breθ], but between voiced sounds it gains some **voicing** (*e**th**ics* ['eθ̬ɪks]). /**ð**/ is **fully voiced** betwen voiced sounds (*lea**th**er* ['leðəʳ], *al**th**ough* [ɔːɫ'ðəʊ]), but it loses some of its voicing [ð̥] when occurring in initial position (***th**ere* [ð̥eə]) and it is completely devoiced in final position (*clo**the*** [kləʊð̥], *wi**th*** [wɪð̥]).

Other allophonic realisations with **lip-rounding** (***th**ought* ['θʷɔ˙t], *soo**the*** [suːðʷ]) or **lip-spreading** (***th**in* [θʲɪn], ***th**is* [ðʲɪs]) will also emerge in the vicinity of rounded [uː ʊ ɒ ɔː w] and spread [iː ɪ j] vowels or semi-vowels, respectively (see § 5.2.3).

In addition, /ð/ may be pronounced as [**z**], with an alveolar place of articulation, at close-knit word boundaries in rapid speech if preceded by /z/ (*Is **th**ere some?* ['ɪz zeə 'sʌm]). Both dental fricatives may also be elided in consonant clusters preceding /s z/ (*twelf**th**s* [twelfs], *clo**th**es* [kləʊz]) to ease difficulties of articulation (see § 5.4).

Spellings

Table 24: *The spellings of RP /θ ð/*

/θ/	/ð/
<th> **th**in /θɪn/, **th**rough /θruː/ au**th**or /'ɔːθə/ ca**th**edral /kə'θiːdrəl/ nor**th** /nɔːθ/, wor**th** /'wɜːθ/	<th> **th**en (weak) /ðen/ ra**th**er (strong) /'rɑːðə/ wor**th**y /wɜːði/ <the> brea**the** /briːð/

There are some pronunciation hints that may be helpful when deciding whether the <*th*> spelling is pronounced as /θ/ or /ð/. In initial position, the digraph *th* is pronounced /ð/ in most function words and adverbs (***the***, ***th****is*, ***th****eirs*, ***th****an*, ***th****ere*, ***th****us*, ***th****en*) with the exception of ***th****rough* /θru:/; but in most other words it is pronounced /θ/. In medial position, it tends to be pronounced /ð/ (*bo****th****er*, *bro****th****er*, *ei****th****er*, *ga****th****er*, *o****th****er*, *ra****th****er*), but there are a few exceptions which have /θ/ such as *pan****th****er* /ˈpænθə/, ***eth****er* /ˈi:θə/ and compounds of ***th****ing* /θɪŋ/ (*every****th****ing*, *some****th****ing*, etc.). In final positions, the *th* spelling is usually pronounced /θ/, with two exceptions, ***with*** /wɪð/ and *smoo****th*** /smu:ð/; whereas in some other cases both [ð] and [θ] pronunciations can be heard (*boo****th*** [bu:ð], [buˑθ], *beque****a****th* [bɪˈkwi:ð], [bɪˈkwiˑθ]). Generally, however, [**ð**] – [**θ**] pronunciation differences usually serve to mark noun [**θ**] – adjective or verb [**ð**] contrasts, or otherwise they identify noun-verb cognates, spelt with final ***th*** and ***th****e*, respectively, as illustrated in the following examples:

Noun	Adjective	Noun	Verb
Nor**th** /nɔ:θ/	nor**th**ern /ˈnɔ:ðən/	ba**th** /bɑ:θ/	ba**the** /beɪð/
Sou**th** /saʊθ/	sou**th**ern /ˈsʌðən/	brea**th** /breθ/	brea**the** /bri:ð/
wor**th** /wɜ:θ/	wor**th**y /ˈwɜ:ði/	shea**th** /ʃi:θ/	shea**the** /ʃi:ð/
		soo**th** /su:θ/	soo**the** /su:ð/
		wrea**th** /ri:θ/	wrea**the** /ri:ð/

Regional and social variants

Dental fricatives have no significant variants in RP. In London speech /ð/ may be pronounced as labio-dental [v] *mo****th****er* [ˈmʌvə], or with such alveolar articulations as [l] (*all* ***the*** [ɔ:ɫ lə]) and [n] (*in* ***the*** [ɪn nə]), when /ð/ occurs initially in weak forms after /t/ and /n/ at close-knit word-boundaries (Kerswill 2003).

Further allophonic realisations may be heard in Irish English when both dental fricatives are realised as dentalised plosives [t̪ d̪] (***th****ank* [t̪ænk]), although word-finally they can be pronounced as fricatives (*pa****th*** [pʰæθ]) (Wells 1982: 428–431; Cruttenden 2014: 199; Hickey 1984: 240; Hughes 2005: 116).

Comparison with Spanish and advice

The [**θ**] sound produced in most of Spain (*caza* 'hunting' [ˈkaθa]) makes an acceptable equivalent of RP /θ/, even though the Spanish sound is fully interdental and is produced with considerably more friction.

[**ð**], on the other hand, does not have phonemic status in Spanish, but is used as an allophone of [d] in all positions except before a pause and after a nasal (*cada* 'each' [kaða] (Navarro Tomás 1966 [1946]; Quilis and Fernández 1982). A common mistake of SSLE is therefore to pronounce [d] in the place of [ð] in words such as ***th**e*, ***th**en*, ***th**eir*, ***th**em*, ***th**ere*, etc. This error should be avoided because, although it may not be critical for understanding, it may hinder comprehension.

Finally, it should be kept in mind that the main cue to distinguish between **word-final** [θ] and [ð̥] is that the vowels that precede the voiceless phoneme (*tee**th*** [ti·θ]) are shorter than those occurring before the voiced one (*tee**the*** [ti:ð̥]) (Finch and Ortiz Lira 1982: 69; Gallardo del Puerto 2005: 201; Estebas Vilaplana 2009: 77–79; Sedláčková 2010: 59; Mott 2011: 257; Gleason 2012; Cruttenden 2014: 173).

Further practice

AI 4.9 The spellings of RP /θ/. Further practice

thin /θɪn/	**th**rough /θru:/	**th**ink /θɪŋk/
heal**th**y /ˈhelθi/	twenty-**th**ird /ˈtwenti θɜ:d/	clo**th** /klɒθ/
too**th** /tu:θ/	ba**th** /bɑ:θ/	

King Ar**th**ur sat on his **th**rone.
/kɪŋ ˈɑ:θə sæt ɒn ɪz θrəʊn/

I **th**ink this **th**ing is too **th**in.
/ˈaɪ θɪŋk ðɪs ˈθɪŋ z tu: θɪn/

The ba**th** is only **th**irty-**th**ree inches wide.
/ðə bɑ:θ s ˈəʊnli ˈθɜ:ti θri: ˈɪntʃɪz waɪd/

The **th**irty-**th**ree **th**ieves **th**ought that they **th**rilled the **th**rone **th**roughout **Th**ursday.
/ðə ˈθɜ:ti θri: θi:vz ˈθɔ:t ðət ˈðeɪ θrɪld ðə θrəʊn θru:ˈaʊt ˈθɜ:zdi/

AI 4.10 The spellings of RP /ð/. Further practice

this /ðɪs/	**th**en /ðen/	ra**th**er /ˈrɑ:ðə/
o**th**er /ˈʌðə/	tee**th**ing /ˈti:ðɪŋ/	**th**ere /ðeə/
smoo**th** /smu:ð/	clo**the** /kləʊð/	

I breat**he** ra**th**er fast when I'm ba**th**ing.
/ˈaɪ briːð ˈrɑːðə fɑːst wen aɪm ˈbeɪðɪŋ/

I'll do **th**is work here **th**en, and **th**at work **th**ere.
/aɪl də ðɪs ˈwɜːk hɪə ðen | ənd ðət ˈwɜːk ðeə/

It was **th**e coldest day of **th**e year.
/ɪt wəz ðə ˈkəʊldɪst deɪ əv ðə jɪə/

Don't bo**th**er to ga**th**er all the leaves and hea**th**er.
/dəʊnt ˈbɒðə tə ˈgæðər ɔːl ðə liːvz ənd ˈheðə/

There **th**ose thousand thinkers were thinking: how did the o**th**er three thieves go through?
/ðeə ðəʊz ˈθaʊzn̩d ˈθɪŋkəz wə ˈθɪŋkɪŋ ˈhaʊ dɪd ði ˈʌðə θriː θiːvz gəʊ θruː/

4.2.2.3 Alveolar fricatives: RP /s z/ vs. PSp /s/

IPA Symbols

s Lower-case S.
z Lower-case Z.

Identification

/**s**/ Fortis voiceless alveolar fricative.
/**z**/ Lenis voiced alveolar fricative.

Allophones

/**s**/	/**z**/
[s̬] 'voiced'	[z̥] 'devoiced'
[s̠] 'retracted'	[z̠] 'retracted'
[s̟] 'advanced'	[z̟] 'advanced'
[sʷ] 'labialised'	[zʷ] 'labialised'
[sʲ] 'palatalised'	[zʲ] 'palatalised'
[z] 'voiced alveolar fricative'	

Description

To pronounce /**s**/, the blade (and tip) of the tongue (Bladon and Nolan 1977) are quite close to the alveolar ridge and the side rims of the tongue are placed against the upper side teeth. The soft palate is in its raised position so that the outgoing lung air is released through an oral passage that has the shape of a narrow groove in the centre of the tongue – as opposed to the slit of dental fricatives –, producing friction (Gimson 1994: 170; Collins and Mees 2009: 89; Cruttenden 2014: 202). For this reason /s z/ are technically known as **grooved fricatives** (Stone 1990; Stone et al. 1992) (see § 2.3.2.3.). /s/ shortens the long vocalic sounds that precede it (*cease* [siˑs], *grass* [gɹɑˑs]), and is pronounced with more muscular energy than its voiced counterpart.

/**z**/, in turn, is pronounced in the same way as /s/, but has potential voice and is produced with less energy than its voiceless counterpart /s/, without affecting the length of previous vocalic and sonorant sounds (*seize* [siːz]).

See the animations and videos under RP /s/ and /z/ (compared with Spanish /s/) in the Sound Bank of the EPSS Multimedia Lab.

Environment and main allophonic realisations

RP /s z/ can occur in all word positions. /**s**/ remains voiceless initially (***s**in* [sɪn]) and finally (*cat**s*** [kæts], but between voiced sounds it gains some **voicing** (*e**ss**ay* [eˈs̬eɪ]). /**z**/ is **fully voiced** betwen voiced sounds (*ea**s**y* [ˈiːzi], *hu**s**band* [ˈhʌzbənd]), but it loses some of its voicing [z̥] when occurring in initial position (***z**inc* [z̥ɪŋk]) and it is completely **devoiced** in final position (*doe**s*** [dʌz̥]).

In addition, /s z/ will have **retracted** realisations [̠] before /r/ and in the vicinity of a back vowel [uː ʊ ɒ ɔː] or semivowel [**w**] (*horse-riding* [hɔː s̠ˈɹaɪdɪŋ] *newsreel* [ˈnjuːz̠ɹiːl]), or **advanced** realisations [̟], before a **front** vowel [iː ɪ] or glide consonant [j] (***s**eal* [s̟iːɫ], ***z**ero* [ˈz̟ɪərəʊ]) (see § 5.2.7). In the same contexts, i.e. in the vicinity of rounded [uː ʊ ɒ ɔː w] and spread [iː ɪ j] vowels or semi-vowels, the realisations of /s z/ will involve **lip-rounding** (***s**oon* [sʷuːn], ***z**oo* [zʷuː]) and **lip-spreading** (***s**ee* [sʲiː], ***z**eal* [zʲiːɫ]) respectively (see § 5.2.3).

Spellings

Table 25: The spellings of RP /s z/

/s/	/z/
<s> / <'s> / <s'> cat**s** /kæts/ a cat**'s** tail /ə ˈkæts teɪl/ cat**s'** tails /kæts teɪlz/	<s> / <'s> / <s'> boy**s** /ˈbɔɪz/ a boy**'s** brain /ə ˌbɔɪz breɪn/ boy**s'** brains /ˈbɔɪz breɪnz/
<se>[74] fal**se** /fɔːls/, goo**se** /guːs/	<se> / <es> / <-ese>[75] plea**se** /pliːz/, go**es** /gəʊz/ Chin**ese** /tʃaɪˈniːz/ Portugu**ese** /ˌpɔːtʃʊˈgiːz/
<ss> mi**ss** /mɪs/, mi**ss**ile /ˈmɪsaɪl/	<ss>[76] de**ss**ert /dɪˈzɜːt/, sci**ss**ors /ˈsɪzəz/

74 As you can see in Table 25, word final <-se> may be pronounced either /s/ (*el**se*** /els/, *cea**se*** /siːs/) or /z/ (ri**se** /raɪz/, rai**se** /reɪz/).

75 The adjective and noun suffix *-ese* is always pronounced /iːz/.

76 <ss> is pronounced /z/ in approximately five words (e.g. *po**ss**ess* /pəˈzes/, *di**ss**olve* /dɪˈzɒlv/, hu**ss**ar /hʊˈzɑː/ and the two other words included in Table 25), its NP being /s/.

<c> / <ce>[77] **c**entre /ˈsentə/, coun**c**il /ˈkaʊnsl̩/ roman**ce** /rəʊˈmæns/, sau**ce** /sɔːs/ on**ce** /wʌns/ ri**ce** /raɪs/	<z> / <ze>[78] **z**oo /zuː/ bree**ze** /briːz/, ma**ze** /meɪz/ sei**ze** /siːz/
<sc> / <sce> a**sc**end /əˈsend/ acquie**sce** /ˌækwiˈes/	<zz> ja**zz** /dʒæz/ pu**zz**le /ˈpʌzl̩/
<z> blit**z** /blɪts/	<x> **x**ylophone /ˈzaɪləfəʊn/
<x> / <xe> /ks/ si**x** /sɪks/, a**x**le /æksl̩/ a**xe** /æks/	<x> /gz/ e**x**am /ɪgˈzæm/, e**x**ist /ɪgˈzɪst/ Ale**x**ander /ˌælɪgˈzɑːndə/

Before moving on to the next heading, let us focus on some pronunciation hints. The noun suffix *-ism* is always pronounced [ɪzəm] or [ɪzm̩], as in *athletic**ism*** ([æθˈletɪˌsɪzəm], [æθˈletɪˌsɪzm̩]), *capital**ism*** ([ˈkæpɪtəlɪzəm], [ˈkæpɪtəlɪzm̩]), *Marx**ism*** ([ˈmɑːksɪzəm], [ˈmɑːksɪzm̩]), *rac**ism*** ([ˈreɪsɪzəm], [ˈreɪsɪzm̩]). In addition, there exist /s/-/z/ alternations in pronunciation, which usually trigger verb-noun or adjective contrasts that tend, but need not be signalled orthographically with <-se>/<-ce> spellings respectively, as can be seen in the following examples:

Verb	**Noun or Adjective**
abuse /əˈbjuːz/	/əˈbjuːs/
advi**s**e /ədˈvaɪz/	advi**c**e /ədˈvaɪs/
close /kləʊz/	/kləʊs/
devi**s**e /dɪˈvaɪz/	devi**c**e /dɪˈvaɪs/
diffuse /dɪˈfjuːz/	/dɪˈfjuːs/
excuse /ɪkˈskjuːz/	/ɪkˈskjuːs/
house /ˈhaʊz/	/ˈhaʊs/
use /ˈjuːz/[79]	/ˈjuːs/

Nevertheless, there exist some exceptions to the spelling-pronounciation correlations just described. For instance, although the *se* spellings of *licen**se*** and *practi**se*** serve to distinguish these verbs from the nouns *licen**ce*** and *practi**ce***, both verbs and nouns have the same pronunciation with a final /**s**/ (/ˈlaɪsn̩s/, /ˈpræktɪs/). Likewise, *decrea**se***, *increa**se***, *promi**se*** and *relea**se*** are also pronounced with final /s/ regardless of their use as verbs or nouns (/dɪˈkriːs/, /ɪnˈkriːs/, /ˈprɒmɪs/, /rɪˈliːs/). In contrast, *fu**se*** and *surpri**se*** are always pronounced with final /**z**/ (/fjuːz/, /səˈpraɪz/).

77 Word final <-ce> is always pronounced /s/, never /z/.
78 Word final <-ze> is always pronounced /z/, never /s/.
79 Note, however, that in the habitual auxiliary *used to* it is always /juːst/.

Turning to the <-*(e)s*> endings corresponding to regular plurals, possessive nouns and the third person singular simple present tense of regular verbs, they may have three pronunciations, [**s**], [**z**] and [**ɪz**] or [**əz**], which are predictable from the last sound of the base to which they are attached. If the noun or verb ends in a sibilant consonant /**s z ʃ ʒ tʃ dʒ**/, then the ending is realised as [**ɪz**] or [**əz**]:

church /tʃɜːtʃ/	church**es** /ˈtʃɜːtʃɪz/
garage /ˈgærɑːʒ/	garag**es** /ˈgærɑːʒɪz/
George /dʒɔːdʒ/	Georg**e's** /ˈdʒɔːdʒəz/
lass /læs/	lass**es** /ˈlæsɪz/
lash /læʃ/	lash**es** /ˈlæʃɪz/
noise /nɔɪz/	nois**es** /ˈnɔɪzɪz/
clash /klæʃ/	clash**es** /klæʃɪz/

When the noun or verb ends in a vowel or a voiced non-sibilant consonant, the ending is pronounced [**z**]:

Bob /bɒb/	Bob'**s** /bɒbz/
eagle /ˈiːgl̩/	eagle**s** /ˈiːgl̩z/
fee /fiː/	fee**s** /fiːz/
say /seɪ/	pay**s** /peɪz/
prism /ˈprɪzəm/	prism**s** /ˈprɪzəmz/

If the noun or verb ends in a voiceless non-sibilant consonant, the ending is realised as [**s**]:

belief /bɪˈliːf/	belief**s** /bɪˈliːfs/
cough /kɒf/	cough**s** /kɒfs/
opposite /ˈɒpəzɪt/	opposite**s** /ˈɒpəzɪts/
sixth /sɪksθ/	sixth**s** /sɪksθs /
thank /θæŋk/	thank**s** /θæŋks/

Finally, attention should be paid to some vestiges of the Old English pronunciation rule according to which fricative consonants should be voiced in intervocalic position. As a result, some singular nouns ending in /**ð**/ exhibit /**ðz**/ plural patterns, while the rest either admit plurals with both [**θs**] and [**ðz**] pronunciations or otherwise only have /**θs**/ plurals, as shown below:[80]

80 In some of these nouns alternative pronunciations may also be heard but they fall outside mainstream RP (see fn 9). Another instance of the fossilization of this Old English phonotactic rule explains the pronunciation of *house-houses* /haʊs/-/ˈhaʊzɪz/ as no other singular noun ending in /s/ forms its plural in this way in modern English.

plurals with /ðz/	**plurals with [ðz] or [θs]**	**plurals with /θs/**
mouth-mouth**s** /maʊθ/-/maʊðz/	truth-truth**s** /truːθ/-[truːðz], [truːθs]	death-death**s** /deθ/-/deθs/
path-path**s** /pɑːθ/-/pɑːðz/	bath-bath**s** /bɑːθ/-[bɑːðz], [bɑːθs]	month-month**s** /mʌnθ/-/mʌnθs/
youth-youth**s** /juːθ/-/juːðz/	lath-lath**s** /lɑːθ/-[lɑːθs], [lɑːðz]	moth-moth**s** /mɒθ/-/mɒθs/
	cloth-cloth**s** /klɒθs/-[klɒθs], [klɒðz]	myth-myth**s** /mɪθ/-/mɪθs/

Regional and social variants

In regional varieties of RP, while /nz/ and /ndz/ clusters are kept distinct by most speakers (*wi**n**s-wi**nds**, fi**n**es-fi**nds***), the pronunciation of the cluster /ns/ as /nts/ with an **epenthetic** (or additional) alveolar plosive is widespread, thereby neutralizing to /nts/ pronunciations the distinctions between such words as *assista**nce**-assista**nts**, mi**nce**-mi**nts**, pla**ns**-pla**nts*** (see § 5.5). Similarly, in clusters consisting of s + /m/ or /ŋ/ an epenthetic plosive that is homorganic with the nasal may also be heard (*Sa**ms**on* [ˈsæmsən] [ˈsæmpsən], *Ki**ngs**ton* [ˈkɪŋstən] [ˈkɪŋkstən]). In addition, in South-West England /s/ may be replaced by /z/ in word-initial position (***s**erve* [z̥ɜːv]) (Cruttenden 2014: 202–203).

Comparison with Spanish and advice

Although the RP /**s**/ and the Andalusian and Latin American variety of [s] may be regarded as acceptable equivalents, both being made with the blade of the tongue raised towards the alveolar region, the type of [s] produced in the rest of Spain is **apical**: the stricture is made between the tongue tip and the alveolar ridge. Since apical [s] has a slight [ʃ] quality, the [s]-[ʃ] contrast should be practised. Besides, it should be noted that [s] is usually dropped and replaced by [h] in pre-consonantal and final positions in Latin-American Spanish (Argentina, Chile, Central America) and in Andalusian and Canary Spanish, which does not occur in RP. Speakers of Spanish should also avoid the addition of a vowel before any of the clusters beginning with /s/ (***s**cale* / skeɪl/). A good practice in this case is to pronounce a long [sss] before the adjacent consonant.

The potential problems of RP /**z**/ should not concern its articulation because in PSp and in some varieties of Latin-American Spanish [z] occurs as an allophone of /s/ before voiced consonants (e.g. *mi**s**mo* 'same' [ˈmizmo]), and it is the sound found in such Catalan words as *ca**s**a* 'house' [ˈkaza]. The difficulty rather resides in that in English /s z/ have phonemic status and show a much freer occurrence than the Spanish equivalent sounds, of which only /s/ has phonemic nature. As a result SSLE may find it difficult to produce and perceive the differences between /s/ and /z/, and misunderstandings may occur since such English words as ***Sue*** /suː/ – /sjuː/ and ***zoo*** /zuː/ may be pronounced in the same way ([suː]).

To grasp the /**s**/ – /**z**/ distinction is of utter importance because these two sounds are very frequent in English. They are used together with /**ɪz**/ (or /**əz**/) to mark **plurals** (*leg**s*** /legz/), the third person singular of verbs (*eat**s*** /iːts/) and the possessive case (George'**s** /ˈdʒɔːdʒɪz/), as well as in auxiliary verbs (*doe**s**n't* /ˈdʌznt/ and *i**s**n't* /ˈɪznt/) and many grammatical words, among other contexts. SSLE usually pronounce <s> <es> spellings as [s] (*[dʌsnt] and *[ɪsnt]) or *[is] (Sedláčková 2010: 59; Estebas Vilaplana 2009: 107–109), which are close to the devoiced allophones [z̥] [ɪz̥] of the target pronunciations. However, SSLE should try to attain [z] and [z̥] (by weakening), lengthening at the same time the sound preceding it (*bag**s*** [bæːgːz̥]). In contrast, when pronouncing [s] the previous vocalic and sonorant sounds should be shortened (*back**s*** /bæˑks/).

In addition, the differences with the other sibilants or fricatives should also be practised, especially if they occur successively within the same word or phrase (e.g. *deci**s**ion* /dɪˈsɪʒn̩/, ***s**ci**ss**or**s*** /ˈsɪzəz/, *thou**s**and* /ˈθaʊzn̩d/, *enthu**s**ia**s**m* /ɪnˈθjuːzɪæzəm/, etc.) (Finch and Ortiz Lira 1982: 69; Estebas Vilaplana 2009: 73–76; Cruttenden 2014: 203).

Further practice

AI 4.11 The spellings of RP /s/. Further practice

pea**ce** /piːs/	**c**entre /ˈsentə/	**s**illy /ˈsɪli/
mer**c**y /ˈmɜːsi/	ca**st**le /ˈkɑːsl̩/	flee**ce** /fliːs/
cour**se** /kɔːs/	roman**ce** /rəʊˈmæns/	

Some **s**ay **S**uzan is **s**illy, but Ali**ce** is **s**illier.
/səm ˈseɪ ˈsuːzn̩ z ˈsɪli | bət ˈælɪs ɪz ˈsɪlɪə/

I**ce** in jui**ce** is ni**ce**.
/aɪs ɪn dʒuːs ɪz naɪs/

Six terrori**sts** a**ss**a**ss**inated the prin**ce**'s **s**on.
/sɪks ˈterərɪsts əˈsæsɪneɪtɪd ðə ˈprɪnsəz sʌn/

Six **s**ick hick**s** nick **s**ix **s**lick brick**s** with pick**s** and stick**s**.
/sɪks sɪk hɪks nɪk sɪks slɪk brɪks wɪð pɪks ənd stɪks/

AI 4.12 The spellings of RP /z/. Further practice

pea**s** /piːz/	**z**ebra /ˈzebrə/	flea**s** /fliːz/
di**zz**y /ˈdɪzi/	cra**z**y /ˈkreɪzi/	eye**s** /aɪz/
free**ze** /friːz/		

Zebra**s** are like horse**s** but striped.
/ˈzebrəz ə ˈlaɪk ˈhɔːsɪz bət straɪpt/

Zoo**s** are cra**z**y place**s**!
/zuːz ə ˈkreɪzi ˈpleɪsɪz/

Ro**s**a play**s** the **x**ylophone outside.
/ˈrozə pleɪz ðə ˈzaɪləfəʊn ˌaʊtˈsaɪd/

A noi**s**y noi**se** annoy**s** an oyster.
/ə ˈnɔɪzi nɔɪz əˈnɔɪz ən ˈɔɪstə/

Deni**se** see**s** the fleece, Deni**se** see**s** the flea**s**.
/dəˈniːz ˈsiːz ðə fliːs | dəˈniːz ˈsiːz ðə fliːz/

At least Deni**se** could snee**ze** and feed and free**ze** the flea**s**.
/ət liːst dəˈniːz kəd sniːz ənd fiːd ənd friːz ðə fliːz/

4.2.2.4 RP palato-alveolar fricatives /ʃ ʒ/

IPA Symbols

ʃ Esh.
ʒ Ezh.

Identification

/ʃ/ Fortis voiceless palato-alveolar fricative.
/ʒ/ Lenis voiceless palato-alveolar fricative.

Allophones

/ʃ/
[ʃ̬] 'voiced'
[ʃʷ] 'labialised'
[ʃʲ] 'palatalised'
[ʒ] 'voiced palato-alveolar fricative'

/ʒ/
[ʒ̊] 'devoiced'
[ʒʷ] 'labialised'
[ʒʲ] 'palatalised'
[ʃ] 'voiceles palato-alveolar fricative'
[dʒ] 'voiced palato-alveolar affricate'

Description

The nasal resonator being shut off by raising the soft palate, the tip and blade of the tongue makes a light contact with the alveolar ridge, and the front of the tongue is raised in the direction of the hard palate while the side rims of the tongue are in contact with the upper side teeth. The pulmonic air stream escapes causing friction through a more diffuse and extensive area (compared with /s z/) between the tongue and the roof of the mouth.

As a fortis voiceless consonant produced without vocal fold vibration, **/ʃ/** shortens the vocalic and sonorant sounds that precede it (*mousta**che*** [məˈstɑ·ʃ], *dou**che*** [du·ʃ]). **/ʒ/**, in turn, is pronounced with less energy, and as a lenis voiced consonant, it may show different degrees of vocal fold vibration depending on the context, but it does not reduce the length of preceding sounds (*rou**ge*** [ruːʒ], *gara**ge*** [ˈgærɑːʒ]).

See the animations and videos under RP /ʃ/ and /ʒ/ in the Sound Bank of the EPSS Multimedia Lab.

Environment and main allophonic realisations

/ʃ ʒ/ may occur in all contexts, albeit the particularly weak functional load of /ʒ/. It shows a more restrictive distribution than its voiceless counterpart because it only exists word-finally in French loanwords, and it is rarely found word-initially and never occurs in word-initial consonantal clusters. Besides, /ʒ/ may be pronounced as [dʒ] word-finally in fully anglicised forms, and it may alternate with [ʃ] word-medially unless these different pronunciations alter the meanings of the words (*mea**s**ure* /ˈmeʒə/ vs. *me**sh**er* /ˈmeʃə/).

/ʃ/ remains voiceless initially (***sh**ed* [ʃed]) and finally (*fini**sh*** [ˈfɪnɪʃ], but between voiced sounds it gains some **voicing** (*mi**ss**ion* [ˈmɪʃ̬n̩], *ra**sh**ly* [ˈræʃ̬li]). **/ʒ/** is completely **voiced** when it occurs between voiced sounds (*mea**s**ure* [ˈmeʒə]), but in all the other cases it is devoiced (***g**enre* [ˈʒ̊ɑːnrə], ***g**endarme* [ˈʒ̊ɒndɑːm], *rou**ge*** [ɹuːʒ̊]). As regards lip position, the realisations of /ʃ ʒ/ will involve **lip-rounding** (*su**g**ar* [ˈʃʷʊgə], *rou**ge*** [ɹuːʒʷ]) and **lip-spreading** (***sh**eer* [ʃʲɪə], ***g**igolo* [ˈʒʲɪgələʊ]) in the vicinity of rounded [uː ʊ ɒ ɔː w] and spread [iː ɪ j] vowels or semi-vowels, respectively (see § 5.2.3).

Spellings

Table 26: The spellings of RP /ʃ ʒ/

/ʃ/	/ʒ/
<sh> **sh**ip /ʃɪp/, bru**sh** /brʌʃ/ publi**sh**er /ˈpʌblɪʃə/	<si> vi**si**on /ˈvɪʒn̩/, fu**si**on /ˈfjuːʒn̩/
<si>, <ssi> expan**si**on /ɪkˈspænʃn̩/ profe**ssi**on /prəˈfeʃn̩/	<s> + <u> / <z> + <u> ca**s**ual /ˈkæʒʊəl/ sei**z**ure /ˈsiːʒə/
<s> / <ss> + <u> **s**ugar /ˈʃʊɡə/, pre**ss**ure /ˈpreʃə/ a**ss**ure /əˈʃɔː/	
<ti> / <t> + <i> na**ti**on /ˈneɪʃn̩/, func**ti**on /ˈfʌŋkʃn̩/ nego**t**iate /nɪˈɡəʊʃieɪt/	
<ci>, <ce> deli**ci**ous /dɪˈlɪʃəs/ o**ce**an /ˈəʊʃn̩/	
<sci> / <sc> + <i> / <e> con**sci**ous /ˈkɒnʃəs/ *fascist* /ˈfæʃɪst/ cre**sc**endo /krɪˈʃendəʊ/	
French / German Loanwords <ch> / <che> ma**ch**ine /məˈʃiːn/ qui**che** /kiːʃ/ <chsi> /<sch> fu**chsi**a /ˈfjuːʃə/, **sch**edule /ˈʃedjuːl/ **sch**muck /ʃmʌk/, **sch**maltz /ʃmɔːlts/	**French loanwords** <g> / <ge> **g**enre /ˈʒɑːnrə/, re**g**ime /reɪˈʒiːm/ massa**ge** /ˈmæsɑːʒ/, bei**ge** /beɪʒ/ <j> bi**j**ou /ˈbiːʒuː/ dé**j**à vu /ˌdeɪʒə ˈvuː/ **j**e ne sais quoi /ˌʒə nə seɪ ˈkwɑː/

Regional and social variants

/ʃ ʒ/ have no significant regional or social variations. The most remarkable one is that, while Conservative RP speakers prefer to use [s] or [z] + /i/ or /j/ sequences, alternative pronunciations may be heard in two contexts: (1) before /uː/ or /ʊə/, where there are fluctuations between /ʃ ʒ/ pronunciations and those with [s] or [z] + /j/ (***tissue*** [ˈtɪʃuː] [ˈtɪsjuː], ***usual*** [ˈjuːʒʊəl] [ˈjuːʒwəl]; (2) before other vowels, where a similar variation exists between /ʃ/ and /si/ or /sj/ (*ratio* [ˈɹeɪʃɪəʊ]

[ˈɹeɪsjəʊ], *negotiate* [nɪˈgəʊʃieɪt] [nɪˈgəʊsjeɪt]). In certain words before /ə/, however, pronunciations with the sequences [s] or [z] + /i/ or /j/ are preferred, especially in comparatives (*Parisian* [pəˈrɪzɪən], *easier* [ˈiːzɪə]) (Cruttenden 2014: 205).

Comparison with Spanish and advice

As Spanish lacks /ʃ ʒ/ in its phonemic inventory, these two phonemes tend to be substituted by other sounds (Dale and Poms 1986; Swan and Smith 2001; Catford 1987; Avery and Ehrlich 1992; Estebas Vilaplana 2009: 64–66; Gleason 2012; Cruttenden 2014: 206).

/ʃ/ tends to be pronounced as [s] or [tʃ], and so such words as ***sh**ow* /ʃəʊ/ or *Wa**sh**ington* /ˈwɒʃɪŋtən/ may be wrongly pronounced as *[tʃou] and *[ˈwosɪntən]. To avoid such mispronunciations, learners could try to produce the /ʃ/ sound corresponding to the <*x*> spelling in Galician and Catalan (*Caixa*) or to <*ch*> in the Andalusian accent spoken in Cádiz.

Similarly, instead of **/ʒ/**, speakers of Spanish commonly use [ʃ] or even [s], and so instead of *divi**si**on* /dɪˈvɪʒn̩/, *plea**s**ure* /ˈpleʒə/ or *lei**s**ure* /ˈleʒə/, such pronunciations as *[diˈvɪsion], *[pleʃə] and *[lesur] may be heard. SSLE of Basque origin may have no difficulty in producing this sound as it is used in some Vizcayan dialects (García Lecumberri and Elorduy 1994).

Further practice

AI 4.13 The spellings of RP /ʃ/. Further practice

shin /ʃɪn/	**sh**oot /ʃuːt/	ca**sh** /kæʃ/
na**ti**on /ˈneɪʃn̩/	ma**ch**ine /məˈʃiːn/	pu**sh** /pʊʃ/
wa**sh** /wɒʃ/	deli**ci**ous /dɪˈlɪʃəs/	sta**ti**on /ˈsteɪʃn̩/

I wi**sh** the sun would **sh**ine like in A**s**ia.
/ˈaɪ wɪʃ ðə sʌn wʊd ʃaɪn ˈlaɪk ɪn ˈeɪʃə/

The magi**ci**an **sh**owed me the way to the sta**ti**on.
/ðə məˈdʒɪʃn̩ ʃəʊd miː ðə ˈweɪ tə ðə ˈsteɪʃn̩/

She sells sea**sh**ells on the sea**sh**ore.
/ʃi selz ˈsiːʃelz ɒn ðə ˈsiːʃɔː/

Shy **Sh**elly says **sh**e **sh**all sew **sh**eets.
/ʃaɪ ˈʃeli ˈsez ʃi ʃə səʊ ʃiːts/

AI 4.14 The spellings of RP /ʒ/. Further practice

genre /ˈʒɑːnrə/	vi**si**on /ˈvɪʒn̩/
lei**s**ure /ˈleʒə/	massa**ge** /ˈmæsɑːʒ/
gara**ge** /ˈɡærɑːʒ/	u**s**ual /ˈjuːʒʊəl/

That televi**si**on is unu**s**ual.
/ðət ˈtelɪˌvɪʒn̩ z ʌnˈjuːʒʊəl/

My pullover is bei**ge** and orange.
/maɪ ˈpʊləʊvə z beɪʒ ənd ˈɒrɪndʒ/

You must take some deci**si**ons.
/ju məst teɪk səm dɪˈsɪʒn̩z/

4.2.2.5 RP glottal fricative /h/

IPA Symbols

h Lower-case H.
x Lower-case X.
ɦ Hooktop H.

Identification

/**h**/ Fortis voiceless glottal fricative.

Allophones

[**ɦ**] Voiced glottal fricative.

Description

To articulate RP /**h**/ the soft palate is in its raised position and there is friction at the glottis and through the oral cavity, but as the vocal folds do not vibrate there is no distinctive opposition with a voiced counterpart as in the other English fricatives. The glottal fricative is always found before vowel sounds and it may be regarded as a strong, voiceless onset to the subsequent vowel because it has the same articulation (i.e. position of the tongue, lips, soft palate and configuration of the pharynx) as that of the vowel following it. As a result, /h/ will exhibit different types of friction (patterns of resonance) depending on the quality of the subsequent vowel (e.g. ***he*** /hiː/, ***who*** /huː/, ***hard*** /hɑːd/).

See the animation and video under RP /h/ (compared with Spanish /x/) in the Sound Bank of the EPSS Multimedia Lab.

Environment and main allophonic realisations

/h/ occurs only in word-initial and word-medial positions. It remains voiceless word-initially, but between voiced sounds it may have some voicing, the result being a breathy vowel or a voiced glottal fricative [ɦ], especially when initial in accented syllables, as in *a**h**ead* [əˈɦed], and *be**h**ind* [bɪˈɦaɪnd], and less frequently in unaccented syllables, as in *any**h**ow* [ˈeniɦaʊ] and *boy**h**ood* [ˈbɔɪɦʊd].

Spellings

Table 27: The spellings of RP /h/

/h/
<h> **h**elp /help/, **h**ard /hɑːd/
silent <w> + <h> (only before <o> **w**ho /huː/, **wh**ole /həʊl/

Note, however, that the spelling <h> may also be silent word-initially, as in such words as ***h**eir* /eə/, ***h**our* /ˈaʊə/, ***h**onour* /ˈɒnə/, ***h**onest* /ˈɒnɪst/, which must therefore be preceded by the forms of the indefinite and definite articles used before vowels (/ən/, /ði/), but also word-medially, as in *ex**h**ibit* /ɪgˈzɪbɪt/, *ex**h**ilarate* /ɪgˈzɪləreɪt/, *shep**h**erd* /ˈʃepəd/, *ve**h**ement* /ˈviːəmənt/, *ve**h**icle* /ˈviːɪkl̩/ (see § 7.4.1.2).

Regional and social variants

Initial /h/ tends to be dropped in **basilectal**[81] forms of most accents of Britain and Australia, and as a result such minimal pair distinctions are lost as *hill – ill, high – eye, hair – air,* which are pronounced as [ɪl], [aɪ], and [eə], respectively (Hughes *et al.* 2013). Although such *h*-dropping tends to be socially unacceptable, in General RP function words frequently lose initial /h/ in unaccented, non-initial positions in connected speech (see § 5.8). It may also occur that a glottal stop replaces initial /h/ (see § 5.2.8.2), and so *a **h**ill* may be pronounced as [ə ˈʔɪl] (Cruttenden 2014: 208).

Comparison with Spanish and advice

As Spanish does not have the glottal fricative as a distinctive phoneme, in order to avoid the usual mistake to pronounce a velar fricative [x] instead of [h] (García Lecumberri 1999, 2000), SSLE should make the effort of completely devoicing the following vowel, as in ***h**en* [e̥en]. Only in the series /hju/, as in ***h**uge* /hjuːdʒ/, can a fricative noise also be made resulting from a stricture in the mouth (Finch and Ortiz Lira 1982: 70).

81 The term **basilectal** is applied to a linguistic variety that is most remote from the prestige language (the **matrilect** or **acrolect**) and may also be contrasted with the intermediate varieties (or **mesolects**) (Crystal 2008: 51).

Similarly, as already noted, a correct distinction should be made between those minimal pairs differing only in pronunciations with and without initial /h/ (***h****ill* – *ill*), while being well aware of the RP tendency to elide initial /h/ in unaccented function words in connected speech, as will be further discussed in Section 5.8 (Cruttenden 2014: 208).

Further practice

AI 4.15 The spellings of RP /h/. Further practice

help /help/	**wh**o /huː/	**h**ip /hɪp/
be**h**ind /bɪˈhaɪnd/	**h**appy /ˈhæpi/	**h**unt /hʌnt/
how /ˈhaʊ/	**h**eaven /ˈhaʊ/ˈhevn̩//	

Hallo, **h**ow are you? **H**ungry?
/həˈləʊ | ˈhaʊ ə ju | ˈhʌŋgri ||/

Are you **h**oping to stay at a **h**otel?
/ə ju ˈhəʊpɪŋ tə steɪ ət ə ˌhəʊˈtel ||/

How **h**igh is that **h**ill?
/ˈhaʊ haɪ z ðət hɪl ||/

4.2.3 Affricates: RP /tʃ dʒ/ vs. PSp /tʃ/

The manner of articulation of affricates is quite similar to that of plosives, taking place in three steps, as follows. Firstly, the articulators come into contact, in such a way that the active articulator is moved towards the passive articulator. Secondly, a complete closure is produced so that the lung air cannot go out of the mouth, but is stopped at the point in the mouth where the articulators meet; the soft palate is in its raised position, which means that the lung air cannot be released through the nose either. The vocal folds may or may not vibrate during this compression stage. Thirdly, the articulators are separated, and so the lung air goes out of the mouth slowly, producing a slight friction, which is not so strong as that of fricative sounds (see also e.g. Gimson 1984: 172–177; Roach 2005: 54; Collins and Mees 2003: 163–166; Collins and Mees 2009: 44–45, 80–82; Cruttenden 2014: 186–191).

Any plosive whose release stage is produced in this way and is articulated approximately at the point where the plosive is made may be called an **affricate**. In English, in addition to the weakening of plosives by affrication (discussed in § 5.2.8.1), eight affricate series result from this type of release: [**tʃ dʒ tɹ dɹ ts dz tθ dð**]. Of these only /**tʃ dʒ**/ are considered to have phonemic status because they can be contrasted as sound complexes in all word positions with a change of meaning. The former posits an additional medial distinction between close-knit [tʃ] (***butcher*** /ˈbʊtʃə/) and disjunct [t] + [ʃ] (***lightship*** /ˈlaɪtʃɪp/) realisations, friction being shorter in the former. Besides, both **/tʃ dʒ/** have commutability restrictions. In the case of /tʃ/, the plosive element may be commutated within the same syllable with zero or /l/ (as in ***watch***, ***wash***, ***Welsh***), and the fricative element, with zero and /s r j w/ (as in ***catch***, ***cat***, ***cats***, and ***chip***, ***tip***, ***trip***, ***tune***, ***twin***). For **/dʒ/** the commutability is restricted to zero in word-medial positions, in the case of the plosive element (***ledger***, ***leisure***), and to zero and /r j w z/, in the fricative (as in ***jest***, ***dam***, ***dressed***, ***dune***, ***dwell***, and ***hedge***, ***head***, ***heads***).

With more commutability possibilities but a more restricted distribution excluding final positions, **[tɹ]** and **[dɹ]** are normally regarded as series of two separate sounds /t d/ + /r/, in which the plosives have retracted realisations [t̠] [d̠] and /r/ will have different realisations depending on its occurrence in close-knit or disjunct contexts. In close-knit sequences, involving two sounds within one syllable, /r/ is voiced and fricativised (or produced with audible friction) [dɹ̝], if preceded by /d/ (***draft*** [dɹ̝ɑˑft], but it is devoiced and fricativised [ɹ̝̊] after /t/ (***mattress*** [ˈmætɹ̝̊ɪs]); whereas in disjunct sequences, where there is a syllable boundary between the two sounds, /r/ is approximant and voiced (***footrest*** [ˈfʊtɹest]). **/ts dz/** (***cats*** [kæts], ***bids*** [bɪdz], ***outset*** [ˈaʊtset]) are more restricted as they do not occur in initial positions (unless in foreign words) and only doubtfully in close-knit medial contexts (***curtsey*** [ˈkɜːtsi]); whereas **/tθ dð/** are even more restricted, with very few word-final occurrences (***eighth*** [eɪt̪θ] ***width*** [wɪt̪θ]).

Acoustically, as already detailed in Section 2.4.3, affricates show the characteristics of their components: a break for the stop combined with a high-frequency noise for the fricative.

IPA Symbols

tʃ T-Esh ligature.
dʒ D-Ezh ligature.
ʝ Curly-tail J.

Identification

/tʃ/ Fortis voiceless palato-alveolar affricate.
/dʒ/ Lenis voiced palato-alveolar affricate.
/ʝ/ Lenis voiced palatal fricative.

Allophones

/tʃ/	/dʒ/
[tʃ̬] 'voiced'	[d̥ʒ̊] 'completely devoiced' in word-final positions
[tʃʷ] 'labialised'	[d̥ʒ] 'partially devoiced' in word-initial positions
[tʃʲ] 'palatalised'	[dʒʷ] 'labialised'
	[dʒʲ] 'palatalised'

Description

To articulate RP /**tʃ**/ the tip and blade of the tongue are in contact with the alveolar ridge and the front of the tongue with the hard palate. The lung air is stopped behind the complete closure formed by the two articulators and then it is released slowly, so friction is produced. As a fortis consonant, it is produced with more energy than its voiced counterpart and with the vocal folds wide apart, thereby reducing the length of previous vocalic and sonorant sounds as in *por**ch*** [pɔ˙tʃ] and *na**t**ure* [ˈne˙ɪtʃə].

/**dʒ**/ is pronounced in the same way as /tʃ/ but the vocal folds may vibrate during all or part of both the stop and fricative stages. As a lenis consonant, it is articulated with less muscular energy than its fortis counterpart. Aspiration does not take place in the production of this sound, nor does it shorten the length of preceding vocalic or sonorant sounds (lar**ge** [lɑːdʒ]).

See the animations and videos under RP /tʃ/ and /dʒ/ (compared with Spanish /tʃ/) in the Sound Bank of the EPSS Multimedia Lab.

Environment and main allophonic realisations

RP affricates can appear in all possible contexts, but they differ from plosives in that they never lose their (fricative) release stage.

/**tʃ**/ remains voiceless initially (***ch**in* [tʃɪn]) and finally (*cat**ch*** [kætʃ], but between voiced sounds it gains some **voicing** (*furni**t**ure* [ˈfɜːnɪtʃ̬ə]). /**dʒ**/, on the other hand, is **fully voiced** between voiced sounds (*pi**g**eon* [ˈpɪdʒən]), but it loses some of its voicing when it occurs word-initially (***g**ender* [ˈd̥ʒendə]), and it may be completely **devoiced** in word-final positions (*villa**ge*** [ˈvɪlɪd̥ʒ̊]).

Another set of allophonic realisations involve the position of the lips, with **lip-rounding** (***ch**oose* [tʃʷuːz], ***j**ob* [dʒʷɒb]) or **lip-spreading** (***ch**eese* [tʃʲiːz], *villa**ge*** [ˈvɪlɪdʒʲ]) in the vicinity of rounded and spread vowels or semi-vowels, respectively (see § 5.2.3).

Lastly, in such consonant clusters as /ntʃ/ and /ndʒ/ occurring in word-final positions the medial stop may be omitted (*lun**ch*** [lʌnʃ], *stran**ge*** [streɪnʒ]).

Spellings

Table 28: The spellings of RP /tʃ dʒ/

/tʃ/	/dʒ/
<ch> ti**ch** /tɪtʃ/ **ch**ild /tʃaɪld/	<g> / <ge> **g**eneral /ˈdʒenrəl/ colle**ge** /ˈkɒlɪdʒ/
<tch> ma**tch** /mætʃ/	<dg> / <dge> bri**dg**es /ˈbrɪdʒɪz/ bri**dge** /brɪdʒ/
<tu> fu**tu**re /ˈfjuːtʃə/	<j> con**j**unction /kənˈdʒʌŋkʃn̩/
<ti>, <te> ques**ti**on /ˈkwestʃən/ righ**te**ous /ˈraɪtʃəs/	<dj> a**dj**acent /əˈdʒeɪsənt/
Rare cases (Loanwords) <c> cello /ˈtʃeləʊ/ <che> avalan**che** /ˈævəlɑːntʃ/	**Rare cases** proce**d**ure /prəˈsiːdʒə/ sol**d**ier /ˈsəʊldʒə/ exa**gg**erate /ɪgˈzædʒəreɪt/ nostal**gi**a /nɒˈstældʒə/

Regional and social variants

In RP there exist fluctuations between [tʃ dʒ] and [tj] [dj] pronunciations in the onset of both unaccented (*cul**t**ure* [ˈkʌltʃə] – [ˈkʌltjə], *sol**d**ier* [ˈsəʊldʒə] – [ˈsəʊldjə]) and accented syllables (***t**une* [tʃuːn] [tjuːn] – ***d**une* [dʒuːn] [djuːn]). [tj] [dj] pronunciations are associated with careful, Conservative RP, whereas the [tʃ dʒ] pronunciations are well established in RP and they tend to be preferred by younger speakers. No such alternations occur in most accents of GA because they have lost the /j/ element following /t d/ sequences, which are realised as [tuː] [duː] (***t**une* [tʰuːn] – ***d**une* [duːn]), and so neither [tj] [dj] nor [tʃ dʒ] pronunciations are heard.

In addition, some RP speakers omit the stop element in the clusters [ntʃ] [ndʒ] in word-final positions (*Fren**ch*** [frenʃ], *stran**ge*** [streɪnʒ̊]), while [dʒ] is increasingly simplified to [ʒ] (*lie**ge*** [liːʒ̊]), in accented-syllable final positions, and occasionally to [d], in unaccented positions (*dan**g**erous* [ˈdeɪndrəs]) (Finch and Ortiz Lira 1982: 71; Cruttenden 2014: 190–191).

Comparison with Spanish and advice

As /tʃ/ has phonemic status in Spanish, but its voiced counterpart does not, the main difficulty for SSLE involves **/dʒ/**. In Latin-American Spanish (Argentina,

Uruguay and Chilean) the voiced palatal fricative /ʝ/ is realized as a fricative [ʒ] or an affricate [dʒ] as a result of "**žeísmo**", especially in <y> spellings after /n/ (*cón**y**uge* 'partner') and /l/ (*el **y**ate* 'the yacht'), as well as in emphatic pronunciations of some words (***y**o* 'I' [dʒo], *o**y**e* 'listen' [odʒe]). [dʒ] is also used in Catalan in such words as *in**j**ust* [ɪn'dʒust], although in English the sound has a much freer distribution. Besides, among younger Spanish speakers the phenomenon of "**šeísmo**" has been detected, whereby [ʝ] is devoiced to [ʃ] or, in emphatic pronunciations, it is devoiced and affricated to [ʧ]. Likewise, in Andalusian accents /tʃ/ may be replaced by [ʃ].

It should be noted, however, that "**lleísmo**" [ʎe'izmo], or the pronunciation that distinguishes between /ʝ/ (spelled "y") and the palatal lateral approximant /ʎ/ (spelled "ll") is attested sparingly in the dialects of Spanish (broadly, restricted to parts of Northern Spain and of the Andean highlands of Ecuador, Paraguay and Bolivia) and is a recessive feature of modern Spanish. Most varieties of Spanish (most of Spain, Argentina, Chile, Venezuela, Perú, Ecuador and Colombia) are characterized by "**yeísmo**" [ɟ͡ʝe'izmo]. This is a pronunciation in which /ʝ/ and /ʎ/ are merged into the former phoneme with the resulting loss of the palatal lateral approximant, so that <ll> and <y> spellings represent the same sound /ʝ/, usually realized as a palatal approximant (in word initial, as in ***y**eso* 'plaster' ['ʝeso], and intervocalic position, as in *ho**y**o* 'hole' ['oʝo]) or affricate [ɟ] (after a nasal or lateral consonant, as in *un **y**eso* 'a plaster' [uń 'ɟeso], or in emphatic pronunciations, as in ***y**o* 'I' [ɟo]) (Avezado 2009).

From the aforementioned it can be concluded that, although for some SSLE the pronunciation of [dʒ] should pose little or no difficulty because this sound exists in their phonetic inventories, for most SSLE, who do not have it in their native Spanish accents, it may be hard to reproduce. As a consequence, the English voiced palatal affricate (***j**et* /dʒet/) may be mispronounced as a as a palatal lateral approximant (*['ʎet]), as a voiced palatal fricative (*['ʝet]), or affricate (*['ɟet]), or very frequently by a palatal approximant (*[jet], *en**j**oy* *[ɪnjɔɪ], ***j**ust* *[jʌst]), based mainly on the wrong assumption that <j> spellings have to be pronounced as [j]. These mispronunciations create communication problems that result from the neutralisation of the /**dʒ**/ – /**j**/ contrast that exists in English between such words as ***j**et* /dʒet/ – ***y**et* /jet/ and ***j**ot* /dʒɒt/ – ***y**acht* /jɒt/.

When affricates come together in connected speech, the plosive element of the first affricate may be omitted (*Du**tch** **ch**eese* [dʌʃ 'tʃi:z], *chan**ge** **g**es**t**ures* ['tʃeɪnʒ 'dʒestʃəz], *loun**ge** **ch**air* ['laʊnʒ 'tʃeə]). In these cases, especial care should be taken not to omit the fricative element of the first affricate as pronunciations with such omissions would be judged as unacceptable.

Special attention should also be paid to the /**tr**/ and /**dr**/ sequences because of the retracted place of articulation of the plosive and the fricative or devoiced (when following /t/) quality of /r/, taking care not to confuse them with /tʃ/ (***trees*** – ***cheese*** [tʰɹ̥ʲiːz] – [tʃʲiːz]) and /dʒ/ (***draw*** – ***jaw*** [d̥ɹʷɔː] – [d̥ʒʷɔː]), respectively. Similarly, in order to distinguish [tʃ] and [d̥ʒ̊] in word-final positions, SSLE should remember to shorten the length of the vowel preceding [tʃ] (*sear**ch*** – *sur**ge*** [sɜˑtʃ] – [sɜːd̥ʒ̊]).

Production and discrimination exercises are required to distinguish in all possible contexts /tʃ/ and /dʒ/, as well as /tʃ dʒ/ and [ʃ ʒ]. A good starting point could be to pronounce the [tj] [dj] sequences but moving the tongue forward (Finch and Ortiz Lira 1982: 69; Pennock Speck 2001; Gallardo del Puerto 2005: 202; Estebas Vilaplana 2009: 67–70; Cruttenden 2014: 191–192).

Further practice

AI 4.16 The spellings of RP /ʧ/. Further practice

chin /tʃɪn/	**ch**oose /tʃuːz/	**ch**eese /tʃiːz/
lec**t**ure /ˈlektʃə/	kit**ch**en /ˈkɪtʃɪn/	fu**t**ure /ˈfjuːtʃə/
wa**tch** /wɒtʃ/	tea**ch** /tiːtʃ/	

He tea**ch**es Du**tch**.
/hi ˈtiːtʃɪz dʌtʃ/

I like **ch**eese, **ch**erries and **ch**ips very mu**ch**.
/ˈaɪ ˈlaɪk tʃiːz | ˈtʃerɪz ənd tʃɪps ˈveri ˈmʌtʃ/

There's a **ch**icken in the kit**ch**en.
/ðeəz ə ˈtʃɪkɪn ɪn ðə ˈkɪtʃɪn/

If Stu **ch**ews shoes, should Stu **ch**oose the shoes he **ch**ews?
/ɪf ˈstuː tʃuːz ʃuːz | ʃəd ˈstuː tʃuːz ðə ʃuːz hi tʃuːz/

AI 4.17 The spellings of RP /ʤ/. Further practice

gin /dʒɪn/	**g**enerous /ˈdʒenərəs/	con**j**unction /kənˈdʒʌŋkʃn̩/
le**dg**er /ˈledʒə/	ad**j**acent /əˈdʒeɪsənt/	bri**dge** /brɪdʒ/
ba**dge** /bæʤ/	colle**ge** /ˈkɒlɪdʒ/	

Germans are **g**enerally **g**enerous.
/ˈdʒɜːmənz ə ˈdʒenrəli ˈdʒenərəs/

Just sit on the e**dge** of the bri**dge**.
/dʒʌst sɪt ɒn ði edʒ əv ðə brɪdʒ/

A lar**ge** ma**j**ority voted for the **j**u**dge**.
/ə lɑːdʒ məˈdʒɒrɪti ˈvəʊtɪd fə ðə dʒʌdʒ/

4.2.4 Nasals: RP /m n ŋ/ vs. PSp /m n ɲ/

In RP there are three nasal phonemes **/m n ŋ/**. Articulatorily, the manner of articulation of **nasals** (also known as **nasal stops**) resemble that of **plosives** (or **oral stops**) in that in both groups an active articulator comes into contact with a passive articulator so that a complete closure of the oral chamber is made. The main difference between oral and nasal stops is the position of the soft palate. While in plosives it is raised, and so the airstream escapes through the mouth, in nasals it is lowered so that the lung air is unimpededly released through the nasal cavity, for which they are regarded as **continuants**, giving the sound the resonance provided by the nasopharyngeal cavity. Nasals are also referred to as **frictionless continuants**, because no audible friction is produced in their articulation, as it occurs with other continuants such as fricatives. In addition, nasals are considered to be **vowel-type sounds** because they are normally **voiced**, which means that the vocal folds do vibrate in the compression stage. As a consequence, they neither present remarkable voiced/voiceless oppositions, nor reduce the length of the previous sound. Another feature that evidences the vocalic nature of nasals is their capability to become **syllabic**, frequently /n/ (*eleven* [ɪˈlevn̩]), less frequently /m/ (*happen* [ˈhæpm̩]) and occasionally /ŋ/ (*thicken* [ˈθɪkŋ̍]), thereby conveying the syllabic prominence that characterises vowels, as already explained in Section 1.3.3.3.

As regards place of articulation, English nasals and plosives have again the same areas of articulation. **/m/** is **bilabial** (like /p b/), the two articulators being the lower lip (active articulator) and the upper lip (passive articulator); whereas **/n/** is **alveolar** (like /t d/) and **/ŋ/ velar** (like /k g/), the two articulators being in the former case the tip of the tongue (active articulator) and the alveolar ridge (passive articulator), and in the latter case the back of the tongue (active articulator) and the soft palate (passive articulator). As a consequence, if the nasal passage is blocked, as when having a cold, nasals (*manner* /ˈmænə/) may be realised as voiced plosives ([ˈbædə]). /n/ shows the highest number of allophonic realisations because, as already explained about other alveolar consonants, its place of articulation is particularly liable to be affected by that of the following consonant.

Turning to their main acoustic features, as also detailed in Section 2.4.3, nasals are characterised by the absence of energy around 1,000 Hz, the presence of a low-frequency resonance or "murmur" below 500Hz, and abrupt transitions from and into the neighbouring sounds (see also e.g. Gimson 1984: 193–198; Roach 2005: 58–61; Collins and Mees 2003: 167–168; Collins and Mees 2009: 54–57, 84–87; Cruttenden 2014: 209–217).

IPA Symbols

m Lower-case M.

n Lower-case N.

ŋ Eng.

Identification

/**m**/ lenis voiced bilabial nasal.

/**n**/ lenis voiced alveolar nasal.

/**ŋ**/ lenis voiced velar nasal.

Allophones

[**m**]	[**n**]	[**ŋ**]
[m̥] 'devoiced'	[n̥] 'devoiced'	[ŋ̊] 'devoiced'
[mʷ] 'labialised'	[nʷ] 'labialised'	[ŋʷ] 'labialised'
[mʲ] 'palatalised'	[nʲ] 'palatalised'	[ŋʲ] 'palatalised'
[m̩] 'syllabic'	[n̩] 'syllabic'	[ŋ̍] 'syllabic'
[ɱ] 'labio-dental'	[ɱ] 'labio-dental'	
	[n̠] 'retracted' 'post-alveolar'	[ŋ̄] 'retracted'
	[n̟] 'advanced'	[ŋ] 'advanced'
	[n̪] 'dental'	
	[m] 'bilabial'	
	[ŋ] 'velar'	

Description

In order to pronounce /**m**/ the two lips are in contact forming a closure, whereas to produce /**n**/ and /**ŋ**/ the closure is made between the tip of the tongue and the alveolar ridge, and the back of the tongue and the soft palate, respectively. Simultaneously, in all three cases the soft palate is in its lowered position so that the lung air goes out through the nose, adding the resonance of the nasal cavity to those of the oral and pharyngeal cavities.

As voiced phonemes, nasals are produced with varying degrees of vocal fold vibration and they do not shorten the length of preceding vocalic or sonorant sounds (***bean*** [biːn]).

See the animations and videos under RP /m/, /n/ and /ŋ/ (compared with Spanish /m n/) in the Sound Bank of the EPSS Multimedia Lab.

Environment and main allophonic realisations

While /m n/ can occur in all positions, /ŋ/ is restricted to syllable codas, after short vowels /ɪ æ ɒ ʌ e/, either word-medially or word-finally. Phonologically, Roach (2005: 59–60) explains that it is difficult to work out a rule as to how to pronounce word-medial and word-final <nk> <ng> spellings: either as /ŋ/ or as /ŋk/ or /ŋg/ combinations, respectively. Roach suggests that **<nk> spellings** should always be pronounced as **/ŋk/** (*linking* /ˈlɪŋkɪŋ/, *sink* /sɪŋk/), whereas **word-medial <ng>** may have either **/ŋ/** pronunciations, if the digraph occurs at the end of a morpheme (*singing* /ˈsɪŋɪŋ/, *singer* /ˈsɪŋə/, *hanger* /ˈhæŋə/), or **/ŋg/** pronunciations, if it appears in the middle of a morpheme (*anger* /ˈæŋgə/, *finger* /ˈfɪŋgə/). When the **<ng>** spelling occurs in **word-final position**, **[g]** is **never pronounced** (*long* /lɔŋ]). There exist, however, two important **exceptions** to these tendencies. **Comparative** and **superlative** forms are pronounced with medial **/ŋg/**, instead of /ŋ/ (*longer* /ˈlɒŋgə/, *longest* /ˈlɒŋgɪst/), despite consisting of two morphemes and having morpheme-final <ng>, and therefore they "behave" as single-morpheme words.

We have seen that these three nasals are generally voiced. But, as occurs with other voiced phonemes, they are only **fully voiced** between voiced sounds (*amber* [ˈæmbə], *annoy* [əˈnɔɪ], *finger* [ˈfɪŋgə]). **Devoiced** allophones may be heard in word-initial and word-final positions (***mummy*** [ˈm̥ʌmi], ***autumn*** [ˈɔːtəm̥], ***bacon*** [ˈbeɪkən̥], ***hang*** [hæŋ̊]), as well as when nasals follow a voiceless consonant (*smart* [sm̥ɑːt], *sneeze* [sn̥iːz], *bacon* [ˈbeɪkŋ̊ˈ]).]))

In addition to their **syllabic** realisations, which, as already noted, can occur in the three nasals (*rhythm* [ˈrɪðm̩], *cotton* [ˈkɒtn̩], *taken* [ˈteɪkŋ̍]), although /n/ records the highest incidence, both /m/ and /n/ may have **labio-dental** realisations **[ɱ]**, if they are followed by the labio-dental fricatives /f/ or /v/ either within words or in close-knit word-boundaries (*comfort* [ˈkʌɱfət], *circumvent* [ˌsɜːkəɱˈvent], *infant* [ˈɪɱfənt], *envy* [ˈeɱvi]). Also word-medially or at word-junctures /n/ may have a **dental** realisation when it occurs before and after dental fricatives (*ninth* [naɪn̪θ]) and a **post-alveolar** allophonic when followed by /r/ (*inroad* [ˈɪn̠ɹəʊd]). Likewise, [ŋ] and [m] can be two other allophonic variants of /n/, when it is followed by either a **velar** (*ten coins* [teŋ ˈkɔɪnz]) or a **bilabial** consonant (*in bed* [ɪm ˈbed] in close-knit word boundaries, respectively; and [m] may also be heard when word-final /n/ is preceded by bilabial /p b/ (happe**n** [ˈhæpm̩̥], carbo**n** [ˈkɑːbm̩̥].

The last set of allophonic realisations that affect the three nasals involve the position of the lips, with **lip-rounding** (*mob* [mʷɒb], *no* [nʷəʊ], *long* [lɒŋʷ]) or **lip-spreading** (*mule* [mʲjuːl], *mining* [ˈmaɪnʲɪŋʲ]) in the vicinity of rounded and spread vowels or semi-vowels, respectively (see § 5.2.3).

Spellings

Table 29: The spellings of RP /m n ŋ/

/m/	/n/	/ŋ/
<m> mother /ˈmʌðə/ damage /ˈdæmɪdʒ/	<n> plan /plæn/ bend /bend/	<ng> sing /sɪŋ/ longing /ˈlɒŋɪŋ/
<mm> mummy /ˈmʌmi/ immense /ɪˈmens/	<nn> planning /ˈplænɪŋ/ connect /kəˈnekt/	<n> (+ /k/ or /g/) sink /sɪŋk/ bangle /ˈbæŋgl̩/
<m> + silent <b> **bomb** /bɒm/, **climb** /klaɪm/	silent <g> + <n> benig**n** /bəˈnaɪn/, **gnaw** /nɔː/	
	silent <k> + <n> **know** /nəʊ/ acknowledge /əkˈnɒlɪdʒ/	
Rare cases <m> + silent <n> **solemn** /ˈsɒləm/, **column** /ˈkɒləm/ silent <l> + <m> **calm** /kɑːm/, **balm** /bɑːm/ silent <g> + <m> diaphra**gm** /ˈdaɪəfræm/	**Rare cases** silent <m> + <n> **mnemonic** /nɪˈmɒnɪk/ silent <p> + <n> **pneumatic** /njuːˈmætɪk/ **pneumonia** /njuːˈməʊnɪə/	**Rare cases** <ngue> **tongue** /tʌŋ/

Regional and social variants

Neither /m/ nor /n/ have important social or regional variants. The most remarkable feature concerns the alternations between [ŋ] and [ŋg] pronunciations where RP would have /ŋ/ (e.g. ***singing*** [ˈsɪŋɪŋ] – [ˈsɪŋgɪŋg], which are typical of the north-west of England (e.g. Lancashire, Derbyshire, Cheshire and Staffordshire).

Comparison with Spanish and advice

English /**n**/ and /**ŋ**/ pose a problem for speakers of Spanish as regards their phonemic status. In Spanish [ŋ] occurs as an allophone of [n] before velars (e.g. *hongo* 'fungus' [ˈoŋgo]). Its occurrence without an intervening velar is only registered in Central American Spanish, as well as in South American Spanish (Peruvian, Ecuadorian), where [ŋ] is used as a common realisation of /n/. The most common error for SSLE is to produce [n] instead of [ŋ], and so English gerunds, for example, such as *linking* [ˈlɪŋkɪŋ], *watching* [ˈwɒtʃɪŋ], *playing* [ˈpleɪɪŋ] and *coming* [ˈkʌmɪŋ], may be pronounced with a final [n], as in *[ˈlɪŋkɪn], *[wɒtʃɪn], *[pleɪɪn] and *[ˈkʌmɪn], which may cause intelligibility problems derived from the loss of the [ŋ] – [n] phonemic contrast that exists in English (*ran* /ræn/ – *rang* /ræŋ/).

Turning to /**m**/, whereas in English it may occur in all possible contexts, in Spanish its occurrence in word-final positions is highly restricted, since cases like ***álbum*** are exceptional and the final nasal is often pronounced as an alveolar *[alβun] rather than a bilabial.

SSLE should therefore be aware of the need to pronounce word-final /m/ appropriately, keeping in mind the distinct phonemic nature of English /n/ and /ŋ/: the former may occur in all possible contexts, and the latter word-medially or word-finally, whether or not it is next to another velar (Finch and Ortiz Lira 1982: 64, 69; Gallardo del Puerto 2005; Estebas Vilaplana 2009: 82–85).

Further practice

AI 4.18 The spellings of RP /m/. Further practice

met /met/	**m**onth /mʌnθ/	bo**mb** /bɒm/
si**mm**er /ˈsɪmə/	a**m**ber /ˈæmbə/	so**m**eone /ˈsʌmwʌn/
Pa**m** /pæm/	albu**m** /ˈælbəm/	

Mu**mm**y's photo was in the albu**m** all the ti**m**e.
/ˈməmiz ˈfəʊtəʊ wəz ɪn ði ˈælbəm ɔːl ðə ˈtaɪm/

We'll discuss it in the foru**m**.
/wil dɪˈskʌs ɪt ɪn ðə ˈfɔːrəm/

Now it's the **m**onth of **M**ay, it's getting war**m**.
/naʊ ɪts ðə mʌnθ əv meɪ ɪts ˈgetɪŋ wɔːm/

AI 4.19 The spellings of RP /n/. Further practice

net /net/	**n**ever /ˈnevə/	**kn**ow /nəʊ/
si**nn**er /ˈsɪnə/	fi**n**d /faɪnd/	a**n**t /ænt/
pe**n** /pen/	**n**o**n**e /nʌn/	pla**n** /plæn/

No, it's **n**ever **n**ice there.
/nəʊ | ɪts ˈnevə naɪs ðeə/

No **n**ews is good **n**ews.
/nəʊ njuːz ɪz gʊd njuːz/

They fou**n**d a **n**ice **n**ew **n**a**nn**y for the baby.
/ˈðeɪ faʊnd ə naɪs njuː ˈnæni fə ðə ˈbeɪbi/

Ni**n**e **n**ice **n**ight **n**urses **n**ursi**n**g **n**icely.
/naɪn naɪs naɪt ˈnɜːsɪz ˈnɜːsɪŋ ˈnaɪsli/

AI 4.20 The spellings of RP /ŋ/. Further practice

si**ng**er /ˈsɪŋə/	to**ngue** /tʌŋ/	a**n**gry /ˈæŋgri/
pi**ng** /pɪŋ/	u**n**cle /ˈʌŋkl̩/	thi**n**ki**ng** /ˈθɪŋkɪŋ/
si**n**k /sɪŋk/	hu**n**gry /ˈhʌŋgri/	

I heard a loud ba**ng**, and someone si**ng**i**ng** a so**ng**.
/ˈaɪ hɜːd ə laʊd bæŋ | ənd ˈsʌmwʌn ˈsɪŋɪŋ ə sɒŋ/

I'm goi**ng** to the ba**n**k.
/aɪm ˈgəʊɪŋ tə ðə bæŋk/

The si**ng**er, when he was you**ng**er, broke his fi**ng**er.
/ðə ˈsɪŋə | wen hi wəz ˈjʌŋgə | brəʊk ɪz ˈfɪŋgə/

4.2.5 Approximants

This section focuses on four RP consonantal phonemes **/l r j w/** that share the same manner of articulation described as **open approximation** (see also Gimson 1984: 193–198; Roach 2005: 58–61; Collins and Mees 2003: 168–171; Collins and Mees 2009: 54–57, 84–87; Cruttenden 2014: 209–217). This means that these four sounds require a constriction which is typically greater than that required for a vowel, but they are produced with an approximation of the articulators which is too open to cause any friction (unlike that of fricatives, which is characterised as **close approximation**), for which they (together with vowels)[82] are also referred to as **frictionless continuants** (see 2.3.2.2).

/r j w/ are characterised as **central approximants** in that the airstream passes straight along a central/median/mid-sagittal channel through the vocal tract, whereas **/l/** is the only **lateral approximant** of the RP phoneme inventory, because the air flows across the lowered side rims of the tongue around some central obstruction, so that the action of the side rims against the upper molars can be felt, as well as the contact made between the tongue tip and the alveolar ridge (Ashby 2011: 50). Accordingly, in what follows it will be shown that, considering manner of articulation, /l/ is categorised as **alveolar**, whereas /r/, /j/ and /w/ will be classified as **post-alveolar**, **palatal** and **labial-velar**, respectively.

Distributionally, approximants behave very similarly. They are the **second** and **third elements** of two of the most recurrent initial consonant clusters in English: **C** + **/l r w j/** and **/s/** + **/p t k/** + **/l r j w/**. In both contexts approximants

82 In some analyses, [h] is also considered an approximant as the voiceless equivalent of the vowel following (Crystal 2008:32).

are devoiced, if they are preceded by a voiceless consonant (*clay* [kl̥eɪ], *try* [tɹ̥aɪ], *quick* [kw̥ɪk], *fuel* [ˈfj̊uːəl], *spray* [spɹ̥ei], *stewed* [stj̊uːd]), and they are shortened, like long vowels and vocalic glides, if followed by a voiceless consonant (so compare *kilt* [kɪɫˑt] with *killed* [kɪɫːd]).

Acoustically, as already detailed in Section 2.4.3, approximants exhibit a voicing bar along with formant-like structures that resembles those of vowels, and show the following most remarkable characteristics (O'Connor *et al.* 1957; Cruttenden 2014: 225, 220):

(1) /**r**/ may be identified in spectrograms by its steepingly rising transitions (for F1, F2, F3 and F4) to a following vowel.
(2) For most realisations of /**l**/ F3 is high and weak (around 2500 Hz) and transitions from and to vowels tend to be slower than those for nasals although faster than those for glide consonants.
(3) /**j**/ and /**w**/ have a two- or three-formant structure similar to that of [iː] and [uː] respectively, and their steady state is even shorter than that of the other two approximants (around 30 msecs).

In order to be able to devoice /**l r j w**/, SSLE could try to produce them as if they were whispered. It should be kept in mind that, as a side-effect of aspiration, this devoicing effect is blocked in two contexts: (1) when an /s/ precedes the consonant cluster; and (2) when the syllable is not stressed. So compare, *cream* [kʰɹ̥iːm] and *plastic* [ˈpl̥æstɪk], which show fortis plosive aspiration and approximant devoicing, with *scream* [skɹiːm] and *plasticity* [plæˈstɪsɪti], where there is neither aspiration nor approximant devoicing (Estebas Vilaplana 2009: 100–101).

4.2.5.1 Liquids: RP /r l/ vs. PSp /r ɾ l ʎ/

/l/ and /r/ are grouped together because both are **liquid approximants**, that is, both are **apico-alveolar** approximant sounds that are made by placing the tip of the tongue on the alveolar ridge (cf fn 5) (see also Gimson 1984: 193–198; Roach 2005: 58–61; Collins and Mees 2003: 168–172; 176–181; Collins and Mees 2009: 54–57, 84–87; Cruttenden 2014: 209–217; Walsh-Dickey 1997).

IPA Symbols

r	Lower-case R.
ɹ	Turned R.
ɾ	Fish-hook R.
l	Lower-case L.

Identification

/ɹ/ [ɹ] Voiced post-alveolar approximant.
/r/ Voiced post-alveolar trill.
/ɾ/ Voiced post-alveolar tap.
/l/ Voiced alveolar lateral approximant.

Allophones

/ɹ/	/l/
[ɹ] 'post-alveolar approximant'	[l] 'clear' or 'palatal'
[ɹˠ] 'velarised alveolar approximant'	[ɫ] 'dark' or 'velar'
[ɻ] 'retroflex'	
[ɾ] 'alveolar tap'	
[ɹ̝] 'voiced fricative'	
[ɹ̥] 'devoiced' / 'voiceless fricative'	[l̥] [ɫ̥] 'devoiced'
[ɹʷ] 'labialised'	[lʷ] 'labialised'
[ɹʲ] 'palatalised'	[lʲ] 'palatalised'
[ʋ] 'voiced labio-dental approximant'	[ɫ̪] 'dental'
[ʀ] 'voiced uvular trill'	[ɫ̠] 'retracted' or 'post-alveolar'
[ʁ] 'voiced uvular fricative fricative'	[ɫ̃] [l̃] 'nasalised'

Description

For the articulation of RP /ɹ/, the nasal resonator is shut off by raising the soft palate. The tip of the tongue is slightly retroflected close to, but does not touch, the rear part of the alveolar ridge, while the centre of the tongue is hollowed and the back rims are touching the upper molars, no contact being made with the roof of the mouth at any time. The vocal folds do vibrate and no friction is produced when the lung air goes out of the mouth. Although lip position is largely determined by that of the following vowel, English speakers tend to pronounce this sound with rounded lips (Roach 2005: 63).

/l/, on the other hand, is pronounced with a complete median closure of the oral chamber by placing the tip (and blade) of the tongue in the alveolar ridge, and a partial lateral closure, that is, an opening on one or both sides of the mouth which is not radical enough to produce friction. As the soft palate is in its raised position shutting off the nasal resonator, the lung air is released laterally on both sides, or on one side, if there exists a unilateral closure between the side-rims and the upper side teeth. As it is also produced with vibration of the vocal folds, /l/ is classified as a voiced phoneme and therefore it does not affect the length of the previous sound (*feel* [fiːɫ]).

In addition, to pronounce **dark** [ɫ] the back of the tongue is raised in the direction of the soft palate, producing a velarised resonance close to that of back vowels, ranging in closeness from [ʊ], [ö] or [ɤ] to [ɔ] or [ʌ]; whereas the

clear [l] variant is characterised by a front vowel resonance, which results from raising the front of the tongue in the direction of the hard palate. These articulatory differences have acoustic correlates in that the values of F1 (low) and F2 (weak) are quite far apart (around 300 and 1600 Hz) for clear [l], whereas they are close together (around 400 and 600 Hz) for dark [ɫ].

See the animations and videos under RP /r/ and /l/ (compared with Spanish /r ɾ l/) in the Sound Bank of the EPSS Multimedia Lab.

Environment and main allophonic realisations

Since RP is a **non-rhotic accent /r/** is normally pronounced only syllable-initially before vowels or glides (*red* /red/, *arrow* /ˈærəʊ/) (see fn 8). As a result, it does not sound when it is followed by a consonant or when it occurs in syllable-final or word-final positions (*far* /fɑː/, *farm* /fɑːm/). However, when a word ends in the spelling <r> and the following word begins with a vocalic sound, then /r/ is pronounced as an instance of so-called **linking /r/** (*He wore a suit* /hi ˈwɔːr ə ˈsuːt /, *far away* /fɑːr əˈweɪ/, *there are* /ðər ˈɑː/) (see § 5.5). Sometimes speakers use a linking /r/ in words where there is no <r> spelling (*He **saw** a car* /hi ˈsɔːr ə kɑː/), in which case we speak of **intrusive /r/**. However, intrusive /r/ should be avoided as it indicates an uneducated pronunciation.

A **retroflexed** [ɻ], curling the tip of the tongue backwards towards just behind the alveolar ridge, is often heard both before and between vowels (*road* [ɻəʊd], *far off* [fɑːɻ ɒf]), *very* [ˈveɻi])), in which case the vowel is said to be **r-coloured** or **rhotacised** (see fn 64) and the degree of retroflexion varies depending on regional, social and stylistic factors (Wells 1982: 432). /r/ may also be realised as a voiced **alveolar tap** or **flap** [ɾ], and so a short single tap being made with the tip of the tongue on the alveolar ridge, in intervocalic positions (*very* [ˈveɾi]), or the dental ridge, before /θ/ and /ð/ (*three* [θɾiː], *thread* [θɾed], *with rage* [wɪð ɾeɪdʒ]), the central hollowing of the tongue being retained.

Both within words and between close-knit word-boundaries, /r/ has a **fricative allophone**, which is **voiced** when it follows /d/ [**dɹ̝**] (*draft* [dɹ̝ɑˑft], *bedroom* [ˈbedɹ̝uːm], *wide range* [waɪd ɹ̝eɪndʒ]) and shows different degrees of **devoicing** when it follows a fortis plosive (*upright* [ˈʌpɹ̥aɪt], *try* [tɹ̥aɪ], *cream* [kɹ̥iːm]). Likewise, devoiced realisations will occur when /r/ follows a voiceless consonant (*friar* [ˈfɹ̥aɪə], *necessary* [ˈnesəsɹ̥i], *surf-riding* [ˈsɜːfɹ̥aɪdɪŋ]), as well as in word-initial positions (*red* [ɹ̥ed]). Considering the position of the lips, variants with tight **lip-rounding** (*room* [ɹʷuːm]) or some degree of **lip-spreading** (*read* [ɹʲiːd]) will also occur in the vicinity of rounded and spread vowels or semi-vowels, respectively.

Turning to **/l/**, it can occur in all positions in the word, but it has two allophonic variants depending on its place of occurrence. It is **clear** [l] before vowels or before palatal /j/ (*love* [lʌv], *peculiar* [pɪˈkjuːlɪə]), and it is **dark** [ɫ] before consonants and in final position (*milk* [mɪɫk], *mill* [mɪɫ]. **Dark *l*** [ɫ] has the effect of retracting and lowering the articulation of the preceding front vowel, so that [i:ɫ] pronunciations, for example, usually have a centring glide and for many RP speakers there is no contrast with [ɪəɫ] (*reel* – *real*) and they can pronounce words such as *feel* either as [fi:ɫ] or [fɪəɫ]. Similarly, before [ɫ] the second elements of vowel glides tends to be dropped or is otherwise reduced to [ᵊ] or [ᵘ] (*failed* [feᵊɫd], ***aisle*** [aᵊɫ], ***owl*** [aᵘɫ], ***boils*** [bɔᵊɫz], ***cruel*** [ˈkru:ᵊɫ]), as already noted in Section 3.3.

Both clear and dark *l* are voiced, but they are **devoiced** after voiceless consonants (***flee*** [fl̥i:], *bottle* [ˈbɒtɫ̩̊]. Moreover, when preceded by /p/ or /k/ in a stressed syllable (***play*** [pl̥eɪ], ***climb*** [kl̥aɪm]), the devoicing of /l/ sounds like a kind of aspiration of the plosive. Adjacent to nasals, /l/ is nasalised [ɫ̃] (***signalman*** [ˈsɪgnɫ̃mən]), and considering the place of articulation, as already seen in the description of other alveolar sounds, [ɫ] tends to approach that of the following consonant, both within words and in close-knit word-boundaries. Hence, if [ɫ] occurs next to /θ ð/ it will have a **dental articulation** [ɫ̪] (*health*, *feel that* [heɫ̪θ fi:ɫ̪ ðæt]), and it will be **post-alveolar** [ɫ̠] before /r/ (*already* [ɔ:ɫ̠ˈɹedi], ***all*** *roses* [ɔ:ɫ̠ˈɹəʊzɪz]). Lip position is, as usual, another parameter of allophonic variation so that allophones with either **lip-rounding** (***loo*** [lʷu:], *cool* [ku:ɫʷ]) or **lip-spreading** (***lea*** [lʲi:], ***eel*** [i:ɫʲ]) will occur in the vicinity of rounded and spread vowels or semi-vowels, respectively.

Under the conditions explained in Section 1.3.3.2, both /r/ and particularly /l/ (mostly dark) may be syllabic (*generous* [ˈdʒenɹ̩əs], ***memory*** [ˈmemɹ̩i], ***petal*** [ˈpetɫ̩], ***bottle*** [ˈbɒtɫ̩]).

Spellings

Table 30: The spellings of RP /l r/

/r/	/l/
<r> round /ˈraʊnd/, staring /ˈsteərɪŋ/	<l> (including <le>) let /let/, feel /fɪl/, **middle** /ˈmɪdl̩/
<rr> starring /ˈstɑ:rɪŋ/, sorry /ˈsɒri/	<ll> **fill** /fi:l/, **allow** /əˈlaʊ/
silent <w> + <r> **write** /ˈraɪt/, **wreath** /ri:θ/	**Rare cases** silent <s> + <le> **isle** /aɪl/
<r> + silent <h> **rhyme** /raɪm/ **rhythm** /ˈrɪðəm/	

Note that there are words that are spelt with a single <l> in British but normally have a double l <ll> in American English (*dial(l)ing, distil(l), enrol(l), fulfil(l), signal(l), instal(l)ing, travel(l)ing*) whereas in the following cases <l> spellings are always silent.

calm	/kɑːm/	half	/hɑːf/	talk	/ˈtɔːk/
could	/kʊd/	salmon	/ˈsæmən/	would	/wʊd/
folk	/fəʊk/	should	/ʃʊd/		

Regional and social variants

Originating in basilectal London accents and then spreading to the Southeast and further away (e.g. Derby, Milton Keynes, Middlesborough), the labialisation of /**r**/ is so extreme that there exists a widespread tendency to substitute it (and also /w/) by /ʋ/, **a voiced labio-dental approximant**, although this is also a feature of early child language and has often been considered as a speech defect in adults (Cruttenden 2014: 225; Foulkes and Docherty 2000). In addition, either a **voiced uvular trill** [ʀ] or a **voiced uvular fricative** [ʁ] are residual *r*-variants of the north-east of England and Lowland Scottish English.

Unlike in RP, in **rhotic English accents** (most American, Scottish, West England and Irish English and much of the rural areas of the South and South-west of England), the phoneme /r/ is pronounced both in syllable initial and syllable-final positions, and so a distinction is made between such words as *court-caught* and *poor-paw* which are homophones in RP. Broadly speaking, in these rhotic accents prevocalic /r/ is generally pronounced as a **velarised alveolar continuant** [ɹ] ([ɹˠ]), but postvocalic **retroflex** [ɻ] (*bird* [bɜːɻd], *farm* [fɑːɻm], *lord* [lɔːɻd]) is increasingly frequent and may become the mainstream pronunciation. Another feature of these accents resulting from their rhoticity is the absence of linking-/r/ and intrusive-/r/ (Wells 1982: 431–432; Hickey 2007: 320).

Moving on to the lateral approximant, in the speech of London there exists a tendency either to omit **dark** [ɫ] or to substitute it by a vowel in the region of [ö], a centralised close-mid back rounded vowel, or [ɤ̈], its unrounded counterpart (***sell*** [seö] – [seɤ̈]). Besides, the distributionally-based clear [l] and dark [ɫ] distintion that works in RP does not apply to other English accents. In SSE, the North of England and Wales, GA, Australian English and New Zealand English, dark [ɫ] is pronounced in all positions. In contrast, in South Wales and on Tyneside, as well as in West Indian English and southern Irish English clear [l] is found in all positions, although in the latter accent postvocalic dark [ɫ] may also be heard among young speakers (Wells 1982: 431; Hughes 2005: 114; Hickey 2007: 321; Cruttenden 2014: 220–221).

Comparison with Spanish and advice

Whereas RP is a non-rhotic accent in which /**r**/ is generally pronounced only before vowels and glides and is mostly realised as an approximant sound (no contact being made with the roof of the mouth), Spanish is a rhotic language which has two "***r*-phonemes**" involving two different types of tongue-palate contact: tap [ɾ] (as in *pero* 'but'), trill [r] (as in *perro* 'dog'). These phonemes are contrastive only in intervocalic position. Their contrast is neutralised in post-nuclear position (*cardo* 'thistle') (Quilis and Fernández 1996), elsewhere they occur in complementary distribution: [r] is used word-initially and after consonants, as well as an emphatic alternative to [ɾ] in word-final positions (Mott 2011: 258–259), although some experimental studies suggest a preference for a tap [ɾ] in all these contexts except for word-initially (Blecua 1999). In addition, both Spanish phonemes are described as **retroflex**, whereas in English not all instances of /r/ are retroflected.

Hence a common mistake for SSLE is to use the two Spanish *r* sounds ([ɾ] or [r]) instead of English post-alveolar approximant /r/, which does not cause misunderstandings but gives a very strong foreign accent (García Lecumberri and Elorduy 1994; García Lecumberri 1999, 2000; Gallardo del Puerto 2005). To avoid such replacements and pronounce RP /r/ correctly, SSLE are advised to round their lips, but being careful not to exaggerate this gesture as too much rounding would make this consonant sound too much like [w], and try to produce a central vowel of the /ə/ /ɜː/ type. Likewise, to get as close as possible to native RP pronunciation, SSLE should not pronounce pre-consonantal and pre-pausal <r> spellings, but rather should consider them as indications to lengthen or diphthongise the previous vowel(s) (Cruttenden 2014: 227–228). Nevertheless, in connected speech word-final <r> spellings should normally be pronounced as instances of linking /r/ in the appropriate phonetic contexts (see § 5.5).

Now regarding the lateral approximant, while English has only one such phoneme with two main allophones (**clear and dark *l***), Spanish has two lateral phonemes: the alveolar one [**l**] (***la***, ***el*** [la] [el] 'the') and the palatal one [**ʎ**] (*ca**ll**e* [ˈkaʎe] 'street'), although the latter is increasingly delateralised resulting in a merger with the central palatal approximant [j] ([ˈkaje] or as a voiced palatal plosive [ɟ] word-initially (***ll**amo* 'I call' [ˈɟamo]), so that for many speakers the following pairs are homophones: *ha**ll**a* 'have' (pres subj) – *ha**y**a* 'beech', *o**ll**a* 'pot' – *ho**y**a* 'hole', *ma**ll**a* 'net' – *ma**y**a* 'mayan', *po**ll**o* 'chicken' – *po**y**o* 'stone bench'.

Since in Spanish [l] is clear in all positions, when speaking in English SSLE should be careful to pronounce this sound only in syllable-initial positions before vowels or /j/, producing the dark variant elsewhere. To articulate dark [ɫ] the tip of the tongue should not be curled backwards, the most essential feature being a slight rounding of the lips of the [o] or [ɔ̝] quality, this sound being similar to the *l* used in Catalan in such words as ***lámina*** 'sheet', 'slice' ['łamina] or ***sal*** 'salt' [sał] (Finch and Ortiz Lira 1982: 64; Estebas Vilaplana 2009: 88–96; Mott 2011: 258–259; Cruttenden 2014: 222).

Further practice

AI 4.21 The spellings of RP /r/. Further practice

right /raɪt/	sta**rr**ing /ˈstɑːrɪŋ/	t**r**ain /treɪn/
b**r**ight /braɪt/	**wr**ite /ˈraɪt/	t**r**emble /ˈtrembl̩/
sta**r**ing /ˈsteərɪŋ/	**rh**yme /raɪm/	

These **r**ecent songs are **r**eally surp**r**ising.
/ðiːz ˈriːsnt sɒŋz ə ˈrɪəli səˈpraɪzɪŋ/

Who **wr**ote the ly**r**ics?
/huː rəʊt ðə ˈlɪrɪks|/

Roberta **r**an **r**ings a**r**ound the **R**oman **r**uins.
/rəˈbɜːtə ræn rɪŋz əˈraʊnd ðə ˈrəʊmən ˈruːɪnz/

AI 4.22 The spellings of RP /l/. Further practice

lamp /læmp/	**l**ake /leɪk/	**l**ent /lent/
e**l**even /ɪˈlevn̩/	a**l**ready /ɔːlˈredi/	fi**ll** /fɪl/
ta**ll** /tɔːl/	fee**l** /fiːl/	**l**ent /lent/

Lots of **l**akes are sp**l**endid for sai**l**ing.
/lɒts əv leɪks ə ˈsplendɪd fə ˈseɪlɪŋ/

A**l**most a**ll** anima**l**s are sti**ll** beautifu**l** when they are o**l**d.
/ˈɔːlməʊst ɔːl ˈænɪml̩z ə stɪl ˈbjuːtəfl̩ wen ˈðeɪ ər əʊld/

One of the **l**ove**l**iest f**l**owers is ca**ll**ed **l**i**l**y of the va**ll**ey.
/wʌn əv ðə ˈlʌvlɪɪst ˈflaʊəz ɪz kɔːld ˈlɪli əv ðə ˈvæli/

Li**l**y **l**ad**l**es **l**itt**l**e **L**etty's **l**enti**l** soup.
/ˈlɪli ˈleɪdl̩z ˈlɪtl̩ ˈletiɪz ˈlentl̩ suːp/

4.2.5.2 Glide consonants /j w/

In RP there are two **/j w/ glide consonants**, also known as **semi-vowels** or **semi-consonants** (see fn 13). This means that both phonemes are **phonologically** like **consonants** but **phonetically** like **vowels** (see also Gimson 1984:

211–216; Roach 2005: 63–64; Collins and Mees 2003: 172–176; Collins and Mees 2009: 92–94; Cruttenden 2014: 228–235).

Phonologically, /**j**/ and /**w**/ behave like consonants in that they can only occur in the **margins** (onset positions) of syllables, either individually or as part of a consonant cluster. Their consonantal nature is also reinforced by the fact that articles adopt their consonantal forms before /j/ or /w/ (*the **u**niversity* [ðə ˌjuːnɪˈvɜːsɪti], *a **w**oman* [ə ˈwʊmən]), and it will be shown that their allophones are affected by the same phenomena as those undergone by other consonants. From a phonetic point of view, however, /**j**/ and /**w**/ are vowel-like in that they involve a rapid movement or glide from a position similar to [iː] (with spread or neutral lips) or [uː] (with rounded lips) respectively on to a vowel of a longer duration, the actual point of departure being affected by the nature of the following sound.

IPA Symbols

j Lower-case J.
w Lower-case W.

Identification

/**j**/ lenis voiced palatal approximant.
/**w**/ lenis voiced labial-velar approximant.

Allophones

/**j**/
[**j̊**] 'devoiced fricative'
[**ç**] 'voiceless palatal fricative'
[**tʃ**] [**dʒ**] 'affricated'
[**ʃ**] [**ʒ**] 'fricativised'

/**w**/
[**w̥**] 'devoiced'
[**ʍ**] 'voiceless labial-velar fricative'

Description

For the articulation of RP /**j**/ the soft palate is in its raised position shutting off the nasal resonator, the vocal folds vibrate, and the front of the tongue is raised towards the hard palate to approximately the position for an [i] or [ɪ]-type vowel. This is a rapid vowel-like glide on to a vowel of longer duration and prominence, its starting point being of a closer or more open variety according to the degree of openness of the following vowel. When it occurs in consonant clusters, the consonant preceding /j/ will have a **palatalised articulation** with some degree of lip-spreading (*ar**g**ue* [ˈɑːgʲjuː].

Like /j/, /**w**/ produces a crescendo glide that varies its starting point according to the degree of closeness of the following vowel that has greater prominence. The soft palate is also in its raised position shutting off the nasal resonator and the vocal folds vibrate. But in this case the tongue is raised towards the soft palate, to approximately the position for an [u] or [ʊ]-type vowel, and this glide is accompanied by strong lip-rounding. For this reason [w] is said to have a **double articulation** as it involves a combination of two strictures of equal rank: labial and velar open approximation. When it occurs in consonant clusters, the consonant preceding /w/ will be noticeably **labialised** undergoing strong lip-rounding (*language* [ˈlæŋgʷwɪdʒ].

See the animations and videos under RP /w/ and /j/ (compared with the Spanish sequences /wa we wo wi/ and /ja je jo ju/ respectively) in the Sound Bank of the EPSS Multimedia Lab.

Environment and main allophonic realisations

Both /j/ and /w/ occur only in pre-vocalic positions at the beginning or in the middle of words, but never at the end of a word. /**j**/ has a **devoiced** realisation after voiceless consonants [j̊], but there exists an additional fricative component when /j/ occurs after /p t k/ initially in stressed syllables (*pure* [pj̊ʊə], *tumult* [ˈtj̊u:mʌlt]. It may also be realised as a **completely devoiced palatal fricative** [ç̊] similar to the German *ich-Laut*, usually in the sequence /h/ + [j] in a restricted number of words (***hew*** [çu:], ***hu****ge* [çu:dʒ], ***hu****man* [ˈçu:mən], ***hu****mour* [ˈçu:mə]), although on the phonetic pattern /p t k/ + /j/ there are fluctuations between [hj] and [ç] pronunciations.

The sequences /tj/, /dj/, /sj/ and /zj/ are normally coalesced into [tʃ], [dʒ], [ʃ] and [ʒ] in word-medial syllables and at close-knit word-boundaries (*e****du****cated* [edʒʊˈkeɪtɪd], *woul****d*** ***y****ou* [ˈwʊdʒu], *a****ssu****me* [əˈʃu:m], *pre****su****me* [prɪˈʒu:m]), but they may also be heard in stressed onset positions (***tu****ne* [tʃu:n], ***du****ne* [dʒu:n]). These pronunciations, however, are not always accepted in Conservative RP and may be stigmatised as "lazy speech" (see also § 5.3 for details on assimilation). A **junctural** [ʲ] may be pronounced to reinforce the boundary between syllable- or word-final [i: i eɪ aɪ ɔɪ] and a following vowel (*s****ee****ing* [ˈsi:ʲɪŋ], *s****igh****ing* [ˈsaɪʲɪŋ], *m****y*** ***ear*** [maɪ ˈʲɪə]). **A glottal stop** may also be heard as an alternative to junctual [ʲ] (*my ear* [maɪ ˈʔɪə]).

Now considering /**w**/, it has like /j/ a partially **devoiced** allophone [w̥] when it follows a voiceless consonant. But when it follows /t k/ in stressed syllable-initial positions, the devoicing is complete so that a **voiceless labial-velar fricative** [ʍ] is produced (*t****w****in* [tʍɪn], ***qu****estion* [ˈkʍestʃən], *con****qu****est* [ˈkɒŋkʍest]). A **junctual** [ʷ] may be pronounced to reinforce the boundary between syllable- or word-final [u: u əʊ aʊ ɔɪ] and a following vowel (*d****o****ing* [ˈdu:ʷɪŋ], ***no a****sking* [nəʊ ˈʷɑ:skɪŋ]), which may be replaced by a **glottal stop** (*no* ***a****sking* [nəʊ ˈʔɑ:skɪŋ]).

Spellings

Table 31: The spellings of RP /j w/

/j/	/w/
<y> **y**es /jes/, law**y**er /ˈlɔːjə/	<w> **w**in /wɪn/
<i> p**i**ano /pɪˈænəʊ/, on**i**on /ˈʌnjən/	<w> + silent <h> **wh**en /wen/, **wh**y /waɪ/
<u> <ui> (as part of /juː/ or /jʊə/) ab**u**se /əˈbjuːs/, end**u**re /ɪnˈdjʊə/ n**ui**sance /ˈnjuːsns/	<u> (usu. <qu> /kw/) q**u**ite /kwaɪt/, q**u**iet /ˈkwaɪət/ lang**u**age /ˈlæŋgwɪdʒ/
<ue> (as part of /juː/) (usu. Fr loanwords) arg**ue** /ˈɑːgjuː/, resid**ue** /ˈrezɪdjuː/ barbec**ue** /ˈbɑːbɪkjuː/	
<ew> / <eu> (as part of /juː/) (usu. Fr loanwords) neph**ew** /ˈnefjuː/, st**ew** /stjuː/ adi**eu** /əˈdjuː/, f**eu**d /fjuːd/	
Rare cases <e> b**e**auty /ˈbjuːti/ azal**e**a /əˈzeɪliə/, but also /əˈzeɪljə/	

As shown in Table 31, RP /j/ is very common as part of the sequences /juː/ and /jʊə/. The latter may be pronounced as [jɔː] (see § 3.3.2). The following fluctuations between [juː] and [uː] pronunciations should also be borne in mind (Jones 1975: 209–210; Gimson 1984: 192; Cruttenden 2014: 230). After /tʃ dʒ r/ [uː] pronunciations tend to be preferred, but [juː] is retained after plosives, /f/, /v/, and /h/ (*queue* /kjuː/, *few* /fjuː/, *view* /vjuː/, *huge* /hjuːdʒ/), as well as when /l/ is preceded by an accented vowel (*value* /ˈvæljuː/, *curlew* /ˈkɜːljuː/). Elsewhere both /juː/ and /uː/ and may be heard, although /uː/ grows increasingly common (and is the NP in AE) after /n/, /l/ and /s/ in accented syllables (*neutral* /ˈnuːtrəl/, *lute* /luːt/), whilst /juː/ remains predominant after /s z θ l/ (*consume* /kənˈsjuːm/, *enthusiasm* /ɪnˈθjuːzɪæzəm/).

Note that the letter <w> is silent in word-initial <swo>, <wr> spellings (*sword* /sɔːd/, *wrist* /rɪst/).

Regional and social variants

In East Anglia /j/ may be dropped after all consonants, whereas in GA it is not pronounced following /t d θ ð n/ and so such words as *tune, dune* or *duty* will have [uː] pronunciations. In Irish English **yod-dropping** also occurs in stressed syllables after alveolar sonorants (***new*** [nuː]). In certain areas of Wales the [h] + [j] sequence is reduced to [j] (Wells 1982: 436; Hickey 2007: 307).

The most remarkable variant of /**w**/ concerns the spelling <wh>. It is pronounced as a voiceless labial-velar fricative [ʍ] mainly in American English, SSE and Irish, thereby marking a contrast between ***wear*** /weə/ and ***wh****ere* /ʍeə/, ***wh****ich* [ʍɪtʃ] and ***w****itch* [wɪtʃ]). [ʍ] may also be heard in Conservative RP and in formal declamatory styles (Wells 1982: 229, 432; Hickey 2007: 319).

Comparison with Spanish and advice

Most descriptions of the Spanish phonemic system do not include [j] and [w] as these two sounds are considered as allophones of /i/ (***ni****eve* 'snow' [ˈnjeβe]) and /u/ (***hu****evo* 'egg' [ˈweβo]) (Alarcos Llorach 1961; Navarro Tomás 1966 [1946] Quilis and Fernández 1982). Although the articulation of these two sounds should involve no problem, SSLE may find it problematic to pronounce them correctly because of the different phonetic status that they have in English and Spanish, and due to the influence of orthographic pronunciation. Since in Spanish words that begin with <y> may be pronounced with as a voiced palatal fricative [ʝ], a voiced palato-alveolar affricate [dʒ], a voiced palatal lateral [ʎ] or even a voiced palatal plosive [ɟ] (word-initially) (***y****a* 'already' [ʝa], [dʒa], [ʎa], [ɟa]), it is common for SSLE mispronounce RP /**j**/ as [ʝ], [dʒ] or even [ʎ] or [ɟa]), so that such words as ***j****am* /dʒæm/ and ***y****am* /jæm/ are often confused. SSLE should therefore remember that the spelling <y> in English corresponds to /j/, not to [ʝ], [dʒ], [ʎ] or [ɟ].

RP /**w**/, on the other hand, may be mispronounced as a [b], or quite frequently, [g] or [ɣ] may be inserted before the sound itself, so that English words like ***wh****en* [wen] or ***wh****isky* [ˈwɪski] may be mispronounced as *[ˈgwen] and *[ˈgwɪski]. As in RP no sound is inserted before word-initial [w], SSLE should try to avoid the insertion of an initial [g] in this context.

Particularly troublesome for SSLE are the English sequences [ji], [jɪ], [wu], [wʊ]. The reason is that in Spanish, [j] and [w] may occur before all vowels except [i] and [u], whereas in English /j w/ may be found before all vowels, including /i, ɪ, u, ʊ/. For this reason, SSLE tend to wrongly pronounce words such as ***y****ear* /ˈjiə/ as *[iər], *[ʝiər], *[dʒiər] or *[ʎiər] and ***w****oman* /ˈwʊmən/ with initial [gu-], [ɣu-], [u-].

To pronounce RP [**j**] correctly, the front of the tongue must be raised to the closest variety of [i] without producing friction, and then glide quickly to a more open quality. In the case of RP [**w**] articulation should begin with strong lip-rounding and with the tongue being raised as for a very close variety of [u] without producing friction, and then a glide should be quickly made to a more open articulation. Moreover, as both [j w] can occur word-initially, SSLE should refrain from producing an epenthetic consonant before them (Mott 2011: 131; Sedláčková 2010: 59; Estebas Vilaplana 2009: 71–73, 86–87; Pennock 2001; Cuenca-Villarín 1996; Finch and Ortiz Lira 1982: 64, 71).

Further practice

AI 4.23 The spellings of RP /j/. Further practice

yellow /ˈjeləʊ/	**y**es /jes/	**y**esterday /ˈjestədi/
f**e**w /fjuː/	**u**se /ˈjuːs/	un**u**sual /ʌnˈjuːʒʊəl/
p**i**ano /pɪˈænəʊ/	n**e**w /njuː/	val**u**able /ˈvæljʊəbl̩/

Are **y**ou **u**sed to **u**sing online n**e**wspapers?
/ə ju ˈjuːst tə ˈjuːzɪŋ ˈɒnˌlaɪn ˈnjuːspeɪpəz/

Is **y**our friend a law**y**er **y**et? **Y**es, **y**esterday he was given a job for a **y**ear in New **Y**ork.
/ɪz jə frend ə ˈlɔːjə jet | jes | ˈjestədi hi wəz ɡɪvn̩ ə dʒɒb ˈfɔːr ə jɜːr ɪn njuː jɔːk/

AI 4.24 The spellings of RP /w/. Further practice

what /ˈwɒt/	**w**indow /ˈwɪndəʊ/	q**u**estion /ˈkwestʃən/
q**u**ick /kwɪk/	**wh**ile /waɪl/	**w**oman /ˈwʊmən/
when /wen/	q**u**ite /kwaɪt/	

This **w**et **w**eather **w**orries me, I **w**onder **wh**en it **w**ill stop.
/ðɪs wet ˈweðə ˈwʌrɪz miː | ˈaɪ ˈwʌndə wen ɪt wɪl stɒp/

The first sound in ‘**w**ood’, ‘**w**oman’, and ‘**w**ool’ is the same as in ‘**w**ed’, ‘**w**omen’ and ‘**w**ell’.
/ðə fɜːst ˈsaʊnd ɪn wʊd | ˈwʊmən | ənd wʊl z ðə seɪm əz ɪn wed | ˈwɪmɪn ənd wel/

Wise **wh**ales keep a**w**ay from the **w**indy **w**est coast.
/waɪz weɪlz kiːp əˈweɪ frəm ðə ˈwɪ ndi westkəʊst/

While **w**e **w**ere **w**alking, **w**e **w**ere **w**atching **w**indow **w**ashers **w**ash **W**ashington’s **w**indows **w**ith **w**arm **w**ashing **w**ater.
/waɪl wi wə ˈwɔːkɪŋ | wi wə ˈwɒtʃɪŋ ˈwɪndəʊ ˈwɒʃəz wɒʃ ˈwɑːʃɪŋtənz ˈwɪndəʊz wɪð wɔːm wɒʃ ˈwɔːtə/

Further reading

As in the previous chapter, we recommend Cruttenden (2014, Chapter 9), Roach (2005, Chapters 4, 6 and 7), Collins and Mees (2003: 139–188) and Gimson (1984, Chapter 8) for an examination of English consonants. More specialised and technical analyses may be found in Ashby (2005, Chapters 9 and 10), Ashby and Maidment (2005, Chapters 6 and 8), Ladefoged (2005, Chapters 11 and 14,) and Ladefoged and Maddieson (1996, Chapter 10) and Laver (1994, Chapters 11 to 14). A more advanced account of the acoustic features of consonants is offered by Hayward (2000, Chapter 7).

For more thorough descriptions of consonantal phonemes in Spanish, the reader is again referred to Martínez Celdrán and Fernández Planas (2007), Navarro Tomás (1991[1918], 1966 [1946]), Quilis and Fernández (1982), Quilis (1985, 1993), and Alarcos LLorach (1961 [1983]), as well as to Martínez Celdrán and Fernández Planas (2003), Colina (2009) and Gil (2007), to mention but a few basic references. To learn more about the acoustics of Spanish consonants, good references to consult are Cabrera Abreu and Vizcaíno Ortega (2009), Martínez Celdrán (1998) and Quilis (1981).

Lastly, additional accounts of RP in contrast with those of Spanish or addressed to SSLE may be found in the aforementioned (mostly) well-established studies: Estebas Vilaplana (2009, Chapters 2 and 3), Monroy Casas (1980, 1981, 2012, Chapters 1 and 2), Mott (2011, Chapters 5 and 12), Núñez Méndez (2005), Finch and Ortiz Lira (1982, Chapter 7), Sánchez Benedicto (1980) and Stockwell and Bowen (1965); whereas issues of acquisition of English consonants by speakers of Spanish are discussed in Gallardo del Puerto (2005), Dale and Poms (1986), Coe-Guerrero (1981), among many others.

Exercises

1. Passive transcription. Read aloud the following passage given in broad transcription, paying special attention to the consonant sounds. Then write it out in ordinary spelling.
   / fənɒˈlɒdʒɪkli / ˈsɪləbl̩z kən bi lʊkt ət ˈteɪkɪŋ ˈɪntə əˈkaʊnt ðə ˈpɒsəbl ˌkɒmbɪˈneɪʃnz əv ˈfəʊniːmz ðət ər əˈlaʊd ɪn ə gɪvn̩ ˈlæŋgwɪdʒ // sɪˈlæbɪk ˈstrʌktʃə ˈdɪfəz frəm wʌn ˈlæŋgwɪdʒ tu əˈnʌðər ɪn tɜːmz əv sʌtʃ pəˈræmɪtəz əz ˈhaʊ meni ˈkɒnsənənts kən əˈkɜːr ɪn ði ˈɒnsets ənd ˈkəʊdəz əv ˈsɪləbl̩z / ɔː ˈweðə ˈvaʊəlz kən əˈkɜː wɪðˈaʊt ˌkɒnsəˈnæntl̩ ˈɒnsets / ˈsɪləbl̩z wɪð ˈzɪərəʊ ˈɒnsets / ɔː ˈweðə bəʊθ ˈəʊpn̩ / ˈendɪŋ ɪn ə ˈvaʊəl / ənd kləʊzd / ˈendɪŋ ɪn ə ˈkɒnsənənt / ˈsɪləbl̩z ə ˈpɒsəbl̩ //

2. Provide words that have the specified fricative and affricate sounds in initial, medial and final the positions: /f, v, θ, ð, s, z, ʃ, ʒ, ʧ, ʤ, h/
3. Stops: /p, b, t, d, k, g, m, n, ŋ/. Read aloud the following words given in broad transcription and then write them out in ordinary spelling.

1. /ˈgɑːdn̩ /	2. /æd/	3. /ˈbegɪŋ/	4. /ˈkɒfɪŋ/	5. /ˈtempə/
6. /ˈræbɪt/	7. /ˈsɪnə/	8. /ˈbʌtə/	9. /ˈkɒfɪn/	10. /bæg/
11. /ˈsɪŋə/	12. /wɒt/	13. /mɒb/	14. /ˈnɔːti/	15. /ˈmeɪkɪŋ/
16. /sʌŋ/	17. /ˈbæŋə/	18. /pɑːm/	19. /sɪŋk/	20. /gæp/

4. Fricatives: /f, v, θ, đ, s, z, ʃ, ʒ, h/. Read aloud the following words given in broad transcription and then write them out in ordinary spelling.

1. /briːf/	2. /θaɪ/	3. /ədˈvaɪs/	4. /ˈvɜːʒn̩/	5. /suːð/
6. /ədˈvaɪz/	7. /ˈpleʒə/	8. /ˈmʌðə/	9. /ˈiːzi/	10. /ruːʒ/
11. /ˈzenɪθ/	12. /briːv/	13. /ˈmæʃɪŋ/	14. /ðeə/	15. /ˈʃerɪ/
16. /ˈhɪsɪŋ/	17. /ˈmeθəd/	18. /bɪˈheɪv/	19. /feɪs/	20. /ˈsʌfə/

5. Affricates and Approximants: /ʧ, ʤ, l, r, j, w/. Read aloud the following words given in broad transcription and then write them out in ordinary spelling.

1. /bæʧ/	2. /kwiːn/	3. /weɪz/	4. /bæʤ/	5. /ˈrɪəli/
6. /njuː/	7. /rɪəl/	8. /jes/	9. /ˈlɒri/	10. /ʧɑːʤ/
11. /eʤ/	12. /eʧ/	13. /ˈwɒʧɪŋ/	14. /ʤæm/	15. /jɔːnd/
16. /ʤeɪn/	17. /ˈkwaɪət/	18. /juːs/	19. /ʧɜːʧ/	20. /ʤuːs/

6. Mixed consonant sounds. Identify the following words from their transcription. Read them aloud first, and then write the spelling.

1. /ʧeɪn/	2. /ɜːʤ/	3. /ˈrɪŋɪŋ/	4. /ˈrɪbn̩/	5. /fjuː/
6. /kəʊld/	7. /ˈkɒlə/	8. /ʤʌg/	9. /ˈnɪəlɪ/	10. /ˈiːvnɪŋ/
11. /ˈlɪsənɪŋ/	12. /sniːz/	13. /ˈplʌmə/	14. /sæŋ/	15. /ˈθaʊzənd/
16. /vjuː/	17. /ˈpɪkʧə/	18. /ˈhʌzbənd/	19. /əˈraɪvl̩/	20. /ˈbriːðɪŋ/
21. /ˈfjuːʧə/	22. /ˈpʌzl̩d/	23. /liːg/	24. /mʌʧ/	25. /ˈleɪzi/
26. /ˈstrʌgl̩/	27. /ˈbʌtn̩/	28. /streɪt/	29. /ˈbeɪkn̩/	30. /ʤeɪn/

7. /t, θ, ð/. Classify the words given below in spelling into three columns. Note that there is word which does not fit in any column.

eighth	method	then	outhouse	both
third	the	this	time	three
though	soften	through	brother	eight

8. /n/-/ŋ/. Classify the words given below in spelling into two columns. Note that there are two words which do not fit in either column.

long	alone	autumn	ginger	finger
funny	sink	sinner	singer	anchor
angry	fin	hymn	danger	clingy

9. /s, z, ʃ, ʒ, ʧ, ʤ/. Classify the words given below in spelling into six columns. Note that there are two words which do not fit in any column.

school	general	miss	dessert	raise
sugar	equation	Japan	aisle	cello
fashion	journal	science	scene	accept
gym	beds	leisure	prison	chore
nature	machine	Celtic	treasure	jelly
picture	muscle	vision	bets	mission

10. Transcription. Transcribe the following words, paying special attention to fricative and affricate sounds (broad transcription).

these	fifth	behave	scissors	feathers
season	measure	lashes	pleasure	mash
breath	lose	wish	thin	lazy
witch	offering	loose	breathe	over
rush	rouge	match	laugh	gem

11. Transcribe the following sentences.
   1. The grassy fields are closed to the cows
   2. The face of her niece looks satisfied in the picture.
   3. Zoom in a thousand times!
   4. The famous Irish mansion near the station hides a shocking treasure.
   5. There was confusion and division after the 'Prestige' issue.
   6. My brother bought our mother this smooth leather jacket.
   7. She thanked both authors with enthusiasm and a thoughtful smile.
   8. You have a very good view of the valley and the river.
   9. Photographs of African elephants for sale.
   10. Whose behaviour is honest and honourable in his household?

12. Homophones. The following transcriptions represent a pair of homophones (unless otherwise stated). Give their spellings.

1./ˈmɑːʃl̩/	2. /ˈmedl̩/	3. /raɪt/ (4)	4. /rɪŋ/
5. /hɜːd/	6. /reɪn/ (3)	7. /ˈneɪvl̩/	8. /ˈmʌsl̩/
9. /ʃɪə/	10. /reɪz/	11. /sʌm/	12. /ˈsteɪʃnri/

13. A contrastive exercise. Pronounce the following words given in spelling as if they were English words first, and then Spanish. Explain what makes them different in terms of the initial consonant:

    pan ten kilo red rural van

14. Contrastive exercise. Aspiration. Try and pronounce the following English words, paying special attention to the /p, t, k/ phonemes:

    palm pool train top class cot

    Now, pronounce the following English words, in which the plosives are in a different position:

    spam spell strain stop scatter school

    Can you tell the difference between the plosives in both series? Now, pronounce the following similar Spanish words: *palma pulpo tren tope clase cota*. Which of the two series above do these resemble more? Finally, try and swap the English aspirated plosives by the Spanish counterparts, and viceversa, achieving a foreign effect.

15. English /h/ *versus* Spanish /x/. Pronounce both sounds in turn, going from one to the other – i.e. from glottal to velar and back again: /h/-/x/-/h/-/x/-/h/-/x/. Now, pronounce the English word 'ham' and the Spanish word 'jamón'; now interchanging the initial phonemes so that each word is pronounced as if in the 'fashion' of the other language – i.e. with a foreign accent. On the basis of this activity, explain what makes someone sound foreign.

16. There are certain consonant sounds in English which are not part of the Spanish repertoire, even if the actual letter does exist. This is the case of /b/ and /v/, for example. Pronounce the following words carefully, paying attention to the sounds /b/ and /v/, in different positions in the word. Give their transcription.

bat	vat
beer	veer
berry	very
best	vest
burbs (short for *suburb*)	verbs
lobes	loaves
rebel	revel
dribble	drivel
curb	curve
dub	dove

17. The /s/ – /ʃ/ contrast that exists in English does not occur in Spanish. Proceed in the same way as in exercise 16.

save	shave
see	she
seal	she'll
seat	sheet
single	shingle
seen	sheen
sock	shock
sew	show
crust	crushed
gust	gushed
crass	crashed
diss	dished
gas	gashed
plus	plushed
plus	plushed
puss	pushed

Chapter 5

5 Segment Dynamics: Aspects of Connected Speech

5.1 Introduction

In this chapter we are not going to look at sounds in isolation, but rather our attention is centred on connected sequences of sounds in words and larger units. The term **connected speech** refers to an "utterance consisting of more than one word" (Gimson 1984: 255). One of the distinctive features of connected speech is that when uttered in a chain speech sounds affect each other and their features change in such a way that allophonic variations, or different realisations of phonemes, occur as a result of the operation of a number of (**allophonic**) **rules** which, in general, can be described as **simplification rules**. Speakers often have to find a balance between two conflicting factors: ease of articulation and distinctiveness (Boersma 1998). Listeners expect to hear words as different and distinct from one another as possible, but, at the same time, speakers generally prefer to reduce articulatory effort whenever possible, and so they tend to resort to simplification mechanisms so as to convey only the phonetic information that is felt necessary. Although there can be a great deal of variability in how words are pronounced and there are many factors at work in such process (Bell *et al.*, 2003; Shockey 2003), listeners rarely experience difficulty in understanding. What follows describes two different kinds of connected speech phenomena that are involved in phonetic variation:

(1) those affecting sounds within words and/or at word (syllable and morpheme) boundaries, as in the case of **coarticulation** (Section 5.2.), **assimilations** (Section 5.3), **elision** (Section 5.4), **linking** (Section 5.5) and **juncture** (Section 5.6).
(2) those affecting the word as a whole, which is the case of **gradation** (including **neutralisations** of **weak forms**) (Section 5.7), and variations in **accentual patterns**, the latter being illustrated in Chapter 6 together with other prosodic features of speech.

5.2 Co-articulation and allophonic variations of vowels and consonants

When we speak, as already explained, sounds are uttered in sequence (one after the other) in an articulatory continuum. As a result, features of one segment (or sound) may be found in an adjacent segment. When this occurs the label **coarticulation** is generally used to refer to "patterns of coordination, between the articulatory gestures of neighboring segments, which result in the vocal tract responding at any one time to commands for more than one segment" (Manuel 1999: 179; Crystal 2008: 82). Another label that is employed to describe this phenomenon is **coproduction** to emphasise that there exists temporal co-occurrence or overlap in the articulation of two (or more) gestures (Byrd 1996: 210). Examples of coarticulation are the production of labialised (*cool* [kʷuːɫ]) or palatalised (***k**ey* [kʲiː]) allophones, which are produced when consonants are in contact with rounded vowels and front spread vowels, respectively. These types of allophonic alternations may be found within the word, and also at word boundaries, as shown in Table 32 that summarises the main allophonic realisations of consonants (Gimson 1984: 283–298; Cruttenden 2014: 270–322). For an exhaustive description of the allophonic variations of each RP vowel and consonant, please refer to the relevant (sub)sections in Chapters 3 and 4.

5.2.1 Lengthening and clipping

In English long (pure) vowels and vowel glides (diphthongs and diphthongs plus schwa) are equivalent in length and are subject to the same variations of quantity. All undergo **pre-fortis clipping** (Denes 1955; Wiik 1965: 114; Monroy Casas 1980: 75) and therefore are reduced in length if they precede a fortis consonant (e.g. *pl**a**ce* [pleˑɪs] vs. *pl**ay**s* [pleːɪz]). The reduced forms show a considerable shortening of the vowel or the first element of the glide (half-long [ˑ]) (Petterson and Lehiste 1960). As already remarked, not only vowels but also any sonorant consonant is vulnerable to pre-fortis clipping before a fortis consonant. So comparing *se**n**t* [senˑt] and *se**l**f* [seɫˑf] with *se**n**d* [senːd], *se**l**ves* [seɫːvz], the /en/ and /el/ sequences are shorter in the first pair of words as a result of pre-fortis clipping.

In addition, length reduction may also derive from so-called **rhythmic clipping**, which occurs when the duration of a stressed vowel is reduced as a result of the addition of one or several syllables to the same **foot**.[83] Compare the durations of the stressed vowel in *r**ea**d*, *r**ea**der* and *r**ea**dership*, where the stressed syllable has progressively less duration as progressively more syllables follow within the same stress group, so that the first instance of [iː] in *r**ea**d* is longer than the second [iˑ] in *r**ea**der*, and this, in turn, is longer than the third [iˑ] in *r**ea**dership* (Fudge 1984: 20).

83 Crystal (2008: 193) defines the term "foot" as "the unit of rhythm in languages displaying isochrony, i.e. where the stressed syllables fall at approximately regular intervals throughout an utterance."

Table 32: Main allophonic variations of consonants

Type	Within the word			At word boundary
place of articulation	/t/: post-alveolar in *tray* [t̠ɹ̥eɪ] /k/: advanced in *king* [k̟ɪŋ̟] /n/: dental in *ninth* [naɪn̪θ] /m n/: labio-dental in *comfort* [ˈkʌɱfət]			/t/: dental in *not those* [ˈnɒt̪ðəʊz], /d/: dental in *hide this* [ˈhaɪd̪ðɪs] /m n/: labio-dental in *men fight* [meɱ faɪt] /s/: retracted in *horse-riding* [hɔ: s̠ˈɹaɪdɪŋ]
voice	/r/: devoiced in *upright* [ˈʌpɹ̥aɪt], /w/: completlety devoiced in *twin* [tʍɪn] /l/: devoiced in *climb* [kl̥aɪm] /j/: devoiced in *pure* [pj̊ʊə] /m n ŋ/ slightly devoiced in *smart* [sm̥ɑ:t] st], *sneeze* [sn̥i:z], *bacon* [ˈbeɪkŋ̊]			/r/: devoiced in *at rest* [ətˈɹ̥est] /w/: devoiced in *at once* [ətˈw̥ʌns] /l/: devoiced in *at last* [ətˈl̥ɑ:st] /j/: devoiced in *thank you* [ˈθæŋkj̊u:]
lip position	**lip-spreading**		**lip-rounding**	**lip-rounding**
	/p/	*pea* [pʲi:]	*pool* [pʷu:l]	
	/t/	*tea* [tʲi:]	*too* [tʷu:]	*at one* [ətʷˈwʌn]
	/k/	*keep* [kʲi:p]	*cool* [kʷu:ɫ]	*pack one* [ˈpækʷwʌn]
	/m/	*mule* [mʲju:l]	*mob* [mʷɒb]	*come once* [ˈkʌmʷwns]
	/n/	*noon* [nʲu:n]	*no* [nʷəʊ]	
	/ŋ/			*long one* [ˈlɒŋʷwʌn]
	/l/	*lea* [lʲi:]	*loo* [lʷu:]	*will we* [ˈwɪɫʷwi:]
	/r/	*read* [ɹʲi:d]	*room* [ɹʷu:m]	
	/f/	*feel* [fʲi:l]	*fool* [fʷu:ɫ]	
	/s/	*see* [sʲi:]	*soon* [sʷu:n]	*this way* [ðɪsʷˈweɪ]
	/h/	*he* [hʲi:]	*who* [hʷu:]	
	/ʃ/	*sheer* [ʃʲɪə]	*sugar* [ˈʃʷʊgə]	
nasal resonance	Nasalisation of vowels preceding /m n/ in *ham* [hæ̃m] Nasalisation of vowels surrounded by or surrounding nasals: *man* [mæ̃n] Nasalisation of /l/ before or after nasals: *signalman* [ˈsɪgnl̃mən]			Nasalisation of vowels when there is a nasal in the adjacent word, *come along* [kʌ̃m ə̃ˈlɒŋ], especially if another adjacent nasal occurs in the word containing the vowel: *bring in* [brĩŋ ĩn] Nasalisation of approximants: *tell me* [ˈtel̃mi:]

The **clipping-effect** is more noticeable if reduced realisations are contrasted with those occurring in **lengthening** environments (i.e. open word-final syllables), where long (pure) vowels and vowel glides may have **extra-long realisations** [::] (*play* [ple::ɪ]).

AI 5.1 Allophonic variation of vowels

Below are listed more examples of (1) extra-long [::], (2) normally-long [:], and (3) reduced [ˑ] **allophonic realisations** of English vowels and glides:

[iː]	[iː:]: *tea* [tiː:], *see* [siː] [iː]: *team* [tiːm], *seed* [siːd] [iˑ]: *meet* [miˑt], *leak* [liˑk]	Compare: *see* [siː:] *seed* [siːd] *seat* [siˑt]
[ɜː]	[ɜː:]: *purr* [pɜː:], *myrrh* [mɜː:] [ɜː]: *girl* [gɜːl], *word* [wɜːd] [ɜˑ]: *skirt* [skɜˑt], *work* [wɜˑk]	Compare: *purr* [pɜː:] *purl* [pɜːl] *pert* [pɜˑt]
[ɑː]	[ɑː:]: *car* [kɑː:], *star* [stɑː:] [ɑː]: *calm* [kɑːm], *starred* [stɑːd] [ɑˑ]: *cart* [kɑˑt], *start* [stɑˑt]	Compare: *are* [ɑː:] *aren't* [ɑːnt] *art* [ɑˑt]
[ɔː]	[ɔː:]: *poor* [pɔː:], saw [sɔː:] [ɔː]: *poured* [pɔːd], *sawed* [sɔːd] [ɔˑ]: *port* [pɔˑt], *sought* [sɔˑt]	Compare: *core* [kɔː:] *cored* [kɔːd] *caught* [kɔˑt]
[uː]	[uː:]: *blue* [bluː:], *two* [tuː:] [uː]: *pool* [puːl], *food* [fuːd] [uˑ]: *fruit* [fruˑt], *Luke* [luˑk]	Compare: *shoe* [ʃuː:] *shoed* [ʃuːd] *shoot* [ʃuˑt]
[eɪ]	[eː:ɪ]: *day* [deː:ɪ], *bay* [beː:ɪ] [eːɪ]: *fade* [feːɪd], *game* [geːɪm] [eˑɪ]: *eight* [eˑɪt], *face* [feˑɪs]	Compare: *say* [seː:ɪ] *save* [seːɪv] *safe* [seˑɪ f]
[eə]	[eː:ə] *there* [ðeː:ə], *pear* [peː:ə] [eːə] *chairs* [ʧeːəz], *cared* [keːəd] [eˑə] *scarce* [skeˑəs]	Compare: *scare* [skeː:ə] *scares* [skeːə] *scarce* [skeˑəs]
[aɪ]	[aː:ɪ]: *fly* [flaː:ɪ], *die* [daː:ɪ] [aːɪ]: *mine* [maːɪn], *hide* [haːɪd] [aˑɪ]: *fight* [faˑɪt], *like* [laˑɪk]	Compare: *tie* [taː:ɪ] *time* [taːɪm] *tight* [taˑɪt]
[aʊ]	[aː:ʊ]: *how* [haː:ʊ], *cow* [kaː:ʊ] [aːʊ]: *town* [taːʊn], *loud* [laːʊd] [aˑʊ]: *shout* [ʃaˑʊt], *mouse* [maˑʊs]	Compare: *allow* [əˈlaː:ʊ] *allows* [əˈlaːʊz] *a louse* [ə laˑʊs]
[əʊ]	[əː:ʊ]: *go* [gəː:ʊ], *toe* [təː:ʊ] [əːʊ]: *home* [həːʊm], *road* [rəːʊd] [əˑʊ]: *goat* [gəˑʊt], *both* [bəˑʊθ]	Compare: *row* [rəː:ʊ] *robe* [rəːʊb] *rope* [rəˑʊp]
[ɔɪ]	[bɔː:ɪ]: *boy* [bɔː:ɪ], *toy* [tɔː:ɪ] [bɔːɪ]: *void* [vɔːɪd], *coin* [kɔːɪn] [bɔˑɪ]: *choice* [ʧɔˑɪs]	Compare: *joy* [ʤɔː:ɪ] *join* [ʤɔːɪn] *joist* [ʤɔˑɪst]

[ɪə]	[ɪ::ə]: *dear* [dɪ::ə], *here* [hɪ::ə] [ɪ:ə]: *beard* [bɪ:əd], *weird* [wɪ:əd] [ɪ·ə]: *pierce* [pɪ·əs], *fierce* [fɪ·əs]	Compare: *fear* [fɪ::ə] *fears* [fɪ:əz] *fierce* [fɪ·əs]
[ʊə]	[ʊ::ə]: *poor* [pʊ::ə], *moor* [mʊ::ə][84] [ʊ:ə]: *cured* [kjʊ:əd], *moored* [mʊ:əd] [ʊ·ə] (rhythmic clipping): *security* [sɪˈkjʊ·ərɪti]	Compare: *pour* [pʊ::ə] *poured* [pʊ:əd]

5.2.2 Voicing and devoicing

Voicing refers to the auditory result of the vibration of the vocal folds (Crystal 2008: 515). We have seen that **voiced sounds** are produced while the vocal folds are vibrating, whereas **voiceless** or **unvoiced sounds** are articulated with no such vibration. Likewise, voicing is the term applied to describe the phenomenon whereby voiceless phonemes (/p/, /t/, /k/, /ʧ/, /f/, /θ/, /s/, /ʃ/, /h/) have **voiced allophonic realisations** (annotated as [̬] or [ˇ] in intervocalic positions and between voiced sounds (e.g. *matter* [ˈmæt̬əʳ]).

We have also explained that the opposite phenomenon exists in English. In particular phonetic environments (word-initially and word-finally, as well as between voiceless sounds including close-knit word boundaries), sounds which are normally voiced (/**b**/, /**d**/, /**g**/, /**ʤ**/, /**v**/, /**ð**/, /**z**/, /**ʒ**/, /**m**/, /**n**/, /**ŋ**/, /**w**/, /**l**/, /**r**/, /**j**/) are articulated with less vibration than elsewhere and are said to be **devoiced** (symbolised with an under- [̥] or over-ring [˚]) (*pi**g*** [pɪg̊], *gi**v**e* [gɪv̥], *brea**th**e* [bri:ð̥], hi**s** [hɪz̥], ***G**eor**g**e* [d̥ʒɔ:d̥ʒ̊]); whereas they are fully voiced if they occur between vowels (*la**b**our* [ˈleibəʳ]). Approximants are also devoiced if they are preceded by a fortis plosive in consonantal clusters, both within a word and at close-knit word boundaries. This occurs in e.g. ***quiet*** [ˈkw̥aɪət] *try* [tɹ̥aɪ], *play* [pl̥eɪ], *pure* [pj̊ʊə], *at **l**ast* [ətl̥ɑ:st], *at **o**nce* [ətw̥ʌns], *thank **y**ou* [θæŋkj̊u:], where the aspiration of fortis plosives, whatever its degree, is manifested as devoicing of the subsequent approximants. It should be noted, however, that **approximants** are only slightly devoiced when they are preceded by a fortis consonant in an unstressed syllable (*chaplain* [ˈtʃæpl̥ɪn]), while **nasals /m n ŋ/** are also slightly devoiced if they are preceded by voiceless plosives (*certain* [ˈsɜ:tn̥̩], ***s**moke* [sm̥əʊk], ***bacon*** [ˈbeɪkŋ̊̍]).

In addition, when clusters of lenis consonants occur in a devoicing environment, both sounds lose some degree of vocal fold vibration, but it is the one nearer to the devoicing factor that becomes completely devoiced and, for practical purposes, it is the only one that is marked as devoiced in allophonic

84 Remember, however, that *poor* and *moor* are generally pronounced with /ɔ:/ (see § 3.2.4).

transcriptions. Thus, although in ***pigs*** [pɪgz̥] both [g] and [z] lose some of their voicing because they occur word-finally, it is only [z̥] that is marked as completely devoiced, as it occurs immediately before silence (Lombardy 1999; Shockey 2003; Ernestus *et al.* 2006).

5.2.3 Lip shape

Consonants may be modified by having a **secondary articulation** under the influence of the **lip position** adopted for the articulation of adjacent vowels or semivowels (see § 2.3.2.5) (Shockey 2003; Cruttenden 2014: 308–310). Two types of allophones are derived from this process:

Labialised articulations [ʷ], which involve lip-rounding with the accompanying elevation of the tongue back and occur next to rounded vowels /**ɒ ɔː ʊ uː**/ and the rounded semi-vowel [**w**] (Ladefoged and Maddieson 1996: 368). Within words, the effect is most noticeable in the consonants preceding the rounded vowel or semivowel, which explains that only these consonants tend to be marked as labialised in narrow transcriptions (***bog*** [bʷɒg], ***bloo**m* [blʷuːm], ***pork*** [pʷɔˑkʷ], ***rude*** [ɹʷuːdʷ], ***soon*** [sʷuːnʷ], ***up**ward* [ˈʌpʷwəd], *w**hose*** [hʷuːzʷ]). At word boundaries, the semi-vowel [w] exerts some degree of labialisation on the preceding consonant (***that** one* [ˈðætʷ wʌn], *wro**ng** one* [ˈɹʷɒŋʷ wʌn]), but a rounded vowel in an adjacent word does not seem to exert the same labializing influence (e.g. in *W**ho** takes this?* the [uː] of *who* does not labialise the [t] of *takes*, but it does labialise the preceding [hʷ]).

Palatalised articulations [ʲ], which are produced with lip-spreading and raising of the front of the tongue under the influence of adjacent spread vowels /**ɪ iː**/ and the palatal semivowel [**j**], either within words and at close-knit word boundaries (Barry 1992). As in the case of labialisations, palatalisations are more noticeable in the consonants preceding /ɪ iː j/ than in consonants following them, which explains that only the former tend to be marked in narrow transcriptions (***bee*** [bʲiː], ***cute*** [kʲjuˑt], ***pea*** [pʲiː], ***fin*** [fʲɪnʲ], ***read*** [ɹʲiːdʲ]).

5.2.4 Nasal resonance

Vowels and vocalic series have **nasalised** [˜] allophonic articulations, i.e. are articulated with nasal resonance by lowering the soft palate, in the vicinity of a nasal consonant (Cohn 1990). This tendency can be more noticeable in varieties of English other than RP such as GA, where nasalisation not only occurs in vowels next to nasal consonants but also in vowels which are not in contact with any nasal sound, which infuses some American accents with an overall nasal quality (***He drives too fast*** [hĩ draĩvz tũː fæ̃st]) (Estebas Vilaplana 2009: 85).

For practical purposes, these will only be marked when they are particularly noticeable, that is, when occurring between nasals or when a nasal follows them, within words (***man*** [mæ̃n], ***singer*** [ˈsĩŋə], ***ton*** [tʌ̃n], ***ham*** [hæ̃m]). Somewhat reduced nasalisations occur in the same contexts between words (***bring in*** [brĩŋ ĩn], ***for*** *me* [fə̃ miː], *pretty mean* [ˈprɪtĩ ˈmĩːn]), but they can affect the vowel of an adjacent word that is only preceded, but not followed by a nasal (*come along* [kʌ̃m ə̃ˈlɒŋ]).]).

Consonants can also be produced with nasal resonance. **Approximants** may be nasalised broadly in the same phonetic environments as vowels (*helmet* [ˈhel̃mɪt], ***tell*** *mum* [ˈtel̃ ˈmʌ̃m]), while **plosives** have a **nasal release** in consonantal clusters when followed by a nasal consonant (see § 2.3.2.5, 2.4.1, 5.2.6).

5.2.5 Aspiration

We have seen that in English aspiration refers to the audible breath that may accompany the articulation of fortis plosives in specific phonetic contexts (see § 4.2.1). Though varying in intensity, for teaching purposes we only recognise two degrees of the aspiration effect: **aspirated** [**pʰ tʰ kʰ**], in syllable-initial stressed position (***pan*** [pʰæn]), or **unaspirated** [**p⁼ t⁼ k⁼**], when preceded by [s] (***ski*** [sk⁼iː]), in unaccented syllables (***police*** [p⁼əˈliːs]), and in both word and syllable final positions (*tap* [tʰæp⁼]). But if fortis plosives are followed by approximants, especially in syllable-initial stressed position, then the aspiration of the former is manifested, regardless of its degree, as approximant devoicing [l̥ ɹ̥ j̊ w̥] (e.g. ***play*** [pl̥eɪ], splendid [ˈspl̥endɪd], *try* [tɹ̥aɪ], *strange* [stɹ̥eɪndʒ], *obscure* [əbˈskj̊ʊə], *quite* [kw̥aɪt⁼]). In more detailed analyses, **pre-aspiration** after the consonant may be distinguished from **post-aspiration** (aspiration after the consonant), as both features may occur in a language (e.g. Gaelic).

🎧 AI 5.2 Aspiration of voiceless plosives

It has also been explained that the acoustic correlate of aspiration is the **Voice Onset Time** (VOT), that is, the interval that exists between the release of a fortis plosive and the voicing of the following vowel or sonorant. Broadly, aspirated voiceless plosives have positive VOTs and therefore trigger **delayed onsets to voicing**. In contrast, (de)voiced and unaspirated voiceless plosives, with negative and zero VOTs respectively, produce **non-delayed onsets to voicing**.

5.2.6 Types of release

This feature is considered with regard to the plosive group only. In terms of type of release, plosives have three different allophonic realisations that stand in complementary distribution, that is, they occur in mutually exclusive environments:

(1) **Non audible release [p˺ t˺ k˺ b˺ d˺ g˺]** in consonantal clusters, if followed by another plosive or by an affricate either within a word (*act* [æk˺t], *picture* [ˈpɪk˺tʃə]).

(2) **Nasal release [pⁿ tⁿ kⁿ bⁿ dⁿ gⁿ]**, when the plosive is followed by a nasal consonant both between and within words (*top nine* [tɒpⁿ naɪn], *submerge* [səbᵐˈmɜːdʒ]).

(3) **Lateral release [pˡ tˡ kˡ bˡ dˡ gˡ]**, if the plosive is followed by a lateral consonant both within and between words (e.g. *little* [ˈlɪtˡɫ̩], *bad leg* [bædˡ leg]).

For further details on the types of release exhibited by plosive consonants, the reader is referred to Sections 2.3.2.5 and 4.2.1.

5.2.7 Place of articulation

The degree of openness or backness of a vowel and the actual place of articulation of a consonant is conditioned by its phonetic environment. Besides having **closer** [˔] or **more open** [˕] realisations, English vowels may also have **more advanced** [˖] or **more retracted** [˗] realisations depending on regional variants, or otherwise on the place of articulation of the adjacent consonant which may be produced further to the front in the oral chamber (e.g. ***loop*** [lu̟ˑp] where [u̟] is more fronted due to the presence of the following bilabial consonant) or further to the back (e.g. *result* [rɪˈzʌ̠ɫt] where [ʌ̠] results from the influence of [ɫ]). Consonants, on the other hand, may also have more advanced [̟] or more retracted or backed [̠] places of articulation both in consonantal clusters or in C + V series if the second element has a more advanced or a more retracted, or backed, place of articulation respectively, both within a word and at close-knit word boundaries.

For practical purposes, more advanced/retracted places of articulation will only be signalled in those cases in which it is most noticeable, that is, when there exists a succession of two opposite articulatory points in the oral chamber:

(1) When a **velar consonant** is followed by a **(post)alveolar approximant**, it will have a **post-velar articulation** (*gray* [g̠ɹeɪ]), but when there is an adjacent **front vowel** [iː ɪ] or **glide** [j] (*key* [k̟iː]), the place of articulation is **pre-velar**.

(2) When a **bilabial** or an **alveolar consonant** is followed by a **post-alveolar approximant** in consonantal clusters (***brush*** [b̠ɹʌʃ], *unreal* [ʌn̠ˈɹɪəl], *ballroom* [ˈbɔˈl̠ɹuːm], ***tray*** [t̠ɹeɪ], ***dry*** [d̠ɹaɪ]) and when they are next to a **back vowel** [**uː ʊ ɒ ɔː**] or semivowel [**w**] (***pool*** [p̠ʰuːɫ], ***tool*** [t̠ʰuːɫ]), they are produced with **post-bilabial** and **post-alveolar** places of articulation, respectively.

Other allophonic realisations concerning place of articulation that can be found both within words and at (close-knit) word boundaries and that should be marked in allophonic transcriptions are the following:

(3) Within the nasal group:
   a. Labio-dental realisations [**ɱ**] of /**m n**/ if followed by /**f v**/ (*nymph* [nɪɱ̊f], *infant* [ˈɪɱ̊fənt], *Tom Ford* [ˈtɒɱ̊ ˈfɔːd]).
   b. Bilabial realisations [**m**] of /**n**/ before a bilabial consonant (***in** bed* [ɪm ˈbed]).
   c. Velar realisations [**ŋ**] of /**n**/ before a velar consonant (***ten** coins* [teŋ ˈkɔɪnz]).

(4) Dental realisations [̪] of alveolars /**t d n l**/ before a dental consonant /**θ ð**/ (***tenth*** [ten̪θ], ***not** those* [ˈnɒt̪ðəʊz], ***hide** this* [ˈhaɪd̪ ðɪs], ***al**though* [ɔl̪ˈðəʊ]).

For more details on the allophonic variants of RP sounds involving degree of openness and backness, in the case of vowels, and the place of articulation of consonants resulting from processes of coarticulation, please refer to the corresponding sections of Chapters 3 and 4 (Shockey 2003; Cruttenden 2014: 308–310; Gow *et al.* 2007).

5.2.8 Lenition and fortition

The term **fortition** is used in phonology to refer to a strengthening in the overall force of a sound, whether diachronically or synchronically. Typically, fortition involves the change from a fricative to a stop, an approximant to a fricative, or a voiced to a voiceless sound. **Lenition** refers to the opposite phenomenon whereby the overall strength of a sound is weakened, as it occurs in the change from a stop to a fricative, a fricative to an approximant, a voiceless sound to a voiced sound, or a sound being reduced (lenite) to zero (Crystal 2008: 197, 274). English illustrations of both phenomena have already been introduced in Section 2.3.2.1 and are now summarised in the two following sections.

5.2.8.1 Affrication and fricativisation

Plosives are said to be **affricated** when they are articulated with a slow, fricative release but in the same articulatory region. In this type of lenition, plosives have affricated variants that are followed by the brief corresponding fricative [**pᶲ bᵝ tˢ dᶻ kˣ gˠ**], or they may even be replaced by the fricative sound in rapid speech, especially in intervocalic positions (*imported* [ɪmˈpɔˑtˢɪd], [ɪmˈpɔˑsɪd]) (Shockey 2003; Collins and Mees 2009: 154; Cruttenden 2014: 172; Ashby 2011: 135; Buizza and Plug 2012). /p b/ are rarely affricated. **Affrication is particularly associated with alveolar plosives**, both in strongly accented positions (***time*** [ˈtˢaɪm], ***dime*** [ˈdᶻaɪm]), in weakly accented syllables /t d/ (***to*** [tˢə], *reading* [ˈriːdᶻɪŋ]), and in final positions (*heart* [hɑˑtˢ]). Occasionally, with velar plosives affrication may also be heard, particularly in emphatic or hesitant speech in stressed phonetic contexts (*come on* [ˈkˣʌm ɒn], ***good*** [ˈgˠʊd]), or, more frequently, with /k/ in weakly accented or word-final syllables (*black tea* [blækˣ tˢiː]. In English, the production of affricated plosives with homorganic fricative release regardless of the phonetic environment is a characteristic of regional pronunciation, especially of Liverpool (or Scouse) accent.

A different type of lenition involves the **fricativisation of approximants**, as a result of which /r/ is realised as / [ɹ̝] (*draft* [dɹ̝ɑˑft] or [ɹ̝̊] (*try* [tɹ̝̊aɪ]), /l/ as [l̥] (*climb* [kl̥aɪm]), j as [j̊] or [ç], and /w/ as [w̥], as already detailed in Section 4.2.5.

5.2.8.2 Glottalisation and glottaling

Glottalisation is the cover term for any articulation involving a simultaneous glottal constriction, especially a glottal stop (plosive) (Crystal 1988: 213). The **glottal stop** [ʔ] is pronounced with the vocal folds coming into contact and with no vibration, so that there is a glottal closure and the lung air is compressed at that point. The airstream is released out of the oral cavity upon the sudden separation of the vocal folds. The compression stage consists of silence, which is auditorily perceived by the sudden cessation of the preceding sound or by the sudden initiation of the following sound. The preceding sound is shortened as it occurs with the other voiceless plosives. In RP, [ʔ] does not contrast with other plosives to produce differences in meaning, but rather it occurs as secondary articulation to fortis plosives and affricates. These are then said to be **glottalised**, or produced with a **glottal reinforcement** (or **fortition**), in which case a corresponding closure – and its corresponding release – is made either before or simultaneously with the oral closure of the plosive or affricate release (Christophersen 1955; O'Connor 1952; Roach 1973).

Pre-glottalisation[85] is regularly used in RP to reinforce stressed syllable-initial vowels either to mark a syllable boundary or to add emphasis to the word, whatever the preceding stop, as shown in the examples below:

geometry [dʒɪˈʔɒmətri]
disorder [dɪsˈʔɔːdə]
It is **empty** [ɪts ˈʔempti]
I haven't seen **anybody** [ˈaɪ ˈhævn̩t ˈsiːn ˈʔenibɒdi]

An extended use of **glottalisation** in RP, though not subscribed to by conservative speakers, consists in reinforcing [**p t k**] when a vowel, nasal or lateral precedes them and they are followed by another consonant or a pause; **affricates** are also glottalised in theses contexts as well as between vowels:

actor	[ˈæ͜ʔktə]	with glottalisation	[ˈæktə]	without glottalisation
mat	[mæ͜ʔt]	with glottalisation	[mæt]	without glottalisation
ma**tch**es	[ˈmæ͜ʔʧɪz]	with glottalisation	[ˈmæʧɪz]	without glottalisation

In the same phonetic contexts, **glottaling** may also occur. Regarded as the next stage to glottalisation, it involves the **replacement** of a fortis plosive, usually /**t**/ and less frequently /**p k**/, by a glottal stop, no oral closure being made (Fabricius 2002). The glottaling of /t/ in word-final positions and before syllabic [ɫ̩] and [n̩] is acceptable in Estuary English (*foot-rest* [ˈfʊʔɹest], ***bottle*** [boʔɫ̩], *meet me* [miːʔ miː]. Word-medially, however, the use of [ʔ] for /t/ remains stigmatised in RP (*waiter* [ˈweɪʔə], *Britain* [ˈbrɪʔn̩]). Glottaling of final /p k/ is not so common in RP. Its occurrence is restricted to homorganic consonant clusters within words and at close-knit word-boundaries (*soap powder* [ˈsəʊʔ ˈpaʊdə]). In Cockney and other regional (South East) urban dialects /t/ glottaling is heard in the same positions as RP, but more frequently and also in wider contexts such as word-medially and intervocalically (*potato* [pəˈteɪʔəʊ]). /p k/ may also undergo glottal replacements (***supper*** [ˈsʌʔə], ***ticket*** [ˈtɪʔɪt]) in the same phonetic environments but they seem to retain their bilabial and velar closures. In addition, in Cockney speech [ʔ] may ocassionally replace fricatives such as final /f/ and initial /h/ (***half** a minute* [ˈʔɑːʔ ə ˈmɪnɪʔ], *You **hate her*** [ju ʔeɪ ʔə]) (Gimson 1980: 168 ff; Finch and Ortiz Lira 1982: 56; Wells 1982: 341, 344, 347, 416; Roach 2005: 55; Cruttenden 2014: 182–186).

Glottalisation and glottaling are essential features for SSLE (and other learners) to master. They are such prevalent features of RP that their correct use really makes a foreigner's speech sound more native.

---

85 Tyneside is unique in showing **post-glottalization**, i.e. the addition of glottal reinforcement to a preceding plosive, in intervocalic positions (*water* [ˈwɔːtʔə]) (Cruttenden 2014: 185).

5.3 Assimilation and phonemic variations

Assimilation of sounds is a process that takes place in connected speech whenever a sequence is particularly awkward to pronounce given its phonetic environment. We speak of **assimilation** when **a phoneme** is actually **replaced** by **another phoneme** as a result of phonetic conditioning usually at the word-boundary level, but also word-internally (Collins and Mees 2003: 203–216, 327; Collins and Mees 2009: 120–123, 274; Cruttenden 2014: 312–313). Assimilations occur both in formal and in informal speech, even though assimilated forms are more frequent in casual speech. Assimilations are blocked in slow speech and when the speaker makes a pause between words.

There are different types of assimilation, attending to two parameters, which may interact in such a way that various possible combinations of assimilation processes are observed in connected speech, as will be shown in the following sections:

(1) **Direction of influence**: one sound may affect either the preceding one or the following one; or two sounds may actually affect each other to the extent of both of them being replaced. The process is known as **regressive assimilation** (**redressive, leading**, or **anticipatory**) when sound 2 affects sound 1, or put differently, when a sound affects the preceding one so that the latter is anticipating articulatory features of the sound after it. The direction of influence is therefore backwards, from right to left, as in *white plane* [waɪp ˈpleɪn], where boldtype is used to highlight the spelling of the sound being assimilated. In contrast, the process is called **progressive assimilation** (**lagging** or **perseverative**) if sound 1 affects sound 2. In other words, a sound affects the following one so that the second sound carries articulatory features from the previous one. In this case the movement is from left to right, as in *happen* [ˈhæpm̩]. A third possibility is that two sounds may reciprocally affect each other to the extent of producing a different sound. This is a case of **coalescent**, or **reciprocal assimilation**, as in *Would you?* [wʊdʒu], giving place to the emergence of the affricate [dʒ].

(2) **Type of influence**: regardless of whether the assimilation is leading, lagging or reciprocal, this process may affect the assimilated sounds in different ways. **Place of articulation** is affected when the assimilated sound exhibits a different place of articulation from the original one. For example, an alveolar consonant may become bilabial in the vicinity of a bilabial sound. **Manner of articulation** can also be affected. The most common process is that of **nasalisation**, whereby a sound becomes nasal in the vicinity of another nasal sound. The **quality of the voice** can also be affected. This usually affects voiced sounds, which may become voiceless in the vicinity of voiceless sounds. We shall see that two of these changes may actually take place at the same time, such as place and manner.

AI 5.3 Assimilation

5.3.1 Variations of place of articulation

This process affects mostly alveolars, which become de-alveolarised and replaced by bilabials, velars or palate-alveolars, in a process which most native speakers are usually not aware of. Changes in the place of articulation can take place in leading, lagging or reciprocal directions, as we can see below.

5.3.1.1 Regressive assimilation

Word-final alveolars /t, d, n, s, z/ adopt the place of articulation of the following consonants, without changing their voice, as can be seen in the following table, which summarises some of the most usual cases:

Table 33: Regressive assimilation

Articulation Sound 1	Followed by Sound 2	Regressive assimilation	New place of articulation	Example
i. Alveolar	**Bilabial**		**Bilabial**	
/t/	/p b m/	⇐	[p]	that pot [ðæp pɒt] white-board [ˈwaɪpbɔːd]
/d/	/p b m/	⇐	[b]	add me [æb mi]
/n/	/p b m/	⇐	[m]	ten pens [tem penz] unplugged [ʌmˈplʌgd]
ii. Alveolar	**Velar**		**Velar**	
/t/	/k g/	⇐	[k]	that car [ðæk kɑː]
/d/	/k g/	⇐	[g]	good guy [gʊg gaɪ]
/n/	/k g/	⇐	[ŋ]	ten cats [teŋ kæts]
iii. Alveolar	**Palato-alveolar**		**Palato-alveolar**	
/s/	/ʃ ʧ ʤ j/	⇐	[ʃ]	this yacht [ðiʃ jɒt]
/z/	/ʃ ʧ ʤ j/	⇐	[ʒ]	has Sheila? [hæʒ ˈʃiːlə]

5.3.1.2 Progressive assimilation

Changes in the place of articulation of phonemes in progressive processes are not very frequent, the most usual context being when a plosive is followed by a syllabic nasal, in which case the nasal may undergo assimilation to the place of articulation of the preceding plosive.

Table 34: Progressive assimilation

Articulation Sound 1	Followed by Sound 2	Progressive assimilation	New place of articulation	Example
i. Bilabial /p b/	**Nasal** /n/	⇒	**Bilabial** [m]	cup **and** saucer [kʌp **m** ˈsɔːsə]
ii. Velar /k g/	**Nasal** /n/	⇒	**Velar** [ŋ]	bake **and** fry [beɪk **ŋ** fraɪ]

5.3.2 Variations in the manner of articulation.

These are usually nasalisations, involving alveolars in very rapid speech, especially when close to the negative *n't*. The following table summarises the most common regressive nasalisations:

Table 35: Regressive nasalisations

Articulation Sound 1	Followed by Sound 2	New manner of articulation	Example
/d/	/n/	[n]	ba**d** news [bæ**n** njuːz]
	/g/	[ŋ]	woode**n** gate [ˈwʊd**ŋ** geɪt]
	/m/	[m]	goo**d** mum [gʊ**m** mʌm]
/v/	/m/	[m]	o**f** mine [ə**m** maɪn]

5.3.3 Variations in voicing

Changes in voicing are often due to regressive assimilations, whereby a word-final voiced fricative followed by a word-initial voiceless fricative may be realised as the corresponding voiceless fricative, as is illustrated in Table 36.

Table 36: Regressive assimilations: voicing

Articulation Sound 1	Followed by Sound 2	New manner of articulation	Example
/ð/	Voiceless	[θ]	wi**th** threats [wi**θ** θrets]
/z/	Voiceless	[s]	it wa**s** supposed [ɪt wɒ**s** səˈpəʊzd]
/v/	Voiceless	[f]	you'**ve** finished [juː**f** ˈfɪnɪʃt]

Change of voicing is affected by progressive assimilation in the case of the /s/ and /z/ morphemes, represented by /S/ in Table 37 below, used in the formation of the plural of nouns, the genitive case, the third-person singular of the present tense of verbs, and also the /t/-/d/ ending of the past and participle of regular verbs, represented by /T/ below. In these cases, if the root of the word ends in a voiceless sound, then the morpheme assimilates to the voiceless variety, whereas a voiced consonant at the end of the root will have as an effect of an assimilation to the voiced variety as a realisation of the morpheme.

Table 37: Progressive assimilations: voicing

Archiphoneme and Morphemic meaning	Allomorphic or Morpho-phonemic variation	Example
{plural} /S/ {present} {genitive}	→ /s/ 'voiceless' / C [-voice] _ ⇒ → /z/ 'voiced' / C [+voice] _ ⇒	cats, Pip's, asks /kæts/ /pɪps/ /ɑ:sks/ dogs, Bob's, saves /dɒgz/ /bɒbz/ /seɪvz/
<ed> /T/ {simple past} {past participle}	→ /t/ 'voiceless' / C [-voice] _ ⇒ → /d/ 'voiced' / C [+voice] _ ⇒	asked, parked /ɑ:skt/ /pɑ:kt/ saved, combed /seɪvd/ /kəʊmd/

5.3.4 Coalescent assimilation

Coalescent assimilation is a cover term for the reciprocal assimilation of two underlying phonemes, usually involving place and manner assimilation at the same time, resulting in a third phoneme (Collins and Mees 2003: 328; Cruttenden 2014: 313). As shown in Table 38, in English coalescent assimilation is typically derived from the **palatalisations** of **stops** and **fricatives**, generally in close-knit word boundaries, as illustrated in Table 38 below.

Table 38: Coalescent assimilation

Articulation Sound 1	Followed by Sound 2	New place and manner of articulation Sound 3	Example
i. Alveolar	**Palatal**	**Palato-alveolar**	
/t/	/j/	[tʃ]	won't you? [ˈwəʊntʃu:]
/d/	/j/	[dʒ]	did you? [ˈdɪdʒu:]
/s/	/j/	[ʃ]	It's your book! [ɪtʃɔ: bʊk]
/z/	/j/	[ʒ]	Has your book come? [həʒɔ: bʊk kʌm]

One common case is when an unvoiced [**ʧ**] or voiced [**dʒ**] **palato-alveolar affricate** results from the fusion of correspondingly an alveolar unvoiced [**t**] or voiced [**d**] plosive and a palatal approximant [j], which becomes a voiceless [**ʃ**] or voiced [**ʒ**] palato-alveolar fricative, respectively (Harris 1994: 118). Hence, attention should be paid not to use [**dʒ**], for instance, when the sound preceding [j] is [t], as in *let you*, which in rapid speech should be pronounced as [ˈleʧu] not [ˈledʒu]. Another frequent example of coalescent assimilation also illustrated in Table 38 occurs when a voiceless /**ʃ**/ or voiced /**ʒ**/ palato-alveolar fricative results from the merging of [sj] and [zj], respectively.

5.4 Elision

This phenomenon refers to the loss of sounds, particularly at word boundaries or very close to them (Collins and Mees 2009: 114; Cruttenden 2014: 313–314). Deletion of phonemes tends to occur both in formal and casual speech, and is more likely to happen the faster the speed of delivery is. **Consonants** are elided in the weak forms of some grammatical words:

(1) Loss of /**h**/ in pronominal weak forms such as /ɪ/, /ɪm, /ə/ for *he, him, her,* or in some auxiliaries, such as ***h****ave,* ***h****as,* ***h****ad* realised as /əv/, /əz/, /əd/, respectively.

(2) Loss of /**t**/ in one of the weak forms of *mus****t*** /məs/, as well as in other words in which syllable-final /t/ is preceded by another consonant of the same voicing and it is followed by a consonant other than [h] (*las****t*** /lɑːst/, which may be pronounced as [lɑːs] with [t] elision).

(3) Loss of /**d**/ in the weak form of *an****d*** /ən/ and /n/; also in the weak form of ***d****oes*, which may be pronounced as /z/ or /s/. Syllable-final [d] elisions can also occur when this sound is preceded by another consonant of the same voicing and it is followed by a consonant other than [h], either across words or within a word (*col****d*** /kəʊld/ which may be pronounced as [kəʊl] with [d] elision).

In addition, **omission of alveolar plosives** may also occur in the following contexts:

(4) When word-final /**t**/ or /**d**/ are followed by initial either /t/ or /d/, the resulting cluster may be simplified by elision of the **first plosive** of the two, as in *I've go****t*** *to go* /aɪv gɒtə gəʊ/, *wha****t*** *does he like,* /wɒdəz hi laɪk/, *I coul****d*** *do it* /aɪ kə duː ɪt/, *he shoul****d*** *talk* /hi ʃə tɔːk/;

(5) The /**t**/ of the negative /nt/ is often removed, especially in two-syllable words, when followed by a consonant, as in *I shouldn'****t*** *carry it* /aɪ ʃʊdn̩kæri ɪt/;

(6) /**t**/ or /**d**/ may be elided when they occupy the middle position in a group of three consonants, most usually in the following contexts: (1) Voiceless continuant + /t/ or voiced continuant + /d/ (e.g. /st/, /ft/, /ʃt/, /nd/, /ld/, /zd/, /ðd/, /vd/) followed by a word-initial consonant (cf. *finished late, hold tight, caused losses*). (2) voiceless plosive or affricate + word final /t/ or voiced plosive + affricate + /d/ (/pt/, /kt/, /ʧt/, /bd/, /gd/, /ʤd/), followed by an initial consonant in the next word (e.g. *picked one, looked fine, stopped speaking*). This process may affect the past tense distinction, which is often resolved by contextual cues. Note that this elision process does not usually take place if the third consonant is /h/ or /j/, and that middle /k/, rather than /t/, is elided in the sequence /skt/, as in *asked* /ɑːst/.

There are, however, some contexts in which plosives are **not generally elided**. Word-final /**t**/ and /**d**/ are retained before /**h**/ as in *reached home* /riːʧt həʊm/ or *round here* /raʊnd hɪə/; or they may be kept in a **coalesced form** (/**ʧ ʤ**/), when followed by /j/ as in *caught you* /ˈkɔːʧə/ or *lend you* /ˈlenʤə/. Word-final /nt/ and /lt/ do not normally involve elision either. In this case, /t/ is normally replaced with /ʔ/ as in *He spelt it wrong* /hi spelʔ ɪt rɒŋ/.

Other examples of consonant elision include: elision of /**v**/ in *of* before /**ð**/ (*one of them* /wʌn ə ðem/); elision of the **consonant before** /**θ**/ in numerals (*sixth* /sikθ/), and the elision of **dental fricatives** in some common nouns (*clothes* /kləʊz/, *months* /mʌnz/).

Let us now have a look at **vowel elisions**. The most frequent instance is the elision of /**ə**/ occurring in two main contexts:

(1) When it is preceded by a word-final consonant and followed by a continuant, which normally becomes syllabic, as in *got another* /gɒt ˈn̩əðə/;

(2) When final /ə/ is followed by a linking /r/ plus word-initial vowel, as in *after an hour* /ˈɑːftrən aʊə/.

Elision may also affect the second element of a closing diphthong when followed by a syllable beginning with a vowel, whether word-internally (resulting in **neutralisation**, see § 5.7.2), as in *tower* /taʊə/ → /tɑːə/ → /tɑː/, or at word boundary, as in *try another* /traɪ əˈnʌðə/ → /tra əˈnʌðə/ → /trɑː ˈnʌðə/. It can be concluded, as noted by Ortiz and Lira (1982: 79), that the most frequent vowel elisions occur before /r/, /l/ or /n/.

AI 5.4 Elision

5.5 Linking

Linking (adjective / noun) or **liaison** (noun) are terms used in phonology to refer to one type of transition between sounds, where a sound is introduced at the end of a word if the following syllable has no onset, usually for ease of pronunciation (Crystal 2008: 280, 285). In English a **word-final post-vocalic /r/** may be added to those words ending in /ɑː ɔː ɜː/ and /ə/, either single or in glides, when followed by a syllable beginning with a vowel, whether at morpheme or word boundary (Collins and Mees 2009: 118–120; Cruttenden 2014: 315–318) (see also Section 4.2.5.1). Now, this **linking /r/** may be 'historically justified', i.e. it has existed in earlier stages of the language (e.g. *her invoice*), as indicated by the spelling, which is usually retained. This /r/ link is optional, although very frequent, between words, but pronounced when it occurs word-internally, that is, the root of the word ends in /aː ɔː ɜː ə/ plus <r> and the suffix begins with a vowel (e.g. *occur* + *-ing* > *occurring* /əˈkɜːrɪŋ/). Linking /r/ is present in both formal and informal speech.

Linking /r/ should be distinguished from what is known as the "**intrusive /r/**". This takes place when this linking function of /r/ is analogically extended to words in which the /r/ is not present in spelling at all (*drawing* /drɔːrɪŋ/), although the phonetic environment in which it occurs is similar to the one in which a linking /r/ arises. This link is very common after /ə/, as in *vanilla ice* /vəˈnɪlər aɪs/. Intrusive /r/ is stigmatised as uneducated and therefore it should be avoided. In its place, some speakers may produce a glottal stop or a glide.

5.6 Juncture

The phonetic boundary features between morphemes and words, which can help separate between otherwise identical units, are known as **juncture** (Cruttenden 2014: 318–319). The most common type of juncture is known as **open or plus juncture**, and it refers to that which takes place between words. In phonetic transcription open juncture is transcribed [+].

Let us examine one example to see how juncture features operate in order to distinguish between two otherwise phonemically identical sequences. Consider the sequences *that stuff* and *that's tough* (taken from Crystal 2008: 258). A broad transcription illustrating connected speech will render both sequences as: /ðætstʌf/. However, if *that stuff* is meant, with the boundary between /t/ and /s/, the pronunciation of the initial /s/ will be powerful and the /t/ will be unaspirated; whereas if *that's tough* is meant, the placement of the boundary between the /s/ and the /t/ means that the /s/, which is now final, will be less energetic, and the /t/, now in initial position, will be aspirated. Other well-known examples include: *I scream-ice cream*: /aɪ skriːm/ or /aɪs kriːm/; *a name-an aim*: /ə neɪm/ or /ən eɪm/; *why chop-white shop*: /waɪ tʃɒp/ or /waɪt ʃɒp/.

5.7 Vowel gradation

The terms **vowel gradation** or **ablaut** are generally used in historical linguistics to refer to the relationship between verb forms based on variations in the root vowel, as in *ring, rang, rung* (Crystal 2008: 216). Here by **"vowel gradation"** we mean the process whereby some function words exhibit more than one quantitative and qualitative pronunciation pattern depending on whether they are unaccented (the most usual form) or accented (in special situations or said in isolation), and so they have correspond **weak** or **strong pronunciations** or **forms** depending on the phonetic context. In contrast, lexical words (nouns, adjectives, adverbs, main verbs) usually retain prominence based on the occurrence of a full vowel even when there is no pitch prominence, even if they are monosyllabic. This implies that they tend to have the same quantitative pattern in connected speech as in isolation.

5.7.1 Weak and strong forms

In English **weak pronunciations** are much more frequent than strong ones, and so they should be regarded as **basic**, with occasional use of strengthening. However, it should be borne in mind that, while some function words have no weak form at all (*on* /ɒn/, *off* /ɒf/, *when* /wen/), others have more than one weak form. In the latter case the choice of one weak form over another usually depends on the phonetic context, but the effect of the phonetic environment may differ substantially from one accent or style to another. The 53 weak forms listed in Table 39 below, which can be compared with other lists proposed by Cruttenden (2014), Ortiz Lira (2008), García Lecumberri and Maidment (2000) or Kenworthy (1987) containing 55, 37, 44 and 35 entries, respectively, are typical of **careful colloquial RP** (Gimson 1980: 297) and are characterised by the following features:

(1) Reduction in **length** (***be*** [bi] instead of [biː]).
(2) **Vowel reduction** or **obscuration** towards weak vowels (***are*** [ə] instead of [ɑː]).
(3) **Elision of vowels** (***is*** [z] instead of [ɪz]).

(4) **Elision of consonants** (***him*** [ɪm] instead of [hɪm]). Function words with elided /h/ are more common than the unelided ones (except in sentence-initial position, where only the latter are possible). For this reason SSLE are advised to pronounce and transcribe aitchless forms, as well as to counteract their tendency to mispronounce RP glottal fricative /h/ as a velar fricative [x].

(5) In those function words which have **alternative weak pronunciations**, one with a **schwa/vowel** and another one with **schwa/vowel delition** (as in the case of, for example, *and, can, does, was* and *will*), the former generally occurs before vowels and the latter before consonants.

Table 39: Weak and strong forms

	WEAK **basic**	**STRONG** **exceptional**
a	[ə]	[eɪ]
am	[əm m]	[æm]
an	[ən]	[æn]
and	[ənd ən n̩][86]	[ænd]
are	[ə]	[ɑː]
as	[əz]	[æz][87]
at	[ət]	[æt]
be	[bi]	[biː]
been	[bin]	[biːn]
but	[bət]	[bʌt]
can (aux. v)	[kən kn̩][88]	[kæn]
could	[kəd]	[kʊd]
do[89]	[du də] auxiliary verb	[duː] full verb / emphatic use of auxiliary verb
does	[dəz dz z s][90] auxiliary verb	[dʌz] full verb / emphatic use of auxiliary verb sometimes sentence initially

86 The pronunciation [ənd] is slightly more formal than [ən]. *And* is frequently reduced to [n̩] in rapid speech after [t d f v θ ð s z ʃ ʒ] (*fish* ***and*** *chips* /ˌfɪʃ n̩ ˈtʃɪps/)

87 *As* generally has a weak pronunciation, the strong form is only used in sentence/utterance initial position when followed by an unstressed word. So compare ***As*** *far as I am concerned* /əz ˈfɑːr əz ˈaɪ əm kənˈsɜːnd/ with ***As*** *I was tired* /æz aɪ wz ˈtaɪəd/).

88 The weak realization of the modal auxiliary *can* is normally [kən], but it may be pronounced [kn̩] if it is followed by a vowel (*What* ***can*** *I do?* /ˈwɒt kən aɪ ˈduː/ vs. *What* ***can*** *you do?* /ˈwɒt kn̩ ju ˈduː/).

89 The auxiliary verb *do* is pronounced [du] before vowels and [də] before consonants (***Do*** *I know you* /du ˈaɪ ˈnəʊ ju/ vs. ***Do*** *you know me?* /də ju ˈnəʊ miː/).

90 Unless in emphatic contexts (*Mary* ***does*** *know* /ˈmeəri ˈdʌz ˈnəʊ/), the auxiliary form *does* is normally pronounced [dəz] before vowels (***Does*** *it sell well?* /dəz ɪt ˈsel ˈwel/) and [dz] before consonants (*What* ***does*** *he know* /ˈwɒt dz hi ˈnəʊ/).

	WEAK **basic**	**STRONG** **exceptional**
for	[fə]	[fɔː]
from	[frəm]	[frɒm]
had	[həd əd d] auxiliary verb	[hæd] full verb / emphatic use of auxiliary verb
has	[həz əz z] auxiliary verb	[hæz] full verb / emphatic use of auxiliary verb
have	[həv əv v] auxiliary verb	[hæv] full verb / emphatic use of auxiliary verb
he	[hi iː ɪ]	[hiː]
her	[hə ə ɜː][91]	[hɜː]
him	[ɪm]	[hɪm]
his	[ɪz]	[hɪz]
is	[s z]	[ɪz]
just	[dʒəst] when meaning 'only', 'simply' unstressed time adverb (with pres. perfect v)	[dʒʌst] when meaning 'exactly', 'precisely' stressed time adverb (with pres. perfect v)
me	[mi]	[miː]
must	[məst məs][92] when expressing 'obligation'	[mʌst] when expressing 'deduction'
not	[nt]	[nɒt]
of	[əv]	[ɒv]
our	[ɑː]	[ɑː aʊə]
or	[ə]	[ɔː][93]
saint	[sənt sən sn] when followed by the name of a saint	[seɪnt] when the word occurs on its own
shall	[ʃəl ʃl̩ l̩][94]	[ʃæl]
she	[ʃi]	[ʃiː]
should	[ʃəd əd d]	[ʃʊd]

91 These three weak forms have a linking-*r* when they are followed by a vowel. [ɜː] or [hə] are the usual pronunciations when *her* functions as a determiner (*I brought* ***her*** *orchids* /ˈaɪ ˈbrɔːt ɜː ˈɔːkɪdz/, while as an object it is usually pronounced [ə] or [hə] (*I gave* ***her*** *the orchids* /ˈaɪ geɪv ə ði ˈɔːkɪdz/).

92 The weak form of *must* may be reduced to [məs], with the [t] elided, when the next words begins with a consonant.

93 *Or* is generally pronounced [ɔː] and it has linking-r pronunciations when followed by a word beginning with a vowel (*two* ***or*** *eleven* /tuː ɔːr ɪˈlevn̩/).

94 *Shall* is often weakened to [ʃəl] before a vowel (***Shall*** *I come?* /ʃəl aɪ ˈkʌm) and to [ʃl̩] before a consonant (*I* ***shall*** *come tomorrow* ˈaɪ ʃl̩ kʌm təˈmɒrəʊ).

	WEAK basic	STRONG exceptional
sir	[sə] when followed by a name	[sɜː] when the word occurs on its own
some	[səm sm̩] 'an unspecified amount / number'	[sʌm] 'a small / certain amount of something' pronoun
than	[ðən ðn̩][95]	[ðæn]
that	[ðət] conjunction and relative pronoun	[ðæt] demonstrative and adverb
the[96]	[ðə ði]	[ðiː]
their[97]	[ðə]	[ðeə]
them	[ðəm ðm̩ əm m]	[ðem]
there	[ðə] existential pronoun	[ðeə] adverb (homophone of *their*)
to	[tə tu][98]	[tuː]
us	[əs s]	[ʌs]
was	[wəz]	[wɒz]
we	[wi]	[wiː]
were	[wə]	[wɜː]
who	[hu u] unstressed relative	[huː] NP (either stressed or not)
will	[wl̩ l̩]	[wɪl]
would	[wəd əd d]	[wʊd]
you	[ju]	[juː]
your	[jə] used only occasionally (LPD)	[jɔː] normal pronunciation

95 *Than* is generally pronounced [ðən] before words beginning with a vowel (*rather* ***than*** *eating* /ˈrɑːðə ðən ˈiːtɪŋ/) and [ðn̩] before words starting with a consonant (*shorter* ***than*** *legs* /ˈʃɔːtə ðn̩ legz/).

96 *The* is pronounced [ðə] before words beginning with a consonant, and [ði] when it is followed by a vowel. The strong pronunciation [ðiː] is heard when the article is emphasised for some reason.

97 *There* normally takes the strong pronunciation [ðeə], but it can be weakened to [ðə], especially when followed by a word beginning with a vowel, and both forms have a linking-*r* when they are followed by a vowel (*She caressed* ***their*** *arms* /ʃi kəˈrest ðeər ɑːmz/ /ʃi kəˈrest ðər ɑːmz/).

98 The stranded version of *to* is usually [tu] rather than [tuː] (EPD). [tuː] is used restrictively in some fixed expressions such as *to and fro*, as well as in contrastive contexts (*The letter was* ***from*** *him not* ***to*** *him* /ðə ˈletə wəz ˈfrɒm ɪm nɒt ˈtuː ɪm/). In addition, it should be noted that *to* and *into* have two weak forms: [tə] and [ɪntə] are used before consonants (***to/into*** *the house* /tə ˈɪntə ðə ˈhaʊs), while [tu] and [ɪntu] occur before vowels (***to/into*** *a house* /tu ˈɪntə ə ˈhaʊs). In GA, however, these distinctions do not apply, because schwa pronunciations are heard in all contexts.

In rapid casual speech, there is a tendency for reduction and obscuration of vowels, both in grammatical words which do not usually have a weak form, and even in some lexical items as well. For example, the pronoun ***I*** in *I didn't know* /ə/ or the possessive *my* in *I love* ***my*** *baby* /mə/). The words *any* and *many,* as in *How* ***many*** *have you got?* /haʊ mnɪ əv ju gɒt/. Concerning lexical words, these may show reduction of the short vowel (/ɪ ʊ ʌ æ ɒ/) or the diphthong /əʊ/ to /ə/, in unaccented positions close to a primary accent, as in *You sit over there,* with the verb *sit* as /sət/ or *He's going to buy it,* with *going to* as /ˈgənə/.

Strong forms, on the other hand, are produced in slow formal or solemn speech, as well as in the following contexts (Lillo 2009: 81–96):

(1) When a function word is **stressed** for one or several of the following reasons:
  a. It is being **quoted**, as in *Spell the word* ***"was"*** /ˈspel ðə ˈwɜːd ˈwɒz/, where /ðə/ is weak, whereas /wɒz/ is used in its strong form.
  b. It is **emphasised**, as in *I'd like milk* ***and*** *coffee, please* /aɪd ˈlaɪk ˈmɪlk ˈænd ˈkɒfi |ˈpliːz/, where the speaker emphasises that s/he wants to have both milk and coffee.
  c. It is **contrasted,** as in *The book isn't for* ***them,*** *it's for* ***us*** /ðə ˈbʊk ˈɪznt̩ fə ˈðem | ɪts fər ˈʌs/, where /ðə, ɪznt̩, fəʳ/ are weak in this context, whereas /ðem/ and /ʌs/ exhibit their strong form for reasons of contrast.

(2) When a preposition or auxiliary verb is **stranded** or is left on its own, with no object or full verb after it, usually in sentence-final position. This occurs in *Where are you going* ***to?*** /ˈweər ər ju ˈgəʊɪŋ ˈtuː/, where /ər/ and /ju/ are weak in this context, whereas the preposition /tuː/ is strong as it comes in final position. Likewise, in the exchange A: *Are you Mary?* B: *Yes, actually I* ***am.*** /ə ju ˈmeəri | jes | ˈæktʃuəli ˈaɪ ˈæm/, the auxiliary /ˈæm/ has a strong pronunciation because it is stranded in utterance final position. However, stranded auxiliaries and prepositions may occur non-finally, but still in these cases they tend to have a strong pronunciation, as in ***I can,*** *of course* /ˈaɪ ˈkæn | əv ˈkɔːs/, or *Peter was lauged* ***at*** *by his classmates* /ˈpiːtə wəz ˈlɑːft ˈæt baɪ ɪz ˈklɑːsmeɪts/.

(3) The negative contractions of (auxiliary and primary) verbs are always stressed and therefore have the same vowels as the strong form of their affirmative counterparts *aren't* /ɑːnt/, *couldn't* /ˈkʊdnt/, *hadn't* /ˈhædnt/, *hasn't* /ˈhæznt/, *haven't* /ˈhævnt̩/, *mustn't* /ˈmʌsnt/, *shouldn't* /ˈʃʊdnt/, *wasn't* /ˈwɒznt/, *weren't* /wɜːnt/.

5.7.2 Neutralisation of weak forms

As we have seen in section 5.8.1. and in Table 39, certain grammatical words may have different pronunciations depending on whether or not they are accented in the utterance (Cruttenden 2014: 305–307). This leads to confusion, since two words with different pronunciations, when said slowly or in isolation, may show the same pronunciation when said quickly in connected speech. This process of reduction to a common weak pronunciation is known as **neutralisation**. The consequent ambiguity is usually resolved by context and grammar. Tables 40 and 41 below (adapted from Gimson 1984: 279–80) show some of the most common neutralised forms and their full correspondences.

Table 40: Neutralisation of weak forms

Neutral form	Correspondences	Examples
/ə/	are, a	*The bottles **are** new* /ðə ˈbɒtlz ə nju:/ *He bottles **a** new wine* /hi ˈbɒtlz ə nju: waɪn/
	a, her	*She loves **a** girl* /ʃi lʌvz ə gɜ:l/ *She loves **her** girl* /ʃɪ lʌvz ə gɜ:l/
	or, of	*Five **or** six people turned up* /faɪv ə sɪks ˈpi:pl̩ tɜ:nd ʌp/ *Five **of** them turned up* /faɪv ə ðem tɜ:nd ʌp
	are, or	*Hens **are** rare* /henz ə reə bɜ:dz/ *Hens **or** rare birds* /henz ə reə bɜ:dz/
	are, of	*Three books **of** his* /θri: bʊks ə hɪz/ *Three books **are** his* /θri: bʊks ə hɪz/
/əv/	*have (aux.), of*	*A few **have** my books* /ə fju: əv maɪ bʊks/ *A few **of** my books* /ə fju: əv maɪ bʊks/
/ðə/	*there, the*	***There** sounds as…* /ðə saʊndz əz/ ***The** sound is…* /ðə saund əz/
/s/	*is, has, does*	*It'**s** going* /ɪts ˈgəʊɪŋ/ *It'**s** gone* /ɪts gɒn/ *What'**s** (=does) it mean?* /wɒts ɪt mi:n/
/z/	*is, has, does*	*Where'**s** she going?* /weəz ʃi: ˈgəʊɪŋ/ *Where'**s** she gone* /weəz ʃi: gɒn/ *Where'**s** she come from?* /weəz ʃi: kʌm frɒm/
/əz/	*as, has*	***As** white **as** a sheet* /əz waɪt əz ə ʃi:t/ *Who **has** a sheet?* /hu: əz ə ʃi:t/
/ən/	*and, an*	*Green **and** orange* /gri:n ən ˈorɪndʒ/ *Eat **an** orange* /i:t ən ˈɒrɪndʒ/
/n/	*and, not*	*He hid **and** shut up* /hi hɪd n̩ ʃʌt ʌp/ *Didn'**t** he like it?* /dɪd n̩ hi: laɪk ɪt/
/d/	*had, would*	*She'**d** set my hair* /ʃɪd set maɪ heə/ *She'**d** set my hair* /ʃɪd set maɪ heə/

Table 41: Neutralisation matrix

	a	*an*	*and*	*are*	*as*	*does*	*had*	*has*	*have*	*is*	*not*	*of*	*or*	*the*	*there*	*would*
A				/ə/												
an			/ən/													
and		/ən/									/n/					
are	/ə/												/əʳ/			
as								/əz/								
does								/s/ /z/		/s/ /z/						
had																/d/
has					/əz/	/s/ /z/				/s/ /z/						
have												/əv/				
is						/s/ /z/		/s/ /z/								
not			/n/													
of									/əv/							
or				/ər/												
the															/ðə/	
there														/ðə/		
would							/d/									

5.8 Advice to learners

Studies in second language acquisition of English have shown that, although certain connected speech phenomena such as velarisation (Martínez-Dauden and Llisterri 1990; Moore 2008) and palatalisation (Keys 2002), for example, may occur both in the L1 and the L2, it is not necessarily the case that they will be easily acquired in the second. Likewise, it has been observed that the application of the rules concerning connected speech phenomena, as in the case of secondary articulations, may be more difficult for some sounds or phonetic contexts than for others, much in the same way that connected speech phenomena can be more difficult to reproduce for some speakers than for others. At a more general level, it has thus been concluded that the acquisition of segment dynamics is partly affected by language-specific variation (Strange,

Weber, Levy, Shafiro and Nishi 2002), as well as by general production constraints generated by individual vocal tract configurations (Fowler and Saltzman 1993). Be that as it may, what previous work unanimously suggests is that non-native speakers must learn the general parameters of connected speech variability from the language environment.

Foreign learners often learn English pronunciation on a basis of isolated word forms. However, in conversations and specially in colloquial speech, native speakers frequently modify words as described in the foregoing sections. It may not be necessary for SSLE to reproduce all the special context forms that have been described, but those aiming at a native speaker competence should be aware of the features that characterise more casual pronunciation, in particular the proper use of weak forms, liaisons, elisions and the co-articulatory and assimilatory tendencies (especially those of [n], [t], [d], [s] and [z]) that apply in certain contexts given the high frequency with which these processes occur in English. Nevertheless, elisions should be avoided when the dropping of a sound triggers the loss of a grammatical or semantic meaning (tense, number, possession, etc.). An excess of pre-vocalic glottal stops should also be discouraged (Cruttenden 2014: 321; Estebas Vilaplana 2009: 118–127).

Further reading

Readers wishing more detail on connected speech phenomena and other related issues such as transcription and segmentation should consult, for example, Cruttenden (2014, Chapters 11 and 12), Ashby (2011, Chapter 9), (Lodge 2009, Chapters 4 to 7), Ogden (2009, Chapter 3), and Ladefoged (2005, Chapter 16). In addition, we also recommend Shockey (2003) because it focuses on the phonetic and phonological features that characterise conversational English such as reduction, syllabicity and weak forms, among others, and it also presents experimental studies that illustrate how casual speech is produced and perceived.

Turning to long established texts particularly addressed to SSLE, descriptions of connected speech phenomena may be found in Monroy Casas (1980, 1981, 2012, Chapter 2), Estebas Vilaplana (2009, Chapters 4), Mott (2011, Chapter 6), Finch and Ortiz Lira (1982, Chapter 8), Sánchez Benedicto (1980) and Stockwell and Bowen (1965), among others.

Exercises

1. Render the following text given in narrow (phonetic) transcription into ordinary spelling.[99]
   [ð̥eːːɹ ɔːɫ̥ l̥ʲɪvd̥ tʰəˈg̟eðəɹ̥ ĩn̥ ə sm̠ʷɔːɫ̥ haˑʊs ĩn̥ ð̥ə ˈv̥eɹʲi ˈsẽnt̬ʰəɹ̥ ɒv̥ ə d̥ɑˑk pʰaːĩn̥ w̥ʊd̥ // ˈĩnt̬ʰə ð̥ʲɪs p̟ˡleˑɪs ð̥ə sʌ̃n̥ ˈn̥evə ʃõn̥ b̥ʲɪˈk̬əz̥ ð̥ə ʃeːɹd̥ʷ w̥əz̥ t̠ʰʷuːː d̥ʲiˑp / ə̃n̥ n̥əʊ w̥ʲĩnd̥ ˈevə k̟ʰeːĩm̥ ð̥eə ˈaːɹðə / b̥ʲɪˈk̬əz̥ ð̥ə b̥aːʊz̥ w̥ə t̠ʰʷuːː θʲɪk / səːːʊ ð̥æt ɪt w̥əz̥ ð̥ə m̥əˑʊst ˈs̠ʷɒlʲɪt̬ɹ̩ʲi ə̃n̥ kʰʷwaˑɪət pˡleˑɪs ĩn̥ ð̥ə w̥ɜːld̥ / ə̃n̥ ð̥ə fʲɪˈl̠ʷɒs̬əf̬əz̥ w̥əɹ̥ ˈeːɪbˡɫ̩ tʰə h̟ʲɪəɹ̥ iˑʧ ˈʌðə ˈθʲĩŋk̟ʰʲĩŋ̊ ɔːɫ̥ d̥eːːɪ l̠̥ʷõŋ̊ / ɔːː ˈm̥eˑɪk̟ʰʲĩŋ ˈspʲiˑʧ̬ʲɪz̥ tʰə iˑʧ ˈʌðə //]
2. Allophonic variation of vowels. Classify the following words under the right heading: normal length, clipping, lengthening and extra length.

code	steep	pit	bed	higher
wool	coat	soothe	turn	thief
pea	search	claim	cord	niece
tear	through	big	wound	south
breath	sang	enough	blob	car

3. Allophonic variation. Give the allophonic transcription of the following words:

appeal	vocalic	accomplish	middle	pointing
Spain	acknowledge	leaked	thank you	acclaims
care of	behave	it took	cold	either of

4. Render the following text into narrow (phonetic) transcription, paying special attention to all the allophonic variations of both vowels and consonants.
   When the little boy found that the light did not move he drew closer to it, and at last, emboldened by curiosity, he stepped right into it and found that it was not a thing at all. The instant that he stepped into the light he found it was hot, and this so frightened him that he jumped out of it again and ran behind a tree. Then he jumped into it for a moment and out of it again, and for nearly half an hour he played a splendid game of tip and tig with the sunlight. At last he grew quite bold and stood in it and found that it did not burn him at all, but he did not like to remain in it, fearing that he might be cooked.[100]

99 The Project Gutenberg EBook of The Crock of Gold, by James Stephens http://www.gutenberg.org/files/1605/1605-h/1605-h.htm.
100 Same as in Exercise 1.

5. Assimilation. Identify instances of assimilation in the following sequences and explain each case. Try and pronounce them without assimilation. Does it seem to affect speech speed?

1. white paper	2. stand by	3. bath salts	4. gold plate
5. in question	6. seven pots	7. that ghost	8. nice shells
9. newspaper	10. good cook		

6. Elision. Identify possible cases of elision in the following words and sequences. Explain them. Now try and pronounce the words without the elision: does it sound natural?

1. stand there	2. I don't know	3. next please	4. postman
5. stand here	6. stand aside	7. picked one	8. asked him
9. picked two	10. give me one	11. but came	12. can't hurry

7. In the following passage given in orthography, try and identify the places where either linking or intrusive *r* might occur and comment on each case.

In these people the children were deeply interested. They used to go apart afterwards and talk about them, and would try to remember what they looked like, how they talked, and their manner of walking or taking snuff. After a time they became interested in the problems which these people submitted to their parents and the replies or instructions wherewith the latter relieved them. Long training had made the children able to sit perfectly quiet, so that when the talk came to the interesting part they were entirely forgotten, and ideas which might otherwise have been spared their youth became the commonplaces of their conversation.[101]

8. In the following passage, given in orthography, try and identify all the grammatical words susceptible of use in their weak form. Comment on whether the weak or the strong form is used and why.

Brother, these are weighty reflections, and I do clearly perceive that the time has come for you to stop. I might observe, not in order to combat your views, but merely to continue an interesting conversation, that there are still some knowledges which you have not assimilated – you do not yet know how to play the tambourine, nor how to be nice to your wife, nor how to get up first in the morning and cook the breakfast. Have you learned how to smoke strong tobacco as I do? or can you dance in the moonlight with a woman of the Shee? To understand the theory which underlies all things is

---

101 Same as above.

not sufficient. It has occurred to me, brother, that wisdom may not be the end of everything. Goodness and kindliness are, perhaps, beyond wisdom. Is it not possible that the ultimate end is gaiety and music and a dance of joy? Wisdom is the oldest of all things. Wisdom is all head and no heart. Behold, brother, you are being crushed under the weight of your head. You are dying of old age while you are yet a child.[102]

102 Same as above.

Chapter 6

6 Beyond the Segment: Stress, Rhythm and Intonation

6.1 Introduction

So far, we have dealt with what is usually referred to as **segmental** phonetics and phonology, that is, the articulatory, acoustic and auditory properties of discrete segments or speech sounds and the phonological processes involved in their production, paying particular attention to the sounds of RP in comparison with those of PSp. It is time now to go beyond the individual segment in order to study the features that extend over and above a sequence of segments, occurring at a higher level of the utterance. These features are known as **supra-segmental** or **prosodic**, namely, **stress** at sentence level, **rhythm** and **intonation. Prosodic** units are chunks of speech, which may not coincide with grammatical units, whose boundaries are marked by the breathing processes of inhalation and exhalation, gradually delineating a contour in which pitch declines and vowels lengthen over the duration of the unit, until both pitch and speed are reset at the boundary of the next unit. This is what gives languages and dialects their idiosyncratic **prosody** or melody. In this chapter we will explore their phonetic realisation and perception and how they fit into the phonological system of English – i.e. how they can affect meaning (Collins and Mees 2003: 226–275; Collins and Mees 2009: 123–148; Roach 2005: 93–203; Crystal 2008: 393; Cruttenden 2014: 239–269).

6.2 Stress and rhythm

Stress is a relative concept, which may be defined in terms of production and reception, as the degree of force, or relative emphasis, which is given to a syllable in a word in isolation (**word stress** or **lexical stress**) or to certain words within a longer utterance (**prosodic stress** or **sentence stress**),[103] and which means that stressed syllables are then perceived as more forceful than others. However, it must be noted that prominence does not simply imply a more forceful articulation, i.e. an increase in loudness, but it is due to a concurrence of other phonetic features, such as pitch, length of the vowel in the stressed syllable, and subsequent changes in the quality of not only the vowels affected, but also the consonants and their articulation. In this unit, we are going to see that when

103 We avoid the use of the term 'sentence' to refer to the stress words take in connected speech, so as not to link the notion of 'utterance' in general to a particular grammatical category.

words are put together in utterances, they are subject to rhythmical variations, usage conventions and the intentions of the speaker. This means that words which in isolation would always be stressed, as seen in Chapter 5, may lose their stress when they are considered in connected speech because of the presence of stronger stresses in surrounding syllables; and likewise, words which would normally not be stressed, may be stressed for a certain effect (Finch and Ortiz Lira 1982: 87–90; Crystal 2008: 454–456; Roach 2005: 93–103).

6.2.1 Stress-timed languages versus syllable-timed languages

Stress and rhythm are closely connected. **Rhythm** is the periodic repetition of an event, that is, at regular intervals of time. English is a **stress-timed language** whereas Spanish is **syllable-timed** (Crystal 2008: 456; Collins and Mees 2003: 241–242; Cruttenden 2014: 271–272). The difference between these two rhythms may be comparable to what in music is known as *legato*, or 'tied together', and *staccato* or 'detached'. This means that in English stressed syllables recur at equal intervals of time, regardless of the number of unstressed syllables between them, which normally get shortened or phonetically weakened as they are fitted in quick succession between stresses. This can be seen in two different ways by considering the following examples:

(1) ˈSusan had ˈbought her the ˈapples in the ˈmarket.
|| ˈsuːzn̩ həd ˈbɔːt hə ði ˈæpl̩z ɪn ðə ˈmɑːkɪt ||

(2) a. ˈJohn ˈcame ˈhome at ˈfive.
|| ˈdʒɒn ˈkeɪm ˈhəʊm ət ˈfaɪv ||

b. The ˈboys aˈrrived at the ˈschool at ˈseven.
|| ðə ˈbɔɪz əˈraɪvd ət ðə ˈskuːl ət ˈsevn̩ ||

In example (1), we can observe that since the stresses occur at equal intervals, the syllables in between have to take roughly the same time to be pronounced, even though there are only two syllables between *su-* and *bought* or *bought* and *a*, and yet there are three syllables between *a* and *mar* and only one after *mar*. This is what is meant by stress-timed: stress rules the time taken to pronounce unstressed syllables. In examples (2a) and (2b) we see that although (2a) contains a total of five syllables and (2b) has exactly double, the two utterances should take roughly the same amount of time to pronounce, since they each contain four stresses.

A side-effect of English stress-timed rhythm is **vowel weakening**, whereby vowels are shifted to the central part of the CVS (Carr 2012: 33) in unstressed syllables resulting in the production of weak vowels /ɪ ʊ e ə/ that are located in that area. Thus, it can be seen in the phonemic transcriptions of (1) and

(2) above, as well as in all previous and subsequent ones, that most unstressed syllables have one of these weak vowels, mostly /ə/.

Syllable-timing, on the other hand, means that syllables are repeated periodically, taking approximately the same time, regardless of whether they are stressed or not, producing the "machine gun" effect of Spanish speech. To give similar examples to the English ones above, consider (3) and (4) below:

(3) Suˈsana venˈdrá el ˈsábado a las ˈcinco.
'Susan will come on Saturday at five.'

(4) a. ˈElla ˈcanta ˈbien.
'She sings well.'

b. Los ˈtigres y aˈquellos eleˈfantes
'The tigers and those elephants'

In (3) because there is one syllable between *drá* and *sá* and there are four syllables between *sá* and *cin*, the latter sequence will take more time to pronounce than the former. For this same reason, (4a) with five syllables will take less time to pronounce than (4b), with ten, even though they both exhibit the same number of stresses: in this case, the rhythm is syllable-driven and, as a result, no vowel weakening takes place. Therefore, it is extremely important for Spanish speakers to pronounce English utterances paying attention to phonic groups, trying to join together unstressed syllables with stressed ones into a single one, in a *legato* manner.

6.2.2 Word stress

We have mentioned the phonetic features of stress, but now we must consider whether stress has a **phonemic function** serving to distinguish words that otherwise would be homophones. Lexical stress is phonemic in English and Spanish. For example, the noun *ˈincrease* and the verb *inˈcrease* are distinguished by the positioning of the stress on the first syllable in the former, and on the second syllable in the latter. Likewise, many pairs of compound words and word sequences are distinguished by means of stress (*blackbird* vs *black ˈbird*; *ˈpaper bag* vs *paper ˈbag*); and to provide further examples of English and Spanish, words such as *insight* and *incite* in English, or in the Spanish *compro* and *compró* are only distinguished by the position of the stress – that is, the stress falling on the first syllable in the former and on the second in the latter, respectively.

We are going to look at stress placement within the word in isolation, what is known as **citation form**, which is not the way we normally speak words aloud. By doing this, we can focus more clearly on the different levels of stress within the word, before we see how this may be affected when words are spoken together in connected speech.

6.2.2.1 Levels of stress

It is possible to distinguish up to five different **levels of stress** within a polysyllabic word, but for practical purposes we are going to distinguish only three, which is what most dictionaries do: **primary**, **secondary** and **unstressed**. Every polysyllabic word has a primary stressed syllable and everything else remains unstressed, with another syllable possibly carrying **secondary stress**, which is not always predictable. The standard notation of stress in transcription, a superscript straight comma before the accented syllable with a primary stress, and a subscript one for secondary stress as is already familiar in this book. In monosyllables the stress is not generally marked. (Collins and Mees 2003: 229–230; Roach 2005: 95–100).

6.2.2.2 Placement of stress

The position of the stress in a given word is not as predictable in English or Spanish as it is in other languages, like Czech or Polish, for example, which have clearer guidelines or rules. However, certain rules seem to be in operation given the fact that native speakers have no difficulty in assigning the right stress to an unfamiliar word. Such guidelines work on the basis of **four parameters**, which can help identify where to place the stress in any given word in English. These are:

(1) the **morphological structure** of the word: is it simple, i.e. containing only one grammatical unit, or complex, either by derivation with prefixes and/or suffixes or compounding?
(2) the **grammatical category** of the word (noun, adjective, verb, etc.)
(3) the **number of syllables** of a word.
(4) the **phonological structure** of those syllables.

However, any attempt at a complete prescriptive system of all the rules deriving from the application of the above parameters would be much too complex in the context of foreign language learning. For that reason, while still following the above considerations, we will be looking at the most frequent patterns which may prove useful for students. A first division of words focuses on **word length**, two and three syllable words being considered **short** on the one hand, and words with more than three syllables being considered **long**, regardless of their morphological structure. We want to avoid morphological considerations as much as possible, which in turn have a lot to do with etymology and the origin of words, as they would complicate the general picture unnecessarily for present purposes. These rules apply to major lexical words only.

AI 6.1 Stress in polysyllables

(1) Short words (maximum three syllables)

As a very general rule, there is a general tendency for stress to fall on the first syllable of nouns with two or three syllables; however, if that syllable is weak then the stress is shifted to the next syllable on the right. The tendency for simple verbs and adjectives of two or three syllables is different as they tend to carry stress on the final syllable, unless this is weak, in which case stress will be placed on the penultimate syllable (second from the end); if this is also weak, stress will then be shifted to the first syllable. Note that the diphthong /əʊ/ is never stressed when final (Finch and Ortiz Lira 1982: 90–94; Collins and Mees 2003: 231; Roach 2005: 96–100).

Table 42: General tendencies in stress patterns: 2 and 3 syllable words

	2 syllables	3 syllables
Nouns	ˈbottle ˈmorning	ˈprinciple ˈquality
Verbs	aˈpply, aˈttract,	conˈsider conˈtribute
Adjectives	aˈlone unˈknown	imˈportant

Following this general tendency, quite a few words in English which can function as both verbs and nouns exhibit this contrastive stress pattern: nouns tend to be stressed on the first syllable and verbs on the last. This is known as **variable stress** or **stress switch.** Note that in this case those words functioning as adjectives are stressed on the first syllable as well, not on the second, to distinguish them from verbs. This stress switch may also be associated to a change in the quality of the vowels (Cruttenden 2001: 233; Roach 2009: 87).[104]

AI 6.2. Variable stress

(2) Long words (more than three syllables)

A very strong tendency is for long words in general to carry the stress on the **antepenultimate syllable** – i.e. the third from the end- as in *e ˈmergency, an*

104 Some exceptions are: *ˈcomment* (vb), *a ˈddress* (n.), *reˈsearch* (n.). Note also: *ˈminute* (n.) but *mi ˈnute* (adj.), *ˈinvalid* (n) but *inˈvalid* (adj.).

Table 43: Most common pairs of words with variable stress

	Verbs	Nouns/Adjectives
accent	/ækˈsent/	/ˈæksent/
abstract	/æbsˈtrækt/	/ˈæbstrækt/
attribute	/æˈtrɪbjuːt/	/ˈætrɪbjuːt/
compact	/kəmˈpækt/	/ˈkɒmpækt/
compound	/kəmˈpaʊnd/	/ˈkɒmpaʊnd/
concert	/kənˈsɜːt/	/ˈkɒnsət/
conduct	/kənˈdʌkt/	/ˈkɒndʌkt/
conflict	/kənˈflɪkt/	/ˈkɒnflɪkt/
construct	/kənˈstrʌkt/	/ˈkɒnstrʌkt/
content	/kənˈtent/	/ˈkɒntent/
contest	/kənˈtest/	/ˈkɒntest/
contract	/kənˈtrækt/	/ˈkɒntrækt/
contrast	/kənˈtrɑːst/	/ˈkɒntrɑːst/
convert	/kənˈvɜːt/	/ˈkɒnvət/
convict	/kənˈvɪkt/	/ˈkɒnvɪkt/
decrease	/dɪˈkriːs/	/ˈdiːkriːs/
desert	/dɪˈzɜːt/	/ˈdezət/
dictate	/dɪkˈteɪt/	/ˈdɪkteɪt/
escort	/ɪˈskɔːt/	/ˈeskɔːt/
exploit	/ɪkˈsplɔɪt/	/ˈeksplɔɪt/
export	/ɪkˈspɔːt/	/ˈekspɔːt/
extract	/ɪkˈstrækt/	/ˈekstrækt/
frequent	/frɪˈkwent/	/ˈfriːkwent/
import	/ɪmˈpɔːt/	/ˈɪmpɔːt/
incense	/ɪnˈsens/	/ˈɪnsəns/
increase	/ɪnˈkriːs/	/ˈɪnkriːs/
insert	/ɪnˈsɜːt/	/ˈɪnsət/
insult	/ɪnˈsʌlt/	/ˈɪnsʌlt/
invite	/ɪnˈvaɪt/	/ˈɪnvaɪt/
object	/əbˈdʒekt/	/ˈɒbdʒɪkt/
perfect	/pəˈfekt/	/ˈpɜːfɪkt/
perfume	/pəˈfjuːm/	/ˈpɜːfjuːm/
permit	/pəˈmɪt/	/ˈpɜːmɪt/
pervert	/pəˈvɜːt/	/ˈpɜːvɜːt/
produce	/prəˈdjuːs/	/ˈprɒdjuːs/
progress	/prəˈgres/	/ˈprəʊgres/
project	/prəˈdʒekt/	/ˈprɒdʒekt/
protest	/prəˈtest/	/ˈprəʊtest/
rebel	/rɪˈbel/	/ˈrebəl/
record	/rɪˈkɔːd/	/ˈrekɔːd/
refund	/rɪˈfʌnd/	/ˈriːfʌnd/
refuse	/rɪˈfjuːz/	/ˈrefjuːs/
reject	/rɪˈdʒekt/	/ˈriːdʒəkt/
segment	/segˈment/	/ˈsegmənt/
subject	/sʌbˈdʒekt/	/ˈsʌbdʒɪkt/
torment	/tɔːˈment/	/ˈtɔːment/
transfer	/trænsˈfɜː/	/ˈtrænsfə/
transplant	/trænsˈplɑːnt/	/ˈtrænsplɑːnt/
transport	/trænsˈpɔːt/	/ˈtrænspɔːt/
update	/ʌpˈdeɪt/	/ˈʌpdeɪt/

ˈticipate, iˈronical. In words with three or more syllables secondary stress is frequent, usually when the primary stress falls on the third syllable or later. Here it is normal for secondary stress to be marked on one of the preceding syllables (normally not the one immediately preceding the primary stress). For example, *ˌinter ˈjection* and *ˌevo ˈlution*, which have their primary stress on the third syllable, consequently take secondary stress on their first syllables; *ˌorgani ˈzation* and *a ˈssoci ˈation* both have primary stress on the fourth syllable, but have secondary stress on the first and second syllables respectively. If the primary stress falls on the third or fourth syllable from the end, that is, quite early in the word, the secondary stress will then fall on a later syllable: *ˈMedite ˌrranean.*

Although so far we have been considering short and long words in general, it may prove useful to pay some attention to their morphological structure, since some very general guidelines for stress placement can be observed. Very briefly, a word may become complex by means of two different processes: by **affixation** of either a **prefix** before the basic form of the word, or stem, as in *in-adequacy*, or a **suffix** after it, as in *contrast-ive*; and also by **compounding**, of two independent stems, as in *basket-ball*. In the case of **prefixes**, a very general tendency is for primary stress to fall on the syllable following the prefix, as in *de ˈcrease ex ˈclaim, i ˈllegal, re ˈform and un ˈreliable*, for example -except for a large number of nouns and adjectives, such as *ˈabstract*, *ˈcontract*, *ˈexchange* or *ˈprodigal.* **Suffixation** is slightly more complex, but since most suffixes are easily recognisable by students, it seems worthwhile to have a look at their most frequent stress patterns. Suffixes may be divided in two groups: (a) those that do not affect the stress pattern of the stem, in (3), and (b) those that cause stress shift of some sort, exemplified in (4). Note that for practical purposes single and double endings are not differentiated, and that stems may not necessarily be obvious “English” words, but vestiges of older words of other origins, like Latin or Greek. Note also that there will be a secondary stress on a previous syllable in the case of long words (Finch and Ortiz Lira 1982: 94–97; Collins and Mees 2003: 232–237; Roach 2005: 104–111; Cruttenden 2014: 242–248).

AI 6.3 Suffixes which do not affect the pronunciation of the stem

(3) Suffixes that do not affect the stress pattern of the stem

<-able>	ˈlaughable, ˈperishable, reˈmarkable, unforˈgettable
<-age>	ˈcarriage, ˈmarriage, ˈpackage, perˈcentage
<-al>	ˈfloral, ˈordinal, ˈnatural, ˈnaval
<-cy>	ˈjuicy, ˈcurrency, ˈdelicacy, ˈintimacy

<-dom>	archˈbishopdom, ˈfreedom, ˈkingdom, ˈprincedom
<-en>	ˈchristen, enˈlighten, ˈmadden, ˈwiden
<-er>	ˈgardener, ˈlecturer, ˈplumber, ˈsilencer
<-ful>	ˈbeautiful, ˈharmful, ˈgraceful, forˈgetful
<-fy>	ˈclassify, ˈglorify, iˈdentify, ˈnotify
<-hood>	ˈchildhood, ˈfalsehood, ˈlikelihood, ˈwomanhood
<-ing>	ˈboring, conˈfirming, enterˈtaining, imˈproving
<-ise/ize>	aˈpologise, ˈcivilize, ˈnormalize, rˈealise
<-ist>	exˈtremist ˈfinalist ˈjournalist ˈoculist
<-like>	ˈchildlike ˈfactorylike ˈlifelike ˈwarlike
<-less>	ˈaimless, ˈbottomless, comˈpassionless, ˈuseless
<-let>	ˈbooklet, ˈeyelet, ˈpiglet, ˈquadruplet
<-ling>	ˈduckling, ˈlordling, ˈyearling
<-ly>	biˈlingually, iˈdeally, ˈlovely, ˈscholarly
<-ment>	aˈgreement, ˌdisaˈppointment, ˈpunishment, ˈvestment
<-ness>	ˈcalmness, ˈcheerfulness, ˈfaithfulness, ˈsadness
<-ous>	auˈtonomous, conˈtemptuous, ˈdangerous, ˈvigorous
<-ship>	ˈcitizenship, ˈfellowship, ˈfriendship, ˈscholarship
<-ure>	ˈcapture, deˈparture, ˈfailure, ˈsignature
<-wise>	ˈclockwise, ˈlengthwise, ˈlikewise, ˈotherwise
<-y>	ˈairy, ˈrocky, ˈfunny, ˈnoisy

Note: <-ish>

(4) Suffixes which affect stress placement: two groups

a. Suffixes which tend to attract the primary stress to the **syllable preceding** them; this means that the original primary stress *may* be shifted to the last syllable of the stem, just before the suffix. There may also be changes in the quality of vowels.

AI 6.4 Stress shifting suffixes

<-ative>	aˈffirmative, comˈparative, deˈmonstrative, imˈperative
<-cient>	deˈficient, eˈfficient, proˈficient, suˈfficient
<-ciency>	coefˈficiency, deˈficiency, improˈficiency, suˈfficiency
<-eous>	ˌadvanˈtageous, couˈrageous, misceˈllaneous, ˈrighteous
<-graphy>	ˌbibliˈography, ˌcinemaˈtography, disˈcography, phoˈtography
<-ial>	adˈverbial, coˈllegial, confiˈdential, meˈmorial
<-ian>	Augusˈtinian, Caˈnadian, cosmeˈtician, dictaˈtorian
<-ic>	alcoˈholic, Aristoˈtelic, cateˈgoric, magˈnetic

<-ical>	acaˈdemical, aposˈtolical, matheˈmatical, synˈtactical
<-inal>	ˈcriminal, meˈdicinal, oˈriginal, ˈvirginal
<-ion>	adminisˈtration, compliˈcation, conˈception, exˈtension
<-ious>	laˈborious, inˈfectious, luˈxurious, reˈligious
<-ital>	ˈcapital, ˈorbital, reˈcital, ˈvital
<-itous>	caˈlamitous, feˈlicitous, forˈtuitous, uˈbiquitous
<-itude>	ˈaltitude, fˈortitude, ineˈxactitude, ˈmultitude
<-itive>	deˈfinitive, ˈprimitive, reˈpetitive, ˈsensitive
<-ity>	aˈcidity ambiˈguity Chrisˈtianity seˈxuality
<-ive>	conˈtemplative, diˈgestive, imˈpressive, reˈflexive
<-ual>	biˈlingual, conˈtextual, eˈventual, spiˈritual
<-ular>	moˈlecular, parˈticular, quaˈdrangular, ˈcircular
<-uous>	conˈtinuous, imˈpetuous, inconsˈpicuous, temˈpestuous
<-wards>	ˈbackwards ˈforwards ˈhomewards ˈoutwards

b. Suffixes which attract the primary stress to **themselves**, that is, the original primary stress is shifted to the actual suffix.

AI 6.5 Stress carrying suffixes

<-ade>	cruˈsade, lemoˈnade, masqueˈrade, oranˈgeade
<-ain>	doˈmain, orˈdain, planˈtain, teˈrrain
<-atic>	diploˈmatic, dogˈmatic, idioˈmatic, systeˈmatic
<-ation>	accuˈsation, circuˈlation, derivˈation, falsifiˈcation
<-ee>	absenˈtee, briˈbee, interˈviewee, refuˈgee
<-eer>	auctioˈneer, domiˈneer, mountaiˈneer, puppeˈteer
<-ental>	fundaˈmental, governˈmental, instruˈmental, occiˈdental
<-ential>	eviˈdential, influˈential, resiˈdential, toˈrrential
<-esce>	efferˈvesce, fluoˈresce, lumiˈnesce, phosphoˈresce
<-ese>	Bologˈnese, Cantoˈnese, Chiˈnese, Japaˈnese
<-esque>	araˈbesque, burˈlesque, pictuˈresque, romaˈnesque
<-ette>	disˈquette, kitcheˈnette, luˈnette, vinegaˈrette
<-etic>	apoloˈgetic, geˈnetic, homiˈletic, paˈthetic
<-iety>	anˈxiety, proˈpriety, soˈciety, vaˈriety
<-ique>	anˈtique, criˈtique, mysˈtique, uˈnique
<-ition>	acquiˈsition, compoˈsition, eˈdition, prepoˈsition
<-oon>	baˈlloon, ponˈtoon, raˈtoon, saˈloon
<-self, -selves>	herˈself, itˈself, ourˈselves, themˈselves
<-ution>	absoˈlution, constiˈtution, dissoˈlution, soˈlution

(5) Compounds

Let us now focus on **compounding**. Knowing the general tendencies which operate in the stressing of compounds will make it much easier for the student to sound more native-like. A compound word is one which is made up of two (less frequently three) independent words, which may be written as one word or as two, with or without a hyphen, and which act together as one grammatical and semantic unit: *blackbird, week-end, paper clip*. The grammatical structure of the word, together with certain lexical aspects, will prove very useful in guessing whether the stress falls on the first or the second element. Compounds with the stress on the first element tend to be single-accented, like those presented in (5.1), whereas compounds with the stress on the second element tend to have a secondary stress on the first, which are listed under (5.2).

An important prosodic phenomenon that affects compounds and long words in English is **stress shift**. We have mentioned above that English is a stress-timed language, unlike Spanish, which is syllable-timed. Because of this, two stressed syllables in a row are avoided, increasing the distance between stresses whenever possible. This means that, as we shall see later when dealing with the nuclear stress of an utterance, compounds, and other long words, with a primary stress on the last syllable and an earlier secondary stress will shift the primary stress to the first syllable in the vicinity of another stress in the utterance. For example: consider the compound *New York* in:

(5) I am in New ˈYork and ˈNew York ˈCity is huge

(5.1) Compounds that have the primary stress on the first element:

a. Most of those made up of two single-syllable words, especially when written as one word: *ˈairport, ˈfootball, ˈblackboard, ˈcowboy.*
b. Those in which the second element indicates the performer of the action, of the pattern "noun+agent noun": *ˈtypewriter, ˈbaby-sitter, ˈpainkiller, ˈrecord-player.*
c. Those in which the first noun delimits the meaning of the second, indicating its purpose or "what type of thing", of the pattern "–ing verb/noun + noun": *ˈchewing ˌgum, ˈhearing ˌaid, ˈfiling ˌcabinet, ˈnail ˌpolish, ˈtimeˌtable, ˈnews ˌpaper, ˈtoothˌbrush.*
d. Those nouns with the pattern "adverb/preposition + noun": *ˈbypass, ˈinside, ˈafterthought, ˈovercoat.*
e. Those nouns with the pattern "adjective + noun" (*ˈblackboard, ˈgrandchild, ˈnobleman, ˈshorthand*) with some exceptions (*prime ˈminister, best-ˈseller, mobile ˈphone*).

f. Those nouns resulting of the combination "verb + noun": *ˈbreakfast, ˈcookbook, ˈhangman, ˈpushchair.*
g. Those nouns resulting from the combination "verb + particle" or "particle + verb" (*ˈhold-up, ˈincome, ˈmake-up, ˈoutset*) with some excepctions (*lie ˈdown*).

(5.2) Compounds that have the primary stress on the second element, with usually a secondary stress on the first element

The following types of nouns receive primary stress on the second element and secondary stress on the first. Note also that resulting compound adjectives and verbs also carry stress on the second element.

a. Those nouns which include in the first element the ingredient or material that the second element is made of. Food items constitute a very numerous group, with the exception of compounds of *–bread, -cake* and *-paste*: *apple ˈpie, gold ˈring, glass ˈjar, paper ˈbag* (cf. *ˈpaper clip*).
b. Those nouns which include some sort of location, positioning or time in the first element:
   (i) Location: a compound which has the name of a country, region or town as first element: *Irish ˈcoffee, Spanish ˈomelette, Yorkshire ˈpudding, French ˈkiss.*
   (ii) Compound place names generally: names of roads and areas within the town, including suburbs and districts and names of cities (*Church ˈRoad, St Peter's ˈSquare, Nelson's ˈAvenue, Botany ˈBay*), except those compounds ending in the actual word *street* (*St ˈPeter's Street*).
   Also included in this category are the names of geographical and architectonic features, such as names of parks and gardens, as well as bridges, tunnels, buildings and stations (*Abbey ˈWood, Castle ˈGreen, Bedford ˈPark, Tower ˈBridge, Clapham ˈJunction, Westminster ˈCathedral, Rose ˈCottage*), including parts of these buildings (*back ˈdoor, clock ˈtower, loo ˈwindow, front ˈgate, faculty ˈlibrary*). Note, however, that compounds with *room* have stress on the first element (*ˈbedroom*), with some exceptions (*front ˈroom*).
   (iii) Other compounds including location references with second-element stress are the names of publications, like newspapers and magazines, and associations, such as sports clubs or choirs (*ˌSunday ˈExpress, ˌKent ˈMessenger, ˌCroydon ˈAthletic, ˌInverness ˈSociety*).
   (iv) Positioning: *right ˈwing, upper ˈclass, high ˈchurch.*
   (v) Time: *ˌChristmas ˈDay, ˌJanuary ˈsales, ˌevening ˈpress, night ˈbus, Old ˈEnglish.*
c. Nouns and adjectives with a numeral as the first element: *first ˈclass, ˌsecond-ˈhand, third ˈworld, forty-ˈsix.*

d. Nouns with the structure "participial adjective + noun": *barbed ˈwire, split ˈsecond, ˌpromised ˈland, broken ˈpromise.*
e. Nouns of the pattern "-ing + noun" in which the *-ing* suggests a characteristic of the noun but does not indicate its function as above: *leading ˈarticle* is not an article for leading (cf. *ˈsewing ˌmachine*, or a machine that aids the activity of sewing), *ˌdrinking ˈwater.*
f. Adjectives with the pattern "adjective + -ed/-ing form", especially when used predicatively (*long-ˈlived, big-ˈheaded, bad-ˈtempered, good-ˈlooking, hard-ˈworking, easy-ˈgoing*).
g. Nouns of the pattern "noun in -er/-ing + adverb/preposition": *passer-ˈby, washing-ˈup.*
h. Noun + adjective combinations: *brand-ˈnew, snow-ˈwhite, world-ˈwide.*
i. Compounds which function as adverbs: *North-ˈEast.*
j. Compounds which function as verbs, with an adverb as first element: *down ˈgrade.*

(6) Difference between free phrases and compounds

We have seen so far that most compounds take primary stress on the first element, especially in the case of an adjective as first element. In this case we are dealing with a real compound, a word which functions as one both semantically and grammatically. But sometimes these compounds may be confused with free phrases. Consider, *greenhouse* and *green house*: the former is a particular type of building made of glass for growing and protecting plants, whereas the second sequence refers to a house which is painted green. The difference between both sequences is signalled by accent only: the compound has primary accent on the first element, the free sequence on the second element, with secondary stress on the first.

Phrases	**Compounds**
black ˈbird	ˈblackbird
dark ˈroom	ˈdarkroom
green ˈhouse	ˈgreenhouse

6.2.3 Prosodic stress

As we have seen, prosodic stress is the stress given only to certain words in an utterance. The general tendency for English is that **lexical** or **content words**, which carry a lot of information, such as nouns, adjectives, adverbs and verbs, keep their primary stress, whereas **grammatical** or **structural words**, which carry a light information load, (articles, personal, reflexive and relative pronouns, possessive adjectives, prepositions, conjunctions and auxiliary verbs) lose it. Consider the following example, in which subscript $_L$ and $_G$ stand for lexical and grammatical words, and where the general stress tendency is marked with ˈ:

AI 6.6 Prosodic stress

$_{G}$We $_{G}$shall $_{L}$disˈtinguish $_{L}$phoˈnetics $_{G}$from $_{L}$phoˈnology $_{G}$for $_{L}$methodoˈlogical $_{L}$ˈreasons $_{G}$and $_{G}$because $_{G}$it $_{L}$ˈseems $_{L}$ˈtrue $_{G}$that $_{L}$phoˈnetics $_{G}$can $_{G}$be $_{L}$ˈstudied $_{G}$without $_{L}$ˈever $_{L}$ˈreally $_{L}$ˈgoing $_{G}$into $_{L}$phoˈnology, $_{G}$while $_{L}$phoˈnology $_{G}$is $_{L}$ˈclosely $_{L}$deˈpendent $_{G}$on $_{L}$phoˈnetics $_{G}$for $_{G}$the $_{L}$ˈdata $_{G}$on $_{G}$which $_{G}$it $_{L}$reˈlies $_{G}$to $_{L}$purˈsue $_{G}$its $_{L}$ˈarguments.

However, exceptions to this overriding principle governing prosodic stress are observed in English, following rhythmical constraints, usage conventions and the intentions of the speaker. This means that certain lexical words may lose their stress whereas some structural words may be stressed, as we shall see (Finch and Ortiz Lira 1982: 115–116; Cruttenden 2001: 250; Collins and Mees 2003: 238–239).

6.2.3.1 Rhythmical variations

Beat adjusts the number of stresses in an utterance, which in turn modifies the speed delivery of the unstressed syllables. Two adjacent full stresses is not a common beat pattern in English. This is why

(1) In sequences of three content words, all of which could be stressed, the middle one tends to be unstressed, as long as it has no more than two syllables: *a ˈcheap old ˈblanket, a ˈcheap tatty ˈblanket, a ˈcheap ordiˈnary ˈblanket.*

For the same reason, phrasal verb sequences may vary their stress patterns according to neighbouring stresses:

a. Transitive phrasal verbs: *ˈtake off your ˈcoat, ˈtake your ˈcoat off, ˈtake it ˈoff.*

b. Intransitive phrasal verbs: *ˈsit ˈdown!, ˈdon't sit ˈdown!, You may ˈsit down ˈhere.*

(2) In double-stressed words, whether simple or compound, the stress which is nearest another one in the utterance is lost or weakened:

ˈcar-ˈpark: He went to the car-ˈpark, the ˈcar-park is full.

ˈHeathˈrow: at ˈHeathrow ˈairport, the ˈtrain to Heathˈrow

For the same reason, double-stressed adjectives, when used attributively, lose their primary stress and when used predicatively lose their secondary stress:

ˌhand-ˈmade: a ˈhand-made ˈquilt, the ˈquilt is hand-ˈmade

(3) In some single-stressed words, a shift of stress may take place when used before another stressed word, for example, attributively:

ˈalready: She's ˈalready ˈleft, she's ˈhome alˈready
prinˈcess: a ˈletter from the prinˈcess, a ˈletter from ˈPrincess ˈAnne

6.2.3.2 Usage

Certain parts of speech, actual words and phrases depart from the default stress pattern outlined above through ordinary usage. This is why:

(1) *wh*-interrogatives, demonstrative adjectives and pronouns, possessive pronouns and negative anomalous finites are usually stressed. Note that exclamatory *what*, though, is usually unstressed, as in *ˈWhy ˈcan't ˈthat ˈdog of ˈyours ˈeat ˈthis?*
(2) The verb *to be*, even when used as a full verb, is usually unstressed, except in final position, as in *She is ˈhere* (vs. *ˈHere she ˈis*) or *It was in the ˈhouse* (vs. *ˈThat's ˈwhere it ˈwas*).
(3) Comment phrases are usually unstressed, as in "*ˈCome on!*", *he said*, "*Let's ˈgo.*"
(4) Certain nouns when used in a very broad, general sense are usually unstressed (e.g. *I ˈdon't underˈstand ˈcertain things, I've ˈmet such a ˈlot of people*).
(5) The word street in street-names is usually unstressed, such as *ˈLeicester Street* (vs. *ˈLeicester ˈSquare*) or *ˈKensington Street* (vs. *ˈKensington ˈGardens*).

6.2.3.3 Emphatic and contrastive patterns

Added meaning, highlighting emphasis or contrast, is achieved by altering the default stress pattern of an utterance. This is why:

(1) Some grammatical words receive stress, as in *He ˈphoned me* (vs *ˈHe ˈphoned me* =it was him, not anybody else) or *He ˈlived in ˈLondon* (vs *He ˈlived ˈin ˈLondon*, not "near" London).
(2) Anaphoric elements, which have just been repeated literally or referred to by a direct equivalent, are usually left unstressed, as shown in the examples included in (6) below:

(6) a. A: You ˈdidn't ˈtell me.
B: No, I ˈknow I didn't.

b. They ˈvisited his ˈmother and ˈwhen they ˈleft his mother, they ˈcried.

c. A: Would you ˈlike some ˈcoffee?
B: No, ˈthanks, I ˈhate the stuff.

Note that when the repeated elements in the utterance are used to express contrast they are usually both left unstressed, with the stress falling on the contrasting words, as in *You didn't 'tell me and I didn't 'ask you*. And if the anaphoric element changes function, then they are both stressed, as in *They 'visited his 'mother and 'when 'his mother smiled, they 'cried*.

6.2.4 Nuclear stress

Although we have seen that various words can carry stress in an utterance – regardless of whether or not they would carry it when pronounced in isolation – only one of those words carries what is known as the **nuclear stress** in the utterance. It is an observable fact of English that in connected speech, and particularly in what are called broad focus sentences, in which the most important element is generally presupposed, **nuclear stress** falls on the stressed syllable of the last important word of the utterance. In other words, the final stressed syllable of an utterance carries the nuclear stress. We will mark this typographically by highlighting it in bold. This is known as the **nuclear stress rule**. Consider example (7) below, in which the nuclear stress does not fall on the last syllable, but the last stressed syllable:

(7) What would you like me to **put** it in?

A common mistake by Spanish speakers is to place the nuclear stress on the accented syllable of the **last** word, whether it is an important word or not, that is, even if it is a grammatical word. For example, Spanish speakers will often pronounce *I went with **her** or *I saw **him**, with a stressed *it* or *her*.

Once again, there are exceptions to this rule, so that the nuclear stress may be brought forward to an earlier position in the utterance, that is, it may be fronted. This fronting process is observable in:

(1) Event or presentation utterances, particularly with intransitive verbs, or with transitive verbs followed by fairly predictable objects, as represented in (8):

   (8) a. He noticed the baby **cried**. vs The **ba**by cried.

   b. He knew he drove the **car**. vs He **dro**ve the car.

(2) Utterances ending in an adverbial:

   (9) I hate **Mon**days. vs She came to **Man**chester on Monday.

(3) *wh*-utterances in which the *wh*-word functions as a modifier of a noun.

   (10) What did you **take**? vs **What** train did you take?

   Notice in this case that if the utterance is longer, then the nuclear stress falls in its default syllable:

   (11) What train did you take e**ven**tually?

Nuclear stress may also be displaced for reasons connected with narrow focus, with the intention of giving the utterance some special meaning. Thus, stress is displaced in the following contexts:

(1) Whenever the last important word is obvious in the context of utterance. For example, when reading a story to a child and while pointing to the picture of a piglet in the book, we would not say *This is a very naughty* ***pig****let*, but *This is a very* ***naugh****ty piglet.*

(2) For pragmatic reasons, distinguishing degrees of emphasis or contrast in sentences. Consider the utterances included in (12), which differ only in the placement of the nuclear stress:

(12) a. **I** didn't see him yesterday = 'perhaps you did'

b. I **didn't** see him yesterday = 'I certainly did not'

c. I didn't **see** him yesterday = 'perhaps I spoke to him or emailed him'

d. I didn't see **him** yesterday = 'perhaps it was someone else I saw'

e. I didn't see him **yesterday** = 'perhaps it was the day before'

(3) Cases involving anaphoric reference, as seen before in the context of the distressing process of some words, are also affected by fronting of the nuclear stress, as in *I would go with John but I don't really* ***like*** *John.*

Now, anaphora may be presented in a very subtle way, and only the stress pattern will throw light on the possible pragmatic interpretations of such an utterance. Consider the example *Jane said she'd been delighted long enough and Margaret offended her.* The nuclear stress rule tells us that nuclear stress falls on the last stressed syllable, which seems to be the word *offended*. However, we also know that anaphoric references tend not to be stressed; so, if Jane's comment that she's d been delighted long enough is considered to be offensive in the context, then the word *offended* is an anaphoric reference, in which case it would not be stressed, which means it obviously does not carry the nuclear stress of the utterance, but this is displaced to an earlier position, namely, to the stressed syllable of the word *Margaret*, as shown in (13a) below. Now, if Jane's comment is innocent and fair, then *offended* is introducing a completely new idea and is therefore eligible for stress, and because of its position in the utterance it would carry the nuclear stress, as it does in (13b).

(13) a. Jane said she'd been delighted long enough and **Mar**garet offended her. (Jane's comment is offensive)

b. Jane said she'd been delighted long enough and Margaret o**ffen**ded her. (Jane's comment is fair)

6.3 Intonation

We are all familiar with the fact that languages are not spoken in a monotone; in fact, one can easily recognise an automated, or robot-like voice, as in an onboard navigation satellite system or your mobile assistant, and in fact we tend to find it particularly annoying when someone speaks in a "monotonous" voice, an adjective which has acquired pejorative implications. What makes the difference between human and this automated kind of language is a question of **pitch**, which is what gives human language its melody. Pitch refers to the speed of vibration, more strictly speaking, the **frequency of vibration**, that is, the number of vocal cord movements per second (see § 1.2.2).

We can distinguish, for example, four basic levels of pitch, 1 to 4 or Low, Mid, High and Extra High, respectively. When we speak, our voice travels on a line of declination, or downward scale, in which we introduce changes from one step to another, that is, **rises** and **falls** in the line of declination. This change of pitch level is basically what intonation is; however, to define intonation solely on the basis of this vocal fold activity would not render a complete picture, since together with pitch variation, other features such as loudness, rhythmicality and tempo make up the melody, or intonation, of human languages. Intonation is also a question of perception, as speakers are not always aware of producing it. Have you not experienced someone guessing where you come from on the basis of your accent, even if you are not aware of having one? However, having said that, some people are very good at producing voice impressions, taking into account various features, including idiosyncratic intonation (Tench 1996: 1–16; Collins and Mees 2003: 245; Roach 2005: 167–168; Wells 2006: 1–12; Cruttenden 2014: 299).

Pitch variation has two distinctive functions. In the first place, pitch can help distinguish between different words which share the same phonemes; that is, **tone**, as it is known, is meaningful in that it distinguishes between the lexical, or "dictionary" meaning, and the grammatical, or inflectional meaning of words. This is the case of **tone languages**, in which each **toneme** is a lexically distinct variant of a given syllable so that they are phonetically distinguished from each other only by the tone of the vowel. Tonal languages are very common in Africa, the Far East and Central America, which means that as many as 70% of the world's languages are tonal. This is, however, rarely the case in Europe and elsewhere in the Asiatic continent. Tonal languages may operate either on a **register** basis, that is, tones are distinguished by their pitch level relative to each other, which usually falls on monosyllables, or in the case of polysyllables on the whole word, as is the case of many African languages, or else on a **contour** basis, as is the case of the most widely-spoken tone language, Mandarin Chinese, in which each tone is made up of internal rising and falling movements of pitch, so in the case of polysyllables, each syllable carries a different tone (Tench 1996: 3; Collins and Mees 2003: 246; Roach 167–169; Wells 2006: 4; Crystal 2008: 369–370).

This brings us to the second function of pitch variation. If we think of English, we can easily observe how the word *No*, for example, may be produced with different intonation patterns under different circumstances, but its dictionary meaning of "negative reply", for example, always stays the same. In most languages in Europe, this pitch movement, or intonation, plays a very important role since it can affect the way in which an utterance is understood in terms of speaker's attitude, grammatical structure, organisation of the information, and intended illocutionary force, as we will see.

Three related systems make up English intonation. These are: **tonality**, **tonicity** and **tone.** The first step in assigning prosody to a series of phonemes is to decide on the tonality: this has to do with chunking, or the splitting up of the spoken chain into manageable, meaningful units, or intonation groups. Once this is done, tonicity has to do with the stressing of the relevant syllable in each intonation group, that is, the nucleus of the group is located. Finally, tone has to do with pitch variations in the nucleus. These aspects of intonation all contribute together or in isolation to the correct delivery of any given utterance.

Out of the several **intonation marking** methods possible, we propose one which is user-friendly while showing as much information as possible about the intonation patterns under analysis. By user-friendly, we mean that it is an in-text system with a reduced number of simple symbols which should make it easy to read from a script in spelling (which would therefore have no punctuation marks, which are the nearest orthographic equivalent of intonation), and to transcribe, both manually and in type, as follows:[105]

Table 44: Proposed intonation marking system

Markup	Symbol	Further distinctions	Symbol
tone boundary	|	end of utterance	||
Fall	\	high fall low fall	ˋ ˎ
Rise	/	high rise low rise	ˊ ˏ
fall-rise	\/	rise-fall	/\
primary accent	ˈ	secondary accent	ˌ
nucleus	**bold type**		
onset	°		

105 Please note that no orthographic punctuation is used in the examples throughout this section.

6.3.1 Intonation groups and Tonality

In English, only a small number of particularly prominent syllables carry the tone in an utterance, which means that a unit larger than the syllable is needed in order to describe intonation patterns. So, we speak of **intonation groups**, or **intonation** or **tone units**, which are defined as the basic unit of speech melody, making up one complete pattern of intonation, usually lasting between one or two seconds. This chunking or breaking up of the spoken chain into separate intonation groups, which may or may not coincide with syntactical units, is known as **tonality** (Tench 1996: 31–49; Wells 2006: 187–205). Intonation groups are separated by **tone boundaries**, which are represented graphically by either a single bar (if there is a close connection between them) or a double bar (if not). Tone boundaries are not always easy to identify and it would, indeed, be simplistic to measure the length of an intonation group in terms of syllables. For practical purposes, let us say that, at the end of every clause there is an intonation boundary, and that, basically, a grammatical clause often represents one intonation group within the sentence: || Part of the sea wall in Lytham co**llapsed** | and the railway line was badly **da**maged ||. This means that phonology, grammar and semantics are brought together by means of what is known as **neutral tonality**.

Between coordinate clauses we usually place a boundary mark, as shown in (14), but usually not when there is an elided element, whether it be the subject or an object, which is the same for both clauses, as shown in (15):

(14) || They played two more pieces | and the audience was delighted ||

(15) a. || They played two more pieces and received a standing ovation ||
b. || They played and sang two more pieces ||

Note that (15b) is potentially ambiguous. If an intonation boundary is placed after the first verb, as in (16), it is suggested that they played first (only instrumental) and then they sang two more pieces:

(16) || They played | and sang two more pieces ||

However, other smaller grammatical units may represent an intonation group, as we often place intonation boundaries between phrases within a clause as well. We can talk of **marked tonality** when intonation units do not coincide, for several reasons, with whole clauses, as in the following cases

(1) When the boundary between intonation units is placed between a long noun phrase and a verb phrase, as exemplified in (17):

(17) || Wet and windy weather in the **a**rea | will continue until the end of **Fe**bruary ||

(2) When an intonational boundary is located within smaller phrases, such as (sentence) adverbs or adverbial phrases, either initially or in the middle of a clause, as shown in (18):

(18) a. || Un**for**tunately | waves crashed over the harbour in **Black**pool ||

b. || After all this heavy **rain** | a major salvage operation was **laun**ched ||

(3) When vocatives are used, particularly in initial position; if they occur in any other positions, they constitute the tail to what precedes them, as in (19):

(19) a. || **Kim** | have you seen the news to**day** ||

b. || **Anne** | as you **know** | is on **sick leave** ||

c. || Have you seen the **news** Kim ||

(4) Pseudo-cleft sentences involving *what*:

(20) || What I **saw** | was his big friendly **smile** ||

(5) Parenthetic material in general, such as non-defining relative clauses:

(21) || I met my **bro**ther | who arrived by **train** ||

(6) Also, question tags of the "checking" type, which are added to a clause in order to confirm the validity of the proposition expressed in the main clause, have their own separate intonation group, as in (22):

(22) a. || They are not coming after **all** | **are** they ||

b. || She left all her luggage be**hind** | **didn't** she ||

(7) Question tags of the "copying" type, that is, showing an understanding of the value of the proposition, tend to be incorporated into the same intonation unit as the main clause, as it occurs in (23):

(23) || The police found out who gave the false a**larm** did they ||

(8) Occasionally, and usually for reasons of emphasis or for some special effect, a tone boundary may be inserted between successive words in the same grammatical unit or even within one word:

(24) a. || **I** | am not **going** ||

b. || **To** | **mo** | **rrow** ||

Tonality does vary according to whether the speech is being read aloud, and is therefore more carefully planned, or if it is spoken spontaneously. In the first case, intonation groups are usually longer and may therefore contain more stressed syllables than just the nuclear tone; whereas in unprepared speech the groups are shorter and usually have just one accent. Style and tonality are also closely related, since a formal pompous style will pause more often, and have more stressed syllables overall, than ordinary speech, as shown in (25a) and (25b) below:

(25) a. || Where have you **been** ||
b. || /**Where** | /**have** | /**you** | /**been** ||

6.3.2 Structure of intonation groups and tonicity

Every intonation group consists of a series of stressed and unstressed syllables. Typically, one of the stressed syllables carries the change in pitch on the declination scale we introduced earlier on, which makes it more prominent, in terms of longer duration and extra loudness. Consider (26) below, with these stressed syllables shown in bold type, others with just the usual stress mark:

(26) || Des'pite the '**war**nings | some 'residents were not '**lea**ving ||

The words *warnings* and *leaving* are the most prominent or salient words in each intonation group in this utterance, given the change in pitch on the syllables /wɔː/ and /liː/, with extra duration and loudness, however subtle this may be to the ear. This maximal prominence is what is referred to as **tonicity**, and the corresponding intonation pattern is called the **nuclear tone**. The most prominent syllable in an intonation group is the **nucleus. Neutral tonicity** tends to indicate a broad focus, i.e. all the information in the clause is new, and in this case the nucleus falls on the stressed syllable of the last lexical item in the group, i.e. at or near the end of the intonation group, and the function is to initiate pitch movement. This type of tonicity is also used when the focus is narrow but the new information is included at the end of the clause, which is its usual position anyway. **Marked tonicity**, on the other hand, happens when the nucleus falls on a lexical item which is not final, or on a grammatical item, and therefore signals this as new information, thus narrowing the focus.

We find marked tonicity when expressing a contrast, both between lexical items or grammatical items, or even between morphemes, as in (27) to (30):

(27) a. I would love a holiday by the **sea.**
b. And I would **hate** a holiday by the sea.

(28) Forget what **they** want and think of what **we** want.

(29) He doesn't live **in** Madrid but **near** Madrid.

(30) The price of houses is not **in**creasing, but **de**creasing.

Marked tonicity is also employed in spoken discourse to avoid placing the nucleus of two subsequent intonation groups on the same actual lexical element, as when giving your phone number, for example: 5 38**6** 7**4**6. Note that if the last digit of the second group was not 6, then the group would carry neutral tonicity, as in 38**6** 7**49**.

Another context for marked tonicity to occur is in the presence of a final intransitive verb of movement or happening, which generally is rather empty of full lexical meaning, as contrasted in (31a) and (31b) below:

(31) a. **He**len's going.

b. Helen's **pho**ning.

Nuclear tones show variation, as illustrated by the syllables /wɔː/ and /liː/ above, which do not seem to have the same pattern, as we shall see. Any syllables after the nucleus are known as the **tail**, and by definition are usually unstressed and continue the pitch movement that was initiated at that point. There may also be other syllables before the nuclear tone, which can be unstressed or weakly stressed. The first stressed syllable before the nucleus is known as the **onset**, and is graphically signalled by placing the symbol ° before it. The stretch between both syllables is the **head** of the intonation group. Any unstressed syllables preceding either the onset, or the nucleus in the absence of an onset, constitute the **pre-head**, i.e. an intonation group may have a pre-head and no head, if there are no stressed syllables at all before the nucleus (Finch and Ortiz Lira 1982: 119–122; Tench 1996: 53–73; Cruttenden 2001: 256–257; Collins and Mees 2003: 248–252; Wells 2006: 93–184; Roach 2009: 130–133).

The general pattern of an intonation group, then, can be summarised as follows, with optional elements given in brackets: (pre-head) (onset) (head) nucleus (tail). So, going back to example (26) above, the analysis of its internal structure, represented in (32) below, gives us a more complete picture of each intonation group:

(32) Des°pite the /**war**nings | some °residents were not **lea**ving||[106]

	Des°pite the /**war**nings	some °residents were not **lea**ving
Pre-head	des	some
Onset	pite	re
Head	the	sidents were not
Nucleus	war	lea
Tail	nings	ving

106 If instead of 'some residents were not leaving' in the second intonation group, the sequence was 'they were not leaving', the stretch 'they were not' would be a pre-head and there would not be an onset, or stressed syllable before the nucleus, nor a head, i.e. no stressed syllables would precede the nucleus.

6.3.3 Intonation patterns and tone

The pitch movement initiated by the nucleus, i.e. the tone, or colloquially the tune, of intonation, is what is most often perceived by the ear, and what gives spoken utterances their melodic flavour. The pitch of the voice on the tonic syllable may move downwards or upwards, producing simple primary falling or rising patterns, or a combination of both in complex fall-rises, and the less common rise-falls. Let us have a look at these in turn, paying special attention to the intonation typically associated with statements, commands and questions, as well as the most usual intonation group combinations (Finch and Ortiz Lira 1982: 125–128; Tench 1996: 73–106; Collins and Mees 2003: 259–273; Wells 2006: 15–93; Roach 2005: 162–167; Cruttenden 2014: 278–280).

6.3.3.1 Simple tones: falls and rises

These are prototypically associated with statements and commands in the first case, and questions in the other; however, the inherent connotations of these two tones may be used to modulate them, as we shall see.

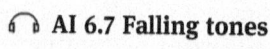

AI 6.7 Falling tones

(1) Falls

The most usual intonation pattern in RP English, a falling movement, always changes the melody to a low pitch, either from a high position, in which case we talk of a **high fall**, or else from mid pitch downwards, producing a **low fall.** The tail is low. A fall is considered a neutral tone, denoting a sense of conclusiveness, i.e. as if there is nothing else to follow. In the example below, if the utterance \No, with a falling intonation, is an answer to a previous question, it means that this negative reply is a final decision. The symbol used for a high fall is placed higher up just before the word which carries the nuclear tone, whereas the sign for a low fall is placed at the foot of the nucleus.

Table 45: High tones

Markup	High Fall	Low Fall
Nucleus only	ˋ**No**	ˎ**No**
Nucleus last	I said ˋ**No**	I said ˎ**No**
Nucleus + Tail	ˋ**No** more	ˎ**No** more

A falling tone is the commonest for **statements**, **wh-questions** and **commands**. Broadly speaking, a high fall makes them sound more lively and positive, with energetic connotations of interest and animation, whereas a low fall projects deliberation and distance, even coolness, as shown in (33):

(33) a. \ Philip is coming tomorrow
b. \ When is Philip coming
c. \ Give me that chair

Note that a yes/no question, which is usually pronounced with rising intonation, acquires the pragmatic force of a command when pronounced on a fall. This command will be more or less friendly depending on whether it is on a high fall or a low fall, as illustrated in (34):

(34) a. / Will you ˊ come here (question)
b. \ Will you ˋ come here (command; friendly)
c. \ Will you ˎ come here (command; distant)

(2) Rises
Rising patterns, a lot less frequent in RP English than falls, always work upwards to a mid or high pitch, either from a low position, known as **low rise**, which is more common, or from a mid pitch, or **high rise**. A rise is generally understood as a prompt for conversation to continue or to mean that there is something else to follow. In the example below, /No, with a rising intonation, can be used as a negative answer to a question and at the same time inviting more information on the part of the first speaker. The symbol used for a high rise is placed higher up just before the word which carries the nuclear tone, whereas the sign for a low fall is placed at the foot of the nucleus.

Table 46: Rise tones

Markup	Low Rise	High Rise
Nucleus	ˏ**No**	ˊ**No**
Nucleus last	I said ˏ**No**	I said ˊ**No**
Nucleus + Tail	ˏ**No** more	ˊ**No** more

A low rising intonation is the commonest for **yes/no questions**, whereas a high rise signals surprise or doubt, and is also common in **echo questions**, i.e. repeating what has just been asked, as illustrated in (35):

(35) a. Do you like / ˏ chocolate.
b. Do you like / ˊ chocolate.
c. (Do you like chocolate) / Do I like ˊ chocolate (thinking Hmmm. . .of course, I do!)

Although normally pronounced on a falling pattern, as we have just seen, both wh-questions and commands when pronounced on a rising pattern convey a warm and gentle tone, which in the case of commands adds a sense of non-finality. Compare the sequences in (36):

(36) a. Now | go / ˋ upstairs (high fall, as above)
b. Now | go / ˎ upstairs (low fall, as above)
c. Now | go / ˏ upstairs (low rise)

Initial clauses, lists of items and parenthetical information are usually pronounced with a rising tone, given their non-final condition, as shown in (37):

(37) a. After all the effort they / put into it the whole project was \ abandoned.
b. Pack your / tent / pegs a / mallet a / torch a / sleeping bag and your \ boots.
c. He's so / attractive if you see what I / mean that I can't \ help it

6.3.3.2 Complex tones: fall-rises and rise-falls

Complex tones are not typically associated with particular grammatical or pragmatic categories; rather, their inherent connotations may be superimposed on any of them, as we can see below.

(1) Fall-rise

A fall-rise pattern shows movement from a high position down to low and up to mid pitch, with the fall on the nuclear syllable and the rest of the movement spreading over the tail, if there is one. It conveys a sense of hesitation or reservation, also implying doubt or partial agreement (as in e.g. I wouldn't call it \/ perfect).

This tone may be used to highlight two elements in an utterance, which is particularly useful both in *wh-* and *yes/no* questions, as the auxiliary verb would not normally be stressed, as shown in (38):

(38) a. When \/ did he come?
b. \/ Is he going?

(2) Rise-fall

This unusual pattern moves up from mid to high pitch and down to low. If there is a tail, the movement can be completed in two different moves: either the rise falls on the accented syllable and the tail is produced at low pitch; or else, the accented syllable is produced at mid pitch which is then followed by a falling tail. The connotations of this pattern are those of the expression of strong feelings, such as surprise, doubt and (dis-)approval, adding a patronising effect, as in (39):

(39) Oh I don't know /\ whatever.

For the sake of comparison, in the example below, \/ *No*, with a fall-rise pattern, is a negative answer which is expressing doubt or partial agreement, whereas /\ *No*, with a rise-fall pattern, may express strong surprise, for example, when listening to some unbelievable news.

Table 47: Complex tones: Fall-rises and rise-falls

Markup	Fall-rise	Rise-fall
Nucleus	\/ **No**	/\ **No**
Nucleus last	I said \/ **No**	I said /\ **No**
Nucleus + Tail	\/ **No** more	/\ **No** more

6.3.4 Functions of intonation

So far we have seen what intonation is and how melody is made up of three interrelated systems – tonality, tonicity and tone-, which give it structure. Now we must turn to how intonation is used and what functions it plays. We are all familiar with the monotonous speech of answering machines, so it is obvious enough that intonation *does* something to the spoken chain when delivering a message. Most speakers seem to think that the only role of intonation is to express attitude, but this is not its only function. Four main functions of intonation can be highlighted, namely (a) **attitudinal**, (b) **accentual** or **focusing**, (c) **grammatical**, and (d) **discourse** and **pragmatic**. The attitudinal function has to do with the expression of speaker's emotion and this is done by means of tone, and more specifically, by deviations from the default or neutral tones, which are normally associated with particular illocutionary forces. The accentual or focusing function is connected with the narrowing of focus on new information, but is also related to issues of emphasis and contrast. This is done by means of tonicity, in particular by shifting tonic stresses away from the default positions. The grammatical function of intonation means that it helps disambiguate potentially ambiguous utterances, both at clausal and phrasal levels, by using tonality to alter intonation group boundaries as appropriate. Finally, intonation has an important role in the organisation of information in discourse, on the one hand, and in the encoding of the communicative functions of utterances on the other, for which all three intonational systems are at work (Tench 1996: 16–29; Collins and Mees 2003: 256–258; Wells 2006: 11–12; Roach 2005: 183–203; Cruttenden 2014: 284–298).

Although intonational systems also operate in Spanish, and in some cases with some similarities, we cannot emphasise enough how important it is that intonation is properly taught to foreign students, since the "wrong" overall melody is more often a serious cause of linguistic misunderstanding, and even social misfortune, than the incorrect articulation of phonemes.

6.3.4.1 Attitudinal function

Most speakers associate intonation with the expression of feelings and emotions, which are added to the semantic content of what is being said, to such an extent that attitude is a key factor in conversation – we have often heard "it's not what you say, but the way you say it". Intonation is a means of revealing attitude in speech, whether it be towards the listener, the actual message or the situational context, and it certainly gives away something about the speaker. However, it must be borne in mind that the expression of emotion in speech may be actually impossible, as in chorus community prayer, for example, or out of place, as in weather forecasting or, to a certain extent, in newsreading. Attitude is often expressed in colloquial, spontaneous conversation, but even in this context it is an optional component.

Speakers have a variety of intonational resources which can be used to express emotion. **Sequential** elements, such as those aspects which are connected with tonicity and tonality, like shifting the nuclear stress, chunking the spoken chain into relevant units or measuring pauses, all contribute for a special effect. **Prosodic elements** include variations in loudness and speed, different voice qualities, and particularly pitch range, that is, changes in the width of the tones used. As we saw in Section 6.3.3. above, tones have neutral forms, which are mainly used to perform the grammatical, discursive and pragmatic functions of intonation, which we shall analyse below in more detail. It is mainly the complex tones and variations in the width of the pitch range of simple tones that are used to encode intonational attitude.

(1) A fall-rise is associated with the expression of uncertainty, hesitation, and surprise. It may reveal the speaker as distant and detached or as if appealing to the listener's reconsideration, with strict and stern undertones, showing reservation.

(2) A rise-fall indicates the speaker is impressed, but also proud and conceited, as if mocking the listener, with a ring of dismissal. It is used for the expression of sarcasm and indignation. Compare the examples in (40):

(40) a. ˅ what (fall-rise: reservation, surprise)
b. ^ what (rise-fall: arrogance, patronizing)

(3) A high fall and a low rise are considered neutral tones, whereas a low fall and a high rise have an attitudinal function. A low fall is associated with boredom and resignation, disclosing a phlegmatic speaker, who is dispassionate, dull and detached; whereas a high rise suggests excitement, curiosity and eagerness, showing a speaker who seems to be concerned, enthusiastic or interested. Consider the examples in (41):

(41) a. ˎ what (low fall: boredom) *vs* ˋ what (high fall: unmarked, neutral)
b. ˊ what (high rise: interest) *vs* ˏ what (low rise: unmarked, neutral)

AI 6.8 Attitudinal function of intonation

Finally, **paralinguistic features**, otherwise known as **body language**, are often revealing of speaker's attitude. Facial expressions, like raising an eyebrow, and other body movements, such as shrugging a shoulder, play an attitudinal function and are an expression of emotion and the speaker's inner state of mind, which may be accompanied by tears, laughter, coughing, and so on. Kinesics has proved most insightful in detecting lies in court, incriminating suspects, for example, in situations in which other forms of linguistic analysis fail to be useful.

The attitudinal function of intonation is so highly valued by speakers that efforts are made to express this function in writing. Whereas tonality may be shown by the use of commas or question marks, and tonicity may rely on the use of bold and italic fonts, the orthographic expression of attitude is not an easy task. This may explain the recent development of a "dictionary" of **emoticons**[107], a graphic representation of attitude in everyday conversations in texting and chatting contexts.[108] Prosodic elements and, specially, facial expressions and vocal effects are reflected in these little faces, a metacommunicative

---

107 Emoticons have gone as far as not only encoding prosody, but almost becoming a new language altogether, to the extent that complete messages can be given by using only these icons – the advantage being the mutual intelligibility among speakers of different languages – at the expense of misunderstandings if icons are not interpreted correctly.

108 Before emoticons existed, efforts were made to convey attitude by means of 'icons' constructed on the basis of the combination of certain graphic characters available in an ordinary keyboard, such as :), which suggests a smile and possibly an associated rising tone.

device which speakers eagerly use in order to make their attitudinal connotations clearer, and thus avoid the risk of misunderstandings, particularly in a medium which makes use of much abbreviated written language and hardly any punctuation, with messages overlapping in time and many times without a very clear context. Consider the following Whatsapp conversations:

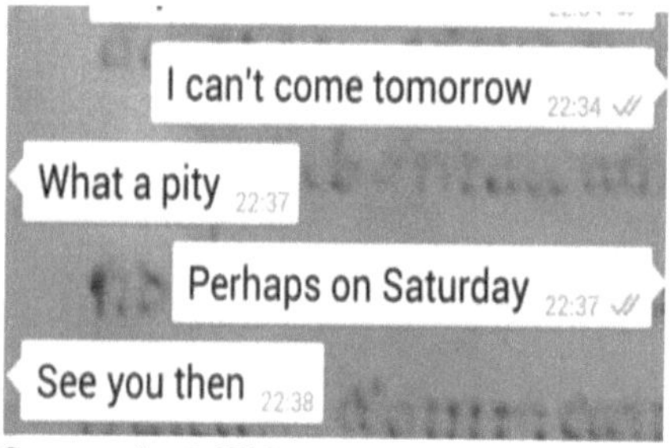

Conversation 1. With no emoticons

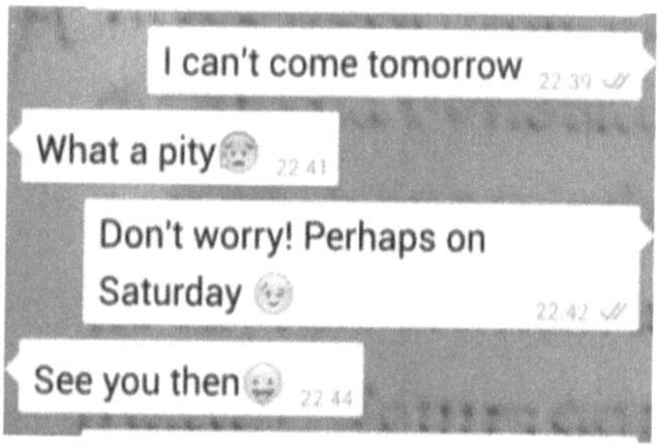

Conversation 2. With emoticons.

Figure 50: Whatsapp Emoticons as a graphic representation of attitude

Conversation 1 is a mere transaction of information about the impossibility of going the next day. The only expression nearing emotion is encoded in the semantics of the Speaker B's answer, 'what a pity', which could have been said with sarcasm, annoyance or impatience, but Speaker A does not know. His only reply is a factual postponement until Saturday, which could have been said on an inconclusive low rise, to which B closes with an emotionless farewell greeting. Conversation 2, instead, illustrates Speaker B showing emotion: the choice of an icon with the mouth curving downwards and a tear, denotes a high fall, expressing concern and worry. This clue is retrieved by Speaker A, who is then prompted to respond with a reassuring "Don't worry!" before the inevitable postponement until Saturday, which is however suggested with a friendly and knowing icon, complete with a smile and a wink, suggesting probably a lively and definite high fall tone, which is the cue for the animated final goodbye.

6.3.4.2 Accentual function

We saw in section 6.2.3. that nuclear stress may be displaced within a given utterance for various reasons. This prominent syllable we called the nucleus of the intonation group. This shifting of the nucleus will result in the highlighting of the information the speaker wishes to focus on. This is referred to as the accentual or focusing function of intonation and is related to tonicity. The nucleus of the intonation group may be used to signal a narrow focus on a piece of new information when everything else is given, or treated as given or implied – i.e. recoverable from the linguistic context, the conversational situation, common ground between speakers or general knowledge. In this case, marked tonicity functions to mark narrow focus on items which are not final lexical items (also see § 6.3.2. above).

Consider, for example, the sequences in (42), where you can see how the focus of information changes as we shift the nucleus:

(42) a. I only bought one carton of **milk**.
b. I only bought one **car**ton of milk.
c. I only bought **one** carton of milk.
d. I only **bought** one carton of milk.
e. I **on**ly bought one carton of milk.
f. **I** only bought one carton of milk.

Other contexts of use in which intonation plays an accentual function are, as we have already seen, when contrast or emphasis is needed or the lexical content of the utterance requires it. Ambiguity can also be resolved by tonic shifting, as occurs in (43):

(43) a. || He had ˈreasons to \ **give** || (= he wanted to give, with an implied direct object, which is implied, for example, money)
b. || He had \ ˈ**rea**sons to give || (= he had some reasons that he wanted to give; *reasons* is the direct object of *give* in this case).

In this case, as we shall see in the following subsections, tonicity often combines with tonality, if a new intonation group is created, and tones, which are added to the new groups, and these processes may result in the production of different syntactic structures, attitudes and even speech acts.

AI 6.9 Accentual function of intonation

6.3.4.3 Grammatical function

This is mostly related to tonality: two structures which are parallel on the surface can be disambiguated by producing them with different intonation boundaries, which will have an effect on the syntactic function of some elements and the meaning of the overall utterance – a fact which is not always reflected orthographically. If a new intonation group is created, shifting of tonic stresses and the addition of new tones may have to be considered. Therefore, the three systems of intonation -tonicity, tonality and tone- often combine and have a role in this grammatical function of intonation. We will illustrate this by means of a selection of some of the most common cases. Please note that some of the examples could be dealt with under more than one heading. The following arrangement is for ease of reference.

AI 6.10 Grammatical function of intonation

(1) Vocatives

Vocatives at the beginning of an utterance tend to have their own intonation group, are stressed and are said on a rising tone. Final vocatives, on the other hand, are usually said as the tail of the previous group. Consider the sequence, *Mary my neighbour is coming tomorrow*, which has two possible interpretations, illustrated in (44):

(44) a. || Mary | my neighbour is coming tomorrow ||
b. || Mary my neighbour | is coming tomorrow ||
c. || Mary | my neighbour | is coming tomorrow ||

(44a) illustrates a case of an initial vocative: the speaker is addressing Mary to let her know that her neighbour, whose name we do not know, is coming the next day; in (44b) the speaker is saying – it is not known who he is talking to- that a neighbour of his called Mary – and not any other Mary he may know- is coming. That is, (44b) is a case of a defining use of the appositional element. In (44c), in turn, by placing an extra boundary after *Mary*, the appositional element becomes non-defining.

Consider now (45), where the possible vocative comes at the end of the clause:

(45) a. || **Help** | John || vocative
b. || Help **John** || direct object

Because final vocatives tend to be tails of the previous group, ambiguity rises as this element could be taken to be the direct object of the verb, as in (b). By placing an intonational boundary between both elements, *help* is shown to be a noun addressed to someone called John, whereas it is not known who the command to help John in (b) is addressed to.

(2) Appositions

Tonality is the key factor, as we have just seen, in disambiguating appositions from other structural units, as in, for instance, the sequence *They called John a doctor*, offering two possible appositive structures presented in (46):

(46) a. || They called John | a doctor ||
b. || They called John a doctor ||

In (46a), the verb is a mono-transitive one, with *John* as the direct object and *a doctor* as an apposition to this, so that the meaning of the utterance is that 'they called John, and John is a doctor'. In (46b), we have a case of a ditransitive verb, with *John* as the indirect object and 'a doctor' as the direct one, the meaning being ‘they called a doctor for John’. There is a third meaning which cannot be distinguished intonationally: ‘They ascribed a doctorate to John’.

(3) Relative clauses

Tonality signals the defining or non-defining nature of relative clauses. For instance, a sentence like *My friends who live in Lancaster arrived yesterday*, could broadly show two different intonational patterns, illustrated in (47), which denote different syntactic structures:

(47) a. || My /**friends** | who °live in /**Lan**caster | a°rrived \ **yes**terday ||

b. || My °friends who live in /**Lan**caster | a°rrived \ **yes**terday ||

The interpretation of (47a) is that of a non-defining relative clause, meaning that my friends arrived yesterday, and they all happen to live in Lancaster, implying by means of the appositional clause that all the friends I have are those who live in Lancaster. The interpretation offered in (47b) is that of a defining relative clause, functioning as a post-modifier of the head noun *friends*, denoting that it is only those friends of mine who live in Lancaster that arrived yesterday, but implying that I may have other friends elsewhere, and who have nothing to do with “arriving yesterday”.

(4) Transitive *versus* intransitive verb complementation

In the utterance, || They’re leaving Susan ||, the main verb, *leaving*, can be interpreted as transitive or intransitive:

(48) a. || They’re leaving Susan ||

b. || They’re leaving | Susan ||

If the utterance is said as one single intonation group, as in (48a), then the verb is transitive and *Susan* is its direct object. However, as mentioned above, if *Susan* is a final vocative, in which case it is normally the tail of the group, then an extra intonational boundary has to be added for disambiguation purposes, as in (48b).

Now consider an apparently similar example:

(49) a. || They’re leaving all of them ||

b. || They’re leaving | all of them ||

Although (48) looks very similar to (49), syntactically, the function of the element *all of them* cannot be that of vocative, but it is a case of a postposed subject, as a kind of explanation. This means that it would be actually possible to find a context in which an utterance, given a particular selection of lexical items, posed a three-way distinction. Consider the following sequences:

(50) a. They’re leaving my friends.

b. She’s leaving Susan.

Tonality can help disambiguate between the direct object function of the final noun phrases and the other two functions, but it is not enough to differentiate between the vocative and the postposed subject functions, with an intonational boundary before them in both cases. Tonicity does not help either, as both groups are very small and therefore carry the tonic stress on the same syllable regardless of the function. It is tone, in this case, which plays the crucial role. A falling tone in the first intonation group, denoting the finality of the statement, will suggest the vocative meaning, whereas a rising tone, denoting more information to come, will suggest the postposed subject meaning. Compare the sequences in (51):

(51) a. || They're \ leaving | \ my friends || *versus* They're / leaving | \ my friends ||

b. || She's \ leaving | \ Susan || *versus* She's / leaving | \ Susan ||

(5) Phrasal verbs versus verb + prepositional phrase

Phrasal verb constructions can create ambiguity, even if the particle is prepositional in both cases, as we can see in the following example:

(52) a. || He looked | after my sister ||

b. || He looked after my sister ||

Although in both cases the sequence *after my sister* is a prepositional phrase, (52a) shows an intransitive use of the verb *look* with the PP as a time adverbial, which is shown by an intonation boundary between them, whereas in (52b) *look* is a prepositional verb with the PP as a verb complement.

(6) Reflexive versus emphatic pronouns

This is another case showing how tonality alone is not enough to disambiguate between two potentially ambiguous structures. The grammatical distinction between the structures (a) transitive verb + direct object (reflexive), as in *I* ***hurt*** *myself*, and (b) (intransitive) verb + subject complement (emphatic), *I'll send the letter* ***myself***, rely on tonicity, as the pronoun belongs in the same intonation group as the verb regardless of the function. In the transitive version it is the verb that carries the tonic syllable, but in the subject complement one, the reflexive pronoun, which could be given its own intonation group for further emphasis. Compare (53a), transitive, and (53bi) and (53bii), subject complement, the latter version, with a greater pause and two intonation groups, also adding the connotation of an afterthought.

(53) a. || I have never **taught** myself ||

bi. || I have never taught my**self** ||

bii. || I have never **taught** | my**self**.

(7) Double-verb constructions

Some "verb + to-infinitive" constructions are potentially ambiguous, and placing a pause and creating and extra intonation group aids understanding. Consider the following example:

(54) a. || She stopped to eat peanuts ||

b. || She stopped | to eat peanuts ||

The interpretation rendered by (54a), with one single intonation group, illustrates a transitive double-verb construction, with *peanuts* as the direct object, with the meaning 'cease', that is, she 'ceased peanut eating', equivalent to "she stopped eating peanuts". (54b), however, shows an intransitive use of the verb *stop* and the sequence *to eat peanuts* as a purpose clause, that is, she stopped doing whatever it was she was doing at that moment, in order to eat peanuts. In fact, the two examples illustrate opposite meanings, as in (54a) she did not eat peanuts, but in (54b) she did.

(8) Negative context

In the context of a negative main clause followed by an adverbial clause of reason (introduced by *because*) or of result (introduced by *so that*), tonality helps resolve the potential ambiguity between parallel structures which, in fact, as in the previous subsection, denote opposite meanings. Consider (55) below:

(55) a. || I didn't buy because he advised me ||

b. || I didn't buy | because he advised me ||

In (55a), the reason clause, embedded in the same intonation group as the main verb is functioning as an adjunct to the verb, and the implication of the whole sentence is that 'I did buy' but *not* as a result of following his advice, but for some other reason. In (55b), however, the reason clause is a sentence adjunct, or comment clause, and the implication is, in fact, that I **didn't** buy and that was because he advised me not to.

(9) Comment clauses and parenthetical information

Something similar to the above is the case in the following examples, in which comment or parenthetical information is given their own intonation group to differentiate them from a transitive interpretation, as shown in (56):

(56) a. || You know | I don't like it ||

b. || You know I don't like it ||

(56a) shows the discourse marker *you know* as a separate element, the main clause being "I don't like it", whereas (56b) shows the main clause "You know etc", in which "I don't like it" is a clausal direct object. Something similar happens in (57):

(57) a. || Their suggestion | to go by plane | was rejected ||
b. || Their suggestion to go by plane | was rejected ||

(57a) is a case of parenthetical information, the implication being that they only had one suggestion to make, which was "to go by plane", and this was rejected. (57b) shows the sequence "to go by plane" as a noun modifier, which implies that they may have had other suggestions, but it was this particular one the one, and not the others, that was rejected.

(10) Attachment of adverbials

Adverbial mobility is a frequent source of ambiguity, and one which is very much exploited in humour. Appropriate tonality can help recover the meaning intended. Let us examine the following series of examples:

(58) a. || Those who left | soon managed to get the lifts ||
b. || Those who left soon | managed to get the lifts ||

(59) a. || I was asking for the book I had seen | in the library ||
b. || I was asking for the book I had seen in the library ||

(60) a. || I saw the man | with the telescope ||
b. || I saw the man with the telescope ||

(61) a. || I saw the man | crossing the river ||
b. || I saw the man crossing the river ||

In example (58) the ambiguity is resolved by shifting the boundary to a position before or after the adverb, which indicates that the adverb is a modifier of the verb *managed*, in the main clause, in the (a) version, or of the verb *left*, in the relative clause, in the (b) version, with the consequent change in meaning: (a) means that the people that left managed to get a lift soon, whereas (b) means that only those who were quick enough to leave managed to get a lift. In contrast, examples (59) to (61) illustrate in the (a) versions adverbial expressions as modifiers of the immediately antecedent element, namely, "seen in the library", "man with a telescope", "man crossing the river", whereas in the (b) versions, these adverbials belong higher up in the syntactic branching, that is, "asking in the library", "saw with a telescope" and " I crossing the river".

(11) Final adjuncts: manner versus comment

Tonicity resolves the ambiguity of single intonation groups of the type:

(62) a. || He fell un**for**tunately ||
b. || He **fell** unfortunately ||
c. || He **fell** | un**for**tunately ||

(62a) illustrates the case of the adverbial of manner within the verb phrase, which carries the tonic syllable of the one single intonation unit, whereas in (62b), *unfortunately* is a comment adjunct, added to the whole clause; the tonic syllable of the intonation group falls on the verb. In (62c) this interpretation is further reinforced by giving the adverb its own intonation group, which means it would then also carry a nuclear stress.

(12) Coordinated phrases

Tonality is at work to disambiguate meanings in coordinated structures of different type, as represented in the following examples:

(63) a. || I love chicken | risotto | and pie || (= I love three things)

b. || I love chicken risotto | and pie || (= I love two things, but only the risotto has chicken in it).

c. || I love chicken | risotto and pie || (= I love two things and both of them have chicken in them).

(64) a. || The woman | and the girl in blue | are in my group || (only the girl is in blue; we don't know about the woman).

b. || The woman and the girl in blue | are in my group || (= both the girl and the woman are in blue).

(65) a. || I washed | and polished the floor || (= *washed* is intransitive, whereas *polished* is transitive, i.e. *the floor* is the direct object of *polished* only; it is a case of two coordinated clauses).

b. || I washed and polished the floor || (= both *washed* and *polished* are transitive, sharing the direct object *the floor*, that is, coordination takes level within the verb phrase and between the two heads).

So far we have seen how intonation plays a role in the way we speak, which is superimposed on the actual message, to the extent that two similar messages can be delivered in different ways if we produce changes in the tonality, tonicity, and/or tone of an utterance. So, for example, if we consider an utterance like *Take the keys*, there are many different possible intonation units in which it could be "packed", as shown in (66):

(66) a. \ **Take** \ the **keys**

b. **Take** the keys

c. Take **the** keys

d. Take the **keys**

e. \ Take \ **the** keys

Tonality determines the number of intonation units that are made: for instance, one, as in (66b) to (66d), or two, as in (66a) and (66e). **Tonicity** allows us to shift the stress, which could fall on any of the three words, depending on the desired meaning. The three utterances in (66b) to (66d) above each illustrate a different shade of meaning of the utterance, which relies on shared ground between speakers. So (66b) means 'take' and not 'send them by post' for example; (66c) means 'you know exactly which ones and what is special about them'; and (66d) suggests the keys as opposed to "a piece of wire, which could damage the lock". In (66e) tonality and tonicity are combined, rendering an interpretation that combines those of (66b) and (66c), both carrying intonational prominence on being packed in corresponding intonation units.

Tone will determine the attitude in which the command is uttered; as a fall, the difference lies on the variation of pitch, so that if said on a neutral high fall it sounds more lively and energetic than if said on a low fall, which shows signs of boredom and dullness, as in (67b), where (67c) shows that, again, the desired selection of tones can be combined with the intonation grouping intended and also the tonicity required:

(67) a. ˋ Take the keys (= high fall: lively and cheerful)
b. ˎ Take the keys (= low fall: boring and dull)
c. ˎ Take \ **the** keys

However sophisticated the system may seem to be so far, these are not all the possibilities that intonation allows, because we still have to consider at least one more major function, namely, the discourse and pragmatic functions.

6.3.4.4 Discourse function

Discourse organisation consists in the chunking of information units into manageable pieces, deciding what elements count as old or given information in a message, and what count as new, and presenting all of this in some kind of order to the listener. Furthermore, conversation, in particular, is ruled by a series of norms that both speakers observe. Syntax and semantics tend to provide enough clues for discourse to be well organised, but intonation plays a very substantial role in these processes, either by supporting the existing layout or, most decisively, by disambiguating between otherwise equal utterances, where syntactic and semantic features alone fail to transmit the desired meaning, or by encoding an intended effect. The different prosodic elements of intonation often combine, as we have seen repeatedly in this section, but we can say that tonality has more to do with the first aspect of breaking up the spoken chain into information units; tonicity is related to questions of focus and old versus new information; and tones support decisions concerning the staging of the information into major or leading units, and "minor" or "trailing" ones. Since the role of intonation in discourse is very much connected with other functions, such as the accentual and the grammatical functions already discussed, here we will take a brief look at some of the most relevant situations in which intonation plays this discourse function specifically.

AI 6.11 Discourse function of intonation

(1) Chunking
Divisions into more than one intonation group of a sequence which would normally constitute one unit may obey a series of reasons, for example, the addition of an afterthought or the wish to reinforce a marked theme, as represented in (68):

(68) a. || She is arriving tomorrow | by plane ||
b. || By plane | she is arriving tomorrow ||

Tonality also supports the addition of parenthetical information:

|| She is arriving | weather permitting | by plane ||

(2) New versus old information
Neutral tonicity, as we have seen, means that the nuclear stress in an utterance falls on the tonic syllable of the last lexical item. If this item also represents **new information**, generally located at the end of an utterance, then the utterance is not marked. However, if new information is located elsewhere in the utterance, or is a grammatical element instead of a lexical item, then the stress is shifted accordingly, since we tend to stress new information, as illustrated in example (69):

(69) || Did you meet Peter and Paul? No | I met **Mark** and Paul ||

(3) Broad versus narrow focus
Neutral tonicity is the one we use to bring an **utterance** into **broad** focus, that is, we place the nuclear stress on the tonic syllable of the last lexical item, as in (70):

(70) || She is arriving tomorrow by **plane** ||

In addition to this, the linguistic system of English allows us a series of syntactic operations whereby only part of what is being said is brought into **narrow focus**, which is accordingly reinforced by a shift of the nuclear stress. Two such possibilities are represented in (71):

(71) a. Who arrived first? || **Ann** I think || (fronting)
 b. || It was **Ann** that arrived first || (*it*-cleft)

However, it may also happen that a narrow focus results from tonicity alone, as in (72), where the nuclear stress is unexpectedly shifted to initial position, instead of final position, because the final and medial slots are occupied by repeated material (Given information), and so the "unmarked", or "neutral", tonicity option is to place the focus on the initial constituent that carries New information:

(72) Who arrived first? || **Ann** arrived first ||

(4) Staging of information

We organise our discourse into chunks to which we give **more** or less importance, that is, some are dependent on others. The order in which these are given to the listener is irrespective of their importance. Tone helps signal this relationship. An independent chunk in an utterance tends to be said always on a fall, whereas dependent stretches are usually said on a non-fall, either a rise or a fall-rise, indicating that more information is to come – if they are preceding the independent or main element- or that they have just been added to the previous sequence and belong with it – when following it. When the dependent element comes first, the tone is usually a fall-rise, whereas if it comes after the main one, the tone is a rise, as shown in (73):

(73) a. || There was complete silence when she \ **left** ||
 b. || When she \/ **left** | there was complete \ si**lence** ||
 c. || There was complete \ si**lence** | when she / **left** ||

If we compare (73a), the neutral version of this utterance, with the other two versions we will be able to notice the nuances in meaning that the different tones add. In (73b), the independent element is in the leading position and is therefore said on a fall-rise, whereas in (73c), where it comes after the main element, the tone is a rise.

The function of the initial dependent fall-rise, preceding a falling tone, is to highlight a theme; if the theme is marked this will almost invariably have its own intonation group anyway, as shown in (74a) and (74b) below; but if theme is not marked, then the choice of a fall-rise will not only highlight it but almost inevitably give it its own intonation group, as illustrated in (74c) and (74d):

(74) a. || This / **mor**ning | my friend came || (= marked theme; neutral tone)
b. || This \/ **mor**ning | my friend came || (= marked theme, marked tone)
c. || My friend came this \ **mor**ning || (= unmarked theme; neutral tone)
d. || My \/ **friend** | came this \ **mor**ning || (= unmarked theme; marked tone)

Finally, we would like to mention again the question of lists. We have already seen that the usual tone between items in a list is a rise, and that the final element is said on a fall. This is the case of a closed list. However, if a list ends in a rise, this means the list is open and that there may be more information to come, even if it is not said. Something similar happens when giving choices, as shown in (75):

(75) a. || We have va /**nil**la | or \ **cream** ||
b. || We have va /**nil**la | or / **cream** ||

It is from the tone alone that we know that the choice of icecream flavours in (75a) is limited to two, whereas in (75b) there are, or may be, more flavours, which have not been mentioned yet.

The same takes place in alternative questions, represented in (76): in (76a) the question ends on a final fall, which implies the speaker is conceiving of only two possible places for the listener to stay, whereas the final rise of (76b) allows the listener to give a different answer.

(76) a. || Are you staying in / **Lon**don | or in \ **Man**chester ||
b. || Are you staying in / **Lon**don | or in / **Man**chester ||

6.3.4.5 Illocutionary function

Intonation, particularly by means of the tone system, helps encode the illocutionary force of an utterance, so that it is delivered as a command, a question or a statement, for example. This is because there is not a one-to-one relationship between grammatical categories (declaratives, interrogatives, imperatives and verbless constructions) and illocutionary categories (statements, questions, commands and exclamations). This means that, although the interrogative mood usually encodes a question, and vice versa, a question is normally asked in the interrogative form, the linguistic system is flexible enough to allow for other combinations. Consider, for example the illocutionary category "command", as in (77a), which may be expressed by means of an interrogative, or the grammatical category "declarative", as in (77b), which may actually encode a question:

(77) a. Will you sign here, please? (interrogative = command)

b. I wonder when she's coming (declarative = question)

Given this state of affairs, the grammatical structure of an utterance alone is not always indicative of its communicative function. Thus, it is easy to see now that intonation, and tones in particular, plays a crucial role not only in expressing the communicative function intended but, specially, in disambiguating between pragmatic categories which share the same surface grammatical structure, as can be seen in (78a) and (78b) (using example (66) above):

(78) a. \ **Take** the keys (= command)

b. / Take the keys (= question; suggestion)

c. ˎ **Take** / the **keys**

(78c), on the other hand, shows that the discourse and illocutionary functions of intonation can also combine with the other three and therefore, as seen above, new meanings are possible: the first low fall command, denoting boredom and dullness, is followed by a question about the keys, which suggests 'have you got them?' or even 'will you give them back to me?'; and, in any case, in this example, even more so than in the previous ones, the command *to take* is not necessarily related to *the keys*, as it could well refer to 'taking something else'.

In addition to the main four illocutionary functions that have been mentioned, there are others such as requesting, promising, threatening, complimenting, suggesting, offering, praying, greeting, cursing, insulting, and so on, the list is almost never-ending. All of them are brought together under the cover-term **speech acts**, which refer to what language is used for, given the fact that when we use language we are actually doing something with it. As an illustration, let us look at the following identical utterances, which are both said on a rising tone:

(79) a. Can you / lend it to me?

b. Can you \/ lend it to me? (fall-rise = request)

The modulation allowed by the fall-rise helps define the illocutionary force of (79b) as a request rather than a simple question on a simple rising tone, as in (79a).

Despite its richness, the tone system of the language is not sophisticated enough to enable each possible speech act to have its own characteristic melody. Hence, what the tone system does, by variations and combinations of the basic falling and rising movements, is to allow for generalisations about the position the speaker adopts towards the listener along a cline from the power associated with falling tones to the deference related to the rising ones.

In this section we will look at the main pragmatic categories, namely, statements, questions, commands and exclamations, and the role different tones play. We have already seen, in section 6.3.3. above, that the intonation patterns of English fall within two wide categories: falling and rising patterns, depending on the final movement in the nucleus of the intonation group. Falling tones tend to indicate finality, in the sense of conclusiveness, which is to say that they are used to disclose information the speaker has or to express his feelings, which, in other case, enables him to exert a certain sense of authority or dominance over the listener. Rising tones, on the other hand, indicate incompleteness, doubt and withholding of information, they are a prompt for conversation to continue and generally allow the speaker to show deference to the listener. Typically, **statements**, **commands** and **exclamations** are associated with falling tones, and **questions** with rising ones, as illustrated in the examples above, with departures from this signalling a different communicative function or modulating speaker's attitude.

(1) Statements

a. **The definitive fall.** The neutral, unmarked or default tone for a statement is a fall, also known as a definitive fall, which means that what is said is a complete statement, definitive and final, which the speaker is expressing with confidence and resolution, as in

   (80) || *I saw him* \ *in* ***Lon****don* ||

   However, statements can be said on other tones, which have pragmatic connotations, that is, they add an extra layer of meaning which is not explicitly said, but implied.

b. **The fall-rise.** A complete independent statement said on a fall-rise indicates that the speaker has some reservations about what he is saying, whether these are made explicit or not, that is, he is implying something else, which may or may not be left unsaid. Compare example (80) with (81), which has an implicational fall-rise:

   (81) || I saw him \/ in **Lon**don ||

   In this case, the reservation is not explicit, which means that it is left to the listener to resolve it: perhaps there was a "secret" reason for him to be in London, or else he should have been somewhere else, and so on. By using this tone, which is rising at the end, the speaker is somehow inviting the listener to either ask for what the reservation is or to offer it himself, depending on the degree of shared common ground between them:

(82) || I saw him \/ in **Lon**don || What do you mean?

I know, perhaps he was visiting Ann.

This fall-rise can also be used for reasons of contrast, as in:

(83) || I saw him in \/ **Lon**don (= not in **Man**chester)

One particular context of use of this fall-rise is in contrasting negative statements, whether the positive part is explicitly said or not. The above example would normally be said like this:

(84) || I saw him \ in **Lon**don | not in \/ **Man**chester

A fall-rise is also used in tentative statements, in which the speaker does not wish to commit himself or is not completely sure about what he is saying. It also softens an otherwise more abrupt fall:

(85) || How much money do you want? \/ **Twen**ty pounds ||

This is the reason why it is also used in corrections which are made to sound more polite or friendly, as in (86a), and also in partial agreements, as in (86b):

(86) a. So, you're name is Mary \/ **Su**san ||

b. Did you enjoy the film? || The \/ **mu**sic was good || (= not the rest of the film)

c. **The rise.** A rising tone in statements, known as the **high raising terminal, uptalk** or **backpack**, is a feature that entered the language in the 80s and spread quickly via the younger generations who, as is speculated, picked it up when travelling or watching foreign TV comedies. Because of the most usual meaning of a rise, typically used in yes/no questions, it sounds strange in a statement which is supposed to be final and conclusive, and a lot of people still find it annoying, as it is not quite clear whether the speaker is actually disclosing information, requesting it, being tentative or simply, most annoying, checking whether the listener knows what he is talking about. This leaves the listener in a position in which he does not always know whether he has to answer a possible question or just follow the conversation, as in:

(87) A. Where's the church?

B. || Past / **Sains**bury's. . . .||

Speaker A is not sure whether Speaker B is actually checking whether he knows where Sainsbury's is. The rise also suggests that something else is to follow, so Speaker A is waiting for more information, but if this is a case of uptalk, then, as far as speaker B is concerned, that was all there was to be said.

A rise may be used in contradictions, but it sounds more unfriendly, as if on the defensive, than a definitive fall or the tentative fall-rise, as we have seen above:

(88) You are late.

a. || \ No || (= neutral)

b. || \/ No || (= polite, deferential)

c. || / No || (= brusque, protesting)

Any of the tones above can be used not only for complete independent statements, but also in short answers to yes/no questions, for example, with all the nuances of meaning discussed above.

Finally, we have already spoken about the lack of a one-to one relationship between grammatical and pragmatic categories. So far, we have seen declaratives functioning as statements, and vice versa, all the instances of statements in this section remain statements regardless of the tone used. However, a declarative on a rise is no longer a statement, but a question, and this is why we will deal with it in the following section:

(89) || You are coming / to**mo**rrow ||

(2) Questions

There are questions of different types, and they do not all have the same tones. We will look at some of the most often used.

(2.1) *Wh*-questions

a. **The definitive fall.** Information questions, introduced by *wh*-words, are often pronounced on a fall, with a conclusive intonation. The reason for this lies in the fact that the presupposition enclosed in the proposition means that the speaker already knows at least part of the information, and therefore can use a more definitive tone:

(90) || When are you \ **co**ming ||

The final element is the presupposition, i.e. the fact that [you are coming] is being disclosed, and is consequently pronounced with falling intonation.

b. **The rise.** A rising tone, whether it is a simple rise or a complex fall-rise, adds the overtones of deference and sympathy which are typically **associated** with it. This is known as the **encouraging rise**:

(91) || When are you / coming ||

With this rising intonation, the question sounds much more friendly and welcoming than with the neutral default fall we have seen above.

(2.2) Yes/No questions

a. **The yes/no rise.** The neutral tone for a yes/no question, or polarity question, whether it is in the positive or in the negative, is a rise, known as **the yes/no rise**. The speaker is genuinely asking something for which he does not know an answer and is, therefore, encouraging the conversation to continue:

(92) a. || Are you / **co**ming ||

b. || Aren't you / **co**ming ||

This is also the case when the interrogative is actually encoding a request and not a question proper:

(93) || Will you lend me your / **car** ||

b. **The fall-rise.** A fall-rise can be used make it even clearer that the interrogative is a request as opposed to a plain question in those cases in which there are no other illocutionary force indicators. Also, it sounds more persuasive than a simple rise. Contrast the following two examples:

(94) a. Will you \/ lend it to me || (= requesting; persuasive)

b. Will you / lend it to me || (= asking for a yes/no answer

c. **The insistent fall** is a yes/no question that is said on a fall. This makes the speaker sound more aggressive or formal:

(95) || Are you \ **co**ming ||

It is also used when the question has to be repeated if the listener has not heard properly, denoting some boredom or fastidiousness on the part of the speaker:

(96) A. || Are you / **co**ming ||
B. -Sorry, did you say something?
A. Are you \ **co**ming

(2.3) Declarative questions

Note that, as mentioned above, there are cases in which it is the tone, rather than the grammatical form, that makes an utterance a question. So we can talk of **declarative questions**, which are also pronounced on a yes/no rise. The above example could be issued as:

(97) || You are / **co**ming ||

The reasons for choosing one grammatical form or the other may have to do with politeness issues -the declarative being perhaps less invasive- or with how much the speaker is assuming to be already true – the declarative implying that the speaker thinks he already knows the answer.

(2.4) Echo questions

These typically repeat all or part of the words of the previous speaker, whether these were a statement, a question of whatever type, or a command, in order to query them, ask for a repetition or to simply check understanding. Echo questions are said on a rise:

(98) A. I'm coming tomorrow|

B. || Coming / to**mo**rrow ||

(99) A. When are you coming?

B. || When am I / **co**ming ||

(100) A. Are you coming tomorrow?

B. || Am I / to**mo**rrow ||

(101) A. Come tomorrow!

B. || Come / to**mo**rrow ||

This rise is known as the **pardon-question rise** and is also used whenever we want to enquire about any element in the previous utterance, either by using one of the "pardon" words, such as **sorry** or **pardon**, quoting the actual element that is being checked, or changing it into a wh-word, which may or may not be fronted:

(102) || I'm coming tomorrow / Sorry ||

a. Coming / to**mo**rrow

b. Coming / **when**

c. When are you / **co**ming

d. / **You** are coming

Notice that if the query focuses narrowly on one of the elements of the previous utterance, there may be also a shift of stress. Examples (102a) to (102c) focus broadly on the previous utterance, questioning the whole of it, whereas in (102d) the speaker focuses on the element *I* only.

(2.5) Tag questions

Tag questions, variable reduced syntactic structures consisting of only an auxiliary verb and a pronoun, are usually added to the end of a statement in colloquial English. This is done on a polarity basis, in such a way that if the statement is positive, then the tag is negative, and vice versa, a negative statement is followed by a positive tag. This type is known as **balanced** or **reverse polarity tag questions**. More rarely, the tag and the statement may show the same polarity, in which case we talk of **unbalanced tag questions** or **copy tags**. Consider the following examples:

(103) a. Monica plays the flute, doesn't she? (statement = positive; tag = negative)
b. Martin can't drive a car yet, can he? (statement = negative; tag = positive)
c. Andrea will phone later, will she? (statement = positive; tag = positive)
d. Angie doesn't really like the project, doesn't she? (statement = negative; tag = negative)

Now, what is interesting about these tags is that their intonation is pragmatically determined, that is, tag questions may encode two different illocutionary forces -their grammatical form remaining the same-, and therefore act either as a question proper or else as a (request for) confirmation on the information which is given in the statement: in the first case, the speaker is not sure about the truth condition of the statement, whereas in the second, the speaker is only checking for confirmation of what he already suspects is true. Intonation, then, plays a disambiguating role, conveying the pragmatic force of the tag. As already discussed in Section 6.3.3.1, a rising tone is open-ended and denotes a true question, whereas a falling one, with its sense of finality, is the usual one in statements. Therefore, tags of the first type are said on a rise, and tags of the second type are said on a fall. Please note that the nucleus of the tag intonation group always falls on the verb and never on the pronoun, which is a common mistake among learners of English. Compare the following examples:

(104) a. || He is not going back to Africa | / **is** he || = rising tone: true question
b. || He is not going back to Africa | \ **is** he || = falling tone: request for confirmation

The less usual unbalanced tags do not often have a separate intonation group, but if they do they are then said on a low rise. Consider the examples in (105):

(105) a. || He is going back to \ **Africa** is he || (most usual intonation pattern)
b. || He is going back to Africa | / **is** he ||
c. || He is not going back to Africa | / **isn't** he ||

The above also applies to tags added to commands -as they show the same polarity-, which have the illocutionary force of a request, not a question. If pronounced on a rise, a positive tag softens the force of the command, whereas a negative one, also on a rise, conveys a more demanding attitude on the part of the speaker, as in:

(106) a. || Bring those boxes nearer to me | / **will** you ||

b. || Bring those boxes nearer to me | / **won't** you ||

AI 6.12 Tag questions

Resembling tag-questions, but actually uttered by a different speaker and with the same polarity as the previous one, elliptical short questions may be used as answers to a previous questions o statement, in order to keep a conversation going. The neutral tone for these is a yes/no rise, as in (107a) and (107b), whereas an insistent fall will denote hostility, scepticism or even contempt, as it occurs in (107c):

(107) a. || I didn't really like it / **Didn't** you ||

b. || I have decided to stop it / **Have** you ||

c. || I have decided to stop it \ **Have** you ||

(3) Commands

a. **The fall.** The neutral tone for a positive command is a fall, as in || *Speak* \ ***softly*** ||.

b. **The rise.** The illocutionary force of a command may be softened by the use of rising intonation. It can also act as a reminder of a previously issued order or as gentle encouragement to get on with it, as in || *Speak* / ***softly*** ||.

c. **The fall-rise.** In much the same way a fall-rise turned a question into a request, a command becomes a warning if said as in (108a), or it may be used in negative commands, as in (108b):

(108) a. || Speak \/ **soft**ly | or I'll call the po**lice** ||

b. || Don't speak so \/ **loud**ly ||

(4) Exclamations

a. **The fall.** The neutral tone for the expression of emotion in exclamations, interjections and greetings is the fall, regardless of their grammatical form, as shown in (109). Two common greetings are always said on a fall, namely *Hi!* and *Cheers!*

(109) a. || How \ **love**ly ||

b. || \ **Awe**some ||

c. || Isn't that \ **good** ||

d. || \ **Thank** you ||

b. **The rise**. Exclamations and greetings on a rise denote a more friendly, approach-based attitude, and are also used as cues to encourage the continuation of the conversation, as exemplified in (110a) to (110d). Note, however, that, contrary to expectation, *thank you* on a rise denotes a routinary attitude, as shown in (110e).

(110) a. He/**llo** ||

b. Good / **bye** ||

c. Good / **even**ing ||

d. O/ **K** ||

e. Thank / **you** ||

6.3.4.6 Other functions

Intonation also plays other roles in our everyday life, such as aiding our memory – what is referred to as the psychological function- or signalling our social position. For example, it is often the case that people find it much easier to memorise phone numbers in a certain sequence but not in others. If you are used to saying your phone number in groups of three digits with their particular cadence you will find it more difficult when trying to give your number in pairs. Socially, it is also a well-known feature that newsreaders, for example, have a characteristic intonation, which makes them different from priests. Even within newsreaders, television and radio reporters, who rely solely on voice, sound different; also, whether reporting a happy item of news or a dramatic event, their voice, i.e. their intonation, is crucial for a professional delivery.

6.4 The prosody of English and Spanish compared and advice

6.4.1 Stress and rhythm

English is a stress-timed language whereas Spanish is syllable-timed, as we saw above in section 6.2.1. Added to this, difficulties in word and sentence stress will cause the rhythm to be different in the productions of SSLE, who will tend to treat English as a syllable-timed language instead of giving it the stress-timed rhythmic distribution which is natural in native speech.

Whereas Spanish word stress can be decided simply in relation to the syllables of words and their endings according to some straightforward rules, placement of stress in English is, indeed, a very complex issue. Although the learning of word accentual patterns is not as large a task as might be imagined considering that in conversations monosyllables may account for more than 80 per cent of words, the accent of polysyllabic words should be learnt when they are first acquired (Cruttenden 2014: 333). There is no simple way of predicting which syllable or syllables must be stressed. One obvious difference between the two languages is the fact that Spanish indicates stress through accent marks, whereas English does not. Therefore, whenever foreign speakers learn a new word, they must learn it individually with its stress. Incorrect placement of stress may be a major cause of intelligibility problems and of foreign diction. There are some tendencies in Spanish, which, if carried over into English, may lead to incorrect stress placement. Particular problems can appear with multisyllabic **cognates**, or "related words between two languages that are similar or identical in form and meaning" (Knorre 2009: 8), as illustrated in the examples given below extracted from Sedláčková (2010). 30–40% of all words in Spanish are cognates of English (Knorre 2009: 8).

Table 48: Accentuation disparities between English and Spanish cognates

Word class	Stress in English	Stress in Spanish
Noun	ˈanimal ˈdoctor ˈnation ˈoptimism ˈstudent voˈcabulary	aniˈmal docˈtor naˈción optiˈmismo estuˈdiante vocabuˈlario
Adjective	eˈffective inˈtelligent imˈportant ˈordinary ˈterrible	efecˈtivo inteliˈgente imporˈtante ordiˈnario teˈrrible
Verb	exˈport inˈvite inˈsist ˈoperate ˈsignify	exportar inviˈtar insistir opeˈrar significar
Adverb	eˈxactly	exactaˈmente

As can be seen from Table 48, whereas in English stress is most commonly placed on the first syllable, in Spanish the two most frequent patterns are those in which the stress is placed either on the penultimate or on the last syllable. In addition, you can see that, unlike English, Spanish has a written accent mark when demanded by the Spanish accentuation rules, that is, in **proparoxytone** 'esdrújulas' words and **oxytone** 'agudas' words ending in vowels, <n> and <s>.

English prosodic stress falls on the last lexical word in the utterance, i.e. the word that carries the most relevant meaning, whereas Spanish systematically places it on the last stressed syllable of the sentence, regardless of whether this last word is lexical or grammatical. Therefore, a common mistake by Spanish learners is that represented in (111) below, where no emphasis on the stressed words is at all meant:

(111) a. *I went with **her**

b. *I love **you**

Contrastive uses of sentence stress pose problems for Spanish learners and may give rise to pragmatic misunderstandings. This is because new information is typically presented after given information, receiving more stress, as it is considered to have more prominence in the sentence (and in the wider context of the conversation) than information already known to the listener. The different meanings expressed in English through sentence stress are conveyed in Spanish through other resources such as word order or the use of particular words. For example, while in English sentence stress serves to differentiate between *Mary went to the* ***shop*** (as an answer to *what did Mary do?*) and ***Mary*** *went to the shop* (as an answer to *who went to the shop?*), Spanish has different means to mark these contrasts, as in *Fue a la tienda*, with ellipsis of the subject in the first case, or *Fue María*, with subject-verb inversion in the second.

The following points may serve as general guidelines in order to avoid interferences concerning stress and rhythm (Finch and Ortiz Lira 1982: 87–117; Estebas Vilaplana 2009: 138–181):

(1) Every English word has a definite place for stress: it is most commonly placed on the first syllable but many words are stressed on the second syllable. Some words (mostly compounds) may have two stressed syllables.

(2) The placement of stress is English depends on the grammatical category of the word.

(3) The weight of the syllable (i.e. whether the vowel is short or long as well as the number of consonants that follow it) plays an important role as well.

(4) Stress rules for simple words are mostly unpredictable and they are so complex that it seems easier to treat stress placement as an inseparable part of the word and learn it when the word itself is learnt. Rules for complex words' stress placement are much easier than those for simple words (see § 6.2.2.2. above). Problems may arise with compound words. Because Spanish uses word order to show contrast, learners may be unfamiliar with the use of stress to mark the distinction between noun compounds and nouns with an adjective modifier, of the '*blackbird* and *black* '*bird* type. Spanish often stresses the second element of compound words, which

means that speakers may incorrectly use the same stress pattern in English compounds.

(5) A most important aspect concerning English stress is the effect it has on the quality of vowels. Whereas Spanish maintains a strong vowel quality in both stressed and unstressed syllables, in English vowel weakening occurs, as already noted, so that unstressed syllables are usually produced with a weak vowel [ə i u ɪ ʊ], although some strong vowels can also appear in unstressed syllables. As an illustration, consider the word *potato* /pə ˈteɪtəʊ/, where the two unstressed syllables contain weak [ə] and strong [əʊ]. Vowels can also be omitted in unstressed syllables giving place to syllabic consonants, as already explained in Section 1.3.3.3). SSLE should pay particular attention to vowel weakening in order to improve their English pronunciation, as well as to prevent communication problems because in some contexts vowel weakening has a contrastive effect. Consider, for example, the difference between *exercise* /ˈeksəsaɪz/ and *violet* /ˈvaɪələt/, on the one hand, with vowel weakening to /ə/ of the first and second syllables, respectively, and *exorcise* /ˈeksɔːˌsaɪz/ and *violate* /ˈvaɪəleɪt/, on the other, where no such weakening occurs (Fudge 1984).

(6) While in Spanish polysyllabic words have only one stressed syllable, in English especially long words tend to have more than one stressed syllables which may have either a primary or a secondary stress. One frequent mistake for SSLE is to produce English double (*understand* /ˌʌndəˈstænd/) or multiple (*misrepresent* /ˌmɪsˌreprɪˈzent/) stressed words with one single stress, which results in a rather strange foreign accent.

(7) In English there exist a number of (normally disyllabic) words whose grammatical category (verb or noun/adjective) is distinguished by the location of the stress (*suspect* /səˈspekt/ (v.) vs. /ˈsʌspekt/ (n)). SSLE should avoid producing such words with the same stress distribution, whatever their grammatical category, usually by placing the stress on the first syllable [ˈsaspekt].

(8) We have already seen that in English phrases and compounds, which may be written differently (as two separate words, as two words separated by a hyphen or as one word), can be distinguished by the location of the stress: the latter tend to receive only (one) primary stress on the first element (*greenhouse* /ˈgriːnhaʊs/), while phrases have two stresses, a pre-primary stress on the first word and a primary stress on the last word if it is the head (*green house* /ˌgriːn ˈhaʊs/. One common mistake for SSLE is to pronounce both sequences with a phrasal stress pattern, that is, with two stresses. This may lead to obvious misunderstandings. In the case in point a listener may interpret that the referent is ‘a house painted in green’ when what is actually intended is ‘a place that is full of plants and vegetables’.

Let us now consider rhythm. We have explained that English has **stress-timed rhythm**, that is, stress occurs at approximately equal intervals so that the duration between stressed syllables tend to be approximately the same, regardless of the number of intervening unstressed syllables. In contrast, Spanish has a **syllable-timed rhythm**, in which syllables are produced at more or less regular intervals so that that the duration of each syllable is fairly similar, irrespective of whether it is stressed or unstressed. Consequently, for a speaker of Spanish sentences like *ˈMary could ˈsee* and *ˈMary could have been ˈseen* differ in duration, that is, the higher the number of syllables, the longer the sentence. For an English speaker, in contrast, both last approximately the same amount of time since what matters in English is the number of stresses, not the number of syllables. Bearing this in mind, if SSLE want to sound natural when speaking in English particular attention should be paid to the following:

(1) English stress-timed rhythm should be reproduced by reducing the duration of the unstressed syllables and producing (or omitting) weak vowels in unstressed vowels, as well as the weak forms of function words, instead of pronouncing syllables with similar duration without changing the quality of unstressed vowels. A good way to start acquiring English rhythm is through singing songs and reciting nursery rhymes. The tempo used can be marked by clapping. If the tempo is quicker, then more unstressed syllables should be produced between stresses to be able to keep the same rhythm.

(2) Another aspect derived from English stress-timed rhythm is that when a phrase consists of three content (mainly mono- or disyllabic) words occurring in a sequence, the one in the middle normally loses the stress (*little young boy* /ˌlɪtl̩ jʌŋ ˈbɔɪ/) to contribute to keeping a more even rhythmic pattern. Instead, SSLE tend to stress either just the word in the middle [lɪtl̩ ˈjʌŋ bɔɪ] or each of the three words [ˈlɪtl̩ ˈjʌŋ ˈbɔɪ], which sounds awkward to the native ear.

(3) A further consequence of English stress-timed rhythm, **stress-shift** occurs in English but not in Spanish. It is the phenomenon whereby the stress of a word is shifted to the front to avoid the production of two consecutive or close stressed syllables. Thus, words like *Japanese* /ˌdʒæpəˈniːz/, which has two stressed syllables, one with a secondary stress (the first) and another one with a primary stress (the third), if followed by another word which starts with a stressed syllable such as *noodles*, the primary stress will be shifted to the syllable that originally carries the secondary stress (*Japanese noodles* /ˈdʒæpəniːz ˈnuːdl̩z/). In contrast, SSLE normally pronounce such sequences without stress shift (*Japanese noodles* [ʤapaˈniːz ˈnuːdl̩z]), which again causes a strong foreign accent. To minimise this effect, the application of the stress-shift rule is recommended.

6.4.2 Intonation

Intonation patterns employed by English speakers differ from those of Spanish speakers, as we have seen, mainly regarding the much wider range of pitch that English uses: higher highs and lower lows are reached, and more often. As a result, Spanish may be perceived as rather monotonous and not so melodic as English. This way, the English speaker may get the wrong impression that the Spanish speaker lacks involvement or interest in the conversation; but most importantly, since intonation plays a series of linguistic functions, wrong melodic movement may lead to the conveyance of a wrong message. Some areas which are particularly problematic for Spanish speakers are: pitch range, since Spanish speakers seem to use too narrow a pitch range; final falling pitch movement, which may not sound low enough; and the rise-fall pattern, which is difficult for learners to produce, especially on short phrases or monosyllables (Sedláčková 2010: 42–46; 74–76; Gutiérrez 2005; Gutiérrez and Conde 1990; Finch and Ortiz Lira 1982: 56).

In both languages, the two main melodies are based on rising and falling tones and combinations thereof; but, whereas in English, utterances begin at an overall high pitch, in Spanish utterances begin at a lower one; and while in English there is a large pitch change on the most emphasised word, in Spanish, the major pitch change usually takes place on the first stressed syllable. In practical terms, this means that in an English utterance such as *I am going to the shop*, the higher pitch used at the beginning would gradually lower until the end of the utterance, where the word *shop* would be given the most emphasis. If the same sentence was pronounced with a Spanish melody, most probably it would begin at a low pitch, which would then be raised on the first stressed syllable of the sentence, i.e. *going*.

As far as the intonation contours for statements and questions are concerned, English and Spanish differ substantially, which means that interferences may occur. The following areas are problematic:

(1) Statements

Both English and Spanish use a final falling pitch for statements. But in clauses with two intonation units English frequently uses the fall-rise pattern, which is not the case in Spanish. Compare the following:

(112) a. || Todavía no ha llegado el \ tren ||
ai. || The train has not \ arrived yet ||
b. || Si encuentras las llaves \ dímelo ||
bi. || If you find the \/ keys | let me \ know ||

(2) Interrogatives

English and Spanish intonation contours for interrogatives depend on the type of question. For present purposes, we distinguish between *yes/no* questions and *wh*-questions.

(2.1) *Yes/no* questions

English *yes/no* questions end in a rising pitch when the speaker does not know the answer to the question:

(113) a. || Is he / handsome ||

b. || Do you want some / coffee ||

In addition to the rising tone pattern, English also employs a falling tone if the speaker expects confirmation (e.g. in some tag questions), or if the speaker is sure that the answer to the question is positive:

(114) a. || The weather is \ good | \ isn't it ||

b. || Is he \ coming ||

In contrast, Spanish *yes/no* questions always rise at the end:

(115) Es el libro / interesante ||

'Is the book interesting?'

The pitch is high on the first stressed syllable, then the contour line remains the same until the last stressed syllable where it rises again. Therefore, Spanish learners are expected to face problems maintaining the correct (falling) intonation pattern in English *yes/no* questions when the answer is expected to be positive.

(2.2) *Wh*-questions

Wh-questions in Spanish have a tendency to rise on the final syllable, whereas they are pronounced on a falling tone in English. This is a cause for frequent mispronunciation.

(2.3) Tag questions

Since in Spanish tag questions are always pronounced with a rising intonation, SSLE generally use a rise in English tag questions, regardless of their function, when in English, as already noted, they are generally uttered with a falling contour, if asking for agreement, or with a rising intonation, if asking for information. SSLE should hence become aware that if used for different purposes, as information- or confirmation-seeking devices, tag questions in English should have correspondingly different intonation patterns, rising in the first case or falling in the second.

Although the correct acquisition of the attitudinal functions of English intonation is one of the most difficult areas for SSLE, some effort should be made to master at least some of its uses, in particular those of fall-rise in, for instance, warnings, contradictions and reservations. Also relevant for learners aiming at a native-like RP is the tonal quality of this accent, which mainly derives from the types of pre-nuclear patterns that are used, most frequently involving a series of glides-down. A series of glides-up will sound comically enthusiastic, and it should be avoided in long sequences of syllables on a low level, which will be perceived as bored or even surly. SSLE should therefore make every effort to employ the tonality, tonicity and tone (pitch) range used by native English speakers in order to avoid giving the overall impression that their speech is monotonous or otherwise being "accused" of not showing enough enthusiasm or interest. Consider, for instance, thanks-giving exchanges such as A: *–**Thank** you*. B: *–Thank **you***. By choosing a contrastive accentuation pattern focusing on *you* speaker B wants to emphasise that it is him/her, not A, who must be grateful. In order to succeed in such a challenging task, some training may be necessary to exercise the learners' acting abilities, as well as their empathy and imagination (Cruttenden 2014: 335; Sedláčková 2010: 75; Estebas Vilaplana 2009: 182–234).

Further reading

Most manuals for learners of English phonetics and phonology tend to include one or two chapters on stress, rhythm and intonation. Our experience tells us that this topic is still the "poor relation" in a general phonetics and phonology course for foreign students. This is not necessarily for lack of information on the topic: quite to the contrary, it is often the case that too much detail is given on certain aspects – such as the morphological structure of words in order to get accentuation right, or the intricacies of the internal structure of the English tone unit, for example – which make this an even more difficult and complicated area of practice for foreign learners. So, if you wish to go into further details along these lines, please refer to Gimson (1984, Chapters 9 and 10), Cruttenden (2014, Chapters 10 and 11) and Collins and Mees (2003: 123–132), (2009: 226–284), the latter two offering many interesting and practical exercises on stress and rhythm, and intonation.

Roach (2005) offers an extensive and accessible analysis of English prosody, which has served as inspiration for this chapter: Chapter 10 focuses on the nature, levels and placement of stress within the word, whereas complex word stress is dealt with in Chapter 11, and intonation is extensively treated in Chapters 15 to 19.

For a thorough study following Halliday's functional linguistic treatment of intonation, the reader is referred to Tench (1996) and Wells (2006). In their aim at describing intonation objectively and with precision, both authors provide a descriptive framework of intonation as a system composed of tonality, tonicity and tone, known as "the three T's", which we have also adopted here. Based on these parameters, they give special attention to the crucial role intonation plays in expressing meaning, providing clear explanations of some of the key functions of intonation, namely the attitudinal, grammatical and discourse functions, as well as what we have labelled pragmatic. They both give many illustrative examples throughout, and an extensive collection of useful exercises, both written and recorded.

Finally, descriptions of English prosody in contrast with that of Spanish or addressed to SSLE can be found in Monroy Casas (2012, Chapters 3, 4 and 5, 1980, 1981), Mott (2011, Chapters 7 to 10), Estebas Vilaplana (2009, Chapters 5 to 8), Gutiérrez (2004a, b, 2005), Gutiérrez and Conde (1990), Finch and Ortiz Lira (1982, Chapters 9, 11 and 12), and Sánchez Benedicto (1980, Chapter 5), to mention but a few.

Exercises

1. Choose six pairs of words from Table 43 in Chapter 6. Write two sentences to illustrate their different stress patterns. Mark them and then read the sentences aloud carefully.
   Example: *insult* I don't like ˈinsults vs She inˈsults everyone when she's angry
2. Explain the stress shift processes in the following words. Group those that show the same pattern:
   kingdom demonstrative magnetic journalist idiomatic evidential
3. Place the stress on the following words with suffixes; find the (possible) correlate root:

carriage	advantageous	lemonade	cinematography
memorial	alcoholic	domain	glorify
delicacy	original	widen	dogmatic

4. Place primary and secondary stresses on the following compounds; justify your answer:

low classes	front door	onlooker	London Bridge
Christmas holiday	fifty-four	St Therese Cathedral	pencil sharpener
kitchen window	lemon juice	Ivory Coast	blackmail
grandson	guesswork	greenhouse	downpour

5. Stress all the words that carry prosodic stress in the following utterances, using the labels L for lexical words, and G for grammatical words, commenting on the exceptions that you find.
    1. The man who came and asked for her sounded rather foreign.
    2. That thick book on the lower shelf is not mine.
    3. The child himself had told me before.
    4. What lovely weather but how cold it is!
    5. Who was the man that was talking to you before the class?
    6. She said that their car would not start again.
6. Stress the relevant syllables in the following constructions with phrasal verbs:
    1. bring down the box / bring the box down / bring it down
    2. it blew up / it then blew up / it blew up suddenly
    3. give back the book / give the book back / give it back
    4. fill in the form / fill the form in / fill it in
    5. she dressed up / she couldn't dress up / she dressed up nicely
    6. he gave up / he won't give up / he gave up abruptly
7. Provide your own examples to illustrate the stress modifications the following words suffer because of rhythmic constraints: shop-window, first-floor, afterlife.
8. Place prosodic stress on all the possible syllables in the following utterances. Explain your choices.
    1. Don't let down your brother, she said, and pay him back.
    2. I didn't know where you've been!
    3. What a dark room! I can´t see a thing.
    4. The old blue car broke down in Queen Street.
    5. He offered her some cake but she hates sweet things.
    6. Nick went to the supermarket.
9. Place the nuclear stress in the following utterances, explaining the exceptions.
    1. Put it in the box.
    2. Put it in the box near it.
    3. Put it in the box (complaining that he was putting it outside the box)
    4. Go with him!
    5. The actors appeared.
    6. What did you buy?
    7. What detergent did you buy?
    8. What detergent did you buy yesterday?
    9. The pictures, he said, were extraordinary.

10. The train was very late (about ten minutes).
11. The train was very late (over an hour).
12. I saw her.

10. Place the nuclear stress on all the possible words in the following utterance and explain the differences in meaning:

    Ruth gave me only one book

11. Explain the pragmatic implications – i.e. implicit meaning – produced by the possibility of shifting the nuclear stress in the following utterance:
    1. The boy raised his fist and the teacher threatened him.
    2. Carol told the actor how well he had performed and then he praised her.

12. Analyse the internal structure of the intonation groups in the following utterances, on the basis of the structure given in Chapter 6: (pre-head) (onset) (head) nucleus (tail)
    1. I don't know
    2. I don't know her
    3. I don't know her name
    4. Who do you live with?
    5. Where do you live?
    6. Do you live in London?

13. Add the various optional elements (pre-head, onset, head and tail) to the following intonation groups, which consist of a nucleus only, in a variety of combinations, e.g. pre-head + nucleus; pre-head + nucleus + tail, or nucleus + tail, and so on. Mark up the new group using the appropriate symbols.

    1. John 2. take 3. now 4. green 5. two

14. Consider these two conversations. Describe the possible intonation pattern of the utterances "What a pity", "Perhaps on Saturday" and "I will try on Saturday" using graphic notation, and paying special attention to the use of emoticons. Justify your decisions.

Conversation A

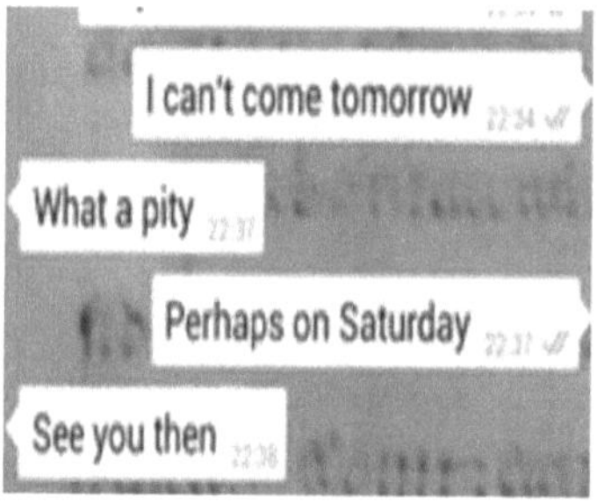

Conversation B

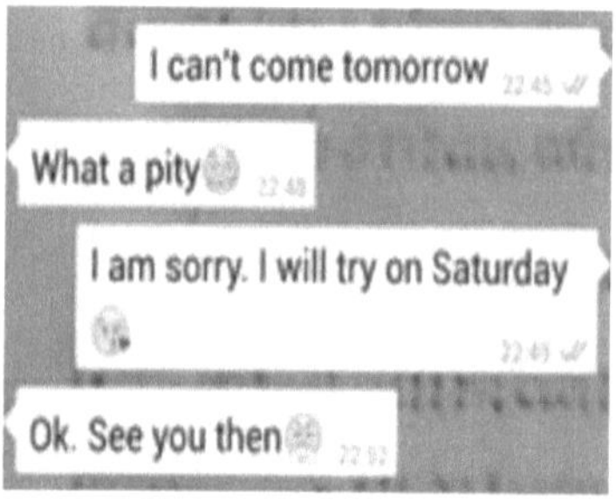

15. Explain the difference between both answers to the question:
    Do you know about Susan's new job?

    Answer A: /No.
    Answer B: \No.

16. Spanish is described as a syllable-timed language, whereas English is stress-timed, as we have seen in Chapter 6. This can make it difficult for Spanish speakers to sound natural in English, and vice versa. Pronounce the following sentences with Spanish syllable-timing first, and then with the correct English stress-timing pronunciation.
    1. Tropical storms have been migrating northwards, a paper in Nature says.
    2. The Facebook Translation Department will make Bolivian a language option.
    3. More than 500 museums, galleries and historic spaces across France are keeping their doors open.
    4. In September 2012 a man in his forties was found dead in Shetland Avenue a suburban street in West Nottingham.

Chapter 7

7 Predicting Pronunciation from Spelling (and Vice Versa)

7.1 Introduction

The main aim in this chapter is to help SSLE to increase the probability of correctly guessing the pronunciation of words that they read but are not familiar with. The problem is not, as some people say, that there are no rules relating spelling with pronunciation, but rather that there are very many of them, as well as very many exceptions, and also that surprisingly few people seem to know or understand the rules. This applies not only to **speech-to-text** rules (regarding how to spell, which will also be briefly dealt with at the end of the present chapter), but to **text-to-speech** ones as well (how to pronounce). The more rules one knows, and the better one understands and applies them, the more words one will find to have a pronunciation that is predictable. And it is of course important to avoid applying the text-to-speech rules that apply to Spanish but not to English. For example, the spelling <au> almost never represents the sound /aʊ/, and <c> never represents /θ/.

It is perhaps especially in the case of vowels that text-to-speech is complicated. For this reason, we will begin with a description of how the vowel-spelling system works (Section 7.2) and this will be followed by the spelling-to-sound correspondences of consonants (Section 7.3). In particular, we will see how it seems less chaotic if one relates it to syllable division (the syllabic structure of words). We will deal with stressed vowels first, and leave unstressed ones until later. But firstly, brief comment is needed about the way vowels are classified. If we are studying speech sounds in isolation, a classification should be based on phonetic criteria, but if we want to understand how the orthography functions, and to know the spelling patterns that apply to different groups of sounds, then a classification should be in terms of such groups. The chapter closes with a summary of the sound-to-spelling correspondences of English sounds (Section 7.4) because they have already been described and exemplified in more detail in Chapters 3 and 4, in the **Spelling** subsection of each sound entry.

7.2 Spelling-to-sound correspondences of vowels

This section describes the spelling-to-sound correspondences of stressed (Section 7.2.1) and unstressed (Section 7.2.2) vowels. This is followed by a discussion of silent V letters (Section 7.2.3).

7.2.1 Stressed vowels

The spelling-to-sound correspondences of stressed vowels are described in this section considering seven parameters: (1) syllable division (Section 7.2.1.1), (2) the contrast between "heavy" and "r-tense" vowels (Section 7.2.1.2), (3) vowels following /w/ (Section 7.2.1.3), (4) occurrence of lax instead of tense vowels (Section 7.2.1.4), (5) occurrence of tense instead of lax vowels (Section 7.2.1.5), (6) the contrast between lax and "heavy" vowels (Section 7.2.1.6), and (7) occurrence in digraphs (Section 7.2.1.7).

7.2.1.1 Syllable division

As already explained in Section 1.3.3, both in spelling and in pronunciation, a syllable ending in a consonant (C) is described as **closed**, and a syllable ending in a vowel (V) is described as **open**. Let us consider for the moment that, as a basic rule, the V in a closed syllable is a **lax** one (/æ e ɪ ɒ ʌ ʊ/), as in the word *plan*, while the V in an open syllable is a **tense** one (/eɪ iː aɪ əu juː uː/), as in *no*, as illustrated in Table 49. All lax Vs are short, pure ones, except that /æ/ is long in some words if followed by certain voiced Cs. All tense Vs are long pure ones, or else diphthongs.

Table 49: Vowels in closed and open syllables

Example	Type of syllable: open / closed	Type of V	Pronunciation
plan	closed	lax	/plæn/
no	open	tense	/nəu/

Now, *plane* is **pronounced** as one syllable (as final <e> is almost never pronounced), but **orthographically** the word is to be considered as consisting of two syllables and as having the syllabic structure <pla.ne>. So, although the spoken word is /pleɪn/, which is a closed syllable, the first **written** syllable (spelt <pla>) is open, and it is this detail of the spelling that tells us that the V is tense and that the word is therefore /pleɪn/, as shown in Table 50. In fact, this is of course one of the main functions (although not the only one) of final mute <e>, and one might say that the orthography, curiously, seems to obey the principle of syllable division more consistently than the phonology does.

Table 50: Orthographic syllable division

Example	Orthographic syllable division	1st syllable: open/closed	Type of V	Pronunciation
plane	pla.ne	open	tense	/pleɪn/

The above assumes that a C is to be considered as part of the same syllable as a following V letter (if there is one), whether a spoken counterpart of the second written V is pronounced or not. It should also be made clear that if there are two or more C letters, then as many of these that can begin a word begin a syllable. For example, many words begin with <st>, so *waste* has the structure <wa.ste>, which indicates the pronunciation /weɪst/.

Silent <e> is not the only V letter that shows that a previous one very probably represents a tense V sound, as shown in Table 51:

Table 51: Tense vowels in non-final syllables

Example	Orthographic syllable division	1st syllable: open/closed	Type of V	Pronunciation
planing	pla.ning	open	tense	/ˈpleɪnɪŋ/
wasting	wa.sting	open	tense	/ˈweɪstɪŋ/
pastry	pa.stry	open	tense	/ˈpeɪstrɪ/

On the other hand, no word or syllable ever begins (neither in spelling nor in pronunciation) with <nd>, which is only one of various C clusters that do not begin a word or syllable, nor with a **double C**, which is usually one C written twice (<dd>), as well as a few other letter combinations (<ck>). So in both cases the syllable boundary "splits" the C cluster, leaving the earlier syllable closed, which implies a lax V, as displayed in Table 52, therein lies the difference between such words as *backing* = bac.king /ˈbækɪŋ/ and *baking* = ba.king /ˈbeikɪŋ/.

Table 52: Lax vowels in non-final syllables

Example	Orthographic syllable division	1st syllable: open/closed	Type of V	Pronunciation
bandit	ban.dit	closed	lax	/ˈbændɪt/
planning	plan.ning	closed	lax	/ˈplænɪŋ/

7.2.1.2 The letter <r> and other V sounds: "Heavy" and "r-tense"

<ar> is the usual spelling of /ɑː/. <r> is basically a C letter, which (whether it represents a /r/ sound or not) "closes" an orthographic syllable in many words like *star*, *star.ring*, *star.red*, just as other C letters close syllables that include a lax V (*plan*, *plan.ning*, *plan.ned*). *Start*, like *pant*, is also a closed syllable, and in *star.ting*, like in *pan.ting*, the C cluster is split, again leaving the earlier syllable closed (since neither words nor syllables ever begin with <rt> or <nt>).

/ɑː/, /ɜː/ and /ɔː/ are what will be called here a **heavy** V (to avoid the ambiguous word "long"). Certain other V sounds are spelt with a V letter followed by <r>, but where the syllable is open, as in *sta.re, sta.ring, sta.red* (cf. *pla.ne, pla.ning, pla.ned*), in which case the sounds /eə ɪə ɑɪə jʊə/ will be called **r-tense**. This label reflects the fact that <r> is part of the spellings of words in which such sounds occur, although they are represented, just like tense Vs, in orthographically **open** syllables, which mark them as r-tense instead of heavy. The above examples of words with heavy and r-tense Vs are presented again in the following table:

Table 53: Heavy and r-tense vowels

Example	Orthographic syllable division	1st syllable: open/closed	Type of V	Pronunciation
star	star.	closed	heavy	/stɑː/
starring	star.ring	closed	heavy	/ˈstɑːrɪŋ/
start	start.	closed	heavy	/stɑːt/
starting	star.ting	closed	heavy	/ˈstɑːtɪŋ/
stare	sta.re	open	r-tense	/steə/
staring	sta.ring	open	r-tense	/ˈsteərɪŋ/

So, in short, <a> usually represents /æ/ or /eɪ/ depending on whether the orthographic syllable is closed or open, while <ar> usually represents /ɑː/ or /eə/, again depending on the type of orthographic syllable. The pattern is similar with the other Vs, as is reflected in Table 54, where the following variations should be clarified:

(1) Variations regarding sounds in the <o> column:

a. Before **dark l** [ɫ] (but in no other cases), the tense V [əu] (spelt <o>) is replaced by [ɒʊ] (the diphthong in Galician words like *cousa* 'thing'), as in *cold, pole,* if it is not followed by a V sound in the same morpheme. So it can be said that the <o> spelling of *hole* and *hope* have different pronunciations that are different allophonic realizations ([ɒʊ] [əu]) of the same phoneme /əu/.

b. The letter sequences <aul>, <awl> and <al> represent [ɔːl]. However, in the latter case, <al> tends to represent [ɔːl], if <l> is not followed by a V, in words that are Germanic and/or monosyllabic; but it represents approximately [æ] or [aː], if it is followed by [ɫ], in a few non-Germanic words such as *banal, canal, algebra,* and just syllabic /l̩/, when <al> is word-final and unstressed as in *final.*

c. Note that the words *for, fort* (with "heavy" spellings) and *fore, story* (with "r-tense" spellings) all have the same [ɔ:] sound. Presumably, previously different sounds have merged, in most idiolects.

(2) Variations regarding the <u> column:

a. There are two lax sounds often spelt with <u>: over twenty roots (i.e. excluding derivatives) have the V sound /ʊ/, and over fifty have /ʌ/.

b. Over fifty of <o> spellings are pronounced /ʌ/.

c. There are also two tense sounds spelt with <u>: /ju:/ and /u:/. But /ju:/ does not occur after /r/, nor after /C l / (i.e. l preceded by another C).

Table 54: Vowels of the four groups

Type of orthographic syllable	Type of V sound	Spellings with vowel letters				
		<a>	<e>	<i> / <y>	<o>	<u>
closed (not by <r>)	lax	æ plan planning	e pet petty	ɪ pin pinned	ɒ hop hopping	ʌ or ʊ cut put cutter putting
open	tense	eɪ plane planing	i: Pete Peter	aɪ pine try final fined	əu (or [ɒʊ]) hope hole	ju: or u: cute rude
closed by <r>	heavy	ɑ: star start starry tarry	3: her referring	3: stir stirred	ɔ: for fort boring	3: fur furry
open, but <r> follows V letter	r-tense	eə stare staring	ɪə revere adherent	aɪə tire tyre spiral tired	fore story	jʊə pure fury

AI 7.1 Pronunciation of the letter <a>

The above observations and tables may be said to represent the primary or most basic text-to-speech rules for vowels. Of course, how to pronounce words that we read is not always so simple, as there are various types of "departures" from the above (or exceptions to them), as indicated below. But in many cases, exceptions to a rule have something in common which is the basis of a secondary rule or "sub-rule". In other cases deviation is arbitrary and not predictable by rule.

7.2.1.3 Different V sounds after /w/

Although the lax Vs spelt <a> and <o> are usually /æ/ and /ɒ/ respectively and the heavy Vs spelt <ar> and <or> are usually /ɑː/ and /ɔː/, they are different after /w/, in <w> (*world*) and <qu> (*quarter*) spellings.

Table 55: Sounds after RP /w/

Spelling	Pronunciation	Examples	Exceptions
a	ɒ	wand, wander, what, quantity, warrior	*/æ/ before a velar:* wax, wag(gon), swang
o	ʌ	won, wonder, worry (*also* one wʌn/)	wobble
ar	ɔː	war, warm, quarter	
or	ɜː	work	(s)wore, (s)worn.

7.2.1.4 Lax instead of tense

The following lists a number of cases in which a lax V is pronounced where the spelling suggests tense V (see also § 7.2.3):

(1) The word *natural*, derived from *nature* (with /eɪ/), has lax /æ/ instead of /eɪ/, even though the <t> is not doubled. This violation of the syllable division principle is due to **trisyllabic laxing** (i.e. laxing of a tense V in the antepenultimate syllable of suffixed words), a pronunciation change which occurred after spellings were established. Other word-pairs like *nature* – *natural* include: *serene* – *serenity, fable* – *fabulous, Bible* – *biblical.*

The same phenomenon has occurred in many penultimate syllables, especially where -*ic* has been added to a monosyllable, as in *cone* – *conic* (also in numerous words spelt with a digraph, e.g. *please* – *pleasant*), as well as in some monosyllabic derived words, especially the past forms of several irregular verbs (*dream* – *dreamt*). In such cases one might call the phenomenon **disyllabic laxing** and **monosyllabic laxing** respectively (see § 7.2.7 for a discussion of other examples of laxing). Note that in words ending in <ic>, the penultimate syllable is nearly always stressed and includes a lax V even if the word is mono-morphemic (*comic*), or is a derivative but from a word without any tense V (*atomic*).

(2) Other written words wrongly suggest tense Vs because of **graphotactic constraints**, i.e. spelling "rules" that serve no purpose and simply mislead readers. The letter <v> and certain others are virtually never doubled, so for example /lɪvɪŋ/ is misleadingly spelt <living> instead of *<livving>.

(3) C letters are almost never doubled after a V digraph, but single as in *looking* (<loocking> would be a less ambiguous spelling.) A few exceptions are foreign words that have kept their original spellings, e.g. *chauffeur* (cf. Spanish *chofer*).

(4) Doubling is also missing in some words with irregular V spellings, e.g. *coming*, *money*. But notice, however, that the <rr> in *worry*, as well as the /ʌ/ sound spelt <o> can be considered regular after <w>.

7.2.1.5 Tense instead of lax

In the following cases a tense V is pronounced where the spelling suggests lax V:

(1) The spellings of words like *find* seem, at least at first sight, to wrongly imply a lax V in so far as only one V letter is written. On the other hand, addition of final <e> (like in *plane*) would not make the word conform to spelling rules either, since the syllable division would be <fin . de> which implies a lax V like in the word *bandit*. By contrast, a few word-spellings like *most* and *post*, which end in C clusters that can be initial, would indeed be less misleading with <e> added (cf. *waste* with the syllable division *wa . ste*). On the other hand, it seems that all the common English words spelt with final <-ind> are pronounced with /aɪ/ (except *wind* when meaning 'moving air'), so the learning effort is negligible.

(2) Note also that word-final <-es> is pronounced /iːz/ instead of /ɪz/ when it is the plural ending of Latin words ending in <is> (*crisis*, *crises*).

(3) It was mentioned above that <v> is virtually never doubled. To add to the confusion, it is never word-final either, so /lɪv/ is spelt <live> instead of *<liv>. One cannot therefore guess purely from spellings whether the V before a <v> is lax, as in *have* and *giving*, or tense, as in *save* and *arriving*.

7.2.1.6 Lax vs. heavy

Although <r> is used to spell heavy and r-tense Vs, it is also of course used to spell the C sound /r/, which can follow a lax V. How can one know that in *preferring* the penultimate V is /ɜː/ but in *herring* it is /e/? Quite simply, *preferring* is the gerund of *prefer*, in which <er> clearly represents /ɜː/ since no words end in /er/ in RP (SSBE), and addition of an ending such as *-ing* does not change the V sound in the root. However, there is no verb *her*, and *herring* is in fact a mono-morphemic noun and the V is lax. *Tarry* as an adjective derived from *tar* is /tɑːrɪ/ but as a mono-morphemic verb is /tærɪ/ (cf. also *fur # ry hurry* ⊣).[109] Accordingly, the relevant part of Table 54 could be extended as follows:

Table 56: Vowels of the four groups (extended)

closed by <r>	**heavy or**	ɑː star.ry tar.ry	ɜː prefer.ring	ɜː stir.red	ɔː bo.ring	ɜː fur.ry
	lax	æ ⊢marry⊣ ⊢tarry⊣	e ⊢herring⊣	ɪ ⊢mirror⊣	ɒ ⊢horrid⊣	ʌ ⊢hurry⊣

7.2.1.7 Digraphs

Vs are usually tense, whether the syllable is open or closed, if a V digraph (two consecutive V letters) is written. For example, <ai> represents /eɪ/ as in *rain*, and <oa> /əu/ as in *road*. Digraphs are in fact an alternative way of indicating that a V is tense, or r-tense as in *stair* if a digraph is followed by <r>. Although this complicates the orthography, an advantage is that homophonous words are distinguished in writing, as in *plane* – *plain* and *stare* – *stair*, thus reducing confusion for readers.

There are many exceptions to the rule that a V spelt with a digraph is tense. <ea> is usually /iː/ as in *please*, but it is often /e/. However, most examples of the latter are cases of disyllabic laxing as in *pleasant*, *breakfast*, (derivatives of *please*, *break*) or monosyllabic laxing as in *dreamt*, or else words in which <ea> is followed by <d> or <th> (*bread*, *breath*, *feather*). As a result, there exist some homographs (*lead*, *read*) much in the same way that the pronunciation of some digraph cannot be guessed, as in the case of <oo>, which may have a pronunciation with lax /ʊ/ (*soot*, *hood*) or one with tense /uː/ (*boot*, *food*).

A few other letter sequences function as V digraphs even though they do not consist of two V letters. <ew> is a frequent spelling of /juː/, <ow> of /əu/, and <igh> of /aɪ/ (*few*, *know*, *sigh*). Note that <aw> is another spelling of /ɔː/, even though this sound is not a tense one but a heavy one.[110]

There are two diphthongs that are always spelt not according to syllable division but with digraphs: /aʊ/ and /ɔɪ/. The former is spelt <ow> or <ou>, and the latter <oy> or <oi>. Regarding text-to-speech, there is a problem in that <ow> often represents /əu/ (as mentioned above), and <ou> often represents /uː/ or /ʌ/ as in *group* and *cousin*.

---

109 The symbol # here represents a boundary between morphemes, while the special brackets ⊢, ⊣ are a convenient way of indicating **no** morpheme boundary, i.e. a monomorphemic word.
110 Non-finally, <au> is usually written instead of <aw>, and so compare *pause* with *paw*.

Word-final V digraphs virtually always represent tense V sounds (assuming final stress). Their use is in general somewhat redundant, since lax Vs do not occur in stressed word-final position, so a single V letter would be understood as probably representing a tense V anyway.

To conclude this section on stressed vowels, Tables 57[111] to 59 list the main stressed sounds of each of the common digraphs (and some less common and/or longer spellings) when not followed by <r>, as opposed to the pronunciations of digraphs followed by <r> that are registered in Table 52 above.

Table 57: V letter followed by other V letter or <w>

Spellings	Pronunciation	Examples	Comment	More examples	Exceptions
ae	i: e	formulae haemorrhage	(esp if Latin pl. end)	anaemia	
ai, ay	eɪ	plain, play			/e/ said /i:/ quay
au w	ɔ: ɔ:	cause law	(not usu bf V:) (/əw/ away)		/ɑ:/ aunt, laugh
ea	i: e	meat head	freq bf <d, th>	please pleasure, feather	/ɪə/ idea, really
ee	i:	meet			
ei, ey	i:	receive, key			/i:/ or /aɪ/ (n)either /aɪ/ height, /eɪ/ weigh(t), they /e/ leisure
eu	ju:	feud(al)		pseudo-	
ew	ju: u:	dew grew	/j/ omitted af /r, ʧ/ or C+l	few, chew, blew sewer	/əu/ sew
ie	aɪ i:	lie believe	Syl. final, if only <l> letter bf <ie> non-final		/ɪ/ sieve
oa	əu	road			/ɔ:/ in (a)broad
oe	əu	toe			/u:/ in shoe
oi, oy	ɔɪ	noise, toy			

111 In this chapter the following abbreviations are used: *af* = after/following, *bf* = before/followed by, *freq* = frequently, and *usu* = usually.

Table 57: (continued)

Spellings	Pronunciation	Examples	Comment	More examples	Exceptions
oo	uː	food			/ʌ/ blood, flood /ʊ/ hood
ou	aʊ uː ʌ	noun group cousin	(see also *ough* below)	county, south soup, youth country, couple, southern, young	
ow	aʊ əu	now know		bow, brown bow, own	/ɒ/ knowledge
ue	juː uː	due rude	/j/ omitted af /r/ or C+l	true, blue, clue	
uy	aɪ	buy		guy	
ye	aɪ	rye	final	good-bye, dye	
Exceptions in foreign words not fully anglicised					
ai oi	aɪ wa	balalaika bourgeois	Russian French		
Rare digraphs					
ao	eɪ	gaol /ʤeɪl/ also spelt *jail* chaos /ˈkeɪɒs/, where <ao> represents /eɪ/ + /ɒ/			
eo	iː əu	people yeoman			

Table 58: V followed by (V)C(C)

Spell.	Pron.	Examples	Comment	More examples	Exceptions
al	ɑː	almond	bf <m> in same morpheme	balm	
igh	ɑɪ	sigh, sight			
augh	ɔː ɑːf	daughter laugh(ter)		caught draught	
ough	ɔː uː əu aʊ ʌf ɒf ʌp	ought through (al)though plough enough cough hiccough	only before <t> also spelt <hiccup>	 dough rough, tough	/ɑʊ/ drought
oul	ɒʊɫ	shoulder			/ʊ/ could

Table 59: Digraphs + <r>

Spelling	Pronunciation	Examples
air	eə	Air, airie
ear	ɪə eə ɜː ɑː	ear, year, tear (n) bear, tear (v) early, earth, pearl, search heart(y), hearth
eer	ɪə	beer, career, -eer mountaineer
ier	ɪə	pier, frontier
oar	ɔː	oar
oir	waɪə	choir (homophone of <quire>)
oor	ɔː	door
our	ɔː aʊ ɜː	four, mourn our journey, journal(ism/ist), adjourn

7.2.2 Unstressed vowels

For help with deciding which syllables are stressed and which are not, see Chapters 5 and 6. Here we shall briefly consider how to guess the correct V sound in an unstressed syllable, based on its spelling. SSLE will already realise that the **reduced** or **weak** V /ə/ is the most usual sound but not the only one.

As a general rule, the vowel sound in an unstressed syllable depends on what the sound *would* be if the syllable were stressed, and this is often indicated by the spelling, and/or by the pronunciation of a related word with a different stress pattern. E.g. the <pp> in *suppose* shows that the <u> would, if stressed, be the short vowel /ʌ/ – as it indeed is (although not fully stressed) in the word *supposition* – and the weak (unstressed) version of the short vowels /æ, ɒ, ʌ / (and often /e/) is /ə/. /ɑː ɔː ɜː/ also tend to weaken to /ə/ (cf. *confirm* vs *confirmation*). But there is a tendency for /əu juː uː/ to be shortened without being weakened to /ə/. Hence the <u> in *argue* and *argument* would probably be /juː/ if stressed (as suggested by the spelling), but if it is not stressed, then it is a shortened /ju/ sound rather than /ə/. Similarly, /huː/ (*who*) is weakened to /hu/, not /hə/.

The sound /ɪ/, apart from being one of the (stressed) lax Vs, is also another weak V which for example "replaces" /eɪ/ in the unstressed ending spelt <age>, as in *village*. It is also a very frequent alternative to schwa when the V spelling in an unstressed syllable is <e>, as in *believe*, which is pronounced either /bəli:v/ or /bɪli:v/.

7.2.3 Silent V letters

It was mentioned earlier that **word-final <e>** is nearly always **silent** (i.e. it does not itself represent a sound), except in words with no other V letter (e.g. *he* /hi:/, *the* /ðə ði:/) and in a group of words mostly from Greek (and often similar in Spanish), as in *apostrophe* /əˈpɒstrəfi/, where the V in the previous syllable is neither stressed nor tense. Elsewhere, final <e> acts as a marker indicating that:
(1) the previous V is tense (*fate* /feɪt/, *face* /feɪs/) or r-tense if the intervening C is silent <r> (*fare* /feə/);
(2) pre-final <c> represents /**s**/ instead of /k/, irrespective of whether the previous V is tense or lax (*ice* /aɪs/, *office* /ˈɒfɪs/);
(3) pre-final <g> represents /**ʤ**/ instead of /g/ (*rage* /reɪdʒ/).

Likewise, in regular past forms and some plural forms, **non-final <e>** is usually written but silent (*washed* /wɒʃt/, *clothes* /kləuðz/). However, in some cases a silent <e> is added to show that a word ending in single <s> is not being used as a plural noun (or 3rd person verb ending), as in *tense* /tens/, in which case the <s> is voiceless.

Finally, an unstressed V in the second of three syllables is very often silent, the word being pronounced as two syllables instead of three, as in *chocolate* /ˈʧɒklɪt/, *business* /ˈbɪznɪs/, *general* /ˈʤenrl̩/.

7.3 Spelling-to-sound correspondences of consonants

This sections explains the spelling-to-sound correspondences of RP consonants, taking into account the parameters of voicing (Section 7.3.1.1), as well as the effect of "silent" C letters (Section 7.3.1.2). After this, a summary of these tendencies is presented (Section 7.3.2), in addition to other pronunciation details (Section 7.3.3).

7.3.1 Voicing and "silent" C letters

7.3.1.1 Voicing

As regards voicing, special attention should be paid to the following:
(1) <c> always represents an unvoiced sound (/k/ or /s/, or very rarely /ʧ/).
(2) <x> is pronounced /ks/ (unvoiced), unless it is immediately followed by a stressed vowel sound in the same word, in which case it is voiced /gz/. (Cf. /ɪkˈspekt, ˈtæksi/ vs /ɪgˈzæm/)

(3) <s> in final <rse> is nearly always unvoiced (*course*).
(4) <s> between vowel letters is usually (but not always) voiced (*close* when verb but not when adjective).

As already noted in Chapters 4 and 5, those voiced consonants that have unvoiced counterparts (i.e. /b d ɡ v ð z ʒ ʤ/) are **not** usually completely voiced at the end of words, but only what we might call semi-voiced. So, to help our listener avoid confusion between, for example, *card* and *cart*, or *ride* and *write*, we pronounce the preceding vowel (if it is a supposedly long one) in a shorter manner than usual. In this way, there are two small differences between the words, instead of only one, the difference in length being often more audible than the difference in voicing.

AI 7.2 Pronunciation of the letter <g>

7.3.1.2 Silent C letters

Silent letters in any given word are those that do not themselves represent any sound. Besides, **graphotactic constraints**, whereby in some words a letter is written, or else omitted, for no valid purpose so that <v>, for example, is virtually never doubled but always followed by a V letter (pronounced or silent),[112] SSLE should be aware of the following points concerning silent consonants (C) in RP:

(1) For a reader, perhaps the most useful function of both silent letters and the availability of different spellings for one sound is to distinguish **homophones** from each other (*son/sun* /sʌn/, *hour/our* /ˈaʊə/, *rite/write/right/wright* /raɪt/).
(2) **Silent <r>** is the regular way of indicating that the preceding V is "heavy" (*car* /kɑː/), unless <r> is followed by silent <e>, in which case the previous V is nearly always r-tense (*care* /keə/). But remember that syllable-initial <r> or <rr> is of course not silent (*caring* /ˈkeərɪŋ/, *starring* /ˈstɑːrɪŋ/, *marrying* /ˈmærɪɪŋ/).
(3) **Initial <h>** is silent in some words, especially if a very similar word, with <h>, exists in Spanish (***h**eir* /eə/, ***h**our* /aʊə/, ***h**onour* /ˈɒnə/, ***h**onest* /ˈɒnɪst/) (see § 4.2.2.5). Otherwise, /h/ is usually pronounced (***h**air* /heə/, ***h**at* /hæt/, ***h**ead* /hed/, ***h**orrid* /ˈhɒrɪd/, ***h**armony* /ˈhɑːməni/).

112 Graphotactic constraints also affect vowels. One, for instance, requires <u> to be almost always followed by another letter, as <e> in *argue* /ˈɑːgjuː/.

(4) In certain **compound words** in which the first part (in isolation) ends in a C sound and the second begins with another one, certain letter pairs are pronounced complete (as in *timetable* /ˈtaɪmˌteɪbl̩/), while others are not, as in *grandson* /ˈgrænsʌn/, where the <s> is pronounced but the <d> is silent. Similarly the <d> before <k> in *handkerchief* /ˈhæŋkətʃɪf/ is silent. In *black-guard* /ˈblægɑːd/ <ck> is silent but <g> is pronounced.

(5) **C-doubling**: one might wish to consider one member of the doublet as pronounced and the other as silent. A double C between Vs marks the previous one as most likely lax. So, compare *planning* /ˈplænɪŋ/ with *planing* /ˈpleɪnɪŋ/, <a> is lax in the former word, but tense in the latter. On the other hand, doubling often simply reflects a Latin word, part of whose prefix (*sub*) became silent, resulting eventually in English spellings like *succumb* /səˈkʌm/, instead of *subcumb*.[113]

(6) Many words begin or end with **consonant digraphs** (or **trigraphs**) consisting of a sequence of two (or three) consecutive consonant letters, both of which presumably used to be pronounced but no longer are. Usually one letter has its usual pronunciation and the other is silent and has no practical function. Take for instance the digraph <ch> in the word *character* /kærɪktə/: it would be pronounced the same without the <h> letter (which simply reflects Greek origin). In other cases, the digraph has a pronunciation that is not the same as either letter in isolation, as in the case of <ng> (*sing* /sɪŋ/). Cases like this suggest that there are not enough single letters in the alphabet to distinguish each sound in the language.

There are also cases of a digraph that is "shared" by two very similar words, one of which is longer and with full digraph pronounced, the other being shorter and with only one digraph part pronounced. This is what occurs to the second <b> in *bomb* /bɒm/: it is silent in this word because it occurs in word-final position, but it is audible word-medially, as in the verb *bombard* /bɒmˈbɑːd/, so the connection between the words is more obvious. Similarly, the <n> of *autumn* is silent /ˈɔːtəm/, but it is pronounced in *autumnal* /ɔːˈtʌmnəl/.

In the following list, silent letters mostly in digraphs and trigraphs are grouped according to their position in the word. You will see that usually, the **first** or **last letter** of a word-initial and a word-final digraph are silent, but there also exist other possibilities:

---

113 A double consonant also indicates that the preceding syllable is probably stressed (ˈ*offered* vs. *reˈferred*). When <s> is doubled, it is nearly always /s/, while <s> can be /s/ or /z/.

AI 7.3 Silent letters

a. **Initial silent letter in word-initial two-consonant clusters:**
- <cz> *czar* /zɑː/
- <gn> *gnash* /næʃ/, *gnaw* /nɔː/, *gnome* /nəʊm/
- <kn> *knead* /niːd/, *knee* /niː/, *knell* /nel/, *knife* /naɪf/, *knit* /nɪt/, *knight* /naɪt/, *knock* /nɒk/, *knot* /nɒt/, *know* /nəʊ/, *knickers* /ˈnɪkəz/
- <pn> *pneumonia* /njuːˈməʊnɪə/, *pseudo-psyˈchology* /ˌsjuːdəʊ saɪˈkɒlədʒi/
- <wh> *who* /huː/, *whom* /huːm/, *whose* /huːz/, *whole* /həʊl/, *whore* /hɔː/
- <wr> *write* /raɪt/, *wrist* /rɪst/, *wrong* /rɒŋ/

b. **Second silent letter in word-initial two-consonant clusters:**
- <ch> *chaos* /ˈkeɪɒs/, *character* /ˈkærəktə/, *chronic* /ˈkrɒnɪk/, *echo* /ˈekəʊ/
- <gh>, <kh> *ghost* /gəʊst/, *ghastly* /ˈgɑːstli/, *khaki* /ˈkɑːki/
- <tw>, <sw> *two* /tuː/, *sword* /sɔːd/
- <wh> *what* /ˈwɒt/, *where* /weə/, *when* /wen/, *why* /waɪ/ *wharf* /wɔːf/

c. **Penultimate silent letter in syllable-final and word-final two-consonant clusters:**
- <bt> *debt* /det/, *debtor* /ˈdetə/, *doubt* /daʊt/
- <ct> *indict* /ɪnˈdaɪt/
- <gn> *align* /əˈlaɪn /, *reign* /reɪn/, *phlegm* /flem/, *diaphragm* /ˈdaɪəfræm/
- <lk>, <lf> *chalk* /tʃɔːk/, *folk* /fəʊk/, *calf* /kɑːf/
- <lm> *alm* /ɑːm/, *calm* /kɑːm/, *almond* /ˈɑːmənd /, *salmon* /ˈsæmən/
- <pt> *receipt* /rɪˈsiːt/
- <sc> *viscount* /ˈvaɪkaʊnt/
- <sl> *isle* /aɪl/, *island* /ˈaɪlənd/ *aisle* /aɪl/

d. **Last silent letter in word-final two-consonant clusters:**
- <mn> *autumn* /ˈɔːtəm/, *column* /ˈkɒləm/, *solemn* /ˈsɒləm/, *damn* /dæm/, *hymn* /hɪm/, *condemn* /kənˈdem/
- <mb> *bomb* /bɒm/, *crumb* /krʌm/, *climb* /klaɪm/, *comb* /kəʊm/, *tomb* /tuːm/

e. **Two silent letters in syllable-final and word-final two-consonant clusters:**
- <gh> *dough* /dəʊ /, *though* /ðəʊ/, *through* /θruː/, *plough* /plaʊ/, *thorough* /ˈθʌrə/, *high* /haɪ/, *daughter* /dɔːtə/

f. **Two pre-final silent letters before word-final consonants:**
- <gh> *bright* /braɪt/, *height* /haɪt/, *weight* /weɪt/, *fought* /ˈfɔːt/, *caught* /ˈkɔːt/

g. **Other distributions of silent letters:**
- <b> *subtle* /ˈsʌtl̩/
- <c> *muscle* /ˈmʌsl̩/
- <f> *twelfth* /twelfθ/

- <**g**> *champa**g**ne* /ʃæmˈpeɪn/
- <**k**> and <gh> ***k**ni**gh**t* /naɪt/
- <**l**> (and 2nd <o>) *co**lo**nel* /ˈkɜ:nl̩/
- <**p**> *cu**p**board* /ˈkʌbəd/, ***p**sa**l**m* /sɑ:m/ (and <l>)
- <**s**> *bourgeoi**s*** /ˈbʊəʒwɑ:/, *debri**s*** /ˈdeɪbri:/
- <stm>, <stl> *Chris**t**mas* /ˈkrɪsməs/, *lis**t**en* /ˈlɪsn̩/, *this**t**le* /θɪsl̩/, *cas**t**le* /ˈkɑ:sl̩/, *fas**t**en* /ˈfɑ:sn̩/
- <**t**> *balle**t*** /ˈbæleɪ/, *ricoche**t*** /ˈrɪkəʃeɪ/
- <**th**> *as**th**ma* /ˈæsmə/
- <**w**> *ans**w**er* /ˈɑ:nsə/
- <**x**> *grand pri**x*** /grænd ˈpri:/
- <**z**> *che**z*** /ˈʃe/

h. **Curiosities:**
- *ha**lf**penny* /ˈheɪpni/
- *scissors* /ˈsɪzəz/
- *corpse* /kɔ:ps/, *cor**ps*** /kɔ:/
- *cough* /kɒf/, *rough* /rʌf/, *laugh* /lɑ:f/, *laughter* /ˈlɑ:ftə/
- <ham> /əm/, *Birmin**gham*** /ˈbɜ:mɪŋəm/
- <ically> /ɪklɪ/, *magically* /ˈmædʒɪkl̩i/

7.3.2 Summary

Table 60 summarises the main text-to-speech correspondences regarding consonants.

Table 60: Consonants: Text-to-speech correspondences

Spell.	Pron.	Examples	Comment	More examples	Exceptions
b	b	but			
c	k s	cat cent	bf <a,o,u, C> bf <e,i,y>	clip icy	/ʧ/ in Italian words: cello, concerto
ch	ʧ ʃ k	chip chic chemist	French words Greek words	which, such machine chronic	
d	d	did			see below: "Regular grammatical endings"
f	f	fit			of → /ɒv/

Table 60: (continued)

Spell.	Pron.	Examples	Comment	More examples	Exceptions
g	g ʤ	get general	see 7.4.3 below: "Other details of pronunciation"	got gin	
h	h	here	after C letter in same morpheme, usu it is a part of a digraph (<ch>, <ph>, <sh>, <th>, <wh>)		
j	ʤ	jam			
k	k	kiss			
l	l ɫ	lip apple	bf V sound "dark l" if not bf V sound	old	
m	m	mum		album	
n	n ŋ	noon bank	bf velar (/k g/)		
ng	ŋ ŋg	sing anger	morpheme-medial, or in comparative adj.	singer younger	
p	p	pop			
ph	f	phone	(within morpheme: /ph/ uphill)		/p/ shepherd
qu	kw k	queen boutique	bf V sound bf /ɔ:/ or bf final <e> or /ə/	quality quarter conquer	
r	r	red	bf V		
s	s z ʃ ʒ	course phase sugar pleasure	VsV rare, but see <si>	cats dogs sure	/s/ case
sh	ʃ	fish	(within morpheme: /sh/ mishap)		
si	ʃ ʒ	mansion vision	af /n, l/ af V	emulsion evasion	

Table 60: (continued)

Spell.	Pron.	Examples	Comment	More examples	Exceptions
ss	s	mass			/z/ scissors
ssi	ʃ	passion			
t	t	at			
th	θ ð ð	thin feather then	initial or final in lex. word: unvoiced medial or final in lex. word: strongly voiced in non-lexical word: weakly voiced	bath bathe rather, with	
ti	ʃ	station	start of unstressed syll	militia	
v	v	vet			
w	w	wet	(bf V)		
wh	h w	who why	only bf <o> elsewhere	whole when, what	
x	ks ks gz	taxi expect exam	af stress bf C immediately bf stressed V		
y	j	yes	(bf V)		
z	z	zoo			

AI 7.4 Pronunciation of the sequence <ough>

7.3.3 Other details of pronunciation

SSLE should pay special attention to the following details of English pronunciation:

(1) Regular grammatical endings:

a. <-ed> = /t d ɪd/. The regular past ending spelt <ed> (simple past or past participle) is only pronounced /ɪd/ if the final sound of the infinitive is /t/ or /d/ (as in 'hated, divided'). Elsewhere it is /t/ following any unvoiced C, or /d/ following any V or voiced C.

b. Exceptions: Some words ending in <ed> are pronounced with /ɪd/ instead of /t/ or /d/ if we use them to express an adjectival rather than verbal meaning. Compare *He has* ***aged*** /eɪʤd/ with *an* ***aged*** *man* /eɪʤɪd/.

c. <-(e)s> = /s z ɪz/. The plural or third person or possessive endings, spelt <s, es, 's, s'>, are only pronounced /ɪz/ if the final sound of the basic word is /s, z, ʃ/ (as in *wishes*). Elsewhere they are /s/ following any unvoiced C, or /z/ following any V or voiced C.

d. This also applies to the contracted form of *is* or *has* (cf. <it's> vs. <he's>).

AI 7.5 Pronunciation of the *-ed* ending

(2) Concerning <g> and <gg>:

a. Initial <g> before <e, i, y> generally represents /ʤ/ if a very similar word with the letter <g> exists in Spanish (*general, geranium, gel, gin*), but elsewhere it is pronounced /g/ (*get, gimlet, give*).

b. <gg> is nearly always /g/, as in 'hugged' (but /ʤ/ in 'suggest, exaggerate')

(3) Clear [l] vs. dark [ɫ]: the /l/ phoneme is realised as [ɫ] (**dark *l***, similar to Catalan l) when not followed by a V sound in the same word. So compare *mild* and *pearl* (with dark l) and *silly* (with clear or palatal l).

7.4 Sound-to-spelling correspondences

As implied at the start of this chapter, there is no denying that the relationship between English spelling and pronunciation is very complicated, in both directions: not only how to pronounce what we read but also how to spell words whose pronunciation we know. There are various reasons for this, such as the following:

(1) the pronunciation of very many words has changed since their spellings were established;

(2) English includes many words from different languages and therefore different spelling systems; and

(3) the syllabic structure of words has special relevance, as was explained earlier in this chapter.

Understanding and remembering what we have seen so far will help us, even though in the "opposite direction" – for example while we must remember to **pronounce** the word <work> with /ɜː/ instead of with /ɔː/, we must also remember to **spell** /wɜːk/ with <or> instead of with <er>. Similarly (and more importantly because far more words are affected), we of course need to remember not only that a V followed by a double C letter is nearly always lax (i.e. short), but also (again, in the "opposite direction") that if a V is short we must usually write a double C letter after it, if another V follows. Furthermore, the existence of **homophones** complicates even more the mapping of sound-to-spelling correspondences because different word spellings are assigned to the same pronunciation.

AI 7.6 Some English homophones

It should therefore come as no surprise that the problem of how to predict the correct spellings of English words is too complex to be fully dealt with in the present volume. What follows here is a guide to only the **main** spellings of each sound, in table form, with examples and indications for choosing the most probable one according to characteristics of the words. Section 7.4.1 focuses on vowels, and Section 7.4.2 on consonants. For a more thorough and detailed description, the reader is referred to Rollings, A. G. (2004) *The Spelling Patterns of English.*

7.4.1 Vowels

Tables 61 to 65 list the most important sound to spelling correspondences that apply to stressed vowels and diphthongs. Table 61 focuses on lax vowels. Note that stressed lax Vs are never word-final. A double C marks the preceding V as lax.

Table 61: Lax vowels: Sound-to-spelling correspondences

Sound	Spelling	Word-final	Final (or only) syl.	Non-final syl.	Comments
æ	a		plan	planning	
e	e		invest	penny mended	
	ea		head	heading	no double C af. V digraph
ɪ	i		six	kitten	
	y			syntax	(syl/sym/syn-)

Table 61: (Continued)

Sound	Spelling	Word-final	Final (or only) syl.	Non-final syl.	Comments
ɒ	o		hot	hotter	
	a		wand	wander	only af <w>
ʌ	u		cut	cutter	
	o		won	worry	esp. af. <w>.
	ou		touch	cousin	no double C af. V digraph
ʊ	oo		wood	booking	no double C af. V digraph
	u		put	pushing	<sh> is never doubled

Table 62 below concentrates on tense vowels. Note that underlined letters mark the preceding V as tense. An entry in col. 2 like "a..." means that for <a> to be read as tense, a further V letter in the word is needed (as in *plane* or *planing*).

Table 62: Tense vowels: Sound-to-spelling correspondences

Sound	Spelling	Root-final	Final (or only) syl.	Non-final syl.	Comments
eɪ	a...		plane	planing	
	ai		plain	plainer	
	ay	play, plays, played			
iː	e...		phoneme	legal	
	ea	sea	meat	eaten	
	ee	see	meet		
	ei			ceiling	only af <c>
	ie			believe	not af <c>

Table 62: (continued)

Sound	Spelling	Root-final	Final (or only) syl.	Non-final syl.	Comments
aɪ	i...		fine	final	
	y	try		trying	
	ie	tie, tied, tried			
	igh	sighs	sight	sighing	
əu	o...		phoneme	vocal	
	ow	know	known		
	o	no, so		only	
juː	u...		cute		
	ew	dew			
	ue	due			
uː	u...		rude	super	
	ew	blew			
	ue	blue			
	oo		food		

Table 63: Heavy vowels: Sound-to-spelling correspondences

Sound	Spelling	Root-final	Final (or only) syl.	Non-final syl.
ɑː	ar	far	farm	army
	a		pass, calm	bf <CC>
ɜː	er	prefer	perm	hermit
	ir	fir	affirm	dirty
	ur	fur	nurse	furnish
	ear	yearn	learn	early
ɔː	or	nor	north	order
	ore	adore	adored	
	our	your	court	
	aw	law	lawn	awful
	au		cause	autumn

Table 64: R-tense vowels: Sound-to-spelling correspondences

Sound	Spelling	Root-final	Final (or only) syl.	Non-final syl.
eə	are	fare	prepare	careful
	air	fair	repair	fairy
ɪə	ere	here		hereby
	ear	fear	feared	fearing
aɪə	ire	fire	fired	fireman
	yre	tyre		tyrant
ɔː	ore	adore	adored	boring
jʊə	ure	pure		fury

Table 65: Other diphthongs: Sound-to-spelling correspondences

Sound	Spelling	Root-final	Final (or only) syl.	Non-final syl.
aʊ	ou		noun	
	ow	now	brown	
ɔɪ	oi		noise	
	oy	toy		royal

Turning to unstressed vowels, the following sound to spelling correspondences should be borne in mind, which are further illustrated in Tables 66 and 67:

(1) Although the schwa sound is spelt in many different ways, a very large number of words are very similar to Spanish ones and spelt with the same V letters (e.g. <u> in *s**u**poner* implies <u> in *s**u**ppose*).

(2) Another frequently available clue to the spelling of an unstressed syllable is the pronunciation of a similar and related but differently stressed English word. For example <u> pronounced /ʌ/ in *s**u**pposition* implies <u> pronounced /ə/ in *s**u**ppose*, and similarly <o> in *supp**o**se* implies <o> in *supp**o**sition*.

Table 66 below gives one or two examples of each of the main spellings of /ə/, in each of the five word-positions (where applicable). The same rationale is applied to Table 67, which comprises spellings of unstressed /ɪ/.

Table 66: Schwa /ə/: Sound-to-spelling correspondences

Spelling	Word-initial	After C in initial syllable	Medial syllable	Before C in final syllable	Word-final
a	a among	canal	eatable	moderate (adj.)	drama
e		believe, rely	moderate	twentieth newest	the
i			edible, funnily		
o	obey	polite	holocaust, synonym	purpose, method	
u	upon	suspect	industry	autumn	
ai				certain	
ou		courageous		famous	
ar	arrive			northward	liar, burglar
er		perhaps		concert	never, miner
ir			confirmation		
or					actor, minor
our					colour
ur		pursue			murmur
re					theatre
ure					measure
ough					thorough

Table 67: Unstresed /ɪ/: Sound to spelling correspondences

Spelling	Word-initial	After C in initial syllable	Medial syllable	Before C in final syllable	Word-final
a				village	
e	embrace	befriend	telegraph	forest, careless	the (bf V) simile
ey					money
i	imply	disturb	vanity, happiness		taxi
ie				ladies	movie
y		symphonic	polyglot, anonymous	analyst	happy

7.4.2 Consonants

To close this chapter, Table 68 offers the most important sound-to-spelling correspondences that apply to RP consonants.

Table 68: Consonants: Sound-to-spelling correspondences

Pronunciation		Spelling	Examples	Comments
p		p	pip	
	b	b	bib	
t		t ed	tact tacked	reg. past ending
	d	d ed	did rained	reg. past ending
k kw		c k qu	cot kiss queen	not bf <e, i, y> bf <e, i, y>
	g	g gu	got guitar	bf <e, i> in Romance words
f		f ph	fill philosophy	in Greek words
	v	v	van, give, gave giving, driving	never word-final, never doubled
θ		th	thin	
	ð	th	this, father	
s		s c ss	sent cent, peace press(ing)	
	z	z s	zip pens, peas, present	
ʃ		sh ssi ti	she mission station	
	ʒ	si	vision	
ʧ		ch tch	cheap watch(ed)	morpheme-final
	ʤ	j g	jet general	bf <e, i> in Romance words
m		m	ram	
n		n	ran	
ŋ		ng	rang	af lax V
l		l	led	
r		r	red	bf V
h		h	head	bf V
w		w	wed	bf V
j		y	yes	bf V

Further reading

Works focusing on spelling as well as pronunciation include the following: Vallins (1965), Venezky (1970), Williamson (1980), Carney (1994), Yule (1982) and Smith (1980 a, b). The last three concern the English spelling reform, Yule being in favour and Smith against it. This chapter draws heavily on Rollings (1998, 2004): the former focuses on so-called "marking devices", which could be broadly described as letters that are not pronounced but indicate something about a word, whereas the latter offers an in-depth exploration of the spelling patterns of English.

Readers interested in knowing more about the orthographic interlanguage of Galician-Spanish undergraduates are referred to Doval-Suárez (2004). This volume pays special attention to the exploration of spelling errors in as far as they are indicators of the learners' use of strategies. The author's main assumption is that writing processes are also ruled by a grammar, and as a consequence, that learning to spell is a hypothesis-testing process.

Exercises

1. How many syllables (spoken and written) are there, in the words spelt as follows? Transcribe each word.

can	cite	happy	enrage
haste	carrying	ringer	pasted

2. Are the first (or only) syllables, both spoken and written, open (O) or closed (C), in the following words? Transcribe each word.

tales	baking	runner	open	linking
tasty	legal	optical	stare	young

3. Are the stressed syllables lax (L) or tense (T), in the following words? Transcribe each word.

nation	national	cone	conic	mean	meant
define	definitive	reduce	reduction	go	gone
duchess	table	gratitude	breakfast	moon	pleasantly

4. Is the vowel in the first syllable of these words lax (L) or heavy (H)? Transcribe the first vowel sound under it.

her	starring	herring	story	marriage	carrot
purred	lorry	large	stirred	hurry	form

5. /ʊ/ or /ʌ/? Formulate pronunciation rules valid for 15 of the following words. One of the words does not have the vowel that we would expect. Which? Another has a more eccentric spelling/pronunciation relationship. Which, and what is eccentric about it?

bull	cut	push	sugar	curry	bullet	bus	running	uncle
custard	fully	dull	cushion	butter	pulpit	nutty	pull	

6. How many pronunciation "rules" would be needed to cover all the following words? Try to formulate them.

   born wore port work torch world sworn worst

7. What is the difference between all the shorter words and all the longer words?

ad	be	in	I	no	we	so	by	hi	to	oh	or	lo
add	bee	inn	eye	know	wee	sow	buy	high	two	owe	oar	low

8. Transcribe phonemically the following words:
   1) Concentrate on whether the stressed vowel is tense or lax.

      plan planing planning serenity comedy comic

   2) Notice the different pronunciations of the spelling <ough>.

      plough cough thorough dough ought through enough hiccough

9. Heteronyms. Write two transcriptions of each written form:

1. tear	2. wind	3. record	4. wound	5. object	6. bow
7. desert	8. blessed	9. excuse	10. lives	11. bass	12. close

10. Write the listed words below orthographically:
    1) Silent letters.

1. /ˈɒnɪst/	2. /ˈwenzdei/	3. /nɪˈmɒnk/	4. /saɪˈkɒlədʒgi/
5. /sɑːm/	6. /ˈθʌmneɪlz/	7. /ˈbɪskɪt/	8. /lɪsn̩/

    2) Homophones. Write two (or three) spellings of each spoken form.

1. /eə/	2. /pleɪn/	3. /tuː/	4. /weə/	5. /aɪl/
6. /weɪst/	7. /breɪk/	8. /meɪl/	9. /beə/	10. /nəʊ/
11. /ˈɔːltə/	12. /hɪm/	13. /baʊ/	14. /reɪn/	15. /raɪt/
16. /dɪˈzɜːt/	17. /rəu/	18. /əˈlaʊd/	19. /aʊə/	20. /njuː/

Further exercises

Passages for Phonemic Transcription

Render the following passages into broad phonemic transcription (answers may be found in the Answer Key).

Transcription Passage 1

It was a glorious morning in early June; the dew still hung heavy on each grass blade and leaf, making rainbow tapestries that defy description, as the waking sunbeams stole into the heart of each round drop and nestled there; the fresh, cool air was sweet with the breath of a thousand flowers; a beautiful bird chorus filled the earth with riotous melody as the happy-hearted songsters flitted from tree to tree saying, "Good morning," to their neighbors. Through a mass of rosy clouds in the east, the sun struggled up over the hilltop and smiled down on the sleeping village of Parker as if trying to coax the dreamers to arise and behold the beauties of the dawning day. In the barn-yards of the little farms scattered around about the town roosters were crowing, hens were clucking, cattle lowing, and horses stamping and neighing, eager for their breakfast.

Adapted from Project Gutenberg's At the Little Brown House, by Ruth Alberta Brown MacArthur (http://www.gutenberg.org/cache/epub/23785/pg23785.txt)

Transcription Passage 2

It is with the most contending feelings of pleasure, pride, and sorrow that I rise to return you thanks in the name of myself and the Royal family for the kind terms in which you, Sir Charles, have proposed our health, and for the very cordial way in which this distinguished assembly has received it. I cannot on this occasion divest my mind of the associations connected with my beloved and lamented father. His bright example cannot fail to stimulate my efforts to tread in his footsteps: and, whatever my shortcomings may be, I may at least presume to participate in the interest which he took in every institution which tended to encourage art and science in this country, but more especially in the prosperity of the Royal Academy. Adverting to my marriage, I beg you to believe how grateful I feel for, and I may be permitted to add how sincerely I appreciate, the sentiments you have expressed with reference to the Princess. I know that I am only speaking her mind in joining her thoughts to mine on this occasion. We neither of us can ever forget the manner in which our union has been celebrated throughout the nation; and I should be more than ungrateful if I did not retain the most lasting as well as most pleasing recollection of the kind expressions and reception which my attendance at your anniversary meeting has evoked this evening."

The Project Gutenberg EBook of Speeches and Addresses of H. R. H. the Prince of Wales: 1863-1888, by Edward VII (http://www.gutenberg.org/files/32848/32848-h/32848-h.htm)

Transcription Passage 3

When the lamp went out by my bed I woke up with the early birds. I sat at my open window with a fresh wreath on my loose hair. The young traveller came along the road in the rosy mist of the morning. A pearl chain was on his neck, and the sun's rays fell on his crown. He stopped before my door and asked me with an eager cry, "Where is she?" For very shame I could not say, "She is I, young traveller, she is I."

It was dusk and the lamp was not lit. I was listlessly braiding my hair. The young traveller came on his chariot in the glow of the setting sun. His horses were foaming at the mouth, and there was dust on his garment. He alighted at my door and asked in a tired voice, "Where is she?" For very shame I could not say, "She is I, weary traveller, she is I."

It is an April night. The lamp is burning in my room. The breeze of the south comes gently. The noisy parrot sleeps in its cage. My bodice is of the colour of the peacock's throat, and my mantle is green as young grass. I sit upon the floor at the window watching the deserted street. Through the dark night I keep humming, "She is I, despairing traveller, she is I."

The Project Gutenberg EBook of The Gardener, by Rabindranath Tagore (http://www.gutenberg.org/cache/epub/6686/pg6686.txt)

Transcription Passage 4

The spring returned at last, and the starry monarch reappeared, but his golden crown was gone, and he himself well-nigh unrecognisable. He was entirely red. The meadows were no longer green, the sky was no longer blue, the Chinese were no longer yellow, all had suddenly changed colour as in a transformation scene. Then, by degrees, from the red that he was he became orange. He might then have been compared to a golden apple in the sky, and so during several years he was seen to pass, and all nature with him, through a thousand magnificent or terrible tints – from orange to yellow, from yellow to green, and from green at length to indigo and pale blue. The meteorologists then recalled the fact, in the year 1883, on the second of September, the sun had appeared in Venezuela the whole day long as blue as the moon. So many colours, so many new decorations of the chameleon-like universe which dazzled the terrified eye, which revived and restored to its primitive sharpness the rejuvenated sensation of the beauties of nature, and strongly stirred the depths of men's souls by renewing the former aspect of things.

The Project Gutenberg EBook of Underground Man, by Gabriel Tarde (http://www.gutenberg.org/cache/epub/33549/pg33549.txt)

Transcription Passage 5

The public relations of civil society towards religion attracted in the eighteenth century – especially in the earlier part of it – very universal attention. Of the various questions that come under this head, there was none of such practical and immediate importance as that which was concerned with the toleration of religious differences. The Toleration Act had been carried amid general approval. There had been little enthusiasm about it, but also very little opposition. Though it fell far short of what would now be understood by tolerance, it was fully up to the level of the times. It fairly expressed what was thoroughly the case; that the spirit of intolerance had very much decreased, and that a feeling in favour of religious liberty was decidedly gaining ground. Meanwhile, in King William's reign, and still more so in that of his successor, there was a very strongly marked contention and perplexity of feeling as to what was really meant by toleration, and where its limits were to be fixed. Everybody professed to be in favour of it, so long as it was interpreted according to his own rule. The principle was granted, but there were few who had any clear idea as to the grounds upon which they granted it, and still fewer who did not think it was a principle to be carefully fenced round with limitations.

The Project Gutenberg eBook, The English Church in the Eighteenth Century, by Charles J. Abbey and John H. Overton (http://www.gutenberg.org/cache/epub/16791/pg16791.txt)

Transcription Passage 6

In my school vacations I used occasionally to visit an old sailor friend, a man of uncommon natural gifts, and that varied experience of life which does so much to supply the want of other means of education. He must have been a handsome man in his youth, and though time and hardship had done their utmost to make a ruin of his bold features, and had made it needful to braid his still jetty black locks together to cover his bald crown, his was a fine, striking head yet, to my boyish fancy. I loved to sit at his feet, and hear him tell the events of sixty years of toil and danger, suffering and well-earned joy, as he leaned with both hands upon his stout staff, his body swaying with the earnestness of his speech. His labors and perils were now ended, and in his age and infirmity he had found a quiet haven. He had built a small house by the side of the home of his childhood, and his son, who followed his father's vocation, lived under the same roof. This son and two daughters were all that remained to him of a large family.

The Project Gutenberg eBook, Autumn Leaves, by Various, Edited by Anne Wales Abbot (http://www.gutenberg.org/cache/epub/17189/pg17189.txt)

Transcription Passage 7

The young wife's letters gave no untrue expression of her state of feeling, yet there were times when the dream-like sensation which pervaded her outlook on the new surroundings disturbed her. The spell of the East was strong; the tropical life, the vivid colouring, the brown-skinned multitudes, the waving palms, all seemed to belong to a bright pageant in which she was only a passing spectator. And now, with the simple sense of duty which had marked the only daughter of the Pinkthorpe Rectory, she was asking herself whether it was right to yield so entirely to the wooing of the magic present. Even her weekly journal from home seemed to deepen the glamour; all in that dear distant home was transfigured by its glow; never had the tender affection of father and mother felt so precious, and who would have believed that the couple of schoolboy brothers would prove so much more demonstrative in their first letters than in the days when she had painted their wickets, made sails for their boats, and was their willing helper in all school preparations? And again the unexpected was on its way.

The Project Gutenberg EBook of A Bottle in the Smoke, by Milne Rae (http://www.gutenberg.org/cache/epub/40517/pg40517.txt)

Transcription Passage 8

As civilisation advances there is a continual change in the standard of human rights. In barbarous ages the right of the strongest was the only one recognised; but as mankind progressed in the arts and sciences intellect began to triumph over brute force. Change is a law of life, and the development of society a natural growth. Although to this law we owe the discoveries of unknown worlds, the inventions of machinery, swifter modes of travel, and clearer ideas as to the value of human life and thought, yet each successive change has met with the most determined opposition. Fortunately, progress is not the result of pre-arranged plans of individuals, but is born of a fortuitous combination of circumstances that compel certain results, overcoming the natural inertia of mankind. There is a certain enjoyment in habitual sluggishness; in rising each morning with the same ideas as the night before; in retiring each night with the thoughts of the morning. This inertia of mind and body has ever held the multitude in chains. Thousands have thus surrendered their most sacred rights of conscience. In all periods of human development, thinking has been punished as a crime, which is reason sufficient to account for the general passive resignation of the masses to their conditions and environments.

The Project Gutenberg eBook of History of Woman Suffrage, Volume I,
Edited by Elisabeth Cady Stanton, Susan B. Anthony, and Matilda Joslyn Gage
(http://www.gutenberg.org/cache/epub/28020/pg28020.txt)

Transcription Passage 9

I was opening my mouth to answer, when I suddenly became aware that the noises were now definitely louder. Noises faint, but not blurred any longer. Noises which weren't really noises, but were actually voices!

I grabbed Stoddard by the arm.
"Listen!" I ordered.

We stood there silently for perhaps half a minute. Yes, there wasn't any question about it now. I knew that the faint sounds were those of human voices.

"Good heavens!" Stoddard exclaimed.
"Rats, eh?" I said sarcastically.
"But, but–" Stoddard began. He was obviously bewildered.

"There's a sort of central pipe and wiring maze up here," I told him, "due to the plans we were forced to follow in building this house of yours. Those faint voices are carried through the pipes and wires for some reason of sound vibration, and hurled up here. Just tell me where you keep your radio, and we'll solve your problem."

Stoddard looked at me a minute.
"But we don't own a radio," he said quietly.

The Project Gutenberg EBook of Rats in the Belfry, by John York Cabot
(http://www.gutenberg.org/cache/epub/32900/pg32900.txt)

Transcription Passage 10

"Good day, Mr. Kingston," she responded, looking very pink and bright, and a little flurried as she returned his salutation. She had the daintiest complexion that ever adorned a youthful face, and whenever she was startled or embarrassed, however slightly, she blushed like a rose. Mr. Kingston, accustomed to appraise the charms of his female friends with an almost brutal impartiality, was unjustifiably touched and flattered by this innocent demonstration. He was really very glad he had remembered who she was before he had lost so good an opportunity for looking at and talking to her.

"I don't think it is a very fine afternoon," she remarked presently, as the gentleman seemed to find himself for once a little at a loss for a subject; and she smiled at him through her blushes, which went and came suddenly and delicately, as if they were breathed over her by the air somehow. "It has been looking grey, like rain, ever since we started; and it is rather cold, don't you think?"

"Is it? Ah! so it is. But we must expect cold weather in May. I suppose it is rather strange to you to be finding winter coming on at this season?"

"No. Why should it be strange to me?"

"I thought -I am sure somebody told me- that you were recently out from England."

The Project Gutenberg EBook of A Mere Chance, Vol. 1 of 3, by Ada Cambridge (http://www.gutenberg.org/cache/epub/38083/pg38083.txt)

Answer key

Exercises Chapters 1 to 7

Chapter 1

1. Sound in general is defined as a sequence of waves produced by an oscillation of pressure which is propagated through a solid, liquid, or gas, and is composed of frequencies within the range of hearing, which for the human ear must be between about 20 Hz to 20,000 Hz ("hertz" being 'one cycle per second'). Human beings may produce different sounds with their vocal apparatus: some are "noises" and others are "speech". A "noise" is defined as a sound which is especially not wanted, unpleasant or loud. A "speech sound", or phoneme, on the other hand, is a sound which is considered to be the smallest segmental unit of sound employed to form meaningful contrasts between utterances. Therefore, if we compare the various noises and the speech sounds that humans produce with their vocal apparatus, we soon realise that the former are not linked to any actual language, whereas the latter are. This means, for example, not only that a sneeze or a hiccough or a cry do not, in themselves, mean anything (pragmatic implications are not considered here, such as baby's cry = 'hunger or discomfort', or cough = 'I'm cold', and so on), whereas speech is meaningful, but also, it means that we can understand a sneeze, a hiccough or a cry in *any* language, whereas we will not understand the speech sounds of a language different from our own unless we have had some training.
2. Phonetics can be justified as a branch of Linguistics if we understand it as the integrated study of not only the properties of human sound (both speech and otherwise, from an articulatory, acoustic and perceptional perspective), but also as the study of the concrete realisations of those sounds in the pronunciation system of a particular language. Moreover, phoneticians also have an interest in particular realisations of languages, reflected in accents and dialects. Therefore, in a forensic examination, the fact that the phoneticians have phonological expertise is extremely important because they will be able to tackle issues pertaining dialectology (for example, /h/-dropping or the /ʊ/-/ʌ/ alternation), accent (particular intonation patterns) and phonotactic constraints (use of glottal stops), for example. Further general linguistic knowledge will prove most useful, as the researcher will be able to pinpoint other linguistic characteristics of the voice under examination, such a particular grammatical feature (for example, the absence of third-person singular –s morpheme), a lexical peculiarity (does the person use

the term "trainers" or "sneakers"?), register variations (levels of formality in the diction), sociolinguistic variables concerning age or education, for example (does the person say "frock" or "dress", or does he confuse "teach" and "learn"?). All of these linguistic features, as opposed to just the phonetic properties of sound, when analysed in combination, will provide extra support for the identification of a given voice.

3. Contrastive distribution is illustrated by changing any of the three phonemes in /pɪt/ for any others, so that different words are produced, even if they are nonsense words, the question being that meaning is altered, as in: /bɪt/ – /pæt/ – /pɪn/, in which the first, middle and final phonemes have been changed with regards to the original /pɪt/. Complementary distribution accounts for the fact that different allophones may be used in a particular phonetic context. In the case of [pʰɪt], we know that the initial /p/, for example, shows aspiration in English RP because it is a stressed syllable-initial voiceless plosive. Lack of aspiration, as in /pɪt/ would "only" result in the production of a foreign effect, as if a Spanish-speaker had pronounced it, but meaning, although arguably impaired, would not be altered.
4. When used in contrastive distribution in the sequence above, /s/ does not render a word of English – **san*. However, the fact that **san* does not actually mean anything is irrelevant; what is important is that it does *not* mean the same as any other words in the series and is therefore not eligible for replacement, whereas, for example, /pæn/, showing an unaspirated /p/ could replace [pʰæn/], as we have seen in Exercise 3.
5. What both characters have in common is that they both speak English, but their poor articulation needs training of some sort: Inspector Clouseau, who is French, requires an "accent trainer" so that he can pass off as an American; whereas Eliza Doolittle, although she is English, would like to climb the social ladder.
   1) This scene in *Pink Panther* illustrates aspects connected with the phonetics-phonology interface in their relation with accent and the foreignness effect; phonological to start with, as the coach is focusing in the achievement of the correct intonation patterns and fluency, the session proceeds to a more phonetic analysis as the different units of the sentence are broken down more and more to the level of the individual phonemes. Phonology comes into account again when the /h/ of "hamburger" is shown in contrastive distribution with /d/ in "damburger". What is at issue here, when Clouseau pronounces the whole sentence again at the end, is the fact that certain phonemes are idiosyncratic of certain languages, and their substitution, while not affecting meaning

necessarily, will reveal the fact that the speaker is not native, an aspect which is crucial for this character, "so as not to allow suspicion".

2) The film *My fair lady* is a sociolinguistic study which focuses on class and status as social parameters and the phonetics-phonology interface as a linguistic discipline. This scene focuses on phonetics, specifically on the correct articulation of the vowel sounds, which, in Eliza's case, are more similar to noises than linguistic speech; this aspect is further reinforced by her exaggerated sneeze and shouting, which are also fed into the spectrograph (see exercise 1 above for 'noise' and 'speech' sounds). The consequences of incorrect phonetic articulation are seen when Eliza meets her father and her vowels are heard again in the context of ordinary conversation. Again, her poor phonetic articulation is focused on when she produces a yelling noise while she pulls her tongue out. There is a shift from phonetics to phonology when her speech is contrasted with Dr Higgings', as he uses the kind of /aɪ/ phoneme she uses in the context of the word /seɪ/; phonological implications are further reinforced when the articulation of vowels is integrated in the context of the connected speech of English, in the well-known "the rain in Spain falls mainly in the plain". Further implications of the importance of good diction will be displayed later on in the film, when sociolinguistic variables also come into play.

6. In the pronunciation of the English sequence by a native Spanish speaker, the following features might be observed, which would reflect Peninsular Spanish diction:

(1) We have some ham sandwiches ready for tea in the garden

- Regarding vowels: the /æ/, /ʌ/ and /ɑː/ in *have, some, ham, sandwiches* and *garden* (the vowels are all equally levelled to Spanish /a/); in *tea* (the vowel would be neither short nor long).
- Regarding consonants: the /x/ in *have* and *ham*; the /r/ in *ready* and *garden*; the /t/ in *tea*.

In the pronunciation of the Spanish sequence by a native English speaker, the following features may be observed, typical of RP diction:

(2) El perro está en la jaula y no quiere comer.

- Regarding vowels: /əʊ/ in *perro* 'dog'; /aː/ in *está*; an extra long /e/ in *comer* 'to eat' (this is so given the presence of final <r>, which would not be pronounced in RP.
- Regarding consonants: The /l/ in *el* (darker than in Spanish); the /p/ and /r/ in *perro* (/p/ aspirated; /r/ as a tap); the /t/ in *está* 'is' (alveolar as opposed to dental, thus producing a clicking effect); the /h/ in *jaula* 'cage' (very aspirated); the /k/ in *quiere* 'wants' (aspirated); the /r/ at the end of *comer* would be missing.

7. three / θri:/ CCV tax /tæks/ CVCC table /ˈteɪbl̩/ CVCC
awe /ɔ:/ V checking /ˈʧekɪŋ/ CVCVC

8. /æ/ pat-pet /ɑ:/ card-cord /ɜ:/ curt-cart /ɪ/ pit-peat
/ɔ:/ port-pot /ʊ/ pull-pool /əʊ/ cold-called /eə/ pear-pearl
/t/ tin-din /g/ got-cot /v/ vat-bat /θ/ thin-this
/ʃ/ posh-podge /ʤ/ gin-chin /h/ ham-am /r/ rot-lot
/j/ yet-jet

9. initial consonant 1. /k/ 2. /s/ 3. /j/ 4. /ð/
medial consonant 5. /ʃ/ 6. /t/ 7. /ʧ/ 8. /v/
final consonant 9. /ŋ/ 10. /s/ 11. /θ/ 12. /l/
vowel 13. /ɔ:/ 14. /ʌ/ 15. /ɜ:/ 16. /ɪ/

10. /θr/: /θret θri: θrɪl θru: θraɪv θrəʊt θrəʊ/
/ʃr/: /ʃred ʃri:k ʃrɪmp ʃrʌg ʃraɪn/

11. /sk/: /skæb sketʃ skɪn skɔ: sku:l skɜ:t skʌl skeɪt skeə skaʊt skweə skwi:z/
/sl/: /slæm ˈslendə sli:p slɒb slu: slɜ:p sleɪv slaɪd sləʊ ˈsləʊgən/
/sm/: /smɑ:t smel smɪθ smɒg smɔ:l smaɪl sməʊk/
/sn/: /snæp snɪf sni:z snɒb sneɪl sneə snəʊ/
/sf/: /sfɪə/
/sp/: /spæm spɑ: ˈspeʃl̩ spend spi:k spɑ:k spɪn ˈspɪrɪt spi:d spi:tʃ spɔ:t spu:n speɪn speə spaɪs spɔɪl spəʊk/
/st/: /stæk stænd stɑ: ˈstedi stem sti:m stɪk stɪl sti:l stɒk stɒp stɔ:m stu:l ˈstju:dn̩t stɜ: ˈstʌdi steɪ staɪl stəʊn/
/skr/: /skræp skrɪpt skru: skri:m skri:n/
/spl/: /splæʃ splɪt ˈsplendɪd/
/spr/: /spræŋ spred sprɪŋ spreɪ/
/str/: /stræp stres stri:t strɪkt strɒŋ streɪndʒ straɪk/

12. /ft/: /drɑ:ft left gɪft sɒft/
/kt/: /ækt əˈfekt dɪˈpɪkt dɪˈdʌkt/
/lt/: /belt bɪlt fɔ:lt/
/ld/: /bɪld fi:ld əʊld kəʊld gəʊld təʊld tʃaɪld waɪld wɜ:ld/
/nt/: /kɑ:nt sent tent mɪnt wɒnt hʌnt seɪnt paɪnt pɔɪnt/
/nd/: /hænd send frend wɪnd pɒnd fʌnd faɪnd faʊnd saʊnd paʊnd/

13. Phonetics is a branch of linguistics that comprises the study of the sounds of human speech, or – in the case of sign languages – the equivalent aspects of sign. It is concerned with the physical properties of speech sounds or signs (phones): their physiological production, acoustic properties, auditory perception, and neurophysiological status. Phonology, on the other hand, is concerned with the abstract, grammatical characterisation of systems of sounds or signs.

Chapter 2

1. There exist three types of ingressive sounds, which are lingual or velaric ingressive (from the tongue and the velum), glottalic ingressive (from the glottis), and pulmonic ingressive (from the lungs). This kind of inhaled speech is not a common phenomenon, but it is normally associated with the Scandinavian languages, usually in discourse markers such as feedback words (*yes, no*) or cries of pain or sobbing. In English an ingressive sound may be used to express surprise, and in Portuguese it is common in interjections. If you want to listen to a sample of ingressive speech, please visit http://ingressivespeech.info.
2. Some of the most frequent are:
   - **Laryngitis** is the inflammation of the larynx and has the following symptoms: hoarseness or no voice at all, dry and sore throat, coughing, difficulty in swallowing, sensation of swelling in the larynx, actual swollen nodes in the throat, fever, difficulty in eating or breathing, and so on.
   - **Chorditis** is the inflammation of the vocal cords.
   - **Vocal fold nodules** are masses of tissue growing on the vocal folds, which reduce or obstruct their ability to create the rapid changes in air pressure needed to produce human speech. These affect adult females and children more than adult males, producing hoarse and painful speech, with frequent vocal breaks and reduced vocal range. Professionals who exercise their voice a lot (singers, teachers, etc) have to be particularly careful not to stress their vocal cords.
   - **Vocal fold cysts** are sac-like formations of fluid on the vocal folds, which can deteriorate the quality of human speech production. These may cause conditions such as **diplophonia**, where the vocal folds produce multiple tones at the same time, or **dysphonia**, which is the impairment of the quality of voice by means of hoarseness or a breathy sound.
   - **Vocal cord paresis** is the weakness of the vocal folds, with symptoms such as hoarseness, reduction in vocal volume or fatigue, pain in the throat, shortness of breath, aspiration resulting in coughing (due to the fact that food or liquids go down the trachea), and so on.
   - **Spasmodic dysphonia** is the condition whereby involuntary movements of one or more muscles of the larynx, which either slam together and stiffen, or else fall wide open, make it difficult for the vocal folds to vibrate properly and produce voice.

- **Puberphonia** is the persistence in males of the unusually high-pitched voice of adolescence, even after puberty, in the absence of any organic cause, when laryngeal growth and a consequent increase in the length of the vocal folds should have taken place, given an increase in the testosterone levels.

3. Communication disorders refer to all aspects of speech production, from cognitive aspects of communication (e.g. attention, memory, problem-solving, etc) to phonation processes (articulation, voice, fluency, etc) and other aspects of language (phonology, morphology, syntax and so on). Among the most frequent conditions that a speech therapist has to deal with in connection with the production of speech sounds are:
   - **Stuttering**, or stammering, which is the interruption of the flow of speech by involuntary repetitions of sounds, from one phoneme to a whole phrase, as well as by unusually long pauses in which the patient is unable to produce a sound (for the consequences of this condition watch the film *The King's Speech*, based on the true story of King George VI, afflicted most of his life by a stutter which robbed Britain of a commanding voice at the very moment that Hitler stood to threaten Europe).
   - **Cluttering** is characterised by a rapid speaking rate and erratic rhythm, as well as by other linguistic defects, such as poor syntax or grammar and the use of words not connected with the sentence.
   - **Muteness**, or mutism, is a complete inability to speak, even though most patients may be able to hear, either because they were born mute or have problems with those parts of the body required for speech (the throat, vocal cords, lungs, mouth, or tongue, etc.), or else they became mute later in life as a result of injury or disease, or even by a major traumatic incident in his life. Being mute is often associated with deafness as people who have been unable to hear from birth may not be able to articulate words correctly. One particular type of mutism, related to social interaction, is known as **selective mutism**, or the inability to speak in specific situations which produce anxiety, whereas they may speak fluently in more relaxed environments. Solutions for mute patients include the use of machines that make their vocal cords vibrate, allowing them to speak; also, the acquisition of sign language, using manual communication and body language to convey meaning. (for further information, please visit the site of the British Deaf Association at http://www.bda.org.uk/).

- **Apraxia of speech** may result from stroke or be developmental, and involves inconsistent production of speech sounds and rearranging of sounds in a word (*potato* may become *topato* and next *totapo*).
- **Some other speech sound disorders** involve difficulty in producing specific speech sounds (most often certain consonants, such as /s/ or /r/), and are subdivided into **articulation disorders**, characterised by difficulty in learning to produce sounds physically (also called phonetic disorders) and **phonemic disorders**, characterised by difficulty in learning the sound distinctions of a language, so that one sound may be used in place of many. However, a combination of both types is not infrequent.

4. The articulation disorders featured in these examples can be classified and explained as follows:
   - **Substitutions**

   (1) Gliding of liquids: /l/ becomes /w/: *wittle* and *wamb* instead of *little* and *lamb*; and /r/ becomes /w/ in *wosy*, *wabbit*, *wed* and *wadio* instead of *rosy*, *rabbit*, *red* and *radio*.

   (2) Velar fronting: the velar phonemes /k/ and /g/ are pronounced nearer the front of the mouth, as alveolar /t/ and /d/, respectively: *dood*, *dirl* instead of *good* and *girl*; *tar* and *toming* instead of *car* and *coming*.
   - **Omissions**

   (3) Final consonant deletion: in *coo*, *buh*, *ree*, *boo* and *poo* instead of *school*, *bus*, *read*, *book* and *spoon*. Notice that *school* and *spoon* also feature the following disorder:

   (4) Cluster reduction: two consonants reduced to one, as in *coo*, *poo* and *boken* instead of *school*, *spoon* and *broken*.

5. Speech recognition applications include:
   - **Voice User Interfaces** (VUIs), such as in voice dialling or computer software applications (so as to avoid problems connected with keyboard and mouse use). Remote controls and keypads from televisions to microwave ovens and photocopiers could also be substituted by a VUI device.
   - **Controlling a machine** by simply talking to it (e.g. answering a phone call while driving or taking a picture with your mobile phone).
   - **Domotics** (or home automation) refers to the control of domestic appliances through voice commands. These may include from centralised control of lighting to HVAC (heating, ventilation and air conditioning) appliances, for example, or from pet feeding to garden watering, offering convenience, energy efficiency and security, integrating all the different electrical devices in a house by means of a computer network

which allows remote access from the internet. This can be particularly useful for elderly and disabled persons, who might otherwise require caregivers or institutional care.

- **Training for air traffic controllers** (ATC), avoiding the need for a pseudo-pilot to engage in a voice dialog with the trainee controller.
- **Further applications** can be found in the fields of healthcare; in the military environment (high-performance fighter aircraft, helicopters, battle management); in aerospace; in automatic translation, court reporting, hands-free computing, pronunciation evaluation, video games, and so on.

For a very funny example of how voice recognition technology is still far from perfect, watch the sequence *Two Scotsmen in a lift* at http://www.youtube.com/watch?v=6twPKXNrUxY, where the difficulties of regional accents in voice-recognition systems are exploited.

6. Whereas normal human speech, or speaking quietly, is produced with enough pulmonary pressure provided by the lungs in order to create phonation in the glottis and larynx, a shout is produced when the air is passed through the vocal folds with greater force. Singing is defined as the production of musical sounds with the voice, by means of tonality and rhythm. Tonality refers to the hierarchical pitch relationships between sounds, that is, these are ordered on a frequency-related scale. Rhythm has to do with the regulated succession of strong and weak elements, including silences. In this sense, rapping or chanting, which may be defined as "rhythmic speaking", are different from normal speech in terms of rhythm, whereas they differ from singing in terms of tonality, using only one or two pitches or reciting tones.
7. Yes, they are. Phonation takes place at the larynx and glottis, whereas articulation takes place in the mouth. Because phonation and articulation are independent processes, we are able to produce phonemes (articulate) with different phonation types; this means that we are still able to articulate sounds even if we have a sore throat (hoarse voice), or in a low voice (whisper). In fact, we are able to articulate sounds with no voice at all, which may be decoded by means of lip-reading.
8. Phonetically, a consonant is realised by two articulators in the mouth coming into contact, an active one which moves towards and/or touches a passive one. Think of the articulation of any consonant sound and think about which articulators are at work. The production of a vowel sound, however, does not involve articulators moving in the mouth, except for the tongue, the height and backness of which determine that a given vowel

sound is produced. The only function of the lips is to shape the air column as it comes out of the mouth.

Phonemically, a vowel sound can function as the nucleus of a syllable, which in English and Spanish means that it can actually constitute a syllable by itself (/e/ in ***elephant*** or ***elefante***), whereas a consonant sound cannot. Think, for example, how most monosyllables used to catch someone's attention in a loud voice will be based on either open syllables (therefore, ending in a vowel sound, which can be easily prolonged in time), or else a single vowel (e.g. *eh!*).

9. The word *would* was probably chosen because of the articulatory characteristics of the vowel sound /ʊ/, which features extreme lip-rounding and protruding, as in kiss-giving, for example. The same comic effect would not have been achieved with spread or neutral lips, as in the word /laɪk/ following in that same sentence. Notice, though, that when dubbed into Spanish, the phonemes chosen for that particular moment, are /sie/ from the word 'quisiera', a translation of 'I would'. However, this is not a very fortunate choice since there is no lip-rounding or protruding in the articulation of /ie/, which should be produced with spread to neutral lips. In fact, the scene looks strange just at that point. A better translation would have been 'me gustaría', focusing on the articulation of /gus/, therefore giving a version which is much more similar to the original one, from a pragmatical point of view. (Watch the scene in Spanish at http://www.youtube.com/watch?v=7oOSvUlk2Uk).

10. In the pronunciation of the English sequence by a native Spanish speaker, the following features might be observed, which reflect Peninsular Spanish diction:

    (1) We have some ham sandwiches ready for tea in the garden

    - Levelling of vowels: the fact that Spanish only features five pure vowel sounds will affect the production of English vowels with a tendency to assimilate those that are fairly similar; thus, /ɪ/ and /iː/ will be levelled to [i] in *ready* and *tea*, and /ʌ/, /æ/ and /ɑː/ will be levelled to [a] in *some*, *ham* and *garden* (as well as *have* and *sandwiches*).
    - Regarding consonants, those that have a similar enough Spanish counterpart will exhibit the Spanish features, producing a /x/ in *have* and *ham* which will be more velar than English /h/; the Spanish /r/ is rolled in initial position and in post-vocalic and post-consonantal positions, therefore the /r/ sounds in *for* and *garden* will not only be pronounced, but rolled, rather than tapped. Also in *ready*. Spanish does not have a voiced sibilant /z/, which means that most Spaniards will substitute

this for an unvoiced /s/, making no difference, as in the plural *sandwiches*, in which the final /z/ will be pronounced the same as the initial /s/. The articulation of the Spanish /t/ and /d/ as dental, and not alveolar, will be reflected in /tiː/ and /ˈredi/. The fact that /ð/ does not exist in Spanish accounts for the pronunciation /d/ in the article *the*.

In the pronunciation of the Spanish sequence by a native English speaker, the following features might be observed, typical of RP diction:

(2) El perro está en la jaula y no quiere comer.

- English dark /l/ will be incorporated in the article *el* 'the', whereas it would be clear in Sp.
- English syllable structure will affect the pronunciation of certain vowel sounds in open syllables, which will become either diphthongs, such as /əʊ/ in *perro* 'dog' or *no*, or unusually long vowel sounds, as in /aː/ in *está* 'is' o /eː/ in *comer* 'to eat'.
- The initial /p/ in *perro* and the initial /k/ in *quiere*and *comer* will be aspirated, whereas they are not in Spanish.
- The /r/ phoneme in *perro* and *quiere* will be pronounced the same, that is, as a tap, whereas the first one should be a continuous trill and the second one a flap.
- The /t/ sound in *está* will be alveolar rather than dental, therefore producing something of a clicking effect to Spanish ears.
- The /x/ of *jaula* will be very weak, as in English *ham*.

Chapter 3

1. None of the organs conforming the three systems involved in speech production have speech as their main original function – for example, the lungs are for breathing, the vocal cords are for preventing choking, the tongue is for eating and tasting, the nose for breathing and smelling, and so on-, but they have been adapted to produce communicative sounds, as is explained in what follows.
2. The difference between /ɪ/ and /iː/, and /ʊ/ and /uː/ is not based only on length of duration – or quantity – but also on quality. And this is the reason why a different symbol, in addition to the length marks, is used.

   The quality of a vowel is determined by several articulatory features, such as tongue height, tongue backness and lip shape. The differences between /ɪ/ and /iː/, and /ʊ/ and /uː/ are summarised below (please refer to Chapters 2 and 3):

	Tongue height	Tongue backness	Lip shape	Length
/iː/	close	front	tightly-spread	tense and long
/ɪ/	near-close	near-front	slightly-spread	lax and short
/ʊ/	close-mid	back	closed liprounding	lax and short
/uː/	close	back	very closed liprounding	tense and long

3.

1. cheese	2. biscuit	3. peach	4. still
5. bitch	6. week; weak	7. jeans; genes	8. lettuce
9. leave	10. keen	11. even	12. peace; piece
13. these	14. physics	15. mist; missed	16. guilt; gilt
17. police	18. leader	19. key; quay	20. leap

4.

/ɪ/	women /ˈwɪmɪn/	wanted /ˈwɒntɪd/	village /ˈvɪlɪʤ/
	minute /ˈmɪnɪt/	rich /rɪʧ/	Sunday /ˈsʌndi/
	tip /tɪp/	private /ˈpraɪvɪt/	city /ˈsɪti/
	build /bɪld/	busy /ˈbɪzi/	pretty /ˈprɪti/
/iː/	please /pliːz/	complete /kəmˈpliːt/	reach /riːtʃ/
	tea /tiː/	piece /piːs/	meat /miːt/
	receive /rɪˈsiːv/	people /ˈpiːpl̩/	field /fiːld/
	sheet /ʃiːt/	sleep /sliːp/	key /kiː/
Odd one out:	pleasure /ˈpleʃə/		

5.

1. necklace	2. honour	3. preface
4. breakfast	5. earn; urn	6. heard; herd
7. birth; berth	8. earth	9. work
10. berry; bury	11. girl	12. weather; whether
13. word	14. red; read	15. journey
16. colour	17. mother	18. urge
19. bird	20. church	21. pearl; purl

6.

/e/:	best /best/	head /hed/	friend /frend/	many /ˈmeni/
	bury /ˈberi/	breath /breθ/	them /ðem/	dead /ded/
/ə/:	river /ˈrɪvə/	mother /ˈmʌðə/	conservation /ˌkɒnsəˈveɪʃn̩/	stomach /ˈstʌmək/
/ɜː/:	nurse /nɜːs/	turn /tɜːn/	skirt /skɜːt/	thirst /θɜːst/
	pearl /pɜːl/	work /wɜːk/	journey /ˈdʒɜːni/	search /sɜːʧ/
	worm /wɜːm/	world /wɜːld/	church /tʃɜːtʃ/	

Odd one out: afraid /əˈfreɪd/

7. 1. stuff 2. father; farther 3. apples
4. borough 5. staff 6. blood
7. bank 8. love 9. remarks
10. aren’t; aunt 11. drank 12. none; nun
13. son; sun 14. basket 15. answer
16. one; won 17. salmon 18. ant
19. drunk 20. country 21. laughs

8. /æ/ badge /bædʒ/ packet /ˈpækɪt/ bad /bæd/ man /mæn/
/ɑ:/ aunt /ɑ:nt/ hard /hɑ:d/ laugh /lɑ:f/ garden /ˈgɑ:dn̩/
bath /bɑ:θ/ past /pɑ:st/ half /hɑ:f/ father /ˈfɑ:ðə/
grass /grɑ:s/ park /pɑ:k/ glass /glɑ:s/ heart /hɑ:t/
/ʌ/ duck /dʌk/ month /mʌnθ/ hut /hʌt/ Monday /ˈmʌndeɪ/
uncle /ˈʌŋkl̩/ blood /blʌd/ love /lʌv/ country /ˈkʌntri/
Odd one out: bother /ˈbɒðə/

9. 1. port 2. coarse; course 3. swan
4. water 5. saw; sore 6. gone
7. talk 8. caught; court 9. ward
10. altar; alter 11. raw; roar 12. what; watt
13. walk 14. cost 15. salt
16. baugh; bore 17. awe, ore; or 18. because
19. poor; paw; pore; pour 20. warn; worn 21. your; yore

10. /ɒ/: doctor /ˈdɒktə/ wander /ˈwɒndə/ potter /ˈpɒtə/
salt /sɒlt/ sausage /ˈsɒsɪdʒ/ wash /wɒʃ/
because /bɪˈkɒz/ watch /wɒtʃ/ knowledge /ˈnɒlɪdʒ/
/ɔ:/: horse /hɔ:s/ law /lɔ:/ forty /ˈfɔ:ti/
porter /ˈpɔ:tə/ caught /ˈkɔ:t/ war /wɔ:/
cause /kɔ:z/ bought /ˈbɔ:t/ fault /fɔ:lt/ daughter /ˈdɔ:tə/
Odd one out: wonder /ˈwʌndə/

11. 1. pull 2. flew; ‘flue 3. root; route
4. group 5. book 6. soon
7. fruit 8. rude; rood 9. wolf
10. good 11. Luke 12. look
13. would; wood 14. foot 15. shoe
16. bush 17. juice 18. food
19. choose 20. through; threw 21. cruise; crews

12.	/ʊ/	butcher /ˈbʊtʃə/	wolf /wʊlf/	full /fʊl/	foot /fʊt/
		pull /pʊl/	put /pʊt/	cook /kʊk/	sugar /ˈʃʊgə/
		woman /ˈwʊmən/	good /gʊd/	cushion /ˈkʊʃn̩/	
	/uː/	fruit /fruːt/	June /dʒuːn/	true /truː/	rude /ruːd/
		soon /suːn/	move /muːv/	food /fuːd/	pool /puːl/
		clue /kluː/	grew /gruː/	moon /muːn/	fool /fuːl/
		Jew /dʒuː/			
	Odd one out:	butler /ˈbʌtlə/			

13.	1. rain; reign; rein	2. time; thyme	3. noise
	4. home	5. house	6. loud
	7. own	8. brown	9. throw
	10. road; rode	11. boy; buoy	12. day
	13. they	14. wait; weight	15. die; dye
	16. cry	17. fright; freight	18. coin
	19. hate	20. isle; I'll	21. eight; ate

14.	/eɪ/	break /breɪk/	favour /ˈfeɪvə/	weight /weɪt/	
		aid /eɪd/	plain /pleɪn/	say /seɪ/	
	/aɪ/	sign /saɪn/	mile /maɪl/	sky /skaɪ/	
		height /haɪt/	buy /baɪ/		
	/ɔɪ/	toy /tɔɪ/	voice /vɔɪs/	boy /bɔɪ/	point /pɔɪnt/
	/əʊ/	road /rəʊd/	toe /təʊ/	know /nəʊ/	though /ðəʊ/
	/aʊ/	plough /plaʊ/	mouse /maʊs/	town /taʊn/	
		around /əˈraʊnd/	brown /braʊn/		
	Odd one out:	said /sed/			

15.	1. dear; deer	2. bear; bare	3. poor
	4. where; wear; were	5. pear; pair	6. fair; fare
	7. sure	8. here; hear	9. beard
	10. fear	11. hair; hare	12. rare
	13. moor	14. hero	15. tour

16.	/ɪə/	real /rɪəl/	idea /aɪˈdɪə/	weird /wɪəd/	year /jɪə/
		fierce /fɪəs/	cheer /tʃɪə/	peer /pɪə/	
	/eə/	share /ʃeə/	mayor /meə/	where /weə/	
		stare /steə/	parents /ˈpeərənts/	hair /heə/	
	/ʊə/	jewel /ˈdʒuːəl/	jury /ˈdʒʊəri/	cruel /krʊəl/	
		cure /kjʊə/	sure /ʃʊə/	tour /tʊə/	
	Odd one out:	clean /kliːn/			

17.	1. friar; fryer	2. player	3. lower
	4. loyal	5. tower	6. layer
	7. flower; flour	8. royal	9. iron
	10. slower	11. drier	12. greyer

18. /aɪə/	liar /ˈlaɪə/	higher /ˈhaɪə/	fire /ˈfaɪə/
	hire /ˈhaɪə/	quiet /ˈkwaɪət/	
/eɪə/	layer /ˈleɪə/	gayer /ˈgeɪə/	
/ɔɪə/	joyous /ˈdʒɔɪəs/	soya /ˈsɔɪə/	
/əʊə/	widower /ˈwɪdəʊə/	mower /ˈməʊə/	
/aʊə/	towel /ˈtaʊəl/	sour /ˈsaʊə/	shower /ˈʃaʊə/
Odd one out:	quite /kwaɪt/		

19.
1. || ʃɪ wəz ˈprɪtɪ ˈbɪzɪ ɪn hə ˈleʒə taɪm ˈsɜːvɪŋ tiː tə ˈɪŋglɪʃ ˈtiːʧəz ||
2. || ʃɪ hæd ðə ˈləðə ˈʤækɪt kliːnd bʌt kept ðə ˈswetər ɒn ||
3. || maɪ ɑːnt ɑːskt ðə mæn huː həd pʊt ðiː ˈæpl̩z ɪn ðə ˈbɑːskɪt ən hiːˈɑːnsəd bæk ||
4. || maɪ ˈʌŋkl̩ ən maɪ ˈjʌŋgə ˈkʌzn̩ ræn pɑːst miː ||
5. || ðə mʌŋk dɪd nɒt hæv ˈeni ˈmʌni fə ðə bʌs tə ˈglɒstə ||
6. || maɪ tʌŋ æn maɪ ˈstʌmək wʊd lʌv ðət ˈhʌni ||

20. 1. not, knot 2. fought, forth 3. earn, urn 4. you, ewe, yew 5. threw, through 6. root, route 7. lose, loos 8. would, wood 9. coarse, course 10. what, watt 11. steal, steel 12. caught, court 13. colonel, kernel 14. warn, worn 15. crews, cruise

Chapter 4

1. Phonologically, syllables can be looked at taking into account the possible combinations of phonemes that are allowed in a given language. Syllabic structure differs from one language to another in terms of such parameters as how many consonants can occur in the onsets and codas of syllables, or whether vowels can occur without consonantal onsets (syllables with zero onsets), or whether both open (ending in a vowel) and closed (ending in a consonant) syllables are possible.

2.

Initial	**Medial**	**Final**	
1. /f/	fan	infer	laugh
2. /v/	van	having	save
3. /θ/	thanks	anthem	tooth
4. /ð/	those	other	bathe
5. /s/	son	ask	taps
6. /z/	zoo	cousin	tabs
7. /ʃ/	shoe	cushion	push
8. /ʒ/	genre	version	beige
9. /ʧ/	chip	matching	watch
10. /ʤ/	John	suggest	bridge
11. /h/	house	ahead	–

3.	1. garden	2. ad; add	3. begging	4. coughing	5. temper
	6. rabbit	7. sinner	8. butter	9. coffin	10. bag
	11. singer	12. what	13. mob	14. naughty	15. making
	16. sung	17. banger	18. palm	19. sink	20. gap

4.	1. brief	2. thigh	3. advice	4. version	5. soothe
	6. advise	7. pleasure	8. mother	9. easy	10. rouge
	11. zenith	12. breve	13. mashing	14. their; there	15. sherry
	16. hissing	17. method	18. behave	19. face	20. suffer

5.	1. batch	2. queen	3. ways; weighs	4. badge	5. really
	6. new; knew	7. real	8. yes	9. lorry	10. charge
	11. edge	12. etch	13. watching	14. jam	15. yawned
	16. Jane	17. quiet	18. use	19. church	20. juice

6.	1. chain	2. urge	3. ringing	4. ribbon	5. few
	6. cold	7. collar	8. jug	9. nearly	10. evening
	11. listening	12. sneeze	13. plumber	14. sang	15. thousand
	16. view	17. picture	18. husband	19. arrival	20. breathing
	21. future	22. puzzled	23. league	24. much	25. lazy
	26. struggle	27. button	28. straight	29. bacon	30. Jane

7. /t/: outhouse, time, eight
/θ/: eighth, method, both, third, three, through
/ð/: then, the, this, though, brother
Odd one out: soften /ˈsɒfn̩/

8. /n/: alone, ginger, funny, sinner, fin, danger
/ŋ/: long, finger, sink, singer anchor, angry, clingy
Odd one outs: autumn /ˈɔːtm/; hymn /hɪm/

9.

/s/	/z/	/ʃ/	/ʒ/	/ʧ/	/ʤ/
school	dessert	sugar	equation	cello	general
scene	raise	mission	vision	picture	japan
miss	beds	fashion	leisure	chore	journal
science	prison	machine	treasure	nature	gym
bets					jelly
accept					
muscle					

Odd one outs: Celtic /ˈkeltɪk/; aisle /aɪl/

10.	/ðiːz/	/fɪfθ/	/bɪˈheɪv/	/ˈsɪzəz/	/ˈfeðəz/
	/siːzn̩/	/ˈmeʒə/	/ˈlæʃɪz/	/ˈpleʒə/	/mæʃ/
	/breθ/	/luːz/	/wɪʃ/	/θɪn/	/ˈleɪzi/
	/wɪʧ/	/ˈofərɪŋ/	/lʊs/	/briːð/	/ˈəʊvə/
	/rʌʃ/	/ruːʒ/	/mæʧ/	/lɑːf/	/ʤem/

11. || ðə ˈgrɑːsi fiːldz ɑː kləʊzd tə ðə kaʊz ||
	ðə feɪs əv hə niːs lʊks ˈsætɪsfaɪd ɪn ðə ˈpɪʧə	
	zuːm ɪn ə ˈθaʊzn̩d taɪmz	
	ðə ˈfeɪməs ˈaɪrɪʃ ˈmænʃn̩ nɪə ðə ˈsteɪʃn̩ haɪdz ə ˈʃɒkɪŋ ˈtreʃə	
	ðə wɒz kənˈfjuːʒn̩ ən dɪˈvɪʒn̩ ˈɑːftə ðə ˈprestiːʒ ˈɪʃuː	
	maɪ ˈbrʌðə bɔːt aʊə ˈmʌðə ðɪs smuːð ˈleðə ˈʤækɪt	
	ʃi θæŋkt bəʊθ ˈɔːθəz wɪθ ɪnˈθjuːzɪæzəm ənd ə θɔːtfl̩ smaɪl	
	ju hæv ə ˈveri gʊd vjuː əv ðə ˈvæli ən ðə ˈrɪvə	
	ˈfəʊtəgrɑːfs əv ˈæfrɪkn̩ ˈelɪfənts fə seɪl	
	huːz bɪˈheɪvɪə ɪz ˈɒnɪst ən ˈɒnərəbl̩ ɪn ðɪs haʊshəʊld	

12. 1. martial, marshal 2. medal, meddle 3. right, rite, write, wright 4. ring, wring 5. heard, herd 6. rain, rein, reign 7. naval, navel 8. muscle, mussel 9. sheer, shear 10. raise, rays 11. some, sum 12. stationary, stationery

13. English initial plosives /p, t, k/ are aspirated, whereas Spanish ones are not. English /ɪ/ is a post-alveolar central approximant, whereas the Spanish /r/ is an alveolar trill. (Notice that the second /r/-sound in the word 'rural' in Spanish is a single alveolar flap). Finally, the English letter <v> represents the sound /v/, which is distinct from /b/. In Spanish, both letters represent the same sound, /b/.

14. The English plosives /p, t, k/ in initial position are aspirated, but they lose this aspiration when following another consonant in the same syllable, ie. they are no longer initial, as is the case in the second series. Since Spanish plosives do not have aspiration, the English plosives in the second series resemble Spanish plosives. Notice that failure to produce initial aspiration of English plosives can lead to misunderstanding, as there are many minimal pairs of the 'pear, bear' type: if the voiceless plosives are pronounced unaspirated, particularly in the case of /p/, they will sound like their voiced counterparts to an English ear.

15. Spaniards tend to pronounce a velar fricative /x/ for an English glottal /h/ sound, whereas English speakers tend to use the glottal fricative /h/ when trying to pronounce a Spanish /x/. For further details on the articulation of these two sounds, please visit the Sound Bank in the EPSS Multimedia Lab.

16. /bæt/ /væt/
/bɪə/ /vɪə/
/ˈberi/ /ˈveri/
/best/ /vest/
/bɜːbz/ /vɜːbz/
/ləʊbz/ /ləʊvz/
/rɪˈbel/ /ˈrevəl/
/drɪbl̩/ /drɪvl̩/
/kɜːb/ /kɜːv/
/dʌb/ /dʌv/

17. /seɪv/ /ʃeɪv/
/siː / /ʃiː/
/siːl/ /ʃiːl/
/siːt/ /ʃiːt/
/ˈsɪŋgl̩/ /ˈʃɪŋgl̩/
/siːn/ /ʃiːn/
/sɒk/ /ʃɒk/
/səʊ/ /ʃəʊ/
/krʌst/ /krʌʃt/
/gʌst/ /gʌʃt/
/kræs/ /kræʃ/
/dɪs/ /dɪʃ/
/gæs/ /gæʃ/
/plʌs/ /plʌʃ/
/pʊs/ /pʊʃ/

Chapter 5

1. They all lived together in a small house in the very centre of a dark pine wood. Into this place the sun never shone because the shade was too deep, and no wind ever came there either, because the boughs were too thick, so that it was the most solitary and quiet place in the world, and the Philosophers were able to hear each other thinking all day long, or making speeches to each other.[114]

---

114 The Project Gutenberg EBook of The Crock of Gold, by James Stephens. http://www.gutenberg.org/cache/epub/1605/pg1605.txt

2.

Normal length	Clipping	Lengthening	Extra length
code	steep	bed	higher
pit	coat	wool	pea
soothe	thief	big	tear
turn	search	wound	through
claim	niece	sang	car
cord	south	blob	
breath			
enough			

3. [əˈp̆ʰʲiːɫ̥] [v̥əˈʊˈk̬ʰælʲɪk] [əˈk̬ʰʷõmp̆ˡlʲɪʃ] [ˈm̥ʲɪdˡɫ̩] [ˈp̄ʰʷɔːĩnt̬ʰʲɪŋ̊]
[speːĩ n̥] [əˈk̟̬ⁿˈn̠ʷɒɫʲɪd̊ʒ] [lʲi·k̟˺t] [ˈθæ̃ŋk̬ʲju] [əˈk̟̬ˡleːĩmz̥]
[ˈk̟ʰeːəɹ əv̥] [b̥ʲɪˈɦ̟eːɪv̥] [ɪt˄ ˈt̠ʰʷʊk] [kʰəːʊ̟ld̥] [ˈaːɪðəɹ əv̥]

4. [w̥ẽn̥ ð̥ə ˈl̥ʲɪt̬ˡɫ̩ b̠ʷɔːːɪ faːʊ̃nd̥ ð̥æt ð̥ə l̥aˑɪt d̥ʲɪd̥ n̠̊ʷɒt m̠̊ʷuːv̥ h̟ʲɪ d̥ɪʷuːː ˈk̟ˡləˑusə t̠ʰʷʊ ɪt / ə̃nd̥ ət l̥ɑˑst / ĩmˈbəːʊldⁿn̩d̥ b̥aːːɪ ˌk̟ʰʲjʊəɪiˈɒs̬ɪt̬ʲi / h̟ʲɪ ˈstep˺t ɹ̥aˑɪt ˈĩnt̬ʰə ɪt ə̃n̥ faːʊ̃nd̥ ð̥æt ɪt w̥əz̥ n̠̊ʷɒt ə θʲĩŋ̊ ət ɔːɫ̥ // ð̥ɪ ˈĩnstə̃nt ð̥æt h̟ʲɪ ˈstep˺t ˈĩnt̬ʰə ð̥ə l̥aˑɪt h̟ʲɪ faːʊ̃nd̥ ɪt w̥əz̥ hʷɒt / ə̃n̥ ð̥ʲɪs səːːʊ ˈfɹaˑɪt̬ⁿn̩d̥ h̟ʲĩm̥ ð̥æt h̟ʲɪ ˈd̥ʒʌ̃mp˺t aˑʊt ɒv̥ ɪt əˈg̟ẽn̥ ə̃n̥ ɹ̥æ̃n̥ b̥ʲɪˈɦaːĩnd̥ ə tɪʲiːː // ð̥ẽn̥ h̟ʲɪ ˈd̥ʒʌ̃mp˺t ˈĩnt̬ʰə ɪt fəɹ̥ ə ˈm̥əːʊ̃mə̃nt ə̃nd̥ aˑʊt ɒv̥ ɪt əˈg̟ẽn̥ / ə̃n̥ fə ˈn̥ʲɪəli hɑˑf ə̃n̥ aʊə h̟ʲɪ pˡleːɪd̥ ə ˈspˡlẽndʲɪd̥ g̊eːĩm̥ ɒv̥ tʰʲɪp ə̃n̥ tʰʲɪg̥ ẘ̟ʲɪð̥ ð̥ə ˈsʌ̃nlaˑɪt // ət l̥ɑˑst h̟ʲɪ g̊ɪʷuːː kʰʷwaˑɪt b̥əːʊld ə̃n̥ st̠ʷʊd̥ ĩn ɪt ə̃n̥ faːʊ̃nd̥ ð̥æt ɪt d̥ʲɪd̥ n̠̊ʷɒt b̥ɜ̃ːn̥ h̟ʲĩm̥ ət ɔːɫ̥ / b̥ət h̟ʲɪ d̥ʲɪd̥ n̠̊ʷɒt l̥aˑɪk tə ɹ̥ʲɪˈmeːĩn̥ ĩn ɪt / ˈfʲɪəɹʲĩŋ̥ ð̥æt h̟ʲɪ m̥aˑɪt b̥ʲi ˈkʰʷʊk˺t //][115]

5. (1) Alveolar stop regressive place assimilation. The alveolar stops /t, d, n/ may become bilabial – i.e. there is a change in the place of articulation- when followed by a bilabial stop, /p, b, m/, and that is why it is a case of regressive assimilation. There is no change in voicing, so /t/ changes to /p/, /d/ to /b/ and /n/ to /m/, as in: *white paper, stand by, gold plate, seven pots.*

(2) Alveolar stop regressive place assimilation. The alveolar stops /t, d, n/ may become velar – i.e. there is a change in the place of articulation- when followed by a velar stop, /k, g/, and that is why it is a case of regressive assimilation. Note that /ŋ/ is not mentioned as it does not occur as syllable initial. There is no change in voicing, so /t/ changes to /k/, /d/ to /g/ and /n/ to /ŋ/, as in: *that ghost, good cook, in question, in gear.*

---

115 Same as above.

(3) Alveolar fricative regressive place approximation. The alveolar fricatives /s, z/ may become post-alveolar fricatives /ʃ, ʒ/ – i.e. there is a change in the place of articulation- when followed by a post-alveolar fricative /ʃ, ʒ/ or a palatal approximant /j/, and that is why it is a case of regressive assimilation. There is no change in voicing, as in: *nice shells*.

(4) Dental fricative regressive place approximation. The dental fricatives /θ, ð/ may become alveolar fricatives /s, z/ – i.e. there is a change in the place of articulation- when followed by a alveolar fricative /s, z/, and that is why it is a case of regressive assimilation. There is no change in voicing, as in: *bath salts*.

All the above sequences cause more effort and take longer to pronounce when produced with no assimilation; compare [waɪpˈpeɪpə] with /waɪt peɪpə/. For more details, please refer to the EPSS Multimedia Lab exercises. Unit 5. Audio exercises.

6. (1) In *stand there*: alveolar plosive elision, /d/, since /d/ is in the coda of the syllable, is preceded by another voiced consonant and is followed by a consonant other than /h/. Compare with *stand aside* or *stand here*, which exhibit no elision since /d/ is followed by a vowel and /h/, respectively. /d/ is not elided in *add one* since it is not preceded by a consonant.

(2) In *next please, postman*: alveolar plosive elision, /t/, since /t/ is in the coda of the syllable, is preceded by another consonant and is followed by a consonant other than /h/. Compare with *asked him*, which exhibits no elision since /t/ is followed by a vowel or /h/. /t/ is not elided in *but came* since it is not preceded by a consonant.

(3) /t/ is elided in *I don't know* although it is preceded by a consonant of different voicing since it is part of a negative contraction. This is also the case even if the following sound is /h/ or a vowel, as in *can't hurry* or *can't answer*.

(4) /t/ is elided in the sequence /tt/, as in *picked two*.

(5) Labio-dental fricative elision, /v/, at rapid tempo before /m/, as in *give me one* and *of mine*.

If pronounced without elision, diction sounds extra careful, almost affected. To see how these are pronounced, please refer to the Multimedia Web exercises. Unit 5. Audio exercises.

7. In these people the children were deeply interested. They used to go apart afterwards and talk about them, and would try to remember what they looked like, how they talked, and their **manner of** walking or taking snuff. **After a** time they became interested in the problems which these people

submitted to their parents and the replies **or instructions** wherewith the latter relieved them. Long training had made the children able to sit perfectly quiet, so that when the talk came to the interesting part they **were entirely** forgotten, and ideas which might otherwise have been spared their youth became the commonplaces of their conversation.[116]

All instances of linking /r/ are highlighted in bold; this means that a letter *r* is in the spelling, before a vowel sound in the following word.

8. Brother, these are[1] weighty reflections, and[2] I **do**[3] clearly perceive that[4] the[5] time has[6] come for[7] you[8] to[9] stop. I might observe, not in order to[10] combat your[11] views, but[12] merely to[13] continue an interesting conversation, that[14] there[15] are[16] still some[17] knowledges which you[18] have[19] not assimilated – **you**[20] do[21] not yet know how to[22] play the[23] tambourine, nor how to[24] be nice to[25] **your**[26] wife, nor how to[27] get up first in the[28] morning and[29] cook the[30] breakfast. Have[31] **you**[32] learned how to[33] smoke strong tobacco as I **do**[34]? or can[35] **you**[36] dance in the[37] moonlight with a woman of[38] the[39] Shee? To[40] understand the[41] theory which underlies all things is not sufficient. It has[42] occurred to[43] **me**[44], brother, that[45] wisdom may not be the[46] end of[47] everything. Goodness and[48] kindliness **are**[49], perhaps, beyond wisdom. Is it not possible that[50] the[51] ultimate end is gaiety **and**[52] music **and**[53] a dance of[54] joy? Wisdom is the[55] oldest of[56] all things. Wisdom is all head and[57] no heart. Behold, brother, you[58] are[59] being crushed under the[60] weight of[61] your[62] head. You[63] are[64] dying of[65] old age while you[66] are[67] yet a child.[117]

   Notice the following strong forms:

   (1) Auxiliaries:
   - *do* in 3: emphatic use in a positive statement; in 34: pro-form, with the lexical verb, *smoke*, elided, therefore in a stranded position.
   - *are* in 49: before a pause

   (2) Personal pronouns:
   - *you* in 20, 32 and 36: emphatic use, as in accusation, and as we shall see, as a contrast to the narrator.
   - *me* in 44: before a pause

   (3) Possessive adjective *your* line 26: the same as for *you*.

   (4) Conjunction *and* in 52 and 53: slow and meaningful enumeration, almost as if thinking aloud.

116 Same as above.
117 Same as above.

All the others are used in their weak forms, as they are not particularly emphasised nor placed in stranded positions, as follows:

(1) Auxiliary verbs:
- *have*, in its various forms, is weak when used as an auxiliary, as in 6, 19, 31, 42.
- *are*: 1, 16, 59, 64, 67.
- *can*: 35

(2) Conjunctions:
- *and*: 2, 29, 48, 57
- *that*: 4, 14, 45, 50
- *but*: 12

(3) Prepositions:
- *for*: 7
- *of*: 38, 47, 56, 61, 65

(4) Existential *there*: 15; *Some*, as the plural of *a*, in 17; Possessive adjective *your*, in 11 and 62.

(5) Note that some words have their weak form determined by the phonetic context: *the* /ðə/, in 5, 23, 28, 30, 37, 39, 41, 60, but /ðɪ/ in 46, 51, 55; *do* /dʊ/ in 21; *to* /tʊ/ in 40, but /tə/ in 9, 10, 13, 22, 24, 25, 27, 33, 43; *you* /jʊ/ in 58, 63, 66, but /jə/ in 8, 18.

Chapter 6

2. (a) Suffixes that do not affect the stress pattern: *-dom*: *king* > *ˈkingdom*; -ist: *ˈjournal* > *ˈjournalist*.

   (b) Suffixes which affect stress placement by attracting the primary stress to the syllable preceding them; this means that the original primary stress *may* be shifted to the last syllable of the stem, just before the suffix. There may also be changes in the quality of vowels: *-ative*: *ˈdemonstrate* > *deˈmonstrative*; *-ial*: *ˈevident* > *eviˈdential*; *-ic*: *ˈmagnet* > *magˈnetic*.

   (c) Suffixes which affect stress placement by attracting the primary stress to themselves, that is, the original primary stress is shifted to the actual suffix: *-atic*: *ˈidiom* > *idioˈmatic*.

3. ˈcarriage < ˈcarry advanˈtageous < adˈvantage lemoˈnade < ˈlemon ˌcinemaˈtography < ˈcinema meˈmorial < ˈmemory alcoˈholic < ˈalcohol doˈmain < dome ˈglorify < ˈglory ˈdelicacy < ˈdelicate oˈriginal < ˈorigin ˈwiden < wide dogˈmatic < ˈdogma

4. Low ˈclasses: the first element denotes positioning
   Front ˈdoor: the first element denotes positioning
   ˈOnlooker: adverb/preposition + noun combination
   London ˈBridge: the first element includes location.
   Kitchen ˈwindow: the first element denotes a part of a building.
   Fifty-ˈfour: the first element is a numeral
   St Therese ˈCathedral: name of architectonic feature
   ˈPencil sharpener: the second element indicates the performer of the action
   Christmas ˈholiday: the first element denotes time
   Lemon ˈjuice: the first element is a numeral
   Ivory ˈCoast: name of geographical feature
   ˈBlackmail: adjective + noun combination
   ˈGrandson: adjective + noun combination
   ˈGuesswork: verb + noun combination
   ˈGreenhouse: adjective + noun combination
   Downˈpour: verb with adverb as first element
5. 1. $_G$The $_L$man $_G$who $_L$came $_G$and $_L$
      asked $_G$for $_G$her $_L$sounded $_L$rather $_L$foreign.
   2. $_G$That $_L$thick $_L$book $_G$on $_G$the $_L$lower $_L$shelf $_G$is $_L$not $_L$hers.
   3. $_G$The $_L$child $_G$himself $_G$had $_L$told $_G$me $_L$before.
   4. $_G$What $_L$lovely $_L$weather $_G$but $_G$how $_L$cold $_G$it $_L$was!
   5. $_L$Who $_G$was $_G$the $_L$man $_G$that $_G$was $_L$talking $_G$to $_G$her $_L$friend $_G$before $_G$the $_L$class?
   6. $_G$She $_L$said $_G$that $_G$their $_L$car $_G$would $_L$not $_L$start $_L$again.
6. 1. ˈbring down the ˈbox / ˈbring the ˈbox down / ˈbring it ˈdown
   2. it ˈblew ˈup / it ˈthen blew ˈup / it ˈblew up ˈsuddenly
   3. ˈgive back the ˈbook / ˈgive the ˈbook back / ˈgive it ˈback
   4. ˈfill in the ˈform / ˈfill the ˈform in / ˈfill it ˈin
   5. she ˈdressed ˈup / she ˈcouldn't dress ˈup / she ˈdressed up ˈnicely
   6. he ˈgave ˈup / he ˈwon't give ˈup / he ˈgave up ˈabruptly
7.

ˈshop-window:	The ˈshop-window is dirty	vs	He looked at the shop-ˈwindow
ˈfirst floor:	A ˈfirst floor office	vs	The office is on the first ˈfloor
ˈafterlife:	An ˈafterlife experience	vs	They believe in afterˈlife time

8. 1. ˈDon't let ˈdown your ˈbrother, she said, and ˈpay him ˈback. Negative 'don't' is usually stressed; Comment phrase 'she said' is usually unstressed; the sequence 'pay him back' is an example of transitive phasal verb as in exercise 6 above.
   2. I ˈdidn't know ˈwhere you've ˈbeen! Negative 'didn't' and wh-interrogative usually stressed; verb 'to be' in final position

3. What a ˈdark room! I ˈcan't see a thing: introductory 'what' is usually unstressed; negative 'can't' is usually stressed, the word 'thing' used in a general sense is usually unstressed.
4. The ˈold blue ˈcar ˈbroke down in ˈQueen Street: 'blue' is the middle word in a series of three lexical words. The word 'street' in street names is usually unstressed.
5. He ˈoffered her some ˈcake but she ˈhates sweet things.'
6. ˈNick ˈwent to the superˈmarket.

9. 1. Put it in the **box.** Nuclear stress falls on the last stressed syllable.
   2. Put it in the **box** near it: Nuclear stress falls on the last stressed syllable.
   3. Put it **in** the box: the preposition 'in' carries the nuclear stress in order to show the contrast established between inside the box and outside it.
   4. **Go** with him!: This is the default nuclear stress, that is, in the last stressed syllable, not the final syllable necessarily.
   5. The **ac**tors appeared: it is a presentation utterance
   6. What did you **buy**? The wh-word is not adjectival, so it does not carry the nuclear stress, which falls in the default last stressed syllable
   7. **What** detergent did you buy?: the wh-word is adjectival and there is no other syllables after the verb.
   8. What detergent did you buy **yes**terday?: the utterance is now longer than in 7 above (after the main verb), therefore the nuclear stress falls in the last stressed syllable.
   9. The pictures, he said, were ex**traor**dinary
   10. The train was very **late**: this is the default nuclear stress; cf. 11
   11. The train was **ve**ry late: for added emphasis, to illustrate the fact that the delay was more than reasonable.
   12. I **saw** her: default nuclear stress, on the last stressed syllable.

10. **Ruth** only gave me one book: It was Ruth, not Mary
    Ruth **gave** me only one book: She didn't lend it to me
    Ruth gave **me** only one book: to me, not to you
    Ruth gave me **only** one book: she gave me one book and nothing else
    Ruth gave me only **one** book: not two or three
    Ruth gave me only one **book**: not a DVD

11. 1. The boy raised his fist and the teacher threatened him
    2. Carol told the actor how well he had performed and then Tom praised her.

    The two utterances are very similar in that they illustrate cases of subtle 'anaphoric' references. In 1, if the fact of raising his fist is considered to be a threat on the part of the boy, then the word *threatened* is a kind of anaphoric reference (referring back to 'raised his fist'), and would not therefore be stressed and so the nuclear stress would fall on the previous lexical word, *teacher*. On the other hand, if the fact of raising his fist is not considered a menacing sign, then the word *threatened* is not anaphoric and is therefore introducing a new concept. It therefore carries the nuclear stress in the first syllable. Similarly in 2, if Carol's telling the actor how well he had performed is considered an act of praise on her part, then it is the case that this is anaphorically referred to in the word *praised*, and therefore, once again, it is unstressed, with the nuclear stress of the utterance falling on the stressed syllable *Tom*; however, if telling someone how well he has performed is not considered an act of praise, then the word *praised* would carry the nuclear stress, as above.

12.

	Pre-head	**Onset**	**Head**	**Nucleus**	**Tail**
1.	I don't			ˈknow ||	
2.	I don't			ˈknow	her ||
3.	I don't	°know	her	ˈname ||	
4.	Who do you			ˈlive	with ||
5.	Where do you			ˈlive ||	
6.	Do you	°live	in	ˈLondon ||	

13. For example:

Pre-head	Onset	Head	Nucleus	Tail
Was it			ˈJohn ||	
Was it			ˈJohn	then ||
Do you	°like		ˈJohn ||	

14. What a \ˈpity || (= Conversation A; exclamation; default intonation; represented in messaging language with no emoticons).
   (1) What a /ˈpity || (= Conversation B; exclamation; friendly tone; encouraging more to follow; with emoticon showing concern).
   (2) Perhaps on \ˈSaturday || (= Conversation A; definitive fall; default tone)
   (3) I will try on / ˈSaturday || (= Conversation B; friendly and helpful, as indicated in the kissing emoticon, following the invitation implicit in the rising tone of the previous utterance – also indicated in the emoticon; inviting any other suggestions if Saturday is not OK, as suggested by the more extended answer, "OK. See you then", also followed by another emoticon.

15. Answer A shows a rising tone, which means that, while still a negative statement, it invites more conversation to follow; pragmatically, it is a question asking for more information while at the same time confirming the lack of knowledge. Answer B, on the other hand, shows falling intonation, which means that the negative answer is a statement, and one which is final and

definite, fulfilling the function of confirming the lack of knowledge but not inviting the first speaker to continue. This tone may be appropriate as part of an investigation session, for example, but it sounds matter-of-fact like, almost rude, in the course of everyday friendly conversation, as it implies a lack of interest.

16. A Spanish speaker is likely to pronounce each syllable equally, which will produce a 'machine-gun' effect to English ears.

Chapter 7

1. Number of syllables: (spoken, written)

can (1, 1)	cite (1, 2)	happy (2, 2)	enrage (2, 3)
/kæn/	/saɪt/	/hæpi/	/ɪnˈreɪdʒ/
Haste (1, 2)	carrying (3, 3)	ringer (2, 2)	pasted (2, 2)
/heist/	/ˈkærɪɪŋ/	/ˈrɪŋə/	/ˈpeɪstɪd/

2. Open vs. closed syllables (spoken, written)

tales (C, O)	baking (O, O)	runner (C, C)	open (O, O)	linking (C, C)
/teɪlz/	/ˈbeɪkɪŋ/	/ˈrʌnə/	/ˈɒəpn̩/	/ˈlɪŋkɪŋ/
tasty (C, O)	legal (O, O)	optical (C, C)	stare (O, O)	young (C, C)
/ˈteɪsti/	/ˈliːgl̩/	/ˈɒptɪkl̩/	/steə/	/jʌŋ/

3. Lax vs. tense vowels

T L T L T L:	/ˈneɪʃn̩/	/ˈnæʃnəl/	/kəʊn/	/ˈkɒnɪk/	/miːn/	/ment/
T L T L T L:	/dɪˈfaɪn/	/dɪˈfɪnətɪv/	/rɪˈdjuːs/	/rɪˈdʌkʃn̩/	/gəʊ/	/gɒn/
L T L L T L:	/ˈdʌtʃɪs/	/ˈteɪbl̩/	/ˈgrætɪtjuːd/	/ˈbrekfəst/	/muːn/	/ˈplezntli/

4.

H	H	L	H	L	L
/ɜː	ɑː	e	ɔː	æ	æ/
H	L	H	H	L	H
/ɜː	ɒ	ɑː	ɜː	ʌ	ɔː/

5. /ʊ/ vs. /ʌ/: pronunciation rules
   1. Before <l> or <sh>, <u> is regularly pronounced /ʊ/ as in *bull*.
   2. Elsewhere, <u> is regularly pronounced /ʌ/ as in *cut*.
   3. Exceptionally, *dull* is pronounced /dʌl/
   4. Doubly exceptional is *sugar*, in which not only <u> before <g> represents /ʊ/, but also, <s> represents /ʃ/.

This may be expressed more formulaically, and differently ordered, as follows:

1. <u> ⇒ /ʌ/ Main rule: <u> is pronounced /ʌ/ as in *cut*.
2. ʌ → ʊ /__ <l, sh> Secondary rule: /ʌ/ is replaced by /ʊ/ (i.e. <u> is pronounced /ʊ/) before <l> or <sh>, as in *bull*.
3. <u> ⇒! ʌ /__ <l> 'Listing rule': <u> represents /ʌ/, despite being followed by <l>, in 'dull' etc.
4. <u> ⇒! ʊ /__ <g> Listing rule: <u> represents /ʌ/, despite being followed by <g>, in 'sugar'.
5. <s> ⇒! ʃ Listing rule: <s> represents /ʃ/ in 'sugar'

(Note: 'Listing rules' are not truly rules, but exception lists expressed as rules.)

6. 3 'rules' for pronouncing <or>:
   1. <or> ⇒ /ɔː/ Main rule: e.g. born, port, torch.
   2. ɔː → ɜː /w__ Secondary rule: after <w> e.g. work, world, worst.
   3. <or> ⇒! ɔː /w__ Listing rule: <or> can irregularly represent /ɔː/ after <w> e.g. wore, sworn; worn, swore.

7. Short homophones
   The shorter words are "function" or "non-lexical" words (auxiliary verb, prepositions, pronouns, short adverb, conjunction, exclamation, abbreviation). "Content" or "lexical" words (nouns, non-aux verbs, adjectives, and also numbers) are always spelt with at least 3 letters. This distinction is considered by many to help fast reading.

8. 1. /plæn/, /ˈpleɪnɪŋ/, /ˈplænɪŋ/, /səˈrenətɪ/, /ˈkɒmədɪ/, /ˈkɒmɪk/
   2. /plaʊ/, /kɒf/, /ˈθʌrə/, /dəʊ/, /ɔːt/, /θruː/, /ɪˈnʌf/, /ˈhɪkʌp/

9.

1. /tɪə, teə/	2. /wɪnd, waɪnd/	3. /ˈrekɔːd, rɪˈkɔːd/	4. /wuːnd, waʊnd/
5. /ˈɒbdʒekt, əbˈdʒekt/	6. /bəu, bɑʊ/	7. /ˈdezət, dɪˈzɜːt/	8. /blest, ˈblesɪd/
9. /ɪkˈskjuːs, ɪkˈskjuːz/	10. /lɪvz, laɪvz/	11. /beɪs, bæs/	12. /kləus, kləuz/

10.

(i) Honest, Wednesday, mnemonic, psychology, psalm, thumbnails, biscuit, listen.

(ii)

1. air, heir	2. plane, plain	3. two, too, to	4. where, ware, wear
5. isle, aisle, I'll	6. waste, waist	7. break, brake	8. male, mail
9. bear, bare	10. know, no	11. altar, alter	12. him, hymn
13. bow, bough	14. rain, rein, reign	15. write, right, rite	16. desert, dessert
17. row, roe	18. aloud, allowed	19. our, hour	20. new, knew

Answer key

Further exercises: Passages for Phonemic Transcription

Transcription Passage 1

|| ɪt wəz ə glɔːrɪəs ˈmɔːnɪŋ ɪn ˈɜːlɪ dʒuːn | ðə djuː stɪl hʌŋ ˈhevi on iːtʃ grɑːs bleɪd ən liːf | ˈmeɪkɪŋ ˈreɪnbəʊ ˈtæpɪstrɪz ðət dɪˈfaɪ dəsˈkrɪpʃn̩ | əz ðə ˈweɪkɪŋ ˈsʌnbiːmz stəʊl ˈɪntə ðə hɑːt əv iːtʃ raʊnd drɒp ən ˈnesl̩d ðeə || ðə freʃ | kuːl eə wəz swiːt wɪð ðə breθ əv ə ˈθaʊzn̩d ˈflaʊəz || ə ˈbjuːtɪfl̩ bɜːd ˈkɔːrəs fɪld ðiː ɜːθ wɪð ˈraɪətəs ˈmelədi əz ðə ˈhæpi ˈhɑːtɪd ˈsɒŋstəz ˈflɪtɪd frəm triː tə triː ˈseɪɪŋ gʊd ˈmɔːnɪŋ tə ðeə ˈneɪbəz || θruː ə mæs əv ˈrəʊzi klaʊdz ɪn ðiː iːst | ðə sʌn ˈstrʌgl̩d ʌp ˈəʊvə ðə ˈhɪltɒp ən smaɪld daʊn ɒn ðə ˈsliːpɪŋ ˈvɪlɪdʒ əv ˈpɑːkər əz ɪf ˈtraɪɪŋ tə kəʊks ðə ˈdriːməz tə ə ˈraɪz ən bɪˈhəʊld ðə ˈbjuːtɪz əv ðə ˈdɔːnɪŋ deɪ || ɪn ðə ˈbɑːnjɑːdz əv ðə ˈlɪtl̩ fɑːmz ˈskætəd əˈraʊnd əˈbaʊt ðə taʊn ˈruːstəz wə ˈkraʊɪŋ | henz we ˈklʌkɪŋ | ˈkætl̩ ˈləʊɪŋ | ən ˈhɔːsɪz ˈstæmpɪŋ ən ˈneɪɪŋ | ˈiːgə fə ðeə ˈbrekfəst ||

Transcription Passage 2

|| ɪt ɪz wɪð ðə məʊst kənˈtendɪŋ ˈfiːlɪŋz əv ˈpleʒə | praɪd | ən ˈsɒrəʊ ðət aɪ raɪz tə rɪ ˈtɜːn ju θæŋks ɪn ðə neɪm əv maɪˈself ən ðə ˈrɔɪl̩ ˈfæmɪli fə ðə kaɪnd tɜːmz ɪn wɪtʃ juː | sə tʃɑːlz | həv prɒˈpəʊzd aʊə helθ | ən fə ðə ˈveri ˈkɔːdjəl weɪ ɪn wɪtʃ ðɪs dɪs ˈtɪŋgwɪʃt əˈsembli həz rɪˈsiːvd ɪt || aɪ ˈkænɒt ɒn ðɪs əˈkeiʒn̩ daɪˈvest maɪ maɪnd əv ðiː əˌsəʊsɪˈeɪʃn̩z kəˈnektɪd wɪð maɪ bɪˈlʌvɪd ən ləˈmentɪd ˈfɑːðə | hɪz braɪt ɪgˈzɑːmpl̩ ˈkænɒt feɪl tə ˈstɪmjʊleɪt maɪ ˈefəts tə tred ɪn hɪz ˈfʊtsteps | ənd | ˈwɒtevə maɪ ˈʃɔːtkʌmɪŋz meɪ biː | aɪ meɪ at liːst prɪˈzjuːm tə pɑːˈtɪsɪpeɪt ɪn ði ˈɪntrəst wɪtʃ hi tʊk ɪn ˈevri ˌɪnstɪˈtjuːʃn̩ wɪtʃ ˈtendɪd tu ɪŋˈkʌrɪdʒ ɑːt ən ˈsaɪəns ɪn ðɪs ˈkʌntri | bət mɔːr ɪˈspeʃəli ɪn ðə prɒsˈperɪti əv ðə ˈrɔɪl̩ əˈkædəmi || ədˈvɜːtɪŋ tə maɪ ˈmærɪdʒ | aɪ beg ju tə bɪˈliːv haʊ ˈgreɪtfʊl aɪ fiːl fɔː | ənd aɪ meɪ bi pəˈmɪtɪd tu æd haʊ sɪnˈsɪəli aɪ əˈpriːʃieɪt | ðə ˈsentɪmənts ju həv ɪkˈsprest wɪð ˈrefrəns tə ðə prɪnˈses || aɪ nəʊ ðət aɪ əm ˈəʊnli ˈspiːkɪŋ hə maɪnd ɪn ˈdʒɔɪnɪŋ hə θɔːts tə maɪn ɒn ðɪs əˈkeɪʒn̩ | wi ˈnaɪðər əv əs kən ˈevə fəˈget ðə ˈmænər ɪn wɪtʃ ˈaʊə ˈjuːnɪən həz biːn ˈselɪbreɪtɪd θruˈaʊt ðə ˈneɪʃn̩ | ənd aɪ ʃəd bi mɔː ðən ʌnˈgreɪtfəl ɪf aɪ dɪd nɒt rɪˈteɪn ðə məʊst ˈlɑːstɪŋ əz wel əz məʊst ˈpliːzɪŋ ˌrekəˈlekʃn̩ əv ðə kaɪnd ɪkˈspreʃn̩z ən rɪˈsepʃn̩ wɪtʃ maɪ əˈtendəns ət jər ˌænɪˈvɜːsəri ˈmiːtɪŋ həz ɪˈvəʊkt ðɪs ˈiːvnɪŋ ||

Transcription Passage 3

|| wen ðə læmp went aʊt baɪ maɪ bed aɪ wəʊk ʌp wɪð ði ˈɜːli bɜːdz || aɪ sæt ət maɪ ˈəʊpn̩ ˈwɪndəʊ wɪð ə freʃ riːθ ɒn maɪ luːs heə || ðə jʌŋ ˈtrævlə keɪm əˈlɒŋ ðə rəʊd

ɪn ðə ˈrəʊzi mɪst əv ðə ˈmɔːnɪŋ || ə pɜːl ʧeɪn wəz ɒn hɪz nek | ənd ðə sʌnz reɪz fel ɒn hɪz kraʊn || hi stɒpt bɪˈfɔː maɪ dɔːr ənd ɑːskt mi wɪð ən ˈiːgə kraɪ | weər ɪz ʃi || fə ˈveri ʃeɪm aɪ kəd nɒt seɪ | ʃi ɪz aɪ | jʌŋ ˈtrævlə | ʃi ɪz aɪ || ɪt wəz dʌsk ən ðə læmp wəz nɒt lɪt || aɪ wəz ˈlɪstləsli ˈbreɪdɪŋ maɪ heə || ðə jʌŋ ˈtrævlə keɪm ɒn hɪz ˈʧærɪət ɪn ðə gləʊ əv ðə ˈsetɪŋ sʌn || hɪz ˈhɔːsɪz wə ˈfəʊmɪŋ ət ðə maʊθ | ən ðə wəz dʌst ɒn hɪz ˈgɑːmənt || hi əˈlaɪtɪd ət maɪ dɔːr ənd ɑːskt ɪn ə ˈtaɪəd vɔɪs | weər ɪz ʃi || fə ˈveri ʃeɪm aɪ kəd nɒt seɪ | ʃi ɪz aɪ | ˈwɪəri ˈtrævlə | ʃi ɪz aɪ || ɪt ɪs ən ˈeɪprɪl naɪt || ðə læmp ɪs ˈbɜːnɪŋ ɪn maɪ ruːm || ðə briːz əv ðə saʊθ kʌmz ˈʤentli || ðə ˈnɔɪzi ˈpærət sliːps ɪn ɪts keɪʤ || maɪ ˈbɒdɪs ɪz əv ðə ˈkʌlər əv ðə ˈpiːkɒks θrəʊt | ən maɪ ˈmæntl̩ ɪz griːn əz jʌŋ grɑːs || aɪ sɪt əˈpɒn ðə flɔːr ət ðə ˈwɪndəʊ ˈwɒʧɪŋ ðə dɪˈzɜːtɪd striːt || θruː ðə dɑːk naɪt aɪ kiːp ˈhʌmɪŋ | ʃi ɪz aɪ | dɪˈspeərɪŋ ˈtrævlə | ʃi ɪz aɪ ||

Transcription Passage 4

|| ðə sprɪŋ rɪˈtɜːnd ət lɑːst | ən ðə ˈstɑːri ˈmɒnək ˌriːəˈpɪəd | bət hɪz ˈgəʊldn̩ kraʊn wəz gɒn | ən hi hɪmˈself wel naɪ ʌnˈrekəgˌnaɪzəbl̩ || hi wəz ɪnˈtaɪəli red || ðə ˈmedəʊz wə nəʊ ˈlɒŋgə griːn | ðə skaɪ wəz nəʊ ˈlɒŋgə bluː | ðə ʧaɪˈniːz wə nəʊ ˈlɒŋgə ˈjeləʊ | ɔːl həd ˈsʌdn̩li ʧeɪnʤd ˈkʌlər əz ɪn ə ˌtrænsfəˈmeɪʃn̩ siːn || ðen/ baɪ dɪˈgriːz | frəm ðə red ðət hi wəz hi bɪˈkeɪm ˈɒrɪnʤ || hi maɪt ðen həv biːn kəmˈpeəd tʊ ə ˈgəʊldən ˈæpl̩ ɪn ðə skaɪ | ən səʊ ˈdjʊərɪŋ ˈsevrəl jɪəz hi wəz siːn tə pɑːs | ənd ɔːl ˈneɪʧə wɪð ɪm | θruː ə ˈθaʊzn̩d mægˈnɪfɪsənt ɔː ˈterəbl̩ tɪnts | frəm ˈɒrɪnʤ tə ˈjeləʊ | frəm ˈjeləʊ tə griːn | ən frəm griːn ət leŋθ tə ˈɪndɪgəʊ ən peɪl bluː || ðə ˌmiːtɪəˈrɒləʤɪsts ðen rɪˈkɔːld ðə fækt | ɪn ðə jɪə ˌeɪˈtiːn ˈeɪti θriː | ɒn ðə ˈsekənd əv sepˈtembə | ðə sʌn həd əˈpɪəd ɪn ˌvenɪˈzweɪlə ðə həʊl deɪ lɒŋ əz bluː əz ðə muːn || səʊ ˈmeni ˈkʌləz | səʊ ˈmeni njuː ˌdekəˈreɪʃn̩z əv ðə kəˈmiːlɪən laɪk ˈjuːnɪvɜːs wɪʧ ˈdæzl̩d ðə ˈterɪfaɪd aɪ | wɪʧ rɪˈvaɪvd ən rɪˈstɔːd tʊ ɪts ˈprɪmɪtɪv ˈʃɑːpnəs ðə riːˈʤuːvəneɪtɪd senˈseɪʃn̩ əv ðə ˈbjuːtiz əv ˈneɪʧə | ən ˈstrɒŋli stɜːd ðə depθs əv menz səʊlz baɪ rɪˈnjuːɪŋ ðə ˈfɔːmər ˈæspekt əv θɪŋz ||

Transcription Passage 5

|| ðə ˈpʌblɪk rɪˈleɪʃn̩z əv ˈsɪvəl səˈsaɪəti təˈwɔːdz rɪˈlɪʤn̩ əˈtræktɪd ɪn ði ˌeɪˈtiːnθ ˈsenʧəri | ɪˈspeʃəli ɪn ði ˈɜːliə pɑːt əv ɪt | ˈveri ˌjuːnɪˈvɜːsl̩ əˈtenʃn̩ || əv ðə ˈveərɪəs ˈkwesʧənz ðət kʌm ˈʌndə ðɪs hed | ðə wəz nʌn əv sʌʧ ˈpræktɪkl̩ ənd ɪˈmiːdɪət ɪmˈpɔːtns əz ðət wɪʧ wəz kənˈsɜːnd wɪð ðə ˌtɒləˈreɪʃn̩ əv rɪˈlɪʤəs ˈdɪfrənsɪz || ðə ˌtɒləˈreɪʃn̩ ækt həd bɪn ˈkærɪd əˈmɪd ˈʤenrəl əˈpruːvl̩ || ðə həd bɪn ˈlɪtl̩ ɪnˈθjuːzɪæzəm əˈbaʊt ɪt | bət ˈɔːlsəʊ ˈveri ˈlɪtl̩ ˌɒpəˈzɪʃn̩ || ðəʊ ɪt fel fɑː ʃɔːt əv wɒt wʊd naʊ bi ˌʌndəˈstʊd baɪ ˈtɒlərəns | ɪt wəz ˈfʊli ʌp tə ðə ˈlevl̩ əv ðə taɪmz || ɪt ˈfeəli ɪkˈsprest wɒt wəz ˈθʌrəli ðə keɪs | ðət ðə ˈspɪrɪt əv ɪnˈtɒlərəns həd ˈveri mʌʧ dɪˈkriːst | ən ðət ə

ˈfiːlɪŋ ɪn ˈfeɪvər əv rɪˈlɪʤəs ˈlɪbəti wəz dɪˈsaɪdɪdli ˈgeɪnɪŋ graʊnd || ˈmiːnwaɪl | ɪn kɪŋ ˈwɪljəmz reɪn | ən stɪl mɔː səʊ ɪn ðæt əv hɪz səkˈsesə | ðə wəz ə ˈveri ˈstrɒŋli mɑːkt kənˈtenʃn̩ ən pəˈpleksɪti əv ˈfiːlɪŋ əz tə wɒt wəz ˈrɪəli ment baɪ ˌtɒləˈreɪʃn̩ | ən weər ɪts ˈlɪmɪts wə tə bi fɪkst || ˈevriˌbɒdi prəˈfest tə bi ɪn ˈfeɪvər əv ɪt/ səʊ lɒŋ əz ɪt wəz ɪnˈtɜːprɪtɪd əˈkɔːdɪŋ tu hɪz əʊn ruːl || ðə ˈprɪnsəpl̩ wəz ˈgrɑːntɪd/ bət ðə wə fjuː hu həd ˈeni klɪər aɪˈdɪə əz tə ðə graʊndz əˈpɒn wɪʧ ðeɪ ˈgrɑːntɪd ɪt | ən stɪl ˈfjuːə hu dɪd nɒt θɪŋk ɪt wəz ə ˈprɪnsəpl̩ tə bi ˈkeəfəli fenst raʊnd wɪð ˌlɪmɪˈteɪʃn̩z ||

Transcription Passage 6

|| ɪn maɪ skuːl vəˈkeɪʃn̩z aɪ juːzd əˈkeɪʒn̩əli tə ˈvɪzɪt ən əʊld ˈseɪlə frend | ə mæn əv ʌnˈkɒmən ˈnæʧrəl gɪfts | ən ðət ˈveərɪd ɪkˈspɪərɪəns əv laɪf wɪʧ dəz səʊ mʌʧ tə sə ˈplaɪ ðə wɒnt əv ˈʌðə miːnz əv ˌeʤʊˈkeɪʃn̩ || hi məst həv biːn ə ˈhænsəm mæn ɪn hɪz juːθ | ən ðəʊ taɪm ən ˈhɑːdʃɪp həd dʌn ðeər ˈʌtməʊst tə meɪk ə ˈruːɪn əv hɪz bəʊld ˈfiːʧəz | ən həd meɪd ɪt ˈniːdfʊl tə breɪd hɪz stɪl ˈʤeti blæk lɒks təˈgeðə tə ˈkʌvə hɪz bɔːld kraʊn | hɪz wəz ə faɪn | ˈstraɪkɪŋ hed jet | tə maɪ ˈbɔɪɪʃ ˈfænsi || ˈaɪ lʌvd tə sɪt ət hɪz fiːt | ən hɪər ɪm tel ði ɪˈvents əv ˈsɪksti jɪəz əv tɔɪl ən ˈdeɪnʤə | ˈsʌfərɪŋ ən wel ɜːnd ʤɔɪ | əz hi liːnd wɪð bəʊθ hændz əˈpɒn hɪz staʊt stɑːf | hɪz ˈbɒdi ˈsweɪɪŋ wɪð ði ˈɜːnɪstnəs əv hɪz spiːʧ || hɪz ˈleɪbəz ən ˈperɪlz wə naʊ ˈendɪd | ənd ɪn hɪz eɪʤ ənd ɪnˈfɜːmɪti hi həd faʊnd ə kwaɪət ˈheɪvn̩ || hi həd bɪlt ə smɔːl haʊs baɪ ðə saɪd əv ðə həʊm əv hɪz ˈʧaɪldhʊd | ən hɪz sʌn | hu ˈfɒləʊd hɪz ˈfɑːðəz vəʊˈkeɪʃn̩ | lɪvd ˈʌndə ðə seɪm ruːf || ðɪs sʌn ən tuː ˈdɔːtəz wər ɔːl ðət rɪˈmeɪnd tə hɪm əv ə lɑːʤ ˈfæməli ||

Transcription Passage 7

|| ðə jʌŋ waɪfs ˈletəz geɪv nəʊ ʌnˈtruː ɪkˈspreʃn̩ əv hə steɪt əv ˈfiːlɪŋ | jet ðə wə taɪmz wen ðə ˈdriːmlaɪk senˈseɪʃn̩ wɪʧ pəˈveɪdɪd hər ˈaʊtlʊk ɒn ðə njuː səˈraʊndɪŋz dɪ ˈstɜːbd hə || ðə spel əv ði iːst wəz strɒŋ || ðə ˈtrɒpɪkl̩ laɪf | ðə ˈvɪvɪd ˈkʌlərɪŋ | ðə braʊn skɪnd ˈmʌltɪtjuːdz | ðə ˈweɪvɪŋ pɑːmz | ɔːl siːmd tə bɪˈlɒŋ tʊ ə braɪt ˈpæʤənt ɪn wɪʧ ʃi wəz ˈəʊnli ə ˈpɑːsɪŋ spekˈteɪtə || ən naʊ | wɪð ðə ˈsɪmpl̩ sens əv ˈdjuːti wɪʧ həd mɑːkt ði ˈəʊnli ˈdɔːtər əv ðə ˈpɪnkθɔːp ˈrektəri | ʃi wəz ˈɑːskɪŋ hɜːˈself ˈweðər ɪt wəz raɪt tə jiːld səʊ ɪnˈtaɪəli tʊ ðə ˈwuːɪŋ əv ðə ˈmæʤɪk ˈprezn̩t || ˈiːvn̩ hə ˈwiːkli ˈʤɜːnl̩ frəm həʊm siːmd tə ˈdiːpən ðə ˈglæmə || ɔːl ɪn ðət dɪə ˈdɪstənt həʊm wəz trænsˈfɪgəd baɪ ɪts gləʊ || ˈnevə həd ðə ˈtendər əˈfekʃn̩ əv ˈfɑːðər ən ˈmʌðə felt səʊ ˈpreʃəs | ən huː wʊd həv bɪˈliːvd ðət ðə ˈkʌpl̩ əv ˈskuːlbɔɪ ˈbrʌðəz wʊd pruːv səʊ ˈmʌʧ mɔː dɪˈmɒnstrətɪv ɪn ðeə fɜːst ˈletəz ðən ɪn ðə deɪz wen ʃi həd ˈpeɪntɪd ðeə ˈwɪkɪts | meɪd seɪlz fə ðeə bəʊts | ən wəz ðeə ˈwɪlɪŋ ˈhelpər ɪn ɔːl skuːl ˌprepəˈreɪʃn̩z || ənd əˈgen ði ˌʌnɪkˈspektɪd wəz ɒn ɪts weɪ ||

Transcription Passage 8

|| əz ˌsɪvɪlaɪˈzeɪʃn̩ ədˈvɑːnsɪz ðər ɪz ə kənˈtɪnjʊəl ʧeɪnʤ ɪn ðə ˈstændəd əv ˈhjuːmən raɪts || ɪn ˈbɑːbərəs ˈeɪʤɪz ðə raɪt əv ðə ˈstrɒŋgɪst wəz ði ˈəʊnli wʌn ˈrekəgnaɪzd | bət əz mænˈkaɪnd prəˈgrest ɪn ði ɑːts ən ˈsaɪənsɪz ˈɪntəlekt bɪˈgæn tə ˈtraɪəmf ˈəʊvə bruːt fɔːs || ʧeɪnʤ ɪz ə lɔː əv laɪf | ən ðə dɪˈveləpmənt əv səˈsaɪəti ə ˈnæʧrəl grəʊθ || ɔːlˈðəʊ tə ðɪs lɔː wi əʊ ðə dɪˈskʌvərɪz əv ʌnˈnəʊn wɜːldz | ði ɪnˈvenʃn̩z əv məˈʃiːnəri | ˈswɪftə məʊdz əv ˈtrævl̩ | ən ˈklɪərər aɪˈdɪəz əz tʊ ðə ˈvæljuː əv ˈhjuːmən laɪf ən ˈθɔːt | jet iːʧ səkˈsesɪv ʧeɪnʤ həz met wɪð ðə məʊst dɪˈtɜːmɪnd ˌɒpəˈzɪʃn̩ || ˈfɔːʧənətli | ˈprəʊgres ɪz nɒt ðə rɪˈzʌlt əv ˌpriːəˈreɪnʤd plænz əv ˌɪndɪˈvɪʤʊəlz | bət ɪs bɔːn əv ə fɔːˈtjuːɪtəs ˌkɒmbɪˈneɪʃn̩ əv ˈsɜːkəmstænsɪz ðət kəmˈpel ˈsɜːtn̩ rɪˈzʌlts | ˌəʊvə ˈkʌmɪŋ ðə ˈnæʧrəl ɪˈnɜːʃə əv mænˈkaɪnd || ðər ɪz ə ˈsɜːtn̩ ɪnˈʤɔɪmənt ɪn həˈbɪʧʊəl ˈslʌgɪʃnəs | ɪn ˈraɪzɪŋ iːʧ ˈmɔːnɪŋ wɪð ðə seɪm aɪˈdɪəz əz ðə naɪt bɪˈfɔː | ɪn rɪˈtaɪərɪŋ iːʧ naɪt wɪð ðə θɔːts əv ðə ˈmɔːnɪŋ || ðɪs ɪˈnɜːʃə əv maɪnd ən ˈbɒdi həz ˈevə held ðə ˈmʌltɪtjuːd ɪn ʧeɪnz || ˈθaʊzn̩dz həv ðʌs səˈrendəd ðeə məʊst ˈseɪkrɪd raɪts əv ˈkɒnʃəns || ɪn ɔːl ˈpɪərɪədz əv ˈhjuːmən dɪˈveləpmənt | ˈθɪŋkɪŋ həz bɪn ˈpʌnɪʃt əz ə kraɪm | wɪʧ ɪz ˈriːzn̩ səˈfɪʃn̩t tʊ əˈkaʊnt fə ðə ˈʤenrəl ˈpæsɪv ˌrezɪgˈneɪʃn̩ əv ðə ˈmæsɪz tə ðeə kənˈdɪʃn̩z ənd ɪnˈvaɪrənmənts ||

Transcription Passage 9

|| aɪ wəz ˈəʊpnɪŋ maɪ maʊθ tʊ ˈɑːnsə | wen aɪ ˈsʌdn̩li bɪˈkeɪm əˈweə ðət ðə ˈnɔɪzɪz wə naʊ ˈdefɪnətli ˈlaʊdə || ˈnɔɪzɪz feɪnt | bət nɒt blɜːd ˈeni ˈlɒŋgə || ˈnɔɪzɪz wɪʧ wɜːnt ˈrɪəli ˈnɔɪzɪz | bət wər ˈækʧuəli ˈvɔɪsɪz || aɪ græbd ˈstɒdəd baɪ ði ɑːm || ˈlɪsn̩ | aɪ ˈɔːdəd || wi stʊd ðeə ˈsaɪləntli fə pəˈhæps hɑːf ə ˈmɪnɪt || jes | ðə ˈwɒznt ˈeni ˈkwesʧən əˈbaʊt ɪt naʊ || aɪ njuː ðət ðə feɪnt saʊndz wə ðəʊz əv ˈhjuːmən ˈvɔɪsɪz || gʊd ˈhevn̩z | ˈstɒdəd ɪkˈskleɪmd || ræts | eɪ | aɪ sed sɑːˈkæstɪkl̩i || bət | bət | ˈstɒdəd bɪˈgæn || hi wəz ˈɒbvɪəsli bɪˈwɪldəd || ðeəz ə sɔːt əv ˈsentrəl paɪp ən ˈwaɪərɪŋ meɪz ʌp hɪə | aɪ təʊld hɪm | djuː tʊ ðə plænz wi wə fɔːst tə ˈfɒləʊ ɪn ˈbɪldɪŋ ðɪs haʊs əv jɔːz || ðəʊz feɪnt ˈvɔɪsɪz ə ˈkærɪd θru ðə paɪps ən ˈwaɪəz fə səm ˈriːzən əv saʊnd vaɪˈbreɪʃn̩ | ən hɜːld ʌp hɪə || ʤəst tel mi weə ju kiːp jə ˈreɪdɪəʊ | ən wil sɒlv jə ˈprɒbləm || ˈstɒdəd lʊkt ət mi ə ˈmɪnɪt || bət wi dəʊnt əʊn ə ˈreɪdɪəʊ | hi sed ˈkwaɪətli ||

Transcription Passage 10

|| gʊd deɪ | ˈmɪstə ˈkɪŋstən | ʃi rɪˈspɒndɪd | ˈlʊkɪŋ ˈveri pɪŋk ən braɪt | ənd ə ˈlɪtl̩ ˈflʌrɪd əz ʃi rɪˈtɜːnd hɪz ˌsæljʊˈteɪʃn̩ || ʃi həd ðə ˈdeɪntiɪst kəmˈplekʃn̩ ðət ˈevər ə ˈdɔːnd ə ˈjuːθfʊl feɪs | ən wenˈevə ʃi wəz ˈstɑːtl̩d ɔːr ɪmˈbærəst | haʊˈevə ˈslaɪtli | ʃi

blʌʃt laɪk ə rəʊz || ˈmɪstə ˈkɪŋstən | əˈkʌstəmd tʊ əˈpreɪz ðə ʧɑːmz əv hɪz ˈfiːmeɪl frendz wɪð ən ˈɔːlməʊst ˈbruːtl̩ ɪmˌpɑːʃɪˈælɪti | wəz ʌnˌʤʌstɪˈfaɪəbli tʌʧt ən ˈflætəd baɪ ðɪs ˈɪnəsn̩t ˌdemənˈstreɪʃn̩ || hi wəz ˈrɪəli ˈveri glæd hi həd rɪˈmembəd hu ʃi wəz bɪˈfɔː hi həd lɒst səʊ gʊd ən ˌɒpəˈtjuːnɪti fə ˈlʊkɪŋ ət ən ˈtɔːkɪŋ tə hə || aɪ dəʊnt θɪŋk ɪt ɪs ə ˈveri faɪn ˌɑːftəˈnuːn | ʃi rɪˈmɑːkt ˈprezn̩tli | əz ðə ˈʤentl̩mən siːmd tə faɪnd hɪmˈself fə wʌns ə ˈlɪtl̩ ət ə lɒs fər ə sʌbˈʤekt || ən ʃi smaɪld ət hɪm θru hə ˈblʌʃɪz | wɪʧ went ən keɪm ˈsʌdn̩li ən ˈdelɪkətli | əz ɪf ðeɪ wə briːðd ˈəʊvə hə baɪ ði eə ˈsʌmhaʊ || ɪt həz bɪn ˈlʊkɪŋ greɪ | laɪk reɪn | ˈevə sɪns wi ˈstɑːtɪd | ənd ɪt ɪs ˈrɑːðə kəʊld/ dəʊnt ju θɪŋk || ɪz ɪt || ɑː || səʊ ɪt ɪz || bət wi mʌst ɪkˈspekt kəʊld ˈweðər ɪn meɪ || aɪ səˈpəʊz ɪt ɪs ˈrɑːðə streɪnʤ tə ju tə bi ˈfaɪndɪŋ ˈwɪntə ˈkʌmɪŋ ɒn ət ðɪs ˈsiːzn̩ || nəʊ || waɪ ʃəd ɪt bi streɪnʤ tə miː || aɪ θɔːt || aɪ əm ʃɔː ˈsʌmbədi təʊld mi | ðət ju wə ˈriːsn̩tli aʊt frəm ˈɪŋglənd ||

References

Abercrombie, D. 1975. *Elements of general phonetics*. Edinburgh: Edinburgh University Press.

Aguilar, L. 1999. Hiatus and diphthong: Acoustic cues and speech situation differences. *Speech and Communication* 28. 57–74.

Alarcos Llorach, E. 1961 [1983]. *Fonología española*. Madrid: Editorial Gredos.

Alcaraz, E. and Moody, B. 1993 (3rd edn.). *Fonética inglesa para españoles*. Alcoy: Editobal Maffil.

Alcina, J. and Blecua, J. M. 1975. *Gramática española*. Barcelona: Ariel.

Allen, E. M. and Munro, M. J. 1995. The perception of English and Spanish vowels by native English and Spanish listeners: A multidimensional scaling analysis. *Journal of the Acoustical Society of America* 97.4. 2540–2551.

Altenberg, E. 2005. The perception of word boundaries in a second language. *Second Language Research* 21.4. 325–358.

Anderson-Hsieb, J. and Kehler, K. 1988. The effect of foreign accent and speaking rate on native speaker comprehension. *Language Learning* 38.4. 561–613.

Arnold, G. F. and Gimson, A. C. 1976 (4th edn.). *English pronunciation practice*. London: Hodder & Stoughton.

Arteaga, D. and Llorente, L. A. 2009. *Spanish as an international language: Implications for teachers and learners*. Clevedon: Multilingual Matters.

Ashby, M. G. and Maidment, J. 2005. *Introducing phonetic science*. Cambridge: Cambridge University Press.

Ashby, P. 2005 (2nd edn.). *Speech sounds*. London: Routledge.

Ashby, P. 2011. *Understanding phonetics*. London: Hodder Education.

Avery, P. and Ehrlich, S. 1992. *Teaching American English pronunciation*. Oxford: Oxford University Press.

Azevedo, M. M. 2009. *Introducción a la lingüística española*. Upper Saddle River, NJ: Pearson Education Inc.

Baker, A. 2007 (3rd edn.). *Ship or sheep? An intermediate pronunciation course*. Cambridge: Cambridge University Press (with 4 audio CDs).

Ball, L. J. and Quayle, J. D. 2009. Phonological and visual distinctiveness effects in syllogistic reasoning: Implications for mental models theory. *Memory and Cognition* 37.6. 759–768. doi:10.3758/MC.37.6.759

Ball, M. J. and Rahilly, J. 1999. *Phonetics: The science of speech*. London: Arnold.

Barry, M. 1992. Palatalisation, assimilation, and gestural weakening in connected speech. *Speech Commun* 11. 393–400.

Baugh, A. and Cable, T. 1993. *A history of the English language*. London: Basil Blackwell.

Bell, A., Jurafsky, D., Fosler-Lussier, E., Girand, C., Gregory, M. and Gildea, D. 2003. Effects of disfluencies, predictability, and utterance position on word form variation in English conversation. *Journal of the Acoustical Society of America* 113. 1001–1024.

Best, C. 1994. The emergence of native-language phonological influences in infants: A perceptual assimilation model. In J. Goodman and H. C. Nusbaum (eds.), *The development of speech perception: The transition from speech sounds to spoken words*. Cambridge: MIT Press. 167–224.

Best, C. 1995. A direct realist view of cross-language speech perception. In W. Strange (ed.), *Speech perception and linguistic experience: Issues in cross-language research*. Baltimore: York Press. 171–204.

Best, C. T. and Strange, W. 1992. Effects of phonological and phonetic factors on cross-language perception of approximants. *Journal of Phonetics* 20. 305–331.

Best, C. T. and Tyler, M. D. 2007. Nonnative and second-language speech perception: Commonalities and complementarities. In B. Ocke-Schwen and M. J. Munro (eds.), *Language experience in second language speech learning: In honor of James Emil Flege*. Philadelphia: John Benjamins. 13–34.

Bladon, R. A. W. and Nolan, F. 1977. A videofluorographic investigation of tip and blade alveolars in English. *Journal of Phonetics* 5. 185–193.

Blecua, B. 1999. Características acústicas de la vibrante múltiple del español en habla espontánea. Actas del I Congreso de Fonética Experimental. Tarragona: Universidad de Barcelona and Universidad de Rovira i Virgili.

Boersma, P. 1998. Functional Phonology: Formalizing the interactions between articulatory and perceptual drives. PhD dissertation, University of Amsterdam.

Boersma, P. and Weenink, D. *Praat: Doing phonetics by computer* (Versión 5.0.20): http://www.praat.org/

Boomershine, A. 2013. Perception of English vowels by monolingual, bilingual, and heritage speakers of Spanish and English. In Ch. Howe *et al.* (eds.), *Selected proceedings of the 15th Hispanic linguistics symposium*. MA: Cascadilla Proceedings Project. 103–118.

Bradlow, A. R. 1995. A comparative acoustic study of English and Spanish vowels. *Journal of the Acoustical Society of America* 97.3. 1916–1924.

Brengelman, F. 1970. Generative phonology and the teaching of spelling. *English Journal* 59. 1113–1118.

Buizza, E. and Plug, L. 2012. Lenition, fortition and the status of plosive affrication: The case of spontaneous RP English /t/. *Phonology* 29.1. 1–38.

Burn, A. 2003. *Clearly speaking: Pronunciation in action for teachers*. National Center for English Language Teaching and Research, Macquaire Universiydney NSW 2109.

Byrd, D. 1992. A note on English sentence-final stops. University of California at Los Angeles. *Working Papers in Phonetics* 86.

Byrd, D. 1996. A phase window framework for articulatory timing. *Phonology* 13. 139–169.

Cabrera Abreu, M. and Vizaíno Ortega, F. 2009. *English phonetics and phonology for Spanish speakers. A workbook*. Las Palmas, Spain: Universidad de las Palmas de Gran Canaria University Press.

Calvo Shadid, A. 2008. Semiconsonantes y semivocales en los diptongos del español: Propuesta de análisis fonológico. *Filología y Lingüística* XXXIV.2. 107–142.

Carlisle, R. S. 1998. The acquisition of the onsets in a markedness relationship. *Studies in Second Language Acquisition* 20. 245–260.

Carney, E. 1994. *A survey of English spelling*. London/New York: Routledge.

Carr, P. 2012 (2nd edn.). *English phonetics and phonology: An introduction*. Oxford: Wiley-Blackwell.

Celce-Murcia, M., Brinton, D. M., Goodwin, J. M. and Griner, B. 2010. *Teaching pronunciation: A course book and reference guide*. Cambridge: Cambridge University Press.

Chang, Ch., Haynes, E., Yao, Y. and Rhodes, R. 2009. The phonetic space of phonological categories in heritage speakers of Mandarin. In M. Elliott *et al.* (eds.), *Proceedings from the 43rd Annual Meeting of the Chicago Linguistic Society: The main session*. Chicago, IL: Chicago Linguistic Society. 31–45.

Chomsky, N. and Halle, M. 1968. *The sound pattern of English. Studies in Language*. New York: Harper and Row.

Christophersen, P. 1955. The glottal stop in English. *English Studies* 33. 156–163.
Clark, J., Yallop, C. and Fletcher, J. 2007. *An introduction to phonetics and phonology.* Oxford: Basil Blackwell.
Coe, N. 2001. Speakers of Spanish and Catalan. In M. Swan and B. Smith (eds.), *Learner English: A teacher's guide to interference and other problems.* Cambridge: Cambridge University Press. 90–112.
Coe-Guerrero, D. L. 1981. Consonantal phonemes in the interlanguage of native speakers of Spanish acquiring English. MA thesis. Iowa: University of Iowa.
Cohn, A. 1990. Phonetic and phonological rules of nasalization. *U.C.L.A. Working Papers in Phonetics* 76.8. 1–224.
Coleman, J. 2005. *Introducing speech and language processing.* Cambridge: Cambridge University Press.
Colina, S. 2009. *Spanish phonology: A syllabic perspective.* Georgetown University Press.
Collins, B. and Mees, I. M. 2003. *The phonetics of English and Dutch.* Leiden/Boston: Brill.
Collins, B. and Mees, I. M. 2009 (2nd edn.). *Practical phonetics and phonology: A resource book for students.* London: Routledge.
Cortés Pomacóndor, S. M. 1999. Production and perception of English sounds by Catalan/Spanish speakers. *Proceedings of the I Congress of Experimental Phonetics.* Tarragona: Universidad de Barcelona. 165–170.
Cortés Pomacóndor, S. M. 2000. Acquisition of two non-native sound contrasts by Catalan speakers. Paper presented at *New Sounds 2000.* Amsterdam, September 2000.
Cruttenden, A. 2014 (8th edn.). *Gimson's pronunciation of English.* London: Edward Arnold.
Crystal, D. 2008 (6th edn.). *A dictionary of linguistics and phonetics.* Oxford: Blackwell.
Cuenca-Villarín, M. H. 1996. Principales dificultades de la pronunciación inglesa para hablantes nativos de español. En M. Martínez Vázquez (ed.), *Gramática contrastiva inglés/español.* Huelva: Servicio de Pulbicaciones de la Universida de Huelva. 309–325.
Dale, P. and Poms, L. 1985. *English pronunciation for Spanish speakers: Vowels.* New Jersey: Prentice Hall.
Dale, P. and Poms, L. 1986. *English pronunciation for Spanish speakers: Consonants.* New Jersey: Prentice Hall.
Delattre, P. 1965. *Comparing the phonetic features of English, French, German, and Spanish.* Harrap & Co, London.
Denes, P. 1955. Effect of duration on the perception of voicing. *Journal of the Acoustical Society of America* 27. 761–764.
Denes, P. B. and Pinson, E. N. 1993 (2nd edn.). *The speech chain: The physics and biology of spoken language.* W. H. Freeman & Co (Sd).
Disner, S. 1983. Vowel quality: The relation between universal and language-specific factors. *UCLA Working Papers in Phonetics* 58.
Docherty, G. J. 1992. *The timing of voicing in British English obstruents.* Berlin: Foris.
Doval-Suárez, S. M. 2004. *The acquisition of L2–English spelling.* Muenchen: Lincom.
Ellis, R. 1985. *Understanding second language acquisition.* Oxford: Oxford University Press.
Ellis, R. 1994. *The study of second language acquisition.* Oxford: Oxford University Press.
Ernestus, M., Lahey, M., Verhees, F. and Baayen, R. H. 2006. Lexical frequency and voice assimilation. *Journal of the Acoustical Society of America* 120. 1040–1051.
Escudero, P. 2000. Developmental patterns in the adult L2 acquisition of new contrasts: The acoustic cue weighting in the perception of Scottish tense/lax vowels by Spanish speakers. University of Edinburgh: M Sc dissertation.

Escudero, P. and Boersma, P. 2004. Bridging the gap between L2 speech perception research and phonological theory. *Studies in Second Language Acquisition* 26. 551–585.

Escudero, P. and Chládková, K. 2010. Spanish listeners' perception of American and Southern British English vowels. *Journal of the Acoustical Society of America* 128.5. 254–260.

Estebas Vilaplana, E. 2009. *Teach yourself English pronunciation*. A Coruña: Netbiblo.

Fabricius, A. H. 2002. Ongoing change in Modern RP. Evidence for the disappearing stigma of *t*-glottaling. *English World-Wide*, 23.1. 115–136.

Fayer, J. M. and Krasinski, E. 1987. Native and nonnative jusdgements of intelligibility and irritation. *Language Learning* 37.3. 313–327.

Finch, D. F. and Ortiz Lira, H. 1982. *A course in English phonetics for Spanish speakers*. London: Heinemann Educational Books Limited.

Flege, J. E. 1989. Differences in inventory size affect the location but not the precision of tongue positioning in vowel production. *Language and Speech* 32. 123–147.

Flege, J. E. 1991. Orthographic evidence for the perceptual identification of vowels in Spanish and English. *Quarterly Journal of Experimental Psychology* 43. 701–731.

Flege, J. E. 1995. Second language speech learning: Theory, findings, and problems. In W. Strange (ed.), *Speech perception and linguistic experience: Issues in cross-language research*. York Press, Baltimore, MD. 233–277.

Flege, J. E. 2003. Assessing constraints on second-language segmental production and perception. In A. Meyer and N. Schiller (eds.), *Phonetics and phonology in language comprehension and production: Differences and similarities*. Berlin: Mouton de Gruyter.

Flege, J. E. and Eefting, W. 1988. Imitation of a VOT continuum by native speakers of English and Spanish: Evidence for phonetic category formation. *Journal of the Acoustical Society of America* 83.2. 729–740.

Flege, J. E. and MacKay, I. R. A. 2004. Perceiving vowels in a second language. *Studies in Second Language Acquisition* 26. 1–34.

Flege, J. E., Bohn, O.-S. and Jang, S. 1997. The effect of experience on nonnative subjects' production and perception of English vowels. *Journal of Phonetics* 25. 437–470.

Flege, J. E., Fox, R. and Munro, M. 1994. Auditory and categorical effects for cross-language vowel perception. *Journal of the Acoustical Society of America* 95. 3623–3641.

Foulkes, P. and Docherty, G. 2000. Another chapter in the story of /r/: Labiodental variants in British English. *Journal of Sociolinguistics* 3. 30–59.

Fowler C. A. and Saltzman E. 1993. Coordination and coarticulation in speech production. *Language and Speech* 36. 171–195.

Fox, R. A., Flege, J. E. and Munro, M. J. 1995. The perception of English and Spanish vowels by native English and Spanish listeners: A multidimensional scaling analysis. *Journal of the Acoustical Society of America* 97.4. 2540–2550.

Fry, D. B. 1947. The frequency of occurrence of speech sounds in Southern English. *Archives Neérlandaises de Phonétique Expérimentale XX*. 103–106.

Fudge, E. C. 1984. *English word-stress*. George Allen & Unwin, London.

Fuller, M. 1990. Pulmonic ingressive fricatives in Tsou. *Journal of the International Phonetic Association* 20.2. 9–14.

Gallardo del Puerto, F. 2005. *La adquisición de la pronunciación del inglés como tercera lengua*. País Vasco: Servicio Editorial de la Universidad del País Vasco.

García Lecumberri, M. L. 1999. Foreign language English sounds in young learners of three different age groups. Paper presented at the *VIII Conference of the International Association of Child Language* (IASCL). San Sebastián-Donostia (Spain), 12–16 July, 1999.

García Lecumberri, M. L. 2000. La pronunciación del inglés como lengua extranjera en escolares de diferentes edades. Paper presented at the Curso de Verano de la Universidad del País Vasco *El factor edad en la adquisción de lenguas extranjeras*. San Sebastián-Donostia (Spain), 10–12 July, 2000.

García Lecumberri, M. L. and Cenoz Iragui, J. 1997. L2 perception of English vowels: Testing the validity of Kuhl's Prototypes. *Revista Alicantina de Estudios Ingleses* 10. 55–68.

García Lecumberri, M. L. and Cenoz, J. 2003. Phonetic context variation versus word perception in a foreign language. En I. Vázquez orta and I. Guillén Galve (eds), *Perspectivas pragmáticas en la lingüística aplicada*. Zaragoza: Asociación Española de Lingüística Aplicada (AESLA). 201–207.

García Lecumberri, M. L. and Elorduy Urquiza, A. 1994. Sistema fonológico de la lengua inglesa I, II y III. *Temario para el ingreso en el cuerpo de profesorado de I de bachillerato*. Madrid: Centro de Estudios Académicos.

García Lecumberri, M. L. and Gallardo, F. 2003. English F1 sounds in school learners of different ages. In M. P. García Mayo and M. L. García Lecumberri (eds.), *Age and the acquisition of English as a foreign language*. Clevendon: Multilingual Matters. 94–114.

García Lecumberri, M. L. and Maidment, J. 2000. *English transcription course*. London: Edward Arnold.

Gass, S. and Varonis, E. M. 1984. The effect of familiarity on the speech comprehensibility of nonnative speech. *Language Learning* 34.1. 65–89.

Giegerich, H. 1992. *English phonology: An introduction*. Cambridge: Cambridge University Press.

Gil, J. 2007. *Fonética para profesores de español: De la teoría a la práctica*. Madrid: Arco/ Libros.

Gimson, A. C. 1980. *A practical course of English pronunciation*. A Perceptual Approach. London: Edward Arnold.

Gimson, A. C. 1984 (3rd edn.). *An introduction to the pronunciation of English*. London: Edward Arnold.

Gimson, A. C. 1994 (5th edn.). *Gimson's pronunciation of English Revised by Alan Cruttenden*. London: Edward Arnold.

Gleason, J. 2012. Beaches and peaches: Common pronunciation errors among L1 Spanish speakers of English. In K. Levelle and J. Levis (eds.), *The confluence of social factors and pronunciation: Accent, identity, irritation and discrimination*. Ames, IA: Iowa State University. 205–215.

Goldsmith, J. 1990. *Autosegmental and metrical phonology*. Basil Blackwell.

Gow, D. W. and McMurray, B. 2007. Word recognition and phonology: The case of English coronal place assimilation. *Papers in Laboratory Phonology* 9. 173–200.

Gussenhoven, C. and Jacobs, H. 2005 (2nd edn.). *Understanding phonology*. London: Arnold.

Gutiérrez, F. 2004a. Acento y debilitamiento vocálico en el inglés de un grupo de estudiantes españoles de Enseñanza Secundaria Obligatoria (ESO). *Porta Linguarum* 2. 111–124.

Gutiérrez, F. 2004b. Contraste entre las vocales átonas del inglés y el español. El debilitamiento vocálico en el inglés de un grupo de hispanohablantes. In E. González and A. Rollings (eds.), *Studies in contrastive linguistics*. Publicaciones de la Universidad de Santiago de Compostela. 211–222.

Gutiérrez, F. 2005. Aprendizaje de la pronunciación del español por anglohablantes. Distorsión rítmica y timing. In C. Butler, M. A. Gómez González and S. Doval (eds.), *The dynamics of language use*. Amsterdam: John Benjamins. 287–306.

Gutiérrez, F. and Conde, C. 1990. Supuestos dudosos en la enseñanza del ritmo inglés a hispanohablantes. In F. Garrudo y F. Comesaña (eds.), *Actas del VII congreso nacional de lingüística aplicada* (Universidad de Sevilla). 265–273.

Haggard, M. 1978. The devoicing of voiced fricatives. *Journal of Phonetics* 6. 95–103.

Handbook of the International Phonetic Association. 1999. Cambridge: Cambridge University Press.

Harris, J. 1994. *English sound structure*. Oxford: Blackwell.

Hayward, K. 2000. *Experimental phonetics*. London: Longman.

Helman, L. A. 2004. Building on the sound system of Spanish: Insights from the alphabetic spellings of English-language learners. *Reading Teacher* 57.5. 452.

Hewlett, N. and Mackenzie Beck, J. 2006. *An introduction to the science of phonetics*. London/New York: Routledge.

Hickey, R. 1984. Coronal segments in Irish English. *Journal of Linguistics* 20. 233–50.

Hickey, R. 2007. *Irish English: History and present-day forms*. Cambridge: Cambridge University Press.

Hill, J. H. and O. Zepeda. 1999. Language, gender, and biology: Pulmonic ingressive airstream in women's speech in Tohono O'odham. *Southwest Journal of Linguistics* 18.1. 15–40.

Hogg, R. and McCully, C. B. 1987. *Metrical phonology: A coursebook*. Cambridge: Cambridge University Press.

Hooke, R. and Rowell, J. 1982. *A handbook of English pronunciation*. London: Edward Arnold.

Hualde, J. I. 2005. *The sounds of Spanish*. Cambridge: Cambridge University Press.

Hualde, J. I. and Prieto, M. 2002. On the diphthong/hiatus contrast in Spanish: Some experimental results. *Linguistics* 40. 217–234.

Huckvale, M. 2008. *SFS Speech Filing System 4.7*, http://www.phon.ucl.ac.uk/resource/sfs/. University College London.

Hughes, A. 2005. *English accents and dialects*. London: Arnold.

Hughes, A., Trudgill, P. and Watt, D. 2013 (5th edn.). *English accents and dialects. An introduction to social and regional varieties of English in the British Isles*. London/New York: Routledge.

Iverson, P. and Evans, B. G. 2003. A goodness optimization method for investigating phonetic categorization. *Proceedings of the 15th International Conference of Phonetic Sciences*, Barcelona, Spain.

Iverson, P. and Evans, B. G. 2007. Learning English vowels with different first-language vowel systems: Perception of formant targets, formant movement, and duration. *Journal of Acoustic Society of America* 122.5. 2842–2854.

Iverson, P., Smith, C. A. and Evans, B. G. 2006. Vowel recognition via cochlear implants and noise vocoders: Effects of formant movement. *Journal of the Acoustical Society of America* 120. 3998–4006.

Jawale, P. 2010. *Speech Analysis using PRAAT*. http://www.ee.iitb.ac.in/daplab/resources/SpeechAnalysisUsingPRAAT.pdf. Jersey: Prentice Hall.

Jones, D. 1967/1976 (3rd edn.). *The phoneme: Its nature and use*. Cambridge: Cambridge University Press.

Jones, D. 1975 (9th edn.). *An outline of English phonetics*. Cambridge: Cambridge University Press.

Katamba, F. 1989. *An introduction to phonology*. Essex, England: Longman.

Katz, W. F. 2013. *Phonetics for dummies*. Hoboken, New Jersey: Wiley, John & Sons, Incorporated.

Kent, R. and Read, Ch. 2002. *The acoustic analysis of speech*. University of Michigan: Singular/Thomson Learning.

Kenworthy, J. 1987. *Teaching English pronunciation*. London: Longman.
Kerswill, P. 2003. Dialectal levelling and geographical diffusion in British English. In D. Britain and J. Cheshire (eds.), *Social dialectology. In honour of Peter* Trudgill. Amsterdam: Benjamins. 223–243.
Keys, K. 2002. First language influence on the spoken English of Brazilian students of EFL. *ELT Journal* 56. 41–46.
Knorre, M. 2009. *Puntos de partida: An invitation to Spanish*. New York: McGraw-Hill.
Knowles, B. 1974. The rhythm of English syllables. *Lingua* 34. 115–147.
Kreidler, Ch. 1989. *The pronunciation of English: A course book in phonology*. Oxford/New York: Basil Blackwell.
Kuhl, P. K. 1993. Early linguistic experience and phonetic perception: Implications for theories of developmental speech production. *Journal of Phonetics* 21. 125–139.
Kuhl, P., Williams, K., Lacerda, E, Stevens, K. and Lindblom, B. 1992. Linguistice experience alters phonetic perception in infants by 6 months of age. *Science* 255. 606–608.
Kurowski, K. 1987. Acoustic properties of place of articulation in nasal consonants. *Journal of the Acoustical Society of America* 81. 1917–1927.
Ladefoged, P. 1996 (2nd edn.). *Elements of acoustic phonetics*. University of Chicago Press.
Ladefoged, P. 2001 (4th edn.). *A course in phonetics*. Orlando: Harcourt Brace.
Ladefoged, P. 2003. *Phonetic data analysis. An introduction to fieldwork and instrumental techniques*. Oxford: Blackwell.
Ladefoged, P. 2005 (2nd edn.). *Vowels and consonants. An introduction to the sounds of languages*. Oxford: Blackwell.
Ladefoged, P. and Maddieson, P. 1996. *The sounds of the world's languages*. Cambridge: Blackwell.
Ladefoged, P. and Zeitoun, E. 1993. Pulmonic ingressive phones do not Occur in Tsou. *Journal of the International Phonetic Association* 23.1. 13–15.
Lado, R. 1957. *Linguistics across cultures*. Ann Arbor, Michigan: Univ. of Michigan Press.
Lado, R. 1965. *Una comparación entre los sistemas fónicos del ingles y del español*. Montevideo: Universidad de la Republica.
Lass, R. 1984. *Phonology: An introduction to basic* concepts. Cambridge: Cambridge University Press.
Laver, J. 1994. *Principles of phonetics*. Cambridge: Cambridge University Press.
Lehiste, I. 1970. *Suprasegmentals*. Cambridge, MA: MIT Press.
Lillo, A. 2009. *Transcribing English: The nuts and bolts of phonemic transcription*. Madrid: Comares.
Lisker, L. and Abramson, A. S. 1964. A cross-language study of voicing in initial stops: Acoustical measurements. *Word* 20. 384–422.
Lodge, K. 2009. *A critical introduction to phonetics*. London: Continuum
Lombardy, L. 1999. Positional faithfulness and voicing assimilation in Optimality Theory. *Natural Language and Linguistic Theory* 17. 267–302.
Macken, M. and Barton, D. 1980. The acquisition of the voicing contrast in English: A study of the voice onset time in word-initial stop consonants. *Journal of Child Language* 7. 41–74.
MacNeilage, P. F., Davis, B. L., Kinney, A. and Matyear, C. L. 2000. The motor core of speech: A comparison of serial organization patterns in infants and languages. *Child Development* 2000.1. 153–163.
Maddieson, I. 1984. *Patterns of sounds*. Cambridge: Cambridge University Press.

Magen, H. 1989. An acoustic study of vowel-to-vowel coarticulation in Enlgish. Ph.D. dissertation, Yale University.
Maidment, J. *Speech Internet Dictionary* (SID) http://blogjam.name/sid/
Malécot, A. 1968. The force of articulation of American stops and fricatives as a function of position. *Phonetica* 18. 95–102.
Mann, V. A. and Repp, B. H. 1980. Influence of vocalic context on perception of the [ʃ]-[s] distinction. *Perception & Psychophysics* 28. 213–228.
Manuel, S. 1999. Cross-language studies: relating language-particular coarticulation patterns to other language-particular facts. In W. Hardcastle and N. Hewlett (eds.), *Coarticulation: Theory, data and techniques*, Cambridge: Cambridge University Press. 179–198.
Martínez Celdrán, E. 1986. *Fonética*. Teide: Barcelona.
Martínez Celdrán, E. 1995. En torno a las vocales del español: Análisis y reconocimiento. *Estudios de Fonética Experimental* 7. 195–218.
Martínez Celdrán, E. 1996. *El sonido de la comunicación humana*. Barcelona: Ariel.
Martínez Celdrán, E. 1998. *Análisis espectrográfico de los sonidos del habla*. Barcelona: Ariel.
Martínez Celdrán, E., Fernández Planas, A. M. 2007. *Manual de fonética española. Articulaciones y sonidos del español*. Barcelona: Ariel.
Martínez Celdrán, E., Fernández Planas, A. M. and Carrera, J. 2003. Illustrations of the IPA: Spanish. Journal *of the International Phonetic Association* 33.2. 255–260.
Martínez-Dauden, G. and Llisterri, J. 1990. Phonetic interference in bilingual speakers learning a third language: The production of lateral consonants. *9th World Congress of Applied Linguistics* 9.
McAllister, R., Flege, J. E. and Piske, T. 2002. The influence of the L1 on the acquisition of Swedish vowel quantity by native speakers of Spanish, English and Estonian. *Journal of Phonetics* 30. 229–258.
Monroy Casas, R. 1980. *Aspectos fonéticos de las vocales españolas*. Madrid: Paraninfo.
Monroy Casas, R. 1981. *Las vocales en inglés y en español: nuevas perspectivas*. Murcia: Servicio de Publicaciones de la Universidad de Murcia.
Monroy Casas, R. 2001. *Systems for phonetic transcription of English: Theory and texts*. Bern: Peter Lang.
Monroy Casas, R. 2012. *La pronunciación del inglés británico simplificada*. Murcia: Editum.
Moore, D. H. Jr. 2008. The perception of English word-final /l/ by Brazilian learners. Unpublished dissertation. Universidade Federal de Santa Catarina.
Morley, J. 1991. The pronunciation component in teaching English to speakers of other languages. *TESOL Quarterly* 25.1. 51–74.
Morrison, G. 2006. L1 & L2 production and perception of English and Spanish vowels: A statistical modelling approach. Doctoral dissertation, University of Alberta, Edmonton, Alberta, Canada.
Morrison, G. 2008. Perception of synthetic vowels by monolingual Canadian-English, Mexican-Spanish, and Peninsular-Spanish listeners. *Canadian Acoustics* 36. 17–23.
Mott, B. 2011 (3rd edn.). *English phonetics and phonology for Spanish speakers*. Barcelona: Servicio de Publicaciones de la Universidad de Barcelona.
Moyer, A. 1999. Ultimate attainment in L2 phonology: The critical factors of age, motivation and instruction. *Studies in Second Language Acquisition* 21. 81–108.
Munro, M. J. 1998. The effect of noise on the intelligibility of foreign-accented speech. *Studies in Second Language Acquisition* 20. 139–154.

Navarro Tomás, T. 1966 [1946]. *Estudios de fonología española*. New York: Las Americas Publishing Company.

Navarro Tomás, T. 1968. *Studies in Spanish phonology*. Miami: University Press.

Navarro Tomás, T. 1991 [1918] (25th edn.). *Manual de pronunciación española*. Madrid: Consejo Superior de Investigaciones Científicas.

Núñez Méndez, E. 2005. *Fundamentos de fonología y fonética española para hablantes de inglés*. Muenchen: Lincom. Europa.

O'Connor, J. D. 1952. RP and the reinforcing glottal stop. *English Studies* 33. 214–218.

O'Connor, J. D., Gerstman, L. J., Liberman, A. M., Delattre, P. C. and Cooper, F. S. 1957. Acoustic cues for the perception of initial /w, j, r, l/ in English. *Word* 13. 24–36.

Ogden, R. 2009. *An introduction to English phonetics*. Edinburgh: Edinburgh University Press.

Ohde, R. N. 1994. Fundamental frequency as an acoustic correlate of stop consonant voicing. *Journal of the Acoustical Society of America* 75. 224–230.

Ortiz Lira, H. 2008. The 37 essential weak-form words. UMCE, USACH. 1–16. Available at http://www.hectorortiz.cl/articulos/weak_forms_may_2008.swf

Pennock Speck, B. 2001. Markedness and naturalness in the acquisition of phonology. En C. Muñoz (coord), *Trabajos en lingüística aplicada*. Barcelona: AESLA. 179–185.

Peperkamp, S., Le Calvez, R. Nadal, J.-P. and Dupoux E. 2006. The acquisition of allophonic rules: Statistical learning with linguistic constraints. *Cognition* 101. B31–B41.

Petterson, G. E. and Lehiste, I. 1960. Duration of syllable nuclei in English. *Journal of the Acoustical Society of America* 32. 693–703.

Pike, K. L. 1943. *Phonetics*. Ann Arbor, Michigan: University of Michigan Press

Quilis, A. 1981. *Fonética acústica de la lengua española*. Gredos: Madrid.

Quilis, A. 1985. *El comentario fonológico y fonético de textos. Teoría y práctica*. Madrid: Arco/Libros.

Quilis, A. 1993. *Tratado de fonología y fonética españolas*. Madrid: Gredos.

Quilis, A. and Esgueva, M. 1983. Realización de los fonemas vocálicos españoles en posición fonética normal. In M. Esgueva and M. Cantarero (eds.), *Estudios de fonética*. Madrid: Centro Superior de Investigaciones Científicas. 159–252.

Quilis, A., and Fernandez, J. A. 1996. *Curso de fonetica y fonologia españolas para estudiantes angloamericanos*. Madrid: Consejo Superior de Investigaciones Científicas (CSIC).

Real Academia Española (RAE). 1973. *Esbozo de una nueva gramática de la lengua española*. Madrid: Espasa-Calpe.

Roach, P. 1973. Glottalization of English /p, t, k, tj/ – a re-examination. *Journal of the International Phonetic Association* 3. 10–21.

Roach, P. 2005 (3rd edn.). *English phonetics and phonology. A practical course*. Cambridge: Cambridge University Press. (with CD).

Roach, P., Sergeant, P. and Miller, D. 1992. Syllabic consonants at different speaking rates: A problem for automatic speech recognition. *Speech Communication* 11. 475–479.

Roca, I. and Johnson, W. 1999. *A course in phonology*. Oxford: Blackwell Publishing.

Rollings, A. 1998. Marking devices in the spelling of English. *Atlantis* XX.1. 129–143.

Rollings, A. 2004. *The spelling patterns of English. Lincom Studies in English Linguistics*. Muenchen: Lincom Europa.

Sánchez Benedicto, F. 1980. *Manual de pronunciación inglesa comparada con la española*. Madrid: Longman Alhambra.

Scragg, D. 1974. *A history of English spelling. Mont Follick Series, Vol. 3*. Manchester: MUP.

Sedláčková, K. 2010. *Some aspects of non-native acquisition of English pronunciation in Spanish speakers*. Brno: Masaryk University MA thesis. Available at http://is.muni.cz/th/160409/pedf_m/DIPL.IS.pdf

Shockey, L. 2003. *Sound patterns of spoken English*. Oxford: Blackwell Publishing.

Skandera, P. and Burleigh, P. 2005. *A manual of English phonetics and phonology*. Tübingen: Narr Franke Verlag.

Smith, P. 1980a. In defence of conservatism in English orthography. *Visible Language* XIV.2. 122–136.

Smith, P. 1980b. Linguistic information in spelling. In U. Frith (ed.), *Cognitive processes in spelling*, New York: Academic Press. 33–49.

Stockwell, R. P., and Bowen, J. D. 1965. *The sounds of English and Spanish*. University of Chicago Press, Chicago, IL.

Stone, M. 1990. A three-dimensional model of tongue movement on ultra-sound and x-ray microbeam data. *Journal of International Phonetic Association* 87. 2207–2217.

Stone, M., Faber A., Raphael, L. J. and Shawker, T. H. 1992. Cross-sectional tongue shape and linguo-palatal contact patterns in [s], [ʃ], and [l]. *Journal of Phonetics* 20. 253–270.

Strange W, Weber A, Levy E, Shapiro V and Nishi K. 2002. Within and across language acoustic variability of vowels spoken in different phonetic and prosodic contexts: American English, North German, and Parisian French. *Journal of the Acoustical Society of America* 112. 23–84.

Subtelny, J., Worth, J. H. and Sakuda, M. 1966. Intraoral pressure and rate of flow during speech. *Journal of Speech and Hearing Research* 9. 498–518.

Swan, M. and Smith, B. 2001 (2nd edn.). *Learner English: A teacher's guide to interference and other problems*. Cambridge: Cambridge University Press.

Tatham, M. and Morton, K. 2011. *A guide to speech production and perception*. Edinburgh: Edinburgh University Press.

Tench, P. 1996. *The intonation systems of English*. London: Cassell.

Tench, P. 2011. *Transcribing the sounds of English. A phonetics workbook for words and discourse*. Cambridge: Cambridge Univeristy Press.

Trask, R. L. 2012. *A dictionary of phonetics and phonology*. London/New York: Routledge

Trubetzkoy, N. S. 1969. *Principles of phonology*. Translated by Christiane A. M. Baltaxe from Grundzüge der Phonologie. Berkeley: University of California Press.

Trudgill, P. 2005. *English accents and dialects: An introduction to social and regional varieties of English in the British Isles*. London: Routledge.

Vallins, G. 1965. *Spelling*. London: André Deutsch.

Varonis, E. M. and Gass, S. 1981. The comprehensibility of non-native speech. *Studies in Second Language Acquisition* 6.2. 226–232.

Venezky, R. 1970. *The structure of English orthography*. The Hague: Mouton.

Volatis, L. E. and Miller, J. L. 1992. Phonetic prototypes: Influence of place of articulation and speaking rate on the internal structure of voicing categories. *Journal of the International Phonetic Association* 92. 723–735.

Walsh-Dickey, L. 1997. The phonology of liquids. PhD Dissertation, UMass Amherst.

Ward, I. 1972. *The phonetics of English*. Cambridge: Cambridge University Press.

Wells, J. C. 1982. *Accents of English Vols. 1–3*. Cambridge: Cambridge University Press.

Wells, J. C. 2000 (2nd edn.). *Longman pronunciation dictionary*. Harlow: Longman.

Wells, J. C. 2005. Goals in teaching English pronunciation. In K. Dziubalska-Kołaczyk and J. Przedlacka (eds.), *English pronunciation models: A changing scene*. Bern: Peter Lang. 101–110.

Wells, J. C. 2006. *English intontion. An introduction*. Cambridge: Cambridge University Press.

Wiik, K. 1965. *Finnish and English vowels*. Annales Universitatis Turkuensis B 94. University of Turku.

Williamson, L. 1980. *The influence of phonetics, semantics, etymology and preference on English spelling*. LACUS. 546–572.

Yule, V. 1982. An international reform of English spelling and its advantages. *Revista Canaria de Estudios Ingleses* 4. 9–22.

Subject Index

www.ingramcontent.com/pod-product-compliance
Lightning Source LLC
Chambersburg PA
CBHW051241300426
44114CB00011B/842
9781501510960